Financing Federal Systems

The Selected Essays of Edward M. Gramlich

Edward M. Gramlich

Dean, School of Public Policy and Professor of Economics and Public Policy, University of Michigan, US

STUDIES IN FISCAL FEDERALISM AND STATE–LOCAL FINANCE

Edward Elgar
Cheltenham, UK • Northampton, MA, USA

© Edward M. Gramlich, 1997

Published by
Edward Elgar Publishing Limited
8 Lansdown Place
Cheltenham
Glos GL50 2HU
UK

Edward Elgar Publishing, Inc.
6 Market Street
Northampton
Massachusetts 01060
USA

A catalogue record for this book
is available from the British Library

Library of Congress Cataloguing in Publication Data
Gramlich, Edward M.
    Financing federal systems : the selected essays of Edward M.
Gramlich / Edward M. Gramlich.
        (Studies in fiscal federalism and state–local finance)
    Includes bibliographical references and index.
    1. Fiscal policy—United States.   2. Intergovernmental fiscal
relations—United States.   3. Local finance—United States.
I. Title.   II. Series.
HJ275.G7   1997
336.73—dc21
                                                                    97–23204
                                                                    CIP

ISBN 1 85898 656 7

Printed and bound in Great Britain by
MPG Books Ltd, Bodmin, Cornwall

Contents

Acknowledgements

The publishers wish to thank the following who have kindly given permission for the use of copyright material.

American Economic Association for articles: 'Public Employee Market Power and the Level of Government Spending', with Paul N. Courant and Daniel L. Rubinfeld, in *The American Economic Review*, **69**(5), December 1979, 806–17; 'Infrastructure Investment: A Review Essay', in *Journal of Economic Literature*, **XXXII**, September 1994, 1176–96 and 'New York: Ripple or Tidal Wave? The New York City Fiscal Crisis: What Happened and What is to be Done?', in *The American Economic Review*, **66**(2), May 1976, 415–29.

The Brookings Institute for articles: 'State and Local Fiscal Behavior and Federal Grant Policy', with Harvey Galper, in *Brookings Papers on Economic Activity*, 1, 1973, 15–50; 'State and Local Budgets the Day after It Rained: Why Is the Surplus So High?', in *Brookings Papers on Economic Activity*, 1, 1978, 191–214; '"A Fair Go": Fiscal Federalism Arrangements', in Richard E. Caves and Lawrence B. Krause (eds), *The Australian Economy: A View from the North*, The Brookings Institution, Washington, 1984, 231–74 and 'Rethinking the Role of the Public Sector', in Barry P. Bosworth and Alice M. Rivlin (eds), *The Swedish Economy*, The Brookings Institution, Washington, 1987, 250–86.

Canadian Tax Foundation for article: 'Canadian Fiscal Federalism: An Outsider's View', in Melville McMillan (ed.), *Canadian Tax Paper No. 91, Volume 2, Provincial Public Finances: Plaudits, Problems and Prospects*, Canadian Tax Foundation, 1991, 403–15.

Federal Reserve Bank of Chicago for article: 'A Report on School Finance and Educational Reform in Michigan', with Paul N. Courant and Susanna Loeb, in Thomas A. Downes and William A. Testa, *Midwest Approaches to School Reform*, Federal Reserve Bank of Chicago, Chicago, 1995, 5–33.

International Economic Review for article: 'State and Local Governments and their Budget Constraint', in *International Economic Review*, **10**(2), June 1969, 163–82.

MIT Press for article: 'The Impact of the Tax Reform Act of 1986 on State and Local Fiscal Behavior', with Paul N. Courant, in Joel Slemrod (ed.), *Do Taxes Matter? The Impact of the Tax Reform Act of 1986*, MIT Press, Cambridge, 1990, 243–75.

National Tax Association for articles: 'Why Voters Support Tax Limitation Amendments: The Michigan Case', with Paul N. Courant and Daniel L. Rubinfeld, in *National Tax Journal*, **XXXIII**(1), March 1980, 1–20; 'The Deductibility of State and Local Taxes', in *National Tax Journal*, **XXXVIII**(4), December 1985, 447–65 and 'Federalism and Federal Deficit Reduction', in *National Tax Journal*, **XL**(3), September 1987, 299–313.

Professor Wallace E. Oates for article: 'Intergovernmental Grants: A Review of the Empirical Literature', in Wallace E. Oates (ed.), *The Political Economy of Fiscal Federalism*, Lexington Books, Lexington, 1977, 219–39.

Regents of the University of California and the University of California Press for article: 'Reforming U.S. Federal Fiscal Arrangements', in John M. Quigley and Daniel L. Rubinfeld (eds), *American Domestic Priorities: An Economic Appraisal*, University of California Press, London, 1985, 34–69.

Russell Sage for article: 'The Spatial Dimension: Should Worker Assistance be given to Poor People or Poor Places?', with Colleen M. Heflin, in Richard Freeman and Peter Gottschalk (eds), *Demand Side Explanations of Earnings Inequality*, Russell Sage, forthcoming.

University of Chicago Press for article: 'Micro Estimates of Public Spending Demand Functions and Tests of the Tiebout and Median-Voter Hypotheses', with Daniel L. Rubinfeld, in *Journal of Political Economy*, **90**(3), June 1982, 536–60.

The University of Wisconsin Press for article: 'Migration and Income Redistribution Responsibilities', with Deborah S. Laren, in *The Journal of Human Resources*, **XIX**(4), Fall 1984, 489–511.

John Wiley & Sons, Inc. for articles: 'Moving into and out of Poor Urban Areas', with Deborah Laren and Naomi Sealand, in *Journal of Policy Analysis and Management*, **11**(2), 1992, 273–87 and 'Cooperation and Competition in Public Welfare Policies', in *Journal of Policy Analysis and Management*, **6**(3), Spring 1987, 417–31.

The Urban Institute for article: 'The Stimulative Effects of Intergovernmental Grants: Or Why Money Sticks where it Hits', with Paul N. Courant and Daniel L. Rubinfeld, in Peter Mieszkowski and William H. Oakland (eds), *Fiscal Federalism and Grants-in-Aid*, Committee on Urban Public Economics and the Urban Institute, Washington, 1979, 5–21.

Introduction

Questions of how to finance federal governmental systems have proliferated in the last several decades. On the academic side, there are now several journals devoted largely to such issues, and hundreds of articles. On the political side, in the United States most of the important domestic policy initiatives of every President since Johnson have involved in one way or other an important change in the structure of fiscal federalism. Around the world, developed economies are continually confronting these questions of federalism as they consider harmonizing trade and tax arrangements, and emerging market economies are confronting the questions as they organize systems to promote growth and development.

I have been writing in this field off and on for three decades now, and am obviously flattered to be asked to gather many of these articles together. Some of my work has been theoretical, some empirical and some diagnostic, both in regards to United States' issues and to fiscal decentralization issues in other countries. This volume contains 23 of these papers: some I worked on alone, some with co-authors, some early, some late, some theoretical, some applied, some domestic, some foreign. It begins with a brief overview of the state of play on fiscal federalism today; essentially a policy maker's guide to issues that arise in the formation of a federal system, annotated to indicate how some of my own (and my co-authors') modest contributions fit into this state of knowledge. Some earlier work on behavioral models for state and local governments follows. This section is in turn followed by a number of essays on particular federalism topics, and a few essays on overall federalism strategies in the United States and certain other countries.

A policy-maker's guide

The topic of fiscal federalism has generally been understood to mean the proper placement, by level of government, of various taxes, spending programs, grants, and regulations. Questions asked include what types of spending should be conducted by what levels of government, what types of taxes should be assessed by what levels of government, how should grants fill in the gaps and/or improve cooperative incentives, and how should regulations be harmonized? On the one hand, taste and other differences between jurisdictions argue for letting the jurisdictions conduct separate policies – governments in jurisdiction x should do what voters in jurisdiction x want. On the other hand, the existence of economies of scale in the provision of public goods, benefit spillovers across jurisdictions and the potential migration of taxpayers and benefit recipients complicate the picture. These factors suggest that individual jurisdictions do not operate in a vacuum, can make things easy or difficult for other jurisdictions and should not behave independently. The tension between cooperation and competition among jurisdictions has always been the key element in analysing fiscal decentralization strategies.

In sorting out these issues, I find it helpful to use Musgrave and Musgrave's

(1989) allocation, distribution and macroeconomics trilogy. Musgrave actually called the last branch the 'stabilization' branch, but these days macroeconomic fiscal management has come to refer to much more than stabilization policy alone, so I use the broader designation.

Allocation
On the spending side, the basic allocation issue involves the spatial domain of benefits from public service or public expenditure programs. Oates (1972) showed how optimal jurisdiction size can be determined by the balance between competing forces – the welfare loss from taste differences, which argues for small jurisdictions, and the welfare gain from burden sharing or economies of scale, which argues for large jurisdictions. His spending decentralization theorem called for public services to be provided by the jurisdiction covering the smallest area over which benefits are distributed. A corollary says that, if the spending decentralization theorem is followed, efficiency can be further promoted by having central government grant programs to insure that those living outside the jurisdiction pay their appropriate marginal share of the benefits of public service. Coasian bargaining among jurisdictions would bring about this latter outcome automatically, but Coasian bargaining is often not feasible with the number of governments existing in most countries today.

Following this logic, public services such as schools, roads and public safety would be provided locally, while transportation networks, national defense and foreign aid would be provided by the central government. This split in spending responsibilities does seem to be broadly realized in most countries with federal governmental systems. Normally the split is supplemented with national matching grant programs to deal with externalities, though as shown below, most real-world matching grant programs here and abroad are not constructed to take advantage of this efficiency.

On the tax side, the key issue is factor mobility. Suppose some factor is mobile across local boundaries but not across national boundaries. Trying to extort fiscal residuals at the local level by having the local government tax the factor more than the value of local services received by the factor will simply drive the factor out of the jurisdiction. But national taxes can and should be imposed on the factor. The lesson is almost the direct opposite of that on the spending side – factors should be taxed by the jurisdiction covering the largest area over which the factor is not mobile, to cut down on mobility distortions. I am not aware that this proposition has ever been named, but if it has not, it might be called the 'tax centralization theorem'.

This disjuncture between spending and tax outcomes leads to what has been called the vertical imbalance problem. If many spending programs are conducted by lower levels of government and most taxes are assessed by higher levels of government, it may be impossible to finance the activities of lower levels of government without grants from the national government. These grants should be general purpose, as opposed to specific purpose, and this whole argument is perhaps the strongest one for central government general purpose grants to local governments.

But, as is routine in this field, there are caveats. One is that even mobile factors may be willing to pay user fees to local governments for the use of their services. User fees automatically solve the spillover problem, because whoever benefits pays, wherever the beneficiary lives (or is incorporated). Second, this argument is not a cause of despair for local governments because not all factors are mobile – factors have location preferences, and mobility costs can be high. Third, there can be rent-seeking inefficiencies, if local officials win re-election by their ability to procure grants rather than by their ability to manage governments. In the end the proper amount and usage of general purpose grants to resolve vertical imbalance issues becomes an empirical issue. All of the following papers on specific jurisdictions grapple with this fundamental issue.

These comments refer to the normative structure of federal systems. My initial way into the topic was by asking not about normative structures but positive behavior (1969). How do states and localities make tax and spending decisions? This work was later elaborated with Harvey Galper (1973) to examine behavioral responses to a variety of stimuli, and again later with Paul Courant and Daniel Rubinfeld (1979, 1980, 1982) to ask about the empirical strength of the famous median voter theorem and the potential inefficiencies (or efficiencies) of tax limitation amendments.

As regards central government grants more specifically, even if there were no vertical imbalance grants, there might still be special purpose grants to correct for benefit spillovers. Especially if the spending decentralization theorem is followed, there will typically be outsiders who benefit from local public spending and should pay some of the costs. Nonpayment means that the supplying jurisdiction will tend to underprovide the services. Obvious examples include outsiders who benefit from an excellent set of highways in nearby states, or downriver communities that benefit from pollution prevention upriver. Coasian bribes are possible, but central government special purpose matching grant programs are more feasible.

Under this rationale, central government grants should be open-ended price subsidies for particular types of spending, with the central government matching rate roughly equal to share of marginal benefits realized outside the jurisdiction. Throughout the world, the very great majority of central government matching grant programs are not of this form, something I have discovered in my fiscal examinations of specific jurisdictions (1984, 1985, 1987, 1991). Here and abroad, existing matching grant programs typically feature very high central government matching rates, much higher than the benefit share of outsiders, with caps on grant amounts to prevent the local recipient from overspending. The cap means that at the margin there is no price subsidy at all to induce the recipient government to consider externalities. If grants are to be used at all, one clear remedy is to realign matching rates and to uncap the grant. Another, developed at length in my paper on infrastructure investment (1994), is to recognize that there are strong political imperatives against ever developing an efficient set of matching grant programs and to switch over to user-fee financing.

I have also worked on the predictive side of the grant question. Both with Galper and alone (1973, 1976, 1978) I have tried to show how matching grant programs typically generate more recipient government spending than non-matching grants, though not as much spending as if the matching grants were uncapped. And, non-matching grants in turn generate more recipient government spending than pure income changes, in contradiction to the then prevailing theory. This difference between the spending effects of non-matching grants and the spending effects of income changes was christened the 'flypaper effect' (money sticks where it hits). Courant, Rubinfeld and I (1979) tried to justify flypaper theoretically, and there are still empirical debates about its importance (see Ladd, 1993).

There is one last, and largely unconscious, way in which central governments often give open-ended price subsidies. If state and/or local taxes are deductible against the national income tax, the marginal tax cost of a dollar of local revenue is the complement of the marginal central government income tax rate. It may be that this slight reduction in local tax cost is an appropriate correction for generalized externalities, but there are certainly distortions. First, there is no obvious reason why the marginal income tax rate equals the benefit share of outsiders, though it may come surprisingly close on average. Second, if many communities do not contain many itemizers of deductions, as poor communities typically do not, the income tax deduction becomes a giveaway to wealthy people in these communities without influencing spending behavior at the margin. These arguments were developed in my paper on federal income tax deductibility (1985).

Distribution

There are generally two types of distributional programs in modern societies – human capital-type programs aimed at helping people earn higher incomes in the long run, and transfer programs aimed at protecting peoples' incomes in the short run. Both types of programs could be lodged at either a higher or lower level of government, and both raise a series of policy issues.

The most prominent human capital program under the purview of local governments is elementary and secondary education. The tradition in most countries is to conduct public schooling at the local level, with opportunities for parental involvement in the operation of schools.

While the local role is an established tradition that is likely to persist, the fact that elementary and secondary education has an important long run impact on the nation's income distribution argues for a broader interest as well. Specifically, since poor people tend to live together in poor communities, these communities would generally spend less on their children's education than rich communities. Not only that, the costs of maintaining schools and of providing for a good learning atmosphere are also likely to be higher in poor communities with difficult crime prevention problems. Without some centralized sources of financing, both factors together would tend to perpetuate society's income differences.

There are essentially three ways to break this vicious circle. One approach, known as the 'foundation' approach, is simply to centralize some base level of spending on public schools, hence at least eliminating spending differences on the bottom side of the distribution. Another is to give general purpose grants to poor jurisdictions to bring their spendable resources up to those in wealthy jurisdictions. But since there is no guarantee that general purpose grants will be spent on education, this approach can be very costly unless flypaper effects are huge. A third approach, known as power equalization, features open-end matching grants with the matching rate set so that on average spending will be equalized, or more equal, across districts. One could also imagine a hybrid approach combining elements of these three. The education paper with Paul Courant and Susanna Loeb (1995) reports on the recent attempt of the state of Michigan to switch from a modified form of the power equalization approach to a modified form of the foundation approach.

Regarding the income transfer side of the distribution issue, the central program is, of course, welfare. Should welfare expenditures be conducted at the national level, as most economists think; the local level, as most politicians think; or as a hybrid reflected in US law prior to 1996?

The key theoretical issue turns out to be the spatial horizon of altruism. Taxpayers give income transfer benefits either as a form of social insurance or because they care about the welfare of their fellow citizens suffering poverty. If the motive is social insurance, over what geographic domain is that to be – do taxpayers want programs that operate throughout their locality, state, or nation? If the motive is altruism more generally, again which fellow citizens are the beneficiaries – those in the same local jurisdiction, state, nation, or common market? If the relevant area is the nation, transfer benefits should be nationwide, or at least there should be a nationwide floor on benefits.

There are further complications on the recipient side. As I tried to show in a paper with Deborah Laren (1984), recipients do seem to migrate across state lines in search of higher transfer benefits, at least in the long run. This raises the long-run cost to any state or locality of setting its own transfer benefits at some generous level its own taxpayers might prefer – the higher benefits attract recipients from other states, thus raising costs and extending the geographic domain of benefits beyond that which the voters might have preferred. Residency requirements might eliminate this distortion, but courts have often thrown out these residency requirements. This all sounds like an externality, and in fact Boadway and Wildasin (1984) have treated these migration costs as an explicit externality. In another paper (1985), I tried to compute how much interstate welfare differentials would be reduced by measures that eliminated the migration inefficiency, finding (to my surprise) that there would still be substantial interstate variation in welfare benefits.

Because of these migration inefficiencies, there are significant costs to leaving welfare entirely to the states with no marginal price incentives, as the United States has decided to do as of 1996. Changes to a foundation grant program for welfare would improve both horizontal equity among welfare recipients and economic efficiency (in the sense that taxpayers could afford to pay their preferred level of support). At the same time, because feelings of taxpayer altruism may be somewhat local, and because local conditions matter in attempts to combine welfare with work, there are also arguments for permitting state initiatives as well and not leaving welfare entirely up to the national government. I tried to show both sides in my 1987 paper.

There are also other aspects of a redistribution policy. In two papers I have tried to discuss the general issue of whether national governments should aid people (as in welfare) or places. One striking finding, shown in my 1992 paper with Laren and Naomi Sealand, is that poor communities have lots of mobility in and out –

they seem like backwaters but in fact small changes in people's moving propensities would lead to large changes in the income composition of the area.

That in turn opens up a new strategy for aiding poor people living in poor areas. Rather than trying to develop the area, which can be costly and has large chances of failure, a strategy of moving poor people to suburban jobs might offer better chances of success, and indeed has been quite successful when it has been tried. The forthcoming paper with Colleen Heflin works out this argument.

Macroeconomics

Musgrave actually called this the stabilization branch of government, but I use the broader term because views about macroeconomics have changed substantially since the 1950s. The traditional closed-economy Keynesian view of macroeconomics was that fiscal policy should stabilize the economy around full employment, period. The modern view, really the open economy view, is that now that economies are generally open, with flexible exchange rates and free mobility of capital, fiscal policy has very weak stabilization effects. National stabilization policy should be the province of monetary policy, not fiscal policy. What fiscal policy should now do is to regulate a country's national saving rate, which determines the composition of its output between consumption and investment and its living standards in the long run. Fiscal policy does have stabilization impacts when exchange rates are fixed, as in Europe, but most of the world has shifted over to flexible rates. Moreover, even when exchange rates are fixed, there are still the old-fashioned objections to countercyclical fiscal policy – fiscal changes are usually made so sluggishly that they may well augment rather than limit business cycles.

In the traditional Keynesian view, stabilization policy should be the province of national, not state or local, governments. Even in this traditional view there was apparently little thought that macro demand or supply shocks might operate differently across different regions of the country – raising output and employment in some areas and lowering these in others. Now that national economies are largely open with flexible rates, it is quite clear that macro shocks can often have these differential effects, and since central government fiscal policy has a limited effect anyway, the time seems right for some new thinking about decentralization strategies.

In a series of papers, one of them unpublished, I have tried to argue that the appropriate way to discharge responsibilities is to let the world economy set real interest rates, have the national government set fiscal policy to determine the nation's saving rate, and then give lower governments the ability to operate some limited fiscal stabilization policies. Since exchange rates are clearly fixed for these lower governments, local fiscal changes should have some effect on local demand. Since shocks are not perfectly correlated across countries, state and local governments can manage their own stabilization policies as they see fit, differently from each other and from the national government.

While this idea has been difficult to sell to economists, there is a sense in which American states have long followed such policies. Many states operate rainy day funds, that build up in good years and run down in bad years, just as if states were following cyclical stabilization policies. Moreover, states can borrow from the national unemployment insurance trust fund in bad years and repay the loans in good years, again to conduct a limited form of stabilization policy.

A final thought

I will not try to sum up the substantive conclusions from these papers, but I will note that these contributions in no sense are only mine. Ten of the 23 papers printed below are co-authored, and each of those co-authors deserves an appropriate share of the credit. More deeply, ideas build on themselves, so thoughts tendered in one paper, and in papers written and discussed elsewhere, get embedded in later papers. I have also had the privilege of working on these issues at government agencies (the Federal Reserve Board, the Office of Economic Opportunity and the Congressional Budget Office), think tanks (the Brookings Institution), and universities (the University of Michigan) alike, and of benefiting from talks and insightful discussions with many valued colleagues at each place. To all, I acknowledge a deep debt of gratitude.

References

Boadway, Robin W. and David E. Wildasin (1984), *Public Sector Economics*, 2nd edition, Little, Brown and Company, New York.

Musgrave, Richard A. and Peggy B. Musgrave (1989), *Public Finance in Theory and Practice*, 5th edition, McGraw-Hill, Maidenhead.

Oates, Wallace E. (1972), *Fiscal Federalism*, Harcourt, Brace, Jovanovich, Inc., New York.

[1]

INTERNATIONAL ECONOMIC REVIEW
Vol. 10, No. 2, June, 1969

STATE AND LOCAL GOVERNMENTS AND THEIR BUDGET CONSTRAINT*

BY EDWARD M. GRAMLICH[1]

THE RECENT SPATE of large-scale econometric models has probed into many previously unexplored corners of the United States economy. But there is one sector still relatively untouched by the model-builders, and strangely enough, it is a sector which today is generating some of the most heated political controversy—that of state and local governments. These governmental institutions are now very much a part of the landscape in the United States, and it behooves econometricians as well as politicians to pay attention to them.

To be sure, there have been many analyses of certain aspects of state and local behavior—both institutional and econometric, on both a micro and a macroeconomic level.[2] Yet none of these analysis have adequately considered the budget constraint under which states and localities operate. These governmental units are genarally required to balance their current operating budgets, and they must pay a default risk premium when they make use of credit markets. As a consequence, one cannot realistically examine state and local expenditure and revenue items in isolation, as previous studies have done. One must rather permit expenditure and revenue policies to be formulated simultaneouly, and allow them to have mutual ramifications.

This study attempts to build such a budget constraint into behavioral descriptions of the components of state and local budgets. The budget constraint turns out to have quite an important bearing on the way state and local budgets respond to external forces such as movements in GNP, interest rates, and federal grants-in-aid. The paper then presents statistical estimate of the budget constraint model. These regression equations were fitted to quarterly national accounts data over the period 1954-64. They explain all state and local budgetary items in the national accounts quite well, and they can either be used by themselves or as part of a broader model of the economy.

1. THE THEORETICAL MODEL

A. *The Current Operating Portion of State and Local Budgets.* One may think of state and local budgetary determination in either of two ways, both

* Manuscript recieved July 11, 1966, revised March 15, 1967.

[1] This paper is part of an economic model-building project sponsored by the Federal Reserve Board, and directed by Albert Ando, Frank de Leeuw, and Franco Modigliani. I would especially like to thank Mr. de Leeuw for his many valuable suggestions. Peter Diamond, Harvey Galper, Patric Hendershott, Paul McGouldrick, James Pierce, Peter Tinsley and Helmut Wendel have also helped me greatly at different stages of the study.

[2] The most comprehensive of these were sponsored by the Brookings Model. See Ando, Brown, and Adams [2]; and Bolton [4].

of which can be solved into similar estimating equations for expenditures and revenues. The first approach proceeds from a utility maximization exercise for the citizens of state and local governments. In addition to the usual public and private good arguments, the state and local utility function also has a term reflecting the statutory constraint against borrowing on current account. The term says that states suffer increasing marginal disutility, the higher their borrowing is relative to their current construction outlays. The planning horizon for construction outlays is longer than one period, and they can be considered as predetermined for the moment.[3]

The one-period constrained utility function can then be written after the fashion of Henderson and Quandt [8].

(1)
$$U = a_1(E - \alpha G) - \frac{a_2}{2}(E - \alpha G)^2 + a_3\alpha G - \frac{a_4}{2}\alpha^2 G^2 + a_5(Y - T)$$
$$- \frac{a_6}{2}(Y - T)^2 + a_7(C - B) - \frac{a_8}{2}(C - B)^2 + \lambda[E + C - G - T - B]$$

where

$E =$ state and local expenditures;
$T =$ state and local taxes;
$C =$ state and local construction outlays;
$B =$ state and local borrowing;
$G =$ federal grants-in-aid;
$Y =$ an income variable, say GNP;
$\alpha =$ the legal matching ratio for matching grants-in-aid;

and where expenditures are decomposed into (a) a term which states are willing to support unassisted by matching federal grants, and (b) a term with different utility parameters which reflect the utility of grant-aided programs. The utility of private goods is expressed by $(Y - T)$. Maximizing with respect to the current policy variables, E, T, and B for a given level of C, G, and Y yields

(2)
$$\frac{\partial U}{\partial E} = a_1 - a_2(E - G) + \lambda = 0 , \qquad \frac{\partial U}{\partial B} = -a_7 + a_8(C - B) - \lambda = 0 ,$$
$$\frac{\partial U}{\partial T} = -a_5 + a_6(Y - T) - \lambda = 0 , \qquad \frac{\partial U}{\partial \lambda} = E + C - G - T - B = 0 .$$

The system can then be transformed into structural equations for expenditure and taxes

(3)
$$E = b_0 + b_1 G + b_2 T$$
$$T = c_0 + c_1 Y + c_2(E - G)$$

---

[3] Throughout the paper construction expenditures are taken as a proxy for state capital investment outlays. A table in [14], page 67, shows that this is a reasonable assumption. The same source, page 150, describes the various statutory restrictions against borrowing on current account.

STATE AND LOCAL BUDGET CONSTRAINTS

where

$$b_0 = \frac{a_1 - a_7}{a_2 + a_8} \ , \qquad b_1 = \frac{a_2\alpha + a_8}{a_2 + a_8} \ , \qquad b_2 = \frac{a_8}{a_2 + a_8} \ ,$$

$$c_0 = \frac{a_7 - a_5}{a_6 + a_8} \ , \qquad c_1 = \frac{a_1}{a_6 + a_8} \ , \qquad c_2 = \frac{a_8}{a_6 + a_8} \ .$$

The utility analysis thus reduces to a scheme where expenditures depend on taxes and taxes on expenditures, with the statutory constraint against current borrowing responsible for the simultaneity. If a_8, the parameter which embodies the statutory constraint, were zero, then b_2 and c_2 would fall out of the analysis. One often overlooked implication of the interdependence of expenditures and revenues, which can be demonstrated by differentiating (3) with respect to either grants or income, is that the state and local response to exogenous variables is more complicated than would be naively recognized. Examples are demonstrated with the regression results in the last section of the paper.

The second derivation of structural equations for expenditures and revenues attempts to reconstruct the budgetary process in a hypothetical state government. By this approach we would have something akin to normal expenditures, which depend on demographic variables, price variables and federal grants; and normal tax revenues which depend on appropriate income variables. Since the state must cover its operating expenditures by taxes and grants-in-aid, it then adjusts both normal expenditures and normal taxes to satisfy the legal constraint.[4]

The budgetary process model can be expressed algebraically as

$$(4) \qquad \begin{aligned} E &= d_0 + d_1 G + d_2[e_0 + e_1 Y - d_0 - (d_1 - 1)G] \\ T &= e_0 + e_1 Y - e_2[e_0 + e_1 Y - d_0 - (d_1 - 1)G] \ . \end{aligned}$$

The parameters d_0 and e_0 include the effects of all variables not yet explicitly considered; d_2 and e_2 are the budget constraint parameters; and the term in brackets is the difference between normal taxes plus grants and normal expenditures. The greater is this term, the greater expenditures eventually will be and the less taxes eventually will be.

This set of equations is then transformed so as to demonstrate the similarity of the two approaches. It can be seen that we reproduce (3) exactly, with

$$(5) \qquad \begin{aligned} b_0 &= \frac{d_0(1 - d_2 - e_2)}{1 - e_2} \ , & b_1 &= \frac{d_1(1 - d_2 - e_2) + d_2}{1 - e_2} \ , & b_2 &= \frac{d_2}{1 - e_2} \ , \\ c_0 &= \frac{e_0(1 - d_2 - e_2)}{1 - d_2} \ , & c_1 &= \frac{e_1(1 - d_2 - e_2)}{1 - d_2} \ , & c_2 &= \frac{e_2}{1 - d_2} \ . \end{aligned}$$

Notice again that if the budget constraint did not exist, $d_2, e_2, b_2,$ and c_2

---

[4] For simplicity we can ignore any explicit dependence of expenditures on income. The system can be transformed into equation (3) regardless of the assumption made on this question.

would be zero.[5]

B. *The Effect of Interest Rates.* Interest rates play a peculiar role in this analysis. Rising rates imply increased borrowing costs, and this substitution effect works against expenditures and in favor of revenues. But aside from public investment projects which can be financed by borrowing, the current budgetary restriction against borrowing is such that one might actually expect the substitution effect to be quite weak. Most states and localities simply are prohibited from borrowing on current account, and interest rates have relatively little influence.

But with every substitution effect there goes an income effect, and it is possible that this one could work in favor of expenditures and against revenues. States and localities are net financial debtors, yet because their asset rates are higher and more volatile than their liability rates, conceivably these governments would actually be richer, spending more and taxing less when rates rise.[6] It is equally conceivable that the income effect, whatever its direction, could dominate the substitution effect and bring about an apparently perverse response to changes in interest rates.

C. *Capital Portion of State and Local Budgets.* Up to now the discussion has centered around the current operating portion of state and local budgets. We turn now to the longer-run motivation for the construction outlays of these institutions.

Again we can assume that there is one component of the capital stock which states are willing to hold without grant assistance from the federal government, and another which is related to these grants. The relationship for the first component is written as a linear function of income (from the reduced form of (3)) and of two cost of capital variables, which in this case are a price ratio and an interest rate.[7]

---

[5] Over the data period covered, the sum of taxes and grants has always been greater than current (net of construction) expenditures. Since the budget constraint parameters are constants and the term in brackets is a variable, the continued surpluses rule out the possibility that $e_2 + d_2 = 1$ (which degenerates the system). It is still possible for $e_2 + d_2 > 1$, which would imply that the term in brackets is consistently negative and that some of the signs of the structural coefficients in (3) could be contrary to those given by the utility analysis. Fortunately the statistical results have rejected this irregularity.

[6] Since the differential between state and local bond yields and other bond yields is due to the tax-exemption of municipalities, state and local liability rates should be some proportion of their asset rates, with the factor of proportion depending upon federal income tax rates. Thus as interest rates rise so will the absolute spread, and even though states and localities are net financial debtors (in 1964 financial liabilities were $96.7 billion and assets $61.9 billion), it is conceivable that earnings on financial assets may increase more than payments on liabilities. This is all the more true because assets are generally more short-term than liabilities.

[7] State and local structures are not taxed and are virtually unsalable, thus eliminating the possibility of capital losses. Jorgenson's formula [10] for the real user cost

(*Continued on next page*)

STATE AND LOCAL BUDGET CONSTRAINTS

$$(6) \qquad \frac{K^*}{P} = g_0 + g_1 \sum_{i=0}^{n} w_i \left(\frac{Y}{P}\right)_{-i} + g_2 \sum_{j=0}^{n} w_j \left(\frac{P_s}{P}\right)_{-j} + g_3 \sum_{e=0}^{n} w_e r_{-e}$$

where K^* is the desired stock independent of grants, P and P_s are price levels for total output and state capital structures respectively, r is some interest rate, the constant reflects demographic forces, and the unspecified lagged weighting patterns reflect the long planning horizon for structures.

Federal grants are statutorily related not to the stock of capital but to the level of construction expenditures. Adding this motivation for construction to the identity that grant-independent construction equals net investment plus replacement gives

$$(7) \qquad \frac{C}{P} = \frac{\Delta K}{P} + \delta \frac{K_{-1}}{P} + g_4 \frac{G}{P}$$

and this can be combined with a stock adjustment relationship for the independent component of state capital

$$(8) \qquad \frac{C}{P} = \beta \frac{K^*}{P} + (\delta - \beta) \frac{K_{-1}}{P} + g_4 \frac{G}{P}$$

where $\Delta K = \beta(K^* - K_{-1})$.[8]

There is relatively little information available on the value of state and local capital. Goldsmith and Lipsey [6] have compiled an annual series extending through 1958, but this series would have to be interpolated and extrapolated to generate the required quarterly and post-1958 data. In addition, of course, there are well-known autocorrelation problems with lagged stock models of this sort. It seems preferable to substitute successively for (8) out of the stock adjustment expression to yield

$$(9) \qquad \frac{C}{P} = \beta \frac{K^*}{P} + (\delta - \beta) \beta \sum_{i=0}^{\infty} (1 - \beta)^i \left(\frac{K^*}{P}\right)_{-i-1} + g_4 \frac{G}{P} .$$

(9) relates construction expenditures to the *level* of current and past determinants of K^* and to the *level* of current grants.[9] The lag in (9) decays exponentially, but it must be combined with the unspecified lag in (6) to give unknown lag patterns for the effect of the determinants of K^* on state and local construction. These lags should then be estimated by a technique which

---

of these structures would thus reduce to $(\delta + r)p_s/p$, with δ a difficult-to-observe constant depreciation rate. Equation (6) takes a linear approximation to Jorgenson's user cost expression. One justification for this simplification is that there is no published price index for state and local structures alone, only for wage and salary dominated total state purchases. It may then be wiser not to let the price ratio interact multiplicatively with the other variables.

[8] This formulation assumes that the replacement of grant-aided capital can be safely ignored.

[9] Construction could also be related to *changes* and *levels* in K^* by rearranging the stock adjustment expression as $K = \beta K^* + (1 - \beta)K_{-1}$, and inserting the first difference of this into (7). But this commonly used procedure contains more independent variables than (8), and is not ideally suited to the situation where the lagged stock must be solved out of the equation.

imposes no *a priori* restrictions on the form of the lag.

A related question concerns the effect of construction expenditures on the tax revenue equations. The budget constraint discussed above applies only to the current portion of state and local budgets, and there is both a theoretical and an institutional reason for the exclusion of construction outlays from the $(E - G)$ variable in (3). The theoretical reason is that public investments most likely create the expectation of higher future incomes, taxes, and user charges, thus requiring less current tax finance.[10] The institutional reason is that while states generally must finance current expenditures by taxation, they are not forced to finance construction in such a manner. At the same time, both considerations imply that current construction outlays would have some influence on revenues.

The best way to handle this problem is to treat as separate independent variables in the tax regressions $E - (1 - \mu)G$ and $C - \mu G$, where μ is the proportion of matching federal grants which states receive by making construction outlays. But it is very difficult to measure the parameter μ even on an annual basis, to say nothing of making quarterly interpolations. I have experimented with calculating μ from the regression results for expenditures, but this procedure generally gave no better results than the idea which was eventually adopted of using $(E + C - G)$ with an expected positive sign and $C/(E + C)$ with an expected negative sign as independent variables in the tax equations.[11]

D. *Dynamics of the Revenue Equations.* A final matter pertains to the dynamics of the revenue equations. My procedure of relating the level of tax revenues directly to expenditures on a quarterly basis assumes a very flexible and frequent adjustment of state and local tax rates. It may be objected that this technique would not predict as well as the exogenous-rate scheme used by Ando, Brown, and Adams [2] if in fact tax rates really are fixed in the short run. It is also possible that my technique may magnify the influence of common trends in tax revenues and bases, and overstate revenue elasticities with respect to their bases.

There are two answers to this objection, one conceptual and one statistical. On conceptual grounds, Table 1 shows that the portion of state and local revenues where one can assume a fixed rate in the short run even for one state is really quite small—only personal income taxes, corporate taxes, and sales taxes (accounting for about 35 percent of total revenue in 1964). All other sources of revenue are generated by a variety of miscellaneous taxes, nontaxes, fees, and tolls where the rate is merely a detail which is set so as

---

[10] See Phelps [12, (55)].

[11] This discussion introduces an additional complexity into the previous budget constraint analysis. The borrowing constraint in (1) should really be written as $C - \mu G - B$, and the adjustment variable in (4) as $[e_0 + e_1 Y - d_0 - d_1 G + (1 - \mu)G]$. The net expenditure variable in the structural equation for taxes (equation (3)) is then $[E - (1 - \mu)G]$, and the parameter b_1 is changed to:

$$\frac{a_2 \alpha + a_8 (1 - \mu)}{a_2 + a_8} = \frac{d_1 (1 - d_2 - e_2) + d_2 (1 - \mu)}{1 - d_2} .$$

TABLE 1

TREATMENT OF STATE AND LOCAL BUDGETS IN THE
NATIONAL ACCOUNTS, 1964

(All figures in billions of current dollars)

Items treated as expenditures		Items treated as revenues	
1. Construction expenditures	16.4	7. Personal taxes	10.6
2. Other purchases	11.0	a. Income taxes	(4.0)
3. Net compensation of employees	31.6	b. Other	(6.6)
		8. Indirect business taxes	41.9
a. Gross compensation of employees	(35.7)	a. Sales taxes	(14.2)
b. *Less*: Social insurance contributions[2]	(4.1)	b. Property taxes	(21.6)
		c. Other	(6.1)
4. Transfer payments	6.5	9. Corporate taxes	1.6
5. Net interest payments	0.8	10. Surplus of government enterprises[3]	3.1
6. *Less*: Federal grants[1]	10.4	Total net revenues	57.2
Total net expenditures	55.9	Budgetary surplus	1.4

[1] Assumed to be exogenous to states.

[2] Treated in national accounts as a revenue but here treated as a deduction from expenditures.

[3] Treated in national accounts as a deduction from expenditures but here treated as a revenue.

to bring in the required amount of revenue. In such cases my technique of short-circuiting the rate is more appropriate.

Another aspect of the conceptual answer concerns the aggregation problem. While it is true that for one state, government tax rates are relatively fixed in the short run, the aggregate state and local sector is composed of thousands of such governments. At any one time it seems likely that many states and localities would be changing their rates in response to factors such as expenditure needs, and aggregating these individual units would then introduce a great deal of short-run flexibility into the tax rates. Thus, even for income and sales taxes it may be more appropriate to work directly in terms of revenue levels rather than going through the intermediate step. Putting this another way, even if one did find that Ando-tpye equations predicted certain types of revenues better, one would still have to explain the tax rates, which are by no means exogenous in the short run for the aggregate state and local sector.

The final choice between these two techniques hinges on statistical grounds. Below I attempt to show that my equations do stand any statistical comparisons very well. Even without such crutches as lagged dependent variables and anticipations data, the revenue equations predict almost perfectly in the short run; and the revenue base elasticities are, if anything, below those calculated by Ando, *et al.*

E. M. GRAMLICH

2.   THE NATIONAL ACCOUNTS BUDGET

The model presented in this paper is designed to deal with state and local behavior as recorded by the national accounts.   This section details the treatment of each budgetary item in the accounts; whether it has been treated as an expenditure, a revenue, or as an item determined entirely outside the budget constraint formulation.   Table 1 gives illustrative information for 1964 (see [15, (68)]).

Federal grants are taken as exogenous to state and local governments. This assumption does a slight disservice to reality because states do have some leeway in influencing the timing and the level of grants within the stipulations laid down by the federal government.   In principle it would be better to take some proxy for the maximum amount the states could receive in any period as exogenous.   But such a variable is not compiled, even for many of the individual grant programs, and it could only be constructed with great difficulty and a large error of measurement.   I have used the simpler approach of assuming grants exogenous as a matter of convenience—with the hope that these grants are such a bonanza to states that the simultaneous eqution bias is not serious.[12]

State and local contributions for social insurance consist almost entirely of taxes on their own employees for pension and sickness programs.   These are merely intra-governmental transactions, and one can equally well describe the behavior of states and localities in terms of net compensation of employees (total compensation less social insurance taxes) as its gross counterpart.   I have thus considered net compensation as the variable to be explained, and have treated social insurance contributions as a deduction from gross expenditures rather than as an independent revenue item.[13]

The surpluses of state and local governmental enterprises are mainly the profits of governmentally sponsored public utilities and turnpike authorities. The rates and tolls determining these profits can be manipulated as easily as can the various tax rates and license fees implicitly represented within other items on the revenue side of the ledger.   For this reason I have considered surpluses of government enterprises to be a positive revenue item rather than the negative expenditure which it is called in the national accounts.

A final item determined outside of the budget constraint formulation is interest payments.   These payments are better thought of as a fixed cost than as item under the purview of current discretionary policy.   They are

[12] Theoretically one could eliminate this bias by the use of a simultaneous estimation technique.   But even here the problem is not solved because we would still need some representation of the true exogenous force in grants-in-aid, and this we do not have.

[13] One would still have to explain social insurance contributions (SIC) and gross compensation in order to predict GNP.   The following quarterly 1954-64 equation does that

$$\text{SIC} = 0.1 + 0.1110 \text{ (Net Compensation Employees + SIC)}$$
$$(0.0009)$$

$$\bar{R}^2 = 0.997 \, , \quad S.E. = \text{Zero} \, , \quad D.W. = 1.009 \, .$$

positively related to market rates on state and local liabilities and negatively related to market asset rates, with the precise form of the relationship being demonstrated below.[14]

The regression uses the variables

I = state and local interest payments;

D = start-of-quarter state financial debt, i.e., financial liabilities less financial assets from the Flow of Funds accounts;[15]

r_s = Moody's state and local bond interest rate (a liability rate);

r_b = three-month U.S. bill rate (an asset rate);

r_c = Moody's corporate bond rate (an asset rate);

R = ruling average interest rate, defined as I/D.

The estimated relationship for quarterly 1954-64 data is:

$$100 \times \frac{\Delta I}{D_{-1}} = \underset{(0.129)}{0.391\Delta R} + \underset{(0.008)}{0.027r_s} + \underset{(0.013)}{0.051(r_s - r_b)} + \underset{(0.027)}{0.075(r_s - r_c)}$$

$$\bar{R}^2 = 0.676, \quad S.E. = 1 \times 10^{-4}(\text{zero at mean } D_{-1}), \quad D.W. = 0.638 \ .$$

The interest rates have been entered in a way intending to minimize multicollinearity. Their coefficients all have the expected sign.

[14] By identity we know that $I = RD$ and that $\Delta I = R\Delta D + D_{-1}\Delta R$. The first term stands for financing the new debt at the old average rate, and the second term for refinancing the old debt. But the average rate is not the observed market rate on new obligations, and we want to explain the relationship between the two rates. Substituting the overall market rate r into the above difference gives the approximation

$$\Delta I = r\Delta D + \gamma D_{-1}\Delta R + u$$

or

$$\frac{\Delta I}{D_{-1}} = r\frac{\Delta D}{D_{-1}} + \gamma\Delta R + \frac{u}{D_{-1}}$$

where $\gamma \neq 1$ and the error term are introduced to correct for the fact that we now have a partly marginal, partly average expression. The true expression in marginal rate terms depends in a complicated way on the amount marginal rates have changed in the past and the proportion of debt which is being refinanced at new rates.

The equation in the text then makes two modifications:

(a) Obviously there is not one true marginal interest rate, but rather a complex of them varying in importance with the importance of different liabilities and assets in state and local balance sheets. I have chosen the three most important entries, and have estimated separate coefficients for the relevant rates.

(b) Quarterly values of D are generated from annual benchmarks by a polynomial interpolation technique. In order to minimize the damage that any inaccuracies could do to the regression, I have let the regression coefficients for the market rates incorporate the near constant $\Delta D/D_{-1}$.

[15] The debt variable is net credit market liabilities less time deposits (see [13], page 1618, line 17 less line 12 for states and localities).

3. STATISTICAL ESTIMATES—EXPENDITURES

The equations for expenditures were estimated by solving for the reduced form of (3), and relating expenditures directly to grants-in-aid, income, and interest rates. This indirect least-squares technique is an appropriate correction for simultaneity because there is only one exogenous variable which appears in the structural equations for revenues but not for expenditures. The expenditure equations then are exactly identified.[16]

However, there are variables which are assumed to affect expenditures but not revenues. The first is prices, both for state and local purchases and for total output (the GNP deflator). These prices are entered in a manner similar to that already described in the section dealing with construction expenditures, and they introduce a clearing mechanism into the markets where states and localities make their purchases. To allow for the possiblity that these markets are not always cleared, the Federal Reserve Board capacity utilization rate was also tested.

The second group of variables added to the expenditure equations are those representing demographic forces. The equations for purchases of goods and services, which are dominated by education, use both the total population and the number of young people (aged one to twenty). The transfer equations, which are dominated by relief payments to aged, needy, dependent children, and others, use total population and the number of people not gainfully employed.

It has already been argued that the lag pattern in the expenditure equations can not be predicted *a priori*. The ideal estimation technique for such a situation is that developed by Shirley Almon [1], and this was used. It was assumed that the weights lie along a third degree polynomial with only the tail-end interpolation point fixed at zero.[17] In every case the equation presented is the one with the shortest lag which gives approximately the highest coefficient of determination. In most cases, aside from construction, the lag was found to be sufficiently short that a simple inclusion of the current level and one or two past changes for the explantory variables worked just as well as the Almon technique[18]—(for which the minimum allowable lag is

---

[16] In this discussion the endogenous variables are state and local expenditures and revenues. Everything else is exogenous. It is, of course, true that a quarterly model of the entire economy would treat income and interest rates as endogenous, but I have broken off the state and local sector from the rest of the larger model. Expanding on an analysis in Johnston [9, (231)], one can express the simultaneous bias in terms of the coefficients giving rise to this bias and the size of equation errors and covariances relative to the variances and covariances of the external variables. Inserting values calculated from preliminary OLS trials, I found that the variances of income and interest rates were so large relative to the errors in these equations that the bias in the coefficients appeared to be negligible.

[17] The precedent for this is Modigliani and Sutch [11].

[18] When the lags are estimated by a level and a change, the lag coefficients can be derived from the transformation,

(*Continued on next page*)

four periods under the conditions specified above).

Two final statistical matters are worthy of mention. The first is that the income variable is meant to approximate state and local income, which I defined as GNP less federal taxes plus federal domestic transfers, interest and subsidies. This variable makes more sense in the utility analysis above. Secondly, the equations presented use the long-term U.S. bond rate instead of the state and local rate as the interest rate variable. I tried both rates, and while they gave quite similar results, the U.S. rate slightly improves the explanatory power of the equations. This indicates that the U.S. rate may give a more realistic indication of the cost of borrowing, even for state and local governments, than does the state and local rate.

The equations were estimated by dividing all dollar flow variables by population and the GNP deflator, and using price and population ratios. These transformations do not completely eliminate the dimension problem, but they do help. Ignoring lags and redefining a_i and b_i, we have regression equations of the form

$$\frac{\text{Purch}}{NP} = a_0 + a_1 \frac{G}{NP} + a_2 \frac{Y}{NP} + a_3 r + a_4 \frac{Ps}{P} + a_5 \frac{N_Y}{N} + a_6 X$$

$$\frac{\text{Transf}}{NP} = b_0 + b_1 \frac{G}{NP} + b_2 \frac{Y}{NP} + b_3 r + b_5 \frac{N_E}{N}.$$

In addition to the variables already defined, we have[19]

N = total population;

N_Y = number of people aged one to twenty;

N_E = employed labor force;

X = FRB aggregate capacity utilization rate;

and we expect a_1, a_2, a_5, b_1 and b_2 to be positive; a_3 on construction, a_6 and b_5 to be negative; and a_3 on current expenditures, a_4, and b_3 to go either way. The coefficient a_4 measures the partial derivative of money purchases with respect to the state and local price level, and it will be positive if states' demand for goods is inelastic.

The quarterly equations for the period 1954–64 are presented in Table 2. I have only presented the final equations, denoting by "n.s." variables which did not satisfy sign or significance tests in previous trials of the equations. The constants, standard errors, and coefficients for interest rates, price and

---

$$m_1 x + m_2 \Delta x + m_3 \Delta x_{-1} = (m_1 + m_2)x + (m_3 - m_2)x_{-1} - m_3 x_{-2}.$$

m_1 is the steady state coefficient, and if the lag is of the declining weight pattern, $0 > m_3 > m_2$.

[19] All variables are taken from standard statistical sources—the *Survery of Current Business* for national accounts information; the *Federal Reserve Bulletin* for interest rates; and the *President's Economic Report* for quarterly demographic information. Charles Waite of the OBE has generously made available to me unpublished quarterly breakdowns of state and local purchases by construction, compensation of employees, and other purchases.

TABLE 2

REGRESSION EQUATIONS FOR STATE AND LOCAL EXPENDITURES, QUARTERLY OBSERVATIONS, 1954-64

Dependent variable	Con-stant	$\frac{G}{NP}$	$\Delta\left(\frac{G}{NP}\right)$ $\Delta_{-1}\left(\frac{G}{NP}\right)$	$\frac{Y}{NP}$	$\Delta\frac{Y}{NP}$	r	Δr	$\frac{P_s}{P}$	$\Delta\frac{P_s}{P}$	$\frac{N_Y}{N}$	$\frac{N_E}{N}$	K	R^2	S.E.	D.W.
1. (Construction)/NP[1]	-132.6	0.303 (0.085)	n.s.	0.007 (0.002)	—	-11.78 (3.00)	—	116.67 (43.62)	n.s.	257.36 (169.47)	—	n.s.	0.949	1.36	1.778
2. (Other Pur.)/NP	-142.6	0.368 (0.078)	-0.255 (0.091)	0.012 (0.006)	n.s.	-5.28 (1.35)	-1.74 (1.46)	-44.92 (28.87)	n.s.	544.90 (125.96)	—	n.s.	0.971	1.18	1.248
3. (Net Comp. Emp.)/NP[2]	-282.2	0.451 (0.099)	-0.206 (0.122)	0.025 (0.007)	0.020 (0.014)	-0.23 (0.10)	—	203.27 (38.71)	-69.77 (52.84)	311.80 (170.58)	—	n.s.	0.995	1.47	1.280
4. (Transfers)/NP	51.8	-0.002 (0.027)	n.s.	0.010 (0.001)	n.s.	0.29 (0.24)	-1.00 (0.47)	—	—	—	-128.48 (15.40)	—	0.974	0.38	1.470
5. (Total Disc. Exp.)/NP[3]	-505.6	1.120	-0.255	0.054	0.020	-17.00	-2.74	275.02	-69.77	1,115.06	-128.48	—	—	—	—

Note: Standard errors below coefficients. All variables tested and found insignificant are excluded from the final equations and denoted by "n.s." The interest rate and income variables were included in Almon form, and only the steady state coefficients and approximate standard errors thereof are reported. The lags for these variables are:

	r	Y/NP
$t-1$	-0.25	0.001
$t-2$	-0.38	-0.007
$t-3$	-0.61	-0.011
$t-4$	-0.89	-0.010
$t-5$	-1.18	-0.007
$t-6$	-1.44	-0.002
$t-7$	-1.62	0.003
$t-8$	-1.69	0.008
$t-9$	-1.60	0.011
$t-10$	-1.32	0.012
	-0.80	0.008

[1] The interest rate and income variables were included in Almon form, and only the steady state coefficients and approximate standard errors thereof are reported. The lags for these variables are:

[2] The interest rate is in Almon form. Its lag is:

t	-5.73
$t-1$	-2.18
$t-2$	2.77
$t-3$	4.90

[3] The sum of rows one through four.

population ratios can be multiplied by 0.1788, the mean of the deflation factor, to convert them to billions of current dollars. Table 2 presents only the steady state values for the Almon terms, consigning the individual period values to footnotes in the Table.

The equations explain expenditures very well. The average adjusted coefficient of determination is over 0.97, and the average standard error is only about $0.2 billion. The Durbin-Watson ratios are also encouragingly high for items which might seem to be as autocorrelated as state and local expenditures.

According to the ideas proposed above, we expect the budget constraint (embodied in the income variable) to operate more strongly on the current expenditure and transfer programs, and less strongly on construction. We also expect interest rates to have a strong negative influence on construction and not much of an influence on anything else. Table 4 (on page 180), which summarizes information on some of the important state elasticities (all calculated at the point of means) in fact gives these results.

The statistical estimates also verify our earlier ideas about lags. Construction expenditures do indeed show a long lag in their response to income and interest rates, and a nonexistent lag in their response to federal grants.[20] It is reassuring that exactly the same search for the lag which maximizes the explanatory power found much shorter lags for the current varieties of expenditures.

The equation for transfer payments creates the impression that states and localities treat these welfare payments very much like fixed costs. Payments depend on the number of people needing them, but on little else. I have left grants-in-aid in the regression despite its unimpressive coefficient in order to capture the full state and local response to federal grants. Simply excluding grants wherever they do not get a positive coefficient would give a biased picture of the sensitivity of total expenditures to grants.

Even though about forty percent of federal grants-in-aid have been for transfer-oriented programs, and even though all grants are conditional on matching state funds, the equation says that states have not increased their transfer payments at all as a result of the increase in federal grants. They have simply taken federal public assistance money, added about one-third more to satisfy the matching requirement, and then reduced other transfer payments by four-thirds of the federal grant. The only effect that these grants have had on states is that they have increased other types of purchases (hopefully not for bureaucrats to process the grants). Of course, this is not to say that grants are a waste of money; it is perhaps desirable that this money be spent in other areas. But it is to say that the amount and stringency of federal regulations on federal grants may not be so very important after all. The states seem to be spending this money as they will almost regardless of how the federal Government says it should be spent.[21]

---

[20] There should also be a long-lagged response to prices and population, but at least the former lag could not be discerned. The population variable was such a smooth trend that the Almon test was not attempted.

4. STATISTICAL ESTIMATES—REVENUES

Since the revenue equations in (3) do not contain some of the exogenous variables in the expenditure equations, these revenue expressions are over-identified. In these cases indirect estimation of the reduced form relation-ship would be an inefficient means of eliminating simultaneity, and (3) was instead estimated directly by two-stage least-squares. The regression equations for state and local expenditures described in the previous section are determined wholly by variables exogenous to the state and local model, and the expenditure predictions given by these equations can be used as the second-stage instrumental variables. Thus in addition to being final equations in their own right, the expenditure equations also represent the first stage of the two-stage relationship for revenues.[22]

The revenue equations were also modified somewhat before estimation. In the first place, both personal taxes and corporate taxes are more closely related to specific portions of income in the legal tax base than to the over-all total. In these two equations income is divided into two terms, one of which is the tax base and the other is income less the tax base. According to the logic of the budget constraint, personal and corporate taxes should bear a negative relationship to income less the tax base. The higher is nontaxable income, the more will indirect taxes increase to meet a given level of expenditures and interest rates, and the less must personal and corporate taxes be increased.

The revenue relationships are actually determined in money terms, and it is sensible to fit them this way. But in the case of both personal taxes and indirect taxes, population would be expected to influence revenues over and above its influence on expenditures (the latter because population has an in-dependent influence on consumption and excise tax revenues, and property values and property tax revenues). In these two instances the equation was expressed in income per capita terms.

The lags in the revenue equations were all quite short, and were handled with a level and a change of the appropriate variable (see footnote 18). Again ignoring lags, we have the following regression equations for tax revenues:

$$\text{Pers. Tx.} \over N = c_0 + c_1 \frac{TPY}{N} + c_2 \frac{(\hat{E} + \hat{C} - G)}{N} + c_3 \frac{\hat{C}}{\hat{E} + \hat{C}} + c_4 r + c_5 \frac{Y - TPY}{N}$$

$$\text{Ind. Tx.} \over N = d_0 + d_1 \frac{Y}{N} + d_2 \frac{(\hat{E} + \hat{C} - G)}{N} + d_3 \frac{\hat{C}}{\hat{E} + \hat{C}} + d_4 r$$

$$\text{Corp. Tx.} = e_0 + e_1 CP + e_2(\hat{E} + \hat{C} + G) + e_3 \frac{\hat{C}}{\hat{E} + \hat{C}} + e_4 r + e_5(Y - CP)$$

$$\text{Surp. G.E.} = f_0 + f_1 Y + f_2(\hat{E} + \hat{C} - G) + f_3 \frac{\hat{C}}{\hat{E} + \hat{C}} + f_4 r \,.$$

[21] These remarks apply only to the effect of grants on the composition of state expenditures, That the matching provisions of grants are still important in affect-ing the total is demonstrated below.

[22] This procedure is the logical way to implement the recommendations of Fisher [5]. It is as if we have rewritten the expenditure relationships in terms of their reduced form, and had considered these the new structural relationships for expendi-tures.

The new variables are

TYP = taxable personal income (NIA personal income less other labor income transfer payments plus qersonal social insurance cost);

CP = corporate profits;

$\hat{E}$ = total state and local nonconstruction expenditures predicted by regressions in Table 2;

$\hat{C}$ = construction expenditures predicted by the regression in Table 2.

All coefficients with subscripts one and two are expected to be positive, all with subscripts three and five to be negative, and those with subscript four to be ambiguous with respect to sign.

The results of these estimations are in Table 3. The mean inflation factor for the equations in per capita terms is 0.1774. Here the average $\bar{R}^2$ is 0.99 and the average standard error is only about $0.1 billion. The Durbin-Watson ratios are not quite as high as before.

All signs are as expected, with the possible exception of those for interest rates. These have a slight negative elasticity in the revenue equations (as if the income effect outweighs the substitution effect), in contrast to the similar slight negative elasticity for non-construction expenditures (as if the substitution effect dominates). But neither of these elasticities is very large, and it may not be unreasonable for the income and substitution effects to work with differing intensities on different budgetary items.

Table 4 also compares revenue elasticities calculated from Table 3 with those presented by Ando, *et al.* As was mentioned above, my base elasticities are about the same as theirs, probably because the expenditure variable serves to eliminate the trend from the tax base coefficients. And as for prediction, even though the Ando equations do predict well, they do not explain as high a proportion of the variance of the dependent variable as do the regressions in Table 3 (in addition to the fact that the Brookings model does not endogenize tax rates). Thus on statistical as well as conceptual grounds one should not be reluctant to use the direct revenue level approach.

5. TESTS AND SIMULATIONS OF THE REGRESSION RESULTS

The regression results of Tables 2 and 3 can then be used to test the budget constraint hypotheses proposed above. Using steady state coefficients, mean values of the deflators, construction ratio, and tax base income shares, and plugging these estimates into equations (3), (4), (5), and footnote 11 gives

$$\alpha = 0.8463, \qquad 0.07\,a_8 \leq a_6 \leq 0.42\,a_8 \text{[23]}, \qquad d_2 = 0.226,$$
$$1 - \mu = 0.7133, \qquad d_1 = 0.846, \qquad e_2 = 0.544,$$
$$a_2 = 1.021\,a_8, \qquad e_1 = 0.210, \qquad d_2 + e_2 = 0.770.$$

[23] The utility function is over-determined with respect to the $a_6 - a_8$ ratio. It can be calculated with either c_1 or c_2. Hopefully the two estimates bracket the real parameter.

TABLE 3

REGRESSION EQUATIONS FOR STATE AND LOCAL REVENUES, QUARTERLY, 1954-64

Dependent variable	Constant	$\frac{Y}{N}$	$\Delta\frac{Y}{N}$	$\frac{TPY}{N}$	$\Delta\frac{TPY}{N}$	$\frac{Y-TPY}{N}$	$\frac{\hat{E}+\hat{C}-G}{N}$	$\Delta\frac{(\hat{E}+\hat{C}-G)}{N}$	$\frac{\hat{C}}{\hat{E}+\hat{C}}$	r	$\bar{R}^2$	S.E.	D.W.
Per capita terms:													
1. Pers. Tx. $\frac{}{N}$	-2.0	—	—	0.027 (0.004)	-0.010 (0.007)	n.s.	0.098 (0.019)	-0.092 (0.046)	-128.60 (13.57)	-1.64 (0.43)	0.996	0.69	1.479
2. Ind. Tx. $\frac{}{N}$	57.5	0.035 (0.007)	-0.021 (0.012)	—	—	—	0.487 (0.053)	-0.220 (0.118)	-269.58 (33.22)	-2.48 (1.05)	0.997	1.68	0.905

Dependent variable	Constant	Y	ΔY	CP	ΔCP	$Y-CP$	$\hat{E}+\hat{C}-G$	$\Delta(\hat{E}+\hat{C}-G)$	$\frac{\hat{C}}{\hat{E}+\hat{C}}$	r	$\bar{R}^2$	S.E.	D.W.
Undeflated:													
3. Corp. Tx.	1.3	—	—	0.018 (0.002)	0.005 (0.003)	-0.006 (0.002)	0.050 (0.014)	-0.040 (0.017)	-3.54 (0.95)	0.11 (0.03)	0.975	0.04	1.637
4. Surp. Govt. Ent.	0.2	0.009 (0.001)	-0.006 (0.003)	—	—	—	-0.013 (0.010)	n.s.	-3.78 (1.06)	-0.10 (0.03)	0.991	0.05	1.005

Note: Standard errors below coefficients. All variables tested and found insignificant are excluded from the final equations and denoted by "n.s."

These calculations tell a rather remarkable story: while the parameter reflecting the diminishing marginal utility of expenditures is 1.02 times the parameter reflecting the increasing marginal disutility of borrowing, the parameter representing the increasing marginal disutility of taxes is only from 0.07 to 0.42 of the borrowing parameter. In other words, on the margin there is a very strong political or legal restriction against current borrowing almost as strong as the feeling against cutting expenditures, and apparently much stronger than the feeling against higher taxes.

The power of the budget constraint is also apparent in the adjustment model.

To begin with, $d_2 + e_2$ is less than one and we do not get the perversity mentioned in footnote 5. The bracketed term in equation (4) is consistently positive, but the budget constraint is strong enough that 77 percent of this "luxury surplus" is distributed, mainly in the form of tax reductions. In both models, then, taxes seem to be the residual decision.

We can also use the regression results to examine the composite state and local response to federal grants, income, and interest rates. Again, the calculations use steady state responses and mean values.

Including construction, states have a marginal propensity to spend matching grants of 1.120, with this additional spending having almost no effect on the construction ratio. The fact that spending has increased more than grants stimulates increased revenues in the amount of 0.073 units. Thus while matching grants do stimulate states' spending, they also increase revenues, and the latter dampens the GNP multiplier for grants. The ultimate reaction is a composite of the pure expenditure multiplier and the balanced budget multiplier.

It is interesting to compare this response with the response to states to the unconditional bloc grants proposed by Walter Heller [7]. Bloc grants do not require matching expenditures, and they would work through the b_2 parameter rather than b_1 in equation (3).[24] They would increase current and capital expenditures directly by 0.280 units (as opposed to 1.120 for matching grants), slightly decrease the construction ratio, and decrease taxes by 0.488 units (as opposed to increase of 0.073 units). Thus there would be a sizeable reduction in the aggregate "fiscal effort" of states and localities (taxes over GNP) associated with bloc grants—especially in comparison with the present grant program. The most damaging aspect of bloc grants is that only $0.280 + 0.488 = 0.768$ units are returned to the economy in the form of higher expenditures and/or lower taxes (as opposed to $1.120 - 0.73 = 1.047$ units for matching grants). While the Heller program may be desirable on other grounds, therefore, these results imply that on purely fiscal grounds untied grants do not appear to be nearly as stimulative as the present matching variety.

[24] This result is derived by writing the utility function in (1) without the term in αG and proceeding as before. Rather than decomposing expenditures into a term more or less forced on states, untied grants simply enter the budget identity as a non-tax source of funds. As such, they can be used either for public or private consumption.

180   E. M. GRAMLICH

TABLE 4

IMPORTANT PARTIAL ELASTICITIES FOR EXPENDITURES AND REVENUES

Budgetary item	Point of means steady state elasticity with respect to:				
	Income	Tax base		Interest rates	Prices[a]
		This study	Ando, *et al.*[b]		
1. Construction	0.242	—	—	−0.621	0.756
2. Other purchases	0.714	—	—	−0.458	−2.112
3. Net compesation of employees	0.505	—	—	−0.007	0.771
(Total purchases)	0.464	—	—	−0.273	0.241
4. Transfers	0.886	—	—	0.039	—
(Total expenditures)	0.502	—	—	−0.237	—
5. Personal taxes	—	1.444	1.679[c]	−0.155	—
6. Indirect taxes	—	0.493	n.a.	−0.053	—
7. Corporate taxes	—	0.745	0.693	0.328	—
8. Surplus of government enterprises)	—	1.824	n.a.	−0.171	—
• (Total revenues)	—	0.664[d]	n.a.	−0.065	—

[a] The price elasticity of demand is defined as

$$\frac{\partial(E/P)P}{\partial P(E/P)} = \left(\frac{P}{E}\right)\left(\frac{\partial E}{\partial P}\right) - 1 .$$

For normal goods it would lie in the range 0 (infinitely inelastic) to $-\infty$ (infinitely elastic). The positive elasticities given here indicate that demand is extremely inelastic.

[b] The $\bar{R}^2$ for Ando's personal and corporate tax equations are 0.95 and 0.97 respectively, both below those shown in Table 3.

[c] A more recent estimate used in the Ando-Goldfeld model [3].

[d] Using total income as a base, and assuming that the marginal income distribution among tax bases is the same as the average for the entire period.

The automatically stabilizing properties of state and local budgets can be calculated in the same way. A rise in income increases current and construction expenditures by 0.054 units, with a slight decrease in the construction ratio. Revenues rise directly because of income and indirectly because of expenditures by 0.098 units. The coefficient of automatic stability, $\partial(T - E - C)/\partial Y$ is then 0.042. That this is positive implies that states do stabilize the economy, but that the stabilizing effect is rather slight. Since the income variable used here is net of federal withdrawals, we can expect the same response with respect to a cut in federal taxes or a rise in transfer payments.

A one percentage point decrease in the U.S. bond rate will eventually increase state spending by $3.03 billion at mean values of the variables. Most of the increase is in construction, and the monetary change will raise the construction ratio by 0.0192 units, a large amount considering the dimension of this variable. The net effect of the direct and indirect impacts on revenues is an increase of $ 2.20 billion, and an increase in the deficit of $ 0.83 billion. The revenue response in this case is substantially less than the spending response because construction outlays are largely insulated from the budget constraint. In addition, of course, the long lag in the construction equation implies that this response will be slower than the fairly rapid response to grants and income.

4. CONCLUSION

Taken as a body, the system of equations for state and local budgets is quite satisfactory. All equations explain a high proportion of the variance of the budgetary items. and most coefficients are very reasonable. These criteria are by no means conclusive, and it is possible that a different theoretical framework would reach different findings. But it is at least interesting that this framework, which has two (and possibly more) justifications, does give such reasonable answers.

It is especially noteworthy that the budget constraint comes through so strongly. This constraint conforms with intuitive notions about how the budgetary process works in lower levels of governments, it is quite important statistically, and it profoundly alters the state and local response to external shocks. Whatever form it takes, one can ill-afford to ignore it in future studies of this sector.

Federal Reserve Board, U.S.A.

REFERENCES

[1] ALMON, SHIRLEY, "The Distribted Lag between Capital Appropriations and Expenditures," *Econometrica*, XXXIII (January, 1965).

[2] ANDO, ALBERT, E. CARY BROWN, and EARL W. ADAMS, "Government Revenues and Expenditures," in J. Duesenberry, *et al.*, eds., *The Brookings Quarterly Econometric Model of the United States* (Amsterdam: North-Holland Publishing Co., 1965).

[3] ANDO, ALBERT and STEPHEN M. GOLDFELD, "An Econometric Model for Stabilization Policies," in A. Ando, *et al.*, eds., *Essays in Stabilization Policies* (Washington: The Brookings Institution, 1968).

[4] BOLTON, ROGER E., "Predictive Models for State and Local Government Purchases," in J. Duesenberry, *et al.*, eds., *The Brookings Model, Some Further Results* (Amsterdam: North-Holland Publishing Co., 1969).

[5] FISHER, FRANKLIN M., "Dynamic Structure and Estimation in Economy-Wide Econometric Models," in J. Duesenberry, *et al.*, eds., *op. cit.*

[6] GOLDSMITH, RAYMOND and ROBERT LIPSEY, *Studies in the National Balance Sheet*, Vol. 2 (New York: National Bureau of Economic Reserch, 1963).

[7] HELLER, WALTER, *New Dimensions of Political Economy* (Cambridge: Harvard University Press, 1966), especially chapter 3.

[8] HENDERSON, JAMES and RICHARD QUANDT, *Microeconomic Theory: A Mathematical Approach* (New York: McGraw-Hill Book Co., 1958).

[9] JOHNSTON, J., *Econometric Methods* (New York: McGraw-Hill Book Co., 1963).

[10] JORGENSON, DALE W., "Anticipations and Investment Behavior," in J. Duesenberry, *et al.*, eds., *op. cit.*

[11] MODIGLIANI, FRANCO and RICHARD SUTCH, "Innovations in Interest Rate Policy," *American Economic Review*, LVI (1966).

[12] PHELPS, EDMUND S., *Fiscal Neutrality Toward Economic Growth* (New York: McGraw-Hill Book Co., 1965).

[13] U. S. FEDERAL RESERVE SYSTEM, BOARD OF GOVERNORS, *Federal Reserve Bulletin* (November, 1965).

[14] U. S. CONGRESS, JOINT ECONOMIC COMMITTEE, *State and Local Public Facility Needs and Financing*, Vol. 2 (1966).

[15] U. S. DEPARTMENT OF COMMERCE, OFFICE OF BUSINESS ECONOMICS, *Survey of Current Business* (August, 1965).

EDWARD M. GRAMLICH*

Brookings Institution

HARVEY GALPER*

Urban Institute

State and Local Fiscal Behavior and Federal Grant Policy

PURCHASES BY STATE AND LOCAL GOVERNMENTS have long been the most rapidly rising component of aggregate demand. While real consumption and investment expenditures have both doubled since the end of the Korean war, and federal purchases have increased barely at all, state and local purchases of goods and services have almost tripled. They have grown at an annual average rate of 5.5 percent and now account for over 10 percent of real gross national product (GNP).

For much of this period, the budgetary surplus for state and local governments hovered very close to zero, being negative as often as positive and never amounting to more than $2 billion. Recently, however, the surplus has grown at a remarkable rate. It was only $0.7 billion as late as

* We have benefited from the comments of several members of the Brookings panel, and also from discussions with Frank de Leeuw, Robert W. Hartman, Larry L. Orr, George E. Peterson, and Robert D. Reischauer. Charles A. Waite has supplied us with unpublished national income accounts data, Joseph Valenza ably assisted with the computer work, Su Nokkeo with data preparation, and Kathryn Breen and Patricia Sachs with the typing. Some of the results in the paper are taken from an Urban Institute study, financed by the Office of Economic Opportunity, on the distributional aspects of urban fiscal behavior. A preliminary report on this project can be found in Harvey Galper, Edward Gramlich, Claudia Scott, and Hartojo Wignjowijoto, "A Model of Central City Fiscal Behavior," forthcoming in the Proceedings of the 28th Congress of the International Institute of Public Finance, 1972.

15

1969 but then began a rapid expansion, reaching $4.8 billion in 1971 and $12.3 billion in 1972—when it attained an annual rate of almost $20 billion in the fourth quarter. Though special factors have accounted for some of this rise, a 1972 report on the fiscal policies of President Nixon and Senator George McGovern predicted that the state and local surplus would rise even higher under both sets of proposals.[1]

Grants to state and local governments from the federal government were undoubtedly responsible for much of the increase in expenditures, and possibly the budget surplus as well. Whereas in 1954 these grants amounted to only $2.9 billion, by 1974 they are expected to reach $41.6 billion, a thirteen-fold expansion.[2] And grants are of current interest not only because of their sheer growth. The recent enactment of general revenue sharing, the administration proposal to convert existing categorical grants to special revenue sharing, and numerous other plans to federalize welfare payments or to provide property tax relief or income tax credits to state and local taxpayers—all indicate that fundamental changes are occurring in the form of federal assistance to states and localities.

The increasing importance of the state and local sector and the changing role of federal grants point to the need for a more thorough understanding of the budgetary behavior of state and local governments, particularly the way in which it is influenced by intergovernmental transfers. To explore this topic, we first estimate a model of state and local fiscal behavior and then use it to examine these policy questions.

We begin by discussing different forms of grant assistance and how they might be expected to affect the budgetary behavior of states and localities differently. These ideas underlie our theory of state and local fiscal behavior, from which we derive a consistent set of estimating equations for state and local expenditures, revenues, and the budget surplus. The independent variables in these equations are federal grants of various types, income, relative prices, previous stocks of financial assets, and demographic variables.

The model is estimated with two separate bodies of data: (1) quarterly time series observations on the entire state and local sector in the national income accounts for the period 1954–72; (2) annual budgetary observations for a sample of ten urban governments for the period 1962–70. While

1. See David J. Ott and others, *Nixon, McGovern, and the Federal Budget* (Washington: American Enterprise Institute for Public Policy Research, 1972).
2. *Special Analyses, Budget of the United States Government, Fiscal Year 1974*, p. 8.

the coverage of the time series sample is more comprehensive, the pooled cross-section data contain information on a wider range of intergovernmental assistance that is more finely disaggregated by function, and therefore helps to sharpen the estimates for certain critical parameters. These empirical results are then used to judge how the state and local sector responds to federal aid of various sorts, especially general and special revenue sharing, and to interpret the recent spectacular increases of the state and local budget surplus.

Federal Grants

Although there is a relatively well-developed theory of the roles played by different types of intergovernmental transfers, most empirical studies in this area have paid little attention to it. They have usually assumed that grants of whatever kind affected state and local government behavior in much the same way, disregarding a theory that postulated they would not. This approach may have yielded acceptable predictions of the growth of state-local spending as long as grants increased in volume without changing in structure, but it is clearly inappropriate now when grant policy is undergoing such a radical restructuring.

The theory of intergovernmental transfers suggests that grants from higher to lower levels of government can be classified into three broad types.

Case A. *Open-end matching grants*, under which the higher level of government pays some portion of the cost of certain state or local expenditures, thus effectively reducing their price, and the lower government is free to take as much of the grant money as it wants at this new price ratio. Federal grants of this type have all been in the welfare area—for public assistance, Medicaid, and social services. The response of expenditures by lower governments to these grants depends on the price elasticity of demand for the relevant good or service: The lower level of government increases total spending (from its own resources plus the grant) by more than the grant—and reduces it on all other goods—if demand is elastic, and increases spending by less than the grant—and raises it on all other goods—if demand is inelastic.

Case B. *Closed-end lump-sum transfers*, under which the higher level of government merely transfers a fixed amount of money to a lower government without any effective restrictions on its use or any change in relative prices. The recently enacted general revenue-sharing program constitutes the first important federal policy of this type, though such programs have existed on the state level. The response of expenditures to these grants depends simply on the lower government's propensity to spend budgetary resources rather than to reduce taxes or add to its surplus. In the normal case, in which both public and private goods have positive income elasticities, lump-sum transfers will stimulate some increased public spending and some tax reduction. Case B grants will also stimulate less total spending per dollar of grant than case A grants if the demand for expenditures is at all sensitive to price changes.

Case C. *Closed-end categorical grants*, through which the higher level of government transfers a limited amount of money to be used for a specific program. These grants are a hybrid of case A and B grants in that the higher government lowers the price of the aided activity but limits the size of the grant. All important grant programs at the federal level except those already noted have been of this type. Without any other restrictions, case C grants can be shown to have expenditure effects somewhere between those of case A and case B grants—less than open-end matching grants because the limitation on funds diminishes the impact of the price reduction, and more than lump-sum transfers because at least some price reduction occurs for the specified activity. If limited to incremental expenditures above some base amount, however, case C categorical grants can increase expenditures by more than open-end case A grants that are not subject to such restrictions.[3]

These straightforward ideas become difficult to apply once diverse types of expenditures are aggregated into functional categories for empirical study. For any one type of expenditure, open-end case A grants will stimulate more spending per dollar of grant than closed-end categorical case C grants without other restrictions, which themselves stimulate more expenditures than lump-sum B transfers. But case C grants could be observed to have a larger impact per dollar on spending than case A grants if existing C grant programs make more use of effort maintenance requirements that confine aid to incremental expenditures in a certain category, or if C grants have been more extensively used to support activities that have not

3. These propositions are described more completely in James A. Wilde, "Grants-in-Aid: The Analytics of Design and Response," *National Tax Journal*, Vol. 24 (June 1971), pp. 143–55.

previously been carried out at the state-local level and are therefore incremental expenditures in effect. The situation is complicated even further because grants have different legal and administrative provisions, and because they go to many different lower governments, special districts, and the like, all with presumably different behavioral responses.

Recognizing that we cannot deal with all of these complexities, we have nevertheless tried to estimate the differing responses to various types of grants, first on an aggregate basis and then with some disaggregation. Our approach is to classify grants into the three types on the basis of information about the nature of the program, then to enter these grants as independent variables in regressions in order to estimate their separate effects. This approach allows us to determine how state and local governments might respond to different types of grants and to changes in the restrictions accompanying them.[4]

In our model, case A open-end matching grants are assumed to reduce the price of the grant-aided goods and services by the fraction $(1 - M_A)$, where M_A represents the federal share of total expenditures in the category and is the exogenous policy instrument. The dollar volume of transfers of the case B type, B, are simply added to the budgetary resources at the command of state and local governments; the size of the grant is then the exogenous variable. With categorical case C grants, the lower level of government is assumed to take the entire grant available (C) and this amount, along with the matching rate (M_C), is used as the exogenous policy instrument to determine the volume of "mandated" expenditures on the good or service supported by the grant, C/M_C. This would be the level of spending for this activity required of the lower government in order to obtain the federal grant. Then the recipient government is assumed, in response to the mandated spending, to reduce its other "discretionary" expenditures on these programs—the amount it was spending in excess of C/M_C. The degree to which lower governments reduce discretionary spending, which we will term the grant displacement effect, determines the location of the impact of case C grants between case A and B grants. If grant displacement

4. In first classifying grants and then estimating their separate effects, our approach differs from that of Martin McGuire, who takes all grants together and estimates the degree to which they reduce prices or increase income. See his "Federal-Local Interactions in the Allocation of Resources" (University of Maryland, Department of Economics, 1972; processed). Since we place no restrictions on the relative responses to different types of grants, our treatment could lead to similar results, though within a framework that permits analysis of the response to changes in grant provisions.

is complete, so that the federal government is simply paying for part of what states and localities would have done anyway, categorical C grants are identical to lump-sum B transfers, and our estimates will reflect this equivalence. If grant displacement is incomplete, C grants will have larger effects on total spending than B grants, and possibly even larger effects than A grants when the effective degree of effort maintenance in the C grant programs is high enough.

A Model of the Determination of State and Local Expenditures, Revenues, and Budget Surplus

These ideas about federal grants can be used to develop a model of the determination of state and local government expenditures, revenues, and budget surplus. The model incorporates an optimization procedure for the decision makers at the state-local level that parallels that used in the development of consumer demand functions for households. We first describe the objectives state and local officials seek in their budgetary policy, and then introduce the budget constraint that limits the attainment of these objectives. Maximizing the preference function subject to the budget constraint leads to a system of equations determining expenditures, revenues, and the budget surplus.[5] The budget constraint ensures that an increase in expenditures must be financed by a grant, a rise in taxes, or a decline in the surplus. Similarly, the equations ensure that exogenous budgetary resources such as grants are completely allocated to all competing uses of funds.

THE OBJECTIVES OF STATE AND LOCAL BUDGETARY POLICY

We assume that state and local government budgetary policy has four main objectives: (1) higher current expenditures, whether locally initiated or resulting from the need to match federal case C grants; (2) higher private

5. This use of a maximization theory for state and local governments is similar to other recent contributions. See James M. Henderson, "Local Government Expenditures: A Social Welfare Analysis," *Review of Economics and Statistics*, Vol. 50 (May 1968), pp. 156–63; Robert P. Inman, "Four Essays on Fiscal Federalism" (Ph.D. thesis, Harvard University, 1971); Thomas E. Borcherding and Robert T. Deacon, "The Demand for the Services of Non-Federal Governments," *American Economic Review*, Vol. 62 (December 1972), pp. 891–901.

disposable incomes, resulting from either higher pretax incomes or lower state and local taxes; (3) greater flows of services from the stock of tangible capital possessed by states and localities; (4) greater flows of services from the stock of net financial assets.

Current expenditures. Decision makers at the state-local level, whether they be government officials or, by virtue of their voting power, private households, are assumed to gain satisfaction both from expenditures mandated by federal categorical grants and from locally initiated discretionary expenditures. Total expenditures (purchases plus transfer payments) can be defined as the sum of mandated and discretionary expenditures through the identity,

(1) $$EXP = E + E_M.$$

Here EXP is total state and local expenditures however financed, E is discretionary expenditures, and E_M is expenditures mandated by the federal grant, defined above to equal C/M_C. Since the volume of mandated expenditures, determined by case C grants and their matching rates, are by definition exogenous, explaining E is tantamount to explaining EXP.

The utility of state and local decision makers is then assumed to depend on the real value of mandated and discretionary expenditures, taken separately, adjusted for a measure of expenditure needs that is discussed below. Formally, utility depends on,

(2) $$Q_1 = E/P_E + \gamma_1 E_M/P_E - N,$$

where P_E is the expenditure price deflator to put the expression in real terms, γ_1 is the grant displacement parameter that allows for a differential utility from mandated as opposed to discretionary expenditures, and N is a variable reflecting minimum expenditure needs.

If the grant displacement parameter, γ_1, is unity, mandated expenditures arising from case C grants and locally initiated discretionary expenditures lead to identical utility per dollar and can be considered perfect substitutes. In this event, categorical grants will turn out to have effects on total spending identical to those of lump-sum transfers. If γ_1 is less than 1, on the other hand, mandated expenditures add less utility per dollar than do local discretionary expenditures; thus they must be only partially substitutable, the grant displacement is incomplete, and the effect of categorical C grants on total spending will be greater than that of lump-sum case B grants.

The term for expenditure needs, N, contains all demographic variables that change the marginal utility of expenditures, and hence spending propensities, without directly altering the budgetary situation of local governments. In principle many variables could meet these criteria; we tried a number of candidates but eventually settled on only three: (1) the number of school age children (*KID*), a proxy for education needs; (2) the number of families headed by females (*FEM*), a proxy for needs for welfare and other social services; (3) the robbery rate (*ROB*), which is the best empirical proxy for needs for expenditures on public safety. We then let N be a function of these three variables and substituted this expression into equation (2) in the maximization exercise.[6]

Private disposable incomes. The objective of higher private disposable incomes makes utility a positive function of pretax income (Y) and a negative function of state and local taxes (T). But allowance must be made for the possibility that equivalent changes in taxes and in pretax incomes will not necessarily lead to the same utility per dollar. If the state or locality could be thought of simply as an aggregation of households that cared only about total disposable income and not about whether its source was higher pretax incomes or lower taxes, the relevant indicator of satisfaction would be ($Y - T$).[7] But this may not be an accurate way to represent the state-local budgetary process if elected representatives imperfectly translate household preferences. In particular, if government officials have some independent influence on budgetary allocations, they would presumably prefer disposable income to rise through a cut in taxes, for which they can take credit, rather than through a rise in pretax earnings, for which they cannot. The community might then operate as if the utility associated with the disposable income objective were a function of

$$(3) \qquad\qquad Q_2 = \gamma_2 Y/P - T/P,$$

where γ_2 sets the relative weight of private incomes and taxes in the preferences of decision makers, and the expression is put in real terms by deflating by the overall price level, P. If γ_2 equals 1, decision makers are indifferent between income increases and tax reductions; if γ_2 is less than 1, they prefer income to rise through a reduction in taxes. The relation be-

6. These "need" variables correspond loosely to the "supply" variables of James C. Ohls and Terence J. Wales, "Supply and Demand for State and Local Services," *Review of Economics and Statistics*, Vol. 54 (November 1972), pp. 424–30. The concept is also used in the work of McGuire, "Federal-Local Interactions," and Inman, "Four Essays."

7. For a more detailed discussion of the conditions under which this proposition holds, see Wallace E. Oates, *Fiscal Federalism* (Harcourt Brace, 1972), Chap. 3.

tween the effect of private income increases and unrestricted lump-sum transfers on public spending will depend on this parameter γ_2. The two have identical effects when the source of the money is immaterial ($\gamma_2 = 1$); and lump-sum transfers, which are already in the public treasury and therefore do not require the painful act of taxation, have a greater impact on spending if γ_2 is less than 1.[8]

The stock of tangible capital. The third objective of state and local budgetary policy is to increase the flow of services from the stock of tangible capital. If this flow is proportional to the actual stock of capital, the utility from this source is also a proportional function of the stock.

To derive the utility expression, we begin with the identity, similar to that used for current expenditures, that total construction expenditures (CON) equals the sum of mandated (I_M) and discretionary (I) construction expenditures,

$$(4) \qquad CON = I + I_M;$$

I_M is again equal to (C_I/M_{CI}), where C_I and M_{CI} equal case C construction grants and their matching ratio, respectively.

Two types of capital can then be distinguished, that resulting from the discretionary expenditures of local governments (KO) and that resulting from mandated spending under current and previous categorical grants for construction (KM). The earlier procedure can be used to define a parameter, γ_3, which measures the capital grant displacement effect in the same way that γ_1 measures the current grant displacement. With this parameter as a utility weight, the capital term in the utility function is proportional to

$$(5) \qquad Q_3 = (1 - \delta)(KO_{-1} + \gamma_3 KM_{-1}) + I/P_I + \gamma_3 I_M/P_I,$$

where δ is the rate of physical depreciation and P_I the price index for new construction, and where the capital stock terms are both in real terms because they cumulate all past investments also measured in real terms.[9]

---

8. We might label this phenomenon the "flypaper" theory of incidence: Money sticks where it hits. Ray D. Whitman, in "Effect of Revenue Sharing Upon State-Local Fiscal Effort: A Revision of Current Theory" (paper prepared for delivery at the 1973 annual meeting of the Public Choice Society; processed), also gives other reasons why γ_2 might not equal 1. The argument in the text is proven formally in Appendix A.

9. Expressions for these two real stocks would be of the form,

$$KO = \sum_{i=0}^{\infty} (1 - \delta)^i (I/P_I)_{-i}; \quad KM = \sum_{i=0}^{\infty} (1 - \delta)^i [(1/M_{CI})(C_I/P_I)]_{-i}.$$

This expression can be written in simpler notation as

$$(6) \qquad\qquad Q_3 = K' + I/P_I,$$

where

$$K' = (1 - \delta)(KO_{-1} + \gamma_3 KM_{-1}) + \gamma_3 I_M/P_I.$$

The stock of net financial assets. The fourth budgetary objective is to increase the flow of services from the stock of net financial assets. Net financial assets are defined here as all components of the net worth of states and localities other than real capital, or as all financial assets less all liabilities. This term in the utility function, Q_4, is simply given by the real stocks of financial assets:

$$(7) \qquad\qquad Q_4 = (FA_{-1})/(P) + (S/P),$$

where FA_{-1} represents stocks in the previous period and S is current net financial saving.

DERIVING THE ESTIMATING EQUATIONS

In the real world a government obviously cannot satisfy all of these goals simultaneously—spend as much as it would like, tax as little as it would like, and maximize stocks of tangible capital and financial assets. Rather, it will have to allocate its limited resources among these competing objectives according to its perception of the highest priorities at that particular time. We describe this process through our optimization procedure.

Mathematically, we maximize the preference function,

$$(8) \qquad\qquad U = F(Q_1, Q_2, Q_3, Q_4),$$

subject to a budget constraint. Since each of the terms in the utility function is assumed to have positive but declining marginal utility, governments will desire a smaller increment of any Q_i the more they already have. Governments are assumed to use the four discretionary components of equation (8)—current expenditures (E), construction expenditures (I), taxes (T), and financial saving (S)—to adjust to movements in the exogenous variables in (8)—expenditure needs (N), expenditures mandated by case C grants (E_M), income (Y), and previous stocks of capital and financial assets (K', FA_{-1})—in such a way as to establish this maximum continually. Solution of this system will lead to a set of estimating equations that describe how discretionary expenditures respond to these independent variables.

The budget constraint in this system is

$$(9) \qquad\qquad X = I + E + S - T,$$

where X (for exogenous budgetary resources) equals the algebraic sum of all nondiscretionary items—lump-sum transfers, interest and principal payments on outstanding debt, and the matching expenditures on categorical case C grants. The precise composition of this variable is demonstrated below and in Appendix A.

The optimization procedure, which is also worked out in detail in Appendix A, leads after a minor simplification to the following set of estimating equations for the four discretionary components:

$$(10) \quad \begin{bmatrix} I/P_I \\ E/P_E \\ -T/P \\ (FA_{-1} + X + T)/P - E/P_E - I/P_I \end{bmatrix} = g\,\{(FA_{-1} + X)/P, \\ (Y/P),\, (E_M/P_E), \\ [P_E(1 - M_A)/P], \\ (R + \delta)(P_I/P),\, K', \\ KID,\, ROB,\, FEM\}.$$

The fourth discretionary variable equals previous stocks of financial assets plus exogenous budgetary resources plus taxes less the two types of expenditures, with everything in real terms. This means that the sum of all four dependent variables is $(FA_{-1} + X)/P$, which is also the first independent variable. Such a system forces this variable to be allocated completely to expenditures, tax reductions, or surplus accumulation, with allocation coefficients that sum to unity across the four equations. These coefficients thus describe how either previous balances or exogenous budgetary resources will be split up among the four possible discretionary uses with all other independent variables held constant. All other independent variables will, on the other hand, have coefficients that sum to zero across the four equations. These coefficients will then change the allocation of any given level of exogenous budgetary resources in response to movements in the independent variables, without changing the overall total.

The lagged stock of financial assets in the budget constraint term gives the model somewhat complicated dynamic properties. If some outside change were, for example, to increase expenditures, either taxes would have to rise or the surplus would have to fall to preserve the budget identity. Whenever the surplus does change, stocks of financial assets will be lowered, leading governments to try to regain them either by increasing taxes or reducing expenditures. When they eventually do this, changes in the stock, or the current surplus, will cease. Financial assets are then acting as a buffer stock, with the surplus responding in the short run but not in the long run to changes in outside forces.

26   *Brookings Papers on Economic Activity, 1:1973*

The remaining independent variables and their expected roles in the budgetary allocation process are described as follows:

Real income (Y/P). Real income will make communities better off and induce them to spend more on public goods and to increase stocks of capital and financial assets, by raising taxes (or reducing negative taxes).

Mandated expenditures under categorical case C grants (E_M/P_E). We use the exogenous amounts and matching ratios of closed-end categorical grants to determine the mandated level of spending under the grant program. States and localities are then free to vary their discretionary spending (E) accordingly. If they reduce discretionary spending, they must also either increase their accumulation of financial assets or reduce taxes.

Relative prices. Relative prices alter discretionary spending and hence either taxes or the surplus. For current expenditures the appropriate price term is $P_E(1 - M_A)/P$, or the relative price of expenditures times the implied price reduction due to case A grants. For construction there are no case A grants; but the relative price term, $(R + \delta)(P_I/P)$, where R is the state and local interest rate and δ the rate of depreciation, allows the budgetary allocation to change in response to the opportunity cost of new investment.

Stocks of tangible capital. The capital stock objective implies that states and localities will invest more the less capital they have, and vice versa. Our theory reflects this by including the previous stock of capital, whether grant supported or not, as an independent variable, which lowers new construction and raises the other uses of budgetary resources. Apart from the residual financing effect, the lagged stock of structures should have a special stimulative effect on current expenditures for maintenance and for the wages of those who work in them.

Demographic terms. Each of these proxies for expenditure needs, *KID, ROB, FEM,* which were described earlier, should increase expenditures and also either increase taxes or reduce the surplus.

Quarterly Time Series Estimates, Aggregate State and Local Sector

NATIONAL INCOME ACCOUNTS DATA

The time series estimates of the model described above are based on data from the national income accounts for the aggregate state and local sector. These data cover the activities of two quite separate governmental

Table 1. National Income Accounts Budget for State and Local General Governments and Social Insurance Funds, 1971

Billions of current dollars

Budget item	Amount
Revenues, total	151.8
General government	142.4
Social insurance trust funds	9.4
Expenditures, total	147.0
General government	145.1
Social insurance trust funds	1.9
Benefit payments	5.0ᵃ
Less: Interest earnings	−3.1
Surplus, total	4.8
General government	−2.7
Social insurance trust funds	7.5

Source: *Survey of Current Business*, Vol. 52 (July 1972), Tables 3.3, 3.7.
a. Includes a small amount of transfers to general government. Figures may not add to totals because of rounding.

bodies, general governments and the social insurance pension funds for state and local employees. The overall budget statement disaggregated into these two components is shown for 1971 in Table 1.

The table indicates that the trust funds accounted for more than the entire state and local surplus in 1971. Indeed, they have been chiefly responsible for growing surpluses in other recent years. Since trust funds are accumulating liabilities for retirement payments in the future, however, the implication of these high and rising surpluses is not clear. A positive trust fund surplus simply means that current inflows exceed benefit payments, but gives no indication whether these inflows are sufficient to meet future needs. Only a comparison of current receipts with those required to maintain the actuarial position of the funds—a measure that does not exist for state and local trust funds in the aggregate nor even for most individual funds—could resolve this question.[10]

What is clear, however, is that the transactions of retirement funds are motivated by quite different considerations from those influencing general governments. Since the model described here is meant to refer only to general governments, we have eliminated all trust fund items from the

10. See William B. Neenan, "Status of and Prospect for Municipal Retirement Plans" (Urban Institute, 1973; processed), for a more detailed description of the problems and prospects for trust funds.

budget identity and will hereafter deal exclusively with general governments. The general government budget for 1971 is given in Table 2.

Revenues consist of income, corporate, sales, and property taxes, along with a small amount of other revenues, plus federal grants. We have separated grants into types A (open-end), B (lump-sum), and C (closed-end categorical), with type C grants divided into those for current expenditures and those for construction. Total expenditures consist of construction and current outlays—each distributed between mandated and discretionary expenditures—and interest payments minus the surplus of government enterprises.

Table 3 then displays the budget divided into its discretionary and nondiscretionary components. Because we have simply transferred various items from one side of the ledger to the other, the budget identity still holds; now, however, it implies that the sum of the four discretionary items—two types of discretionary expenditures plus the budget surplus minus taxes—equals total nondiscretionary budgetary resources, X.

Table 2. National Income Accounts Budget for State and Local General Governments, by Major Revenue and Expenditure Items, 1971

Billions of current dollars

Revenue or expenditure item	Amount
Revenues, total	142.4
Taxes and other	113.1
Federal grants-in-aid	29.3
Open-end (A)	10.8
Lump-sum (B)	0.1
Closed-end categorical (C)	18.4
Construction	8.4
Current expenditures	10.0
Expenditures, total	145.1
Construction	26.2
Mandated by federal C grants	10.5
Discretionary	15.7
Other purchases and transfer payments	120.5
Mandated by federal C grants	11.5
Discretionary	109.0
Interest payments[a]	2.8
Less: Surplus of government enterprises	−4.3
Surplus, total	−2.7
Retirement of long-term debt (gross)	7.8
Cash flow surplus	−10.5

Sources: Table 1 above; *Survey of Current Business* (July 1972), Table 3.3; U.S. Bureau of Economic Analysis, unpublished data. Figures may not add to totals because of rounding.
a. Net of a small trust fund transfer to general government.

Edward M. Gramlich and Harvey Galper 29

Table 3. National Income Accounts Budget for Discretionary and Nondiscretionary Components of State and Local General Governments, 1971

Billions of current dollars

Component	Amount
Nondiscretionary budgetary variable (X)	−5.4
Federal open-end A grants ($M_A\bar{E}$)	8.7[a]
Federal lump-sum B grants (B)	0.1
Less: Drain due to federal closed-end categorical C grants, construction ($I_M - C_I$)	−2.1
Less: Drain due to federal C grants, current expenditures ($E_M - C$)	−1.5
Less: Interest and debt retirement (D)	−10.6
Discretionary budgetary variables	−5.4
Construction expenditures (I)	15.7
Current expenditures (E)	109.0
Cash flow surplus (S)[a]	−12.7
Less: Taxes and surplus of government enterprises (T)	−117.4

Source: See Table 2.

a. An estimate of the income effect of A grants, the matching rate M_A times a previous average of values for expenditures, $\bar{E}$, is included on the nondiscretionary side of the budget. See text for discussion. Since this income effect is different from actual A grants (Table 2), the budget surplus also has been changed.

Three items in the table deserve special mention. Since the level of categorical C grants is exogenous, the expenditures from own sources necessary to match these grants, ($E_M - C$) and ($I_M - C_I$), appear on the nondiscretionary side. These local expenditures are a drain on budgetary resources and thus become a negative component of the budgetary resource variable.

A second matter requiring explanation is our treatment of case A grants. These grants are included in the exogenous term in Table 3 to account for the income effect of the implied expenditure price reduction. Like any other price change, A grants operate through a substitution effect which shifts prices with budgetary resources constant, and an income effect which changes budgetary resources with prices constant. Even when states and localities do not respond to the price reduction implied by case A grants, they are still getting revenue from such grants based on previously planned expenditures which they are likely to use as they do other nondiscretionary funds. To capture this income effect, we have included an A grant term in X, defining it as the current matching rate, M_A, times a previous average of values for expenditures, $\bar{E}$.[11]

11. This adjustment is a way of simplifying an equation system that becomes nonlinear when all prices are not the same. There is also a much smaller income effect working through the interest and debt retirement term, D, for the opportunity cost of investment expenditures. See Appendix A for details.

Finally, we have classified interest payments and the retirement of long-term debt as exogenous—the first because they are determined by current and previous market interest rates and the predetermined stock of debt, and the second because they too depend on the predetermined stock of debt, as well as on its repayment schedule. This dependence in itself would not make debt retirement expenditures exogenous if states and localities were able to prepay or refinance their debt so as to alter its payment schedule. But most of these governmental units are legally prevented from refinancing their long-term debt, and few have been known to prepay it. Thus for these purposes we have lumped debt retirement with interest payments as a negative component of X.

The Estimates

We estimated the model given in equation (8) with seventy-six quarterly time series observations from 1954 through 1972. All variables reflecting dollar flows were in real terms and all prices were entered as ratios, as suggested by the maximization exercise. We deflated all the dollar variables and demographic terms by population to correct for any common trends that might be introduced by sheer growth.[12] Since the response of the state and local sector to outside influences is likely to be sluggish even apart from the lag working through the surplus described above, we have also used distributed lags (denoted by L) for these independent variables, which are difficult to predict and for which we might expect a lag.[13]

12. Another rationalization for this technique might be that expenditure decisions are probably made in terms of real services delivered per capita. We tried to take this reasoning one step further by assuming that tax decisions were made in terms of effective rates on income, and to distinguish between discretionary taxes involving changes in these rates and nondiscretionary taxes involving changes in income. This approach yielded results similar to those presented here but somewhat less reliable statistically, possibly because discretionary and nondiscretionary taxes are difficult to distinguish operationally.

13. The three demographic terms in the quarterly model were all interpolations of annual numbers. Since each of these series was already smoothed, it did not seem worthwhile to use distributed lags for them.

In addition, it is especially important to compute a lag distribution for the expenditures implied by categorical grants. These expenditures are subtracted from total expenditures to compute the discretionary component (see equation 1) at the same time that they are addedas an independent variable in equation (10). This procedure builds a negative bias into the estimates if there is measurement error due to the timing of federal categorical grants. We have attempted to adjust for this kind of error by smoothing our

Estimation of the equations proceeded in two stages. First, each of the four equations for the discretionary variables of equation (10) was estimated separately by ordinary least squares. These initial estimates were used to eliminate independent variables that did not work well in the equation for the dependent variable they should primarily affect, and to measure the shape of the lag distributions, the degree of serial correlation of residuals, and the size of the remaining standard errors. The estimated degree of serial correlation was high enough to justify using all observations in first-difference form. Final coefficient estimates were then obtained from a second regression in which these first differences were stacked in such a way as to impose the budget constraint and ensure that each of the four equations had the same weight in influencing the structure of the coefficients.[14]

The best estimates of this set of equations are given in Table 4. Some of the cells in the table are blank because the relevant coefficient was either insignificant or had an incorrect sign and was dropped from the specification. But the only independent variable that did not have the expected sign in any of the four equations was the relative price for current expenditures. This means that A grants have no price substitution effects in this version.

The coefficients in the table give the impact effect in the first quarter of changes in the independent variables. Because resources not spent or used for tax reduction add to the current surplus, they continue to influence budgetary allocations in future quarters. Ultimate long-run effects are discussed in the next section.

We retained the lagged resources term, L_1/X, despite its relatively low t-ratio because this was the only avenue through which construction responded to changes in budgetary resources. (The current value of X has almost no effect on construction.) But even with relaxed standards of significance, we found no influence of lagged resources on current expenditures and taxes.

---

series for all case C grants before subtracting them from total expenditures, and then using a distributed lag on this smoothed series as the independent variable for categorical grants.

14. The stacking technique is described in Frank de Leeuw, "A Model of Financial Behavior," in James S. Duesenberry and others (eds.), *The Brookings Quarterly Econometric Model of the United States* (Rand McNally, 1965). The stacked equations were then weighted by the inverse of the standard error of the ordinary least squares estimation after correction for serial correlation to ensure that equations with large residuals would not unduly influence the overall coefficients.

Table 4. Coefficients for Time Series Equations Explaining State and Local Government Expenditures, Revenues, and Budget Surplus, 1954–72[a]

Independent variable	Construction expenditures $\Delta\left(\dfrac{I}{POP \cdot P_I}\right)$	Current expenditures $\Delta\left(\dfrac{E}{POP \cdot P_B}\right)$	Negative taxes $\Delta\left(\dfrac{-T}{POP \cdot P}\right)$	Surplus plus net financial assets $\Delta\dfrac{1}{POP}\left(\dfrac{X+T+FA_{-1}}{P} - \dfrac{I}{P_I} - \dfrac{E}{P_B}\right)$
Exogenous budgetary resources and net financial assets $\Delta\left(\dfrac{X+FA_{-1}}{POP \cdot P}\right)$	−0.003 (−0.2)	0.019 (1.4)	0.028 (2.3)	0.956 (47.6)
Lagged budgetary resources[b] $\Delta L_1\left(\dfrac{X}{POP \cdot P}\right)$	0.100 (0.9)	...	...	−0.100 (−0.9)
Mandated C grant expenditures[b] $\Delta L_2\left(\dfrac{E_M}{POP \cdot P_B}\right)$	...	−0.316 (−0.9)	...	0.316 (0.9)
Income[b] $\Delta L_3\left(\dfrac{Y}{POP \cdot P}\right)$	0.072 (4.0)	0.016 (1.1)	−0.108 (−6.0)	0.020 (1.2)
Relative price of capital[b] $\Delta L_4\left(\dfrac{(R+\delta)P_I}{P}\right)$	−3.032 (−1.5)	...	...	3.032 (1.5)
Real capital stock $\Delta\left(\dfrac{K'}{POP}\right)$	−0.121 (−3.3)	0.121 (3.3)	...	...

School children $\Delta\left(\dfrac{KID}{POP}\right)$	5.458 (1.5)	3.492 (1.0)	...	−8.950 (−2.2)
Female-headed families $\Delta\left(\dfrac{FEM}{POP_H}\right)$	...	17.257 (3.0)	−43.627 (−7.3)	26.370 (4.2)
Robbery rate $\Delta\left(\dfrac{ROB}{POP}\right)$	...	24.843 (2.4)	...	−24.843 (−2.4)
Standard error of estimate	2.452	1.390	2.446	3.483
R^2 with first differences[c]	0.119	0.466	0.159	0.984
R^2 with levels[c]	0.831	0.999	0.999	0.998

Sources: Time series equations based on seventy-six quarterly observations, 1954–72. See Appendix B for sources of the underlying data. The numbers in parentheses are t-ratios.

a. The variables here and in all other tables are defined as follows:

I = discretionary construction expenditures, current dollars
E = discretionary current expenditures, current dollars
T = taxes and surplus of government enterprises, current dollars
Y = GNP less federal taxes plus transfers, interest, and subsidies, current dollars
$X = M_A \bar{E} + B + C - E_M + C_I - I_M - D$
M_A = matching rate, open-end A grants, current expenditures
E_M = mandated current expenditures under C grants, current dollars
I_M = mandated construction expenditures, under C grants, current dollars
B = level of closed-end lump-sum B grants, current dollars
C = level of closed-end C grants, current expenditures, current dollars
C_I = level of closed-end C grants, construction, current dollars
$$\bar{E} = 0.25\left(\sum_{i-1}^{4} E_{-i}\right)$$
D = interest payments and retirement of long-term debt, current dollars
P_I = price index, state and local construction
P_E = price index, state and local current expenditures

P = GNP deflator
R = nominal interest rate on municipal bonds, percentage points
δ = annual rate of depreciation, state and local structures, assumed equal to 1.75 percent
POP = total population
KID = population, children 1–19, times 100
FEM = total number of female-headed families, times 100
POP_H = total number of households
ROB = number of robberies, times 1,000
K' = weighted state and local capital stock, real terms, where γ_3, the grant displacement parameter for construction, is set equal to unity.
FA_{-1} = net financial assets, cash flow basis (accumulation of past cash flow surpluses), end of previous period.

b. L_1 is an inverted V lag extending for six periods from t_{-1} to t_{-6} (weights are 0.08, 0.17, 0.25, 0.25, 0.17, 0.08). L_2 is a decay lag extending from t to t_{-8} (weights are 0.4, 0.3, 0.2, 0.1). L_3 and L_4 are rectangular lags extending from t to t_{-7} and t_{-4}, respectively (weights are 0.125 each period for L_3 and 0.2 each period for L_4).

c. The R^2s for first differences and levels were computed by comparing the residual variance (square of the standard error of estimate) with the variance of the appropriate dependent variable, in both first-difference and level forms.

The coefficients for $(X + FA_{-1})$ indicate a very sluggish response of both current expenditures and taxes to changes in previous balances or exogenous inflows of funds. A rise of $1 in some inflow—say, lump-sum transfers—will increase the surplus by $0.96 in the first quarter, with only a slight increase in expenditures and a small reduction in taxes. After one year the surplus will be higher by $0.75, with $0.25 going into expenditure increases and tax reductions; after two years the proportions are about fifty-fifty. Of the two, expenditures approach their equilibrium value very slightly faster than do taxes.

The coefficients for mandated C grant expenditures indicate that the reaction of expenditures would be much faster in this instance. A rise in C grants will immediately increase total expenditures by E_M, as given in equation (1). Then discretionary expenditures will decline by an amount that equals $0.32 per dollar of change in E_M over a period of four quarters. This decline in discretionary spending will also be reflected as a rise in the surplus, which ultimately again raises discretionary expenditures by a small amount. If matching rates are set equal to one, a $1 rise in C grants will stimulate $0.88 total expenditures in the first quarter, about $0.70 in the fourth quarter when the displacement effect has had time to work, and about $0.75 in the eighth quarter, by which time the increase in the surplus has begun to feed back on expenditures.

EQUILIBRIUM CHANGES

Solving these equations for their equilibrium properties once all lags have been played out provides a better idea of their long-run properties. This is done by determining the equilibrium stocks of capital and financial assets and substituting them into the relationships for current expenditures and the negative of taxes. The current surplus is unchanged in this equilibrium, and investment is changed only by altered replacement needs. In these calculations we have added mandated C grant expenditures to discretionary expenditures to produce results in terms of total state and local expenditures, a more familiar concept. The steady-state magnitudes are given in Table 5.

Several results stand out in the table. A dollar of revenue sharing or of any other exogenous budgetary inflow will ultimately raise expenditures by $0.43 and lower taxes by $0.57. The current expenditure response to revenue sharing is roughly five times that of the response to private income,

Table 5. Steady-state Coefficients and Elasticities from Time Series Equations for Total Expenditures and Negative Taxes, State and Local Governments, 1954–72[a]

Dependent variable	Independent variable						
	Exogenous budgetary resources $\dfrac{X}{POP \cdot P}$	Mandated C grant expenditures $\dfrac{E_M}{POP \cdot P}$	Income $\dfrac{Y}{POP \cdot P}$	Relative price of capital $\dfrac{(R+\delta)P_I}{P}$	School children $\dfrac{KID}{POP}$	Female-headed families $\dfrac{FEM}{POP_H}$	Robbery rate $\dfrac{ROB}{POP}$
1. Total current expenditures $\left(\dfrac{EXP}{POP \cdot P_E}\right)$	0.428	0.799	0.095 (1.08)	−1.93 (−0.04)	5.7 (0.81)	26.8 (1.06)	15.7 (0.05)
2. Negative taxes $\left(\dfrac{-T}{POP \cdot P}\right)$	0.573	0.201	−0.095	1.93	−5.7	−26.8	−15.7

Source: Table 4. The numbers in parentheses are the elasticities of total discretionary expenditures with respect to the independent variables.

a. See Table 4 for definition of the symbols.

Note: The relevant parameter reflecting the grant displacement effect, γ_1, is $0.201/0.573 = 0.35$; that reflecting the relative preferences of decision makers for tax reduction γ_2, is $0.095/0.428 = 0.22$.

an extra dollar of which eventually produces only $0.10 of current expenditures in equilibrium. This implies a relative utility weight, γ_2, of 0.22 for income—that is, that income received in the public treasury (X) has a much different effect from income received by private households (Y).

The displacement of categorical matching grants is relatively slight in this version ($\gamma_1 = 0.35$), indicating that categorical case C grants with a matching ratio of unity will increase total spending by $0.80, almost twice as much as does revenue sharing.[15] The expenditure impact is even greater when matching rates are below unity, or when the federal government pays less than the full cost of the expenditure program, because under these circumstances the initial level of mandated spending is higher, with this impact only partly offset by the negative income effect of the budgetary drain due to matching. By way of illustration, if matching rates were equal to their present average federal share of 80 percent ($M_C = 0.8$), total expenditures would increase by $1.00—($0.80)(1/0.8)—through the mandated C grant term in Table 5, to be offset by $0.10—(0.43)($1.25 − $1.00) —through the exogenous budgetary resource drain in Table 5, for a net increase of $0.90. This evidence of a fairly strong impact from categorical C grants appears to conflict with the estimated weak effects on spending of case A grants. However, as mentioned above, such a result could be explained by effective effort maintenance requirements for case C grants, resulting either from legal restrictions or from the fact that case C grants have been used more extensively for new expenditure programs.

The other variables operate in relatively predictable ways. In order to facilitate their interpretation, we have also presented these results in terms of elasticities, or ratios between the marginal coefficients and average ratios, for the relevant concept of discretionary expenditures. The income elasticity of discretionary expenditures is 1.08, implying that state and local discretionary expenditures grow slightly faster than income. The interest rate elasticity of expenditures is very slightly negative because the capital stock, whose operation and maintenance are responsible for some of these expenditures, is negatively related to interest rates. The elasticity of expen-

15. Computation of these values for γ_1 and γ_2 is described in Appendix A and also in the note to Table 5. The effect of displacement ($\gamma_1 = 0.35$) is calculated as follows: The impact of $0.80 is 35 percent of the way between the impact if there were no displacement ($1.00 when $M_C = 1.0$) and the revenue-sharing impact if displacement were complete ($0.43).

ditures with respect to the number of school children is 0.81. This may appear high in view of the fact that only about half of total expenditures are for schools; but some other expenditures for social services, welfare, and public safety also depend partially on numbers of children. The elasticity with respect to the robbery rate is very small, as would be expected from the fact that it should raise expenditures on only a small portion of the expenditure budget. The one variable with a coefficient that seems high is that reflecting families headed by females. Though its effects should also be restricted to certain types of expenditures, it nevertheless has an elasticity of 1.06, suggesting that it may be serving as a proxy for some other influences.

Although these results give some indication of the impacts of different types of grants, a fair amount of uncertainty remains. It is surprising that the impact per dollar of case C grants appears to be greater than that of revenue sharing while the impact of open-end A grants does not. For revenue sharing itself, the results—that somewhat less than half the funds actually will augment expenditures—are reasonably plausible, but the inference arises from a variable that has not included revenue sharing until now and for which the t-ratio is rather low. The next section then compares these inferences with those of the same model estimated with another body of data.

Pooled Cross-section Estimates, Ten Large Urban Governments

The equations presented in this section come from a budgetary model based on data for ten large urban governments. These data have the advantages, first, of permitting identification of aggregation effects, and, second, of including revenue-sharing money from state governments along with their other components of budgetary inflows. With these pooled cross-section data, there is also enough information to disaggregate expenditures into functional categories and thus to estimate separate price substitution effects and the displacement propensities of categorical grants for the different categories.

One of the problems in using local government data is that jurisdictions overlap. Typically, residents in any one area will be served by a city or town government, a county government, and probably, for certain functions, special districts. This makes it very difficult to examine the behavior of any one government in isolation, because it depends crucially on what all the other local governments serving the same geographic area are doing or have done in the past. We have tried to get around this problem by choosing for our sample only jurisdictions that were served by one general government during the estimation period. A relatively homogeneous sample of ten large urban city-county governments met this criterion: Baltimore, Boston, Denver, New Orleans, New York, Philadelphia, Providence, St. Louis, San Francisco, and Washington, D.C. We then defined for these cities a standard discretionary public sector, consisting of education, public safety, social services (health and hospitals, housing), urban support (sewage, sanitation, highways, parks and recreation), and general government, but excluding airports, water transport, mass transit, higher education, and some other items. All expenditures and revenues of general government and special districts within our standard public sector were part of the general government, and only net drains due to these excluded items were deducted from exogenous budgetary inflows (X). Another negative component of X was the cost (net of federal case A grants) of city expenditures on welfare, which are basically set by state laws determining caseloads and payment levels and are therefore exogenous to cities.

A further problem concerns the fact that these large urban governments are typically surrounded by high-income areas that might limit their fiscal flexibility. Cities may feel unable to tax and spend as much as they like because these suburbs offer a potential tax haven to wealthy city residents.[16] We have allowed for this possibility by including real per capita taxes on suburban property in the model, expecting increases in this variable to make city governments more willing to increase their own taxes and expenditures.

Table 6 gives the pooled cross-section equations, using annual first differences stacked as before to impose the budget constraint and to ensure that all equations had the same weight in estimating the coefficients. We have disaggregated discretionary current expenditures into five components, each with its own price (two of which are not significant) and federal and state categorical grant programs (two of which are not present because there are no grant programs in these areas). In addition, no separate data

16. For the original statement that consumers choose among tax and expenditure packages of competing jurisdictions, see Charles M. Tiebout, "A Pure Theory of Local Expenditures," *Journal of Political Economy*, Vol. 64 (October 1956), pp. 416–24.

on investment are available and thus the entire current account surplus, or change in net worth (ΔNW), is included as the last dependent variable, where ΔNW is again defined by subtracting all other discretionary uses of resources from X.[17]

Our attempts to include the level of net worth as one independent variable, and hence ensure that this stock would be unchanged in the long run, were not successful. Although such an equation can be estimated with fairly sensible long-run coefficients, the estimated time period over which this adjustment appears to take place is unreasonably long. Thus for the cross-section results we adopted an alternative specification that merely used the previous change in net worth as one independent variable, and hence did not fully distribute all changes in private income and budgetary resources to current expenditures and taxes. All other independent variables have a direct impact on expenditures and taxes, however, and their long-run effects can be determined apart from the behavior of the surplus.

In contrast to the time series results of Table 4, the equations in Table 6 show significant price substitution terms. Categorical federal grants now have statistically significant displacement effects for education, but not for the other two categories. (The coefficient is large and negative for urban support, but federal grants in this area are very small and the estimate is unreliable.) The suburban tax and robbery variables worked well, but not the school-age population variable, possibly because it is difficult to measure between Census years for individual cities. The variable incorporating the number of families headed by females was not even included because it should mainly affect welfare, which is not endogenous in the cross-section model. Other demographic variables reflecting expenditure needs—such as the proportion of aged people in the population, population density, the poverty population, the nonwhite population—typically did not yield very significant effects.

EQUILIBRIUM CHANGES

The steady-state coefficients for these equations are given in Table 7. For exogenous budgetary resources and income, which had effects on the

---

17. Since our pooled cross-section equations are estimated to only nine time series observations for any one city, using lags on the independent variables imposes a real cost in terms of loss of information. Thus we have not computed direct lags for any variable except grants (see note 13).

Table 6. Coefficients for Cross-section Equations Explaining Local Government Expenditures, Revenue, and Surplus, 1962–70[a]

Independent variable	Education $\Delta\left(\dfrac{E_1}{POP \cdot P_1}\right)$	Public safety $\Delta\left(\dfrac{E_2}{POP \cdot P_2}\right)$	Social services $\Delta\left(\dfrac{E_3}{POP \cdot P_3}\right)$	Urban support $\Delta\left(\dfrac{E_4}{POP \cdot P_4}\right)$	General government $\Delta\left(\dfrac{E_5}{POP \cdot P_5}\right)$	Negative taxes $\Delta\left(\dfrac{-T}{POP \cdot P}\right)$	Surplus $\Delta\left(\dfrac{\Delta NW}{POP \cdot P}\right)$
				Dependent variable			
Exogenous budgetary resources $\Delta\left(\dfrac{X}{POP \cdot P}\right)$	0.099 (1.0)	−0.066 (−1.0)	0.098 (1.0)	0.030 (0.3)	−0.034 (−0.4)	0.363 (2.7)	0.512 (3.6)
Lagged surplus $\Delta\left(\dfrac{\Delta NW_{-1}}{POP \cdot P}\right)$	0.016 (0.3)	...	...	0.033 (0.7)	0.012 (0.3)	0.266 (4.1)	−0.327 (−5.5)
Mandated C grant expenditures[b]							
Education[b] $\Delta L_1\left(\dfrac{E_{M1}}{POP \cdot P_1}\right)$	−0.461 (−3.0)	...	...	...	...	0.461 (3.0)	...
Social services[b] $\Delta L_3\left(\dfrac{E_{M3}}{POP \cdot P_3}\right)$	...	...	−0.417 (−1.2)	...	...	0.417 (1.2)	...
Urban support[b] $\Delta L_4\left(\dfrac{E_{M4}}{POP \cdot P_4}\right)$	...	...	...	−1.278 (−1.2)	...	1.278 (1.2)	...

	(1)	(2)	(3)	(4)	(5)	(6)	(7)
Income $\Delta\left(\dfrac{Y}{POP \cdot P}\right)$	0.017 (2.8)	0.009 (2.3)	0.003 (0.7)	0.013 (2.6)	...	−0.077 (−12.0)	0.035 (5.6)
Prices including A grant effects							
Public safety $\Delta\left(\dfrac{P_2(1 - M_A)}{P}\right)$	...	−0.407 (−3.5)	...	...	...	0.407 (3.5)	...
Social services $\Delta\left(\dfrac{P_3(1 - M_A)}{P}\right)$	...	...	−0.310 (−2.3)	...	...	0.310 (2.3)	...
Urban support $\Delta\left(\dfrac{P_4(1 - M_A)}{P}\right)$	...	...	...	−0.535 (−2.0)	...	0.535 (2.0)	...
Robbery rate $\Delta\left(\dfrac{ROB}{POP}\right)$	...	1.775 (2.5)	2.882 (4.0)	...	...	−4.658 (−5.7)	...
Suburban taxes $\Delta\left(\dfrac{T_S}{POP_S \cdot P}\right)$	0.216 (1.9)	...	...	...	0.189 (1.8)	−0.406 (−3.5)	...
Standard error of estimate	6.834	2.932	4.756	5.696	5.968	12.798	16.175
R^2 with first differences[c]	0.148	0.483	0.276	0.134	−0.039	0.206	0.208
R^2 with levels[c]	0.929	0.966	0.994	0.883	0.648	0.973	0.857

Sources: Cross-section equations based on eighty-four pooled annual observations for ten cities. See Appendix B for sources of the underlying data.

a. See Table 4 for definition of symbols. In addition, NW is net worth, the subscripts from 1 to 5 refer to the appropriate expenditure category, and the "S" subscript refers to the value of the variable for the high-income suburb of the relevant city.

b. L_1, L_3, and L_4 each have weights of 0.67 and 0.33 for t and t_{-1}, respectively.

c. For method of computation, see Table 4, note c.

surplus, we used the pattern of coefficients in the lagged surplus to determine the steady-state effects. Because the other independent variables did not affect the current surplus, their steady-state coefficients are the same as the impact coefficients in Table 6. Again, nondiscretionary expenditures are added in to present the table in terms of total expenditures, and the five functional components are also summed.

The effect of a dollar of revenue sharing on expenditures is weaker than in the time series estimates, with only $0.25 going to expenditures and $0.75 to tax reduction. This effect is still roughly five times the effect of income on expenditures, meaning that γ_2, the utility weight for income, remains about the same as before. The effect of categorical grants on spending is lower than before, however, because the displacement parameters, γ_{11}, γ_{13}, and γ_{14}, are larger than in the time series estimates. Each dollar of C grants now stimulates between $0.54 and $0.58 of additional spending for education and social services and actually reduces spending for the small urban support category. The pattern of these estimates suggests that grant displacement is greater the smaller are federal grants relative to local discretionary expenditures, or the more likely cities are to spend this amount of money on programs even in the absence of grants. These equations also indicate that the three significant price elasticities are in the -0.7 to -0.9 range, which implies that A grants stimulate spending by about $0.80 per dollar (see Appendix A for calculations), or by more than C grants. The one exception to this result is education, where the price substitution effect is absent but where categorical grants do stimulate more spending than lump-sum transfers and A grants. Such a finding is again inconsistent with the theory of grants unless there is a high degree of effective effort maintenance with case C grants for education.

The Impact of Federal Grant Policy on State and Local Expenditures

The results of this paper suggest that lump-sum transfers such as general revenue sharing will, for the first year, show up mainly as an increase in the accumulation of financial assets by states and localities. As stocks of assets rise, governments will be less inclined to expand them further, however, and will gradually use this new wealth to increase expenditures and reduce taxes. Ultimately, after about five years, each dollar of revenue sharing will enlarge state and local spending by about $0.43 according to

Table 7. Steady-state Coefficients and Elasticities from Cross-section Equations for Total Expenditures and Negative Taxes, Local Governments, 1962–70[a]

| | | Mandated C grant expenditures | | | | Prices, including A grant effects | | | | |
| | Exogenous budgetary resources $\left(\dfrac{X^b}{POP \cdot P}\right)$ | Education $\left(\dfrac{E_{M1}}{POP \cdot P_1}\right)$ | Social services $\left(\dfrac{E_{M3}}{POP \cdot P_3}\right)$ | Urban support $\left(\dfrac{E_{M4}}{POP \cdot P_4}\right)$ | Income $\left(\dfrac{Y^b}{POP \cdot P}\right)$ | Public safety $\left(\dfrac{P_2(1-M_A)}{P}\right)$ | Social services $\left(\dfrac{P_3(1-M_A)}{P}\right)$ | Urban support $\left(\dfrac{P_4(1-M_A)}{P}\right)$ | Robbery rate $\left(\dfrac{ROB}{POP}\right)$ | Suburban taxes $\left(\dfrac{T_s}{POP_s \cdot P}\right)$ |
Dependent variable										
1. Total expenditures $\left(\dfrac{EXP}{POP \cdot P_E}\right)$	0.245	0.539	0.583	−0.278	0.049 (0.86)	−0.407 (−0.71)°	−0.310 (−0.74)°	−0.535 (−0.92)°	4.658 (0.06)	0.406
2. Negative taxes $\left(\dfrac{-T}{POP \cdot P}\right)$	0.755	0.461	0.417	1.278	−0.049	0.407	0.310	0.535	−4.658	−0.406

Source: Table 6. The numbers in parentheses are the elasticities of total discretionary expenditures with respect to the independent variables unless otherwise indicated.

a. See Table 4 for definitions of symbols.

b. The equations were estimated using early-period payout coefficients. An alternative equation that ensures the proper equilibrium characteristics gives approximately the same results but does not fit as well.

c. Using E_t as the dependent variable.

Note: The parameter reflecting the relative preference for tax reduction, γ_2, is computed as in Table 5: $\gamma_2 = 0.049/0.245 = 0.20$. The three grant displacement parameters are

$\gamma_{11} = 0.461/0.755 = 0.61$

$\gamma_{13} = 0.417/0.755 = 0.55$

$\gamma_{14} = 1.278/0.755 = 1.69$,

for expenditure categories 1, 3, and 4, respectively.

the time series estimates and by about $0.25 according to the cross-section equations.[18] Although neither set of coefficients is estimated with much precision, together they indicate that a sizable part of revenue-sharing grants will result in reduction of state and local taxes below what they otherwise would have been. It also appears that revenue sharing will have less impact on expenditures than categorical grants but more impact than private incomes.

The estimated effects of categorical grants also differ between the time series and cross-section equations. In the time series versions, there is little evidence that categorical grants displace discretionary expenditures, with the result that grants increase total state and local spending by about $0.90 per dollar at present matching rates. Even this estimate is smaller than those reported by most other studies.[19] More displacement is estimated in the cross-section equations; there, categorical grants for education and social services increase expenditures by about $0.65 per dollar at present matching rates, and grants for urban support do not seem to increase expenditures even as much as do lump-sum transfers. In each case the displacement occurs quickly, so that expenditures and taxes are nearly at their equilibrium values by the end of the first year.

The time series equations revealed no price substitution effects for case A grants, which means that their effects are no larger than those of lump-sum transfers and are even smaller than those of categorical C grants. The cross-section equations did uncover significant, and fairly sizable, price substitution effects in three of the five categories of expenditure. In these categories A grants would stimulate spending by about $0.80 per dollar, or by slightly more than would categorical C grants.

Even if these numbers were perfectly reliable, they still would be difficult to use in appraising current policy actions regarding grants. General revenue sharing, for example, comes as close to being a pure lump-sum transfer as one would want. Yet even here, some restrictions are imposed on the

18. We know of only two other studies that report coefficients for the effect of lump-sum transfers on total expenditures. John C. Weicher, "Aid, Expenditures, and Local Government Structure," *National Tax Journal,* Vol. 25 (December 1972), pp. 573–83, finds this parameter to be higher; McGuire, "Federal-Local Interactions," finds it to be lower.

19. The most recent paper on this topic is Thomas O'Brien, "Grants-in-Aid: Some Further Answers," *National Tax Journal,* Vol. 24 (March 1971), pp. 65–77. A long list of previous studies was summarized in Edward M. Gramlich, "The Effect of Federal Grants on State-Local Expenditures: A Review of the Econometric Literature," National Tax Association, *Proceedings of the Sixty-second Annual Conference on Taxation, 1969* (1970), pp. 569–93.

uses to which local governments can put the money, and expenditures are subject to a minor additional stimulus due to a provision that distributes money partly on the basis of tax effort.[20] Furthermore, somewhat more money per capita goes to poorer governments, which may have higher spending propensities. And, finally, local governments may feel that the distribution could be temporary and that they must spend the money on programs to demonstrate their continuing need. Although the precise influence of these forces is impossible to determine, the estimated range for the equilibrium expenditure impact of $0.25 to $0.43 per dollar of grant—approximately $1.3 billion to $2.3 billion for a general revenue-sharing distribution of $5.5 billion—is probably somewhat low. All things considered, general revenue sharing ultimately should stimulate approximately $2 billion to $3 billion of additional expenditures at the state-local level, after fairly long lags.

The administration proposals to convert categorical grants to special revenue sharing are even more difficult to analyze. The proposed legislation combines many existing narrow categorical grant programs into broad special revenue-sharing grants for education, community development, manpower, and law enforcement. All matching requirements and effort maintenance restrictions are eliminated, as are many of the other restrictions on the uses to which the grant money can be put. In analyzing these proposals, account must then be taken both of the nature of the displacement operating in the particular grant being folded into special revenue sharing and of the types of restrictions included in the legislation.

In the limiting case in which the special revenue-sharing categories are defined so broadly that states and localities have broad scope for internal displacement, and in which other restrictions are minimal, special revenue sharing will operate much like a lump-sum transfer. In this event, converting an average categorical grant to special revenue sharing will reduce state and local spending by about $0.40 per dollar in either the time series or the cross-section estimates, or roughly $2.8 billion in terms of the administration's proposal to convert $6.9 billion of grants.[21] In the other limiting case, in which all present restrictions are continued and the matching rate

20. See Charles J. Goetz, "Federal Block Grants and the Reactivity Problem," *Southern Economic Journal*, Vol. 34 (July 1967), pp. 160–65; and Richard A. Musgrave and A. Mitchell Polinsky, "Revenue-Sharing, A Critical View," *Financing State and Local Governments*, Proceedings of the Monetary Conference Sponsored by the Federal Reserve Bank of Boston, June 1970 (FRBB, 1970), pp. 17–52.

21. *Special Analyses, Budget of the United States Government, Fiscal Year 1974*, Special Analysis N.

(M_C) is simply set at unity, the average reduction in state and local spending would be about $0.10 per dollar in either set of equations, or only $0.7 billion. The real impact should fall somewhere between these extremes, depending on the provisions of special revenue sharing, but will probably fall closer to the higher figure.

Apart from these effects on overall expenditures, the interesting social questions concerning categorical grants and whether they should be converted into special revenue sharing require examination of the programmatic distribution of funds within these overall totals. This paper provides some evidence that such distributional questions are important, for the displacement effects of present categorical grants suggest that states and localities may now to some extent frustrate the implied purpose of the federal grant programs, and may do so to an even greater extent if present restrictions on the use of the money are relaxed. But to determine the implications of such shifts requires a much more detailed and disaggregated study of the operation of individual grant programs.

The Meaning of Recent Movements in the State-Local Budget Surplus

For the postwar period as a whole, state and local general governments have greatly enlarged their stocks of tangible capital, partially by increasing stocks of net financial obligations. Thus even though the net worth of general governments has risen, their national accounts budget has typically been in deficit by about $3 billion annually. This deficit has been almost exactly offset by the retirement fund surplus, which has averaged about the same amount, although these deficits and surpluses have not been identical at all times.

In 1971 and 1972, however, this picture changed radically. The overall state and local surplus reached a postwar high of $3.8 billion in the second quarter of 1970 and then, after slipping back briefly, rose to the remarkable amount of $19.5 billion in the fourth quarter of 1972. This sharp increase has raised some eyebrows, including those of David Ott and his associates, who have wondered whether the federal government was "impoverishing itself while putting the states and local governments as a group in a position of relative fiscal affluence."[22] In this section we use our model to examine the implications of this growth in the surplus.

22. Ott and others, *Nixon, McGovern, and the Federal Budget*, p. 3. This phenomenon has also been noticed by the Office of Management and Budget, though, as might be

Our dynamic theory suggests that changes in the surplus take the brunt of the immediate adjustment of state and local budgets to outside forces. For example, most of any exogenous inflow of funds initially swells the surplus, and only gradually affects expenditures or taxes. Similarly, in the first round, changes in other independent variables, such as income, prices, nondiscretionary expenditures, or the demographic terms, affect the activity to which they are directly related and the surplus; later, they affect other, competing, activities, which are affected by this change in the surplus. Viewed in this light, the surplus is really the mechanism through which the lagged response of the entire state and local budget to an outside change takes effect—or the temporary cushion that allows state and local governments flexibility in planning.

In the long run, by contrast, the surplus is assumed not to respond at all to outside forces. Once states and localities have used exogenous inflows of funds to build up their stocks of net financial assets through short-run surpluses, they have no further need to accumulate or decumulate.

These observations underlie an examination of the experience of the 1970–72 period reported in Table 8. The first row in the table gives the gross surplus on the national income accounts basis of the state and local sector, the series that has caused all the excitement. The second row then gives our quarterly estimate of the surplus of state and local retirement funds, which rose to $8.6 billion in 1972. Earlier we argued that it was difficult, if not impossible, to read this number as an indication of the financial strength of retirement funds, since information about the present value of their contractual obligations is not available; it follows therefore that it indicates little about the financial position of state and local general governments.

The third row gives the general government surplus after retirement fund surpluses have been deducted. Before these numbers can be interpreted, two accounting adjustments must be made for special factors that artificially altered the pattern of the surplus in 1972. The first adjustment undoes the effect of an advance payment of public assistance grants in the second quarter of 1972, which raised the surplus $4.0 billion at annual rates in the second quarter and will reduce it correspondingly in the first quarter of 1973. The second adjustment is for general revenue sharing, which was passed by Congress after the third quarter was over, with a

---

expected, not as a prelude to questioning revenue sharing. See *Budget . . . 1974*, Special Analysis N.

Table 8. Analysis of the Budget Surplus of State and Local Governments, 1970–72
Billions of current dollars at seasonally adjusted annual rates

Description	1970				1971				1972			
	I	*II*	*III*	*IV*	*I*	*II*	*III*	*IV*	*I*	*II*	*III*	*IV*
1. Total national income accounts (NIA) surplus	3.6	3.8	2.9	0.9	2.0	5.0	6.2	6.0	7.1	14.8	9.4	19.5
2. Less: surplus of retirement funds	6.2	6.4	6.6	6.8	7.1	7.4	7.7	8.0	8.3	8.5	8.7	8.9
3. General government NIA surplus	−2.6	−2.6	−3.7	−5.9	−5.1	−2.4	−1.5	−2.0	−1.2	6.3	0.7	10.6
4. Adjustment due to speedup in public assistance payments	...	...	...	...	...	...	...	...	...	−4.0	...	...
5. Adjustment due to retroactive payment of general revenue sharing	...	...	...	...	...	...	...	...	...	...	...	−5.2
6. Adjusted general government NIA surplus	−2.6	−2.6	−3.7	−5.9	−5.1	−2.4	−1.5	−2.0	−1.2	2.3	0.7	5.4
7. Residual (actual less predicted), time series equation	0.4	0.2	−0.7	−2.2	1.1	2.6	1.4	0.1	0.8	3.3	−1.3	−1.2

Sources: Line 1—*Survey of Current Business*, Vol. 53 (April 1973), and Vol. 52 (July 1972), Table 3.4; lines 2–6—derived by authors as explained in the text; line 7—residual from equation in Table 4.

double payment of $10.5 billion ($5.2 billion retroactive, $5.3 billion current) made in the fourth quarter. Table 8 retains the current payment but line 5 and hence line 6 eliminate the fourth quarter retroactive payment from the surplus.

The resulting adjusted general government surplus (line 6) looks much less remarkable than the published series (line 1). There was still a rise, totaling $11.3 billion between the low point in the fourth quarter of 1970 and the high point in the fourth quarter of 1972, but this rise could have been expected over the period. Our equations indicate that in the first quarter of general revenue sharing, more than 95 percent of the $5.3 billion disbursement could be expected to be saved, thus immediately accounting for $4.8 billion of this change in the surplus. In addition over the two-year interval the growth in real income was responsible for another $1.5 billion, and the growth in other grants and the demographic factors (mainly the decline in numbers of school children) for another $4.0 billion; the residual increased only $1.0 billion. In fact, after account has been taken of all of the independent variables in our equation, the 1972 residuals (line 7) do not reveal anything very surprising: They are not very large and are even negative in the last two quarters.

Moreover, even if all of the independent variables remain at their recent levels—and at least the grant and demographic variables should do so—this discussion suggests that the high general government surpluses should be reduced and eventually eliminated. Precisely because state and local governments have used this period to build up their stocks of net financial assets, they are likely to use their new-found financial cushion to allocate their surpluses into higher flows of expenditures or reductions in taxes, with somewhat more going to the latter according to our estimates.[23] Whether one believes this process to be an unwarranted "impoverishment" of the federal government then depends not on the size of the surplus, which should decline, but on whether one prefers his tax reductions and expenditure increases to occur at the state and local or national level.

Conclusion

The aim of this paper has been to assess the role of federal grants and other factors in influencing the budgetary behavior of state and local gov-

23. Notice that this statement applies only to general governments. There is no reason why the trust fund surplus, and therefore the overall state and local surplus,

ernments. It has distinguished among three different types of grants—those that operate only through prices, those that operate only through budgetary inflows, and those that have both price and income effects. It has estimated equations that allow for different responses for the different types of grants, along with income and other demographic factors, all the time ensuring that the estimates are internally consistent from a budgetary standpoint.

Although the results are tenuous and should be accepted with a good deal of caution, we find that pure lump-sum transfers are likely to stimulate between $0.25 and $0.43 of expenditures for each dollar of grant. This range must be adjusted upwards before it is applied to the recently enacted general revenue sharing due to several minor additional stimuli to expenditures in the legislation; thus we would expect $5.5 billion of revenue sharing to increase state-local spending by $2 billion to $3 billion. The administration's proposal to convert $7 billion of categorical assistance to special revenue sharing is, on the other hand, likely to reduce overall state and local spending by $1 billion to $3 billion, according to our estimates.

Further, we do not read much into the recent sharp growth in the state and local budget surplus on the national income accounts basis. Over half the surplus in 1972 was earned by state and local retirement funds; but the surplus is not a good indicator of their present financial health. The remaining portion resulted directly from the initiation of general revenue sharing, cyclical movements in income, and the decline in numbers of school-age children. But even if these forces were to continue, we feel confident that the surpluses would ultimately be reduced in favor of a combination of higher state-local expenditures and lower taxes. If a case is to be made against revenue sharing, it is not that the present state and local budget surplus is too high, but that the prospective mix of additional expenditures and tax reductions has a lower priority than some other federal use of this money.

---

should stop growing. Ott and his associates also seem to be somewhat ambivalent on their outlook for the overall surplus (*Nixon, McGovern, and the Federal Budget*, p. 24).

[3]

EDWARD M. GRAMLICH
University of Michigan

State and Local Budgets the Day after It Rained: Why Is the Surplus So High?

READERS of the financial press will be shocked to find that, in the aggregate, the 78,000 state and local governments in this country are running a hefty budget surplus. These governments had a combined budget surplus of $29.2 billion in 1977, by far the largest ever recorded, and in part offsetting the impact of the one government most noticeably not in surplus (the federal deficit was $49.6 billion in that year). The rise in the state and local surplus has been exceedingly dramatic: at its recession low in the first quarter of 1975 it was $3.7 billion; by the third quarter of 1977 it had risen to $32.9 billion, accounting for over one-third of the national rise in gross saving over this two-year period.

Such large changes in the saving behavior of any sector are interesting in their own right, and they have important macroeconomic implications for short-run stabilization policies and long-run growth. In this report I examine both matters. I first disaggregate the budgetary numbers to explore separately movements in the surplus of state and local pension funds and general governments on both current and capital accounts. I then estimate some time-series equations explaining state and local budgetary magnitudes up to 1974, making out-of-sample extrapolations of these

Note: Mark Greene has helped me understand the Michigan computer, John Gorman the treatment of pension fund surpluses, Serge Taylor environmental impact statements, and Roger Vaughan the local public works bill. I would also like to thank Ronald Ehrenberg, Alan Fechter, Harvey Galper, Robert Hartman, Robert Reischauer, and Daniel Rubinfeld for their comments on an earlier version.

0007-2303/78/0001-0191$00.25/0 © Brookings Institution

equations to see how well recent budget movements can be explained. These extrapolations are used to search out any recent shift in state and local spending and taxing behavior—possibly related to the severe 1975 recession which might have drawn down financial assets to dangerously low levels, possibly to federal policies adopted at that time. Then I examine the behavior of state and local budgets over the 1975 recession and calculate the likely impact of various components of the recently enacted economic-stimulus package.

Recent Movements in the State and Local Surplus

The first matter is the relatively straightforward identification of the source of the recent growth in the surplus. This information is given in table 1. The first column shows the total surplus and the next two divide it into two components, the saving (as measured in the national income accounts) of employees' pension funds (column 2) and that of state and local general governments (column 3). The surplus is larger for the pension funds, but the more dramatic changes, and departures from past experience, are for general governments.

The next three columns show how the surplus of general governments might be split into its current and capital components. The surplus given in the national accounts treats all state and local construction expenditures as outlays, but does not consider retirement of long-term debt (which might be viewed as a proxy for capital consumption) as an outlay. To derive the current operating surplus for state and local governments, the number that cannot be negative for a government under most legal or constitutional restrictions, I have deducted net construction expenditures from total outlays (that is, added column 4 to the general government surplus), and then added debt retirement to outlays (that is, deducted column 5 from the surplus).[1] The resulting numbers in column 6 show that the rise in the surplus has come in roughly equal parts from the current budget (column 6) and the sharp fall in net construction expenditures (column 4).

The proper treatment of employees' pension funds for the present

1. In fact, as the New York City experience has indicated, inventive local officials do not always find it difficult to get around this restriction. They can sometimes borrow short term "in anticipation" of future revenues, or they can hide some current expenditures in the capital account and finance them with long-term debt.

Edward M. Gramlich   193

Table 1. Budget Surplus of State and Local Governments, by Component, Quarterly, 1974–77[a]

Billions of current dollars, seasonally adjusted annual rate

Year and quarter	Total surplus (1)	Social insurance funds (2)	General governments			
			Total (3)	Net construction expenditures[b] (4)	Retirement of long-term debt[c] (5)	Operating budget (6)
1974:1	9.5	9.8	−0.3	26.2	10.3	15.6
2	8.8	10.3	−1.5	28.0	10.5	16.0
3	7.7	10.7	−3.0	27.6	10.7	13.9
4	4.2	11.1	−6.8	27.2	10.9	9.5
1975:1	3.7	11.3	−7.6	25.7	11.1	7.0
2	4.5	11.8	−7.2	26.6	11.3	8.1
3	6.6	12.3	−5.8	27.4	11.5	10.1
4	8.9	13.1	−4.2	27.0	11.7	11.1
1976:1	13.3	13.7	−0.4	25.7	11.9	13.4
2	12.9	14.4	−1.5	23.9	12.0	10.4
3	21.1	14.8	6.2	21.7	12.1	15.8
4	26.5	15.2	11.3	19.3	12.2	18.4
1977:1	27.3	15.4	11.9	16.9	12.3	16.5
2	25.4	15.5	10.0	20.1	12.4	17.7

Sources: *Survey of Current Business*, vol. 57 (July and November 1977), tables 3.4, 3.7, 3.14; and U.S. Bureau of the Census, *Governmental Finances in 1975–76*, series GF 76 no. 5 (Government Printing Office, 1977), and various preceding issues, table 3. Column 3 equals column 1 minus column 2. Column 6 equals column 3 plus column 4 minus column 5. Figures are rounded.

a. Most of the numbers for 1977 are estimates.

b. Construction expenditures minus an interpolated estimate of grants for capital construction. The numbers are treated as expenditures in the national income accounts, but not in the current operating budgets of most state and local governments.

c. Interpolation of annual numbers for the retirement of long-term debt of state and local governments. This item is viewed as a mandated expenditure in the operating budgets of state and local governments but is not treated as an expenditure in the national income accounts.

analysis is something of a mystery. First of all it is not even clear that the recorded surplus is a surplus. It simply measures the cash-flow status of employees' pension funds: in 1977:2, for example, employees' payroll contributions and interest earnings exceeded benefit payments by $15.5 billion. This large surplus reveals nothing about whether the funds are actuarially sound (indeed, many of them are not). The surplus does not even imply that their actuarial position improved in the quarter (which it probably did not). The surplus is simply a cash-flow concept, necessary to make the national income statements balance but not a good measure of the financial health of the trust funds.

The second puzzle regards the ownership of these pension surpluses. The national income accounts make a distinction between governmental and nongovernmental pension funds. Surpluses of nongovernmental pension funds are considered a form of deferred compensation of the employees and are added into personal income and, net of any impact on private consumption, to personal saving. Surpluses of governmental pensions, the largest of which is social security, are treated as public saving. While this distinction may be appropriate for social security, which is owned by its future beneficiaries in only a very remote sense, it seems much more questionable for state and local pensions, which resemble private pension plans in the degree to which they are "owned" by employees.

On both counts, therefore, the meaning of the component of saving in pension funds is ambiguous. On one hand, this total does not represent saving in the usual net-worth sense, and on the other, it appears in the public sector only through an accounting quirk. Accordingly, for the balance of this discussion I will simply ignore pension funds, focusing only on the budgetary behavior of general governments.[2]

Regression Estimates of State and Local Budgets

The approach used to explain recent changes in state and local budgets is to fit an empirical model to a stable period, say 1954–74, and then see if these coefficients predict actual budget changes in a turbulent period, 1975–77. If the equations predict well, there is no surprise in the recent developments: they have followed historical responses to determinants of state and local budgets. If the equations do not predict well, the question is, how have the historical patterns of response changed?

An empirical model explaining the budgetary behavior of state and local general governments can be developed through orthodox utility-maximization principles. Assume that state and local decisionmakers, whether private or public employees,[3] take all wages and prices as given

2. The flow-of-funds accounts already follow this reasoning and omit surpluses of state and local pension funds from government saving.

3. It clearly does matter which they are, but for now I gloss over that issue and simply deal with one aggregate decisionmaker. For a more careful treatment of this issue, see Paul Courant, Edward M. Gramlich, and Daniel Rubinfeld, "Public Employee Market Power and the Level of Government Spending" (University of Michigan, Institute for Public Policy Studies, 1977; processed).

and maximize an objective function dependent on (a) public current consumption; (b) private consumption; (c) the stock of public capital; (d) the stock of public financial assets. After adjusting each of these arguments for the complex ways in which different types of federal grants enter the picture, the respective first-order conditions can be transformed into state and local demand functions in which spending, taxes, and the surplus depend on lagged stocks of capital and financial assets, income, relative prices, federal grants, and demographic need variables. The way in which this is done is essentially that developed by Galper and myself five years ago,[4] with two new wrinkles.

First, the original analysis distinguished between open- and closed-end categorical matching grants (there called case A and case C grants). Since their impacts on spending were found to be quite similar, in this paper the two types of grants are combined and treated as if they were all closed-end grants. The distinction between categorical aid (C grants) and noncategorical aid (B grants) is maintained, however.

Second, since state and local employment has become an object of interest, an employment component is broken out of current expenditures, with the remainder—"all other"—including purchases of nonconstruction goods and nonemployment services and transfer payments.

The arguments in the state and local utility function (Q_i) are then

$$(1a) \qquad Q_1 = E_1/W + \gamma_1 \frac{1}{m_1} G_1/W - N$$

$$(1b) \qquad Q_2 = E_2/P + \gamma_2 \frac{1}{m_2} G_2/P - N$$

$$(1c) \quad Q_3 = E_3/P_k + \gamma_3 \frac{1}{m_3} G_3/P_k + (1 - \delta)K_{-1}/P_k = E_3/P_k + K'/P_k$$

$$(1d) \qquad Q_4 = \gamma_4 Y/P - T/P$$

$$(1e) \qquad Q_5 = F_{-1}/P + S/P.$$

The first two arguments, equations 1a and 1b, relate current consumption to discretionary spending on employment (E_1) and all other (E_2), deflated by the state and local wage rate (W) and the GNP deflator (P), respectively. Total spending in these components can be derived by adding

4. Edward M. Gramlich and Harvey Galper, "State and Local Fiscal Behavior and Federal Grant Policy," *BPEA, 1:1973*, pp. 15–58.

the spending generated by federal categorical grants (G_1 and G_2), multiplied by the inverse of the federal matching ratio (m_1 and m_2) to give the spending mandated on receipt of these grants. In utility terms, however, federal grants may not increase state and local welfare at the same rate as discretionary spending, and the "displacement" parameters γ_i are inserted to adjust for this heterogeneity. The closer the γ_i are to one, the more substitutable are grant-mandated and discretionary spending, and the more state and local governments might be expected to respond to federal categorical grants by cutting back their own spending in that area. The final adjustment in these two arguments is for some as yet unspecified vector of demographic needs (N). The higher the needs—as measured by, say, the welfare or school-age population—the less utility is implied by a given amount of expenditures and the more likely is the district to increase expenditures.

Argument 1c deals with the capital stock. Here, utility depends on discretionary and mandated spending on construction, still deflated by the price of capital goods (P_k). Since the stock of capital is not entirely consumed in one period, however, the lagged stock of capital also adds to utility—$K_{-1}(1 - \delta)$, where δ is the quarterly depreciation rate. The higher this lagged stock, the less occasion to add to it through further current construction. To simplify the model, because $K_{-1}(1 - \delta)$ and construction grants are both exogenous and operate through the same utility parameters, they are combined into one K' term (using for γ_3 an average estimate of γ_1 and γ_2 implicit in the first two arguments).

The fourth argument, 1d, involves private spending. In a world of no illusions and perfect voter control of bureaucrats, γ_4 would equal unity and the private-spending argument would be simply real gross national product after federal taxes (Y/P) less real state and local taxes (T/P). On the other hand, in the real world, in which voters are not perfectly able to control politicians and these bureaucrats and politicians in effect have extra votes, the community might behave as if more utility is gained through a cut in taxes (for which politicians can claim credit) than through a rise in income (for which they cannot). Should this be the case, the "income displacement" parameter γ_4 is less than one, and the source of income becomes important in determining the level of community public and private spending. Changes in private income and noncategorical grants will stimulate exactly the same amount of public spending per dollar when $\gamma_4 = 1$, but noncategorical grants, which are already in the public treasury and do not require the painful act of increasing taxes, will stimulate more public spending when $\gamma_4 < 1$.[5]

The final argument, 1e, describes the stock of accumulated financial assets. As this stock, which includes lagged financial assets (F_{-1}) plus the current surplus (S), becomes greater, there will be less incentive to run further surpluses and more incentive to raise expenditures or lower taxes. In the long run the stock of financial assets, not the flow of new saving, is assumed to adjust to a change in grants, income, or prices, and the flow of saving will return to its level before that change.

Utility maximization in effect determines how states and localities allocate scarce budgetary resources to these five competing claims. Governments maximize

$$(2) \qquad U = f(Q_i), \text{ for } i = 1, \ldots, 5,$$
$$f'(Q_i) > 0, \quad f''(Q_i) < 0,$$

subject to the budget constraint that

$$(3) \qquad S = X + T - E_1 - E_2 - E_3.$$

Here X is exogenous budgetary resources—untied revenue-sharing aid to the community less predetermined expenditures for debt service and less the amount necessary to match categorical grants $G_i - (G_i/m_i)$.[6] Performing the usual algebraic operations leads to the set of estimating equations used below. However, a number of specific problems had to be dealt with in making the actual estimates.

Definition of N. In previous work Galper and I used one variable (the proportion of families headed by females) to measure the population

---

5. Another way to think of this phenomenon is to postulate a "flypaper" effect: money sticks where it hits. The obvious explanation is a bureaucratic one, but there could also be an economic rationale, working through the misperception of the true marginal price of public expenditures in the presence of lump-sum grants. See Paul Courant, Edward M. Gramlich, and Daniel Rubinfeld, "The Stimulative Effects of Intergovernmental Grants: Why Money Sticks Where It Hits" (University of Michigan, Institute for Public Policy Studies, 1977; processed).

6. Were the budget-constraint identity written in terms of total expenditures, it would be

$$S = T - E_1 - \frac{1}{m_1} G_1 - E_2 - \frac{1}{m_2} G_2 - E_3 - \frac{1}{m_3} G_3 + X' + G_1 + G_2 + G_3,$$

where X' is lump-sum transfers less debt-service payments. The exogenous-resources term used in the text is then derived as

$$X = X' + \sum_{i=1}^{3} \left(1 - \frac{1}{m_i}\right) G_i.$$

dependent on welfare and one (the proportion of school-age children in the population) to measure needs for public schooling. When estimated up to 1974, the latter variable no longer was statistically significant, presumably because its steady decline was not reflected in a concomitant drop in spending on public schools. Hence it was no longer included. On the other hand, it has been claimed that state and local employment spending is inherently countercyclical, always rising more in a recession in direct violation of the presumed impact of the budget constraint (unless governments have saved a stock of assets for this rainy day).[7] This hypothesis was tested by including the unemployment rate, with constant demographic weights, as an additional needs variable.

Definition of relative prices. The relative price of compensation expenditures is assumed to be simply W/P, where W is the average wage used to deflate compensation expenditures. For construction, there is the additional complication that benefits are received over time, so that the appropriate price is the annual opportunity cost of capital $(R + 4\delta)P_k/P$, where R is the Aaa municipal bond rate. Attempts to use the Baa rate gave approximately the same results; attempts to use the two rates together did not prove very successful, presumably because of multicollinearity.

Scale of the economy. Since all price-deflated real variables would grow naturally with population size, giving all variables a common trend and possibly introducing heteroskedasticity, all dependent variables and all independent variables except the two relative-price terms and the needs variables are deflated by population.

Autocorrelation. Errors in the state-local sector are strongly autocorrelated, possibly because the quarterly data are not very good and a variety of interpolation techniques are used by the Bureau of Economic Analysis to estimate budgetary variables. To deal with this problem, first differences are used in all estimations, and all statistics on equation fit refer to differences.

Lagged responses. Many of the independent variables should operate through lagged responses. Since there are cross-equation restrictions on coefficients, the lags in the individual equations should be related through the budget identity. I have dealt with this problem by making initial estimates of the equations using the Almon interpolation procedure, and then simplifying those lags to lagged independent variables with constant

7. See, for example, Walter Ebanks, "The Stabilizing Effects of Government Employment," *Explorations in Economic Research*, vol. 3 (Fall 1976), pp. 564–83.

weights (to avoid a proliferation of independent variables). All of the independent variables showed weights so heavily pointed toward the current quarter that I simply used that value except for income (for which the choice was lag weights of 0.67 and 0.33 in t and $t - 1$) and the cost-of-capital variables (for which the lag was rectangular for the current and previous seven periods).[8]

Cross-equation constraints. The variables dealt with here are all components of a budget identity, and it is possible to use the identity to improve the efficiency of the parameter estimates. First, one of the dependent variables in the model is defined so that the sum of all five dependent variables is $(F_{-1} + X)/P$, disposable financial resources. When each of the five equations is estimated using the entire set of independent variables, the sum of the coefficients of $(F_{-1} + X)/P$ across all five equations will be unity and the sum of all other coefficients zero, automatically ensuring consistency of the coefficients with the budgetary identity. But this technique does not give uniformly reasonable coefficients because it is not possible to drop any wrongly signed or insignificant independent variable from any equation without violating the identity constraints. As an alternative, both the original paper and this one use a stacking procedure that permits dropping of individual independent variables from certain equations while maintaining the cross-equation restrictions. This procedure involves running regressions with gigantic independent and dependent variables constructed to embody the budget identity. To ensure that no one stack receives disproportionate weight in forming the overall estimates, each stack is multiplied by the inverse of its standard error.[9]

The estimates using the stacking method are given in table 2. The re-

8. Since the lag on income depends mainly on the response of taxes to income changes, it is mildly surprising that it is so short. The reason seems to be that sales, corporate, and income taxes, which now account for over half of aggregate tax revenues of state and local general governments, respond quickly while revenues from the property tax apparently respond very sluggishly, so much so that their responses may be accounted for by deflating income and taxes by prices and population.

Also in this connection, Galper's and my previous article on this subject contained a separate direct lag on X, to see if the coefficients differed from those for F_{-1}. That variable had a t ratio of only 0.9 ("State and Local Fiscal Behavior," table 4), and on another try the significance level was reduced even further. Hence this time around I dropped it.

9. This procedure appears to have been invented but never written up by Frank de Leeuw. I have an appendix, available on request, that describes how I did it in this case. One can also perform the same operations and impose additional constraints on the cross-equation residuals through the use of a generalized least-squares program, but computer costs would rise sharply.

200   *Brookings Papers on Economic Activity, 1:1978*

Table 2. Coefficients, Derived by the Stacking Procedure, Explaining the Behavior of State and Local Government Budgets, Quarterly Observations, 1954-74

Independent variable[a] and summary statistic	Dependent variable[a]				
	E_1/W	E_2/P	E_3/P_k	$-T/P$	$(F_{-1}+X+T-E_2)/P$ $-E_1/W-E_3/P_k$
Independent variable					
$(F_{-1}+X)/P$	...	0.0136 (1.2)	...	0.705 (6.1)	0.9159 (47.8)
Y/P	0.0269 (4.2)	0.0148 (1.4)	0.0163 (1.3)	−0.0825 (−7.7)	0.0245 n.c.
$\dfrac{1}{m_1}G_1/W$	−0.9032 (−19.6)	...	...	...	0.9032 (19.6)
$\dfrac{1}{m_2}G_2/P$	...	−0.9631 (−21.0)	...	...	0.9631 (21.0)
K'/P_k	0.0274 (11.6)	0.0182 (3.0)	−0.0011 (−0.2)	...	−0.0445 n.c.
W/P	−159.1 (−6.3)	...	...	...	159.1 (6.3)
$(R+4\delta)P_k/P$	...	6.48 (3.4)	−5.53 (−2.2)	...	−0.95 n.c.
FEM	...	7.77 (2.1)	...	...	−7.77 (−2.1)
UR	1.22 (2.7)	0.79 (1.1)	...	...	−2.01 n.c.
Summary statistic[b]					
R^2	0.8272	0.8750	0.0647	0.2668	0.9572
Standard error	1.389	2.068	3.931	4.062	5.133
Durbin-Watson	1.89	1.82	1.88	1.04	1.75

Source: Text equation 1.

a. The first five independent variables and all of the dependent variables are deflated by the total U.S. population. *FEM* is the proportion of U.S. families headed by females, and *UR* is the unemployment rate with constant demographic weights. All other variables are defined in the text. All variables are in first-difference form. The numbers in parentheses are *t* ratios.

b. Summary statistics refer to the first-difference residuals.

n.c. Not calculated.

sults of the equations for employment (E_1), other expenditures (E_2), and the surplus are very similar to single-equation estimates of these relations, with only a few insignificant and unimportant variables dropped and virtually no change in the fit statistics.[10] The single-equation estimates for both the construction (E_3) and tax (T) equations had some independent variables that were significant with the wrong sign, however, and that had to be dropped to give sensible structural equations. These equations suffered an increase ranging from 5 to 15 percent in their standard error in the stacked equations shown in table 2.

Estimated Impacts

Interpretation of the coefficients of these equations revolves around the surplus variable. For example, a rise of \$1 in GNP (second row) initially raises expenditures by \$0.0580 (0.0269 + 0.0148 + 0.0163) and tax revenues by \$0.0825. The difference, \$0.0245, augments the budget surplus in the short run. But this change in the surplus raises next period's stocks of net financial assets (F) by the same amount, and is thereby gradually dispersed to further increases in expenditures and reductions in taxes. In the long run financial stocks rise to a new equilibrium level, the flow of the budget surplus is unchanged, and both expenditures and taxes are higher by \$0.0620.

Table 3 gives short- and long-run coefficients for other important variables. All are computed in a similar manner, except that grant-mandated expenditures are added back to discretionary expenditures to give the results in terms of total expenditures. Estimates of the displacement parameters $(\gamma_1$ and $\gamma_2)$ are very high, so even categorical grants are seen to stimulate only between \$0.09 and \$0.18 of state-local spending per dollar in the short run, and just slightly more in the long run. These impacts are higher than those for untied grants, however, as would be expected because categorical grants have some relative-price effect at the margin. But the long-run impact of untied grants still exceeds that of a change in private income, confirming the existence of a flypaper effect. Finally, the short-run relative-wage elasticity for compensation expenditures is -0.43

10. Note from equation 3 that if all prices $(P, W,$ and $P_k)$ are equal, the fifth dependent variable becomes $(F_{-1} + S)/P$, and since F_{-1}/P is exogenous, the equation explains S/P.

Table 3. Short- and Long-Run Responses of Expenditures and Tax Revenues to Changes in Income and Grants, 1954–74

Per unit change in the independent variable

	Dependent variable			
	Expenditures		Tax revenues	
Independent variable	Short run	Long run	Short run	Long run
Income, Y	0.0580	0.0620	0.0825	0.0620
Untied grants, X	0.0136	0.1617	−0.0705	−0.8383
Categorical grants, G_1[a]				
$m_1 = 1$	0.0968	0.2429	...	−0.7571
$m_1 = 0.8$	0.1136	0.2632	0.0176	−0.7368
$m_1 = 0.5$	0.1800	0.3241	0.0705	−0.6759

Source: Based on equations of table 2.
a. m_1 is the federal matching ratio.

and the long-run elasticity −0.36, again confirming the relatively low implied price elasticities and expenditure impacts of categorical grants.[11]

Forecasts of Recent Changes

The next issue is to see how well these equations forecast recent changes. Have any recent events—say, the particularly severe 1975 recession—encouraged state and local governments to save more because they now believe it will rain harder or more often? To examine recent behavior, constants were added to the first-difference equations of table 2 to make them perfectly accurate in predicting levels in 1974:4, and a ten-quarter dynamic simulation running through 1977:2 was conducted. The simulation is dynamic because the simulated, not the actual, value of the surplus was used in computing subsequent financial stocks.

The results are given in table 4. In the case of compensation, the model overpredicts expenditures by an amount that gradually grows to $3.9 billion by mid-1977. These residuals are a good deal larger than the standard error of the regression equation converted to billions of current dollars (in the last row), but that might be expected when the residuals are strongly autocorrelated. The average new residual each quarter is

11. For what it is worth, the grant impacts identified here are below most others reported in the literature and somewhat below those estimated by Galper and myself last time ("State and Local Fiscal Behavior," pp. 42–46). To find a flypaper effect is, however, quite standard.

approximately what is implied by the fitted regressions, and because these residuals are persistently negative, the level of expenditures gradually drifts off. At its peak, however, this residual is still less than 3 percent of compensation expenditures.

The errors in predicting other expenditures are also modest, though their signs are reversed. This equation simulates quite accurately for a year, and then begins gradually to underpredict expenditures; the error peaks at 8 percent of expenditures. The compensation equation (column 1), and the equation for other expenditures (column 2), are quite accurate in predicting total current expenditures (column 3): here the peak error is only 1.3 percent of expenditures. This seems a rather good performance for a ten-period dynamic simulation, though it has obviously been made possible partly by offsetting errors.

The tax residuals are slightly larger, but not as persistent. The tax equation begins by overpredicting and then, halfway through the simulation period, underpredicts. The largest overprediction is 2.5 percent of tax revenues and the largest underprediction, 2.7 percent. When the tax and current-expenditure residuals are combined, as in column 7, the current surplus is seen to be too high by a maximum of $3.5 billion in 1975:2 and too low by a maximum of $1.4 billion in 1977:1. While both errors are still reasonably small for out-of-period dynamic simulations, there is some tendency for the equations to understate the growth of the current-account surplus. Over the period 1975:1 to 1977:2, the actual current surplus grew by $10.8 billion (table 1) and the predicted surplus by $8.4 billion.

Unfortunately, the relatively minor errors for the current budget do not carry over to the capital budget. The simulation predicts construction expenditures fairly well for four quarters, but then the residuals quickly become very large. The construction equation in table 2 simply cannot explain the nosedive in actual construction expenditures. From the peak in 1975:3 to the trough in 1977:1, actual construction expenditures fell by $8.9 billion in current dollars. This represented a 25 percent decline in current dollars and a 31 percent decline in real per capita terms. Over this period capital grants from the federal government grew by $1.2 billion, which meant that mandated spending grew by $1.5 billion and that the fall in discretionary construction expenditures was even larger, $10.4 billion. The equation in table 2 predicted rising construction, however. Real per capita GNP after federal taxes grew by 4.3 percent over this

Table 4. Dynamic Simulation Errors for Expenditures and Taxes of State and Local General Governments, Quarterly, 1975–77
Billions of current dollars, seasonally adjusted annual rate

Year and quarter	Expenditures					Taxes (6)	Current surplus[c] (7)	Total surplus[d] (8)
	Current			Construction (4)	Total[b] (5)			
	Compensation (1)	Other (2)	Total current[a] (3)					
1975:1	...	0.2	0.2	−1.2	−1.0	−1.7	−1.9	−0.7
2	−0.3	−0.4	−0.7	−0.7	−1.4	−4.2	−3.5	−2.8
3	−1.2	0.3	−0.8	−0.2	−1.0	−4.1	−3.3	−3.1
4	−1.6	0.7	−0.9	−0.8	−1.8	−3.6	−2.7	−1.8
1976:1	−2.3	1.4	−0.8	−3.0	−3.8	−1.2	−0.4	2.7
2	−2.1	3.5	1.4	−5.4	−4.0	0.5	−0.9	4.5
3	−2.7	3.9	1.2	−8.4	−7.2	0.1	−1.1	7.3
4	−3.4	6.0	2.6	−11.8	−9.2	2.6	0.0	11.8
1977:1	−3.3	7.4	4.1	−16.0	−11.9	5.5	1.4	17.5
2	−3.9	8.2	4.3	−15.1	−10.8	4.8	0.5	15.6
Standard error[e]	0.4	0.6	n.c.	1.2	n.c.	1.2	n.c.	1.5

Source: Based on equations of table 2. Figures are rounded.
a. The sum of columns 1 and 2.
b. The sum of columns 3 and 4.
c. Column 6 less column 3.
d. Column 6 less column 5.
e. Fitted equation, converted to billions of current dollars by values of population and prices for 1976.
n.c. Not calculated.

period and the eight-quarter average of current and lagged interest costs on state and local borrowing fell by 62 basis points. Nothing else has an important influence in the equation. Why construction expenditures would have dropped so sharply when both grants and income were rising and interest rates were falling sharply is, to the equation at least, a mystery. The obvious implication of a reasonably well-predicted current-account surplus and a very badly predicted level of construction expenditures is that the predicted overall surplus of general governments is also way off (column 8), with construction accounting for over 90 percent of the largest errors.

The verdict, then, is that there has indeed been an important shift in budget behavior but from an unlikely quarter. Casual reasoning might have suggested that the 1975 recession would have shifted the saving propensity of state and local governments, at least until stocks of financial assets were rebuilt and maybe forever if these governments had come to anticipate more volatility in their revenues. But this does not seem to have happened to any noteworthy degree in the current budget. Out-of-sample simulations of these current operating surpluses predict recent movements at least tolerably well (as well as any ten-period dynamic simulation could be expected to). Where things go haywire is with construction expenditures. Why did construction expenditures take a nosedive in face of rising grants and income and falling interest rates?

What's Ailing Construction?

Attempts to explain a suddenly developing negative residual of $16 billion in the construction equation will, of necessity, have a decidedly ad hoc flavor. I apologize in advance for the lack of rigor in this investigation, but I conduct it anyway to reveal anything that can be learned from an incomplete grilling of the likely suspects.

A first possibility is that the coefficients may simply be misestimated due to some factor such as a short sample period or insufficient variance in the independent variables. One way of checking out this possibility is to estimate the construction equation over the longer period from 1954:1 to 1977:2 to see how the coefficients change and whether the new coefficients improve the simulations at all. Doing so suggests that there have been no important coefficient shifts in any of the other stacked equations (all coefficients are within one standard deviation of their values in table 2), but the coefficients explaining construction do change sharply: the coefficient of income is almost doubled, the coefficient of the capital stock goes from −0.001 to −0.01, and that for interest rates is now very close to zero. Yet even these refitted equations do not help much in the 1975–77 simulation. The largest negative residual is reduced by only $3.2 billion and there are relatively minor changes in the other construction residuals. The unexplained 1976 plunge remains unexplained even if that period is included in the sample.

A second possible explanation is some sort of aggregation problem: perhaps the decline is concentrated in a particular type of construction with a particular explanation. This hypothesis can be broadly checked by using data from the national accounts on the annual breakdown of construction expenditures between education (about 20 percent of the total) and all other. Between 1975 and 1976, real discretionary construction expenditures declined by 19 percent, 22 percent in education and 18 percent in other. According to the Census Bureau's breakdowns in capital expenditures (which at this time are available only through mid-1976), discretionary construction expenditures have fallen at approximately equal rates in highways, water and sewer facilities, and various other categories. More recent and more detailed figures will shed further light; but the scanty evidence so far available suggests that whatever is afflicting construction is afflicting it generally, and is not concentrated in any one category. It seems unlikely that a particular explanation (say, that demographic change is finally cutting into school construction) will suffice.

A third possibility is environmental-impact statements. As a result of the National Environmental Policy Act of 1969, state and local governments are now required to submit such statements on all construction projects financed by federal grants. This legislation should not reduce discretionary construction at all, but various state laws passed at the same time (by California, Michigan, and a few others) could. While there have been some highly visible challenges to projects that dramatize the issue, both the timing and magnitude of any likely effect seem all wrong to explain the residuals in the construction equation. In the first place, only a handful of states have environmental legislation, and even in those states, only a small percentage (5 percent or so) of projects ever get challenged. Second, any slowdown from this source would not have begun suddenly in 1976 but should have been going on for at least four years before that.

Third, the success rate of environmental challenges is actually declining over time. In the early days, it was possible to hold up projects simply because an environmental-impact statement was not submitted; nowadays challengers have to win on the merits of the case. Environmental legislation may be curtailing state and local construction, but all casual evidence indicates that the effect is rather small and not at all concentrated in 1976.

It is not quite so easy to reject the possibility that the nosedive in construction is a delayed reaction to the 1975 recession. There are several variants of this argument. One holds that state and local governments had to restore financial stocks and did so in the only way available to them: by postponing their co nstruction expenditures. A second variant of the argument is that this postponement resulted not from internal reasons but from external credit rationing by lenders. Without putting the matter fully to rest, I should point out that I can find little evidence to support either hypothesis. Regarding internal discipline, the previous statistical estimates indicated that other expenditures and taxes responded to movements in financial stocks (F) and flows (X), but that construction and compensation simply did not (even in the version estimated over the longer 1954–77 period). If no important shift has occurred in those partially sensitive components of the budget as a result of the recession, why should there be such a dramatic shift in a previously insensitive component?

Regarding external rationing, as a result of both the recession and the New York experience, the differential between the rates on Baa and Aaa municipal bonds increased sharply in 1976—from 105 basis points in early 1975 to 190 basis points in late 1976—though it fell back to a normal level of 90 basis points by mid-1977. This spread could indicate that more risky borrowers were being squeezed out of the market, or that the Aaa rate simply underestimated the cost of capital for many borrowers. To assess the simple impact of the higher Baa rate, the previous equations suggest that the maximum effect of this underprediction of rates is less than $2 billion—far short of the residual to be explained—because state and local construction is simply not found to be all that interest sensitive. It is more difficult to assess the impact of any external rationing, but that seems unlikely as the main source of a $16 billion error; the entire volume of new long-term debt floated in 1975 was only $21 billion. Moreover, while new issues of state and local securities did plummet in the New York scare period of late 1975, they have risen very sharply ever since then.

208   *Brookings Papers on Economic Activity, 1:1978*

Another variant of the recession argument works through the lag on income. As mentioned above, the surprisingly short lag on income $(0.67Y + 0.33Y_{-1})$ resulted from a joint search to find the form that worked best for all five budgetary dependent variables. The fact that all other budgetary components might be easier to change than construction may have led to an understatement of the construction lag and to an excessively rapid response of construction to the income growth from late 1975 to 1977. I examined the importance of this problem by redoing the simulations with the actual income lag replaced by an eight-quarter rectangular lag for construction only. The results suggested an improvement, but again very modest, cutting only $1 billion from the peak errors.

There is one final possibility. In July 1976, Congress passed a strange piece of legislation called the Local Public Works Capital Development and Investment Act of 1976, as part of the Public Works Employment Act of 1976. This act, intended to stimulate the economy, gave free money (the federal matching ratio, m, was equal to unity) to state and local governments for projects that could be started within 90 days, almost ensuring that the projects were the sort that might have been constructed anyway. The initial appropriation was $2 billion for the period ending September 30, 1977, with no specific allocation formula, and this generated considerable uncertainty among local governments about how much money they could expect. The Economic Development Administration was flooded with applications, totaling $22 billion for the initial $2 billion appropriation, and did not announce the winners until the end of 1976. Then in 1977, Congress debated round two of this program, for which another $4 billion was allocated through a formula not announced until June, but pertaining only to those governments in the initial queue. All the factors—no matching requirements, limitation to quick-starting projects, and prolonged uncertainty over the recipients—served to maximize the extent to which governments might hold up their own discretionary construction until they could see whether the federal government would pay their entire bill. This time both the magnitudes and the timing match very well the pattern of simulation residuals. These residuals begin in mid-1976, when passage of the bill was imminent, and get very large in the interval between rounds one and two. If there is anything to this explanation for the residuals, the Local Public Works Act should qualify

Congress for a Golden Fleece Award:[12] in the name of stimulating the economy, the government passed a $2 billion program that appears to have caused a postponement of as much as $22 billion in total government spending and a reduction in GNP of perhaps $30 billion![13]

Whatever the resolution of this intriguing puzzle, two points must be emphasized. The first is that all of the likely contributors—recession-induced delays, credit rationing, and the delay in public works—are on their good behavior now. The implication of all of these stories is that the construction residual should begin to disappear, implying a fairly hefty growth in at least this component of aggregate demand in the current year.[14]

Second, the implications of this puzzle for overall long-run economic growth should be examined. Superficially, it seems that the recent high level of NIA saving by state and local governments might imply an increase in national saving, to be desired by those favoring measures to improve long-run U.S. growth potential. But a more careful look at the facts indicates that this is exactly the wrong interpretation. At least for general governments, the appropriate concept of saving is the operating budget surplus, not that measured in the national accounts; and while this has increased recently, there has been no important shift in behavior. State and local general government saving is approximately where it should be in this stage of the business cycle. The dramatic shift has been for state and local construction, which should really be classified as national investment, and it has been a strongly downward one. To the extent that it lasts, the reduced level of properly measured investment demand lowers the probability that any level of high-employment national saving can be met with a like amount of national investment.

12. I should point out that the originator of the Golden Fleece Award, Senator William Proxmire, voted against the Local Public Works Act, taking some political risks in doing so.

13. An examination of the Dodge Construction Potentials (contracts) series for public ownership (roughly five-sixths of which are for state and local governments) weakens this case somewhat. This series shows awards declining in the second half of 1975, before my residuals appeared and also before the Local Public Works Act was an imminent possibility (though Congress was holding hearings on the bill at that time). It is unlikely that the bill could explain this early decline in contracts, though it is still the most likely reason that the decline continued throughout 1976.

14. This supposition is also reflected in the aforementioned contracts series, which shows a very sharp growth in early and middle 1977.

Table 5. Impact of the 1975 Recession on State and Local Budgets, and Effects of Countercyclical Revenue Sharing and Public Service Employment, Quarterly, 1974–77

Billions of current dollars, seasonally adjusted annual rate

Year and quarter	Without revenue sharing[a]					Effects of revenue sharing[b]			Effects of public service employment[b,c]		
	Compensation	Other expenditures	Construction	Taxes	Surplus	Expenditures	Taxes	Surplus	Expenditures	Taxes	Surplus
1974:1	−0.5	−0.3	−0.2	−1.6	−0.6	...	...	...	...	...	...
2	−1.0	−0.6	−0.5	−3.2	−1.1	...	...	...	...	...	...
3	−1.4	−0.7	−0.8	−4.9	−2.0	...	...	...	...	...	...
4	−1.6	−0.8	−1.2	−6.5	−2.9	...	...	...	...	...	...
1975:1	−1.8	−0.7	−1.5	−8.4	−4.4	...	...	...	...	...	...
2	−0.8	−0.1	−1.4	−5.8	−3.5	...	−0.1	1.2	0.1	...	1.2
3	−0.5	...	−1.0	−4.6	−3.1	...	−0.3	2.7	0.3	−0.1	2.6
4	−1.0	−0.4	−1.1	−5.5	−3.0	0.2	−0.6	3.1	0.5	−0.3	3.1
1976:1	−0.9	−0.4	−0.9	−4.0	−1.8	0.2	−0.8	2.7	0.5	−0.5	2.7
2	−0.8	−0.4	−0.9	−3.8	−1.7	0.1	−0.9	2.4	0.4	−0.7	2.3
3	−0.8	−0.4	−0.9	−3.8	−1.7	0.2	−1.1	1.1	0.4	−0.8	1.2
4	−0.9	−0.5	−1.0	−4.3	−1.9	0.2	−1.2	0.9	0.4	−0.9	1.0
1977:1	−1.2	−0.7	−1.1	−4.3	−1.3	0.2	−1.2	1.3	0.5	−1.0	1.2
2	−0.7	−0.7	−1.0	−3.3	−0.9	0.2	−1.3	1.2	0.5	−1.1	1.1

Source: Based on equations of table 2 and on text equation 20.
a. Actual less hypothetical.
b. Values with program less values without.
c. Program is assumed to be the same size as the countercyclical revenue-sharing program to facilitate comparisons.

The Cycle and the Stimulus Program

Recently there has been much discussion of a very old problem concerning state and local finances. Since taxes are based partly on income and there is a limit to budget deficits, state and local governments are vulnerable to recessions and this vulnerability may force them to behave in a procyclical manner, raising taxes and cutting expenditures in a recession. To offset these tendencies, Congress has recently enacted a countercyclical revenue-sharing program featuring payments of approximately $2.5 billion per year to state and local governments in areas of excess (more than 4.5 percent) unemployment; the size of the payment depends on the national unemployment rate and payments stop altogether when this rate falls below 6 percent. Simultaneously, there has been a large expansion of the public service employment component of the Comprehensive Employment and Training Act.

In this section I use the model developed above to examine the impact that these programs might have had if they had been in effect throughout the 1975 recession. The first task is to find the effect of the recession itself on state and local budgets. For this, comparisons are made of the results of two dynamic simulations from 1973:4 to 1977:2, the first using the actual pattern of GNP and the unemployment rate and the second using a hypothetical high-employment path (assuming that the national unemployment rate stayed at its early 1974 value of 5 percent and real GNP grew at a 3.5 percent annual rate throughout). The next step is to find the impact of the countercyclical revenue-sharing program had it been in effect throughout this period. For this purpose, the simulation is redone with exogenous budget inflows (X) expanded by the amount implied by today's law (which was not in effect at the time). The changes due to the recession and to countercyclical revenue sharing are then compared. The final exercise examines the impact of a public service employment grant of the same size as the countercyclical revenue-sharing grant by exactly the same method.

The results of these comparisons are given in table 5. The left panel shows the results of the recession on state and local budgets. Compensation payments were nudged down by the drop in income and up by the rise in unemployment (see the coefficients in table 2). The result was a very modest decline of up to $1.8 billion, only 1.5 percent of compensation expenditures, in this period of peak effect. There were press reports of many layoffs in areas where the economic decline hit hard. According to these equations, however, either many of those employees would have been laid off anyway or layoffs by some governments were offset by above-normal hiring by others.[15]

The decline was also relatively modest for other categories of expenditures, but the budgetary changes were larger for taxes. The tax movements consisted of two independent changes: tax revenues declined because of the automatic fall in receipts, but because the surplus and stocks of financial assets also fell, the model estimates that governments raised tax rates to recapture some of these lost assets. The changes in the table measure the net effect of these two forces.[16] In terms of stocks, by mid-1977 the recession had cost local governments $7.5 billion in financial assets, though of course the number would have been somewhat larger if the discretionary changes in taxes and expenditures had not been made.[17]

The countercyclical revenue-sharing program was assumed to be of the form implicit in the 1977 extension of the program:

$$(7) \qquad X = \bar{X} + 0.5 + 1.2(\overline{UR}_{-2} - 6.0), \quad \overline{UR}_{-2} \geq 6.0$$
$$X = \bar{X}, \qquad\qquad\qquad\qquad\quad \overline{UR}_{-2} \leq 6.0,$$

where $\bar{X}$ is the previous exogenous level of budget inflows, X is the new hypothetical level, and $\overline{UR}_{-2}$ is the national unemployment rate two

15. One perhaps little-appreciated aspect of this decline in compensation expenditures involves the nonentrepreneurial Phillips curve, one of Robert E. Hall's many recent contributions to the literature on the Phillips curve (see his "The Rigidity of Wages and the Persistence of Unemployment," *BPEA*, 2:1975, pp. 301–35). There Hall argues that in a recession, private workers might remain unemployed as they wait for higher-wage nonentrepreneurial jobs to open up. The state and local sector now accounts for 14 percent of total civilian employment and 44 percent of Hall's nonentrepreneurial sector. Given that most workers in this sector are known to have occupational tenure, the fact that total state and local employment *declines* in a recession conceivably means that new hires are interrupted altogether, and that the strategy Hall lays out for unemployed private workers is not very rational.

16. Perhaps because they include these induced tax increases, the cyclical changes in taxes shown in table 5 is a good deal less than that estimated by the Council of Economic Advisers, which presented a full-employment budget for both the federal and the state and local sectors in the *Economic Report of the President, January 1977*, p. 76.

17. This number is derived by cumulating the surplus changes and multiplying by 0.25 to account for the fact that all quarterly budget flows are measured at annual rates.

quarters ago (reflecting the delay in computing payments). Under this payment schedule, there would have been no countercyclical payments at all in 1974 and payments would have averaged $2.6 billion since. The allocation of these payments among expenditures, taxes, and the surplus is shown. There is a very slight rise in expenditures, concentrated in the "other" category, and a larger reduction in taxes. Even by the end of 1977, however, much of the countercyclical money is still going into the surplus. As one indication, by the end of 1977 the countercyclical program would have raised state and local financial assets by $4.2 billion, over half of the recession-induced loss, even though the proportion of expenditures it would have restored is a good deal less (only 8 percent by mid-1977).

Even without a formal evaluation of countercyclical revenue sharing, a few points stand out. The first is that any macrostabilization benefits of the program are, if the equations are to be believed, small indeed. Expenditures do not respond much to new infusions of aid, and such response as occurs is felt with very long lags. Taxes respond more, but to the extent state and local taxes are cut, the program is only marginally preferable to straight federal tax cuts. And a large share of the money seems likely to pad the surpluses of state and local governments, in which case there are no obvious macrostabilization benefits.

But maybe macrostabilization is not the important rationale for the program. Another potential rationale views it as a form of economic-disaster insurance for state and local governments. To a growing extent, these governments are relying on cyclically sensitive revenue sources to pay for relatively predetermined expenditures. If they have not accumulated sufficient stocks of financial assets, they are vulnerable to recession-induced fiscal crises, and this program conceivably could have a role to play in warding off those dangers. The equations here show that there is some, perhaps modest, cyclical variability in financial stocks, and that this variability is importantly reduced by countercyclical revenue sharing. Whether the aid goes in fact to the vulnerable governments and whether it may simply encourage governments not to save for cyclical exigencies are questions that can be dealt with only through more detailed research.

A like evaluation can be made of public service employment. The main difference between the two programs is that public service employment is a categorical grant for employment, paid entirely by the federal government. Rather than varying X, public service employment can be simulated by raising G_1, with m_1 fixed at unity. To make this simulation comparable with that for revenue sharing, I have assumed that the size of the grant is given by equation 7, and have presented the results in the right panel of table 5. These results do suggest a somewhat higher short-run response of expenditures, here concentrated in employment; but even with the categorization and the shorter lag the high displacement parameter in the empirical model implies that there is very little difference between public employment and revenue sharing. Again the main impact is on the surplus, and indeed the path of the surplus is much the same in the two simulations. Until some method can be found to avoid displacement, these results suggest that public service employment will prove disappointing as a direct stimulant to employment.

Implications

The implications of this report can be summarized briefly. The rise in the budget surplus of general governments reflects partly a rise in the operating surplus now that the recession trough has been passed, and partly a sharp fall in construction expenditures. The first component can be explained by and large simply by extrapolating earlier fitted equations, and appears to reflect no important shift in behavior. The drop in construction expenditures, however, simply cannot be explained by a traditional set of variables including such things as income, relative prices, grants, and interest rates. There does seem to have been an important behavioral shift here, one that conceivably represents some sort of delayed reaction to the recession-induced loss of financial assets but more likely is attributable to some questionable properties of the Public Works Employment Act of 1976.

The paper also presents a comparison of the hypothetical budget variables in the absence of the 1975 recession on the one hand and, on the other, with the recession cushioned either by countercyclical revenue sharing or public service employment. This comparison shows, first, that at present these programs are much smaller than would be necessary to neutralize the effects of the recession and, second, that the main impact of the recession is on the tax side. Expenditures appear to have been altered little by the recession, nor are they raised much by either countercyclical revenue sharing or public service employment.

4

81-105

[82]

Micro Estimates of Public Spending Demand Functions and Tests of the Tiebout and Median-Voter Hypotheses

0250-D72

U.S. 3240-H73

9310-R22

Edward M. Gramlich and Daniel L. Rubinfeld

University of Michigan

Responses to questions given to a random sample of Michigan households are used to estimate public spending demand functions. While income and price elasticities are similar to those obtained from aggregate data, positive income elasticities appear to arise because public services are distributed in a prorich manner. A relatively small variance in spending demands among urban and suburban communities in metropolitan areas with substantial public service variety suggests that the Tiebout mechanism works. This interpretation is supported by the fact that actual spending conforms substantially to desired levels in urban areas, but less so in rural areas with little public sector choice.

The existence of micro data on the demand for public goods makes it possible to test several hypotheses that have intrigued public finance economists. The first involves the estimation of parameters in public spending demand functions, specifically whether parameter estimates derived from the usual analyses of local government budgetary aggregates accurately reflect the demands that would be expressed by individual citizens. The second is Tiebout's (1956) now-classic idea that citizens with similar tastes for public goods will live together in

We have benefited from the comments of Theodore Bergstrom, David Bradford, Harvey Brazer, Paul Courant, Arthur Denzau, Martin Feldstein, Gerald Goldstein, Harvey Rosen, Perry Shapiro, Lawrence Summers, and an anonymous referee. We are also appreciative of the highly competent research assistance of Deborah Swift. Work on this project was supported by grants from the National Science Foundation and the Department of Housing and Urban Development.

[*Journal of Political Economy.* 1982, vol. 90, no. 3]

jurisdictions that can then supply these goods with relatively little economic inefficiency. The third is that whatever determines residential location, governments will supply the level of public goods desired by the median voter.

In this paper we use data from a micro survey on demands for public spending to test these hypotheses. The survey, taken by the University of Michigan's Institute for Social Research (ISR), includes 2,001 households in the state of Michigan, sampled randomly immediately after Michigan's 1978 tax-limitation vote. Most questions dealt with why voters voted for or against various tax-limitation amendments, but the survey was also designed to treat these more basic issues of public expenditure demand.[1] The strength of a survey such as this is that a relatively complete array of fiscal, demographic, voting, and attitudinal information is available for a random sample of the state population. These data as well as some direct questions about public sector demand allow one to test the underlying hypotheses. The weakness is that like all other survey data respondents do not have to act on the basis of their answers, and the results are therefore hypothetical.[2]

The first section of the paper gives the demand estimation results. We use standard utility-maximization procedures to derive public spending demand functions that, among other things, depend on both individual and community income. Results of the estimation of these equations to micro spending preferences data are used to try to resolve several issues in the applied public finance literature: the distribution of Buchanan fiscal residuals within a community, an apparent paradox between income-elasticity estimates from aggregated community data and polling data, and why the median-voter theorem works so well.

The next section of the paper tests the Tiebout hypothesis that location decisions permit public goods to be provided with a high degree of economic efficiency. One implication of this hypothesis is that households will group themselves according to their demand for public spending—all those desiring a large public sector will live together, as will all those desiring a small public sector. In statistical terms, the test is accomplished by observing whether the intracommunity variance of public goods demand is smaller than that for the whole statewide sample, either uncorrected or corrected (by regression) for the influence of important independent variables.

The third section goes on to see whether the fiscal taste grouping of

---

[1] The survey is described in Courant, Gramlich, and Rubinfeld (1980).
[2] See Converse (1975) for extensive discussions of the strengths and weaknesses of surveys such as this.

individuals is related to the actual level of public spending provided in the community. In part, this is a necessary complement to the Tiebout test, for if local government fiscal actions were unrelated to the tastes of voters, there would be no reason for individuals to group themselves in a Tiebout-like manner. But this test can even go beyond Tiebout and test the median-voter hypothesis of Hotelling (1929), Bowen (1943), Downs (1957), and others. Does public spending in the jurisdiction reflect the desires of the median voter (from our sample), or are actual spending totals systematically larger or smaller?

I. The Demand for Public Spending

We first develop demand functions for public spending in terms of the ith individual. Let this individual's utility be expressed in terms of the utility obtained from private goods, C_i, and public output, X_i, by

$$U_i = U_i(C_i, X_i). \tag{1}$$

Were all publicly provided goods pure public goods, X_i would be identical for all individuals residing in a community. If publicly provided goods deviate from this archetype, however, we might expect the provision of public goods to vary from individual to individual in the community. There are many ways to describe how it could vary from individual to individual. A convenient approximation first used by Denzau and Mackay (1976) is to let income be the conditioning variable:

$$X_i = (Y_i^{\alpha_1}/Y^*)(E/N), \text{ where } Y^* = \sum_i (Y_i^{\alpha_1}/N). \tag{2}$$

Here Y_i is the individual's income, E the real dollar expenditure on public services, and N the number of consumers of public services. The parameter α_1 reflects the distribution of public services. When $\alpha_1 = 0$, all individuals within the jurisdiction receive the identical level of services E/N. When $\alpha_1 > 0$, the distribution of services is positively related to income (prorich); and when $\alpha_1 < 0$, the distribution is negatively related to income (propoor). Note that, as given by (2), output X is measured in real dollars.

The next question involves the price of public goods. Assume that X is produced according to the Cobb-Douglas production function

$$X = L^{\alpha_3}K^{1-\alpha_3}. \tag{3}$$

The first-order conditions are that $W = \alpha_3 PX/L$ and $R = (1 - \alpha_3)PX/K$, where W is the real wage for public employees, P is the relative gross price for public goods. and R is the rental price of capital, assumed to be constant across jurisdictions. Solving the first-order expressions for L and K, substituting them into the production, and solving for P yields $P = \alpha_4 W^{\alpha_3}$, where α_4 is some constant.

The individual is then assumed to maximize utility subject to the usual budget constraint:

$$
\begin{aligned}
Y_i &= C_i + [(\alpha_4 W^{\alpha_3} H_i)/(V/N)](E/N) \\
    &= C_i + [(\alpha_4 W^{\alpha_3} H_i)/(V/N)](Y^*/Y_i^{\alpha_1})X_i,
\end{aligned}
\tag{4}
$$

where H_i is the value of the individual's property and V is the community tax base. The tax price $(\alpha_4 W^{\alpha_3} H_i N/V)$ measures the price to the consumer of a dollar of real expenditure per capita of public spending. Note that (4) is written as if this price were a *marginal* tax price, so that fixed income tax revenues or fixed categorical or noncategorical grants will not affect it.

Maximizing (1) subject to (4) yields standard demand functions for private consumption C_i and for desired public services X_i. Writing the latter in multiplicative form, as is commonly done, and adding a random-error term to allow for omitted variables, we get

$$
X_i = e^{\beta_0 + \epsilon_i}(\alpha_4 H_i N/V)^{\beta_2} W^{\alpha_3 \beta_2} Y^{*\beta_2} Y_i^{(\beta_1 - \alpha_1 \beta_2)}.
\tag{5}
$$

The parameter β_1 is the individual's income elasticity of demand for public services and β_2 is the price elasticity. But since income terms are now in the price equation, the total elasticity with respect to individual income depends on both the income and price elasticity.

To this point we have not dealt with the congestion problem. To allow for the possibility that the publicly provided goods might be congested, or impure public goods, we modify a procedure employed by Borcherding and Deacon (1972) and Bergstrom and Goodman (1973). This involves rewriting (2) as

$$
X_i = (Y_i^{\alpha_1}/Y^*)(E/N^{\alpha_2}),
\tag{6}
$$

where α_2 is the crowding parameter estimated by the above authors. For α_2 equal to 0, public spending is a pure public good in the Samuelsonian sense (Samuelson 1954). Whatever the value of α_1, as α_2 increases the public goods become more and more crowded. Taking this perspective suggests that our coefficient α_1 may be thought of as an income-crowding parameter, just as α_2 is a population-crowding parameter. We might note, in addition, that more general formulations of the private-public nature of publicly provided goods—such as one allowing public goods to be distributed with house value and including various interaction terms—might also be imagined. However, these somewhat more general approaches were not found to be important in our empirical results, so we do not pursue them here.

We complete the model by accounting for some details of estimation. A first is that the dependent variable, per capita public spending, is actually measured in nominal terms, but we cannot observe a cross-sectional price index for public expenditures. Hence we multiply both sides of the expression by the gross price of public goods used above. A second approximation is to replace Y^* with $\overline{Y}^{\alpha_1}$, where $\overline{Y}$ is mean income in the community.[3] A third adjustment takes account of the fact that individual voters' utility will vary according to a vector of individual characteristics (Z_i) such as the number of children, political affiliation, and so forth. Making these adjustments, we have as our basic public goods demand equation

$$\ln (W^{\alpha_3} E/N) = \beta' + [\beta_1 - \alpha_1(1 + \beta_2)] \ln Y_i + \alpha_3(1 + \beta_2) \ln W$$

$$+ \beta_2 \ln (H_i N/V) + (\alpha_2 - 1) \ln N \tag{7}$$

$$+ \alpha_1(1 + \beta_2) \ln \overline{Y} + \beta_3 Z_i + \epsilon_i,$$

where β' is a constant. Since the dependent variable here is the logarithm of per capita *money* public expenditures, the public wage elasticity is positive or negative as demand is inelastic or elastic. Otherwise the only nonstandard features in the equation are the crowding parameters, α_1 and α_2.

Estimating the Model

Equation (7) can be estimated with either macro or micro data. The usual approach of economists is to use macro data on the overall budgetary behavior of governments and make four additional assumptions: (*a*) The Z_i for individuals cannot be observed and are either assumed to be constant within the jurisdiction or approximated by mean or median values for the community. (*b*) Individual income is set at the median for the community, as if the median voter had median income and as if all other incomes in the community were irrelevant in determining public spending. (*c*) The tax-price term is replaced through a similar assumption. Within a community individual property values are assumed to equal the median residential

---

[3] This approximation is tantamount to assuming that X_i is distributed according to $(Y_i/\overline{Y})^{\alpha_1}$ in eq. (2). We use the form given only to highlight its adding-up features. Clearly our approximation is exact when α_1 equals either 0 or 1. To see what happens in other cases, we can consider varying assumptions about the income distribution. First, if income is uniformly distributed from 0 to maximum income B, the mean of $Y_i^{\alpha_1}$ equals $B^{\alpha_1}/(1 + \alpha_1)$, while (mean $Y)^{\alpha_1} = B^{\alpha_1}/2^{\alpha_1}$. It is clear that for α_1 in the range $(-.5, 1.5)$, $2^{\alpha_1} \approx (1 + \alpha_1)$. Second, we can assume a Pareto distribution, a two-parameter, nonsymmetric distribution of the form $f(Y) = rA^r/Y^{r+1}$ for A positive and r greater than or equal to two. In this case we calculate that the mean of Y^{α_1} is equal to $rA^{\alpha_1+1}/[r - (1 + \alpha_1)]$ while (mean $Y)^{\alpha_1} = A^{\alpha_1} r^{\alpha_1}/(r - 1)^{\alpha_1}$. The two are likely to be approximately equal for $A = 1$ and r large, not unreasonable possibilities.

value, and the community tax price is then usually expressed as the ratio of residential value to total value, as if owners of nonresidential property did not vote in local elections. (*d*) Grants from higher levels of government are introduced to the equation. Typically, just one grant term is added, but in fact several should be. Open-ended categorical grants should have their matching ratio used in the construction of tax prices. Close-ended noncategorical grants should be included in community income, unless there are so-called flypaper effects whereby a dollar of grant spending leads to more public spending than private income at the margin. And close-ended categorical grants should be entered as a separate linear term.[4]

For the sake of comparison, we first follow these conventions and estimate a macro relationship for the 83 counties of Michigan in 1977. The public wage is expressed as the starting salary for teachers and the tax price as the residential share of property values. Categorical and noncategorical grants are treated as separate logarithmic terms, and income is expressed either as county mean income (available in 1976) or as median income (available in 1970). The results are shown in table 1. The income elasticity (β_1) is slightly below that usually found in other studies and the tax-price elasticity (β_2) much below, and not always of the correct sign. The public wage coefficients always have incorrect signs. The crowding terms indicate that public goods are definitely not Samuelsonian, with community population an important determinant of services demand (α_2 is close to one), as is found by both previous studies using the term. In this form it is impossible to identify the α_1 coefficient and thereby tell whether community income is important in determining service demands.[5] Both categorical and noncategorical state and federal grants have fairly strong effects on community spending, much as is found in other studies.

Next we estimate (7) using micro data from our household survey. The dependent variable is derived from a sequence of questions that informed respondents of how local governments in Michigan spend tax dollars; then asked them whether they thought local spending and taxes in their jurisdiction were too large, too small, or about right; and then tried to elicit their preferred percentage change in all budgetary categories. It was stressed to respondents that if they desired a cutback in local spending the outcome would be the same percentage

---

[4] This is all spelled out in Gramlich (1977).

[5] We note that median income works better than mean income. This is a powerful finding because median income was only available for 1970, 7 years before the date of the dependent variable. It might satisfy Romer and Rosenthal's (1978) test of the median-voter hypothesis (median income should work better than any other income), but, as our later discussion will indicate, such an inference cannot be made unambiguously when community income is included in the equation.

TABLE 1

MACRO PUBLIC SPENDING EQUATIONS, 83 COUNTIES OF MICHIGAN, 1977

	Using Mean Income (1976)	Using Median Income (1970)
Independent variable:		
Constant	1.264	−.443
Income	.442 (3.2)	.531 (4.1)
Public wage	−.138 (1.0)	−.059 (.4)
Residential value/ total value	−.058 (.9)	.010 (.2)
Population	.021 (1.1)	.010 (.5)
Categorical grants	.316 (7.6)	.320 (8.0)
Noncategorical grants	.187 (2.8)	.276 (4.0)
Fit statistics:		
R^2	.637	.663
SE	.115	.111
Parameter estimates:		
α_1	N.I.	N.I.
$\alpha_2 - 1$	.021 (1.1)	.010 (.5)
α_3	−.146* (1.1)	−.058* (.4)
β_1	.442 (3.2)	.531 (4.1)
β_2	−.058 (.9)	.010* (.2)

NOTE.—Dependent variable is per capita government spending; all variables in log form; absolute *t*-ratios in parentheses. N.I. = not identified.
* Incorrect sign.

cutback in all local spending and taxes.[6] Respondents' desired level of overall local spending, the dependent variable in the micro equations, was then overall per capita spending in the county multiplied by the adjustment factor. If the *i*th respondent desired a 5 percent cutback, we assumed that the desired spending level was 95 percent of actual local government spending in that county.[7]

The individual independent variables are also taken from our survey, from questions on individual income, tax payments, and from various demographic indicators. The same community variables that appear in the macro equations are also used in the micro equations.

The micro results are shown in table 2. These equations are fitted to

[6] The exact questions were: "Now considering just your local governments which spend mainly on schools, police, fire, parks, and sanitation services—would you favor an across-the-board increase in both local spending and taxes, a decrease in both local spending and taxes, or would you favor no change?" Those who favored a change were then asked: "How much of an increase (decrease) in *both* local spending and taxes would you favor: a 5 percent (increase/decrease), 10 percent, 15 percent, 20 percent (increase or decrease), or what?"

[7] In principle, it is possible to adjust only city spending to get the desired total for a voter. In practice, however, we had so much difficulty in allocating county spending to the various cities, some of which are big enough to have published data, some of which are not, that we simply spread all local spending in a county evenly across all people.

MEDIAN-VOTER HYPOTHESES   543

TABLE 2

MICRO PUBLIC SPENDING EQUATIONS,
1,125 MICHIGAN HOMEOWNER RESPONDENTS, 1978

	Adjusted by Respondent's Answer	Adjusted, with City Dummies	Not Adjusted, with City Dummies
Independent variable:			
Constant	.378	−1.24	−1.80
D, child in public school	.013 (1.7)	.011 (1.5)	−.003 (.7)
D, child in private school	.016 (1.2)	.015 (1.2)	−.005 (.7)
D, over 65	.015 (1.1)	.013 (1.1)	.005 (.8)
D, transfer recipient	.014 (.6)	.005 (.2)	−.002 (.2)
D, black	.010 (.7)	.039 (2.0)	.012 (1.2)
D, other nonwhite	−.048 (1.2)	−.046 (1.2)	−.017 (.8)
D, race not reported	.048 (.8)	.049 (.9)	−.007 (.3)
D, Republican	.001 (.1)	.004 (.5)	.006 (1.4)
D, independent	−.006 (.7)	−.004 (.4)	.005 (1.1)
D, party not reported	.052 (1.0)	.073 (1.5)	.008 (.3)
D, public employee	−.001 (.1)	−.001 (.1)	−.001 (.1)
D, nonresident public employee	.025 (1.5)	.023 (1.5)	.001 (.2)
D, expect real income up	.057 (2.9)	.048 (2.5)	.006 (.6)
D, expect no change real income	.044 (2.2)	.032 (1.7)	.003 (.3)
D, expect real income down	.011 (.6)	.002 (.1)	−.004 (.4)
D, Catholic	−.008 (1.0)	−.003 (.5)	−.003 (.9)
D, Jewish	.015 (.5)	.004 (.1)	.002 (.1)
D, religion not reported	−.020 (1.4)	−.023 (1.7)	−.006 (.9)
Individual income	.001 (.1)	.001 (.2)	.001 (.1)
House value/avg. house value	−.011 (2.2)	−.014 (2.7)	−.004 (1.4)
County income	.285 (5.5)	.347 (4.3)	.408 (9.7)
County public wage	.195 (3.4)	.358 (3.9)	.363 (7.7)
County population	.039 (6.7)	.033 (2.6)	.022 (3.3)
Categorical grants	.201 (15.4)	.178 (5.4)	.200 (11.8)
Noncategorical grants	.226 (11.1)	.265 (9.0)	.271 (17.9)
Fit statistics:			
R^2	.773	.792	.931
SE	.11	.11	.06
Parameter estimates:			
α_1	.288 (5.6)	.352 (4.4)	.410 (9.7)
$\alpha_2 - 1$	.039 (6.7)	.033 (2.6)	.022 (3.3)
α_3	.197 (3.6)	.363 (4.0)	.364 (7.7)
β_1	.286 (5.6)	.348 (4.3)	.409 (10.2)
β_2	−.011 (2.2)	−.014 (2.7)	−.004 (1.4)

NOTE.—Dependent variable is per capita government spending; continuous variables in log form; absolute *t*-ratios in parentheses.

544   JOURNAL OF POLITICAL ECONOMY

the 1,125 respondents who answered the spending-demand questions, with renters omitted because of the difficulty in defining their tax payments and price.[8] Results are given only for the median-income variant, the one that fit best in table 1.

We have shown equations first using spending adjusted by our adjustment factor, then with community dummies included to test whether the dummies really measure individual city or county effects, and then with the dependent variable unadjusted by the answers to our hypothetical question to measure the importance of the adjustment. The independent variables also include a host of dummies (designated by D) to proxy the Z_i factors.

The results agree broadly with those of the macro equations, though there are some interesting differences. In all three equations the population-crowding coefficient α_2 is very close to one, indicating again that public expenditures are not for goods that are public in the Samuelsonian sense. Again the tax-price elasticity is very low, though now it is statistically significant in the first two equations.[9] The public wage coefficients are now of the correct sign, though still lower than they should be if public services have the distributive shares of most private outputs. Community income and grants have very strong and statistically significant effects in all equations, as they did before.

Taking together the Y_i and $\bar{Y}$ terms, the macro income elasticity of about .4 is confirmed in the micro regressions. But virtually all of the positive elasticity is due to *community* income, with individual family income having a coefficient that is very close to zero in all three equations. Our results do suggest a positive income elasticity of demand for public spending, but the increased demand is seen to come in a very special form. As higher-income individuals within a community are surveyed, they do not appear to have any greater taste for public spending. The apparent reason is that higher-income individuals already receive (or perceive that they receive) greater benefits from public spending than do lower-income individuals. Stated differently, if we contrast voters of the same income and tax prices residing in communities of different income but initially the same level of public spending, the voter in a high-income community, for a given level of private goods consumption, will perceive a lower level of public goods consumption and have a higher marginal rate of substitution and demand for public goods.

___

[8] We did some Box-Cox tests for functional form, comparing the fit of log-linear, log-log, linear, and semilog formulations of the model and found that the semilog version used gave a slightly better fit, although the substantive results were not much different. We report the log-log specifications because they are easier to interpret.

[9] We did not incorporate the federal income tax deductibility of the property tax with our measure of price. Had we done so our price elasticity estimate would have been slightly higher.

One other aspect of the individual-income term bears mentioning. A problem in inferring income elasticities from survey results is that only 1 year's income is recorded for respondents. If there were a large transitory component to income, the overall income elasticity would be understated in the micro results but not in the macro community results, because there transitory income deviations are pooled and averaged out. We have no fully satisfactory means of estimating permanent income for the micro equations, but we did try a question borrowed from other ISR surveys on whether the respondent expected real income gains or losses in the next 5 years. As can be seen from the two left-hand columns of table 2, this variable works quite well. Optimists and those who expect no decline want more public spending than those who expect a decline or did not answer the question (the null class). Hence a partial explanation for the low individual-income elasticity is a modified form of the permanent-income hypothesis. Other things equal, individuals who expect real-income growth will desire higher levels of government spending than those who do not.

Some Econometric Issues

Before trying to interpret these results, we take note of several possible econometric problems. One involves the level of information possessed by respondents. When they are poorly informed about the role that tax prices and benefit shares play in determining their utility levels, they might respond to questions as if income and prices did not matter in shaping their demand for public spending. There is no perfect way to control for the information possessed by respondents, but one imperfect way is to stratify the sample according to their education. If more educated respondents are also more informed, their absolute income and price elasticities should be greater than for those without much education. We have tested this hypothesis by simply running the model of table 2 for college-educated respondents, finding micro elasticities that were slightly greater than those given in table 2 but not enough to change the basic interpretation of the results.

A second possibility is that individuals may have differing income elasticities of demand for different budgetary items. Thus the individual-income coefficient might be low because a positive income elasticity of demand for education is canceling a negative income elasticity of demand for welfare. To pursue this issue, we used another sequence included in the survey that asks respondents whether they would like an increase, decrease, or no change in individual budgetary items. Unlike our overall expenditure-demand question, we did not try to measure quantitative preferred changes for these individual functional categories because such a task proved to be difficult in pretesting the questionnaire, and so we were not able to control for the county spending levels for each functional category. As a result, we have not obtained quantitative estimates of micro income and price elasticities. But we can say whether micro-income and tax-price variables are significant determinants of these functional spending desires. The suggestive findings for six functional categories are shown in table 3. We see that micro income does indeed have a positive and significant income elasticity for school spending and a negative and significant elasticity for welfare spending. The relative price elasticities are also significantly negative for schools, parks, and colleges. Hence the micro-income elasticity might have been higher if we had focused on more definable bundles, such as spending for public schools.

This test can be taken one step further. Since welfare benefits are constant throughout the state, the macro-income variable should have a zero coefficient. Including macro income in welfare regressions like those shown in table 3 does lead to this result. But since education benefits are likely to be distributed in a prorich manner, macro income there should, and does, take on a positive coefficient.[10]

Another issue of concern was the choice of unit to which public services are provided. Our tabulated results utilized per capita spending as the dependent variable, even though taxes are paid on a household basis. Since some public services such as education are provided to individuals, such an assumption seems reasonable. But other services are better viewed as household services, in which case per *family* spending might be a better choice for the dependent variable. When we made such an adjustment the price elasticity of demand remained essentially unchanged, but micro-income elasticity rose slightly and became significantly different from zero. Most of the other coefficients were not changed appreciably.

Finally, we were concerned about the correct specification of price in the demand equation. In particular, we attempted to account for the possibility that individuals responded to the reduced marginal tax price of public services created by the statewide property-tax credit program. However, the model with the circuit-breaker adjusted price fit more poorly than the model reported here, suggesting that individuals were not aware of and/or did not respond to the program. Alternatively, we tried a number of different price terms associated with varying assumptions about the impact of commercial and industrial property on tax price. Our model as specified implicitly assumes

---

[10] We do not present these education equations here, but a number of them are given in a paper by Bergstrom, Rubinfeld, and Shapiro (in press) on a related topic.

TABLE 3

MICRO DEMAND EQUATIONS FOR INDIVIDUAL BUDGET ITEMS, 1,125 MICHIGAN HOMEOWNER RESPONDENTS, 1978

Independent Variable	Schools	Welfare	Police & Fire	Roads	Parks	State Universities
Individual income	.108 (2.9)	−.123 (3.4)	−.032 (.8)	−.005 (.1)	.029 (.8)	.044 (1.1)
Residential value/ total value	−.137 (4.2)	.013 (.4)	−.060 (1.8)	−.040 (1.3)	−.060 (−1.8)	−.080 (2.5)
D, child in public school	.100 (3.2)	.010 (.3)	.080 (2.3)	−.030 (.9)	.030 (1.0)	.020 (.7)
D, black	.154 (4.7)	.207 (6.2)	.077 (.5)	.040 (1.3)	.080 (2.5)	.020 (.7)

NOTE.—Dependent variable = 1 if the individual desired an increase in the budget, 0 if no change, −1 if a decrease; all coefficients are standardized β coefficients; absolute t-ratios in parentheses. To save space, we have not presented results for the other independent variables appearing in table 2. None of the macro coefficients could be estimated very well because the dependent variable was not adjusted for county spending levels. The other macro variables that were statistically significant were schools: expect real income up, Jewish; welfare: transfer recipient, Republican, party other, public employee; police and fire: Jewish; roads: expect real income up, expect no change in real income; parks: transfer recipient, public employee; state universities: nonresident public employee, expect real income up, expect no change in real income.

547

that a commercial-industrial tax base reduces tax price, since tax revenues can be used to finance residential public services without encouraging firm outmigration. An alternative specification allowed for the perceived fiscal benefits of a commercial-industrial base to fall to zero (as suggested by Ladd [1975]). Since the price elasticity is small and not very significant, our results were essentially unchanged, but we did note a small worsening in goodness of fit when we used the Ladd assumption.

Interpreting the Results

In this section we digress slightly to show how this finding of a low micro-income elasticity and a high macro–community income elasticity, if true, bears on some current public finance questions.

The first question involves benefit share progressivity. The usual economist's view, to the extent that there is one, appears to be that the benefits of public services are *not* distributed in a prorich manner. The major proponents of this view have been Gillespie (1965), who finds a neutral distribution within communities, and Musgrave and Musgrave (1980), who indicated that state and local purchases, and education in particular, are distributed propoor. This implies that high-income individuals, with higher levels of consumption of private goods, should have a higher marginal rate of substitution for public services. It also implies that if tax shares depend on income, high-income individuals pay a higher fiscal residual (Buchanan 1950) and are more likely to emigrate from the community for fiscal reasons.

In this paper we find some negative evidence for both ideas. If public services are assumed to be normal goods and since high-income individuals do not have a higher marginal rate of substitution than do low-income individuals, these high-income individuals must be consuming more public services than low-income individuals; that is, the within-community distribution of public services must be prorich. The finding corresponds to the possibility noted by Denzau and Mackay (1976) for price-inelastic consumers. It also suggests that the fiscal incentive to migrate because of the presence of fiscal residuals may be overstated. If the income elasticity of property-tax payments within a community is approximately one (as is suggested by several studies and confirmed in our own data set), the benefit side elasticity of approximately .4 suggests that fiscal residuals may be only about half as dependent on income as would be the case if benefit distributions were independent of income. Clearly the impact of such residuals on the migration of high-income individuals from a community will also be smaller.

Since our results do seem to counter the conventional wisdom, at

least as espoused by Musgrave and Musgrave, a more careful examination of the current evidence about within-jurisdiction distributional benefits seems warranted. The evidence Musgrave and Musgrave present relates to education and to medical purchases, both of
which are financed in part at the state level. In addition, their analysis
is based on aggregate data and so does not pretend to control for
within-community spending patterns. Their conclusion about the
propoor pattern of medical expenditures seems consistent with our
knowledge about state and local public hospitals and health care.
However, the conclusion about education involves some strong assumptions and is controversial. To allocate benefits among income
groups, Musgrave and Musgrave simply examine the distribution of
students among households. As a result, the calculation does not take
into account quality differentials among neighborhood schools, nor
does it look at spending differences across communities. Finally, as
they acknowledge, their illustrative calculations are measured solely in
terms of expenditures made without taking into account the value at
which public services are assessed by the recipient of those services.
With a decreasing marginal utility of income, one would expect
higher-income individuals to pay more for education, so that their
calculation is likely to understate the benefits of education received by
those with higher incomes.

A more careful look at other studies by both political scientists and
economists leads us to a different view of the distributional impact of
local expenditures. When dealing with education, which makes up
roughly 57 percent of local budgets, Katzman (1968) examined variations in spending per pupil by neighborhood within several large
cities, as well as variations in factors that might affect school quality.
He found that the distribution of school quality was biased in favor of
upper-income areas. Levy, Meltsner, and Wildavsky (1974) found a
prorich allocation in Oakland, California, compensatory programs
notwithstanding. Other studies of education (Sexton 1961 [Detroit];
Berk and Hartman 1971 [Chicago]; Owen 1972; and Mandel 1974
[Detroit]) all lead to the same qualitative conclusion—a prorich distribution of educational spending within cities.

The evidence concerning other local public services is more spotty
and less conclusive. For police, Bloch (1974 [Washington]) found no
discernible pattern, while Weicher (1971 [Chicago]) found a strong
negative relationship between police expenditures and income up to
the $8,000–$9,000 range (middle income) but a positive relationship
past this point. For fire, Lineberry (1977) found a negative relationship, but his study uses as a measure of output distance from the fire
station, a measure that does not reflect expenditure differentials
across neighborhoods and does not take into account the fact that

citizen use of the system and the value of that use are likely to vary positively with income. For libraries, both Martin (1969 [Chicago]) and Levy et al. (1974) found a prorich distribution. However, for parks the studies are mixed, Gold (1974 [Detroit]) finding a negative relationship between income and benefits and the Community Council of Greater New York (1963) a positive relationship. Finally, for street repairs Antunes and Plumlee (1977 [Houston]) were inconclusive, as were Levy et al. (1974).

One can debate the quality and reliability of each of the studies cited. However, with education making up more than half the budget, and with the studies of most other budgetary items generally inconclusive, a net prorich distribution is at least a likely possibility.[11]

A related empirical issue involves differences between the economist's and noneconomist's views of the demand for public goods. The typical economist's view, based on macro–public goods equations of the sort estimated above in table 1, is that the income elasticity of demand is positive, usually about .6.[12] The usual noneconomist's view, based on polling individuals to find whether they want more, less, or the same amount of spending on public goods, is that implicit income elasticities are zero or sometimes even negative—income cannot explain deviations of desired from actual spending (see, e.g., ACIR 1979; Citrin 1979; or Clark and Ferguson 1981). Our results yield a simple resolution to the paradox. Both studies are right. As community incomes rise, the mean or median voter desires more public goods and public spending rises. But within a community, public services appear to be distributed in a prorich manner, implying that residual desires are uncorrelated with income.

A third idea that takes on a different interpretation is that of the Pareto optimality of the median-voter outcome, a topic dealt with first by Bowen (1943) and recently by Bergstrom (1979). Bowen established the idea that if the distribution of tastes is symmetric, so that the community's median-voter marginal rate of substitution (the result of majority rule) equals the mean marginal rate of substitution (the Pareto efficiency condition), the majority rule is Pareto efficient. Bergstrom argued that this could not be the case if public spending demand depended on income, because income is not distributed symmetrically. This led him to rescue the Bowen proposition through proportional income taxation and a symmetric distribution of "tastes."

[11] The only previous attempt to quantify these distributional results known to us appears in Inman and Rubinfeld (1979). Relying primarily on the studies mentioned above, they estimated a .25 weighted-average elasticity of expenditure benefits with respect to income. This elasticity of .25 is not too different from the .41 elasticity obtained from the survey analysis presented here.

[12] A long list of such studies is cited by Gramlich (1982).

Obviously, if our micro results are right, Bergstrom need not have worried about this problem—since public spending demand does not depend on income within a community, the Bowen majority-rule outcome could be Pareto efficient even without proportional income taxation.

A final point refers more directly to the median-voter proposition. Inman (1978) has shown that most of a sample of Long Island communities behaved "as if" the family with median income were the decisive voter in setting public expenditures. He argues that this finding confirms the median-voter hypothesis. While not necessarily denying that interpretation, the equations shown here offer an alternative possibility. Perhaps communities behave as if the median voter were decisive because of the importance of community median income in setting spending levels. Individual incomes are basically uncorrelated with spending desires, but as the median income in the community rises the community spends more.

II. The Tiebout Hypothesis

Another hotly debated issue in public finance is Tiebout's idea that voters group themselves with others having similar tastes so that public goods can be supplied efficiently. In principle there are many ways in which such an idea could be tested, but in practice the ways of testing the Tiebout hypothesis have been rather limited, and in many ways quite unsatisfactory.

Most attention has been directed at property-value changes, a tradition started by Oates (1969) and taken up by a number of authors, most recently Epple, Zelenitz, and Visscher (1978). The initial Oates article established that property values would be bid up in communities with low tax rates for a given bundle of public goods, or more public goods with a given tax rate. This suggested to Oates that there was a Tiebout-like *mechanism* at work. Economic agents were locating in communities with more favorable budgetary arrangements. Critics of this paper (Edel and Sclar 1974; Hamilton 1976) have argued that in a full Tiebout *equilibrium* property taxes should be simple benefit taxes, and if tax rates were shown to influence property values this would be proof that the system was not in a full Tiebout equilibrium. Epple et al. took this argument farther and showed that Tiebout and non-Tiebout communities could only be distinguished by whether property taxes cause a deadweight loss and hence influence the demand for housing for nonmedian voter individuals (for the median voter the tax rate is determined simultaneously and the econometric test cannot be made). Moreover, they also showed that the property-value test becomes totally nonoperational whenever housing is supplied elastically or community boundaries are changeable.[13]

The data used here suggest a different, and perhaps less ambiguous, way to test the Tiebout hypothesis. If the hypothesis is true, two conditions must hold. (a) Citizens should have grouped themselves together with others with similar tastes for public goods, to eliminate many of the deadweight losses implicit in the communal supply of these goods. (b) The community must in fact supply this community-desired level of public goods. We concentrate on the first condition in this section and the second condition in the next section.

To test the first, we compare the variance of local spending demands within a community with those throughout the state. If there is Tiebout grouping, the within-community variance will be significantly smaller than the entire statewide sample variance.

There are in principle two ways to make the test. The first and most obvious would be simply to compare variances of spending demands within a community and throughout the whole state. The second would be to use regression equations, such as those given in table 2, to control for factors that might influence spending in all districts and then do the test on regression residuals. If, for example, public spending demands depend positively on community income, higher-income communities would be expected to have a smaller intracommunity variance than a statewide sample made up of residents of high- and low-income communities. In this case, the influence of income, and other factors, can be controlled for by the regression and the test made on just the residuals.

Both tests provide somewhat different kinds of information. The residual test asks whether individuals with similar unobservables, pre-

---

[13] A similar test has been devised by Reschovsky (1979). He used power-company data to examine the determinants of location for intracommunity movers and nonmovers, finding that movers were influenced by fiscal variables and nonmovers were not. The criticism would be the same as that directed at Oates: In a full Tiebout equilibrium where property taxes are benefit taxes, we would expect to find fiscal variables unimportant in explaining location. Hence the resident results could be consistent either with a full Tiebout equilibrium or with disequilibrium (as Reschovsky argues). By the same token, in a full equilibrium fiscal variables would affect moving decisions only if taxes were not benefit taxes; hence this finding confirms the Tiebout mechanism but not a Tiebout equilibrium. A different test is provided by Hamilton, Mills, and Puryear (1975). They view education as the primary public good and income as the primary determinant of spending, and attempt to estimate how much income segregation within communities (and thus public goods segregation) there is. They find some evidence that income varies less in suburban communities than in central city communities, and that in SMSAs with a large number of school districts there is less income variation than in those with fewer districts. They conclude that the data provide some mild support for the Tiebout hypothesis.

MEDIAN-VOTER HYPOTHESES   553

TABLE 4

Test of Locational Grouping Hypothesis:
Comparison of Spending Demand
Variances and Residual Variances,
426 Detroit Metropolitan Area Homeowners

Location	Observations (N)	var (PE/N)	F(PE/N)	var (ε)	F(ε)
Wayne County:	201	. . .	. . .	. . .	. . .
Dearborn	21	3,889	8.17**	.005	2.42**
Dearborn Heights	13	26,406	1.20	.041	
Detroit	100	8,644	3.67**	.007	1.73**
Rest of Wayne	67	4,669	6.80**	.005	2.20**
Macomb County:	101	. . .	. . .	. . .	. . .
Roseville	10	880	36.09**	.001	9.31**
St. Clair Shores	10	495	64.17**	.001	10.08**
Sterling Heights	16	639	49.71**	.001	12.10**
Warren	25	7,327	4.33**	.023	.54
Rest of Macomb	40	3,058	10.39**	.007	1.66*
Oakland County:	124	. . .	. . .	. . .	. . .
Pontiac	13	23,104	1.37	.034	.36
Southfield	19	1,722	18.44**	.003	3.90**
Rest of Oakland	92	2,581	12.31**	.004	2.75**

Note.—Countywide expenditure and income data are as follows:

	PE/N	Y	PE/NY
Wayne	1,042	11,351	.092
Macomb	703	12,110	.058
Oakland	791	13,826	.057

* Significant at 5 percent level.
** Significant at 1 percent level.

sumably correlated with public sector demands, live together. The test using direct responses, however, looks at the effect of both observable and unobservable variables. Both tests are shown in tables 4 and 5.

Table 4 focuses on just the Detroit metropolitan area. Three counties—Wayne, Macomb, and Oakland—cover virtually all of the area within 30 miles of downtown Detroit and most of the area within 40 miles. Within this three-county area, it should be possible for all workers to find a residential area consisting of individuals with like tastes in public goods. Indeed, this appears to happen to an overwhelming degree, as is shown by both tests in table 4. The table shows spending demand variances, residual variances, and *F*-tests on each for the 426 respondents living in Wayne, Macomb, and Oakland counties, grouped by community when there are 10 or more respondents and by "rest of county" when not.[14] The countywide expenditure and income figures (in the note to the table) show that there is only a modest countywide dispersion in income (the low is 82 percent of the high) but a greater dispersion in the ratio of public expenditures to income (the low is 62 percent of the high). But what is remarkable about the table is the degree of grouping shown by the residuals. Using either *F*-test, in Wayne County 188 of the 201 (94 percent) respondents live in communities with an intracommunity variance of residual variance significantly smaller than the overall residual variance at the 1 percent level. In Macomb, all respondents do so using the straight variance test; 76 of the 101 respondents (75 percent) do so at the 5 percent level, and 36 of the 101 do so at the 1 percent level using the residual variance test. In Oakland, 111 of the 125 (90 percent) respondents do so at the 1 percent level for either test. Across all three counties 94 percent of the respondents are grouped together at the 1 percent level in the first test, and 79 percent of the respondents are grouped together at the 5 percent level and 88 percent of the respondents at the 1 percent level in the second. These calculations then indicate a very high degree of grouping by expenditure taste residuals in the three-county Detroit metropolitan area.[15]

A first check on this finding is to see whether it obtains in other medium-size communities in Michigan. In principle we would not expect there to be as much grouping in these other communities because there would not be as many fiscally independent jurisdictions to select from in a labor-market area. In fact, there is still a high degree of grouping, as is shown in table 5, which gives the identical information for the four areas with sufficient observations to make such a test. Using the straight variance test all respondents have grouped themselves together, but with the more stringent residual variance test only one-third of the sample observations are so grouped (at both the 5 and 1 percent levels).[16] At least for the residual test, the results are reasonably consistent with a Tiebout interpretation: In

[14] The test of whether two variances σ_1^2 and σ_2^2 are equal is provided by an *F*-test, since s_1^2/s_2^2 (the ratio of the estimated variances) is distributed as *F* with N_1 and N_2 the appropriate degrees of freedom. The test is valid only if the two χ^2 distributions associated with σ_1^2 and σ_2^2 are independent.

[15] The Detroit SMSA extends much farther out, including some counties with exterior borders almost 80 miles from downtown Detroit. We had relatively few observations from these other counties—St. Clair, Lapeer, Livingston, Washtenaw, and Monroe—in our sample, but had we included them in the test our conclusions would be tempered slightly because variances are greater in these outer counties. But still at least two-thirds of the sample observations would be grouped together in the 1 percent test and three-quarters in the 5 percent test.

[16] This percentage would be slightly higher were the next most populous city areas in the sample included (Bay City, Jackson, and Midland), but still not nearly as high as in the Detroit area.

TABLE 5

TEST OF LOCATIONAL GROUPING HYPOTHESIS:
COMPARISON OF SPENDING DEMAND
VARIANCES AND RESIDUAL VARIANCES,
139 NON-DETROIT URBAN MICHIGAN HOMEOWNERS

Location	Observations (N)	var (PE/N)	F(PE/N)	var (ε)	F(ε)
Flint SMSA:	35	. . .	. . .	. . .	. . .
Genessee County	15	4,692	6.77**	.008	1.53
Shiawassee County	20	722	43.99**	.003	3.56**
Grand Rapids SMSA	34	4,045	7.85**	.008	1.46
Lansing SMSA:	43	. . .	. . .	. . .	. . .
Lansing	25	7,310	5.35**	.018	0.68
Rest of Ingham	18	4,264	7.45**	.010	1.26
Kalamazoo SMSA	27	1,648	19.27**	.004	2.82**

** Significant at 1 percent level.

large metropolitan areas, there is quite extensive grouping; in smaller areas, there is some grouping.

III.   The Median-Voter Hypothesis

The other aspect of the Tiebout hypothesis that can be evaluated with these data is the logically complementary one of whether the jurisdictions in question in fact supply the level of public goods desired by these grouped respondents. If they do not, there would not be much point in locating near others with similar tastes, for all voters would be forced to consume nonoptimal levels of public expenditures. Since we are now comparing actual with desired levels of public expenditures, this test generalizes to one involving the median-voter hypothesis: Do communities supply the levels of public expenditures desired by the median voter in their community?

For this we make two changes in the data. Since we are now concerned with correspondence between actual and desired expenditures, we analyze not the residuals in a public expenditure demand equation, as above, but the raw adjustment factors. The ith respondent desiring a 5 percent cutback is recorded as -5.

A second change enables us to run a straightforward test of the median-voter hypothesis. Instead of using homeowner respondents as the sample, we redefine the sample to include only voter respondents. Clearly renter voters should be added to the sample in testing the median-voter hypothesis. By the same token, for tests of the median-voter hypothesis, nonvoting homeowners should be dropped from the sample.

The results of this test are shown in table 6. Respondents are grouped into Detroit metropolitan area, other cities, and other nonurban areas, following the classifications used in tables 4 and 5. For all voters, the table indicates remarkable support for the median-voter hypothesis and also for the idea that voters group themselves because they gain the level of public spending they desire. In the Detroit area, two-thirds of the voters want no change in the level of public spending, and the mean desired level is less than 1 percent below the actual level. Since more than half of the voters favor no change, the median voter obviously favors no change. And in the right-hand column, only 19 percent of the voters favor a level of public spending much different from actual, defined here as a positive or negative change of more than 5 percent. Essentially the same results are obtained for other urban areas in the state: two-thirds of the voters favoring no change and only 19 percent wanting a big increase or decrease.

The results are not as striking for nonurban voters. The median-voter hypothesis still gains convincing support, in that 60 percent of the nonurban voters in the state favor no change in the overall level of public spending, while only 28 percent favor big increases or decreases. But while this supports the median-voter hypothesis, there is not quite as much satisfaction with the overall level of public spending. A slightly smaller proportion of the voters want no change than in urban areas and a slightly larger proportion want a large change. If it is true that the Tiebout mechanism should work less well in large nonurban counties where voters cannot relocate without changing jobs, there should in general be lower levels of satisfaction with government spending and these urban-rural differences would be plausible.

It is possible that with so many voters—two-thirds in urban areas and three-fifths in rural areas—opting for no change, respondents are displaying less dissatisfaction with the public sector than they truly feel. However, it is perhaps still meaningful that the same questioning procedure showed differences between urban and rural areas and that these differences do, if anything, support the Tiebout hypothesis.

IV. Implications

The presence of micro data on public spending demands at least in principle allows several tests to be made of propositions of long-standing interest in the field of applied public finance. For one thing,

TABLE 6

TESTING THE MEDIAN VOTER HYPOTHESIS: DIFFERENCE BETWEEN ACTUAL AND DESIRED SPENDING OF 858 MICHIGAN VOTERS

Place	Homeowner Respondents	Voter Respondents	Want Decrease	Want No Change	Want Increase	Mean Desired Change (%)	Want No Change (%)	Want Big Change* (%)
Detroit metropolitan area:	426	374	49	249	76	-.78	66.6	19.5
Dearborn	21	22	4	14	4	-.23	63.6	13.6
Dearborn Heights	13	11	2	8	1	-5.91	72.7	18.2
Detroit	100	106	12	61	33	-.82	57.5	21.7
Rest of Wayne	67	53	5	37	11	-.23	69.8	20.7
Roseville	10	6	1	5	0	-1.67	83.3	.0
St. Clair Shores	10	6	0	6	0	.00	100.0	.0
Sterling Heights	16	14	0	10	4	2.14	71.4	14.3
Warren	25	23	4	17	2	-1.39	73.9	13.0
Rest of Macomb	40	32	8	20	4	-2.81	62.5	28.1
Pontiac	13	12	2	4	6	3.75	33.3	50.0
Southfield	19	16	2	13	1	-1.81	81.3	12.5
Rest of Oakland	92	73	9	54	10	-.62	74.0	16.4
Other cities:	139	129	23	87	19	-1.10	67.4	18.6
Genessee City	15	15	1	10	4	.67	66.7	.0
Shiawasee City	20	15	3	10	2	-.33	66.7	20.0
Grand Rapids	34	33	9	21	3	-2.58	63.6	24.2
Lansing	25	20	3	13	4	-.25	65.0	25.0
Rest of Ingham	18	23	3	16	4	-.74	69.6	21.7
Kalamazoo	27	23	4	17	2	-1.74	73.9	13.0
Nonurban counties	417	355	78	215	62	-1.81	60.5	28.5

* Want spending changes (up or down) of more than 5 percent.

it appears that spending-demand equations fitted to micro data give approximately the same parameter estimates as those fitted to macro data, though the interpretation of these micro equations can be very different and very illuminating. Positive income elasticities of public spending demand appear to arise because public services are distributed in a prorich manner within communities, implying that, other things equal, residents of higher-income communities perceive that they receive lower levels of spending on public goods and want more. As a consequence, in any given community, there appears to be little difference between the marginal public spending demands of rich and poor respondents, just as public opinion polls suggest. At the same time, respondents who anticipate increases in their own real income do desire somewhat more public spending (or are willing to pay more taxes).

The existence of micro data also permits a different test of the Tiebout hypothesis. Controlling for all the independent variables in a statewide micro–spending demand equation, residuals from the set of observations in urban communities have a significantly smaller variance than in the whole sample in a very high percentage of the cases, indicating that at least in those urban communities there appears to be a high degree of grouping by public spending demands. The obvious explanation for this phenomenon is a Tiebout mechanism, whereby people locate in communities where others want and supply a menu of public goods similar to their own preferred level. This interpretation is supported by three other propositions that can also be established. Actual spending does conform to desired levels in these purportedly Tiebout-like communities, it does so less in rural communities where a Tiebout mechanism is unlikely to operate, and there appears to be less grouping by residuals in small urban labor market areas than in large areas.

References

Advisory Commission on Intergovernmental Relations (ACIR). *Changing Public Attitudes on Government and Taxes.* Washington: Government Printing Office, 1979.
Antunes, George E., and Plumlee, John P. "The Distribution of an Urban Public Service: Ethnicity, Socioeconomic Status, and Bureaucracy as Determinants of the Quality of Neighborhood Streets." *Urban Affairs Q.* 12 (March 1977): 313–32.
Bergstrom, Theodore C. "When Does Majority Rule Supply Public Goods Efficiently?" *Scandinavian J. Econ.* 81, no. 2 (1979): 216–26.
Bergstrom, Theodore C., and Goodman, Robert P. "Private Demands for Public Goods." *A.E.R.* 63 (June 1973): 280–96.
Bergstrom, Theodore C.; Rubinfeld, Daniel L.; and Shapiro, Perry. "Microbased Estimates of Demand Functions for Local School Expenditures." *Econometrica* (in press).

Berk, R. A., and Hartman, A. "Race and District Differences in per Pupil Staffing Expenditures in Chicago Elementary Schools, 1970–71." Evanston, Ill.: Northwestern Univ., Center for Urban Affairs, June 1971.

Bloch, P. "Equality of Distribution of Police Services: A Case Study of Washington." Washington: Urban Inst., 1974.

Borcherding, Thomas E., and Deacon, Robert T. "The Demand for the Services of Non-federal Governments." *A.E.R.* 62 (December 1972): 891–901.

Bowen, Howard R. "The Interpretation of Voting in the Allocation of Economic Resources." *Q.J.E.* 58 (November 1943): 27–48.

Buchanan, James M. "Federalism and Fiscal Equity." *A.E.R.* 40 (September 1950): 583–99.

Citrin, J. "Do People Want Something for Nothing: Public Opinion on Taxes and Government Spending." *Nat. Tax J.* 32 (suppl.; June 1979): 113–39.

Clark, Terry N., and Ferguson, L. "The Middle Class: Policy Preferences and Political Involvement." Manuscript. Chicago: Univ. Chicago, Dept. Soc., 1981.

Community Council of Greater New York. "Comparative Recreation Needs and Services in New York Neighborhoods." New York: Community Council of Greater New York, 1963.

Converse, Philip E. "Public Opinion and Voting Behavior." In *Handbook of Political Science.* Vol. 4, *Nongovernmental Politics,* edited by Fred I. Greenstein and Nelson W. Polsby. Reading, Mass.: Addison-Wesley, 1975.

Courant, Paul N.; Gramlich, Edward M.; and Rubinfeld, Daniel L. "Why Voters Support Tax Limitation Amendments: The Michigan Case." *Nat. Tax J.* 33 (March 1980): 1–20.

Deacon, Robert T. "Private Choice and Collective Outcomes: Evidence from Public Sector Demand Analysis." *Nat. Tax J.* 30 (December 1977): 371–86.

Denzau, Arthur T., and Mackay, Robert J. "Benefit Shares and Majority Voting." *A.E.R.* 66 (March 1976): 69–76.

Downs, Anthony. *An Economic Theory of Democracy.* New York: Harper, 1957.

Edel, Matthew, and Sclar, Elliott. "Taxes, Spending, and Property Values: Supply Adjustment in a Tiebout-Oates Model." *J.P.E.* 82, no. 5 (September/October 1974): 941–54.

Epple, Dennis; Zelenitz, Allan; and Visscher, Michael. "A Search for Testable Implications of the Tiebout Hypothesis." *J.P.E.* 86, no. 3 (June 1978): 405–26.

Gillespie, W. Irwin. "Effect of Public Expenditures on the Distribution of Income." In *Essays in Fiscal Federalism,* edited by Richard A. Musgrave. Washington: Brookings, 1965.

Gold, Steven D. "The Distribution of Urban Government Services in Theory and Practice: The Case of Recreation in Detroit." *Public Finance Q.* 2 (January 1974): 107–30.

Gramlich, Edward M. "Intergovernmental Grants: A Review of the Empirical Literature." In *The Political Economy of Fiscal Federalism,* edited by Wallace E. Oates. Lexington, Mass.: Lexington, 1977.

———. "Models of Excessive Government Spending: Do the Facts Support the Theories?" In *Public Finance and Public Employment,* edited by Robert H. Haveman. Detroit: Wayne State Univ. Press, 1982.

Hamilton, Bruce W. "The Effects of Property Taxes and Local Public Spending on Property Values: A Theoretical Comment." *J.P.E.* 84, no. 3 (June 1976): 647–50.

Hamilton, Bruce W.; Mills, Edwin S.; and Puryear, David. "The Tiebout Hypothesis and Residential Income Segregation." In *Fiscal Zoning and Land*

Use Controls: The Economic Issues, edited by Edwin S. Mills and Wallace E. Oates. Lexington, Mass.: Heath, 1975.

Hotelling, Harold. "Stability in Competition." *Econ. J.* 39 (March 1929): 41–57.

Inman, Robert P. "Testing Political Economy's 'As If' Proposition: Is the Median Income Voter Really Decisive?" *Public Choice* 33, no. 4 (1978): 45–65.

Inman, Robert P., and Rubinfeld, Daniel L. "The Judicial Pursuit of Local Fiscal Equity." *Harvard Law Rev.* 92 (June 1979): 1662–1750.

Katzman, Martin T. "Distribution and Production in a Big City Elementary School System." *Yale Econ. Essays* 8 (Spring 1968): 201–56.

Ladd, Helen F. "Local Education Expenditures, Fiscal Capacity, and the Composition of the Property Tax Base." *Nat. Tax J.* 28 (June 1975): 145–58.

Levy, Frank; Meltsner, Arnold J.; and Wildavsky, Aaron. *Urban Outcomes: Schools, Streets, and Libraries.* Berkeley: Univ. California Press, 1974.

Lineberry, Robert L. *Equality and Urban Policy: The Distribution of Municipal Public Services.* Beverly Hills, Calif.: Sage, 1977.

Mandel, A. S. "The Allocation of Resources inside Urban and Suburban School Districts: Theory and Evidence." Ph.D. dissertation, Univ. Michigan, 1974.

Martin, Lowell A. *Library Response to Urban Change: A Study of the Chicago Public Library.* Chicago: American Library Assoc., 1969.

Musgrave, Richard A., and Musgrave, Peggy B. *Public Finance in Theory and Practice.* 3d ed. New York: McGraw-Hill, 1980.

Oates, Wallace E. "The Effects of Property Taxes and Local Public Spending on Property Values: An Empirical Study of Tax Capitalization and the Tiebout Hypothesis." *J.P.E.* 77, no. 6 (November/December 1969): 957–71.

Owen, John D. "The Distribution of Educational Resources in Large American Cities." *J. Human Resources* 7 (Winter 1972): 26–38.

Reschovsky, A. "Residential Choice and the Local Public Sector: An Alternative Test of the 'Tiebout Hypothesis.'" *J. Urban Econ.* 6 (October 1979): 501–20.

Romer, Thomas, and Rosenthal, Howard. "Political Resource Allocation, Controlled Agendas, and the Status Quo." *Public Choice* 33, no. 4 (1978): 27–43.

Samuelson, Paul A. "The Pure Theory of Public Expenditure." *Rev. Econ. and Statis.* 36 (November 1954): 387–89.

Sexton, Patricia C. *Education and Income: Inequalities of Opportunity in Our Public Schools.* New York: Viking, 1961.

Tiebout, Charles M. "A Pure Theory of Local Expenditures." *J.P.E.* 64, no. 5 (October 1956): 416–24.

Weicher, John C. "The Allocation of Police Protection by Income Class." *Urban Studies* 8 (October 1971): 207–20.

[5]

**Intergovernmental Grants:
A Review of the
Empirical Literature**

Edward M. Gramlich

Intergovernmental grants are a newly discovered object of fascination among public-finance economists. At the policy level, grants have become important because they are viewed as a means by which countries can compromise the desire of the central government to expand services, to equalize local incomes, or to make greater use of the central-government tax base without directly assuming the functional spending responsibilities of lower levels of government. Public-finance theorists have followed this interest, giving now much greater attention to such questions as the underlying rationale for different types of grants, analysis of the lower-government budgetary response to grants, and the development of criteria determining how grant money should be allocated to different areas and types of governments.

There has always been a voluminous empirical literature on the budgetary effects of intergovernmental grants. Until five years ago the dominant species was the "determinants" study of local-government expenditures. The typical determinants study consisted of a regression model explaining local-government expenditures, almost always on a cross-section basis for United States' state or local governments, using independent variables, such as income, population, population density, urbanization, and federal grants. The studies generally showed strong and quite significant coefficients for grants, though the results were accepted less than unanimously because of various conceptual and technical problems with the studies—lack of an underlying theory of the behavior of state and local governments, lack of any attempt to distinguish the different effects of different types of grants, lack of any attempt to deal with the possible simultaneous causation of grants and expenditures. In more recent times, the simple determinants study has given way to a somewhat more thorough analysis that shows at least some recognition of these methodological problems and makes at least some attempt to correct them. There have also been a few attempts to strike out in other directions and estimate the budgetary impact of grants in new and different ways. The upshot, as I will attempt to show, is that now the profession should be able to trust most of the broad empirical results of the grants literature—at least for the United States. As empirical studies in economics go, the remaining reservations to some of these results

219

seem relatively harmless. Despite the fact that many of these broad questions seem reasonably well settled, however, there remain many other questions that have not been treated either extensively or well, and where future work could pay large dividends.

This chapter will attempt to summarize the empirical work on the budgetary impact of intergovernmental grants. The summary will necessarily be brief and will not touch on all contributions made in the area—a sheer impossibility given the volume of the literature (in the past 15 years there have been well over a hundred articles and a few books on this topic). The chapter begins where it ought to—with the theory of grants. It examines the underlying theoretical justification for grants, how different types of grants should affect the budgetary behavior of lower levels of government, how this behavior would be altered when these governments are trying to achieve different objectives, and how the effectiveness of grants in achieving central-government objectives should be evaluated. It then examines the empirical literature, assessing the extent to which these findings do or do not corroborate various theoretical points and the extent to which they have or have not addressed all of the relevant and interesting questions. Finally, it concludes with a few thoughts on where future empirical work on grants ought to be headed.

Justification for Grants

There have been several commonly suggested rationales for intergovernmental grants. In general, they fall into two categories—economic justifications, where one can show that the central government could have efficiency, equity, or stabilization objectives that impinge on local governments in various ways, and political or institutional justifications, where it seems more natural to view the lower level of government as agents of central-government policy.

Economic Justifications

The justification most commonly cited in the literature is benefit spillovers. While various authors state the principle in different ways, the general idea is that not all of the benefits of a local expenditure are captured within the community: therefore, other communities, or the central government acting as their agent, should subsidize the first community's purchase of this good or service. This is done by a Pigovian price-reduction grant, according to which the central government will match all state or local expenditures on the project [see, for example, Break (1967) and Thurow (1966)]. To avoid repeating awkward terms, I will call these open-ended matching grants, which alter the relative prices facing lower levels of government, *case A grants*.

A second justification for grants regards, in one way or another, the distribution of income. Since the benefits of the expenditures of lower levels of government accrue more or less proportionately to all income groups, or are even focused on low-income groups somewhat disproportionately [Gillespie (1965)], there is an innate limit to the degree to which local governments can, on their own, impose progressive taxes. If the net of tax revenues paid to lower levels of government less expenditures benefits received from them becomes too large for any business or income group, that group will simply pick up stakes and locate in some jurisdiction that assesses it a less onerous "fiscal residuum" [the term is Buchanan's (1950)]. Thus it makes perfectly good theoretical sense for state and local taxes to be, on the whole, somewhat regressive,[1] and also for the central government, less concerned by any "flight" of its businesses or high-income groups, to try to rectify the distributional implications by imposing progressive taxes of its own and even sharing to some degree the fruits of these taxes with state and local governments. This line of reasoning could justify a program of central-government unconditional grants or closed-end lump-sum transfers to lower levels of government. I will label these grants, which alter the incomes available to lower levels of government but not the relative prices facing them, *case B grants.*

An extension of this argument could justify a revenue-sharing program more focused on poor jurisdictions. As long as the net fiscal residual for high-income groups is greater than that for low-income groups, as it clearly seems to be on average [Netzer (1974)], it will be more advantageous to locate in high-income than low-income communities. In addition to having high incomes and presumably greater spending on public services, households of any income will face lower tax prices for local public services in high-income communities. If these services—health, education, public safety, or whatever—should from a social point of view be provided at equal cost in the two communities, or more cheaply in low-income communities, the central government will also have a reason for redistributing income among communities—giving to low-income communities and taking away from (or not giving to) high-income communities. This would be another justification for case B grants of a redistributive nature [Musgrave (1961)].[2]

A different type of argument regards economic-stabilization considerations. Conventional Keynesian theory dictates using the monetary and fiscal powers of the government to stabilize private spending and employment in a business cycle. If so, why should the central-government budget not also be used to stabilize local-government public spending and employment? If anything, stability in the services offered by the public sector seems a more worthwhile aim than stability in those offered by the private sector. This consideration would again argue for a program of case B grants to lower levels of governments, with the level dependent on the degree of overall unemployment.[3] The same consideration would, of course, argue for taxes on local governments in a boom period, but rare is the real-world central-government politician who would propose such a thing.

Political-Institutional Justifications

While the foregoing arguments have undoubtedly played some role in the development of central-government grant programs as we now know them, a political-institutional justification has probably played an even more important role in most developed countries. There are very good democratic reasons to try to keep power close to the people by having strong and vigorous local governments. At the same time, central governments have increasingly become more ambitious in trying to establish minimum service or spending levels for different government-provided goods and services. A reasonable way to compromise these partially conflicting objectives is for the central government to give closed-ended categorical grants to local governments. This technique preserves local control over the relevant functional category of expenditures but yet allows the central government to upgrade local spending. It does not, however, allow the local government as much freedom as it would have with an open-ended price-reduction grant: the central government maintains control over its own budget by limiting the total amount of funds available to lower governments. The central government will typically also establish rather tight conditions on the uses to which the money can be put, the degree to which local governments can cut back other spending, and so forth. The most natural way to think of these grants then, as argued by Hicks (1968) and Schultze (1974), may be as a device by which local governments are acting as the agents, or contractors, for the central government in carrying out specified tasks. I will call these grants, which can be thought of as affecting both the relative prices and incomes facing lower levels of government, *case C grants.*

The Impact of Different Types of Grants

Standard indifference-curve theory can be used to indicate the effect of these different types of grants on the budgets of lower levels of government [the earliest example is Scott (1952), the most complete is Wilde (1971)]. For case A grants, which simply imply a reduction in the relative price of the grant-aided good, expenditures will increase by an amount depending on the price elasticity of demand: if expenditure demand is price elastic, total (lower plus higher levels of government) expenditures on grant-aided goods will increase by more than the grant, and expenditures on all other goods will decline; vice versa if expenditure demand is price inelastic. In Figure 12–1, if we represent grant-aided goods or public expenditures, along the abscissa and private goods consumed by the

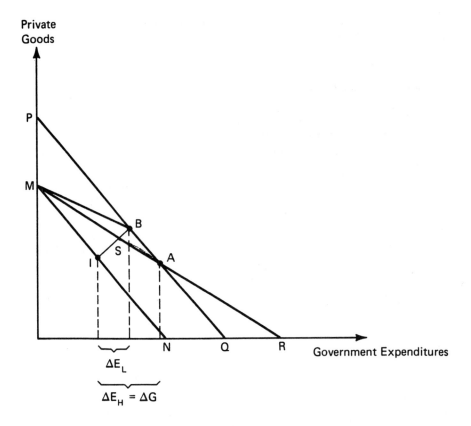

Figure 12-1. The Effect of Grants on Lower-Government Budgets.

community along the ordinate, and if the community was initially located at point I, a reduction in the price of the grant-aided good to MR will increase expenditures by IA, which here is exactly equal to the size of the grant. Thus the partial derivative of expenditures with respect to grants, $\delta E/\delta G$, is equal to unity for this case of a unitary price elasticity of demand. Were price elasticity greater than unity, the community would move to some point along AR and $(\delta E/\delta G) > 1$; were the price elasticity less than unity the community would be on SA and $\delta E/\delta G < 1$; were the price-substitution effect of the change in prices absent, only the income effect would come into play and the community would move along its income-consumption curve to point S. If for purposes of standardization we put everything in terms of a grant of constant size $\Delta G = IA$, the distance ΔE_L (from the income-consumption curve) is the minimum that expenditures should increase in response to an open-ended grant of size ΔG, and ΔE_H is the maximum in the sense that the full price-substitution effect implied by this price elasticity takes place.

Case B grants change the income of the community and not relative prices and, if both public and private goods have positive income elasticities, will move the community to point *B*. The change in expenditures is again ΔE_L, which will usually be less than the grant so the $0 < (\delta E/\delta G) < 1$. The first inequality will be true as long as there is a positive income elasticity of demand for public goods, the second as long as the same condition holds for private goods. Even though the response of expenditures is smaller, however, the local government still has its freedom and enjoys a higher indifference level than with the same sized grant of type A.

Case C grants represent the intermediate possibility, and the community will go somewhere along the line segment *AB* for a grant of size ΔG. If the grant of ΔG reduces the price of public goods to *MR*, the community with unitary price elasticity will go to point *A*, use up all of the grant funds, and have a value of $(\delta E/\delta G) = 1$. Since the community must match central-government money with its own to get the full grant, the fact that the net value of $\delta E/\delta G$ is only one implies that this community is also reducing spending on public goods it would otherwise have undertaken, a phenomenon known in the literature as the "grant displacement" effect.[4] As the central-government matching provisions become more generous and the price of public goods is reduced to *MB*, the community wants more of the grant, the constant funds limit allows the community to take less and less advantage of the price reduction, the community is moved from point *A* to *B*, and the change in expenditures falls from ΔE_H to ΔE_L. As the price of public goods is reduced even further (angle *PMB* is reduced toward 90°), the limit on funds becomes so binding that further price reductions are useless, the community remains at *B*, and the grant becomes like a case B grant with income effects only. Thus, beginning with relatively unfavorable matching ratios, grants of a constant size ΔG in effect pass from case A to case C to case B types as the matching ratio becomes steadily more favorable and the funds limit steadily more binding, ultimately totally dominating and making irrelevant the price reduction.

The same phenomenon can be demonstrated alternatively, this time holding the price ratio constant at MR and varying the central-government funds limit. If the limit is such that the maximum possible grant can exceed ΔG, the limit obviously becomes irrelevant for this community, it stays at *A*, and the grant is case A. As the limit is reduced below ΔG, the community moves along line segment *SA* and the smaller grant would be considered case C. Once the limit on the grant moves the community to *S*, further reductions push the community along *IS* and the grant would be considered case B. The result is again that a case C grant can only become a case A grant when the limit is great enough that it is nonbinding and marginal changes in the price become fully operative; and it can only become a case B grant when the limit is tight enough that marginal changes in the price become irrelevant.

Even though this analysis is devoid of any number of real-world complications, it can already have quite complex empirical implications. The impact of grants on the budgetary position of lower levels of government depends on whether grants alter just the income constraint or that plus the relative prices facing local governments. That in turn depends upon the underlying community price and income elasticities of demand for public goods, the degree of relative price reduction, and the maximum size of grant the central government will allow. The only firm prediction of the model is that for any particular type of good, the expenditure impact, $\delta E/\delta G$, will be greatest for case A grants, next greatest for case C grants, and smallest for case B grants. Even this prediction, however, hinges on the underlying assumption that public goods are reasonably homogeneous and that communities are attempting to maximize some vague phenomenon known as *aggregate community welfare*. If these assumptions are relaxed, as they should be, things become even more complex.

The first assumption to be relaxed is that government expenditures are homogeneous. If they are not, it may become physically impossible for the lower government to displace as many expenditures as would be predicted by the above analysis because the expenditures may not be there in the first place. Similar restrictions on displacement could be obtained if the grant came with effective effort-maintenance provisions that tried to preclude displacement. The result is that if case C grants were for new and nondisplacable programs or with effort-maintenance restrictions, they could in principle show larger expenditure inducements ($\delta E/\delta G$) than would case A grants without such side conditions in the same functional area.

In similar fashion, the joint objectives of the community might be more complicated. The indifference-curve, utility-function-maximization approach to state and local behavior [Henderson (1968), Gramlich (1969a), and others] assumes that the community is rationally trying to maximize some concept of utility that can be that of the median voter or the median voter as somehow perceived by politicians. It does not assume a disharmony of interests between politicians and voters. But if some disharmony exists, different results obtain. In the harmonious world, for example, it should not matter whether the central government cuts taxes or gives revenue-sharing funds to local governments. As long as the income-distributional properties are the same, either measure should increase public spending by the income elasticity of demand, with the remainder going into increased private spending [Oates (1972)]. If a central-government tax cut of $1 would raise local spending and taxes by $0.10, central-government revenue sharing of $1 would also raise local spending by $0.10, lower local taxes by $0.90, and raise total local revenues (taxes plus grants) also by $0.10. As classical economists might say, revenue sharing is a veil for the tax cut.

But what if there is disharmony? What if local politicians feel they can fool the people by not cutting taxes the full $0.90 in response to revenue sharing, even though they would only dare raise them $0.10 in response to a central-government tax cut? Then the initial incidence of the money does become important, revenue sharing is not a veil, and the impact of revenue sharing on case B grants cannot be reliably predicted from the response of public expenditures to private incomes. The phenomenon might be called the *flypaper theory of incidence*: money sticks where it hits.[5]

This interesting case has been generalized by Niskanen (1968) and McGuire (1973). McGuire postulates what might be termed a *greedy politicians model*, where local politicians respond to any grant program by spending all they can get their hands on as long as private households are not made worse off in the process. In this case, all types of grants have identical effects—local-government spending rises by slightly more than the full amount of the grant.[6] McGuire neither necessarily believes nor has tested this model, but this line of reasoning does open up additional possibilities by which the response of lower levels of government to various types of grants may not be easily or rigorously predicted from the "theory."

How Should Grants Be Evaluated?

The preceding remarks provide a fairly clear indication of the type of questions any empirical evaluations of grants should deal with. For case A and C grants, the central government is expressly trying to stimulate spending in a certain area. It then becomes logical to ask how much spending was stimulated, whether the displacement effect mitigated the impact of the grant, whether limitations on central-government spending or effort-maintenance provisions were necessary to restrict the outflow of federal funds or to attain a desired degree of spending, whether matching provisions should be altered, and so forth. These questions have all come up in one way or another in the United States in recent years. A first illustration was the attempt of the Nixon administration to fold several categorical case C grants into special revenue sharing—a closed-ended grant program that defines eligible spending very broadly and thus allows so much displacement that it is probably very close to a case B grant; a second is the recently passed public-service employment provision, which again, because of the many types of employment eligible, is likely to turn into a case B grant and frustrate the attempt of Congress to prevent employment displacement.

Beyond this, of course, there are always the fundamental questions. Whether or not grant program X induced displacement, did it achieve its underlying objective of improving education, training workers, cleaning up the atmosphere, or whatever? Introducing these issues raises the vast questions of program evaluation, which I will not go into here in the interest of brevity. Yet to the extent that the data will support it, it should always be pointed out that expenditures and expenditure impacts are not everything, that what this branch of public finance is and should be all about is whether government programs of whatever type are ultimately doing what they ought to.

For case B grants, the relevant questions become both broader and narrower than simply what lower governments are doing with the money. Since the objective of the program is not so much to encourage spending on a particular program or type of program (though people would be less interested in revenue sharing if local governments were not responsible for many "needed" public services) but to modify the distribution of income, there should be less interest in the question of what local governments are doing with the money. Simply knowing that they got it is enough. But since redistribution is a prime goal, the first important question is to ask which governments in fact did get the money and whether they were the ones that should have gotten it. In the United States, this has led into a whole set of articles on the distributional virtues and anomalies of the new general revenue-sharing legislation [see, for example, Nathan, Manvel, and Calkins (1975), Strauss (1974), Reischauer (forthcoming)]. Much interest also attaches to the question of whether general revenue sharing will heighten citizen interest in local government, rationalize or worsen the somewhat haphazard pattern of overlapping local general governments and special districts, improve management, or whatever. Some have even inquired into whether general revenue sharing will "revitalize federalism," a question that seems likely to have some problems at the definitional level.

The Empirical Work on Intergovernmental Grants

To this point, virtually all empirical work on the effect of grants on lower levels of government has been concerned with the United States.[7] Accordingly, this summary will also limit itself to the United States, though it should obviously be recognized that the lessons are of more general relevance. If U.S. empirical work has been successful, scholars in other countries have a leg up in trying to understand their own grants; if U.S. work is not successful, other scholars can avoid making the same mistakes.

Case A Grants

Although most public-finance discussions of grants begin with case A grants— which reduce the relative prices of designated public services provided by local government—examples of these grants in the United States are relatively rare. At the federal level, the only case A grants are for public assistance ($5.4 billion in fiscal 1974) and medicaid ($5.8 billion), now comprising about 25 percent of total federal government grant expenditures. Some state governments also have case A grants in the area of education and other social services.

Since case A grants are open-ended, the level of the grant is determined simultaneously with and as part of the level of expenditures. Most empirical attempts at estimating the impact of public-assistance grants on expenditures have ignored this complication and have simply regressed the level of expenditures on the level of grants across states, in all cases finding $\delta E/\delta G$ to be greater than unity and, implicitly, the price elasticity of demand to be greater than unity also [see Albin and Stein (1971), Osman (1966), Sacks and Harris (1964)]. It is very likely the case, however, that this high estimated effect represents nothing more than simultaneous-equations bias in the coefficient of federal aid and should not be trusted [Oates (1968), Pogue and Sgontz (1968)]. In the one case where federal-assistance parameters were treated properly [Orr (forthcoming)], using an exogenous indication of the true "after-match" price of welfare within the framework of a theoretically consistent model of income redistribution across states and for different dates, the effective price elasticity of demand for public assistance came out to be –0.23 – implying that welfare grants stimulate a relatively small amount of state and local expenditures. With this elasticity, the implied value of $\delta E/\delta G$ in 1970 is only 0.15.

Most indications are that other case A grants are more stimulative. The evidence is very sketchy for medicaid, where there are not even biased regression studies to use as a guide. The only real examination of medicaid was by Gayer (1972), who tested for changes in the ratio of medicaid expenditures to all state and local expenditures or state and local health expenditures between 1965 (before medicaid) and 1968 (after medicaid was introduced). Although this comparison cannot give very fine-grained results, Gayer did find that after correcting for premedicaid upward trends in expenditures, total state and local expenditures seem to have increased as a result of medicaid but not own expenditures. The implied value for $\delta E/\delta G$ is, in other words, not significantly different from unity. Gayer also found that treatment standards among states have not been equalized as a result of medicaid.

Most evidence on the impact of state case A grants on expenditures also suggests values of $\delta E/\delta G$ between zero and unity. Gramlich and Galper (1973) found values ranging slightly above and below 0.8 in a pooled cross-sectional sample of ten large cities for the categories: urban support, social services, and public safety. Fairly similar results were reported by Inman (1971) for a larger cross section of cities. Feldstein (1975) found price elasticities of demand for education of unity or slightly greater in a study of Massachusetts towns aimed at determining how state matching-grant formulas should be written to neutralize the impact of community wealth on local education expenditures. But Ohls and Wales (1972) found negligible price elasticities of demand (in effect, very small values of $\delta E/\delta G$ for case A grants) across states in all areas except highways. Other cross-sectional studies of local governments, not dealing specifically with grants, have found price elasticities of demand for local services in the neighborhood of unity [Borcherding and Deacon (1972)] or closer to zero [Bergstram and Goodman (1973)].

Case B Grants

The second important type of grant program is that which provides lower levels of government with closed-ended unconditional grant assistance – so-called case B grants. Apart from a few very small programs, these grants had not been used at all by the U.S. government until 1972 when the widely discussed general revenue-sharing program began disbursing approximately $6 billion in aid to state and local governments. In fiscal 1974 these case B grants amounted to 14 percent of total federal assistance to states and localities. Case B grants are also used in several other countries – notably Australia, Canada, and West Germany – generally as part of a treaty or other arrangement dividing up taxing powers between different levels of government. There are also many state case B grants to local general governments or school districts.[8]

Because of the newness of general revenue sharing in the United States, there have not been a great number of statistical studies of its budgetary impact [though many are on the way; the National Planning Association (1974) and and the U.S. National Science Foundation (1975)]. One early attempt at "monitoring" revenue sharing by trained field observers in 63 different state or local governments [see Nathan, Manvel, and Calkins (1975)] concluded that 26 percent of the revenue-sharing money led to new spending, another 15 percent to maintenance of programs that otherwise would have been cut, 30 percent to tax cuts or avoiding tax increases, and the remainder into increases in fund balances and/or avoidance of borrowing. These percentages were essentially the same for states and localities, with local governments spending slightly more – possibly because of certain legal requirements attempting to limit spending reductions for local but not state governments. The results are based on survey data and have all the strengths and weaknesses of such studies – they can be more refined and subtle than regression studies, but they can also be less uniform and harder to validate or disprove. They also have the particular disadvantage that they are monitoring only the very short-run impact of revenue sharing on state-local expenditures. It has been argued, for example, that early responses to federal revenue sharing are contaminated by the fact that lower levels of government may have invested extraordinary proportions of the funds in capital projects because of the fear that the program would be cut off.

Concerning the regression studies, Gramlich and Galper (1973) found in time-series regressions for the aggregate state and local sector up to 1972 that the response of expenditures to changes in unconditional budgetary resources of all sorts implied that about $0.43 per dollar of case B grants would go into expenditures in the long run, very close to the spending impact implied by the survey of Nathan et al. This estimate was a prediction of the impact of revenue sharing before the fact – based on the degree to which such "exogenous" budgetary claims as interest and debt retirement reduced discretionary expenditures –

and while it was not specific to revenue sharing, it also did not have the short-run–long-run problem of Nathan et al. A similar analysis for a pooled cross-sectional sample of 10 large urban governments, this time with some state revenue-sharing money in the budgetary variable, led to coefficients ($\delta E/\delta G$) on the order of 0.25. Other regression estimates in the same general range were made by Feldstein (1975) for state block grants to Massachusetts towns, by Bowman (1974) for West Virginia untied aid to independent school districts, and by Weicher (1972) for untied state school aid to school districts in cities where the district is fiscally independent. At the same time, the coefficients are well below those estimated by Inman (1971) for a panel of cities and again by Weicher for untied aid to municipal governments: both of the latter studies found that almost all case B aid would result in higher expenditures [$\delta E/\delta G$ = 1] with virtually nothing left over for tax reduction. Whether half or all the revenue-sharing money goes into higher expenditures, however, at this point all empirical studies indicate long-run responses appreciably greater than would be implied by the response of expenditures to changes in income—which in vitually all studies comes out to be between 0.05 and 0.10 (implying an income elasticity in the neighborhood of unity). Hence the empirical work to this point strongly suggests that revenue sharing is not a veil for tax cuts—that it does make an appreciable difference in the pattern of expenditures whether the federal government disburses untied aid to state and local governments or makes untied tax cuts benefiting individuals. The results are so striking that the field could well use more theory [perhaps of the Niskanen-McGuire variety] on whether and under what conditions the standard indifference-curve, utility-maximization analysis had better give way to a variant more cognizant of political realities.

In this connection, one of the interesting findings on the probable impact of revenue sharing comes from Weicher (1972). Designers of the general revenue-sharing bill have worried a great deal about which jurisdictions serving a particular area should get the money—should it go to states, counties, towns, villages, overlapping special districts, or whatever? The implication of the veil line of thought is that it does not much matter—if an independent school board gets money, it will lower taxes, allow general governments to raise taxes, and all types of spending will increase; if the school board does not get money, the greater reduction in general government taxes will still allow school boards to raise taxes and again all types of spending will increase. To test hypotheses of this sort, Weicher regressed both municipal and school-district expenditures on a set of variables including cast B state aid to the town and to the other government cross sectionally for 120 large cities with independent school districts. For aid to school districts, he got the expected result that both school and municipal expenditures increase, the former more than the latter, with the total spending coefficient for school aid equal to 0.59—close to that of Nathan et al., Gramlich and Galper, Feldstein, and Bowman. But for untied aid to municipal governments, he found that *school* expenditures increased more, so much so that the total spending coefficient ($\delta E/\delta G$) for case B grants to municipal governments was almost unity. This result, if credible, gives an ambiguous verdict on the veil theory—on the one hand, the theory might be rejected because the net spending impact is so much higher than that for income; on the other hand, it might be accepted because the form of certain types of aid does not appear to matter much. School districts appear to get their cut whether they are or are not directly aided. This finding again should stimulate more examination into the way that governments, particularly overlapping governments, really work.

Case C Grants

Traditionally, the most important type of grant at the federal level has been the closed-ended conditional grant, or case C grant. In fiscal 1974 these grants accounted for $26.8 billion, 61 percent of total grants, in such areas as highways, health, education, manpower, and the environment. The proportion has declined in recent years, however. A few years ago, before the initiation of general revenue sharing and the rapid growth in public assistance and medicaid, it was over 70 percent.[9]

Just as case C grants have received most of the money, they have been the grants ultimately dealt with in most empirical studies of federal aid. The usual approach has been to estimate the spending impact of these grants by regressing the level of total expenditures or expenditures from own funds [as long as one remembers what one is doing, it does not matter which; see Gramlich (1972)] on grants and a set of other independent variables. This technique does not lead to the obvious upward bias in the estimated impact that exists for case A grants, because case C grants are, after all, closed-ended and therefore in principle not simultaneously determined with expenditures. Yet there is a different possible bias relating to the fact that grants are recorded when the money is spent, which is usually the same time that the expenditure is made. There seems to be little question that this type of simultaneous-equations bias led to an excessively high impact of grants on lower-government expenditures in some of the early studies, though more recent studies that have dealt more carefully with simultaneity have not found the bias to be terribly significant [O'Brien (1971) and Horowitz (1968)].

The spending coefficients for federal case C grants on expenditures in 24 recent studies are given in Table 12-1.[10] The estimated values of $\delta E/\delta G$ range between the value of 2.45 for Kurnow, the very first study to use grants as an independent variable, to 0.32 for Bolton, with the mean estimated effect equaling 1.40. If there are any patterns to the results, the early cross-sectional estimates seem to be higher than the later time-series or pooled-cross-sectional estimates and also higher than the amount mandated by the matching formula

Table 12-1
The Impact of Case Grants on Expenditures: Results of Various Regressions Studies for $\partial E/\partial G$

Author	Sample	Date	Dependent Variable	Independent Variable	Result, $\partial E/\partial G$
Kurnow (1963)	48 States	1957	St. Loc. Exp.	Fed. Grants	2.45[a]
Pidot (1969)	81 Large Met. Areas	1962	Met. Exp.	Fed. Grants	2.35
Johnson & Junk (1970)	43 Largest Cities	1967	City Exp.	Fed. & St. Grants	2.02
Osman (1966)	48 States	1960	St. Loc. Exp.	Fed. Grants	1.94
Pogue & Sgontz (1968)	50 States Pooled	1958–64	St. Loc. Exp.	Fed. Grants	1.81[b]
Harlow (1967)	48 States	1957	St. Exp.	Fed. Grants	1.80
Brazer (1959)	462 Cities	1951	City Current Exp.	Fed. & St. Grants	1.74
Petersen (1968)	50 States Pooled	1962–3	St. Loc. Exp.	Fed. current Grants	1.70
Smith (1968)	50 States	1965	St. Loc. Exp.	Fed. Grants	1.66
Booms & Hu (1971)	50 States	1960	St. Loc. Ed. Exp.	Fed. Ed. Grants	1.61
Campbell & Sacks (1967)	48 States	1962	St. Loc. Exp.	Fed. Grants	1.56
Sacks & Harris (1964)	48 States	1960	St. Loc. Exp.	Fed. Grants	1.55
Henderson (1968)	100 Met. Counties	1957	County Exp.	Fed. & St. Grants	1.42
Bahl & Saunders (1966)	48 States	1957–60	St. Loc. Exp.	Fed. Grants	1.36
Horowitz (1968)	50 States	1962	St. Loc. Exp.	Fed. Grants	1.26
O'Brien (1971)	48 States Pooled	1958–66	St. Loc. Exp.	Fed. Grants	1.19
Bowman (1974)	55 W. Va. Counties	1969–70	Loc. Sch. Taxes	Fed. Ed. Grants	1.06[c]
Henderson (1968)	2,980 Non-Met. Counties	1957	County Exp.	Fed. & St. Grants	1.04
Adams (1966)	1,249 Counties	1959	County Taxes	Fed. Grants	0.96[c]
Gramlich & Galper (1973)	76 Quarters	1954–72	St. Loc. Exp.	Fed. Grants	0.90
Ehrenberg (1971)	50 States Pooled	1958–69	St. Loc. Empl. Exp.	Fed. Grants	.79[a]
Gramlich & Galper (1973)	10 City-Counties Pooled	1962–70	Loc. Exp.	Fed. & St. Grants	0.65
Phelps (1969)	16 Years	1951–66	St. Loc. Highway Exp.	Fed. Highway Grants	0.45
Bolton (1969)	40 Quarters	1954–63	St. Loc. Exp.	Fed. Grants	0.32

[a]Estimated in elasticity form and converted to partial derivative using expenditure and grant values for appropriate year.
[b]Regressions were run for each year in the sample. I averaged the seven coefficients, which went as high as 2.04 and as low as 1.31.
[c]Regressions actually used taxes as the dependent variable. In converting to expenditures, I simply added one to the coefficient $[\partial E/\partial G = 1 + \partial T/\partial G]$.

on grants (about 1.3 at present values). These early results are suspect, however, because they imply that not only do federal-grant–supported goods not displace own expenditures at all, they complement own expenditures enough to more than offset the implied reduction resulting from the fact that 0.3 of the grant must be raised from own funds to match it: a possibility that is inconsistent with the fact that the negative income effect of the mandated portion would to some degree reduce expenditures. But even if the very high early estimates of the spending impact are discounted, presumably because of some kind of simultaneous bias, almost all of the regression estimates of the spending coefficients for federal grants remain rather high, usually greater than the estimated effect of case A grants. This in turn implies either that case C grants are given in areas where demand is more price elastic than in the case A grant areas or that grants are given for new types of programs with effective effort-maintenance provisions that prevent much local grant displacement from taking place.

An alternative way of estimating the impact of case C grants on the budgets of state and local governments was developed by Miller (1974). By closely examining highway statistics, he found that all but nine states spend more than is necessary to receive and match closed-end grants under the ABC (non interstate) highway program, indicating that at least small increments in grant funds would not stimulate much spending in all but these nine states. In terms of Figure 12-1, he is finding that the amount of grant funds is so small relative to what states would spend anyway on highways that ABC grants are in effect being converted into case B grants with relatively small spending impacts. This finding does not agree with most of the regression evidence on case C grants. It may not be inconsistent with these findings, however, because the ABC program is much older than most other grant programs and much smaller relative to local expenditures, and it might be natural to expect grant displacement to be much higher. The implication is that if the federal government desires to encourage spending, it can probably do that only by grant programs where the spending output is distinguishable from what the state would have done anyway, where effort maintenance can be effective, and where grants are large relative to existing expenditures. If it wants to encourage somewhat more spending on such areas as highways where states have long been spending large amounts, its grant money will probably get lost in the shuffle anyway and it may as well simply avoid administrative hassles by converting all grants to case B form.

A similar type of finding regards the new U.S. public-service employment program. In some respects, public-service employment might be thought of as a case C grant – it is closed-ended and requires state and local governments to spend in a certain area, i.e., to hire workers. Since the federally funded employment is very small relative to total state and local employment, however, the government may in fact operate much more like a case B grant, because it will be difficult for the federal government to devise effective effort-maintenance provisions insuring that local governments will continue hiring the employees they would have hired otherwise apart from the federal grants (particularly when employment levels are rising over time). The early evaluations of public employment, by Johnson and Timola (1974) and Fechter (1975), indicate that such is the case, that spending and employment propensities are much closer to what might be anticipated under a case B than a case C grant program.

Overall Evaluation

The previous comments suggest the areas where the existing literature is strong and where it is weak. Most of the points have been stressed enough that a detailed recapitulation is not necessary. Yet it is useful to try to put past empirical work into perspective – it has answered this set of questions but not that set. This section indicates very briefly the areas where the work on grants is, in my opinion, reasonably convincing and the areas where there is still much to be done.

Although it is of couse risky to summarize a large number of studies in a few sentences, at the present time empirical work on grants in the United States has basically verified the following four hypotheses:

1. That case A grants generally result in somewhat less spending than the size of the grant, indicating that the price elasticity of demand for most services is probably somewhat less than unity.
2. That case B grants result in some tax reduction and some expenditure increase, with the expenditure increase less than for case A grants, as would be predicted by the theory.
3. That case B grants, on the other hand, stimulate much more spending than central-government tax cuts in the long run, indicating at a minimum the need for some revision in political theories that feature a harmony of interests between bureaucrats and voters.
4. That case C grants stimulate total local spending roughly equal to the grant, generally slightly more spending than is stimulated by case A grants – either because they are given in areas where demand is more elastic, because they are large relative to existing expenditures, or because they come with effective effort-maintenance provisions.

One can always make the claim that researchers on grants should continue working in these areas to refine estimates, test hypotheses in different ways, and so forth. This is as true in the area of grants as in any other area. However, it seems even more important for grant researchers and theorists to extend their investigations into different areas by asking "Why?" and "So what?" The "why" extension would delve into the politicoeconomic theories of bureaucracy indicated in several places. Why does the flypaper theory appear to be correct? Why is the response to central-government grants not as predicted by the harmony-of-interest theory in this case and as predicted by that theory in other cases? Does it or does it not matter whether independent school districts are directly aided, and why? This is an area where it may not be particularly easy to do research, but one can think of many questions regarding grants that can never be convincingly answered without more knowledge of the behavior of government bureaucrats.

A second broad type of extension would move away from the underlying theory and get into questions more relevant for specific legislation. The four hypotheses listed above are broad hypotheses that pertain to grants in general, but they are certainly not universally applicable. Each existing or prospective grant program is obviously unique, and the response of local governments to it will depend on underlying elasticities, the size of the grant, the homogeneity of local expenditures, restrictions on the grant, and any other political factors—in ways that have or have not been laid out above. To get really useful knowledge in this area, legislators must know what specifically will happen with specific changes. The paramount example of the inadequacy of econometric research in this area came recently with the Nixon administration special revenue-sharing proposals: despite all the past work and empirical consensus on the impact of different types of grants, I know of no study that could have convincingly predicted the effects of converting categorical aid to special revenue sharing in any one of the six areas proposed. To predict the effects of this conversion, one simply needed answers to more detailed and specific questions than had been asked before. If econometric research pretends to be policy-relevant, it must extend beyond the broad and general and get into these more specific questions for individual programs.

A third type of extension that also seems warranted is to expand the range of questions asked. To a certain degree, one cannot help but feel that empirical researchers in this area have fallen into the same state of mind that conservative politicians accuse liberal politicians of falling prey to: whereas all liberal politicians can do is "throw money at problems" (this is as alleged but not necessarily my own view), all researchers can do is measure the amount of money thrown. At some point research will have to go beyond the question everybody asks and answers—how much did local spending change—and into some more basic questions, such as whether the right type of spending was encouraged, by the right governments and for the right citizens, and even the ultimate one of whether the spending accomplished its intended objectives. Past empirical work has made a start—it is better to know how much money was spent than nothing—but there is clearly more to grant evaluation.

Notes

1. That they are is shown by Pechman and Okner (1974). When property taxes are allocated according to property ownership, in keeping with the so-

called new view of property-tax incidence, the regressivity is cut markedly. Then state and local property taxes are slightly regressive up to incomes of $20,000, and slightly progressive above that level.

2. If the net fiscal residual were zero for all groups, tax prices for public services would be the same in all communities. But there may still be a reason for case B grants to poorer communities to counter a positive income elasticity of demand for public goods and consequent inequalities of consumption of these goods.

3. The U.S. Congressional Budget Office (1975) has recently made exactly this argument.

4. Sometimes it is called the *substitution effect*, but I use alternative terminology to avoid confusion with the *price substitution effect*.

5. The term was coined by Arthur Okun.

6. Slightly more, because the community is made better off by the increased public spending, and the greedy politicians can then raise taxes slightly without making the electorate either worse off or aware that they are being had.

7. In a few years, it will no longer be possible to make this statement. Expenditure-determinants studies are beginning to appear in Great Britain, though the treatment of grants is still not extensively developed [see Alt (1971) and Ashford (1975)]. The impact of grants on expenditures is also now coming under scrutiny in West Germany, Canada, Australia, and New Zealand.

8. Since school districts cannot easily spend money on, say, highways, there is some doubt as to whether even untied aid to them should be considered a case B grant. In this chapter I do so because school districts still do have the option of lowering taxes in response to case B grants.

9. Strictly speaking, this proportion refers to those grants on which there is a funds limit. Even if there were such a limit, the grant could still be an A grant if undersubscribed. Instances of such undersubscription are, for the United States at least, quite rare.

10. The table omits a few studies that have used either a strange data base or a strange model with some obvious flaw obscuring the effect of grants.

References

Adams, R.F. 1966. The fiscal response to intergovernmental transfers in less developed areas of the United States. *Review of Economics and Statistics* 48:308–313.

Albin, P.S., and Stein, B. 1971. Determinants of relief policy at the subfederal level. *Southern Economic Journal* 37:445–457.

Alt, J. 1971. Some social and political correlates of county borough expenditures. *British Journal of Political Science* 1:49–62.

Ashford, D.E., Berne, R., and Schramm, R. 1975. The expenditure financing decision in British local government. Mimeographed. Cornell University.

Bahl, R.W., and Saunders, R.J. 1966. Factors associated with variations in state and local government spending. *Journal of Finance* 21:523-534.

Bergstrom, T.C., and Goodman, R.P. 1973. Private demand for public goods. *American Economic Review* 63:280-296.

Bolton, R.E. 1969. Predictive models for state and local government purchases. In *The Brookings Model: Some Further Results*, J.S. Duesenberry, G. Fromm, L.R. Klein, and E. Kuh, eds. Chicago: Rand McNally.

Booms, B.H., and Hu, T. 1971. Toward a positive theory of state and local public expenditures: An empirical example. *Public Finance* 26:419-436.

Borcherding, T.E., and Deacon, R.T. 1972. The demand for the services of non-federal governments. *American Economic Review* 62:891-901.

Bowman, J.H. 1974. Tax exportability, intergovernmental aid, and school finance reform. *National Tax Journal* 27:163-174.

Brazer, H.E. 1959. City expenditures in the United States. Occasional paper 66. New York: National Bureau of Economic Research.

Break, G.F. 1967. *Intergovernmental Fiscal Relations in the United States.* Washington, D.C.: The Brookings Institution.

Buchanan, J.M. 1950. Federalism and fiscal equity. *American Economic Review* 40:583-599.

Campbell, A., and Sacks, S. 1967. *Metropolitan America, Fiscal Patterns and Governmental Systems.* Glencoe, N.Y.: The Free Press.

Ehrenberg, R.G. 1973. The demand for state and local government employees. *American Economic Review* 63:366-379.

Fechter, A.E. 1975. Public service employment: Boom or boondoggle? In *Proceedings of a Conference on Public Service Employment.* Washington, D.C.: National Commission for Manpower Policy.

Feldstein, M.S. 1975. Wealth neutrality and local choice in public education. *American Economic Review* 65:75-89.

Fredlund, J.E. 1974. *Determinants of State and Local Expenditures: An Annotated Bibliography.* Washington, D.C.: Urban Institute.

Gayer, D. 1972. The effects of medicaid on state and local government finances. *National Tax Journal* 25:511-520.

Gillespie, W.I. 1965. Effect of public expenditures on the distribution of income. In *Essays in Fiscal Federalism*, R.A. Musgrave, Ed. Washington, D.C.: The Brookings Institution.

Gramlich, E.M. 1969a. State and local governments and their budget constraint. *International Economic Review* 10:163-182.

Gramlich, E.M. 1969b. The effect of federal grants on state-local expenditures: A review of the econometric literature. *National Tax Association Papers and Proceedings* 1969:569-593.

Gramlich, E.M. 1972. A comment on O'Brien's "Grants-in-aid." *National Tax Journal* 25:107-108.

Gramlich, E.M., and Galper, H. 1973. State and local fiscal behavior and federal grant policy. *Brookings Papers on Economic Activity* 1:15-58.

Harlow, R.L. 1967. Factors affecting American state expenditures. *Yale Economic Essays.* Fall 1967:263-308.

Henderson, J. 1968. Local government expenditures: A social welfare analysis. *Review of Economics and Statistics* 50:156-163.

Hicks, U.K. 1968. *Public Finance*, 3d edition. Cambridge: Cambridge University Press.

Horowitz, A.R. 1968. A simultaneous equation approach to the problems of explaining interstate differences in state and local government expenditures. *Southern Economic Journal* 34:459-476.

Inman, R.P. 1971. Towards an econometric model of local budgeting. *National Tax Association Papers and Proceedings* 1971:699-719.

Johnson, G.E., and Timola, J.D. 1974. An evaluation of the public employment program. Technical analysis paper no. 17-A. Department of Labor.

Johnson, S.R., and Junk, P.E. 1970. Sources of tax revenues and expenditures in large U.S. cities. *Quarterly Review of Economics and Business* 10:7-16.

Kurnow, E. 1963. Determinants of state and local expenditures reexamined. *National Tax Journal* 16:252-255.

McGuire, M.C. 1973. Notes on grants-in-aid and economic interactions among governments. *Canadian Journal of Economics* 6:207-221.

Miller, E. 1974. The economics of matching grants: The ABC highway program. *National Tax Journal* 27:221-230.

Musgrave, R.A. 1961 Approaches to a fiscal theory of political federalism. In *Public Finance: Needs, Sources, and Utilization*, National Bureau of Economic Research. Princeton, N.J.: Princeton University Press.

Nathan, R.P., Manvel, A.D., and Calkins, S.E. 1975. *Monitoring Revenue Sharing.* Washington, D.C.: The Brookings Institution.

National Planning Association. 1974. *Proceedings of a Conference on Revenue Sharing Research.* Washington, D.C.

Netzer, D. 1974. State-local finance and intergovernmental fiscal relations. In *The Economics of Public Finance*, A.S. Blinder et al. Washington, D.C.: The Brookings Institution.

Niskanen, W.A. 1968. The peculiar economics of bureaucracy. *American Economic Review, Supplement* (May), 58:293-305.

Oates, W.E. 1968. The dual impact of federal aid on state and local expenditures: A comment. *National Tax Journal* 21:220-223.

Oates, W.E. 1972. *Fiscal Federalism.* New York: Harcourt Brace Jovanovich.

O'Brien, T. 1971. Grants-in-aid: Some further answers. *National Tax Journal* 24:65-77.

Ohls, J.C., and Wales, T.J. 1971. Supply and demand for state and local services. *Review of Economics and Statistics* 54:424-430.

Orr, L.L. 1976. Income transfers as a public good: An application to AFDC. *American Economic Review* 66:359-371.

Osman, J.W. 1966. The dual impact of federal aid on state and local government expenditures. *National Tax Journal* 19:362-372.

Pechman, J.A., and Okner, B.A. 1974. *Who Bears the Tax Burden?* Washington, D.C.: The Brookings Institution.

Peterson, J.E. 1968. The determinants of state and local government capital outlays. Ph.D. thesis. University of Pennsylvania.

Phelps, C.D. 1969. Real and monetary determinants of state and local government capital outlays for highways. *American Economic Review* 59:507-521.

Pidot, G.B. 1969. A principal components analysis of the determinants of local fiscal patterns. *Review of Economics and Statistics* 51:176-188.

Pogue, T.F., and Sgontz, L.G. 1968. The effects of grants-in-aid on state and local spending. *National Tax Journal* 21:190-199.

Reischauer, R.D. 1975. General revenue sharing: The program's incentives. In *Financing the New Federalism*, W.E. Oates, ed. Washington, D.C.: Resources for the Future.

Sacks, S., and Harris, R. 1964. The determinants of state and local government expenditures and intergovernmental flows of funds. *National Tax Journal* 17:75-85.

Schultze, C.L. 1974. Sorting out the social grant programs: An economists criteria. *American Economic Review, Supplement* (May), 64:181-189.

Scott, A.D. 1952. The evaluation of federal grants. *Econometrica*, N.S. 19:377-394.

Smith, D.L. 1968. The response of state and local governments to federal grants. *National Tax Journal* 21:349-357.

Strauss, R.P. 1974. General revenue sharing: How well is it working? *National Tax Association Papers and Proceedings*.

Thurow, L.C. 1966. The theory of grants-in-aid. *National Tax Journal* 19:373-377.

U.S. Congressional Budget Office. 1975. *Temporary Measures to Stimulate Employment: An Evaluation of Some Alternatives*.

U.S. National Science Foundation. 1975. Research applied to national needs: General revenue sharing research program. Mimeographed.

Weicher, J.C. 1972. Aid, expenditures, and local government structure. *National Tax Journal* 25:573-584.

Wilde, J.A. 1971. Grants-in-aid: The analytics of design and response. *National Tax Journal* 24:143-156.

[6]

THE STIMULATIVE EFFECTS OF INTERGOVERNMENTAL GRANTS: OR WHY MONEY STICKS WHERE IT HITS

Paul N. Courant, Edward M. Gramlich, Daniel L. Rubinfeld

The theoretical literature on the impact of intergovernmental grants on state and local fiscal behavior has reached a consensus on some basic propositions. According to this theory, the form in which grant assistance is given is very important in predicting the effect of the grant on local public spending. Nonmatching grants are assumed to alter the income available to jurisdictions without altering the relative price of public goods, and are hence assumed to have an effect on local spending similar to that of any other change in private income in the community. Matching grants, on the other hand, cause relative prices to change and thus are found to stimulate more spending per dollar of grant than nonmatching grants.[1]

Empirically, one of these predictions has passed the statistical test and one has failed. The generally confirmed result is that matching grants stimulate more spending per dollar of grant than do non-matching, revenue-sharing types of grants. Regarding the noncon-firmed hypothesis—that nonmatching grants have spending effects similar to those of other changes in private income—the preponder-

---

1. A good summary of this theory can be found in Wilde (1971).

5

6   Fiscal Federalism and Grants-In-Aid

ance of evidence is that nonmatching grants stimulate much more
local spending per dollar of grant than does income going to private
citizens within the community. The obvious reason for this phenomenon, which we term the "flypaper effect" (money sticks where
it hits), is that bureaucrats and politicians find it easier to avoid
cutting taxes when the government receives revenue-sharing monies
than they do to raise taxes when some exogenous event raises the
income of the community.[2]

The fact that the standard theory of intergovernmental grants has
been only partially supported by empirical studies suggests that some
modifications to the theory may be in order. In this paper we make
two. The first uses orthodox, median-voter assumptions—that the
median voter is a private employee taking all wages and prices as
given—and shows why even in this case the tax price and spending
effects of nonmatching grants and changes in private income may not
be identical. The economic rationale for the flypaper effect hinges on
the inability of voters to perceive the true marginal price of public
expenditures when nonmatching grants are present. Finding this
economic rationale of course does not preclude an additional political
rationale, but it helps to improve the relevance of the economic
theory of grants. The second modification follows the logic of the first,
except that we now investigate tax price and spending behavior for
the case where some voters belong to the public (rather than private)
sector and may possess sufficient power to determine public employee
wage rates and output levels.

These two amendments to the traditional theory are developed in a
model of an economy with two types of governments—an exogenous
federal government and an endogenous local government—and just
one type of grant, consisting of nonmatching aid of a fixed dollar
amount. The model distinguishes between private and public sector
employees, analyzing the optimizing behavior of both.

In the first section of the paper the formal assumptions for both the
private and public employee models are presented. The second
section uses the private employee model to examine the utility-
maximizing behavior of private sector employees when all prices and
wages are taken as given and develops our economic rationalization of
the flypaper effect. The third section then deals with the public
employee case, this time distinguishing between real and nominal

---

2. This empirical literature has been summarized by Gramlich (1977).

Paul N. Courant, Edward M. Gramlich, Daniel L. Rubinfeld   7

flypaper effects because wages may not be exogenous. The final section gives a few concluding observations.

The Formal Assumptions

Consider first a model of community behavior in which the median voter is in the private sector. This private employee is assumed to maximize a utility function whose arguments are private consumption C_p and public output, represented simply by public employment (E_g) following standard accounting conventions. Private consumption goods are bought on a national market at a fixed price (P), and are also produced by the private sector workers in the community (E_p) according to a production function that is homogenous of degree one in E_p. All income earned in the community is assumed to be wage income, earned either by public employees who are compensated at a fixed money rate (W_g) or by private employees compensated at the money wage (W_p), fixed by the homogeneity of the production function and the fact that goods prices are fixed.

The total labor force in the community (E) is the sum of private and public employees:

$$E = E_p + E_g. \tag{1}$$

Total money income earned in the community (W^*E), the gross tax base for both the federal and local government, is the sum of wage income earned by workers in both sectors

$$W^*E = W_pE_p + W_gE_g, \tag{2}$$

where W^* is a wage index.

In the first case (pp. 8–16) we consider the optimization of private employees who choose their desired levels of C_p and E_g, taking W_g, W_p, and P as given. Since W_g is fixed, public employees will be unable to negotiate higher wages and we assume that there will be no incentive for private taxpayers to migrate. This means that the total labor force in the community can be viewed as fixed.[3] However, there could still be an effect of changes in E_g on W^*E through the reallocation of

---

3. Assume for the sake of simplicity that high public sector wages are the only cause of private sector migration. We have dealt with this issue in more detail in an earlier paper where we use models of this sort to examine the real and nominal level of government spending. See Courant, Gramlich, and Rubinfeld (1979).

labor between lower and higher wage sectors. As long as the wage differential is small, however, this effect will be minor and it seems reasonable to expect that private voters will not take account of it in their maximizing calculus. Accordingly we assume that atomistic private voters will treat W^*E as given, despite the fact that general equilibrium shifts in W^*E will be incorporated into the final solution of the model.

In the second case (pp. 16–20) we consider the situation in which public employees have sufficient political-bargaining strength to actually set their own wages. As a result, W_p and P are taken as given but W_g is variable. Then private employees are allowed to migrate out of the community in response to monopolistic public employee behavior. As a result, E can become a negative function of W_g, with the gross tax base varying both through the direct impact on E and the indirect impact of compositional shifts. Public employees are assumed to be aware of these aggregate effects, and thus will incorporate assumptions about changes in W^*E in their maximizing calculus.

The local government must always balance its budget. This is accomplished by the levy of a proportional income tax at a rate which equates income tax revenue plus grant revenue with the level of total public expenditure (W_gE_g) in the community. However, the federal government need not balance its budget and its exhaustive expenditures are assumed to have no impact on local decision making. The federal government influences community behavior by assessing proportional income taxes at the rate t and giving close-ended nonmatching grants of amount B.[4]

Private Employee Optimization

Private sector employees are assumed to maximize utility, subject to the constraint that their expenditures on the consumption good (PC_p) plus their expenditures on public goods at the tax price P_p

---

4. Since we are not forcing the federal budget to be in balance and not treating federal exhaustive expenditures explicitly in the model, we also ignore the fact that the local community must make a federal tax contribution for federal grants. Simply assume that these grants are financed either by a change in exhaustive expenditures or the federal deficit, with no effect on local utility, or that grants are net of the federal tax contribution. Johnson and Tomola (1977) show how the tax contribution effect can be worked into a model of local expenditures.

Paul N. Courant, Edward M. Gramlich, Daniel L. Rubinfeld   9

sum to their income net of federal taxes. Assuming for the moment that the only source of income is wage income, net income is simply $W_p(1 - t)$. The private employee then maximizes

$$U_p = U_p{}'(E_g, C_p) \tag{3}$$

subject to

$$W_p(1 - t) = PC_p + P_pE_g. \tag{4}$$

The general solution is the familiar condition that the marginal rate of substitution be equal to the relative price of the public good:

$$\frac{U_1{}'}{U_2{}'} = \frac{P_p}{P}, \tag{5}$$

where the subscripts of U' denote partial derivatives.

With a proportional income tax, the tax price of public goods that a private sector employee faces will be the net cost of a unit of public goods times the employee's locally taxable share of community income net of federal taxes.[5] Recalling that the net cost of a unit of public goods is W_g, and that nonmatching grants at level B add to community income, the *average* tax price is then

$$P_p = \frac{W_p(1 - t)W_g}{W^*E(1 - t) + B}. \tag{6}$$

Substituting (6) into (4) yields the general expression for the budget constraint as it might be viewed by the private employee:

$$W_p(1 - t) = PC_p + \frac{W_p(1 - t)W_gE_g}{W^*E(1 - t) + B} \tag{7}$$

To examine the effect of grants on local spending, assume that initially $t = 0$ and $B = 0$, and that federal grants at the level B are financed through federal tax rate t which leaves net spendable resources of the community, $W^*E(1 - t) + B = W^*E$, constant.[6] In standard grant theory analysis this type of shift would leave community spending on public output unaffected and there would be no flypaper effect.[7] But in the approach taken here, there can be two

---

5. This was the definition used in Peterson (1973) and Rubinfeld (1977).

6. We make this assumption to simplify the exposition. Unless otherwise stated, the results derived in this section hold in general.

7. See Oates (1972), chap. 3, appendix B, for a good discussion.

10   FISCAL FEDERALISM AND GRANTS-IN-AID

separate effects on E_g:

i) since in the short run the private employee will feel that his/her disposable income had decreased (W_p is fixed but t is increased), the perceived individual budget constraint will involve a loss of income equal to tW_p, and this income effect will lower E_g (assuming that E_g is a normal good);

ii) since the numerator of (6) has declined and the denominator has remained constant, the average tax price of public output will fall. If voters are not able to see that the true marginal price of public output is unchanged, this price effect will raise E_g.

There are, in other words, two misperceptions here, one involving income and one involving price. If the voter is laboring under both misperceptions, the net of these two offsetting influences on E_g would appear to depend on the relative strength of the income and price effects. But this is not so. When we take explicit account of the fact that the net spendable resources of the community have remained constant, the income misperception is eliminated and the remaining price misperception will cause public employment and expenditures to increase.

A graphical presentation of our argument is shown in figure 1. Assume for convenience that the private employee is the median voter in the community and has the usual choice between public and private goods. As before, assume that the federal government has no revenue-sharing program and no federal taxes, so that line MR, the maximum value of private consumption for the consumer, equals W_p. The initial equilibrium for money public expenditure levels is at $W_g E_g^0$ (E_g^0 is denoted by 0 on the graph). Then the central government introduces a revenue-sharing grant to the community of B, simultaneously taxing all income earned in the community at rate t such that aggregate community spending power, $W^*E(1 - t) + B$, is left unchanged at W^*E. Standard grants analysis would predict that this consumer and the community will remain at point 0 because there has been no change in either income or relative prices at the margin for the community. But this may not be the case. In the first instance the consumer is likely to think that the price of public output has fallen and that his income has been reduced to $W_p(1 - t)$ by the federal income tax. He will face the budget constraint represented by line segment ST, and will optimize at point V choosing public expenditures of E_1 (this would be the case when public expenditures demands

Paul N. Courant, Edward M. Gramlich, Daniel L. Rubinfeld   **11**

Figure 1

(assume $P = 1$)

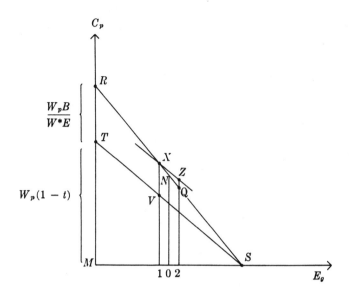

are inelastic and the income effect outweighs the substitution effect). But along ST the consumer is only spending his after-tax private income, not his share of the revenue-sharing grant, and if all consumers do likewise, the local government will run a surplus.

The surplus arises as follows. Given that expenditures have been set at level 1, the line segment $1X$ represents that portion of community resources available for private consumption by the private-sector employee. (Recall that RS represents the true trade-off between public and private expenditures.) However, the private employee has calculated his private consumption to be equal to line segment $1V$. The result, when the government actually spends $W_gE_g^1$, is an unexpected surplus of VX dollars per private employee. In the first instance local officials will presumably compute this surplus at the actual level of public expenditures and mail this consumer his share, a check in the amount of VX.

Since the price of public goods to the consumer has not changed with the return of the surplus, the private employee will then view his constraint line as XZ and vote, say, for expenditure level 2. At this higher expenditure level the government will run a deficit of an amount equal to ZQ for this particular employee. As a result the original rebate check will be reduced and a new budget line drawn. This process will eventually converge towards an equilibrium. The equilibrium point will lie on line RS, the true community resource constraint line, and will be the point of tangency between an indifference curve and a price line parallel to XZ and ST. We will see that at this final equilibrium the rebate the consumer receives will be less than his federal tax payment by the complement of the proportion of income spent on the public sector. Moreover, since community resources are the same as before the policy change, the private good price remains at P, the price of public goods faced by the individual is reduced, and the final level of expenditures must necessarily increase. The trade of revenue sharing for private incomes has *raised* public spending and resulted in what would appear to empirical researchers to be a flypaper effect.[8]

This result can be obtained mathematically if we solve to find the surplus or incremental income, ΔY, to be returned to the private employee so that the final equilibrium occurs at a point which marks his expenditure choice, given income $(W_p + \Delta Y)(1 - t)$ and facing a relative price of public output P_p/P. The incremental income is determined from the community resource constraint which arises in the standard case in which all revenue-sharing funds are allocated to consumers who then make their public or private choice. Since BW_p/W^*E represents the employee's share of revenue sharing money, it follows that

$$W_p \left(1 - t + \frac{B}{W^*E} \right) = PC_p + \frac{W_p W_g E_g}{W^*E} \tag{8}$$

where $W_g W_p/W^*E$ is the true marginal cost of public output. But the

---

8. At this point we can return to a statement made above and say that any compositional effects on W^*E from (2) will also influence the final community-wide equilibrium by adjusting the community-wide resource constraint line. For Walrasian reasons, the local government will find it possible to mail a check for the maximum amount of private consumption individual households can engage in at any level of E_g without unbalancing their own budget. If changes in E_g influence the aggregate constraint line, therefore, these shifts will be incorporated in the rebate checks.

Paul N. Courant, Edward M. Gramlich, Daniel L. Rubinfeld   13

employee's optimization involves the following budget constraint

$$(W_p + \Delta Y)(1 - t) = PC_p + \frac{W_p(1 - t)W_g E_g}{W^*E}. \qquad (9)$$

Combining (8) and (9) to solve for ΔY, we find that (using the fact that $tW^*E = B$):

$$\Delta Y = \left(\frac{W_p B}{W^*E}\right)\left(1 - \frac{W_g E_g}{W^*E}\right)\left(\frac{1}{1 - t}\right) \qquad (10)$$

Thus, the increment to after tax income, $\Delta Y(1 - t)$, is equal to the private employee's share of nonmatching grants, less the fraction of that share spent on public output. If all income in the community is devoted to public output, the income increment is zero. If none of it is spent on public output (and the federal government permits the community to keep the grant), disposable income increases by the employee's share of the grant. Since the increment to income will also be subject to federal taxation, the community-resources constrained income of the employee becomes

$$Y_p(1 - t) = (W_p + \Delta Y)(1 - t) = W_p(1 - t)$$

$$+ \frac{W_p B}{W^*E}\left(1 - \frac{W_g E_g}{W^*E}\right). \qquad (11)$$

Now we are in a position to prove that an increase in t and B which leaves community resources constant will always increase the desired level of public output, E_g. To see this, note that the effect of such a change on $Y_p(1 - t)$ and $P_p E_g$ is of equal magnitude and sign when E_g is held constant. That is, for $d(tW^*E) = dB$ and E_g fixed (from equations [11] and [6]),

$$\frac{dY_p(1 - t)}{d(tW^*E)} = \frac{-W_p W_g E_g}{(W^*E)^2} = \frac{dP_p}{d(tW^*E)} E_g. \qquad (12)$$

Equation (12) implies that the change in disposable income is just equal to the change in expenditure necessary to purchase the initial C_p and E_g pair, implying that the initial bundle is attainable under the changed tax price and disposable income. But if the initial pair was an equilibrium under the initial prices—i.e., if equation (5) held—then it cannot be an equilibrium under the changed price ratio. In particular, if dt is positive, the relative price of public goods will have

14   FISCAL FEDERALISM AND GRANTS-IN-AID

fallen and private employees will demand more public goods than
they did at the initial price ratio. Of course, the increase in demand
for public goods will engender a decrease in $Y_p(1 - t)$ through (11),
and thus the equilibrium level of E_g which is demanded will fall
between the initial level and that which would be demanded if
$Y_p(1 - t)$ remained at the level associated with the initial level of E_g.
But in essence, balanced (federal) budget changes in t and B alter
perceived relative prices while leaving real consumption opportunities
unchanged.

The difference between standard analysis and that given above is
that standard analysis assumes away all illusions. The aggregate
omniscient political authority is assumed to know that the trade of
revenue-sharing and federal taxes does not change relative prices for
the community at large, and is assumed to respond accordingly. But
in real life there is not one aggregate decision maker but a host of
voters who, to the extent that they are guided by economic considerations, would presumably be aware only of their own average tax
prices—not the relative price structure facing the community at the
margin. As long as the government does not incorporate the revenue-
sharing grant in locally taxable income, voters will vote for higher
levels of public expenditures.[9] In terms of the graph, the government
can eliminate this misinformation only by restoring the initial price
line RS. The obvious way of doing this would be to give consumers
the full prorated revenue-sharing grant, making $(W_p + \Delta Y)(1 - t)$
$= W_p(1 - t + B/W^*E)$, and then assessing tax shares on this basis

$$P_p' = \frac{W_p(1 - t + B/W^*E)W_g}{W^*E(1 - t) + B} = \left(\frac{W_p}{W^*E}\right)W_g \qquad (13)$$

so as to make individual budget constraints equal to (8) in the
standard analysis and then to emasculate the price effect. Incidentally,
it is clearly in the community's (perhaps not the bureaucrat's)

9. It is conceivable that over time voters will learn that the level of $Y_p(1 - t)$
is systematically and negatively correlated with E_g, and thus learn that their
true budget constraints are given by equation (8) and line RS in figure 1. But
such learning can only be expected to take place if there are repeated changes
in t and B, and if voters keep records on the effects of such changes and undertake statistical analyses of the relationship between their disposable income
and the behavior of the public sector in response to such changes. To say the
least, the information requirements placed upon individuals in such a scenario
make it implausible.

Paul N. Courant, Edward M. Gramlich, Daniel L. Rubinfeld 15

interest to make this tax price correction, for the switch between revenue sharing and taxing has altered neither tastes nor the boundary of the opportunity set and hence expenditure level 2 is clearly not an optimum. Any deficiencies in the standard analysis are, in other words, descriptive but not normative.[10]

We can also consider the implications of the preceeding analysis if local revenues are raised by property taxation rather than income taxation. Here the extent to which capitalization occurs is the key issue. If the value of nonmatching grants is capitalized into property values, then the local tax base will rise by the amount of such grants, while the local level of disposable income will fall by the amount that federal taxes are increased to finance the nonmatching grants. The numerator of (13) is unchanged and there is no price effect of the type we have considered.[11] To the extent that nonmatching grants are not fully capitalized, the "price-illusion" analysis presented above is appropriate, as some portion of local resources will not be locally taxable. Again, in the short and medium run, incomplete capitalization, and hence the flypaper effect, would seem to be a plausible result.

Finally, we should try to assess the quantitative importance of the flypaper rationale we have identified. The disparity between the estimated marginal propensity of public spending with respect to private income and unconditional transfers is on the order of \$.40: if a community raises public spending by x when private income rises \$1.00, it raises public spending by $x +$ \$.40 when unconditional transfers rise \$1.00 (here the value of x depends on the taste for public and private goods, which is assumed to be different across communities). In the experiment we examine here, the federal government

---

10. In the simple case we have used here to illustrate the problem, an alternative way of making the correction would be to assign tax shares equal to W_p/W^*E, ignoring federal taxes and transfers altogether. That will not work whenever the change in income tax revenues does not equal the change in revenue sharing grants, however. Then (13) must be used.

11. Note that even with complete capitalization, an increase in federal taxes used to finance a nonmatching grant such that community resources are left constant will not be perfectly analogous to the standard case unless each household's annual imputed rental gain from property is just equal to its loss of disposable income. Since this condition will never be met in practice, such a policy change would in general change the distribution of income in a community. If there are income effects on the demand for public goods, this would lead to a change in demand—although the sign of the change is uncertain.

16   Fiscal Federalism and Grants-In-Aid

conducts a balanced-budget change that leaves the community resource constraint unaffected, but which does pivot the price line around the initial point. If the reduction in the perceived price is .1 (B/W^*E goes from 0 to .1) and the price elasticity of demand for public expenditures with community resources held constant is .5, $W_g E_g/W^*E$ will rise by .05. Say that initially $W_g E_g/W^*E$ equals .2, as it does in many communities. The new level of $W_g E_g/W^*E$ is .21, the change in public spending is $.01W^*E$, and the change in B is $.1W^*E$. Hence this change will appear as a difference in the marginal propensity to consume unconditional transfers over private income of as much as .1 for certain communities. We cannot, nor would we want to, explain the entire observed flypaper effect with this phenomenon, but in certain communities with a high level of B, a high level of public spending, and strong price elasticities, these orders of magnitude show that the phenomenon could be a significant force.[12]

Public Employee Optimization

To this point we have examined grant theory under the assumption that the private sector median voter implicitly determined public employment levels. Now we show how the results change when public employees have varying degrees of electoral or bargaining power. We make three sets of assumptions: (a) that public employees have sufficient electoral power to determine their own employment levels; (b) that employees have sufficient bargaining power to determine their own money wages; (c) that employees have enough power to determine both public employment and wages.

In the first case, public employees control (either through voting or through other political processes) the level of public output, but public wages are given exogenously. The median public employee voter then maximizes

$$U_g = U_g'(E_g, C_g) \tag{14}$$

---

12. In a companion paper whose content we were not aware of until the first draft of our own was completed, Wallace Oates explains a much larger share of flypaper effect through a phenomenon that sounds suspiciously like ours. There is a difference, however. Oates' voters misperceive the marginal price even more that ours do—they would consider it line TN in figure 1. We reduce the perceived price by just the reduction in perceived average tax prices; Oates reduces it by the share of expenditures paid for by unconditional grants ($[W_g E_g - B]/W_g E_g$ in our notation). Oates also does not have the community resource constraint built in. See Oates in this volume.

Paul N. Courant, Edward M. Gramlich, Daniel L. Rubinfeld   17

subject to

$$Y_g = PC_g + P_g E_g \tag{15}$$

with

$$P_g = \frac{W_g{}^2 (1 - t)}{W^* E (1 - t) + B} . \tag{16}$$

The solution to this system is essentially the same as before, except that public wages play a dual role—being a component of both the income of public employees and the price they have to pay for public goods. If basic taste parameters are the same, public employees will have a higher demand for public output when $W_g > W_p$ and the income effect outweighs the substitution effect, and a lower demand when the substitution effect outweighs the income effect. As before, there is a flypaper effect when the public employee receives as income some portion of the revenue-sharing grant as long as that grant is not included in the computation of this tax price.

Now consider the second case in which public employees have no control over output, but do have sufficient bargaining strength to raise their wages above that of private employees.[13] To illustrate the nature of the results, we make the strong assumption that public employees can set W_g, and examine the partial equilibrium results when E_g is fixed.

The solution to this case turns out to hinge on the elasticity of the overall tax base, W^*E, with respect to W_g. As long as E_g is fixed, a rise in W_g will increase the money income earned by the public sector, $W_g E_g$, proportionately. But if there is intercommunity migration in response to the rise in W_g, resulting in a fall in $W_p E_p$, the overall tax base, $W_p E_p + W_g E_g$, will not rise in proportion to W_g and may even fall. If we define

$$\eta = \left(\frac{dW^*E}{dW_g} \right) \left(\frac{W_g}{W^*E} \right) \tag{17}$$

as the elasticity of this tax base with respect to the public wages, the above remarks imply that η is strictly less than one and may even be negative.

---

13. Studies of public sector wages indicate that this may be the case for many urbanized areas with strong unions. See Smith (1977) and Ehrenberg and Goldstein (1975) for the general proposition, and Horton (1973) for a description of how it might have already happened in New York City.

The first order condition when E_g is held fixed can be found simply by maximizing C_g with respect to W_g in equations (14)–(16). Using the same assumptions as in the previous section regarding the treatment of rebate checks

$$C_g = W_g\left\{1 - t + \frac{B}{W^*E}\left(1 - \frac{W_g E_g}{W^*E(1 - t) + B}\right)\right\}$$

$$- \frac{W_g(1 - t)W_g E_g}{W^*E(1 - t) + B}$$

or   (18)

$$C_g = W_g\left(1 - t + \frac{B}{W^*E}\right)\left(1 - \frac{W_g E_g}{W^*E(1 - t) + B}\right).$$

If public employees know the size of their tax and revenue-sharing change, they know also that both the aggregate spendable resources and $(1 - t + [B/W^*E])$ will not be affected by the federal policy changes, though of course they must also worry about the fact that increases in W_g could reduce the community tax base W^*E if $\eta < 0$. Their optimal solution is given by

$$\frac{W_g E_g}{W^*E(1 - t) + B} = \frac{1}{2 - \eta}.$$ (19)

If η, the elasticity of the overall tax base with respect to public wages, equals zero, these wages will be set so that the aggregate net public sector wage bill equals just one-half of total community spendable resources. As employees increase their wage beyond this level, the increase in the local tax rate necessary to finance the further wage increases is so great that employees' command over consumption goods actually declines. If $\eta < 0$, the share of resources devoted to the public sector is further reduced by employees' fear of losing tax base when they raise their wages; while $\eta > 0$ the same consideration will raise their wage bill. But as long as $\eta < 1$, which it clearly is as long as $W_p E_p$ does not increase, (19) will be a maximum for public employees and will insure that the public wage bill is less than the level of total output.

Since the optimization condition is stated in terms of the total public wage bill, as the public employee work force expands, increases in W_g must be paid to additional workers, who cost more in terms of necessary tax increases. Hence there is an inverse correlation between the size of the public employee work force and the wage that each can extract. Regarding grants, there is no flypaper effect in this situation. No matter how the government sets tax shares, the employees are assumed to know that aggregate resources are held equal by the federal change, and to set wage policy to take the appropriate fraction.

We note one other interesting feature of (19). If there were no federal taxes or grants, then local tax rates on all income would equal $1/(2 - \eta)$. If the federal government decides to increase its own taxes without a compensatory increase in nonmatching grants, the local public sector is left to take $1/(2 - \eta)$ of a smaller remainder, so that the combined local-federal tax rate is larger than $1/(2 - \eta)$. Generalizing, in a hierarchical federal system with strong employee unions each of which is setting wages on the basis of income left over after the higher level governments take their share, the combined tax rate for all levels of government could get quite large—asymptotically approaching unity in all cases and realistically being well in excess of one-half even when η is close to zero.

The final case where public employees set both wage and employment levels is a composite of the first two. The wage first-order condition (given E_g) is equation (19), and the employment first-order condition (given W_g) is found by maximizing (14) subject to (18). Since public employee households gain their revenue-sharing checks but are not taxed on them at the local level, the employment first-order condition leads them to overconsume public goods, as in the private sector flypaper case. But since optimal wage behavior is set by (19) and is independent of the origin of the community's tax base, there is in effect no *nominal* flypaper effect. Hence the simultaneous solution of the two first-order conditions is that *real* expenditures are larger than before the federal policy change (and larger than if tax prices were computed optimally), that nominal expenditures are exactly the same, and that public sector wages are *reduced* by the so-called flypaper effect. In the private sector optimization case, the unadjusted tax price leads voters to overconsume real and nominal government expenditures; but in the public sector case the same phenomenon leads to overconsumption of public goods and less exploitation of the private sector through high public-sector wage levels. In a welfare sense, the flypaper effect made the private sector worse off when they were determining employment levels and better

20   FISCAL FEDERALISM AND GRANTS-IN-AID

off when public employees were determining both wage and employment levels.

Implications

In this paper we try to amend the standard theory of intergovernmental grants by inquiry into the mechanism by which grant-induced changes in community prices and incomes are actually transmitted to individual voters. In the first half of the paper we find an economic rationale for a well-known empirical puzzle in the grant literature—that a dollar of nonmatching aid seems to stimulate a good deal more local public expenditures than a dollar change in private community income, despite the fact that both should have had exactly the same effect on community-wide relative prices and incomes. The rationale is that in order for the nonmatching grant neutrality to hold, local officials must take the grants into account in computing tax shares, an action that seems quite unlikely. If this is not done, there will be a relative price effect for nonmatching grants which will stimulate expenditures more than private income increases. All of this is, of course, not to deny that there could be other, more powerful, political reasons for the empirical puzzle in addition to the economic rationale we have given.

In the second section of the paper we extend this reasoning to the case where public employees are the median voters. These employees are allowed, successively, control over expenditure levels, wage levels, and both together. Incorrectly viewed relative prices will lead public employees to overconsume public goods just as with their private sector counterparts, but will not affect their wage behavior or the size of the public budget in nominal terms. Hence when public employees control employment as well as wages, the incorrect relative prices will actually aid the private sector—leading to the same sized budget in nominal terms but greater levels of real expenditures and lower levels of public wages.

REFERENCES

Courant, Paul N.; Gramlich, Edward M.; and Rubinfeld, Daniel L. 1979. Public Employee Market Power and the Level of Government Spending. Forthcoming in *American Economic Review*.

Ehrenberg, Ronald G., and Goldstein, Gerald. 1975. A Model of Public Sector Wage Determination. *Journal of Urban Economics* 2: 222–45.

Gramlich, Edward M. 1977. Intergovernmental Grants: A Review of the Em-

Paul N. Courant, Edward M. Gramlich, Daniel L. Rubinfeld   21

pirical Literature. In Wallace E. Oates, ed., *The Political Economy of Fiscal Federalism.* Lexington, Mass.: Lexington Books, 219–39.

Horton, Robert D. 1973. *Municipal Labor Relations in New York City: Lessons of the Lindsay-Wagner Years.* New York: Praeger.

Johnson, George E., and Tomola, James D. 1977. The Fiscal Substitution Effect of Alternative Approaches to Public Service Employment Policy. *Journal of Human Resources* 12: 3–26.

Oates, Wallace E. 1972. *Fiscal Federalism.* New York: Harcourt, Brace, Jovanovich.

Peterson, George E. 1973. The Demand for Public Schooling. Urban Institute Working Paper No. 1207–28. Washington, D.C.

Rubinfeld, Daniel L. 1977. Voting in a Local School Election: A Micro Analysis. *Review of Economics and Statistics* 59: 30–42.

Smith, Sharon P. 1977. Government Wage Differentials. *Journal of Urban Economics* 4: 248–71.

Wilde, James A. 1971. Grants-in-aid: The Analytics of Design and Response. *National Tax Journal* 24: 573–84.

Moving into and out of Poor Urban Areas

Edward Gramlich
Deborah Laren
Naomi Sealand

Abstract

Newly available geographical information from the Panel Study of Income Dynamics (PSID) is used to estimate a variety of relationships involving high-poverty metropolitan census tracts. The longitudinal data from the PSID show a great deal of geographical mobility even for persistently poor adults, with as many as one fourth of certain groups of these entering and leaving poor urban census tracts in a year. At the same time, solution of the transition matrices for various groups—whites and blacks of various income classes, in families with and without children, living in different types of census tracts—in the early 1980s shows the gradual emptying out of poor urban tracts, particularly of whites and blacks in families without children. As a consequence, despite the great degree of geographical "churning," poor urban areas gradually become poorer, blacker, and the home of a larger share of black families with children. Some of these aggregate trends had been noticed by researchers comparing these areas in the 1970 and 1980 censuses; our more up-to-date results demonstrate the relationships between the micro and macro data.

The number of poor people living in poor urban areas grew sharply between the 1970 and 1980 censuses [Jargowsky and Bane, 1991]. The implied increase in the concentration of poor people in poor urban areas could be quite damaging to the long-run income prospects of the poor. Under the starkest of all scenarios, poor people could be trapped both in poverty and in their poor neighborhoods, where they suffer a lack of job opportunities, a lack of upper-class role models, and excessive crime. Perhaps worse, their children could be condemned to very poor schooling, much worse than the schooling provided to others. In this sense it is certainly not good news that a rising share of poor people live in poor urban areas.

Although something like this stark view seems to be quite commonly held, there is surprisingly little empirical evidence to back up most of its underlying postulates. As for the concentration results, there are some technical problems. Jargowsky and Bane also show that the 1970–1980 result is largely

Journal of Policy Analysis and Management, Vol. 11, No. 2, 273–287 (1992)
© 1992 by the Association for Public Policy Analysis and Management
Published by John Wiley & Sons, Inc.   CCC 0276-8739/92/020273-15$04.00

driven by the particular experiences of New York and Chicago. They and Massey, Eggers, and Denton [1989] show that experiences are very different for different definitions of low-income areas, in different regions, for different racial and ethnic groups. The 1970–1980 results may not extrapolate well over decades—the world of the 1980s was very different from that of the 1970s. The whole question of how a region affects a person living there is still quite unresolved; most efforts at pinning this geographical impact down have not shown very clear results [Jencks and Mayer, 1990]. Even the notion that poor people are trapped in poor urban areas is suspect—housing is generally cheap in these poor urban areas, and the fact that many poor people live there could simply reflect the fact that poor people do not have much income to spend on housing.

But perhaps the most serious empirical questions are the longitudinal ones. Previous concentration findings are not longitudinal, so it remains unclear whether the poor people living in poor urban areas are persistently poor, and whether they are the same poor people who lived in the same areas at some earlier date. The ability of individuals to escape from poor areas obviously gives a clue as to how trapped they are. Moreover, the net flows of those who enter and leave these poor urban areas can be used to make inferences about the long-run prospects of the poor areas.

This article uses new longitudinal geographic information to try to resolve these empirical questions. The basic data for individuals come from the Panel Study of Income Dynamics (PSID), a longitudinal time series going back to the late 1960s. The PSID staff has always maintained address files so the survey respondents could be located, but only recently have the census tract and other geographical identifiers been coded for use in research. We use the 1979–1985 segment of this data base, along with 1980 census information on nonelderly poverty rates for the relevant tracts. With this information, we can combine the income and family histories of all PSID individuals with the 1980 poverty rates in all census tracts they resided in over the six-year period.

Our study looks at only a few of the many questions that could be asked with such data. We first use the family income histories to develop measures of permanent income and persistent poverty for all individuals, widely agreed to be improvements on the more common one-year measures of income and poverty status. We show the distribution of persistently poor and nonpoor individuals among metropolitan census tracts characterized by their poverty rates, and nonmetropolitan tracts. We also show the income, racial, and demographic attributes of these high-poverty metropolitan census tracts. We go on to compute geographical transition matrices that tell how likely persistently poor and nonpoor adults living in poor urban areas are to escape these areas, or how likely those living in nonpoor areas are to fall back into poor urban areas. These transition matrices are of direct interest in answering the entrapment questions posed above. The matrices can also be solved for their equilibrium outcomes to illustrate the relationship between micro and macro data. Specifically, we solve the matrices to find the long-run income and racial composition of the urban areas that were poor in 1980.

POOR PEOPLE

It might seem straightforward just to take the PSID sample and see what happens to it. In fact, as anybody who has worked with longitudinal micro data can attest, the questions of what sample is to be examined and how the variables are to be measured can be quite difficult. For this analysis we are interested in adults of various income classes followed longitudinally in their working years. Hence we examine individuals aged 17–64, categorized by their permanent income status. While we do not explicitly follow children in the study, we also categorize adults by whether they do or do not live in families with children. Since for most of the span of the PSID there were trivial numbers of Hispanics, Asians, and Native Americans, we have omitted these groups altogether, and just focus on whites, blacks, and their sum.

Difficulties in measuring income status lead to a rather complex set of decisions. The first step is to define family income. Most poverty statistics are computed from the Current Population Survey (CPS). It is well known that the CPS income definition has two important, though partially offsetting, defects:

- CPS income does not include transfers-in-kind.
- CPS income does not exclude taxes.

With the PSID it is possible largely to correct both defects. We have added the bonus value of food stamps to a family's income and then subtracted federal income and payroll taxes to get a much better proxy for the true disposable income of a family, or its post-tax, post-transfer income.[1] Dividing this post-tax, post-transfer income by the family's poverty needs standard (using the official census definition) adjusts for family size and puts the one-year family income figures on a needs-adjusted basis.

Since the family is the logical unit for computing income-needs status, it would be convenient to use it as the unit of analysis for longitudinal analysis. But changes in family composition over time are so many, and so varied, that it is simply impossible to follow families longitudinally without either restricting the sample to the odd subset of families without major compositional change, or using very arbitrary rules to identify "the same family" over time. What we did instead, and what most other PSID users have been forced to do, is to follow individuals over time and to measure each person's income status for a particular year as that of the family to which he or she belonged in that year.

As mentioned above, there will often be major changes in the composition of the families to which these individuals belong. Such major changes include the divorce or marriage of a head of the family, or the individual leaving home to form a new family unit. Income-needs in years when such major compositional changes occur, as measured by PSID procedures, may not accurately reflect the actual standard of living of the individual in that year. In these cases we keep the individuals in the sample but simply do not record their income for the transitional year.

Another measurement problem involves the time horizon. It is now routinely conceded that a one-year horizon is too short a time to measure true income status—incomes vary too much from year to year, and many of those observed with low incomes for one year are not "poor" in any meaningful

---

[1] Side calculations indicate that our post-tax, post-transfer income averages very slightly more than CPS income for low-income people.

sense. There are many approaches for dealing with what might be termed the permanent income problem, but the simplest, and one used here, is merely to average a family's income-needs ratio over the time it can be measured. When possible, we use both three- and seven-year averages, centered on the year in question.

We use the following strategy to deal with missing data in constructing these three- and seven-year centered income-needs averages. If an individual's income-needs information is missing for the center year, the average is not computed and the individual is not assigned to an income group. If an individual's income-needs information is missing in a year surrounding the center year, we exclude that year's information from the computation of the average, so that in fact some of our three- and seven-year averages use fewer than three or seven years of data. In addition, in constructing these averages, we distinguish years in which an individual is in a family headed by a single person from years in which an individual is in a family headed by two people. If the center year of the average is one in which the individual is in a single-headed (dual-headed) family, the average only uses surrounding years in which the individual is also in a single-headed (dual-headed) family.

Using these conventions, we define persistently poor people as all those individuals in families with a three- or seven-year centered average family income-needs ratio of 1.25 or below, between 6 and 7 percent of the total nonaged adult population for which an income class is designated under the different averaging concepts. Most poverty researchers use income-needs cutoff points of either 1.0 or 1.25. We chose the higher number because the PSID has less underreporting of income than the CPS [Duncan and Hill, 1989], and because 1.0 is also generally viewed as a very austere definition of poverty. We define as "middle income" (not the usual sociological definition of the term) all those individuals in families with a three- or seven-year centered average family income-needs ratio between 1.25 and 3.0, nearly 37 percent of the relevant population for the different averaging concepts. We define as "high income" (again, not the usual sociological definition of the term) all those individuals in families with a centered average family income-needs ratio of at least 3.0, about 57 percent of the relevant population for the different averaging concepts.

POOR PLACES

Two approaches have been used to define poor places. Wilson [1987] and Jargowsky and Bane [1991] have used the straightforward technique of simply categorizing census tracts on the basis of their poverty rate. Ricketts and Sawhill [1988] have tried to construct a more elaborate measure for what they call "underclass" census tracts. These are tracts that are more than one standard deviation above the national mean on four dimensions: receipt of welfare, male labor force nonparticipation, prevalence of single-headed families, and prevalence of high school dropouts. While there is a great deal of overlap in the census tracts classified as poor by these two approaches, there is at least one problem with the Ricketts–Sawhill approach for our purposes. It classifies as nonpoor many very low income southern census tracts in states where public assistance guarantee levels are low. For this reason, we use the more straightforward Wilson–Jargowsky–Bane approach.

Table 1. Distribution of the population, 1979–1984 (sample for 1000 adults, aged 17–64).

| Group | Census tract type | | | | | |
	Poor	Near-poor	Middle	High	Nonmet.	Total
Poor whites	2	1	6	6	14	29
Middle whites	6	5	51	116	104	282
High whites	5	3	60	325	103	496
Unassigned whites	1	1	14	39	18	73
Poor blacks	9	2	5	1	8	25
Middle blacks	13	4	17	6	14	54
High blacks	6	4	8	8	2	28
Unassigned blacks	3	1	4	3	2	13
Total	45	21	165	504	265	1000

Note. Metropolitan census tracts are defined as poor if their nonelderly poverty rate is at least 30 percent, near-poor if their nonelderly poverty rate is between 25 and 30 percent, middle-income if their nonelderly poverty rate is between 10 and 25 percent, high-income if their nonelderly poverty rate is 10 percent or below.

Individuals are defined as poor if in a family with seven-year average income-needs ratio of 1.25 or below, middle-income if in a family with seven-year average income-needs ratio between 1.25 and 3.0, high-income if in a family with seven-year average income-needs ratio of at least 3.0, and unassigned if their family income could not be measured.

Unweighted sample size is 46,937 person-years, 9392 people.

Because at this writing the PSID sample has only 1980 census information, and because the PSID address files could not be located for 1977–1978, we use PSID individuals for the 1979–1985 period only. Our calculations used the PSID sample weights, which are designed to correct for the initial over-sampling of the poverty population and differential attrition over time. Since these weights are scaled arbitrarily, we show all results in terms of a hypothetical probability sample of 1000 individuals.

Table 1 shows the distribution of individuals aged 17–64 (hereafter adults), classified by race and seven-year average income-needs ratios, across census tract types. The note to Table 1 states that the unweighted PSID sample size is 46,937 person-years or 9392 people. Whether one or the other is the proper measure of the true sample size depends on the serial correlation of individual behavior, involving a set of relationships we have not yet attempted to estimate.

Table 1 shows that 4.5 percent of the weighted sample of adults live in metropolitan census tracts with nonelderly poverty rates of at least 30 percent. We call these poor urban tracts. This cutoff point is nearly the same as was used by Wilson, slightly more inclusive than was used by Jargowsky and Bane. But going to the Jargowsky–Bane cutoff point risks getting too small a sample—we are already down to only 4.5 percent of the weighted sample of adults. We do attempt some sensitivity analysis with this cutoff point by defining a sample of near-poor census tracts, with nonelderly poverty rates between 25 and 30 percent and covering 2.1 percent of the weighted sample of adults. Then 16.5 percent of the weighted sample of adults live in metropolitan census tracts with nonelderly poverty rates between 10 and 25 percent. We call these middle-income tracts. Then 50.4 percent of the weighted sample of adults live in metropolitan census tracts with nonelderly poverty rates of 10 percent or less; we call these high-income tracts.[2]

The balance of the weighted sample of adults, 26.5 percent, live in nonmetropolitan census tracts and nontracted areas. These nonmetropolitan tracts and nontracted areas are sufficiently spread out that the normal influence of neighborhood on individuals could be expected to be much weaker, or at least much different, than in urban areas. Moreover, tracts could be identified for only a minority of our nonmetropolitan sample; the remainder were either living in tracts we were unable to identify or in nontracted areas. For both reasons we have simply treated nonmetropolitan areas as a group and have not dealt with the internal migration among them.

Table 1 also shows how people of different incomes are distributed across these census tracts. As already mentioned, across all census tracts, poor adults by the seven-year concept comprise 6 percent of the sample $((29 + 25)/(1000 - 73 - 13))$; blacks comprise 12 percent of the sample $((25 + 54 + 28 + 13)/1000)$. But in poor urban tracts poor adults comprise 26 percent of the sample $((2 + 9)/41)$, blacks 70 percent of the sample $((9 + 13 + 6 + 3)/45)$. Both the poverty and black rates are much higher than for all other areas, including even nonmetropolitan areas. Of course it is this concentration of poor people and blacks in poor urban tracts that forms the crux of the urban poverty problem.

The poor urban tracts can also be examined in demographic terms, as is done in Table 2. This table shows the weighted distribution of adults in poor urban census tracts by age and demographic category—whether the adults living there are white or black, young (aged 17–30) or older (aged 31–64), married male heads, married female heads, and so forth. Focusing on the nonmarried male–female ratios in the summary rows of the table, there seem to be many fewer older nonmarried white males than females. Differential mortality rates could explain some of this difference, but there may well be other factors.

Table 2 shows dramatic differences for blacks: For each age group, the nonmarried male to female ratio is about 20 points lower than for whites. The data are not shown, but the same demographic imbalance is evident for other census tracts.[3]

The literal implication of this demographic imbalance is that part of the reason for the relatively high incidence of female-headed black families is that there are simply not as many nonmarried black males extant, similar to a claim made earlier by Wilson [1987]. Wilson focused on changes over time in the ratio of employed black males to all black females of particular ages for all areas. He did not have information on geography and on whether his males and females were married, and his narrow age categories assumed that people married within fairly narrow age brackets. The calculations in Table

---

[2] It should be noted that in 15 percent of the cases we could not identify the individual's census tract of residence for metropolitan areas. In these cases we measured the nonelderly poverty rate over a larger geographical area.

[3] Regarding the statistical significance of these differences, were the differences computed for random samples of the sample sizes shown, they would be on the margin of statistical significance. But the PSID is a clustered sample, not a simple random sample. Using standard error calculations that take account of the clustered sample design, these differences are *not* statistically significant.

Table 2. Demographic composition in poor metropolitan census tracts, 1979–84 (1000 adults living in poor metropolitan census tracts).

Group	All ages	17–30	31–64	PY
Whites (479 PY, 168 people)				
Married male heads	65	18	47	110
Married female heads	82	32	50	136
Single male heads	40	27	13	69
Single female heads	68	30	38	101
Nonhead males	22	20	2	34
Nonhead females	19	19	0	29
Total	296	146	150	479
Nonmarried males	62	47	15	103
Nonmarried females	87	49	38	130
NM males/NM females (%)	71.3	95.9	39.5	
Blacks (6130 PY, 1634 people)				
Married male heads	118	39	79	849
Married female heads	117	24	93	888
Single male heads	80	54	26	702
Single female heads	229	94	135	2028
Nonhead males	78	74	4	810
Nonhead females	82	75	7	853
Total	704	360	344	6130
Nonmarried males	158	128	30	1512
Nonmarried females	311	169	142	2881
NM males/NM females (%)	50.8	75.7	21.1	

PY = person years.

2 either differ from or improve on Wilson's in many respects, but they tell the same general story.

It would be possible to combine incarceration rates, census or PSID undercount rates, and other such data to find some of the apparently missing nonmarried black males. But such a calculation could miss the point. Those nonmarried black males may be physically "out there" somewhere, but they may also not be very good marriage partners. For marriage purposes the best way to combine the numbers may be as is already done from the PSID. And when that is done, an important factor regarding urban areas, whether poor or not, is the relative absence of nonmarried black males.

MOBILITY: TRANSITION MATRICES

The tabulations so far have shown the population composition for different types of census tracts, but have not directly addressed the mobility issue. The most straightforward way to do this is by analyzing transition probabilities.

One illustration is given in Table 3, which shows mobility patterns for persistently poor adults in families with children, using the seven-year average concept. The top panel of the table, for whites (with an unweighted sample size of 583 person-years or 198 people), shows that a whopping 27 percent of

Table 3. Transition matrices for the persistently poor in families with children, 1979–1984 (seven-year average concept).

Tract type in year T	Poor	Mid.	High	Nonmet.	Total	PY
			Tract type in year $T + 1$			
Whites (583 PY, 198 people)						
Poor	0.728	0.198	0.000	0.073	1.000	19
Mid.	0.030	0.874	0.085	0.010	1.000	131
High	0.000	0.140	0.779	0.081	1.000	126
Nonmet.	0.000	0.006	0.010	0.984	1.000	307
Blacks (2472 PY, 703 people)						
Poor	0.904	0.084	0.010	0.002	1.000	1090
Mid.	0.078	0.880	0.027	0.015	1.000	788
High	0.056	0.226	0.716	0.002	1.000	108
Nonmet.	0.026	0.010	0.005	0.959	1.000	486

Note. For these and other transition calculations, middle-income and near-poor metropolitan census tracts (in the definitions of Table 1) were combined into the middle-income category.
PY = person years.

poor white adults in families with children leave poor urban areas in one year. This is a remarkably high rate of emigration, and while of course there could be all kinds of subtle explanations, on its face it gives a strong vote against the entrapment hypothesis.

Other entries in Table 3 for whites show another high rate of exit from high-income areas, 22 percent. When poor people leave poor areas, they obviously move up, and when they leave high-income areas they obviously move down. But it is also noteworthy that when they leave middle-income areas, they are more likely to move up than down (compare 0.085 with 0.030). Here and elsewhere in the study, the rate of exit from nonmetropolitan tracts is absolutely and relatively quite low. Once people of any racial or income group get to nonmetropolitan areas, that is pretty much where they stay.

These patterns differ in key respects for black adults in families with children, in the bottom panel of Table 3. Now the exit rate from poor urban areas is much lower, 10 percent. This is still a high enough rate of exit to shed doubt on the entrapment hypothesis, but the fact that it is so much lower than for similarly situated whites means that perhaps poor whites and blacks are not similarly situated after all. The other side of the matrix is also inverted: Now poor blacks have a whopping 28 percent rate of exit from high-income areas. And those leaving middle-income areas are now much more likely to move down than up (compare 0.078 with 0.027).

It is difficult to nail down the exact reasons for these differences without going into a complete analysis of regional labor and housing markets. But one simple side-calculation is suggestive. In Table 1 we saw that across the country, poor urban areas were 70 percent black, 30 percent white. Does this mean that each poor urban area is split 70–30, or that this overall number is derived by aggregating nearly uniformly black urban areas and nearly uniformly white urban areas? More nearly the latter, it turns out. Over 75 percent of our sample of whites living in poor urban areas live in areas that are predominantly white; over 90 percent of our sample of blacks living in poor urban areas live in areas that are predominantly black. The clear implication is that any observed racial differences in mobility are more likely due to the characteristics of the place than the person.

Transition matrices for all other groups—poor white and black adults in families without children, middle- and high-income white and black adults in families with and without children, and those for whom we could not assign incomes—are also calculated, though not shown.[4] Middle- and high-income whites are about as likely to exit poor tracts as are poor whites, but less likely to migrate to poor tracts. Middle- and high-income blacks are, if anything, even less likely to leave poor areas than are poor blacks, though they are also less likely to fall back into poor areas when they leave middle-income areas.

These statements refer to the implications of these transition matrices for individuals. It is also interesting to see what the matrices imply for the areas, as can be discerned by solving them out. Focusing on poor metropolitan tracts, suppose the share of any income, racial, or family group living there is P, the same share living in middle-income tracts is M, and the share living everywhere else is $(1 - P - M)$. Using a_{ij} as the coefficients of the transition matrix, the share of this group living in poor metropolitan tracts in the next period is:

$$P_{+1} = a_{11}P + a_{21}M + a_{31}(1 - P - M) \qquad (1)$$

A similar expression can be constructed for the share of the group living in middle- and high-income tracts next period, and the expressions can be solved simultaneously for steady state values of P and M, where $P = P_{+1}$ and $M = M_{+1}$. The solution is:

$$P = (a_{31} + ba_{32})/(1 - a_{11} + a_{31} - b(a_{12} - a_{32})) \qquad (2)$$

where

$$b = (a_{21} - a_{31})/(1 - a_{22} + a_{32})$$

The equation shows that the equilibrium share P depends positively on both the staying probability, a_{11}, and the entrance probabilities, a_{31}, a_{21}, and a_{32}.

One can then repeat the calculations 16 times—for each of the eight racial and income groups for which initial conditions are shown in Table 1, multiplied by two because we split each group into those in families with and without children.

The results of these calculations are presented in Table 4, for both the three- and seven-year average concept. For each average concept, the left column of the pair assumes the existence of 1000 adults aged 17–64 in poor urban tracts in the 1979–1984 period, distributed exactly as the initial conditions of Table 1. As there, the poverty rates in poor metropolitan tracts are about 26 percent, the black rates are 70 percent, and 18–19 percent of the persistently poor live in these poor metropolitan tracts. The right column of the pair gives the equilibrium outcome, a prediction of what will eventually happen to these areas based on the known transition matrices of the early 1980s.

Since for the persistently poor the entrance probabilities (below the princi-

---

[4] All transitions matrices are available from the authors on request.

Table 4. 1979–1984 and equilibrium population composition in poor metropolitan census tracts (1000 adults living in poor metropolitan census tracts, three (3) and seven (7) year average concept).

	Init. (3)	Eq. (3)	Init. (7)	Eq. (7)
Group				
Poor whites, children	14	14	10	12
Poor whites, no children	27	35	27	34
Middle whites, children	59	22	57	49
Middle whites, no children	65	65	62	57
High whites, children	31	18	37	18
High whites, no children	70	32	73	33
Unassigned whites, children	4	4	4	4
Unassigned whites, no children	27	21	27	21
Poor blacks, children	100	99	100	106
Poor blacks, no children	109	116	101	112
Middle blacks, children	142	169	141	168
Middle blacks, no children	147	115	159	120
High blacks, children	55	80	56	69
High blacks, no children	89	53	86	51
Unassigned blacks, children	26	15	25	14
Unassigned blacks, no children	35	36	35	36
Total	1000	894	1000	904
Poverty rate (%)	27.5	32.3	26.2	31.8
Black rate (%)	70.3	76.4	70.3	74.8
Percent of persistently poor in poor urban areas				
Whites	5.1	6.0	5.6	7.0
Blacks	35.3	36.3	35.1	38.1
Total	17.9	18.9	19.4	21.5
Percent of adults in families with children in poor urban areas				
Whites	1.2	0.6	1.2	0.9
Blacks	26.1	29.3	26.1	29.0
Total	4.1	4.0	4.1	4.2

pal diagonal in Table 3) generally exceed the exit probabilities, these calculations show the number of persistently poor in poor urban tracts rising. The same is true for middle- and high-income blacks in families with children. But for all other groups the exit probabilities generally exceed the entrance probabilities and the group sizes fall. In the full equilibrium solution:

- The aggregate population of poor urban areas drops by about 10 percent.
- The poverty rate in poor urban areas rises from about 27 to 32 percent.
- The black rate in poor urban areas rises from 70 to about 75 percent.
- The share of the persistently poor in poor urban areas rises from 18 to 19 percent (three-year) or from 19 to 21 percent (seven-year).
- The share of white children growing up in poor urban areas starts at 1 percent and falls by a large proportion.
- The share of black children growing up in poor urban areas rises from 26 to 29 percent.

To characterize the process simply, most white adults are clearing out of poor urban areas, the one exception being poor whites in families without children. Most black adults in families without children are also clearing out, but all groups of black adults in families with children, even those with high incomes, are entering on balance.

One question that arises immediately is that of sensitivity analysis—how sensitive are our calculations to the income and poverty cutoff points used? Unfortunately they are sensitive, and they have to be. For example, had we used a higher income-needs ratio cutoff point, say 1.5, in defining poor people, we would have had a larger and different sample of poor people. Similarly, had we used a lower poverty rate cutoff point in defining poor places, say 25 percent, we would have had a larger and different sample of poor places. There is no real way to use different cutoff points and replicate results, because the different cutoff points change the nature of the people or areas being studied.

But we can experiment with different cutoff points and see if everything looks reasonable. On the income side, for example, we have computed (but not shown) mobility transition matrices for those with income-needs ratios above 1.25. As said above, these slightly higher-income whites are more inclined to exit poor urban areas than are poor whites, but the slightly higher-income blacks behave about the same as do poor blacks. And it should be stressed that these slightly higher-income adults *are* already included in the equilibrium calculations shown in Table 4—they are just grouped with middle class individuals, not poor individuals.

On the poverty rate side, we have done the complete set of equilibrium calculations for near-poor urban areas, those with poverty rates between 25 and 30 percent. As can be seen from Table 1, initially these near-poor census tracts are noticeably less black and less poor than are the poor urban census tracts. Without showing the full set of numbers, the equilibrium calculations also come out in muted form. There is population loss, but less than for poor urban areas. There is a very slight tendency for these near-poor tracts to get blacker and poorer, but the tendency is not as distinct as for poor urban areas.[5] The results look quite reasonable, but as said above, it is difficult to do more precise sensitivity testing.

Another way to check our results would be to compare them with others in the literature. This cannot be done very precisely either, because all others in the literature refer to the decade of the 1970s, while we use mobility behavior in the 1980s to anticipate future outcomes. But our results are fairly consistent with those of other studies for the 1970s. For example, Jargowsky and Bane [1991] demonstrate that poor urban areas have both lost population and gained poor people, two of our key findings. The picture on Wilson's [1987] "disappearing black role model" hypothesis is more complicated. As Wilson found, many of the upper-income blacks are leaving poor urban areas; exit rates for these groups are between 5 and 10 percent a year. For upper-income blacks in families without children these exit rates exceed entrance rates and the groups show net emigration. But exactly the reverse pattern is observed for upper-income blacks in families with children: Now entrance rates exceed exit rates, and the population of upper-income blacks with children in poor urban areas rises.

---

[5] Detail on these calculations is available on request.

This points to what is perhaps the most disturbing trend of all, not really pointed out by anybody. The numbers in the bottom of Table 4 show a sharp divergence in racial patterns for children. Very few white adults in families with children live in poor urban census tracts, only 1 percent, and this number seems to be dropping sharply. At the same time, more than one-quarter of black adults in families with children live in poor urban census tracts, and this number is rising. If it is true that public schooling is much worse in these poor urban areas, the implied racial disparity in the educational experience of children is definitely not good news for efforts to promote educational equality.

MULTIPLE MOVERS

The transition matrix calculations have aggregated all moves for a pooled sample of adults. Do these calculations reflect the fact that many adults move occasionally, or that some adults move repeatedly?

The importance of multiple movers in shaping our results can be determined as follows. We first make a simple count for individuals—what portion of individuals in a particular group did not move at all in the seven-year period, what portion moved once, and what portion moved more than once. We then measure the impact of the last group, multiple movers, on the equilibrium calculations by excluding these multiple movers in doing all steps of the equilibrium calculations. Comparing these equilibrium calculations with and without the multiple movers gives a precise measure of the impact of the multiple movers.

The simple count of multiple movers by group for the seven-year average concept is shown in Table 5. The results are pretty uniform—only 3 percent of whites and 4 percent of blacks are multiple movers. Never does the share of multiple movers of any group rise above 8 percent. While the results are only shown for the seven-year average concept, the results for the three-year average concept are virtually identical.

But even though multiple moving is relatively rare when measured by individuals, if it occurs by the right amount in the right places it could still affect the equilibrium population densities computed above. And indeed it does slightly. This is shown in Table 6, which gives the results of the recalculation of transition matrices and equilibrium proportions with all multiple movers excluded. For brevity, only the summary ratios are shown in the table.

For the most part, the new equilibria (labeled E3M and E7M) are essentially the same as before. But there are some differences worth noting. The equilibrium share of black adults in poor urban areas is from 2 to 4 points higher when multiple movers are excluded. And the equilibrium share of black adults in families with children is now from 3 to 6 points higher when multiple movers are excluded. This means that some of the apparent exit of black adults in families with children from poor urban areas was due to the repeated moves of those who will soon reenter—not a permanent exit. Hence the exclusion of multiple movers makes the suggested educational disparity results even more alarming.

IMPLICATIONS

As an overall statement, then, there is both good and bad news in these results. The good news is in the micro figures, specifically the reassuringly high exit

Table 5. Number of moves per adult (percent of adults, by number of moves, seven-year average concept).

	No moves	One move	Two+ moves
Group			
Poor whites, children	80.8	11.1	8.1
Poor whites, no children	77.7	17.8	4.5
Middle whites, children	82.9	13.4	3.7
Middle whites, no children	79.1	15.2	5.7
High whites, children	89.0	9.1	1.9
High whites, no children	86.8	10.2	3.0
Unassigned whites, children	84.9	13.3	1.8
Unassigned whites, no children	81.1	16.9	2.0
Poor blacks, children	78.9	14.7	6.4
Poor blacks, no children	78.4	16.3	5.4
Middle blacks, children	77.3	16.0	6.7
Middle blacks, no children	77.1	18.8	4.1
High blacks, children	81.9	15.7	2.4
High blacks, no children	81.9	14.2	3.9
Unassigned blacks, children	81.6	17.1	1.3
Unassigned blacks, no children	80.1	18.2	1.8
Total	81.9	14.4	3.7
By race			
Whites	84.1	12.6	3.3
Blacks	78.9	16.8	4.3
By income			
Poor	78.7	15.4	5.9
Middle	79.1	15.9	5.0
High	86.6	10.7	2.7
Unassigned	81.5	16.8	1.8
By children in family			
With	82.8	13.4	3.8
Without	81.2	15.2	3.6

rates from poor urban areas for people of both races. The bad news comes when one works out the full long-run implications of all exit and entrance probabilities for all groups: Then poor urban areas are seen to be getting poorer and blacker, the home of an even-larger share of the persistently poor, and the home of an ever-larger share of black adults in families with children.

These tabulations illustrate once again the importance of what has come to be known as the "churning" phenomenon. Looked at as overall entities, poor urban areas seem to be changing slowly over time, gradually emptying out and gradually becoming poorer and blacker. But this overall gradual change masks much sharper changes for particular individuals, with as many as one quarter of certain groups leaving or joining these tracts in a particular year. In the past, similar relationships have also been observed for people's income, employment, and family status. Apparently when it comes to the longitudinal status of an individual, nothing is very stable—not income, employment, family status, or even place of residence.

These numbers raise a series of questions for researchers and policymakers alike. For researchers, the questions involve explaining the transition probabilities, the sharp racial differences, and the role of a person's environment

Table 6. 1979–1984 and equilibrium population composition in poor metropolitan census tracts, including and excluding multiple movers (percentage rates, 1979–1984 and in equilibrium).

	I3[a]	E3[b]	E3M[c]	I7[a]	E7[b]	E7M[c]
Ag. pop.	—	−10.6	−9.3	—	−9.6	−12.5
Poverty	27.5	32.3	31.5	26.2	31.8	32.3
Black	70.3	76.4	80.7	70.3	74.8	76.5
Persistently poor in poor urban areas						
Whites	5.1	6.0	4.4	5.6	7.0	6.5
Blacks	35.3	36.3	38.0	35.1	38.1	37.6
Total	17.9	18.9	18.7	19.4	21.5	21.0
Adults in families with children in poor urban areas						
Whites	1.2	0.6	0.6	1.2	0.9	0.7
Blacks	26.1	29.3	35.3	26.1	29.0	32.0
Total	4.1	4.0	4.7	4.1	4.2	4.4

[a] I3, I7 = initial distribution for three- and seven-year average concept.

[b] E3, E7 = equilibrium distribution for three- and seven-year average concept.

[c] E3M, E7M = equilibrium distribution for three- and seven-year average concept with multiple movers excluded.

in shaping behavior. Other questions involve whether geographic movements are beneficial, associated with a rise in income prospects, or harmful. For policymakers, the numbers raise the old question of whether public policy should be focused on poor people or poor places. The high emigration rates reported here would seem to favor aiding people and not places, because people do not seem to be very tied to places. But when one works out the deeper implications, such as the potentially adverse implications of this high degree of mobility for public school education, even these conclusions might be tentative.

The one undisputed implication, however, is that it is clearly wrong to think that because poor urban areas change their shape slowly, the same people are living there year after year. Like molecules, individuals in these slowly changing areas are moving around quite rapidly.

This work was performed under a grant from the Russell Sage Foundation. A number of seminar attendees along the way have made helpful comments, particularly Charles Brown, Gary Burtless, Paul Courant, Sheldon Danziger, Greg Duncan, Doug Massey, Sandy Jencks, and Jeff Lehman.

EDWARD GRAMLICH is Professor of Economics and Public Policy at the University of Michigan.

DEBORAH LAREN and NAOMI SEALAND are Research Associates at the Institute for Social Research of the University of Michigan.

REFERENCES

Duncan, Greg, and Daniel Hill (1989), "Assessing the Quality of Household Panel Survey Data: The Case of the PSID," *Journal of Business and Economic Statistics* 7(4) (October), pp. 441–451.

Duncan, Greg J., and Deborah Laren (1990), "Neighborhood and Family Correlates of Low Birthweight: Preliminary Results on Births to Black Women from the PSID Geocode File," Mimeo.

Jargowsky, Paul A., and Mary Jo Bane (1991), "Ghetto Poverty in the United States, 1970–80," in Christopher Jencks and Paul E. Peterson (eds.), *The Urban Underclass* (Washington, DC: The Brookings Institution), pp. 235–273.

Jencks, Christopher, and Susan E. Mayer (1990), "The Social Consequences of Growing Up in a Poor Neighborhood," in Lawrence E. Lynn, Jr. and Michael McGeary (eds.), *Inner City Poverty in the United States* (Washington, DC: National Academy Press), pp. 111–186.

Massey, Douglas S., Mitchell L. Eggers, and Nancy A. Denton (1989), "Disentangling the Causes of Concentrated Poverty," Mimeo.

Ricketts, Erol R., and Isabel V. Sawhill (1988), "Defining and Measuring the Underclass," *Journal of Policy Analysis and Management* 7(2) (Winter), pp. 316–325.

Wilson, William Julius (1987), *The Truly Disadvantaged: The Inner City, the Underclass, and Public Policy* (Chicago: University of Chicago Press).

[8]

The spatial dimension: should worker assistance be given to poor people or poor places?

(with Colleen M. Heflin)

① Edward M. Gramlich
② Colleen M. Heflin

The basic trends in the 1980s job market suggest a giant mismatch – demand is growing for highly skilled workers. Those workers with the requisite marketable skills then get good job offers and enjoy some combination of rapidly rising employment offers and real wage growth. Those on the other side of the skill distribution, without the requisite marketable skills, suffer the reverse fate – some combination of low employment possibilities and low real wage growth.

For a long time now social scientists have wondered about the role of spatial factors in this process. While it is hard to imagine that spatial mismatch is a main cause of shifts in the entire wage distribution, many less skilled workers do live in areas without good job growth, often in high poverty urban neighborhoods. These spatial factors may be part of the overall problem facing less skilled workers.

The reason that spatial mismatch factors are unlikely to be a main cause of the wage dispersion in the 1980s is that less skilled workers were already concentrated in poor areas, and good manufacturing jobs were already leaving central cities, long before the dramatic spread in the real wage distribution opened up (Wilson, 1987). Only if these spatial trends hit some tripping point in the 1980s would they be an important cause of recent movements in the wage distribution. But at the policy level, even if spatial factors were not prominent causes of recent changes in the underlying wage distribution, programs that improve spatial mobility or reduce the job mismatch could still help mitigate or offset movements in this wage distribution, at least for important subgroups of workers.

In this essay we bring together various strands in the empirical literature to discuss these issues. We focus on one basic causal (or positive) question and one basic policy (or normative) question:

- *Causal* What role has spatial mismatch played in the widening dispersion of real wages for American workers, either in general or for specific groups of workers?
- *Policy* What should be the form of any policy interventions – should there be direct assistance to poor workers or poor places, or should programs target mobility?

We begin on the causal side by reviewing the literature on spatial mismatch. This evidence, unfortunately, is inconclusive about the impact of spatial factors on labor incomes. Since most people worry about spatial issues particularly for high poverty urban areas, we focus on evidence from studies of urban spatial poverty. We then turn to the program side, and discuss programs that aid workers, aid poor places, and improve mobility. We conclude by describing a mixed strategy for dealing with spatial problems.

Causation: spatial mismatch in general

Although the spatial mismatch hypothesis was initially based on empirical observations, it does have a theoretical basis. It starts from the standard urban economics model that has employers locating in the central city and individuals free to locate in the suburbs. This leads to a rent gradient with housing prices declining according to distance from the central city, and to a selection process whereby those with greater taste for housing live further out in the suburbs. If the cross-sectional income elasticity of demand for housing exceeds unity, we would expect to see high income people concentrated in the suburbs and low income people concentrated in central cities, much as is now the case.

But there are at least two important complications that should be introduced to this simple model. One is to recognize that employers too can locate in the suburbs – indeed suburban employment is growing much more rapidly than central city employment in most metropolitan areas. This complication beclouds the clear predictions of the simple urban model – now both high and low income people can be located in both central cities and suburbs.

A second complication is to recognize that not all potential homeowners have free choice of where to live. Suburban zoning restrictions exclude low income people from some suburbs, racial discrimination does likewise for blacks and other ethnic groups, and many young workers or secondary earners live where their family lives. Zoning restrictions and other forms of discrimination should crowd low income people and blacks into the central city and lower their net real wage, by increasing their commuting time from some of their preferred jobs. This net wage reduction could also show up as an employment reduction or mismatch, if for some reason real wages are sticky.

Efforts to test these models empirically have proceeded by comparing distributions of residences and distributions of employment. The first empirical paper by Kain (1968) found that for neighborhoods in Detroit and Chicago employment shares for black adult workers depended positively on black residential shares and negatively on commuting distances. This led to a prediction that black employment shares could be raised slightly if blacks lived nearer to their work.

Kain's initial paper generated so much literature that there are by now a number of summaries of this literature – three good ones are by Kain himself (1992), Jencks and Mayer (1990b) and Holzer (1991). Using data from SMSAs in the 1970s Offner and Saks (1971) overturned Kain's results simply by using different functional forms in their estimating equations. Friedlander (1972), Harrison (1974), Masters (1975), and Danziger and Weinstein (1976) all found little effect of residential segregation on black employment.

More recently, either because of more recent data or different statistical methods, there has been some change. Now the results are mixed. Based on data from the 1980s, Leonard (1987), Price and Mills (1985), Ellwood (1986), and Moss and Tilly (1991) still find little or no effect of spatial factors on black employment and/or incomes. But Farley (1987), Ihlanfeldt (1988), Ihlanfeldt and Sjoquist (1989, 1990, 1991), Kasarda (1989), and Holzer and Vroman (1992) do find that spatial factors have an important impact on relative employment and/or incomes.

There are not yet any mismatch studies based on the 1990 Census, but Jargowsky (1994), Hughes (1995), and Abramson, Tobin, and Vandergoot (1995) do have some disturbing suggestive results from the 1990 Census. In this census there has been a sharp increase in the number and share of blacks living in poor urban areas, along with an increase in the geographical size of these poor areas. Both changes continue trends observed by comparing the 1980 Census with the 1970 Census. This would seem to make it more likely that spatial mismatch problems will be serious in the future, even though they may not have been in the past.

Another important aspect of these mismatch studies is the group under investigation. Most past studies have been based on the employment shares of adult workers, but Ellwood (1986) and Ihlanfeldt and Sjoquist (1989, 1990, 1991) have focused on young male black and white workers. This more pointed focus seems particularly relevant, because the employment problems are much more severe for teenagers, the racial disparities are greater, and teenagers are much more likely to have their residences chosen exogenously by their family, hence mitigating problems of simultaneity. To this point focusing just on teenagers has not narrowed the uncertainty about spatial mismatch much – Ellwood is on the side of the spatial doves and Ihlanfeldt and Sjoquist on the side of the hawks. But it is again possible that differences will become starker in the 1990 Census.

There will no doubt be further work attempting to refine these results with ever more recent and fine-grained data. At the same time, there are a number of serious limitations with these studies. Among the most serious are:

- *Endogeneity* Which comes first, the place of residence or employment? The standard approach has residence determining employment, but there are many scenarios that could reverse the causation. People may determine their residence from their place of employment rather than the other way around.
- *Dynamics* Employers move around a lot, within and across cities. At any point in time some cities may be in the process of adjusting to the move in or out of some large employers: eventually places of residence will adjust but not in the short run. While cross section regressions of the sort run by most investigators may find long run relationships and be relatively immune from these problems, adjustments may take so long that the equilibrium relationship is hard to observe.
- *Heterogeneity* Workers differ in many respects, and studies of employment and residential shares of some groups may not pertain to other groups. Cities differ, and urban models applicable to some cities may be quite inapplicable to others. And time trends differ – things that may be true in one area in 1970 may not still be true by 1980 or 1990. As said above, the time trend problem is a possible explanation for the fact that spatial mismatch problems appear to be getting worse over time; and it may also be that mismatch problems are particularly serious in particular cities.
- *Policy relevance* The early spatial mismatch regressions were fitted to broad

masses of workers such as black and white adult male workers. If there were ever to be spatial labor market programs, one can almost guarantee that budgetary tightness would force these programs to be narrowly-based, selectively affecting particular areas such as urban ghettos or particular groups of workers such as black youths. It is not clear how relevant the entire mismatch literature would be in evaluating these more focused policies.

With all these uncertainties, it may be prudent not to place too much faith in the studies that have attempted to relate employment and/or income differences to spatial characteristics in general. Many of them have never found large impacts of place of residence on employment or income, though some of the more recent studies are beginning to do so. This may be because spatial mismatch problems are gradually worsening, it may be because these problems have always been serious but now they are easier to observe, or it may be because the really difficult problems affecting, say, urban areas or particular groups of workers are becoming more noticeable. And as noted above, whatever the overall verdict on whether spatial mismatch contributed to the wage dispersion, spatial policies could still be an important part of the solution to the problem.

A closer look at poor urban areas
As one reads through the entire spatial mismatch literature, one gets a nagging fear that this literature might be missing the key problem: the existence of possibly dysfunctional systems in a small share of the overall labor market involving high poverty urban areas. It thus makes sense to pay particular attention to the recent literature on these areas.

This literature starts with the observation that the share of poor people located in high poverty urban areas is rising sharply. Reischauer (1987) and Jargowsky and Bane (1991) show the changes between the 1970 and 1980 Census, and Jargowsky (1994) between the 1980 and 1990 Census. Further, Kasarda (1992) has shown that the increase in poverty concentration was correlated with rises in unemployment and other measures of poor work history. Gramlich, Laren, and Sealand (1992b) have shown that medium run (five to seven years) income gains are greater for workers who move out of poor urban areas than for workers who stay; much less for workers who move into poor urban areas than for workers who do not move in. O'Reagan and Quigley (1993) have tied employment rates of parents and children through family networks to job access. Finally, in perhaps the starkest evidence of all, Corcoran, Gordon, Laren, and Solon (1992) have shown that over a longer run the sons of families from poor urban areas do significantly worse than others on a range of labor market outcomes.

These labor market observations are buttressed by other examinations of inner city conditions. Hughes (1988) shows an increase in inner-city isolation and deprivation, as measured by the number of poor black neighborhoods that do not border on integrated or nonblack neighborhoods. Wilson (1987) shows the process by which the emigration of industry and middle class blacks combined with high black male unemployment cause the deterioration of family structures and increased crime and violence in urban areas. Jencks and Mayer (1990a) have shown that in a number of dimensions, from educational attainment to teen pregnancy, those growing up in poor urban areas are likely to be in much worse shape than those not. Freeman (1992) shows the alarming prevalence of crime factors in inner-city life and job markets. Akerlof and Yellen (1994) have demonstrated the weird incentives of the crime problem – not only is crime endemic, but there are pathological situations where it is not even in the interests of ordinary members of the local community to cooperate with the police. Anderson (1990) has documented the social behaviors necessary to survive in poor urban areas and their reliance on a psychology of racial fear, class prejudice, and social distancing. Whatever the impact of spatial mismatch factors for the overall labor force, it is hard to escape the conclusion that things might be reaching a pretty drastic state for poor urban areas.

At the same time, there are grounds for questioning both the pessimistic outlook for poor urban areas and the policy implications of this outlook. Gramlich, Laren, and Sealand (1992a) also find enormous rates of immigration and emigration to and from these areas. Fully one quarter of all poor white adults leave poor urban areas within one year; fully one tenth of poor black adults. The overwhelming majority of these emigrants do not return, though others from nonpoor areas take their places in the poor urban areas. With mobility rates this high, it may not be impossible to imagine programs that change outcomes significantly by altering migration propensities only slightly.

Actual programs
With this background, we now take a look at some actual programs. There are in principle four types – programs that aid poor workers, programs that aid poor places, programs that move poor workers to jobs, and programs that move jobs to workers. We review briefly how each type of program might work, its advantages and disadvantages, and then summarize what there is of any evaluation evidence.

Programs that aid poor workers
One main advantage of direct assistance to low-skilled workers is that the assistance can be made very general. Assistance can be made available to poor workers wherever they live, and can be phased out in a uniform way for more highly skilled workers. This property leads to another advantage – since direct assistance can be phased out for less needy workers, it is likely to be much cheaper than other forms of job assistance.

Making worker aid independent of location may also improve the social outcomes of geographic mobility. If, for example, housing vouchers enable low-skilled workers to live anywhere they could find acceptable housing, they would be more inclined to locate where they wanted, not constrained by program availability. One might predict that many low-skilled workers would leave poor urban areas, lessening the concentration of such workers there, but if that did not happen, these workers would presumably be choosing their place of residence voluntarily, not on the basis of program properties.

But while direct assistance to workers has these desirable aspects, it may not be sufficient to deal with all aspects of urban poverty precisely because there may be spatial factors that impose particular costs – crime, the absence of job networks, poor schooling, and so forth. It is hard to imagine a comprehensive strategy to assist low skill workers that does not entail some direct assistance, but it is also hard to imagine that direct assistance alone will be sufficient.

In the case at hand, the US labor market policy package already features significant programs of direct assistance – minimum wages, the earned income tax credit, and a whole set of training programs. Since these programs are discussed elsewhere in this volume, we will confine our attention to programs involving spatial factors in some way.

Programs that assist poor urban areas
The advantages and disadvantages of programs that aid poor urban areas are almost exactly the reverse of programs that directly aid poor workers. Whereas direct aid can be targeted to needy workers wherever they live, place-based aid cannot be. It by definition affects the residents in the designated target area, and it by definition bypasses residents not living in the target area, however needy they may be. Hence there are inevitable horizontal equity problems across individuals with place-based assistance.

There are also residential distortion effects. Whereas direct assistance lets residential outcomes be determined through individual choice, place-based aid necessarily contains differential subsidies – groups locating in one area get a subsidy and groups locating in another area do not.

Place-based aid can in principle go to either public or private bodies. Since private firms can come and go, they are not tied to the area the way public governments are, and measures to support private firms are discussed below under the heading of mobility assistance. This section considers measures to support the public services in poor urban areas.

There is a straightforward case in favor of such assistance. If the crime problems of poor urban areas are so significant that they impede business and employment activities, what could be more important than measures to improve police protection? Similarly for measures to improve the local public schools, or the functioning of the local labor market. Not only can the public service deficiencies be directly offset, but these public services could in principle be upgraded to combat or compensate for other deficiencies.

Migration affects local public service assistance in a number of ways. Suppose a homeless shelter with decent health and mental care facilities were established in a poor urban area. There could be immigration of poor people from other communities to take advantage of this facility. This eliminates one potential disadvantage of the spatially-targeted assistance, because the benefits are spread more widely than the initial targeting area. At the same time, the assistance could also increase the concentration of poor people in the area, an outcome that works against long run social integration and perhaps even nullifies the effectiveness of the program.

There are two other types of difficulties. One is drawn from long experience studying how local governments respond to federal aid of various sorts, known as the fungibility problem (Gramlich, 1976). Basically, if this aid is general income assistance *or* if it is categorical assistance given in small amounts relative to prior local spending, the aid is unlikely to be spent on the service in question. The federal government may pass a program called local public service assistance, but the assistance may actually be used to cut taxes or to support other functions.

A further difficulty involves the politics of the donor government. While one can set up criteria determining which areas most deserve support for the local public services, these support programs must get passed by real live legislatures consisting of representatives of all areas. These legislatures can be relied on to alter prospective legislation in ways that would not be optimal from a labor market standpoint alone, to cut their own constituents in on the benefits. In this sense there may inevitably be some unnecessary expenditures in any programs to aid poor urban areas.

Given the intrinsic limitations of directly aiding poor workers, and the difficulties in aiding poor places directly, it may also make sense to analyse programs that work on mobility, either trying to move workers to jobs or jobs to workers. We now turn to these.

Moving workers to jobs
Perhaps the most significant advantage of programs that try to move workers to jobs is that they can be done on a limited scale. The programs can focus on particular barriers to mobility, whether housing segregation problems or inadequate commuting networks, and they do not require a radical improvement in the public infrastructure in an area. They may never solve all the problems facing poor workers, but they might be highly productive in their own way.

Unfortunately, there are surprisingly few programs that have tried to move inner city residents to areas of better job prospects. One natural experiment that has received a great deal of attention is the Gautreaux program in Chicago. Gautreaux was created by a consent decree in the aftermath of a judicial finding of widespread discrimination in Chicago's public housing program. It gives applicants for public housing the option to apply for homes in either the city or the suburbs. There are councillors to assist participants in locating housing. A research team then compared outcomes for those leaving the city with those remaining, with all participants being members of black female-headed households (Rosenbaum and Popkin, 1991). Previously employed Gautreaux participants who moved to the suburbs were 14 percent more likely to have jobs than those remaining in the city; previously unemployed participants were 50 percent more likely to be employed. In both cases there were no significant differences in observed wages, but obviously very significant differences in wage incomes. There were also striking improvements in suburban children's high school completion, college attendance, and full time employment (Rosenbaum, 1995).

Two aspects of the Gautreaux results should be specially noted. For one thing, all participants were women, in contrast to the earlier spatial mismatch results that focused largely on males. For another, the results could be influenced by self-selection problems, since the treatment group voluntarily left the city. But while self-selection factors could be influencing the results, that is *only* an interpretation problem if one wants to apply these results to the entire population by, say, forcibly moving nonvolunteers to the suburbs. If only volunteers will be moving to the suburbs, the Gautreaux results should be indicative.

Additional mobility evidence comes from Detroit and Milwaukee, where separate research groups have examined the relationship between commuting times and job outcomes when large employers moved into the suburbs *away from* urban workers. In Detroit, where housing segregation is known to be quite high, white employees with long commutes were found to be more likely to quit their jobs than were white employees with short commutes, presumably because these white workers had other job opportunities. In contrast, increases in commuting times for black employees had no significant impact on quit or move propensities, implying that these employees lost real income (Zax and Kain, 1991a, b). In Milwaukee when a large employer relocated to the suburbs, this relocation greatly increased commuting times for black and Hispanic workers, implying that these workers did not have other job opportunities and suffered losses of real income (Fernandez, 1991). At this point it is too early in the Milwaukee evaluation to assess the impact of commuting time changes on actual patterns of employment.

If mobility assistance seems important from a residential perspective, it also makes sense to examine it from a transportation perspective, since it may be easier to provide transportation networks than to enable people to move. Hughes (1995) discusses several transportation programs. The Wisconsin Department of Transportation has developed a job-ride program that secures city residents rides to jobs or job interviews for up to six months. The Chicago Surburban Job Link program operates a fleet of buses and carpools that now transports from 400 to 600 residents per day to the suburbs. The Southeastern Pennsylvania Transportation Authority works with local businesses to establish subsidized public transportation to particular suburban business parks. Public/Private Ventures is currently engaged in a demonstration project involving ten metropolitan areas funded by a mixture of public agencies and a private foundation. To this point there are no formal evaluations of these demonstration programs.

There are three important themes in these results. One is that surburban housing discrimination against all blacks and Hispanics is still an important phenomenon, a proposition for which there is plenty of confirming evidence (Massey, 1990; Turner, Struyk, and Yinger, 1991). Another theme is that commuting times are important to workers, and the cost or inability to commute does seem to be a barrier in permitting urban black and Hispanic workers to take advantage of suburban jobs. A third theme is that these mobility programs are likely to be relatively attractive – improving job placement while paying only for counselling or transportation, but not massive subsidies for the jobs themselves. All of these themes will come up in our policy section below.

Moving jobs to workers
There are many policies that might fit in this category. Bartik (1994) reviews the experience with a number of present federal and state economic development initiatives. The problem with most from the standpoint of low-skilled workers is that these programs are generally designed to encourage economic development of at least medium- to high-technology firms – if they boost the demand for any labor, it is for highly-skilled labor. They should be viewed more from the standpoint of research and development policy than labor market policy, and in fact Bartik goes

on to argue that the businesses in question generally object to pressures to hire low-skilled workers. These firms, often struggling to get established, have enough to worry about without complicating constraints on their hiring and/or location.

The main policy initiative affecting poor areas are urban enterprise zones (UEZ). Generally these UEZ provide tax incentives and wage subsidies to firms locating in specified areas. Currently the federal government has a small UEZ program, and 37 states and the District of Columbia have also enacted such measures.

On the theoretical side, Quigley (1994) argues strongly against UEZ-type measures, He points out the land intensity of many forms of employment that are moving to the suburbs, and shows how this movement fits into a long term process that is spreading out the population in most central cities. If there is a social problem, it is not this spreading out but rather simply poverty and discrimination. As such, measures that help poor people or help them move or commute to good jobs are desirable, and measures that perpetuate geographic segregation and locate jobs inefficiently are undesirable. He vastly prefers efforts to combat housing discrimination directly to efforts to subsidize jobs made necessary by discrimination.

Ladd (1994) then works through a number of other problems with UEZ legislation. Many of the subsidies are for capital, which might encourage firms to use more capital and highly-skilled labor and less low-skilled labor. Many take the form of reductions in the corporate tax rate, which will not help small firms. Many take the form of property tax abatements, which could largely bypass firms that rent their property. Many take the form of inventory tax credits, which encourage capital-intensive operations like warehouses to locate in the zones. Many take the form of capital gains tax reductions, which may simply bring in venture capital and again bypass small firms. Many work by changing the effective price of labor, which may be unimportant if production conditions or even underlying social conditions make labor demand inelastic.

As for the empirical results, in the early 1980s the United Kingdom offered property and land tax exemptions for firms locating in vacant or deteriorating industrial land (the program has since been discontinued). Ladd reports that survey evaluations found most of the new zone jobs came from surrounding areas, so that the effective cost per new job created was very high, much higher than the cost of the mobility programs discussed above. If it is true that a promising route to urban job creation is by building up surrounding areas, one might even argue that it is preferable in the long run to have unsubsidized jobs in surrounding areas than subsidized jobs in poor urban areas. These subsidies may not last forever.

In this country one of the leading UEZ states is Indiana. Papke (1993) analysed the experience there and found that UEZ designation did increase inventory values and decrease unemployment insurance claims. There was still a high cost per new job created, and still evidence that jobs were stolen from surrounding areas.

Maryland had a program affecting small cities with high unemployment. While there was positive employment growth in the designated areas, employer surveys indicated that this employment growth was not due to the UEZ legislation but rather the apparently exogenous hiring of two new employers. The same question applies to the results for a New Jersey program.

Ladd summarizes all of these studies and computes annual costs per new job across all programs that have been evaluated. These are shown in Table 1 below, and fall in the $40,000 to $60,000 range, a very high number. Moreover, some of these jobs may be stolen from surrounding areas, and as Bartik and Ladd both warn, they may not be the types of jobs ideally suited for workers from poor areas. In contrast to the evaluative evidence on programs that try to move workers to jobs, the evidence on at least these programs that have tried to move jobs to workers is so far pretty negative. Society does not have $40,000 to $60,000 to spend for every new job for poor urban workers.

Table 1   Annual cost per job of UEZ programs

Area	Direct Cost	Net Cost
England	15,000	60,000
New Jersey	13,070	13,070
Indiana	10,170	53,506
Indiana	1,633	43,579
Maryland	Infinite	Infinite

Notes:
The net cost numbers are Ladd's estimates of effective jobs created to UEZ residents, divided by the true cost of the program. The England results are taken from Rubin and Richards (1992). The New Jersey results are from Rubin (1990). The Indiana results are from Papke (1991) and Rubin and Wilder (1989). The Maryland results are from the US General Accounting Office (1988).

Source: Ladd (1994).

A mixed strategy for spatial assistance
Until now the paper has looked at different types of spatial assistance. But there is a sense in which spatial assistance programs are not necessarily substitutes, but could be complementary as well. Suppose, for example, a broader spatial strategy featured some direct assistance to workers, some public service assistance to poor urban areas, and some mobility assistance to help unskilled central city workers find and hold jobs in the suburbs.

The Committee for Economic Development (CED, 1994) recently came out with such a plan. The CED plan contained a number of community-building initiatives, including measures to control guns and crime, some efforts to redress housing discrimination in suburban areas, and some private location subsidies.

Another apparent proponent of a mixed strategy is the Clinton Administration. The Administration supports a number of programs that more or less comprise a mixed strategy for spatial assistance. Some of these initiatives are now under attack from the Republican Congress, and it is not yet clear which measures will survive.

The Administration has promoted direct assistance to workers. There was a large expansion of the Earned Income Tax Credit in 1993. The School to Work Opportunities Act also provides federal seed money to states to combine work with learning.

As for assistance for local public services, the Violent Crime Control and Law Enforcement Act of 1994 contains grants to put up to 100,000 police on the street, primarily in urban areas, and to ban a number of assault weapons. Fungibility skeptics might doubt that this many additional police will be hired, and deeper skeptics might doubt the effectiveness of added police, but these are at least examples of support for local public services. Additionally, the President has established the Community Enterprise Board led by Vice President Gore to co-ordinate programs to distressed communities.

In the domain of moving workers to jobs, the Administration has promoted the Moving to Opportunity Program (MTO). Modelled on the Gautraux project and implemented using a scientific design for evaluation purposes, MTO began in five metropolitan areas – Baltimore, Boston, Chicago, Los Angeles, and New York. Congress has appropriated vouchers and money for counselling assistance in these sites to enable families living in public and assisted housing projects in high poverty areas to move to low poverty neighborhoods. Unlike the Gautreaux program, developed to speed up racial desegregation in Chicago, MTO was focused solely on moving participants from high to low poverty areas. The President has also shown a commitment to fair housing by issuing the first Fair Housing Order in more than a decade, as well as in establishing the Fair Housing Council to oversee its implementation.

While UEZ programs do not fare so well in the hands of the evaluators, the Administration also has a package for location subsidies for private business. The 1993 Empowerment Zone legislation creates six UEZ in big cities, three in rural areas, and 95 enterprise communities. These all combine tax incentives, public investment, and relief from state and local regulations. In total $1 billion in social services and $2.5 billion in tax incentives is provided to selected communities.

Conclusion

While there is little evidence that spatial mismatch problems in general have contributed to the widening of the overall distribution of wages, a closer look at the urban poverty literature suggests that some spatial policies may still be important components of a broader labor market strategy. This strategy should undoubtedly feature some direct assistance to workers, and it might well feature some place-based assistance for the public services of poor urban areas. It could also feature programs that help workers from poor urban areas take advantage of surburban jobs – these programs seem to be very effective without costing much.

A far more difficult question involves programs that attempt to subsidize private firms to locate in poor urban areas. As it stands now, these programs have a number of theoretical deficiencies, they have not fared so well in real world evaluations, and they seem quite costly.

References
Abramson, Alan, Mitchell Tobin, and Matthew VanderGoot (1995), 'The Changing Geography of Metropolitan Opportunity: The Segregation of the Poor in US Metropolitan Areas, 1970 to 1990', *Housing Policy Debate*, 6(1), 45–72.

Akerlof, George A. and Janet L. Yellen (1993), 'Gang Behavior, Law Enforcement, and Community Values', in Henry J. Aaron, Thomas E. Mann, and Timothy Taylor (eds), *Values and Public Policy*, (Washington DC: The Brookings Institution), 173–209.

Anderson, Elijah (1990), *Streetwise: Race, Class and Change in an Urban Community*, Chicago, IL: University of Chicago Press.

Bartik, Timothy J. (1994), *What Should the Federal Government Be Doing About Urban Economic Development?* Kalamazoo, MI: W.E. Upjohn Institute.

Committee for Economic Development (1994), *Rebuilding Inner-City Communities: An Emerging National Strategy Against Urban Decay*, forthcoming, (New York, NY).

Corcoran, Mary, Roger Gordon, Deborah Laren and Gary Solon (1992), 'The Association Between Men's Economic Status and Their Family and Community Origins', *Journal of Human Resources*, **27**(4), 575–601.

Danziger, Sheldon and Mark Weinstein (1976), 'Employment Location and Wage Rates of Poverty-area Residents', *Journal of Urban Economics*, **3**, 127–45.

Ellwood, David (1986), 'The Spatial Mismatch Hypothesis: Are there Teenage Jobs Missing in the Ghetto?', in Richard B. Freeman and Harry J. Holzer (eds), *The Black Youth Employment Crisis*, Chicago, IL: University of Chicago Press, 147–90.

Farley, John E. (1987), 'Disproportionate Black and Hispanic Unemployment in US Metropolitan Areas', *American Journal of Economics and Sociology*, **46**, 129–50.

Fernandez, Robert M. (1991), *Race, Space, and Job Accessibility: Evidence from a Plant Location*, Northwestern University Working Paper.

Friedlander, Stanley L. (1972), *Unemployment in the Urban Core*, New York, NY: Praeger.

Freeman, Richard B. (1992), 'Crime and the Employment of Disadvantaged Youths', in George E. Peterson and Wayne Vroman (eds), *Urban Labor Markets and Job Opportunity*, Washington, DC: The Urban Institute Press, 201–38.

Gramlich, Edward M. (1976), 'A Review of the Empirical Literature on Intergovernmental Grants', in Wallace E. Oates (ed.), *The Political Economy of Fiscal Federalism*, Lexington, MA: Heath Lexington, 219–40.

Gramlich, Edward, Deborah Laren and Naomi Sealand (1992a), 'Moving Into and Out of Poor Urban Areas', *Journal of Policy Analysis and Management*, **11**(2), 273–87.

Gramlich, Edward, Deborah Laren and Naomi Sealand (1992b), 'Mobility Into and Out of Poor Urban Neighborhoods', in Adele V. Harrell and George E. Peterson (eds), *Drugs, Crime, and Social Isolation: Barriers to Urban Opportunity*, Washington, DC: The Urban Institute Press, 241–55.

Harrison, Bennett (1974), *Urban Economic Development*, Washington, DC: The Urban Institute Press.

Holzer, Harry J. (1991), 'The Spatial Mismatch Hypothesis: What Has the Evidence Shown?', *Urban Studies*, **28**(1), 105–22.

Holzer, Harry J. and Wayne Vroman (1992), 'Mismatches and the Urban Labor Market', in George E. Peterson and Wayne Vroman (eds), *Urban Labor Markets and Job Opportunity*, Washington, DC: The Urban Institute Press, 81–112.

Hughes, Mark Alan (1988), *The Underclass Fallacy*, Princeton University Working Paper.

Hughes, Mark Alan (1995), 'A Mobility Strategy for Improving Opportunity', *Housing Policy Debate*, **6**(1), 271–97.

Ihlanfeldt, Keith R. (1988), 'Intrametropolitan Variation in Earnings and Labor Market Discrimination: An Economic Analysis of the Atlanta Labor Market', *Southern Economic Journal*, **55**, 123–40.

Ihlanfeldt, Keith R. and David L. Sjoquist (1989), 'The Impact of Job Decentralization on the Economic Welfare of Central City Blacks', *Journal of Urban Economics*, **26**, 110–30.

Ihlanfeldt, Keith R. and David L. Sjoquist (1990), 'Job Accessibility and Racial Differences in Youth Employment Rates', *American Economic Review*, **80**, 267–76.

Ihlanfeldt, Keith R. and David L. Sjoquist (1991), 'The Effect of Job Access on Black and White Youth Employment: A Cross-Sectional Analysis', *Urban Studies*, **28**, 255–65.

Jargowsky, Paul A. (1994), 'Ghetto Poverty Among Blacks in the 1990s', *Journal of Policy Analysis and Management*, **13**(2), 288–310.

Jargowsky, Paul A. and Mary Jo Bane (1991), 'Ghetto Poverty in the United States, 1970–80', in Christopher Jencks and Paul E. Peterson (eds), *The Urban Underclass*, Washington, DC: The Brookings Institution, 235–73.

Jencks, Christopher and Susan E. Mayer (1990a), 'The Social Consequences of Growing Up in a Poor Neighborhood', in Laurence E. Lynn Jr and Michael G.H. McGeary (eds), *Inner City Poverty in the United States*, Washington, DC: National Academy Press, 111–86.

Jencks, Christopher and Susan E. Mayer (1990b), 'Residential Segregation, Job Proximity, and Black Job Opportunities', in Laurence E. Lynn Jr and Michael G.H. McGeary (eds), *Inner City Poverty in the United States*, Washington, DC: National Academy Press, 187–222.

Kain, John F. (1968), 'Housing Segregation, Negro Employment, and Metropolitan Decentralization', *The Quarterly Journal of Economics*, **82**, 175–97.

Kain, John F. (1992), 'The Spatial Mismatch Hypothesis: Three Decades Later', *Housing Policy Debate*, 3(2), 371–460.

Kasarda, John D. (1989), 'Urban Industrial Transition and the Underclass', *The Annals of the American Academy of Political Science and Social Science*, 501, 26–47.

Kasarda, John D. (1992), 'The Severely Distressed in Economically Transforming Cities', in Adele V. Harrell and George E. Peterson (eds), *Drugs, Crime, and Social Isolation: Barriers to Urban Opportunity*, Washington, DC: The Urban Institute Press, 45–98.

Ladd, Helen F. (1994), 'Spatially Targeted Economic Development Strategies: Do They Work?', *Cityscape: A Journal of Policy Development and Research*, 1(1), 193–218.

Leonard, Jonathan (1987), 'The Interaction of Residential Segregation and Employment Discrimination', *Journal of Urban Economics*, 21, 323–46.

Masters, Stanley (1975), *Black-White Income Differences: Empirical Studies and Policy Implications*, New York, NY: Academic Press.

Massey, Douglas S. (1990), 'American Apartheid: Segregation and the Making of the Underclass', *American Journal of Sociology*, 96, 329–57.

Moss, Philip and Christopher Tilly (1991), 'Why Black Men Are Doing Worse in the Labor Market: A Review of Supply Side and Demand Side Explanations', Social Science Research Council, New York, NY, mimeo.

Offner, Paul and Daniel Saks (1971), 'A Note on John Kain's "Housing Segregation, Negro Employment, and Metropolitan Decentralization"', *The Quarterly Journal of Economics*, 85, 147–60.

O'Reagan, Katherine M. and John M. Quigley (1993), 'Family Networks and Youth Access to Jobs', *Journal of Urban Economics*, 34(2), 230–48.

Papke, Leslie E. (1991), 'Tax Policy and Urban Development: Evidence from an Enterprise Zone Program', National Bureau of Economic Research Working Paper.

Papke, Leslie (1993), 'What Do We Know About Enterprise Zones?', National Bureau of Economic Research Reprint, No. 1817.

Price, Richard and Edwin Mills (1985), 'Race and Residence in Earnings Determination', *Journal of Urban Economics*, 17, 1–18.

Quigley, John M. (1994), 'New Directions for Urban Policy Debate', *Housing Policy Debate*, 5(1), 97–106.

Reeder, Richard J. and Kenneth L. Robinson (1992), 'Enterprise Zones: Assessing Their Rural Development Potential', *Policy Studies Journal*, 20(2), 264–75.

Reischauer, Robert D. (1987), *The Geographic Concentration of Poverty: What Do We Know?*, Washington, DC: The Brookings Institution.

Rosenbaum, James E. and Susan J. Popkin (1991), 'Employment and Earnings of Low Income Blacks Who Moved to Middle Class Suburbs', in Christopher Jencks and Paul E. Peterson (eds), *The Urban Underclass*, Washington, DC: The Brookings Institution, 342–56.

Rosenbaum, James E. (1995), 'Changing the Geography of Opportunity by Expanding Residential Choice: Lessons from the Gautreaux Program', *Housing Policy Debate*, 6(1), 231–69.

Rubin, Barry M. and Craig M. Richards (1992), 'A Transatlantic Comparison of Enterprise Zone Impacts: The British and the American Experience', *Economic Development Quarterly*, 6(4), 431–43.

Rubin, Barry M. and Margaret G. Wilder (1989), 'Urban Enterprise Zones: Employment Impacts and Fiscal Incentives', *APA Journal*, Autumn.

Rubin, Marilyn (1990), 'Urban Enterprise Zones: Do They Work? Evidence from New Jersey', *Public Budgeting and Finance*, 10(4), Winter, 3–17.

Turner, Margery A., Raymond Struyck, and John Yinger (1991), *Housing Discrimination Study: A Synthesis*, Washington, DC: US Department of Housing and Urban Development.

US General Accounting Office (1988), *Enterprise Zones: Lessons from the Maryland Enterprise*.

Wilson, William Julius (1987), *The Truly Disadvantaged: The Inner City, The Underclass, and Public Policy*, Chicago: The University of Chicago Press.

Zax, Jeffrey and John Kain (1991a), 'Commutes, Quits, and Moves', *Journal of Urban Economics*, 29, 153–65.

Zax, Jeffrey and John Kain (1991b), 'The Substitution Between Moves and Quits', *The Economic Journal*, 101, 1510–21.

(U.S.)   173-80

H71   E62

Subnational fiscal policy[1]

One of the least controversial propositions in both public finance and macroeconomics is that only the national government should attempt to conduct stabilization policy. The conventional view, clearly explained by Oates (1972) and never seriously challenged since that time, supposes that demand conditions in a state mirror those in the national economy, that fiscal multipliers for national budget changes are higher than those for the state, and that state debt is external and national debt internal. The inference based on these premises is that it is unwise for a state or subnational government to run its own fiscal stabilization policy.

These premises may have been accurate twenty years ago, but by now each can be seriously questioned:

- The new importance of relative price shocks, whether from the energy sector or exchange rates, implies that demand conditions may not be highly correlated across states (Medoff (1983)). They may not even be positively correlated, meaning that expansionary and contractionary policies may be simultaneously called for in different parts of the country.
- Exchange rate flexibility means that national fiscal changes are offset by changes in the trade balance, while subnational policy changes may be too small to trigger such offsets if demand conditions are not highly correlated.
- The growth of output of services, more likely to be nontradeable than goods, implies that a large share of value added is now produced and consumed inside a subnational jurisdiction such as a state.
- The opening of international capital markets means that all debt, state and national, is effectively external.

The first and second arguments are advantages of conducting fiscal policy at the subnational level, or of decentralizing stabilization policy. The third and fourth arguments neutralize what had previously been felt to be advantages for stabilizing with national, as opposed to subnational, policies.

These arguments all refer to the desirability of having states conduct their own stabilization policy. Another question is raised about the feasibility of such actions, since most states operate under constitutional budget balance restrictions. But therein lies another misunderstanding. Most budget balance restrictions constrain the algebraic sum of the present deficit and the stock of liquid assets. If a state has

[1] Paul Courant, Alan Deardorff, Roger Gordon, and Douglas Holtz-Eakin have made helpful comments and Daniel Polsky provided research assistance.

saved liquid assets, say in a rainy day fund, it is certainly feasible for this state to run a countercyclical deficit. Moreover, a great many states can and do make extensive use of borrowing privileges through their unemployment trust fund (Burtless and Vroman (1984)). In this way it is feasible for states to conduct countercylical policy even if they have not previously saved.

These general comments can be supplemented with one referring to the particular present day situation in the United States. Federal budget deficits are so large, and have proven so difficult to reduce, that very few people would now argue for old-time national fiscal countercyclical policy under any but the worst contractions until these deficits are better controlled. If there are to be attempts at fighting recessions through fiscal policy in the foreseeable future, they will probably have to be at the state level.

On the other side, there are two general considerations that may weaken the argument for subnational stabilization policy. One involves price flexibility – obviously any argument for having state governments try to stabilize their economies presupposes that fiscal policy can be effectively used to stabilize the economy. If it cannot, either because the prompt adjustment of prices maintains employment close to its full employment level in all states or because fiscal authorities just cannot be trusted to improve stability, any case for subnational fiscal policy is similarly weakened. The second concerns migration. If workers costlessly follow jobs around the country, there is no reason to worry about demand conditions in different areas. Moreover, the costs of taking on debt to fight recessions are greater, since many taxpayers will not be there to pay the bills.

In this paper I present a simple model that shows when it is rational for states to try to stabilize their own economies. The private sector is made of of life cycle consumers who optimally vary their expenditures over time in response to changes in state sales tax revenues. States then try to stabilize their economies by varying these sales tax rates so as to minimize a loss function with a cyclical term and debt burden term. The model determines the degree to which states should try to stabilize their own economies, with their response to demand shocks turning out to depend on the size of the state, the effective import propensity, and the cost of debt finance. These parameters can be estimated, and when plugged into the solution formula, they indicate that most states should be trying to stabilize their own economies much more than they do now.

I A model of state stabilization responses

The model used to examine the case for subnational fiscal policy makes several standard assumptions:

- Consumers behave according to the life cycle view, maximizing utility over their remaining lifetime. They do not offset fiscal policy by saving for their heirs.
- Labor is perfectly immobile over the cycle, an assumption that conforms reasonably well to reality (Gramlich (1987)). Capital is perfectly mobile at a fixed world interest rate, and the economy is open to trade across state lines.

- Demand shocks result in business cycles long and predictable enough to be reduced by fiscal policies.
- Prices are either stable, or the stabilization problem can be summarized by the government's choice of a target high employment income level for the jurisdiction.
- States can try to stabilize their economies by minimizing a loss function that depends on deviations of actual income from its desired level and on the cost of external debt.
- States finance their expenditures by proportional sales taxes on all consumption within the state.
- Although demand shocks are transmitted across state borders by changes in imports, states are assumed to be small enough that other states will not engage in strategic behavior. States in effect assume their exports are exogenous.

The basic properties of this model can be well demonstrated with a very simple life cycle model. Using a Cobb-Douglas household utility function and assuming for simplicity that the subjective rate of time preference equals the interest rate, the solution to a life cycle model that incorporates sales taxes into the budget identity is

$$C(1+t) = C_i (1+t_i) \qquad (1)$$

where C is this year's consumption, C_i is consumption in any future year i, t is the current state sales tax rate, and t_i is the anticipated rate for any future year. The equation expresses the simple notion that life cycle consumers try to stabilize consumption over time in the presence of sales taxes. But if consumers expect sales tax rates to rise, they will shift consumption to the present, and vice versa. Underlying growth or decline in consumption over time could easily be incorporated by including differences between the subjective rate of time preference and the interest rate, but the sales tax induced shifting of spending that is important for this model would still remain. In response to this shifting, states can raise or lower aggregate demand in their state by altering sales tax revenues.

Expression (1) can then be substituted into a lifetime income constraint to yield

$$C(1+t) = a(Y + V) \qquad (2)$$

where Y is current income, V is an exogenous variable that sums present net worth and the present value of expected future income, and a is a parameter that depends on the subjective rate of time preference.

Aggregate income in the state comes from the familiar income identity

$$Y = (C + G + X + e)(1-m) \qquad (3)$$

where G is state government spending, X is all other exogenous spending (investment, exports, federal spending, and so on), and m is the state's marginal propensity to import. The presence of G implies that the policy reactions could be solved in terms of government spending as well as sales tax rates, and indeed were in an earlier version of the paper (Gramlich (1987)). The residual e represents a spending shock which for now can be considered either common to all states or particular to a given state, and which is persistent enough that it can be combatted by fiscal policy.

State fiscal planners then try to minimize the loss function

$$L = \{Y^* - Y\}^2 + b\{A^* - A - dA\}^2 \qquad (4)$$

where L is the loss, A is the level of state assets at the start of the period, and dA is the change in assets, or the state government budget surplus. The loss function works by comparing actual levels of income and assets to target levels, though a simple quadratic expression in Y, $-Y^2$, A, and $-A^2$ gives approximately the same results. Both Y^* and A^* can be viewed as exogenous to the stabilization problem. On the basis of its fixed labor force and the fixed return on capital a state works out a realistic high employment income and asset target. Then if there is a negative spending shock its income and assets both fall, and the loss function tells the state how to reoptimize.

Concerning the asset argument, the present value of the consumption loss from any asset shortfall is $(A^* - A)$. Were this shortfall to be made up immediately, the consumption loss would be just $(A^* - A)$. Were it to persist, the annual loss would be $r(A^* - A)$, where r is the interest rate, and the present value when discounted at r would still be $(A^* - A)$. The parameter b, which translates debt burden cost into cyclical cost terms, might then be close to unity for a state with an excellent fiscal history. But if the state has already accumulated a great deal of debt so that marginal cost of further debt issuance is above the interest rate, b might be greater than unity. Or if there is a fear that taxpayers might migrate away from the future interest burden (even though not explicitly assumed in the model), b might again be high. If on the other hand the national government can be induced to increase spending to fight unemployment in a particular state, national taxpayers are bearing the brunt of the debt cost and b would be much less than unity, presumably close to the share of state value added in the national economy.

The state tries to minimize this loss function by altering sales tax rates subject to its own budget constraint

$$dA = tC - G \qquad (5)$$

In doing this, it has to balance its desire to minimize output cycles in its state with its desire to avoid running down its assets. Although the model does not explicitly deal with the question of how a state can distinguish cyclical downturns that can be combatted by policy from trend declines, inclusion of the target asset stock in the loss function provides for automatic regulation. As the stock of assets falls farther and farther away from its target, and its marginal finance cost grows, the state will be led to limit deficits more and stabilize cycles less.

The model is solved by finding the reduced form solution for the endogenous variables Y and dA, substituting into the loss function, differentiating with respect to sales tax rates, and solving for the optimal response of these sales tax rates to demand shocks, whether state or national. The solution is evaluated at the consumption level that generates full employment (C*) to give a concept akin to full employment revenues for the state. Since state policy-makers cannot directly observe the shock term, the useful way to present the results is in terms of the optimal change in full employment revenues per dollar of cyclical change in state income

$$\frac{dtC^*}{dY} = \frac{[1+t-a(1-m)]\,[(1-m)(1+t)\,-\,bat\,(1-a(1-m))]}{[1+t]\,[(1-m)^2\,+\,b(1-a(1-m))^2\,]} \tag{6}$$

When the debt cost parameter b is zero, the optimal state response is to raise full employment revenues by roughly the inverse of the GNP multiplier, as in a standard countercyclical model. But as b rises, the numerator falls and the denominator rises, so the optimal response falls.

Comparing expression (6) with what actually happens in the world, most states now leave their tax rates constant over the cycle, so that *actual* state revenues are cyclical, rising in expansions and falling in contractions (Gramlich (1978)). But expression (6) tells states that they should be doing more than that, raising full *employment* revenues in expansions and lowering them in contractions. One could imagine many reasons why states do not seem to follow such policies. The three most obvious are that:

- Such behavior is easiest when a state starts close to its target stock of assets, and states may be just as myopic as the national government in the way they have run down assets or accumulated debt. The political theory behind this myopia is that it may not make sense for one governor to accumulate assets in a boom, and take the accompanying political heat, so that those assets could be run down by some other governor in a recession.
- Perhaps because of myopia, states' implied b could be very high, giving a solution to (6) that is close to zero.
- States may treat most shocks as national shocks and wait for national monetary or fiscal policies to deal with recessions.

II Parameter values

I now evaluate (6) by inserting standard parameter values. The consumption propensity a can be estimated from micro or macro data. In macro terms it is simply the marginal propensity to consume, a consensus first year estimate of which is about 0.6. It has also been estimated for micro data within the confines of a life cycle model, yielding an income-weighted average of 0.8 (Courant, Gramlich, and Laitner (1984). This same value is close to the optimal value for a consumer of an average age in the early 40s, expecting to work another 20 years and live another 35 years, and to receive constant real income for the balance of her working period and then half that from pensions in retirement. Sensitivity tests on this parameter show it does not alter the value of (6) much, so I split the difference and assume a = 0.7.

The import propensity is a bit trickier because I am here concerned with that for a state. This is not the sort of parameter that shows up in anybody's econometric model, or even in many professional papers. But there is at least one available set of estimates based on input–output and industry shipment data (Regional Science Research Institute (1981)). The seven large states in the United States with a share of national value added between 0.05 and 0.10 have an average import propensity of 0.35. The twenty small states with a share of national value added of less than 0.01 have an average import propensity of 0.5.

There is one other parameter of interest even though it does not explicitly appear in the model. It involves the shock term e, specifically the share of shocks that are national in origin. If shocks are predominantly subnational, states must stabilize on their own, for there is no way the national government can stabilize within all states simultaneously. If shocks are predominantly national, it is not so clear what states should do. They could wait for the national government to stabilize, but it may be rational not to – say if the state knows that the national government will not take aggressive countercyclical action because it has a large debt of its own to contend with. The strategic implications in the latter case are interesting, but are not pursued here for lack of space.

As regards estimation, it is not easy to estimate the share of shocks that are national in origin. It is difficult to use state income data because of widely different trends in state income growth. A more promising approach focuses on state unemployment rates. For each state I fit a 26 year time series regression of the form

$$Uj = f[L(U), Z) \tag{7}$$

where Uj is the unemployment rate for the jth state, U is the national rate, $L(U)$ denotes a lag structure on this national rate, and Z is an unemployment rate trend variable. From this equation I compute two versions of the ratio n, the share of the variance of the dependent variable attributable to the national unemployment rate, or national shocks, for each state:

- n_1 is the simple R_2 from (7).
- n_2 is the share of the variance of the dependent variable attributable to $L(U)$ in estimating (7).

The first share averages 0.81 for all states, slightly above for large states and slightly below for small states. The second share averages 0.73 for all states, slightly below for large states and slightly above for small states. A reasonable summary is that national shocks have generated about three-fourths of all shocks for the average state over the past quarter century. One might anticipate this share to fall with greater flexibility in exchange rates, but for now there is too little experience to test the hypothesis.

These values are substituted in (6) to give response coefficients for a typical large state and a typical small state, all with $a = 0.7$ and $t = 0.1$. Separate responses are computed for the case where there is no burden to the debt ($b = 0$), say because it is assumed by some higher government (for simplicity ignoring the fact that the large state taxpayers will be responsible for a small share of that). The table also gives numbers for a government with an excellent fiscal history ($b = 1$) and for what may be a more normal fiscal history ($b = 2$). It is hard to know exactly what value of b is appropriate, but the various estimates show how sensitive the results are to this key parameter.

	b	m	dY/de	dtC*/dY
Large state	0	0.35	1.11	0.99
	1.0	0.35	1.11	0.55
	2.0	0.35	1.11	0.37
Small state	0	0.50	0.73	1.50
	1.0	0.50	0.73	0.51
	2.0	0.50	0.73	0.30

The numbers in the third column show how the model works by giving the normal fiscal multipliers for a large and small state. Both are reasonably low because of the strong open economy effects, but not zero. The numbers in the fourth column indicate that when $b = 1$, both large and small states should find it optimal to have full employment revenues rise by about half of the dollar change in state GNP following a cyclical shock, half or less of the optimal response in the case where there is no burden of the debt. The response to this unobserved demand shock is greater in the large state, but the response of income to this same shock is greater as well, with the consequence that the two changes roughly offset each other. This fourth column response drops to about one-third when the marginal cost of adding debt is high.

These quantitative estimates illustrate the qualitative statement made above that states should be in the stabilization business much more than they are at present, even if the burden of debt parameter is fairly high. Rather than holding sales tax rates constant and allowing revenues to rise and fall with the cycle, as happens now, the model suggests it would be optimal for states to fight at least their state demand shocks, and perhaps also their national shocks, by having full employment revenues rise and fall with the cycle. And, while such a comment could be made at any time, the importance of the issue is much greater now that the national government seems less likely to fight shocks by fiscal policy.

III Implications

The paper has tried to reexamine the conventional wisdom that states should not try to stabilize their own economies. In an open economy world where demand shocks may not be highly correlated across the country, where national fiscal multipliers may be small because of exchange rate flexibility, and where all debt is effectively external, the conventional wisdom seems seriously misguided. A simple model of the process finds that optimizing states, whether large or small, should be trying to lean against the wind with their fiscal policy substantially more than they do at present.

References

Burtless, Gary and Wayne Vroman (1984), 'The Performance of Unemployment Insurance Since 1979', Industrial Relations Research Association Series: Proceedings of the Thirty-Seventh Annual Meeting, December 1984, 138–47.
Courant, Paul N., Edward M. Gramlich and John P. Laitner (1984), 'A Dynamic Microeconomic Estimate of the Life Cycle Model', in Henry J. Aaron and Gary Burtless (eds), *Retirement and Economic Behavior*, Washington: The Brookings Institution.
Gramlich, Edward M. (1978), 'State and Local Budgets the Day After It Rained: Why is the Surplus So High?', *Brookings Papers on Economic Activity*, 1, 191–214.
Gramlich, Edward M., (1987), 'Subnational Fiscal Policy', *Perspectives on Local Public Finance and Public Policy*, 3, 3–28.
Medoff, James L. (1983), 'U.S. Labor Markets: Imbalance, Wage Growth, and Productivity in the 1970s', *Brookings Papers on Economic Activity*, 1, 87–120.
Oates, Wallace E. (1972), *Fiscal Federalism*, New York: Harcourt, Brace, Jovanovich.
Regional Science Research Institute (1981), 'State Input-Output Models for Transportation Impact Analysis', mimeo.

[10]

Public Employee Market Power and the Level of Government Spending

By PAUL N. COURANT, EDWARD M. GRAMLICH,
AND DANIEL L. RUBINFELD*

Recent budgetary rhetoric emanating from Washington and other governmental capitals suggests a growing fear that public spending is getting out of control. For long periods of time the government budget has grown more rapidly than *GNP* in most mixed economies, and observers of these trends have begun to realize that if this process continues, public expenditures will approach very high shares of *GNP* and income tax rates could get close to unity.[1]

These scare stories are counteracted by the simple question that if government gets too large, why can't voters band together to stop its growth? Rational, informed, democratic voting processes should provide a limit to the size of the public sector; indeed they should insure that the public sector is just as large as the voters want it to be. According to what economists have come to know as the "median voter" theory, it is puzzling to know exactly how government spending could ever get too high or out of control.

There have been several attempts to explain the apparent anomaly. The major focus of previous efforts has been on some aspect of bureaucratic aggrandizement, either broadly or narrowly construed. William Niskanen (1971), for example, presents a model in which bureaucracies desire to obtain as large a budget as possible for the bureau in which they are employed. (See also his 1975 paper.) Despite competition from other bureaus, the size of the overall governmental budget is larger than socially optimal because the nature of the budget process allows bureaus to act as price-discriminating revenue maximizers. Their ability to use their market power is constrained, both by competition from other bureaus and by the preferences of relevant legislative committees. As is implicit in the title of his work, *Bureaucracy and Representative Government*, Niskanen's major concern is with the way in which the institutions of representative government (particularly the *U.S.* federal government) may lead to an overprovision of public services. The model is not directly relevant to the behavior of local governments since it ignores two important constraints on local government spending. One is provided by households' opportunity to vote directly on referenda concerning tax collections, and the other by the ability of households to leave local jurisdictions in response to expenditure-taxation packages which they find to be unsatisfactory.[2]

More general in application than Niskanen's work are a number of papers which focus on the ability of public employees to influence the political process so as to increase both wages and the size of the public sector.[3] The implications of this approach have been discussed by a number of authors, but in each case the underlying model has been left unstated or undeveloped. For example, James Buchanan considers the possible ramifications of the right of public employees to vote when he argues:

*Department of economics and Institute of Public Policy Studies, University of Michigan. We would like to thank Theodore Bergstrom, George Borts, Harvey Brazer, Alan Deardorff, Arthur Okun, A. Mitchell Polinsky, and a referee for helpful suggestions.

[1] Much of this rhetoric is contained in popular articles: see Norman MacRae and Jude Wanniski. The relevant formal empirical literature involves a discussion of Adolph Wagner's law by such authors as Richard Wagner and Warren Weber and Richard Bird.

[2] A related approach, emphasized by political scientists but rarely by economists, concentrates on the voting pressure of the clientele groups of government programs. One economist's treatment of this issue is by Richard Craswell.

[3] The idea was treated in passing by Melvin Reder. See also John Pencavel. The empirical work of such authors as Ronald Ehrenberg and Gerald Goldstein, and Sharon Smith is also indirectly relevant.

Bureaucrats are no different from other persons, and, like others, they will rationally vote to further their own interests as producers when given the opportunity. Clearly their interests lie in an expanding governmental sector, and especially in one that expands the number of its employees. Salaries can be increased much more rapidly in an expanding agency than in a declining or stagnant one. [p. 14]

Buchanan clearly implies that bureaucratic size and market power are highly correlated, but doesn't consider any limits to the growth of government. The dynamics of bureaucratic and governmental growth are also analyzed by Gordon Tullock, who argues that bureaucrats will utilize their market power first to expand the size of the bureaucracy and then to increase wages. Once again, no explicit model is provided to permit consideration of forces that might check the growth of government.

A number of authors have extended the earlier work of Buchanan, Tullock, Niskanen, and others by focusing more specifically on behavioral and motivational differences between public and private employees. For example, Winston Bush and Arthur Denzau cite evidence that voter participation (and presumably support for the public sector) is higher for bureaucrats than for private sector voters, and conclude that higher public sector growth may be the result. A related argument is made in the paper by Thomas Borcherding, Bush, and Robert Spann, who suggest that bureaucrats view public goods as yielding higher (wage) income as well as utility from consumption. If public employees perceive this added dimension as a reduction in the price of public goods, then public employees will opt for a larger public sector.

While certainly not complete, this brief overview of the literature is suggestive. A number of reasons have been given as to why public sector growth might get out of control, without much discussion of the possible checks on governmental growth. As Buchanan and Tullock themselves state, "Presumably there is some limit on this process, but it has not been determined either theoretically or empirically" (p. 150).

In this paper we attempt to respond to the theoretical gap recognized by Buchanan and Tullock by providing a model that permits explicit analysis of some of the issues just raised. The context of the model is a local government beset by growing political and economic power of its own employees on one side, and the threat of mobility of the private sector on the other. As regards the former, it is natural, but not necessary, to view the process in terms of a cohesive public employee union that can bargain for uniform (and high) public wages, and also can choose to vote for a larger public employee work force (though we will see that this particular behavior can be suboptimal). In terms of the classic seller-buyer dichotomy that underlies almost all of economics, to the extent that public employees or their unions gain political power over the budgetary behavior of the jurisdiction, the problem becomes interesting because the suppliers of public goods are in part their own demanders, with the private sector having little to do but pay the bills.

Section I presents the assumptions of the model. Of particular importance is the assumption that public employees have some control over both their own wages and the level of public output. Section II shows how the size of the government budget and its composition between wage rates and employment are determined, first when the private sector workers are the dominant electoral bloc, and then when public sector workers assume control. The main object of interest in this latter case is the ratio of government spending to total income of the community, which will be shown to depend ultimately on the sensitivity of private sector location decisions to the cost of government services. In Section III we deal explicitly with how the competing demands of public and private sector employees might be resolved by a majority rule voting process, noting that public employee bargaining power can alter the level of public employment and public expenditures even when these employees are a minority of the total voting population. This has important implications for the median voter theory, at least in its simplified form, because it argues that even when the median voter is a private employee, the presence of public sector market power will result in a level of public sector expenditures which is influenced by public sector voting power as well as bargaining power. At the same time, the influence of public employees should be a good deal less than is often claimed in the popular press, because the threat of outmigration by private employees constrains the size of the public budget. In addition, for a given public budget, as the employee work force gets large, public wages must fall. Finally, in Section IV, we conclude by summarizing the implications of the analysis for the question of the controllability of public budgets and suggest some further policy issues that might be examined.

I. Assumptions of the Model

To clarify the analysis which follows, we first list the assumptions used in the paper, grouping them by topic.

ASSUMPTION 1. *Employee Optimization:* All actors in the model are employed in either the public or private sector,[4] and maximize utility functions with the arguments private consumption (C) and public output (E_g). The latter is measured exactly by the level of public employment. This assumption is the basis for the voting and private spending behavior of all employees.

ASSUMPTION 2. *Mobility and Tastes:* We assume that all private sector employees have identical tastes for public and private output, and all public sector employees have identical tastes, though the tastes of the public and private employees will in general not be the same.[5] Since a major theme of the paper is the effect of private sector mobility

on the size of the government budget, we assume that although private employees have identical tastes for output, their underlying desires to live in the community vary randomly. When things become sufficiently disadvantageous, those members of the private work force with the weakest desires to live in the community will leave.[6]

ASSUMPTION 3. *Goods and Labor Markets:* We make what might be known as small-country assumptions regarding the behavior of goods and labor markets. Private sector workers produce consumption goods (C) which are sold on a national market at a fixed price which we normalize at unity. All returns from the sale of these consumption goods are distributed equally to the private employees (E_p). Hence the private wage bill W_p (the private money wage) times E_p equals the gross value of private output (C).[7] Over the relevant range, there are no diminishing returns to private sector labor, so W_p remains constant. All private sector workers are assumed to supply labor inelastically as long as they remain in the community.[8]

ASSUMPTION 4. *The Public Sector:* We assume that the government must always balance its budget. Total revenues, the product of a tax rate and the tax base, must equal total expenditures, the product of the number of government employees (E_g) and their

---

[4]Implicit in this assumption is the existence of some mechanism (such as a union) whereby public employees determine who will work in the public sector. It is further assumed that once in the public sector, all public employees get paid the same wage, which, due to the limitation on entry, could exceed the private sector wage. The model could be extended to deal with seniority rules of various kinds.

[5]If an individual changes sectors, he is assumed to acquire the tastes associated with his current sector, either because of a socialization process or because he now has the same interests as others in his current sector.

The assumption of identical tastes within sectors will be relaxed in Section IV, where we consider distributions of tastes. Even there, however, we retain the assumption that if an individual changes sectors his tastes are drawn from the distribution associated with his current sector.

[6]We do not consider the potential mobility of public employees because our major interest is in private sector responses to the exercise of public sector market power. Whatever public employees are likely to do in response to the exercise of such power, it is unlikely that they will leave the community and thus abandon the fruits of their ability to exploit the private sector.

[7]Nonwage income can be incorporated into the analysis by viewing the private wage W_p as the gross pretax income of private workers from all sources, including capital ownership and returns to entrepreneurial services.

[8]It would be possible to incorporate a variable labor supply, but the qualitative results will differ little from those when private workers are free to leave the community.

annual money wage rate (W_g). The nominal tax base is simply total community wage income (both private and public). The tax rate on income is assumed to be proportional and uniform across all employees, though the model could easily be adapted to cases of progressive or regressive taxes. The level of government output (E_g) is determined by the majority voting of utility-maximizing citizens.

ASSUMPTION 5. *Income and the Tax Base*: Since all income in the community is wage income, total income may be represented by an index of wages (W^*) times total employment ($E = E_g + E_p$).[9] Thus,

$$(1) \qquad W^*E \equiv W_pE_p + W_gE_g$$

Note that when government employees have no bargaining power, $W^* = W_g = W_p$. With bargaining power, W_g can exceed W_p, and W^* becomes a weighted average of wage rates in the two sectors.

In the competitive case where employees have no bargaining power, all wages are taken as given and the tax base is fixed and independent of the composition of output between the public and private sector. When employees have bargaining power, upward changes in W_g will alter W^*E for two offsetting reasons: a) since private wage rates are fixed by the price of consumer goods, increases in W_g at a given E_g will tend to raise W^*E through the W_gE_g term; and b) since private employees are allowed to leave the community in response to monopolistic behavior by public employees, declines in E_p at a given W_p will lower W_pE_p and thus W^*E.

II. The Model

The results of the model are described by first calculating outcomes when private

employees are the dominant voting bloc—giving the standard outcome of prevailing public finance theories. We then contrast these results to those that are obtained when public employees are given control over public output, public wages, or both together.

A. *Private Employees*

Private sector employees are assumed to maximize a utility function of the form

$$(2) \qquad U_p = U_p(E_g, C_p)$$

where U_p is the level of utility achieved by private employees when optimizing with respect to the level of public sector employment and private consumption of private employees (C_p). The utility function is maximized subject to the budget constraint

$$(3) \qquad W_p = C_p + P_pE_g$$

where P_p is the price that the private employee must pay for the hiring of an additional public servant, and the private employee is assumed to be a price taker with respect to both private consumption goods and public employment.

The price paid by a private sector employee for a unit of public output is equal to the product of the cost of a public employee (the public sector wage, W_g) times the *share* of community-wide taxes paid by the private sector voter. If taxes are assessed on a per capita basis for all N residents of the jurisdiction, this price (W_g/N) is independent of the income of the private sector employee. However, with our assumption of a proportional income tax,[10] the share of wages the private sector voter must pay is W_p/W^*E, where W^*E is the tax base of the community.[11] The price of a public employee is thus given by

$$(4) \qquad P_p = W_gW_p/W^*E$$

---

[9]In effect, we have assumed that both sectors produce output by means of a constant returns-to-scale one-factor technology. Explicit consideration of two-factor production functions in either one or both sectors would both complicate and enrich the model. For example, one could examine a situation in which factor intensities differed in the two sectors, in which case changes in the allocation of labor would induce changes in the private sector wage. While such possibilities could be important, for the sake of brevity we do not treat them here.

[10]This approximates Joseph Pechman and Benjamin Okner's findings for the *U.S.* local government sector.

[11]If wage rates are fixed in the public sector but not the same in both sectors, changes in E_g voted on by private employees will reallocate labor between the two sectors and make a slight alteration in the nominal tax base of the community and therefore in the tax price for private employees. We assume that private employees are unaware of this effect and simply take W^*E as given.

After substituting (4) into (3), we obtain the budget constraint for the private employee:

$$(5) \qquad C_p = W_p \left(1 - \frac{W_g E_g}{W^* E} \right)$$

The private employee assumes that the tax base $W^* E$ and the prices he faces are not affected by his actions and maximizes (2) subject to (5). Solving the first-order condition yields

$$(6) \qquad \frac{U_1}{U_2} = \frac{W_g W_p}{W^* E} = P_p$$

This is the standard result (appropriate for both voters in political elections and private consumers) that the individual will desire to consume that amount of public goods which equates the marginal rate of substitution with the price ratio.

In the case of the *CES* utility function, for example, the utility function is

$$(7) \qquad U_p = [aE_g^{-r} + (1-a)C_p^{-r}]^{-1/r}$$

and the optimal level of public employment of condition (6) is

$$(8) \quad E_g = \left\{ \left[\frac{a}{1-a} \right]^{-1/(1+r)} \left[\frac{1}{W_p} \right]^{r/(1+r)} \right. $$
$$ \left. \cdot \left[\frac{W_g}{W^* E} \right]^{1/(1+r)} + \frac{W_g}{W^* E} \right\}^{-1}$$

where $r = (1-s)/s$, s being the elasticity of substitution, and a is the distribution parameter. It is easy to show that E_g is homogeneous of degree zero in all prices. In addition, $\partial E_g / \partial W_g$ will always be negative. The desired level of public employment arising from equations (6) and (8) is equivalent to the level of public output resulting from the familiar median voter model in which the median voter is a private employee. (See, for example, James Barr and Otto Davis; Theodore Bergstrom and Robert Goodman; Borcherding and Robert Deacon.)

B. Public Employees

The constrained maximization exercise for public employees is very similar. Employees are assumed to maximize

$$(9) \qquad U_g = U_g(E_g, C_g)$$

subject to

$$(10) \qquad W_g = C_g + P_g E_g$$

where C_g is the private consumption of the public employees and P_g is the tax price facing public employees; i.e.,

$$(11) \qquad P_g = W_g^2 / W^* E$$

At this point an important difference arises between the analysis for the public and private sectors. The difference is that while private sector employees take both public and private wages as given and choose their consumption of public goods (and thereby private goods as well), public employees are assumed to have greater choice. We analyze three cases. First, analogous to the private employee optimum, we consider public sector optimization when the public sector wage (W_g) is fixed. Second, we assume that E_g is fixed, and solve to find the wage rate public employees would set if they had unlimited bargaining power. Third, we combine the first two to find the optimum when E_g and W_g are simultaneously determined. Unless otherwise indicated, in all cases it is assumed that the public sector employees acting in concert are aware of the effects of their policies on the tax price which they face (equation (11)).[12]

For a given value of W_g, the optimal level of public employment for public sector employees is found through a straightforward extension of the private employee optimization exercise by substituting (10) and (11) into (9) and maximizing with respect to E_g:

$$(12) \qquad \frac{U_1}{U_2} = \frac{W_g^2}{W^* E} = P_g$$

or in the case of a *CES* utility function:

$$(13) \quad E_g = \left\{ \left[\frac{b}{1-b} \right]^{-1/(1+r)} \left[\frac{1}{W_g} \right]^{r/(1+r)} \right. $$
$$ \left. \cdot \left[\frac{W_g}{W^* E} \right]^{1/(1+r)} + \frac{W_g}{W^* E} \right\}^{-1}$$

[12]We are implicitly assuming that each public employee is naive in that he does not account for the fact that cuts in public output (i.e., E_g) will imply that there is a certain probability that a given public employee will lose his job and have his wage cut from W_g to W_p. Any attempt to account for this fully would substantially complicate the analysis. However, we might note that our discussion of bargaining strength in Section III does

where b is now the distribution parameter for public employees, but where the elasticity of substitution, $(1/1 + r)$, is the same as in the private case. Comparing (13) with (8), we see that the level of government employment desired by public employees is greater then that desired by private sector employees when

(14) $$(\frac{W_g}{W_p})^r > (\frac{1-b}{b})(\frac{a}{1-a})$$

In the usual case where $r > 0$ (demands for public expenditures are price inelastic), this condition is met with $W_g = W_p$ and $a < b$ (the basic demand shift parameter is higher for public employees), when $a = b$ and $W_g > W_p$ (the income effect of higher public wages outweighs the substitution effect), or when some combination of the two conditions holds. Differentiating both (8) and (13) with respect to W_g, we see further that

(15a) $$\epsilon_p = (\frac{-1}{1+r})(1 + r\frac{W_g E_g}{W^* E})$$

(15b) $$\epsilon_g = \epsilon_p + (\frac{r}{1+r})(1 - \frac{W_g E_g}{W^* E})$$

where ϵ_g and ϵ_p are the price elasticities of demand for public and private employees, respectively. Again, when $r > 0$ the public employee demand elasticity will be less negative than that for private employees because the public wage W_g now has a dual effect, raising the price of public goods while also raising the income of public employees.

The second case we consider assumes that E_g is fixed and finds the wage that government employees would prefer if they had unlimited bargaining power. Obviously the fact that employees prefer this wage does not mean they will get it, but it is still fruitful to go through the case to see how the government wage rate and wage bill will tend to move as employees gain bargaining power. The main limitation on the public sector wage rate in this case is the mobility of the private sector. We assume that there is at least one other accessible community and that public sector wage behavior is not identical in

all jurisdictions.[13] To delineate the behavior of private employees further, we assume that each individual's level of utility attained depends not only on the level of public output and private consumption, but also on the characteristics of the community per se (for example, terrain, accessibility to relatives). To summarize this fact, we assume that each individual obtains a *quasi rent* from residence in the community with its unique characteristics. We also assume that there is a distribution of quasi rents, with the quasi rent for each individual given by A^i so that the actual level of utility of individual i is

(16) $$U_p^i = U_p(E_g, C_p; A^i)$$

where each quasi rent A^i is drawn from a known probability distribution and is strictly separable with respect to the other arguments of the utility function. Assume that each employee decides whether to move by comparing his level of utility U_p^i to the level of utility achievable in the best of all other jurisdictions, $U_p''^i$. If U_p^i is greater than or equal to $U_p''^i$, the private employee remains in the community. If U_p^i is less than $U_p''^i$, emigration occurs.

To simplify the analysis we assume that the parameters A^i are chosen so that private employees can be ranked in terms of the level of quasi rents that they achieve in the original jurisdiction. Specifically, we assume that if $A^i > A^j$ for employees i and j, then $U_p^i - U_p''^i > U_p^j - U_p''^j$. Define A^* to be the minimum value of A^i for all private employees residing in the original jurisdiction, as shown in Figure 1. All citizens with A^i greater than or equal to A^* reside in the community; all with $A^i < A^*$ do not.

Now consider the impact of a change in the public sector wage rate W_g. The gross income earned by public employees ($W_g E_g$) obviously rises, but since the model is open to trade as well as migration, the price of goods sold by the private sector is fixed, as are the gross receipts earned ($W_p E_p$). Hence if there is no

---

implicitly allow for control over the wage, and thus potential public sector benefits, to vary with the current size of the public sector.

[13]As long as it is possible to incorporate entirely new jurisdictions, as it still is in many states, this assumption will be technically fulfilled; and as long as there are many jurisdictions where relative public sector wages are low, the assumption will be fulfilled in practice.

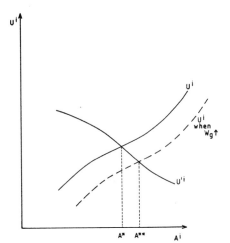

FIGURE 1. MOBILITY OF PRIVATE EMPLOYEES

migration W^*E will rise, but so will the tax rate on private income $W_g E_g / W^*E$. This increase in the tax rate implies that the consumption of private employees, given by (5) will decline, as will the utility of these employees. This outcome is shown graphically in Figure 1 as a downward shift in the U^i schedule. The result is an increase in A^* to A^{**}, the emigration of all private employees with A^i between A^* and A^{**}, a decline in E, and a decline in W^*E if the percentage decline in E exceeds the percentage rise in W^*.

In the more usual case the rise in W_g will lead to a decline in E_g (according to first-order conditions (6) or (12) above). Private employees then lose utility directly from the drop in E_g and indirectly if C_p falls (i.e., the tax rate rises). This in turn will happen whenever $W_g E_g$ rises, or whenever demands for public services are price inelastic.[14]

[14] The tax rate $W_g E_g / (W_p E_p + W_g E_g)$ obviously rises initially whenever $W_g E_g$ does. If $W_g E_g$ falls, there is a mathematical possibility that this fall in the tax rate would lead to a large enough utility *gain* from the increased C_p to offset the utility loss from the fall in E_g and actually encourage in-migration. This case makes no logical sense, however, because if the private sector could actually benefit from a higher W_g, it would already be paying such a wage.

As a general matter, then, we can assert that for relevant values of W_g, E_g, and W^*, private employment and earnings $(W_p E_p)$ will be negatively related to the public sector wage rate. If public sector employees are rational, they will take this mobility explicitly into account in determining their optimum wage levels, by recomputing the price of government services facing their members (equation (11)) as

$$(17) \qquad P_g = \frac{W_g^2}{W^* E(W_g)}$$

where W^*E has been replaced by $W^*E(W_g)$, indicating that the tax base is a function of W_g.

It then becomes important to see how W^*E changes with W_g. There are two offsetting influences: a) the rise in W_g will alter the government wage bill $W_g E_g$ directly; and b) the rise in W_g will reduce private employment E_p and lower the private wage bill and hence the tax base available to public employees. We can summarize these influences by defining the tax base elasticity with respect to public wages as

$$(18) \quad \eta = \frac{dW^*E}{dW_g} \frac{W_g}{W^*E}$$
$$= \left(W_p \frac{dE_p}{dW_g} + E_g + W_g \frac{dE_g}{dW_g} \right) \frac{W_g}{W^*E}$$

where the first term in the parentheses is clearly negative, the second is clearly positive, and the final term is probably negative but could actually go either way depending on who is setting E_g and the value of r (see equation (15b)). The highest η could be is $+1$ (when $dE_p / dW_g = 0$ and when $W_p E_p$ is very small relative to $W_g E_g$), but there appears to be no lower bound on the elasticity.

In the case we are considering, E_g is fixed, the third term in the parentheses drops out, and public employees maximize W_g given this level of E_g. This is tantamount to maximizing

$$(19) \qquad C_g = W_g \left(1 - \frac{W_g E_g}{W^* E(W_g)} \right)$$

which (differentiating with respect to W_g) yields

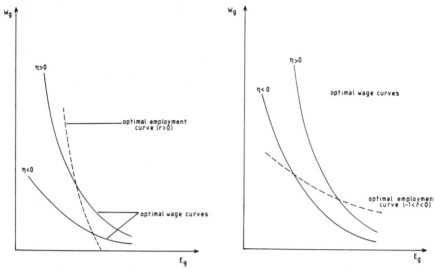

FIGURE 2. OPTIMAL WAGE AND EMPLOYMENT BEHAVIOR WITH MOBILITY

(20)
$$\frac{W_g E_g}{W^* E} = \frac{1}{2 - \eta}$$

Hence the optimum solution is for employees to set the *entire* government budget as a share of the tax base. Other things equal, as the fixed level of government employment rises, the optimum wage declines. Further, when η is close to its highest attainable value of $+1$, the share of the government budget in the total tax base, $W_g E_g / W^* E = t$, is close to unity: public employees take almost all of total output. But as η becomes negative, the share of government declines gradually. Indeed, in the opposite extreme case where the set of A^i for all private workers is sufficiently close to A^*, the private sector is so mobile and has so much bargaining power that the optimum public sector wage could get driven below the private wage. Again, we can rule out this outcome for logical reasons, because as soon as it begins to happen, public sector employees could also quit their jobs and work in the private sector. Hence (20) should be viewed as giving the upper bound on public wages and W_p as giving the lower bound.[15]

Next we consider the third case in which public sector employees are allowed to set E_g and W_g simultaneously. The first-order conditions (12) and (20) are the same, but now they must be solved simultaneously:

(21)
$$\frac{U_1}{U_2} = \frac{W_g}{E_g(2 - \eta)}$$

This simultaneous equilibrium is summarized graphically in Figure 2, where in each panel the dotted line is the expenditure first-order condition (12) and the two solid lines are the

---

[15] With some algebraic manipulation, it can be shown that (21) is exactly equivalent to the first-order condition for the maximization of total tax revenue collected from the private sector, R_p. Since R_p can be written as $t W_p E_p$,

$$R_p = t W_p E_p = \frac{W_g E_g}{W^* E}(W^* E - W_g E_g)$$

$$= W_g E_g \left(1 - \frac{W_g E_g}{W^* E}\right) - E_g C_g$$

When E_g is fixed, as in this case, the revenue taken from the private sector will be exactly proportional to the consumption of public employees, and maximizing C_g is the same as maximizing R_p.

possible wage first-order conditions (20), with the top line showing the situation where $\eta > 0$ and the bottom solid line showing the wage first-order condition when $\eta < 0$. As η becomes negative, the private sector is more mobile and the optimal wage for any E_g is shifted down. But the wage at which the ultimate intersection between the expenditure and wage condition takes place may be shifted either up or down, depending on public employees' price elasticity of demand for E_g (equation (15b)). If demand is inelastic (as in the left-hand panel), a community with a great deal of mobility (i.e., one in which η is negative) will have lower wages and a higher equilibrium level of government output than will a community with enough mobility so that η is exactly equal to zero. But if demand is elastic (as in the right-hand panel), a counterintuitive result arises: here the community with more mobility actually has a *higher* level of wages and a lower level of public employment than the community where not as much mobility is possible. Hence even though private sector mobility will constrain public employee wage demands at any given level of government employment, the full market equilibrium can lead to some surprising readjustments.[16]

III. Voting and Bargaining

In Sections I and II we described the determination by private and public employees of their desired levels of public employment. In this section we outline a resolution to the conflicting desires of private and public employees by introducing a simple majority-rule voting mechanism. In order to enrich the analysis we drop the assumption that the tastes of private and public employees are identical within groups, and instead assume that public and private employees have known distributions of tastes, which are in general different from each

other. Thus, the analysis of desired levels of W_g and E_g now becomes an analysis of the levels desired by the median (or, more generally, the decisive) member of each group, and we assume that the chosen level of public output is equal to the desired level of the median voter.[17]

Consider first the case in which the public sector has a fixed amount of bargaining power and there is no mobility. Real wages in the public and private sectors are not necessarily equal—they could be higher in the public sector—but they are independent of current expenditure demands and the composition of employment in the community. In this case both sectors can be assumed to know W_g and W_p and vote for their optimal level of E_g, given for the private sector in equation (6) and for the public sector in (12) (where these now give the levels chosen by the decisive member of the respective groups). In general the two expressions imply different demands for public employment for three reasons: a) if relative wages differ, incomes differ and the income effect will lead to different public employment demands; b) if relative wages differ, tax prices differ and the substitution effect may lead to different demands; and c) the basic parameters of the utility function may not be the same.

If W_g is in excess of W_p, consideration a) would induce public employees to vote for larger public employment, consideration b)

---

[16]A plausible argument can be made that this case is unstable, while the inelastic demand case is stable. If, for example, moving expenditures were lowered so that η drops, W_g might begin falling as public employees recompute their first-order condition. This moves us toward equilibrium in the left-hand panel of Figure 2 and away in the right-hand panel.

[17]It should be noted that voting is only one of several political mechanisms (say, campaign contributions) which might affect the determination of the level of public employment, and some of the other mechanisms are likely to be more effective from a political point of view. In addition to political mechanisms, there is also the possibility of resolving conflicting demands by using the familiar economic condition for optimal provision of public goods. In the context of our model, this would require finding the public sector wage W_g such that with proportional income taxes the levels of E_g chosen by both public and private employees would be the same; i.e., the tax prices for each group would be the Lindahl prices. In the CES example, this condition can be examined by making inequality (14) an equality and solving for W_g as a function of the relevant parameters. In the case where public employees have some wage-setting power, the notion of a Lindahl solution seems to us to have little meaning, since the level of W_g is the instrument by which one party exploits another, and hence is hardly agreeable to the private employee.

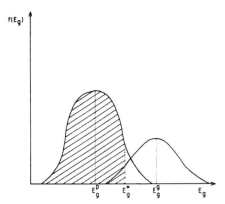

FIGURE 3. DISTRIBUTION OF VOTERS FOR
PUBLIC EMPLOYMENT

suggests smaller, and consideration c) is ambiguous, but probably dictates larger public employment. Regarding the latter, public employees might be sympathetic to the services they produce or have a job security motive where their own security depends on their seniority, which in turn would depend positively on the size of the public employee work force. As long as the substitution effect of higher public wages is small, and public employees have strong tastes for public output, they will vote for larger public employee work forces than will private employees, as shown in Figure 3.[18]

In light of these considerations we assume the median private sector voter will want a smaller public work force (E_g^p) than the median public employee (E_g^g). As long as E_g is less than half of E, there will more private sector workers (larger area) and the voting mechanism will result in an employment level between E_g^p and E_g^g, closer to the median of the private employee distribution, where the shaded area includes exactly one-half of the total voters and E_g^* represents the vote of the median voter of the entire resident population. Note that the median voter is either a private employee with a strong taste for public output (relative to that of other private

workers) or a public employee with a weak taste for public output (relative to that of other public employees).

The question becomes somewhat more intricate when we realize that wage bargaining strength might also be endogenous. Once the public employee work force rises to some critical level, these employees become strong enough to influence elections, and it does not take an extreme cynic to imagine political candidates attempting to bribe unions into supporting the "right" party either with high wage increases or with the promise of institutional changes that facilitate future union bargaining.[19] We might assume that when the public sector is very small, public employee wages are set competitively at W_p, but that as E_g grows, public employees have progressively more power in moving to their desired wage given in (20). But there is a catch here: recall that (20) implies $W_g = W^* E / E_g (2 - \eta)$. As soon as E_g rises to the value of $E/(2 - \eta)$, the *optimal* wage desired by public employees is equal to the wage received in the private sector. Hence the maximum ratio of W_g to W_p will be achievable at a value of E_g between 0 and $E/(2 - \eta)$. This is shown in Figure 4 as a result of a political weighting of the competitive wage line ($W_g = W_p$) and the optimal wage line of expression (20). If $\eta > 0$, the range of E_g/E for which $W_g > W_p$ will extend past $E/2$, implying that public sector workers could simultaneously have a small enough sector to raise their wages and a large enough voting bloc to achieve their wage and expenditure objectives. But in general η is probably less than zero and the optimum economic level of E_g, that at which W_g is maximized, is almost certainly a good deal less than the optimum political level of E_g (where the voting influence is strong enough that workers can achieve their wage first-order condition).

The preceeding discussion is both similar to and different from Tullock's "Dynamic Hypothesis on Bureaucracy." Like Tullock, we have assumed that bureaucrats' political power is endogenous, and can be expected to

---

[18]Note that when utility functions are Cobb-Doublas ($r = 0$), the income and substitution effects exactly offset each other and the respective voting tendencies depend only on consideration c.

[19]That this actually happens in the world can be seen from a discussion of the history of union wage negotiations in New York City, see Raymond Horton and Gramlich.

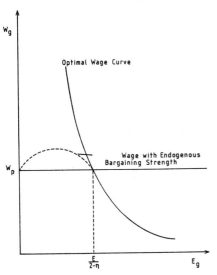

W_g

Optimal Wage Curve

Wage with Endogenous
Bargaining Strength

W_p

$\frac{E}{2-\eta}$ E_g

FIGURE 4. RELATIVE WAGES FOR THE
PUBLIC SECTOR

be increasing in the fraction of the population which is employed in the public sector. But our analysis differs from his in one important respect: he suggests that bureaucrats will use an increasing fraction of their power to raise public sector *wages* as their employment rises. In our model this is not possible beyond some point, because the public employee's own *optimum* wage *decreases* as the level of public employment rises. Furthermore, the downward-sloping optimum wage curve is inherent in the technology of "exploitation" of the private sector—even if all of private sector income could be expropriated and there were no mobility (i.e., η approaches unity), the amount of such income available to each public employee must perforce be decreasing in the number of public employees. Thus, while we agree with Tullock that public employee *political power* will increase in the level of public employment, the ability of public employees to convert that power into high wages will be attenuated both by the mobility of the private sector and by the simple arithmetic of "dividing up the pie."

Putting things in this light implies that even a strong public sector union should

ultimately be controllable. Since the total government budget desired by public employees is constrained by private sector mobility, public sector monopolies interested in maximizing the individual employee's wage will find it economically optimal to aim at a share of total employment that should be substantially less than $E/2$. As long as voting participation rates are the same among public and private sector employees, this assures that the public sector worker-voters will remain a minority. Moreover, there are two other constraints on behavior which temper public employee power even further: a) public employees themselves will be schizophrenic in the sense that their own public-private spending desires (equation (12)) may conflict with the E_g solution of Figure 4; and b) private sector employees may learn that increases in E_g increase the risk that the public sector can move toward its optimal wage curve, and these private employees may take this as another constraint in their own voting.

IV. Implications

At this point it may be helpful to return to the original message and pull together what this model has to say about it. The original fear was that as public servants are hired, they would become a steadily more dominant electoral force, elect politicians who would grant them steadily more market power, and the upshot of the rising levels of E_g and W_g would be steadily greater public budgets and higher tax rates. The public sector becomes dominant and the private sector is struggling, maybe unsuccessfully, for survival.

This model tries to put these fears in perspective by treating them analytically. The major conclusion is that as long as the private sector retains its right to leave the community, and as long as all communities are not suffering high and rising tax rates, public sector monopolies ought to be kept in check by the simple optimizing behavior of these same public employees.[20] It shows further

[20]This does not mean to imply that public sector unions always perform their optimization calculations correctly. A plausible interpretation of the recent history of New York City, for example, would be that the municipal unions' estimate of η was well above the true value of that

that the optimum public wage depends inversely on the size of government employment. Adding public employees may increase the political strength of unions but it also decreases the wage they will desire to attain. Finally, on the demand side, both public and private voters in their expenditure demands will also be price sensitive. As public employees try to enforce higher levels of public sector wages, private voters will force down the share of public employment, which should reduce even more the chance the public sector monopolies will be able to raise wages and exploit the private sector.

REFERENCES

J. L. Barr and O. A. Davis, "An Elementary Political and Economic Theory of Local Governments," *Southern Econ. J.*, Oct. 1966, *33*, 149–65.

T. C. Bergstrom and R. P. Goodman, "Private Demands for Public Goods," *Amer. Econ. Rev.*, June 1973, *63*, 280–96.

R. M. Bird, "Wagner's 'Law' of Expanding State Activity," *Publ. Finance*, No. 1, 1971, *26*, 1–26.

T. E. Borcherding and R. T. Deacon, "The Demand for the Services of Non-Federal Governments," *Amer. Econ. Rev.*, Dec. 1972, *62*, 891–901.

_____, W. C. Bush, and R. M. Spann, "The Effects of Public Spending of the Divisibility of Public Outputs in Consumption, Bureaucratic Power, and the Size of the Tax-Sharing Group," in Thomas E. Borcherding, ed., *Budgets and Bureaucrats: The Sources of Government Growth*, Durham 1977.

J. Buchanan, "Why Does Government Grow?," in Thomas E. Borcherding, ed., *Budgets and Bureaucrats: The Sources of Government Growth*, Durham 1977.

_____ and G. Tullock, "The Expanding Public Sector: Wagner Squared," *Publ. Choice*, Fall 1977, *23*, 147–50.

W. C. Bush and A. T. Denzau, "The Voting Behavior of Bureaucrats and Public Sector Growth," in Thomas E. Borcherding, ed., *Budgets and Bureaucrats: The Sources of Government Growth*, Durham 1977.

R. Craswell, "Self-Generating Growth in Public Programs," *Publ. Choice*, Spring 1975, *21*, 91–98.

R. G. Ehrenberg and G. S. Goldstein, "A Model of Public Sector Wage Determination," *J. Urban Econ.*, July 1975, *2*, 223–45.

E. M. Gramlich, "The New York City Fiscal Crisis: What Happened and What is to be Done?," *Amer. Econ. Rev. Proc.*, May 1976, *66*, 415–29.

Raymond D. Horton, *Municipal Labor Relations in New York City: Lessons of the Lindsay-Wagner Years*, New York 1973.

Norman MacRae, *America's Third Century*, New York 1976.

William A. Niskanen, "Bureaucrats and Politicians," *J. Law Econ.*, Dec. 1975, *18*, 617–43.

_____, *Bureaucracy and Representative Government*, Chicago 1971.

Joseph A. Pechman and Benjamin A. Okner, *Who Bears the Tax Burden?*, Washington 1975.

J. H. Pencavel, "The Demand for Union Services: An Exercise," *Ind. Labor Rel. Rev.*, Jan. 1971, *24*, 180–90.

M. W. Reder, "The Theory of Employment and Wages in the Public Sector," in Daniel S. Hamermesh, ed., *Labor in the Public and Nonprofit Sectors*, Princeton 1975.

S. P. Smith, "Government Wage Differentials," *J. Urban Econ.*, July 1977, *4*, 248–71.

G. R. Tullock, "Dynamic Hypothesis on Bureaucracy," *Publ. Choice*, Fall 1974, *19*, 127–31.

R. B. Victor, "The Effects of Municipal Unionism on Wages and Employment," unpublished doctoral dissertation, Univ. Mich., 1977.

R. E. Wagner and W. E. Weber, "Wagner's Law, Fiscal Institutes, and the Growth of Government," *Nat. Tax J.*, Mar. 1977, *30*, 59–68.

J. Wanniski, "Taxes, Revenues, and the 'Laffer Curve'," *Publ. Interest*, Winter 1978, *50*, 3–16.

parameter. Moreover, in constantly comparing their own wage levels to wage levels in other cities where the size of the public employee work force is smaller, these employees are hurting both the private sector (because the price of public services is raised) and ultimately themselves (because the tax base is falling).

[11]

WHY VOTERS SUPPORT TAX LIMITATION AMENDMENTS: THE MICHIGAN CASE**

PAUL N. COURANT*
EDWARD M. GRAMLICH*
DANIEL L. RUBINFELD*

H71 - 3240
U, S,

ABSTRACT

The paper reports on an attempt to survey a random sample of 2001 respondents in Michigan in 1978 to see why they voted for or against various tax limitation proposals. The results of the survey are that respondents in general do not favor large cuts in public expenditures and taxes—indeed, the median respondent desires no change in the overall level of government spending. Measures to predict the tax limitation vote of respondents based on those preferences were only partly successful—it was found necessary to combine preferences with information about perceptions of the likely impact of the amendments to explain the votes adequately.

IN November, 1978, voters in Michigan were faced with three Constitutional tax limitation proposals on the ballot. In light of the widely perceived "taxpayer revolt" stemming from the then recent passage of Proposition 13 in California, the Michigan proposals provided an ideal natural experiment for attempting to determine why people vote for such proposals; and in particular the nature, causes and extent of voter dissatisfaction with the budget performance of state and local governments. Does this dissatisfaction represent a conservative push toward smaller, or limited, levels of government spending, or does it reflect the feeling that voters may be able to lower their tax bills without undergoing a reduction in public services? In more formal terms, it also provided an opportunity to answer a question that is puzzling in light of the famous median voter theorem: Why would voters add amendments to the Constitution to constrain the behavior of their elected representatives?[1]

*Department of Economics and Institute of Public Policy Studies at the University of Michigan.

The natural reaction of social scientists interested in understanding the motives that underlie the tax limitation movement would be to ask voters, and in this paper we report on our attempt to do that. We conducted a telephone survey of 2001 Michigan residents sampled randomly, in the three weeks immediately after the election. Questions were asked about respondents' voting in the recent election, past voting behavior, political affiliation, income, family characteristics, tax payments, and perceptions about the state of the world and the impact of the proposed amendments. This paper gives the results of our first analysis of these data.[2]

The analysis begins in Section II with normative discussion of the use of tax limitation as a public policy tool, examining the specific Michigan proposals from this standpoint. In Section III we analyze voter tastes for both state and local spending, disaggregated by various demographic and economic characteristics. In Section IV we try to use these spending tastes to predict the tax limitation vote, with surprisingly indifferent success. Then in Section V we construct a more elaborate model of voting behavior, focusing on the importance of interactions between voter tastes and voter perceptions concerning the likely outcome of each of the amendments. We conclude by highlighting some of the implications of this analysis.

II. Tax Limitation as Public Policy

Statewide tax and expenditure limitations generally take one of two forms. They may be constitutional or legislative limitations on the fiscal authority of *local* jurisdictions, or they may be constitutional limitations on the fiscal authority of the *state* legislatures. The distinguishing characteristic is whether the limitation is an attempt to limit the behavior of

1

localities, one's own as well as others, or the behavior of the overall state government.

California's Proposition 13, which rolled back local property tax assessments and placed a ceiling on the tax rates, was clearly the first type of limitation, binding the fiscal behavior of all local governments in the state. The Michigan amendments were more complex than the California one, but they still can be broadly characterized. The Headlee Amendment, which passed with 52 percent of the overall vote, was essentially a limitation on the behavior of the state government. It limited state revenues from own sources to a constant share of state personal income, while prohibiting the state from mandating expenditures to local governments without paying for them. There was also a constraint placed on local fiscal behavior—property tax levies on existing property could not grow at a rate in excess of the inflation rate as measured by the Consumer Price Index without rates being cut automatically. However, these automatic cuts in rates could be prevented by an explicit local referendum on the matter.

The Tisch Amendment, which was defeated with 36 percent of the vote, would have been essentially a local limitation—requiring a large cut in the assessed value of property. In the presence of other restrictions already in the Michigan Constitution, this limitation would have forced property tax revenue cuts in some, though not all, local communities. It also would have placed a slight constraint on the fiscal behavior of the state government by limiting the state income tax rate, but other revenue sources would not have been restricted. Hence the Headlee Amendment was a limit on state taxing behavior with a modest constraint on the behavior of some localities, while the Tisch Amendment drastically limited the fiscal behavior of many localities, did not limit others, and placed a slight constraint on state taxing behavior. The third limitation amendment on the Michigan ballot in 1978, one that we asked about in our survey but are not analyzing here, called for an educational voucher plan to finance

local education but left almost all details of this complex plan unspecified. It received only 25 percent of the vote.

Several authors have recently considered the effects of state imposed expenditure limitations.[3] The papers are concerned mainly with the first type of limitation—statewide restrictions on local behavior—but could be made applicable to an efficiency evaluation of the second type—limitation on the own behavior of the state government. In either case, the passage of tax limitation proposals in Michigan and other states raises the basic question: What "disease" do voters see infecting the behavior of their state and local governments which leads them to opt for such powerful and inflexible "cures" as constitutional limits on revenues and/or expenditures? The literature identifies three motives:

1. Government can be too large because given prices, incomes, and technology, the absolute level of government services provided is greater than that which would be chosen by the median voter. This is the case dealt with in Niskanen's bureaucratic maximizer models, the agenda-setting models of Romer and Rosenthal, and the monopoly models of Denzau, Mackay, and Weaver.[4] Public managers and/or bureaucrats are responsible for the excessive government size.

2. A second way in which government can be considered too large arises when public employees earn wages that exceed competitive levels. In this case public budgets are high because rents are earned by public employees. Here the mechanism responsible for inefficiency is the familiar desire of unions to maximize their own income, a case considered in detail in our earlier work and also by Tullock.[5]

3. A third way in which government might be too large is that it may be inefficient in the sense that bureaucracy functions inside its production frontier. For example, Fiorina and Noll have developed a model in which government is predicted to use suboptimal factor ratios given market prices.[6] In spirit, this case is different from both cases (1) and (2) above, although it shares elements of both—like (1), there is too much absolute

input of real resources; like (2) the average cost of output is too high.

To attempt to establish which of these notions is on the public mind, we have tried to elicit respondents' taste for government spending and perceptions about the likely impact of the tax limitation amendments with a series of survey questions. We first analyze these questions on tastes for public spending, for specific types and in general, both to see how the taste distribution compares with tax limitation votes. We then develop an interactive model that combines tastes with perceptions about the likely impact of the amendments—will it cut spending, lower government wages, or whatever—to illustrate better why voters do and do not support tax limitation.[7]

III. Preferences for Public Expenditure

The most striking empirical result from the survey concerning tastes for public expenditure is that by and large citizens of Michigan are satisfied with current levels of output at both the state and local levels. Indeed, with the exceptions of spending on welfare programs, there is a decided sentiment for expansion (and a stated willingness to pay for expansion) in all of the program areas for which responses were elicited. This is clear from examination of Table 1, which gives information on the public spending preferences of all 2001 survey respondents, following a question sequence that has long been used by the Institute for Social Research.[8]

The first three columns of Table 1 give the program area and the number of persons who favored reductions and constancy in the level of expenditure in the areas, respectively. The column headed "More 1" gives the number of people who favored increased spending but answered no to the question, "If your taxes need to be raised to pay for the additional expenditures for [Program], would you still favor an increase in spending in this area?": The column headed "More 2" gives the number of people who answered yes to that question.[8a] Finally, "mean strong preference" is derived by assigning a value of minus one to those who wanted reduced spending, zero to those who wanted the same or "More 1," and one to those who wanted "More 2," and dividing by the total number of answers to the question.

Thus in every program but welfare, the number of people willing to pay for increases in expenditures exceeded the number expressing a desire for reduction.[9] To the extent that there is a taxpayer revolt in Michigan, it would seem to be a revolt against welfare spending, ironically a type of spending that in Michigan (as in most other states) is financed about equally by the federal and state-local governments.

The preceding interpretation is strengthened when we consider stated preferences regarding state and local

Table 1

Preferences for Spending by Program Area

All 2001 Respondents

Program Area	Less	Same	More 1	More 2	No Response	Mean Strong Preferences[a]
Police/Fire	68	1163	97	615	58	.282
Welfare Spending	1262	499	44	127	69	-.587
School Spending	296	882	108	635	80	.176
College Spending	196	977	126	545	157	.189
Road Maintenance	120	824	295	698	64	.298
Parks & Recreation	209	1117	145	485	45	.141

a. Assigning values of 1 to "More 2," 0 to "Same" and "More 1," and -1 to "Less" in the numerator, and dividing by total number of responses.

spending as a whole. For each of the two levels of government, respondents were informed of the major functional responsibilities of the respective levels, and were then asked if they would favor an across the board increase, decrease, or no change in both spending and taxes, were all spending and tax categories to be changed proportionately. Furthermore, if they favored an across the board increase or decrease in spending and taxes, they were asked to give their desired percentage amount. The results from these questions are summarized in Table 2.

The first six columns give the distribution of desired spending changes, classified into cuts and increases of less and more than ten percentage points. The seventh column gives the implied value for mean strong preferences, computed as before, and the last give the mean and standard deviation of the desired percentage changes. Perhaps the most important result of the Table is that the mean percentage change desired is very close to zero, only −3.53 percent at the state level and −0.22 percent at the local level. These mean changes are small relative to the within group standard deviations, in the last column. Indeed, if a median respondent analysis was applied to this Table, the desired changes would be zero. Since more than half the respondents opt for no change at both levels of government, the median respondent is apparently happy with the status quo at both the state and local levels, implying that the state is in median voter equilibrium.

There is one interesting similarity of these results with those of Table 1, and one interesting difference. The similarity is that respondents were informed in the question that the state government is responsible for the nonfederal portion of welfare spending. Thus the relatively poor showing of the state government relative to localities could be due to the marked desire for reduced welfare spending found in Table 1. The interesting difference is that preferences for overall spending are lower for both levels of government than are preferences for the sum of their parts. While there may be some subtle change in the wording causing this difference, it

is consistent with the modern theory of representative democracy and the economic analysis of logrolling behavior due to Downs, Buchanan and Tullock, and others.[10] With the exception of welfare, there is a strong majority of the population in favor of current or increased levels of spending in each program area. But support for the total is weaker because everyone perceives the possibility of cuts in program areas favored by others. To the extent that logrolling is effective, that is exactly what one would expect to observe.

It is perhaps unwise to take these results too seriously because of the large number of voters opting for the same amount of public spending, over half the sample at both the state and local level. One might argue that some of the voters preferring the status quo were really either uninformed or unable to comprehend the question. To see how sensitive our results were to this possibility we recalculated means and medians with the voters opting for the same amount of spending omitted, obtaining mean and median percentage changes of −7.8 and −8.3 at the state level and −0.5 and 4.5 at the local level. Even this strong correction—surely an overreaction because *some* of those opting for no change must have truly felt that way—did not give very large reductions in desired state spending, and had very modest impacts at the local level. The clear conclusion, in line with what Curtin and Cowan and Citrin have found, is that at least as respondents answer explicit questions, there appears to be a desire for only a modest cutback in state spending and essentially no change in local spending. We might also predict that a statewide tax limitation amendment like Headlee would have a better chance of passage than a local limitation amendment like Tisch, but that gets ahead of our story.

We can then look behind these preferences to see how they vary by demographic and economic characteristics. This is done by using the percentage change responses of Table 2 as dependent variables in cross-section variables. Since we are mainly concerned with the preferences of voters (those of nonvoters are unlikely to be of

Table 2

Preferences for Overall State and Local Spending and Tax Changes

All 2001 Respondents

	Level of Government	
	State	Local
Desired Cut		
More than 10 percent	226	125
Less than 10 percent	402	174
No Change	1027	1190
Desired Increase		
Less than 10 percent	167	368
More than 10 percent	20	51
No Response	159	93
Mean Strong Preference[a]	-.239	.063
Mean Percentage Change	-3.53	-0.22
Standard Deviation	8.83	8.41

a. We categorized the specific quantitative responses to simplify the presentation.

b. Computed as in Table 1 for comparability.

great importance in explaining tax limitation voting behavior) at this point we alter the sample to include those respondents who actually voted on the Headlee or Tisch Amendments (1028 and 1039 respectively). Since we have no value for the dependent variable when voters did not respond to this question, we also must omit nonrespondent voters.

The results for 870 Headlee voter-respondents and 916 Tisch voter-respondents are shown in Table 3. The Table gives the mean desired spending change for each independent variable class, holding constant the influence of all other variables, and compared with the overall mean desired changes for the voter respondents (slightly below the numbers given in Table 2). These comparisons, incidentally, are given for state spending in the case of the Headlee Amendment (because that's what it could limit) and local spending for the Tisch Amendment (because that's what it could limit).

Perhaps the most striking result of Table 3 is the relatively limited variation in the magnitudes of the adjusted means (this is also true for the unadjusted means). Other things equal, federal government employees living in the state

want the least state expenditures, while blacks want the smallest cuts. However, even blacks would like slightly less spending than is now undertaken—and the difference between the two groups is only about 5 percentage points. Likewise for local expenditures: federal government employees are among the most negative and blacks the most positive. In this case, however, blacks do support increases in local spending, as do a few other subcategories of the population.

Despite the relative uniformity of tastes, there are some important differences among groups which are quite interesting and which might conform with *a priori* expectations. First, note that in the case of state spending, tax price bears an inverse relationship with desired spending. The low absolute value of the coefficient for renters supports this interpretation, since renters probably perceive the lowest tax price for public services. The same general result holds for local spending, except that the magnitude of the coefficient of the third tax price variable is slightly out of order. Thus, relative property tax payments clearly matter to voters, and both spending equations are consistent with what one would expect

Table 3

Regressions Explaining Public Spending and Tax Desires

	870 Headlee Voter Respondents Dependent Variable: Desired Percentage Change in State Spending and Taxes		916 Tisch Voter Respondents Dependent Variable: Desired Percentage Change in Local Spending and Taxes	
	Mean = -4.13 St. Dev. = 8.66 R^2 = .07		Mean = -0.86 St. Dev. = 8.00 R^2 = .06	
Independent Variables	Adjusted Mean[a]	Cases	Adjusted Mean[a]	Cases
Children				
None (of age < 18)	-4.98	474	-1.79	498
In private School	-2.55	63	0.19	70
In public school	-3.21	333	0.25	348
	Beta[b] = 0.11		Beta[b] = 0.13	
Marginal Tax Price[c]				
Price < 1.5	-3.85	135	-0.56	129
1.5 < price < 3.0	-4.00	216	-0.75	232
3.0 < price < 4.5	-4.47	172	-2.16	178
price ≥ 4.5	-5.49	187	-1.24	210
Renters	-2.59	160	0.60	167
	Beta = 0.11		Beta = 0.11	
Sex				
Male	-4.91	426	-1.62	431
Female	-3.38	444	-0.19	485
	Beta = 0.09		Beta = 0.09	
Education				
< 12 years	-3.97	120	-0.14	121
12 years	-4.35	307	-0.75	338
13-15 years	-4.46	234	-1.15	241
16 + years	-3.43	204	-1.11	212
No response	-7.25	5	-1.63	4
	Beta = 0.05		Beta = 0.04	

Table 3 (Continued)

Income				
$0 - 10,000	-4.18	164	-1.34	177
$10,000 - 15,000	-2.13	120	-0.51	124
$15,000 - 20,000	-5.12	143	-1.20	152
$20,000 +	-3.93	308	-0.24	316
No response	-5.24	135	-1.58	147
	Beta = 0.11		Beta = 0.07	
Religion				
Protestant	-4.10	524	-0.85	540
Catholic	-4.27	266	-1.04	293
Other	-3.86	80	-0.32	83
	Beta = 0.01		Beta = 0.02	
Race				
White	-4.30	790	-1.03	835
Black	-2.06	66	1.89	68
Other	-5.48	11	-4.90	10
No response	1.10	3	-2.52	3
	Beta = 0.08		Beta = 0.11	
Employment				
Unemployed	-4.30	133	-1.25	153
Local government	-2.89	43	0.31	43
School district	-2.82	72	0.05	74
State university	-3.77	13	2.00	13
State government	-3.73	23	1.32	26
Federal government	-6.99	18	-4.99	20
Private	-4.63	453	-1.14	464
Retired	-2.93	113	-0.45	120
No response	-3.02	2	2.63	3
	Beta = 0.10		Beta = 0.12	
Gloom				
Next 5 years better	-3.60	359	0.25	371
Don't know	-3.43	269	-0.93	288
Next 5 years worse	-5.84	219	-2.55	233
No response	-4.29	23	-0.96	24
	Beta = 0.12		Beta = 0.14	

Table 3 (Continued)

Regressions Explaining Public Spending and Tax Desires

870 Headlee Voter Respondents
Dependent Variable: Desired Percentage Change in State Spending and Taxes

Mean = -4.13
St. Dev. = 8.66
R^2 = .07

916 Tisch Voter Respondents
Dependent Variable: Desired Percentage Change in Local Spending and Taxes

Mean = -0.86
St. Dev. = 8.00
R^2 = .06

Independent Variables	Adjusted Mean[a]	Cases	Adjusted Mean[a]	Cases
Political Party				
Republican	-5.16	305	-0.97	316
Democrat	-2.78	379	-0.58	403
Independent	-5.32	178	-1.41	187
No response	-2.21	8	1.11	10
	Beta = 0.14		Beta = 0.05	

a. The adjusted mean controls for all the other variables included in the model. It is calculated as the overall mean of the dependent variable plus the deviation from that mean associated with the coefficient for each individual subgroup.

b. The beta statistic provides a measure of the overall importance of individual predictors in explaining variation in the dependent variable. It is calculated as a weighted average of the squares of the individual regression coefficients associated with the subgroups of the given predictor variable. (For details, see F. Andrews, J. Morgan, W. Sonquist, and L. Klem, Multiple Classification Analysis, 2nd Edition, Institute of Survey Research, University of Michigan.)

c. The marginal tax price is calculated as the ratio of the individual's assessed house value (in $) to community taxable property base per capita (in $).

from a normal spending demand function, though with rather small price elasticities.

The results for the demographic variables indicate, as expected, that individuals in families are more likely to favor public spending, as are females. It is surprising, however, to find a very weak relationship between education and desired spending. The common view that higher education leads to a taste for relatively more government spending is weakly supported for state spending, but not for local spending. Income, although highly significant, had no clear impact on tastes for public spending. These income results appear to imply a very low income elasticity of demand for public spending, but a careful test (in progress) awaits the inclusion of the level of expenditures that is being altered.

To test the relationship between macroeconomic events such as inflation and unemployment and voter public spending preferences, we defined what we might call a "gloom" variable. This variable distinguished those who thought they would be better off in the next five years from those who felt the reverse. As expected, the pessimists wanted lower public spending (but just a small amount), while the optimists were more neutral. Also we included political affiliation, finding, as expected, that Republicans wanted spending cutbacks at the state level, and, as not expected, that Democrats do also. But, persons affiliated with neither party favored less spending than party members. At the local level political affiliation was unimportant in explaining desired spending changes.

Of greatest interest to us, in light of our concern with the political effects of private versus public sector employment, is the role of the employment status variable. Here we find that private sector voters want less state and local public spending than those in the public sector, especially if one counts federal employees as being in the private sector from the point of view of the political economy of the state of Michigan. But the fact that the marginal effect of employment status on tastes for government spending is of the right sign does not change the fact that the differences are small.

IV. Explaining Votes with Preferences

Until now we have reported and tried to explain state and local public spending demands. The next question is whether these spending demands themselves can predict the vote on the Headlee and Tisch Amendments. We are, in effect, using our survey question to develop an explanation of the vote that is more precise than the one usually given, where individual attributes such as those listed in Table 3 are taken as proxies for spending preferences.[11] To answer this question, we use preferences as independent variables in regressions explaining the vote. Following the procedures adopted above, we use state spending desires as the independent variable explaining the vote on the Headlee Amendment, and local spending desires as the independent variable explaining the vote on the Tisch Amendment. As before, we restrict the sample to those who voted on the respective amendments.

The results are given in Table 4. For each pair (Headlee-State, Tisch-Local), three sets of numbers are given: The share of voters in that class voting for passage, the number of voters in the class, and the t ratio of regression coefficients (not shown) explaining the zero (no vote), one (yes vote) probability of voting for the amendment with just these binary variables.[12] The t ratio tests whether there is a significant difference between those in a given category and those wanting the same amount of spending and taxes. Since the independent variables are in binary form (all favoring an increase are in the dummy class), for this test we are no longer using information telling us by how much voters want to increase or decrease public spending.

The first thing to notice about the table is the difference between actual and reported voting results. The Headlee Amendment actually passed with 52 percent of the statewide vote, but 56.2 of our sample report voting for it. The Tisch Amendment actually received 36 percent of the statewide vote, but only 26.2 percent of our sample voting for it. Part of these discrepancies may be due to sampling bias,

Table 4

Spending Tastes as a Predictor of Votes

Dependent Variable	Headlee and State Spending			Tisch and Local Spending		
	Mean Share	Cases	t Ratio	Mean Share	Cases	t Ratio
Vote on amendment	.562	1028	--	.262	1039	--
Independent Variables						
Desire more spending and taxes	.356	90	2.8	.155	193	2.2
Desire same spending and taxes	.514	510	---	.233	632	--
Desire less spending and taxes	.675	403	4.8	.449	196	6.2
Don't know	.600	15	0.2	.444	9	1.5
No response	.300	10	1.3	.444	9	0.7
Fit Statistics						
Adjusted coefficient of determination	.039			.046		
Votes correctly predicted	.591			.738		
Correct predictions with random assignment[a]	.508			.614		
Improvement over random assignment	.083			.124		

a. Derived by assuming that the percent of yes and no voters assigned is the
    same as the percentage of yes and no voters in the sample, as explained in the text.

but we suspect that even though surveyed immediately after the election, voters are somewhat selective in their recollections about the vote and may not want to admit voting for the losing side.

Concerning the independent variables, the results correspond to prior expectations. Only 36 percent of those desiring more state spending and taxes voted for Headlee, while 67 percent of those desiring less state spending and taxes voted for the amendment. For Tisch the same percentages were 16 and 45 respectively. The fact that 51 percent of those desiring the same spending and tax levels supported Headlee may be surprising if Headlee is interpreted as altering the status quo, but

these voters could have interpreted Headlee as preventing government spending (as a proportion of income) from growing further, and thus *preserving* the status quo.

While these results may or may not be plausible, they are not very powerful. The coefficients of determination adjusted for degrees of freedom are only .039 and .046 respectively, quite low even considering the fact that the conventionally-measured fit statistic is very likely to be substantially less than one in a regression with a 0–1 dependent variable.[13] A more relevant fit statistic can be derived by measuring the percentage of votes correctly predicted by the regression as if one were using discriminant analysis.[14] The Head-lee regression correctly predicts 59.1 per-cent of the votes and the Tisch regression 73.8 percent of the votes.[15] These numbers by themselves are not very meaningful because even a straight random assign-ment of voters would correctly predict close to half the votes for Headlee and even a higher percentage for Tisch (be-cause the mean probability is farther from .5). Hence a better fit statistic can be derived by comparing the proportion of votes correctly predicted with the propor-tion predicted by random assignment. If, for example, .56 of the sample actually voted for Headlee, under a random as-signment of voters $(.56)^2$ percent would be predicted to vote for Headlee and would have voted for it (in the sample); while $(.44)^2$ percent would be predicted not to have voted for Headlee and would not have voted for it (in the sample). The random assignment proportion in the Headlee case then becomes $(.56)^2 + (.44)^2 = .508$. A similar calculation for the Tisch amend-ment indicates that a random assignment model would predict correctly with proba-bility $(.26)^2 + (.74)^2 = .614$. In some sense, then, the Headlee regression has raised the current prediction proportion by only .083 and the Tisch regression has raised it by only .124. The result is that while spending preferences and the vote on tax limitation are correlated as expected, there is a good deal of variation in the vote left to be explained.[16]

V. Perceptions About Tax Limitation

Given that spending preferences alone do not provide a very powerful explanation of tax limitation voting, we now try to do better by interacting spending prefer-ences with perceptions about the likely impact of the limitation amendments. The way in which this is done is by using answers to a series of perception questions about the likely impact of the limitation amendments. The questions followed the format: "Do you think the passage of the Headlee (Tisch) proposal will lead to:

a) a reduction in the overall level of taxes in Michigan

b) a reduction in property taxes

c) an increase in income taxes

d) a reduction in the number of state and local government employees

e) a reduction in the funds available to the local public school system

f) a reduction in the future wage in-creases of government employees."

These questions were followed by the open-ended question of what respondents thought would be the most important impact of the amendment. Perhaps in giving the choices listed in a) to f), the sequence of questions increased the prob-ability of one of our answers being selected as the most important impact, but other responses were possible and were quite frequently given.

Spending preferences and perceptions about the likely impact of the amendments should have an interacting effect on votes. If, for example, a voter perceived that the Headlee amendment would lower public spending and desired less spending, the voter should support the amendment. If the voter had the same perception but desired more spending, the voter should vote against the amendment. We have constructed regression models explaining the vote on both amendments along these lines. The dependent variable was coded as one if the voter voted for the amend-ment and zero if against, just as in Table 4. The independent variables were a series of perception-taste interactions, patterned on the above example. Whenever relevant, the variables were further split according to whether voters were in the public or private sector, and hence would view an outcome such as lower government wages or employment differently. For these purposes all nonworking respondents were considered as private (they would still pay property and sales taxes) as were all working in the federal government (in keeping with our spending taste results above). All those working and nonworking respondents with either the respondent or spouse working in the state or local public sector, about 11 percent of the sample, were considered public.

The results are shown for the Headlee vote in Table 5. The table gives the actual regression, listing the independent varia-bles by group (all, public, or private),

Table 5

Regression Model Explaining Headlee Vote

1028 Headlee Voters
Adjusted R² = .204
Proportion of votes correctly predicted = .736
Improvement over random assignment = .228
Constant, private employees = .525
Constant, public employees = .452

Variable No.	Group	Most Important Impact of Headlee	Perceptions		Cases	Coefficient	t Ratio
			Headlee will	Preferences			
1.	All	Reduce spending	--	More state spending	18	.012	0.1
2.	All	Reduce spending	--	Same state spending	74	.142	2.2
3.	All	Reduce spending	--	Less state spending	66	.302	4.4
4.	Priv.	Reduce taxes	--	Same state spending	80	.139	2.2
5.	Priv.	Reduce taxes	--	Less state spending	78	.212	3.1
6.	Pub.	Reduce taxes	--	Same state spending	27	.288	2.8
7.	Pub.	Reduce taxes	--	Less state spending	13	.333	2.1
8.	All	Increase taxes	--	More state spending	14	-.285	-1.7
9.	All	Increase taxes	--	Same state spending	25	-.157	-1.5
10.	All	Increase taxes	--	Less state spending	32	-.225	-2.2
11.	All	Hurt schools	--	More school spending	11	-.094	-0.6
12.	All	Increase govt. efficiency	--	Govt. wastes much	21	-.358	3.4
13.	All	Increase govt. efficiency	--	Govt. wastes some	22	.201	2.0
14.	All	Increase voter control	--	Trust govt. usually	41	.391	5.0
15.	All	Increase voter control	--	Trust govt. little	36	.441	5.3
16.	All	No change	--	--	102	-.037	-0.6
17.	All	Don't know	--	--	200	-.049	-1.0

Table 5 (Continued)

No.							
18.	Priv.	—	Reduce wage increases	Govt. workers earn more	171	.029	0.7
19.	Priv.	—	Reduce wage increases	Govt. workers earn same	136	.072	1.5
20.	Priv.	—	Reduce wage increases	Govt. workers earn less	27	-.114	-1.2
21.	Pub.	—	Reduce wage increases	Govt. workers earn more	43	-.108	-1.3
22.	Pub.	—	Reduce wage increases	Govt. workers earn same	31	-.167	-1.8
23.	Pub.	—	Reduce wage increases	Govt. workers earn less	27	-.106	-1.1
24.	Priv.	—	Reduce taxes	More state spending	12	.303	2.0
25.	Priv.	—	Reduce taxes	Same state spending	86	.095	1.6
26.	Priv.	—	Reduce taxes	Less state spending	107	.155	2.7
27.	Pub.	—	Reduce taxes	Same state spending	15	.013	0.1
28.	Pub.	—	Reduce taxes	Less state spending	15	-.011	-0.1
29.	Priv.	—	Reduce property taxes	More local spending	38	.126	1.6
30.	Priv.	—	Reduce property taxes	Same local spending	145	.090	1.9
31.	Priv.	—	Reduce property taxes	Less local spending	57	.178	2.5
32.	Pub.	—	Reduce property taxes	More local spending	15	.174	1.4
33.	Pub.	—	Reduce property taxes	Same local spending	28	.094	1.0
34.	Priv.	—	Increase income taxes	More state spending	43	-.048	-0.6
35.	Priv.	—	Increase income taxes	Same state spending	243	-.045	-1.1
36.	Priv.	—	Increase income taxes	Less state spending	184	-.039	-0.9
37.	Pub.	—	Increase income taxes	More state spending	23	-.055	-0.5
38.	Pub.	—	Increase income taxes	Same state spending	73	-.060	-0.8
39.	Pub.	—	Increase income taxes	Less state spending	43	.025	0.3
40.	Priv.	—	Lower govt. employment	Workers work same	103	-.077	-1.5
41.	Priv.	—	Lower govt. employment	Workers work less	203	-.028	-0.7
42.	Pub.	—	Lower govt. employment	Workers work same	34	.030	0.3
43.	Pub.	—	Lower govt. employment	Workers work less	39	.159	1.9
44.	Priv.	—	Reduce school funds	More school spending	81	-.118	-2.1
45.	Priv.	—	Reduce school funds	Same school spending	148	-.141	-3.3
46.	Priv.	—	Reduce school funds	Less school spending	54	-.110	-1.6
47.	Pub.	—	Reduce school funds	More school spending	56	-.259	-3.4
48.	Pub.	—	Reduce school funds	Same school spending	49	-.240	-3.1

perception about the likely impact of the amendment (most important or other), and tastes for public spending and taxes (more, same, or less) or perception about the state of the world (government workers earn more, work harder, etc.). The number of cases in each category is shown, along with the regression coefficient and its t ratio. Whenever the interaction term had less than ten cases, the binary variable was omitted from the regression.[17] Separate constants were estimated for public and private employees through another dummy.

The first thing to be noticed is that the fit is much improved over that in Table 4, when just spending tastes were used without regard to perceptions about the amendment. The adjusted coefficient of determination is now .204, more than five times greater than before. Now 73.6 percent of the votes are correctly predicted, an improvement of .228 over the random assignment naive model. This improvement is almost three times as great as in Table 4.

Most of the regression coefficients are statistically significant and more or less internally consistent, though in some cases puzzles are raised. For example, among the voter-respondents who perceived the most important impact of the Headlee Amendment would be to reduce government spending (variables 1 through 3), those wanting more state spending and taxes were evenly split on the amendment while those wanting less state spending and taxes voted heavily for the amendment (for private employees in this latter case, the proportion of yes votes was the regression constant, .525, plus the coefficient, .302, or .827). Among those who felt the Headlee Amendment would have tax reduction as its most important impact, support was very strong for the amendment (coefficients of variables 4 through 7), even when voters favored the same level of state spending and taxes (as in variables 4 and 6). The obvious rationalization of this behavior is that these voters felt that taxes could be cut without a reduction in spending, either because of supposed efficiency gains or the free lunch illusion. We might go further and even imagine a motive based on the uncertainty about the impact of the amendment: voters feel fairly certain their taxes will be cut, but much less certain that public services affecting them will. Whatever the case, this behavior is mirrored among the 71 cynics who felt the most important impact of the amendment would be to *increase* taxes—these voters were strongly inclined to vote against the amendment even if they wanted more state spending and taxes (variable 8). These types of findings are also reflected in the coefficients of variables representing those who felt that amendment would increase or decrease taxes, even if that were not its most important effect (variables 24 through 39).

Far and away the strongest support for the amendment came from those who felt that it would increase either governmental efficiency (variables 12 and 13) or voter control of government (variables 14 and 15). There are 120 voters in these categories, and ninety percent of them voted for the amendment.

Regarding the wages of public employees, very few voters felt the amendment would have as its *most important* impact the limitation of future government wage increases, but many public and private voters felt the amendment would have that impact. Among public sector voters (variables 21 to 23), votes went against Headlee regardless of whether these workers felt now that public wages were above those for comparable private sector jobs (variable 21). Among private sector voters, those who felt that public wages are higher than private were fairly neutral on the amendment (variable 18), but those who felt that public wages are lower than private were against. Certainly among private sector voters there appears to be little resentment directed against the high wages of government employees, and little occasion to vote for tax limitation on that account. Whether this result would obtain in other states is uncertain: perhaps the union solidarity tradition is very strong in Michigan.

The public employment findings also demonstrate the nonpunitive feelings of private sector voters. Among those who felt the amendment would reduce government employment, voters were neutral to or against the amendment even if they felt that public employees worked less hard than private employees (variable 41). But this time public employees show some mysterious devotion to the common interest: When public employees felt the amendment would lower employment, and that government workers did not work as hard as private workers, they voted for the amendment (variable 43). Presumably they felt the other guy would get laid off.

Finally, among all voters who felt the amendment would hurt schools (variable 11 and variables 44 through 48), voting on the amendment was consistently negative.

The corresponding results for the Tisch regression are given in Table 6. Again the adjusted coefficient of determination is much higher than in Table 4, as is the degree to which the regression improves on random assignment in predicting votes. Since the share of voters reporting voting for the Tisch Amendment is so low (26.2 percent), this regression is more difficult to interpret. The regression constant is .208 for private employees and .254 for public employees, so even a strongly positive coefficient such as .20 may still imply that a minority of voters in the class favor the amendment.

For the Tisch Amendment, voters who perceived that the most important impact of the amendment would be to reduce spending voted against it heavily, especially those who desire more local spending and taxes (variables 1 and 4). Those who saw its most important impact to be reducing taxes were more favorably inclined, though the amendment never got a majority among this group (variables 6 through 11). Variable 6 in particular again demonstrates the possibility that voters perceive a free lunch. As before, those who thought the most important impact of the amendment would be to hurt schools were heavily against it even if they favored less school spending (variable 16), and those who felt it would increase efficiency or control were much more favorably inclined, in the case of variable 17 even giving the amendment a majority.

The public wage findings mirror those

for the Headlee Amendment (variables 21 to 25), though the public employment findings (variables 45 to 49) are more in accord with expectations: here all private employees who think that the amendment will limit government employment are more for it than average, and public employees are more against than average. Among those who think the amendment will reduce taxes, support is generally more positive than average, sometimes in contrast to spending and tax desires (variable 27), sometimes in sympathy (variable 32 and 25).

We can summarize these results by giving a more quantitative notion of the extent to which passage of tax limitation amendments reflects the three motives listed earlier: less public spending, lower public sector wages or government efficiency gains. This is done by taking the amendment that passed, Headlee, and comparing its plurality with that realized among various groups of voters, with the grouping based on voter perceptions of Headlee's most important impact. The net plurality among those who favor less public spending is the net plurality among those who desire lower spending or taxes (variables 3, 5, and 7 in Table 5) and who *perceive* that the amendment will accomplish that, plus the net (negative) plurality among those who with a desire for lower taxes (variables 9 and 10) but with a perception that the amendment will raise them, plus the net (negative) plurality among those who perceive the amendment will lower spending on schools and desire the contrary (variable 11). The net plurality among all of these groups is the plurality gained by Headlee among voters who, on balance, appear to be calling for a smaller, or limited public sector.

The net plurality among those who want lower public sector wages is that for the small number of voters who perceive wage reduction as the most important impact of the amendment and favor that (a number not even large enough to appear as a variable in Table 5). The net plurality among those whose preference could be considered to be inconsistent is that among those who vote for the amendment because it will lower taxes or spending even though

Table 6

Regression Model Explaining Tisch Vote

1039 Tisch Voters
Adjusted R^2 = .235
Proportion of votes correctly predicted = .806
Improvement over random assignment = .192
Constant, private employees = .208
Constant, public employees = .254

Variable No.	Group	Perceptions		Preferences	Cases	Coefficient	t Ratio
		Most Important Impact of Tisch	Tisch will				
1.	Priv.	Reduce spending	--	More local spending	16	-.235	-2.2
2.	Priv.	Reduce spending	--	Same local spending	62	-.104	-1.8
3.	Priv.	Reduce spending	--	Less local spending	20	-.031	-0.3
4.	Pub.	Reduce spending	--	More local spending	18	-.097	-0.8
5.	Pub.	Reduce spending	--	Same local spending	31	-.004	-0.1
6.	All	Reduce taxes	--	More local spending	15	.113	1.0
7.	All	Reduce taxes	--	Same local spending	59	.165	2.8
8.	All	Reduce taxes	--	Less local spending	22	.219	2.2
9.	All	Reduce prop. taxes	--	More local spending	20	-.051	-0.5
10.	All	Reduce prop. taxes	--	Same local spending	78	.148	2.7
11.	All	Reduce prop. taxes	--	Less local spending	38	.219	2.7
12.	All	Increase taxes	--	More local spending	16	.004	0.1
13.	All	Increase taxes	--	Same local spending	51	.053	0.9
14.	All	Increase Taxes	--	Less local spending	16	-.261	-2.5
15.	All	Hurt schools	--	Same school spending	22	-.149	-1.7
16.	All	Hurt schools	--	Less school spending	23	-.095	-0.5
17.	All	Increase efficiency/control	--	Govt. wastes much	26	.401	4.8
18.	All	Increase efficiency/control	--	Govt. wastes some	24	.250	2.9
19.	All	No change	--	--	72	-.035	-0.7
20.	All	Don't know	--	--	179	-.010	-0.3
21.	Priv.	--	Reduce wage increases	Govt. workers earn more	186	.033	0.8

Table 6 *(Continued)*

No.							
22.	Priv.	—	Reduce wage increases	Govt. workers earn same	140	-.014	-0.3
23.	Priv.	—	Reduce wage increases	Govt. workers earn less	37	-.124	-1.8
24.	Pub.	—	Reduce wage increases	Govt. workers earn more	42	-.044	-0.6
25.	Pub.	—	Reduce wage increases	Govt. workers earn same	49	-.070	-1.0
26.	Pub.	—	Reduce wage increase	Govt. workers earn less	33	-.058	-0.7
27.	Priv.	—	Reduce taxes	More local spending	56	.186	2.3
28.	Priv.	—	Reduce taxes	Same local spending	207	.164	3.8
29.	Priv.	—	Reduce taxes	Less local spending	86	.056	0.6
30.	Pub.	—	Reduce taxes	More local spending	29	.058	0.5
31.	Pub.	—	Reduce taxes	Same local spending	57	.042	0.5
32.	Pub.	—	Reduce taxes	Less local spending	14	.635	3.9
33.	Priv.	—	Reduce prop. taxes	More local spending	62	.056	0.7
34.	Priv.	—	Reduce prop. taxes	Same local spending	278	.060	1.4
35.	Priv.	—	Reduce prop. taxes	Less local spending	108	.236	3.1
36.	Pub.	—	Reduce prop. taxes	More local spending	44	.036	0.4
37.	Pub.	—	Reduce prop. taxes	Same local spending	96	-.003	-0.1
38.	Pub.	—	Reduce prop. taxes	Less local spending	18	-.029	-0.2
39.	Priv.	—	Increase income taxes	More state spending	44	-.009	0.1
40.	Priv.	—	Increase income taxes	Same state spending	273	-.095	-2.6
41.	Priv.	—	Increase income taxes	Less state spending	233	-.013	-0.4
42.	Pub.	—	Increase income taxes	More state spending	27	-.042	-0.4
43.	Pub.	—	Increase income taxes	Same state spending	99	-.002	-0.0
44.	Pub.	—	Increase income taxes	Less state spending	51	-.012	-0.2
45.	Priv.	—	Lower govt. employment	Workers work more	17	-.038	0.4
46.	Priv.	—	Lower govt. employment	Workers work same	125	.131	3.0
47.	Priv.	—	Lower govt. employment	Workers work less	253	.070	1.8
48.	Pub.	—	Lower govt. employment	Workers work same	63	-.063	-0.9
49.	Pub.	—	Lower govt. employment	Workers work less	62	-.063	0.9
50.	Priv.	—	Reduce school funds	More school spending	121	-.180	-3.9
51.	Priv.	—	Reduce school funds	Same school spending	233	-.134	-3.7
52.	Priv.	—	Reduce school funds	Less school spending	91	-.024	-0.5
53.	Pub.	—	Reduce school funds	More school spending	76	-.147	-2.0
54.	Pub.	—	Reduce school funds	Same school spending	87	-.158	-2.2
55.	Pub.	—	Reduce school funds	Less school spending	13	-.085	-0.7

they do not favor reductions (variables 1, 2, 4, and 6), plus the plurality among those who perceive the amendment will increase taxes and vote against it, even though they want more public spending (variable 8). These voters either have in mind that the amendment will generate efficiency gains, they may have the uncertainty rationale described above, or they may be searching for the free lunch of tax cuts without spending cuts. The net plurality among those who envision efficiency or responsiveness gains is also taken from Table 5 (variables 12 through 15). For each group Table 7 shows the number of voters, votes for, votes against, and the plurality.

In our sample of Headlee voters, 578 voted for the amendment and 450 against, giving an overall plurality of 128 votes. This plurality was small or negative among those who want lower wages, no change, did not respond, or were in small cell sizes: among all these groups the net plurality was −36 votes. Hence the passage of the amendment can be attributed to the plurality of 128 + 36 = 164 votes among the other groups. Among these groups, those who want a smaller public sector in the sense defined above accounted for a 43 vote plurality, those who are either looking for efficiency gains or a free lunch a 41 vote plurality, and those

who are clearly looking for efficiency or control gains an 80 vote plurality. Hence 3 out of 4 voters responsible for the plurality of the Headlee Amendment were motivated either by a desire for efficiency gains or a free lunch. Only one out of 4 appears to favor a smaller-sized public sector where both spending and taxes are reduced.[18]

Implications

It is undoubtedly unwise to try to read too much into these survey results. Voters may be unwilling or unable to articulate why they voted for an amendment, or whether they favor a larger or smaller public sector. They also may have had in mind a complex package of effects, for any one amendment or for the Tisch and Headlee amendments in combinations that we are unable to test with our questions. And as with any survey, results are always suspect to economists because voters do not have to act on the basis of their answers.

But allowing for these limitations, some suggestive results do appear to be emerging from this attempt to survey voters. One is that there does not appear to be a very widespread feeling that government is too big. More people feel that way

Table 7

Analysis of the Passage of the Headlee Amendment

1028 Headlee Voters
Based on answers to most important impact question
and regression of Table 5

Motive	Variables in Table 5	Cases	For	Against	Plurality
Want smaller public sector	3,5,7,9,10,11	225	134	91	43
Want lower public wages	none	11	5	6	-1
May want free lunch	1,2,4,6,8	213	127	86	41
Want greater efficiency/ control	12,13,14,15	120	100	20	80
Want no change	16	102	44	58	-14
Don't know	17	200	84	116	-32
Small cell sizes	none	157	84	73	11
TOTAL		1028	578	450	128

than the converse, but the differences are not substantial and in any case not strongly related to respondents' votes on the tax limitation amendment. Fundamentally, the tax limitation movement does not appear to be an attempt to correct public sector-private sector spending imbalances.

A second result is that there does not appear to be in the tax limitation movement, at least in its Michigan incarnation, a strong desire to punish public employees. Relatively few private sector voters feel that the amendment will limit government wage increases, and even if they do feel that way, they are not strongly inclined to vote for the amendment. Relatively few private sector voters feel the amendment will lower public employment either, and when voters feel that way, they actually are more inclined to vote against the amendment. Fundamentally, the tax limitation movement does not appear to be seen as an attempt to alter the income distribution between public and private employees.

It is easier to say what this tax limitation movement is not than what it is. The strongest source of support for tax limitation comes from those who think tax limitations will improve voter control of government and/or government efficiency. Had we anticipated such a finding, we would have added questions to probe why and how voters felt this would happen, but for now that matter remains for others to investigate. Another strong source of support comes from those who think the amendment will reduce taxes, even though they have reported not desiring cuts in spending and taxes at that level of government. There it appears that voters are perceiving that their own taxes will be cut without expenditures being cut, either because of supposed efficiency gains, greater uncertainty about the spending side of the budget, or the unending search for a free lunch.

FOOTNOTES

**The survey on which this paper is based was funded by the Office of Policy Development and Research at the Department of Housing and Urban Development. We are grateful to David Puryear and John Ross of HUD for their patience and helpful advice. We have also benefitted greatly from working with Richard Curtin of the Michigan Institute for Social Research, who played the major role in developing the questionnaire and managing the survey. Harvey Brazer, Helen Ladd, Perry Shapiro, and Nicolaus Tideman made helpful comments on an earlier version of the paper. Finally, we have benefitted from the able research assistance of several students: Sue Goldstone, Robert Kleinbaum, James Reschovsky, Deborah Swift, and Michael Wolkoff.

[1]Even though it happened just a year ago, by this time the professional literature is full of references to Proposition 13—see, for example, the June, 1979 Supplement of the National Tax Journal. The median voter theorem and literature on it have been amply described by Robert Deacon, "Private Choice and Collective Outcomes: Evidence from Public Sector Demand Studies," National Tax Journal, December, 1977.

[2]Some of the theoretical underpinnings of this paper and the survey are given in Paul Courant, Edward Gramlich, and Daniel Rubinfeld, "Tax Limitation and the Demand for Public Services in Michigan," National Tax Journal, June, 1979.

[3]See Helen Ladd, "An Economic Evaluation of State Limitations on Local Taxing and Spending Power," National Tax Journal, March, 1978; Geoffrey Brennan and James Buchanan, "The Logic of Tax Limits: Alternative Constitutional Constraints of the Power to Tax"; Gerald S. Goldstein and Mark V. Pauly, "The Effect of Revenue and Tax Limitation on Property Values"; Arthur Denzau, Robert Mackay, and Carolyn Weaver, "Spending Limitations, Agenda Control, and Voters' Expectations"; and Michelle J. White, "Government Response to Spending Limitations," all in the June, 1979, Supplement National Tax Journal; and Paul N. Courant and Daniel L. Rubinfeld, "On the Welfare Effects of Tax Limitations," IPPS Working Paper, University of Michigan, 1979.

[4]See William Niskanen, "The Peculiar Economics of Bureaucracy," American Economic Review, May, 1968; Thomas Romer and Howard Rosenthal, "Political Resource Allocation, Controlled Agendas, and the Status Quo," Public Choice, Winter, 1978; and Arthur Denzau, Robert Mackay, and Carolyn Weaver, "Spending Limitations," op. cit., National Tax Journal, Supplement, June, 1979.

[5]See Paul Courant, Edward Gramlich, and Daniel Rubinfeld, "Public Employee Market Power and the Level of Government Spending," American Economic Review, December, 1979; and Gordon Tullock, "Dynamic Hypothesis on Bureaucarcy," Public Choice, Fall 1974.

[6]Morris Fiorina and Roger Noll, "Voters, Bureaucrats, and Legislators: A Rational Choice Perspective on the Growth of Bureaucracy," Journal of Public Economics, April, 1978.

[7]These hypotheses are slightly different, though obviously related to the "tax shift" vs. "tax cut" hypotheses that were investigated in California by Jack Citrin, "Do People Want Something for Nothing: Public Opinion on Taxes and Government Spending"; and Richard Attiyeh and Robert Engle, "Testing Some Propositions about Proposition 13"; both in the June, 1979, Supplement, National Tax Journal.

[8]These questions were first analyzed by Eva

Mueller, "Public Attitudes Toward Fiscal Problems, *Quarterly Journal of Economics*, May 1963; and later by Richard Curtin and Charles Cowan, "Public Attitudes Toward Fiscal Programs," in B. Strumpel, *et al.*, ed., *Surveys of Consumers*, 1972–3, Institute of Survey Research, The University of Michigan. Jack Citrin, "Do People Want Something for Nothing," *op. cit.*, has also analyzed a similar series of questions in connection with the tax limitation votes, reaching conclusions similar to ours.

[8a]We mechanically adopted the ISR sequence because it was time-tested, without thinking about a weakness that later became apparent. In opting for more, less, or the same levels of public spending, respondents were not explicitly told that less spending implied less taxes. The relatively small number of respondents in the "More 1" column indicates that perhaps this problem is not terribly serious, and in any event we do correct for it in our questions that follow.

[9]The negative attitude toward welfare is confirmed by the fact that 53.9% of the sample stated in response to another question that they felt that *many* of those currently on welfare should not be receiving payments and 38.8% said that some should not be receiving payments.

[10]See Anthony Downs, *An Economic Theory of Democracy*, Harper and Row, 1957; James Buchanan and Gordon Tullock, *Calculus of Consent*, University of Michigan Press, 1962.

[11]In fact, we have tried to develop attributes models explaining the tax limitation vote, and have obtained results that fit about as well as these with preferences. Since we feel we can improve on these equations, we have not presented them for reasons of brevity. A whole series of papers, well-summarized by Robert Deacon, "Private Choice," *op. cit.*, illustrate the "attributes" approach.

[12]We have presented the t-ratios because they are easily interpreted, even though we recognize that with a 0-1 dependent variable in a linear probability model, the error term is not normally distributed and the t-statistics are only valid asymptotically.

[13]See Robert Pindyck and Daniel Rubinfeld, *Econometric Models and Economic Forecasts* (New York: McGraw-Hill), 1976, Chapter 8 for details.

[14]See T. W. Anderson, *An Introduction to Multivariate Statistical Analysis*, John Wiley and Sons, 1958, Chapter 6. The computational equivalence between the 0-1 linear probability model and the discriminant analysis model is given in G. Ladd, "Linear Probability Functions and Discriminant Functions," *Econometrica*, October, 1966.

[15]In computing these percentages we considered a vote correctly predicted whenever its fitted value was greater than .5. Other cutoff values could in general give higher percentages of votes correctly predicted. If, for example, the yes and no distributions had equal variances and numbers of cases, the optimal cutoff value is just midway between the mean of the predicted vote values for the yes and no voters. We have computed these optimal cutoff values for all regressions, in general finding them close to .5. Moreover, fairly sizable changes in the cutoff value in the neighborhood of .5 make very little difference in the percentage of votes correctly predicted.

[16]Even this measure could be improved upon because it assumes that a correct assignment when the predicted probability is .51 is as good as one when the predicted probability is .96, and that a prediction is incorrect when the predicted probability is "only" .49. A better measure would weight outcomes more the farther is a correct or incorrect prediction from .5.

[17]This choice was made mainly for pragmatic reasons to keep down the number of variables, but there is also a methodological rationale: in earlier trials we found that variables with less than 10 cases were extremely unlikely to have statistically significant coefficients (even if their coefficients were large).

[18]At this point enough differences in tax limitation amendments and the nature of our questions have been introduced that it is hard to tell how our results compare with those of Attiyeh-Engle and Citrin for California. Attiyeh-Engle use county aggregate data and find support for their proposition that voters really were opting for a non-marginal cut in both spending and taxes. By contrast, Citrin used micro polling data and found that voters felt they could cut taxes without eliminating public services, much as we do here. It should be noted that the large pre-Proposition 13 state surplus makes this event more likely in California than in Michigan.

[12]

THE DEDUCTIBILITY OF STATE AND LOCAL TAXES**

EDWARD M. GRAMLICH*

ABSTRACT

The paper analyzes the much-debated tax reform proposal to eliminate the deductibility of state-local taxes. This change would appear to hurt high income itemizers and not low income non-itemizers, but for two separate trickle down effects. One involves the possibility that state-local spending will decline as a result of the higher effective tax price; the other the possibility that rich itemizers will leave low income communities. The paper analyzes both effects with micro data on taxes, incomes, and demand for public spending in various communities, and finds them, and the losses to low income people from an elimination of deductibility, to be relatively modest. It also suggests some partial elimination provisions that seem attractive on equity and efficiency grounds.

INDIVIDUALS have been able to deduct state and local taxes from their federal income tax base since the federal income tax was first passed back in 1913. During this seventy year history the only changes in the deductibility provisions occurred in 1964, when license fees and some excise taxes were made non-deductible, and in 1978, when the excise tax on gasoline was made non-deductible.

Although there have been only minor changes in the actual law, there has been a pronounced erosion in the philosophical rationale for the tax deduction. In the early days taxes were viewed as arbitrary changes imposed by some remote government that should be deductible because one should not have to pay a tax on a tax. There are still many Americans who hold that view, but the opinion of economists and others who write about tax reform has shifted. There is an increasing readiness to believe that taxes are ultimately benefit charges, and that they should not be

deductible. If payments for private consumption goods cannot be deducted, the argument goes, payments for public consumption should not be either. In this day when economists and others are alert to provisions that lead to "excessive" levels of government spending, this alleged distortion comes quickly to mind.

Whether related or not to this new view of the deduction, recently there have been a battery of proposals to limit it. In the discussions surrounding the Tax Equity and Fiscal Responsibility Act of 1982, Congress considered eliminating the deduction for sales and personal property taxes. The same option has been prominently displayed by the Congressional Budget Office in several of its reports on possibilities for reducing the federal budget deficit. The Senate Finance Committee has periodically considered partial deductibility of all state and local taxes. Senator David Durenberger has proposed a bill to allow deductions only over some floor. The Bradley-Gephardt tax reform bill permits deduction of state and local income and real property (that means non-personal property) taxes only, and only at their bottom bracket 14 percent rate. The Kemp-Kasten tax reform bill permits deduction of real property taxes only, and only at their standard rate of 25 percent. And the Administration's 1985 tax reform proposal has advocated eliminating deductibility altogether. Such a change is estimated to raise federal revenues by $29 in fiscal 1984, the largest such change in this base-broadening tax proposal.[1]

The political debate on deductibility has featured a strange inversion. It is commonly recognized that almost no low income taxpayers itemize deductions, and hence benefit from the state and local tax provision, while almost all high income taxpayers do.[2] This would appear to make tax deductibility a pro-rich provision and its elimination a pro-poor change. But the main proponents of eliminating deductibility have been Republicans, not generally known for their support of the little

*The University of Michigan

447

man, while the main opponents have been liberal Democrats from high tax states.

There is an obvious self-interest explanation for the Democrats' posture, and conceivably even a deeper point rooted in equity and efficiency considerations. While the first order impact of eliminating the deduction is to hurt rich people, there are two important "trickle down" channels by which elimination could also hurt those with lower incomes:

a) Removal of deductibility raises the tax price of state and local public services and may reduce real spending on them;

b) Removal of deductibility raises the tax price of state and local public services for those rich people who now live in low income communities, which could encourage them to migrate to higher income communities and thereby worsen community income segregation.

The contribution of economists to enlightenment on both questions has been less than impressive. There has been only speculation on the second point, and only indirect empirical evidence on the first.[3]

A second area in which previous discussions of deductibility have been misleading involves efficiency. It is sometimes argued that the tax deduction is an efficient way for the federal government to aid state and local governments because the spending impact is large per dollar of tax loss.[4] This notion of efficiency appears to be much different than an economist's usual notion. The tax reductions are for the most part not costs but transfers between other federal taxpayers and itemizers. And public spending changes are not necessarily good and promotion of private consumption not necessarily bad, as is assumed in the calculation. Other have argued that the tax deduction is inefficient because it imposes a distortion. While this argument gets closer to the traditional economist's definition of efficiency, there are still public goods complications. If, for example, the tax deduction does not change the median amount of spending desired in a community, as is likely to happen in communities with few itemizers, the deduction represents simply a transfer between

federal taxpayers and itemizers with no obvious efficiency implications. If the deduction does raise median spending demands, rich itemizers gain less than federal taxpayers lose, in line with the standard argument, but there is likely to be an offsetting gain both for poor nonitemizers and citizens outside the jurisdiction so that the net efficiency gains or losses are not obvious.

In this paper I try to deal with all of these questions. I use a very simple model to show how the tax deduction works and to analyze the various trickle down and efficiency effects. These effects are then estimated with actual micro survey data on voters. Unlike all previous efforts, these survey data permit income, tax prices, and deadweight losses to be estimated very precisely, both for individual voters and community by community aggregations of these voters. A final section returns to the world of policy, analyzing the effects of some widely discussed alternatives to full elimination of deductibility, along with a few new proposals of my own that try to gain most of the base-broadening revenue from eliminating deductibility without hurting low income people at all.

As a final introductory comment, one point intentionally not dealt with in the paper is the one that most fascinates politicians, involving interstate revenue gains and losses. My aim is to analyze state-local tax deductibility from the standpoint of equity and efficiency. If it shows up poorly on these counts, as it does, there would seem to be little normative relevance to the question of whether this inefficient and inequitable subsidy is now more widely used in some (high tax) states than in other (low tax) states. Such a consideration obviously plays a role in the political horse-trading involving actual changes, but that is a question I do not deal with here.

The Impact of Deductibility on Public Spending

Budget studies of state and local fiscal behavior commonly start with a logarithmic demand expression for public spending. To keep differences between my results and others to an absolute minimum,

I too use this form. Under it, public spending desired by the ith voter can be expressed as

$$E = a_0 P^{-a_1}(Y(1 - t) + Z)^{a_2} \qquad (1)$$

where E refers to i's desired public expenditures, P is the tax price for public goods for this voter, $(Y(1 - t) + Z)$ is i's income after federal taxes, and t is i's marginal federal income tax rate. The Z variable plays two roles: a positive Z yields an approximate linear expression for after-tax income in the presence of progressive marginal income tax rates, and alterations in Z also permit experimentation with deductibility plans that have kinked schedules. For simplicity, all i subscripts have been dropped.

The general expression for the tax price faced by the ith voter is

$$P = S(1 - gt) \qquad (2)$$

where S is the ith voter's marginal tax share times the purchase price (or resource cost) for public services, and g is the deductibility share. With no deductibility of state-local taxes, g = 0; with full deductibility, g = 1; and with partial deductibility $0 < g < 1$. In applying this model, t and $(Y(1 - t) + Z)$ can be measured directly in my micro data set and g and any changes in Z can be determined from the parameters of the deductibility plan.

The gross change in desired expenditures due to deductibility, the first of the trickle down channels, can be determined simply by substituting [2] into [1] and solving

$$\ln E_y - \ln E_n = -a_1 \ln(1 - gt) \qquad (3)$$

where E_y denotes desired spending with deductibility (y = yes) and E_n denotes desired spending without deductibility, all for the ith voter. If this voter does not itemize, deductibility leads to no change in desired spending. But if the deduction were converted to flat rate a partial credit, the gt term would be the same for all taxpayers whether they itemize or not.

To derive the welfare implications of changes in deductibility, it is necessary to find the compensated change in desired expenditures. For both state and local governments about five percent of after-federal-tax income is devoted to public spending. Beginning at E_n, deductibility then leads to an absolute real income gain of $E_n(S - S(1 - gt)) = E_n Sgt$. Since $E_n S$ is about five percent of income, this gain is 5gt percent of income. The income effect of a change in deductibility at the final price ratio can then be approximated by

$$\ln E_y - \ln E_s = .05 a_2 gt \qquad (4)$$

where E_s is desired expenditures from the substitution effect alone, or at the no deductibility indifference curve. Dividing [4] by [3] yields a number that is smaller than $.05 a_2/a_1$, which shows that the income effect change will generally be a very small part of the gross change. In other words, since state and local spending commands such a small share of after-federal-tax income, there will generally be little difference between the compensated and uncompensated spending change, and the gross change will only slightly overstate the true welfare gain to the ith voter from deductibility.

Estimation of compensated willingness-to-pay functions for public services makes it possible to measure efficiency losses from the tax deduction. While the standard view would be that the deduction is inefficient, the reasoning is more complicated in view of the fact that we are analyzing the efficiency of a public good subsidy.

Ignoring the external benefit effect, the ambiguity can be seen most easily in the case where only a small number of voters in a community itemize. In this case there is unlikely to be a change in public spending demands or response to deductibility, and in the first instance the tax deduction can be viewed as a transfer from federal taxpayers to the minority of itemizers within a community. It would only have an efficiency impact if this minority was in some way instrumental in affecting fiscal decisions.

In communities where more voters itemize, there could be a change in median spending demands and then actual spending within the community. To the extent that the deduction increases actual public spending, the normal distortion argument will apply for itemizers: federal taxpayers are forced to pay a subsidy that exceeds the marginal valuation of public goods of these itemizers, and there is a dead-weight loss. But at the same time nonitemizers could actually be moved closer to their desired level of public spending by the deduction, and if so, their gains should be netted against the dead-weight loss for itemizers in making a Kaldor-Hicks evaluation of the distortions implicit in the deduction. And the question becomes even more complicated if these nonitemizers, who are poorer, deserve higher distributional weights on their gains. The efficiency calculation for two representative voters who favor close to the actual amount of expenditures when there is deductibility is illustrated in Figure 1.

Figure 1 determines efficiency changes with deductibility in terms of the difference between the willingness-to-pay and the tax price of various voters. Another way to rationalize the calculation, and understand the conditions necessary for it to work, is in terms of community aggregates. Suppose as a result of the introduction of deductibility public spending in a community changes from E_n to E_y.

Figure 1
The Distortion due to the Tax Deduction

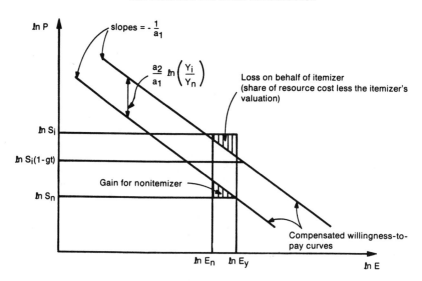

The lower curve is the compensated willingness-to-pay curve for a typical nonitemizer; the upper is the compensated willingness-to-pay curve for a typical itemizer.

E_y is public spending in the community with the tax deduction.

E_n is public spending in the community without the deduction.

The K-H net gain from deductibility for these two representative voters is the gain for the nonitemizer less the loss on behalf of the itemizer. In general, it is the sum of areas under the WTP curves less areas under the S lines between $\ln E_y$ and $\ln E_n$.

The aggregate gain for all voters from this change is

$$AG = \sum_{i=1}^{N} \int_{E_n}^{E_y} f(E)dE \qquad (5)$$

where AG refers to the aggregate gain for all N voters and f(E) is the compensated willingness-to-pay for each voter. The aggregate cost is just the purchase price for a unit of public services times $E_y - E_n$. If tax shares for all voters add to one, the difference between AG and aggregate cost will equal the sum of all gains for non-itemizers less all losses on behalf of itemizers, as is shown in Figure 1. If voter tax shares add to less than one, as could happen if business taxes exceed services or if there are open-ended categorical grants from other governments, the aggregation of triangles across voters will overstate the net gain from deductibility.

The upshot of all this is that even if the usual complications regarding how normal and compensated demand curves should be interpreted are minor, and if externalities and distributional weighting problems are ignored, it is still difficult to tell if the tax deduction is inefficient because of the publicness of the good or service being demanded. It is not evident that deductibility will raise public spending at all, and it is not apparent that even a deduction-induced rise in public spending leads to a net welfare loss—there will be losses for federal taxpayers and smaller gains for rich itemizers, but there could also be efficiency savings for other voters who had previously favored larger public spending.[5]

This model can also be used to address the high income flight issue, the second main trickle down channel. Suppose a rich itemizer lives in a poor community when deductibility is eliminated. Because this itemizer is likely to be in a fiscal minority, there could be no, or little, change in public spending as a result of the federal tax change. Assuming no change in public spending, the itemizer's loss living in the poor community will be

$$L_p = E_pS_p - E_pS_p(1 - gt) = E_pS_pgt \qquad (6)$$

where the p subscript refers to the poor community and L_p is the loss there. The situation for this itemizer is graphed in Figure 2.

If the same itemizer with the same demand for public services were to live in a rich community, there would be three differences:

a) The presence of more wealthy people should make the itemizer's tax share, S, lower. The same result could arise if resource costs are higher in poor communities, as is postulated by Yinger (1985a).

b) The itemizer is likely to be in a fiscal majority in a rich community, and will not have to suffer the dead-weight loss triangle when deductibility is removed.

c) Rich communities spend more than poor communities, so the number of units of public services on which there is a deductibility loss will be greater.

Combining these three effects, the loss induced by loss of deductibility for this itemizer in some hypothetical rich community that forms the best alternative to the itemizer's present residence is

$$L_r = E_rS_r - E_rS_r(1 - gt)$$
$$- \frac{1}{2}(S_r - S_r(1 - gt))\Delta E$$
$$= E_rS_rgt(1 - .5\alpha) \qquad (7)$$

where L_r stands for the loss in this hypothetical rich community, E_r is spending with deductibility in the community, ΔE is the spending change due to the loss of deductibility, and α is the proportionate decline in spending. In this simple model I use S_r to stand for all reasons the tax price might differ in the rich community—a lower tax share, lower resource costs, more congenial public services. The last term in the top expression is an approximation to the dead-weight triangle that is saved because the itemizer should be in the median voter group in the hypothetical community, which I will call the voter efficiency term. The expression is exact when the itemizer's willingnes-to-pay schedule is linear (a reasonable assump-

Figure 2
Losses for Rich Itemizers in Poor and Rich Communities
When the Deduction is Eliminated

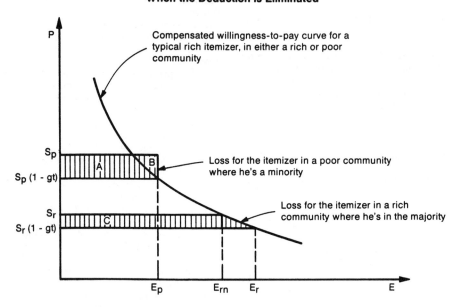

E_p is spending in the poor community, with and without the deduction. Since there are few itemizers in this community, there is no change in public spending.

E_{rn} is spending in the rich community without the tax deduction.

E_r is spending in the rich community with the tax deduction.

With elimination of the tax deduction, the rich itemizer loses area A + B in the poor community and area C in the rich community.

tion for small ΔE) and when the itemizer is the median voter (a reasonable assumption when the itemizer is selecting between a number of communities).

The itemizer's incentive to leave the poor community following the loss of deductibility can now be expressed as a function of the difference between L_p and L_r.[6] Scaling this difference by local tax payments in the poor community yields

$$\frac{L_p - L_r}{E_p S_p} = gt(1 - \frac{E_r S_r}{E_p S_p}(1 - .5\alpha)) \qquad (8)$$

Since S_r is a general proxy measuring all the reasons why public services might be provided on more favorable terms in this hypothetical rich community, the basic public expenditure demand expression in [1] can be used to replace E_r/E_p. Using

$$E_r/E_p = (S_r/S_p)^{-a_1} \qquad (9)$$

from [1], the relative loss becomes

$$\frac{L_p - L_r}{E_p S_p} = gt(1 - (1 - .5\alpha)\left(\frac{S_r}{S_p}\right)^{1-a_1}) \qquad (10)$$

The $(1 - .5\alpha)$ term represents voter efficiency in the rich community, the S_r/S_p term represents the set of changes in tax shares, resource costs, and the utility of public services to the voter across communities, and the elasticity combines this relative price difference into spending differences. As a_1 decreases or as α increases, the voter is more likely to be better off moving when deductibility is eliminated.[7]

Data and Results

I now turn from this general model to an attempt to estimate the empirical impact of changes in deductibility on median spending demands and efficiency. As stated above, these estimates will be derived from micro survey data rather than an attempt to infer behavioral parameters from the aggregate spending behavior of governments, as is usually done. The strength of this approach is that it permits estimation of the entire distribution of changes in spending demands, for rich and poor, in rich and poor communities. An estimate of the change at the median voter point falls out of these predictions and is of independent interest, but obviously another set of assumptions is required to conclude that changes in median spending desires are equal to changes in actual governmental spending.

The data used to make these calculations come from a survey of Michigan voters taken in 1978. This survey asked respondents whether they voted in the November election of that year, when a series of tax limitation amendments to the state constitution was on the ballot. This question permitted segmentation of the sample into voters and non-voters, of which I used only the group that voted. It also asked respondents whether they itemized deductions, permitting identification of the subgroup that would be directly affected by deductibility. It then asked questions about income and tax shares, and I used the income questions and the federal law for 1978 to fill in values for marginal federal income tax rates. Finally, it asked some "budget constrained" questions about respondents'

demand for public service. Unlike the usual questions asked by political scientists, it informed respondents of the types of spending carried out at both the state and local level in Michigan, and told them that *both* spending and taxes would change by the same percentage amount.[8] It asked them their desired percentage, and found incidentally that when done this way, the median voter clearly favored "no change" in overall spending levels at both the state and local level. The specific data and questions used are described in detail in Courant, Gramlich, and Rubinfeld (1980).

The impact of deductibility is computed in a straightforward way. For all those voters who did not itemize in 1978, I assumed that elimination of tax deductibility would have no effect on their tax price and desired level of public spending. For all those voters who did itemize in 1978, I used their income to compute their marginal federal income tax rate and then inserted that value into equation [3]. Most other studies of deductibility have assumed that the price elasticity of demand for public services, a_1, equals .5 so I followed suit, even though the .5 number is generally estimated for particular public services and should be an overestimate of the price elasticity of demand for public services in general.[9]

Sample sizes for itemizers and non-itemizers are shown in Table 1. Of the 2001 total respondents to the survey, 1248 reported voting. Of those, 1170 gave enough information that I could compute their desired spending level before and after deductibility. These voters were disaggregated by place of residence, as shown in the Table. As has been noticed before, the median voter is not an itemizer in large central cities such as Detroit and Lansing, and in rural areas. But the median voter is an itemizer in higher income areas such as the Detroit and Lansing suburbs and in other urban counties encompassing the suburbs of smaller cities throughout the state.[10]

But the question of how changes in deductibility affect state and local spending demands depends only partly on whether the median voter is an itemizer. It also depends on where these itemizers are in

Table 1

Voters Who Did and Did Not Itemize Deductions[a]
Michigan Survey, 1978

Place	Voters who itemized	Voters who did not itemize	Total	Percentage share of voters who itemized
Detroit	59	90	149	39.6
Detroit suburbs[b]	206	126	332	62.0
Lansing	10	18	28	35.7
Lansing suburbs[c]	13	13	26	50.0
Other urban counties[d]	66	64	130	50.8
Rural counties[e]	219	286	505	43.4
Total	573	597	1170	49.0

[a]Includes only those who answered the desired local spending demand questions — 58.5 percent of overall survey respondents and 93.8 percent of those voting. The 6.2 percent nonresponse was divided proportionately between itemizers and non-itemizers, even though more information was required of itemizers.

[b]Wayne, Oakland, and Macomb counties less those voters in the city of Detroit.

[c]Ingham and Eaton counties less the city of Lansing.

[d]Washtenaw (Ann Arbor), Kent (Grand Rapids), Genesee (Flint), Kalamazoo, and Saginaw counties.

[e]All other counties.

Source: Voter survey described in Courant, Gramlich, Rubinfeld (1980).

the taste distribution. If most itemizers initially favor cuts in public spending, elimination of deductibility would make them favor bigger cuts, but the change could have no impact on median spending demands; if some initially favor increases, elimination of deductibility would be more likely to lower median spending demands.

I show the impact of deductibility calculation in light of this subtlety in Table 2 for desired spending and taxes at the state level. The upper panel indicates that with deductibility, the median voter proposition works for all six areas listed: in each case the median voter favors no change in spending and taxes. When deductibility is eliminated and all itemizers get large price increases (1978 federal marginal income tax rates ranged up to seventy percent), median spending demands often fall. In Detroit there are few enough itemizers that there is no change in the median demand for public spending, in the Detroit and Lansing suburbs there is slightly more than a ten percent decrease, and over the rest of the state there is between a six and a ten percent decrease. The overall reduction in median spending demands throughout the state, as calculated exactly from the micro data, is 10 percent, as is indicated at the bottom of the table.

These numbers show only the change in desired state spending and taxes. One has to put much more faith in the median voter proposition to determine whether state spending will actually fall by this amount in a ceteris paribus sense. What can be said is that either it will fall, or state officials will be taking increasing political risks with their voters. Either way the importance of this first trickle down channel should be approximately in proportion to the ten percent state spending reduction, an estimate that is less than half as large as those estimates that have assumed that the median voter itemizes.[11] Using my approach with micro data does not eliminate this trickle down effect, but it certainly lessens it.

The note at the bottom of the table also indicates that the per respondent Kaldor-Hicks distortion from deductibility, assuming no externalities is 1.4 percent of the spending. This distortion is computed in the way described in Figure 1. Voters are assumed to have a willingness-to-pay value just equal to their price at the spending level they prefer, with a logarithmic slope of this willingness-to-pay schedule equal to $-1/a_1$. Assuming that state spending falls just 10 percent, the dead-weight loss is the integral above the willingness-to-pay curve and below the no deduction price line for all itemizers, less that below the willingness-to-pay curve and above the price line for all nonitem-

izers. For ease of interpretation, this estimate is expressed as a per respondent average—whether the expenditures in question are pure public goods or not, the aggregate distortion can be estimated by multiplying the per respondent loss by the number of respondents.

The estimate should obviously be viewed as very crude—to derive it, I simply took the arithmetic average of all trapezoids, as if the Kaldor-Hicks assumption that all gains and losses were equally weighted were appropriate. I was also forced to convert positive or negative dead-weight losses measures in terms of percentages of expenditures for each voter to a common absolute scale in making the calculation. But though the calculation is very crude, it is also indicative—even when per capita state spending is raised as much as 10 percent by deductibility, efficiency losses expressed in the same terms are much less.

The next results are for local spending, again for the six areas shown. The spending drops are smaller because not quite as many voters favor cuts in local spending and taxes. There is again no change in median local spending desired in Detroit and Lansing. Over the rest of the state there is a drop between five and ten percent. Across the whole state, the local spending drop averages five percent, now less than one-fourth as large as the estimates from the literature that assumes the median voter itemizers. And since what local spending reductions there are are concentrated in high income areas, there is only a very slight trickle down effect to lower income people working through local public spending. As before, the per respondent efficiency costs of the tax deduction are quite small, now only 0.6 percent of local spending across the whole state.

A potential criticism of the numbers shown in Table 3 is that the voter sample is taken from those who voted in the widely-publicized November, 1978, election. It is certainly possible that fewer voters would vote in the run-of-the-mill local school millage elections that are very common in Michigan, and that the calculations would thereby be distorted. I

Table 2

Desired State Spending, All Voters
Michigan Survey, 1978

Desired percentage change in state spending and taxes
Median voter group underlined

Place	Cut more than 10	Cut 6 to 10	Cut 1 to 5	None	Raise 1 to 5	Raise 6 to 10	Raise more than 10	Total
(With deductibility)								
Detroit	6	12	6	103	1	8	13	149
Detroit suburbs	43	46	25	171	0	19	14	318
Lansing	4	2	2	16	0	1	1	26
Lansing suburbs	2	6	1	12	0	4	0	25
Other urban counties	18	25	10	71	0	1	6	131
Rural counties	75	86	43	251	1	17	14	487
Total	148	177	87	624	2	50	48	1136
(Without deductibility, $a_1 = .5$)								
Detroit	48	12	5	68	1	4	11	149
Detroit suburbs	172	44	16	72	0	8	5	318
Lansing	8	4	2	11	0	1	0	26
Lansing suburbs	14	2	0	8	0	0	0	25
Other urban counties	59	21	7	42	2	0	2	131
Rural counties	197	80	33	155	2	14	6	487
Total	498	163	63	356	4	28	24	1136

Percentage point increase in median state spending demand with deductibility (as computed exactly from the micro data): 10.0
Per respondent Kaldor-Hicks distortion from deductibility: 1.4 percent of expenditures
Source: Voter survey described in Courant, Gramlich, Rubinfeld (1980). The sample size is slightly smaller than in Table 1 because of nonresponse on the state spending question.

Table 3

Desired Local Spending, All Voters
Michigan Survey, 1978

Desired percentage change in local spending and taxes
Median voter group underlined

Place	Cut more than 10	Cut 6 to 10	Cut 1 to 5	None	Raise 1 to 5	Raise 6 to 10	Raise more than 10	Total
(With deductibility)								
Detroit	7	5	2	87	3	27	18	149
Detroit suburbs	20	16	9	229	3	30	25	332
Lansing	2	2	0	17	0	3	4	28
Lansing suburbs	1	1	1	18	0	3	2	26
Other urban counties	11	8	11	79	0	14	7	130
Rural counties	40	31	28	314	3	41	48	505
Total	81	63	51	744	9	118	104	1170
(Without deductibility, $a_1 = .5$)								
Detroit	37	14	6	54	4	21	13	149
Detroit suburbs	165	32	14	93	3	17	8	332
Lansing	5	8	0	11	0	2	2	28
Lansing suburbs	12	1	1	8	0	3	1	26
Other urban counties	54	12	9	43	1	7	4	130
Rural counties	163	65	37	188	4	25	23	505
Total	436	132	67	397	12	75	51	1170

Percentage point increase in median local spending demand with deductibility (as computed exactly from the micro data):
Detroit and Lansing: zero
Detroit suburbs: 10.0
Lansing suburbs: 5.8
Other urban counties: 7.7
Rural counties: 5.0
Total: 5.0

Per respondent Kaldor-Hicks distortions from deductibility, as a percent of expenditures:
Detroit and Lansing: zero
Detroit suburbs: 1.2
Lansing suburbs: 0.8
Other urban counties: 0.9
Rural counties: 0.5
Total: 0.6

Source: Voter survey described in Courant, Gramlich, Rubinfeld (1980).

examined the possibility by recomputing the numbers in Table 3 for only those who reported voting in the previous school tax election in their district. The sample size is smaller (1079 as opposed to 1170), but otherwise the results are so similar (spending reductions are the same in most areas, averaging 6.7 percent as opposed to 5.0 percent) that a new table is not given.

The Impact on High and Low Income Communities

The second important potential trickle down effect involves income differences within and among communities. Elimination of tax deductibility would lower spending desired by high income voters in all communities. What is not so clear is whether the implications of that spending demand change would be shifted back to the poor living in low income communities.

The first set of results in Table 4. To begin with, the top panel shows that with deductibility median spending demands for high income voters (voters in families with 1978 incomes above $20,000, 14 percent above the overall sample mean) are the same as median spending demands for all other voters (compare Table 4 with Table 3). Whereas richer areas have elsewhere been observed to spend more than poor communities, within communities there is apparently some fiscal shift, or differences in the composition of public services, that encourages high income voters to favor no more public spending than low income voters.[12]

And this is with tax deductibility. When deductibility is eliminated, in the bottom panel, the rich turn into fiscal conservatives. In high income communities such as the Detroit and Lansing suburbs and other urban counties, median spending demands drop more or less along with spending demands of the rich, and the whole spending distribution is shifted left. As was seen previously, that eliminates a distortion of modest size, and presumably has no important distributional costs.

But in lower income communities such as the central cities and the rural areas, there is no important shift in the overall

median spending demand following the elimination of deductibility. The elimination then carries with it no overall efficiency saving, but it now creates a bimodal distribution of desired spending levels, with the rich in these communities favoring lower spending levels. This is likely to lead to a subtle form of intracommunity fiscal tension, to changes in the character of public spending (increasing the bribe for the rich to stay put), or to emigration of the rich.

The model developed above assumed that the outlet for this fiscal tension was the emigration of the rich, and generated an expression for the relative loss faced by rich taxpayers in staying in poor communities. This loss (given by [10] above) was a function of federal tax marginal rates, the drop in spending in the rich community, and the relative price difference for some constant bundle of public services between rich and poor communities.

In Table 5 I attempt to evaluate this loss. To standardize calculations, I confine attention only to itemizing voters with incomes above $20,000 in the Detroit metropolitan area. Detroit, with an average family income of $12,556 in 1978, can be viewed as the poor community; there median spending demanded does not change at all when deductibility is eliminated, just as was assumed in deriving the loss expression. The Detroit suburbs, with family income averaging $21,574, can be viewed as the hypothetical high income suburbs; there median spending demanded drops about ten percent, so α is set equal to .1 for the calculations.

The difficult variable to measure is S_r/S_p, the terms on which public services are provided across communities. If resource costs can be viewed as constant, if overlapping county expenditure can be viewed as equally provided, if higher level grants are not open-ended, and if the character of public services is the same across communities, calculating S_r/S_p with data from the Census of Governments and the voter survey leads to a value of .77.[13] But since the data used to calculate this price ratio are at best imperfect measurements, I have shown results where S_r/S_p is set respectively at .8 and .7.

Table 4

Desired Local Spending, High Income Voters
Michigan Survey, 1978

Desired percentage change in local spending and taxes
Voters in families with income above $20,000
Median voter group underlined
Community income from the sample in parentheses

Place	Cut more than 10	Cut 6 to 10	Cut 1 to 5	None	Raise 1 to 5	Raise 6 to 10	Raise more than 10	Total
(With deductibility)								
Detroit (12556)	3	3	0	<u>16</u>	0	6	2	30
Detroit suburbs (21574)	9	11	3	<u>134</u>	0	16	13	186
Lansing (15371)	1	1	0	<u>6</u>	0	1	1	10
Lansing suburbs (22078)	1	1	1	<u>10</u>	0	1	1	15
Other urban counties (17221)	4	2	5	<u>32</u>	0	6	1	50
Rural counties (16292)	10	13	9	<u>116</u>	0	10	20	178
Total (17544)	28	31	18	<u>314</u>	0	40	38	469
(Without deductibility, $a_1 = .5$)								
Detroit (12556)	<u>22</u>	1	1	4	0	1	1	30
Detroit suburbs (21574)	<u>134</u>	11	4	31	0	4	2	186
Lansing (15371)	4	<u>2</u>	0	3	0	1	0	10
Lansing suburbs (22078)	<u>9</u>	1	1	3	0	1	0	15
Other urban counties (17221)	32	3	3	11	0	4	0	50
Rural counties (16292)	<u>111</u>	13	6	37	0	1	7	178
Total (17544)	<u>312</u>	31	15	89	0	12	10	469

Source: Voter survey described in Courant, Gramlich, Rubinfeld (1980). The sample size is smaller than in Table 1 because of the income filter.

Table 5

Relative Losses in Low Income Communities from Elimination of Deductibility

Detroit city and suburbs
Itemizing voters in families with incomes above $20,000

Income Group ($000)	Marginal federal tax rate for the class (t)	Relative loss in poor community $\left[\dfrac{L_p - L_r}{E_p\,S_p}\right]$			
		Full elimination		Rich only elimination	
		$S_r/S_p = .8$	$S_r/S_p = .7$	$S_r/S_p = .8$	$S_r/S_p = .7$
20-25	.25	.051	.038	-.197	-.211
25-30	.28	.057	.042	-.221	-.237
30-35	.33	.068	.050	-.260	-.279
35-40	.35	.072	.053	-.276	-.296
40-45	.40	.082	.060	-.316	-.338
45-50	.43	.088	.065	-.339	-.363
50+	.53	.109	.080	-.418	-.448
Total	.32	.066	.048	-.252	-.270

[a] Assuming full deductibility, so g=1, a_1=.5, and =.1.

Source: S_r/S_p calculated on basis of Census of Governments data tape and data from the voter survey described in Courant, Gramlich, and Rubinfeld (1980).

The results are as shown. In the full elimination case the relative loss is about five percent of tax payments in the poor community, a noticeable amount but probably small enough to generate very little migration to the higher income communities. The sensitivity of the loss to estimated values of S_r/S_p is also slight.

These calculations refer to a general elimination of tax deductibility. But one might approach the policy problem differently. If a subtle cost in removing deductibility is that a fiscal incentive will be created for the rich to leave poor communities, thus increasing income segregation, it might be possible to use federal tax policy to encourage income mixing. One way to do this would be to eliminate deductibility for rich but not for poor communities. In such a change L_p is by definition set at zero and L_r is just as it was before.

The two columns on the right side of Table 5 give the relative losses to rich itemizers in remaining in poor communities under this differential elimination plan. Now the losses become negative numbers, with shares of tax payments in the poor community equalling about eighty percent of the taxpayer's federal rate, implying much more powerful fiscal incentives for the nonresident rich to immigrate to poor communities. The pre-tax S_p may be high for these rich people, but the post-tax value is definitely not high. And this immigration incentive is only slightly diluted when the pre-tax S_r is arbitrarily lowered.

Intermediate Plans

The intermediate deductibility plan of eliminating deductibility only for high income communities is the one that seems best able to generate both efficiency and equity improvements. Even though this type of measure has not, to my knowledge, been suggested by other commenters, a number of other changes have been suggested. Table 6 reports some general results for them. Since the experience for Detroit and Lansing is usually quite similar, and that for the rest of the state also similar, this table shows results just for those two composite areas. Moreover, since

the income heterogeneity question is relevant only at the local level, and the results for state and local spending are so similar, I have only shown results for desired changes in local spending and taxes. Finally, I only show the percentage change between the median values favored before and after the deductibility change.

The top panel of the table gives just the results described already, for complete elimination of tax deductibility. The second panel can be thought of as showing the results either for partial deductibility with $g = .5$, or as a sensitivity test of how the calculations come out when the assumed tax price elasticity is half as large. Either way, $ga_1 = .25$ and the results are as shown, with changes approximately half those for complete elimination. While it is not surprising that changes turn out to be half as large, it is not preordained either, since the underlying distribution of voter tastes is not rectangular.

The bottom panel of the table shows what might happen under the Bradley-Gephardt tax reform bill. This bill continues the tax deduction for most state and local taxes (sales taxes are no longer deductible, a fact that is irrelevant for these simulations because sales taxes are not local taxes), but makes them deductible only at the bottom bracket marginal federal rate, .14 in their bill. Hence the operative value for gt for all itemizers in the Bradley-Gephardt bill is .14 (similar to a partial credit for all itemizers), a_1 is put back at .5, and the results are as shown. The changes are slightly smaller than with a complete elimination of deductibility for all voters; significantly smaller for high income voters.[14]

The table does not show results for two other approaches for watering down the elimination of deductibility. Under Durenberger's floor approach, state and local taxes up to one percent of adjusted gross income would not be deductible. All those taxpayers with state and local taxes less than this one percent would no longer have the price reduction: for them the Durenberger approach is tantamount to complete elimination of deductibility. Those with state and local taxes of more than one percent of their income, the vast majority, would suffer only a slight decline

Table 6

**Impact of Various Deductibility Limitation Schemes
Michigan Survey, 1978**

Desired percentage reduction in local spending and taxes
at median voter point

Plan and Place	All voters	High income voters
Remove deductibility ($a_1 g = .5$)		
Detroit and Lansing	0	13
Rest of state	7	13
Partial deductibility ($a_1 g = .25$)		
Detroit and Lansing	0	8
Rest of state	3	7
Bradley—Gephardt approach ($gt = .14$)		
Detroit and Lansing	0	7
Rest of state	5	7

Source: Voter survey described in Courant, Gramlich, Rubinfeld (1980).

in their income, but experience no relative price change. For this vast majority of taxpayers, the percentage reduction in state and local taxes is equal to $.01a_2$, where a_2 is the income elasticity. Generally a_2 is estimated at about unity, implying that the Durenberger bill should lower spending desired by most itemizers by one percent, that desired by a few who switch to becoming non-itemizers by more than one percent, and that desired by all others not at all. I do not have the numbers to work all of this out, but the changes in desired local spending and taxes will generally be very slight.

An opposite approach beginning to surface in newspaper reports is to impose a ceiling on the amount of state and local taxes that can be deducted. While the floor approach lowers the income of high income taxpayers but leaves marginal tax prices the same, the ceiling approach alters tax prices but not incomes. The trick-

le down impact on public spending given here will still be operative, but this time without any initial loss for high income itemizers. In this sense it is hard to justify a ceiling on equity grounds.

Implications

Returning to the underlying theme of the paper, eliminating or reducing state and local tax deductibility will raise federal revenue a large amount. Most of the utility loss should be felt by high income taxpayers, with what seem to be minimal trickle down effects. Regarding the first of these trickle down effects, on state and local public spending, the overall responses are on the order of zero to ten percent, much less than estimates used in the political debate. And even these reductions in local public spending would appear to be concentrated in high income communities where most itemizers now live. In poorer communities such as Detroit and Lansing, there are few enough itemizers that median spending demands should not change at all with the elimination of deductibility.

The second important trickle down effect involves the question of whether eliminating deductibility will induce high income taxpayers to leave low income communities. Although it is hard to measure relative prices for public goods across communities, the data again imply that the incentive for the rich to leave poor communities following a general elimination of deductibility seems to be quite modest, again on the order of five percent of local tax payments. But the same model suggests that there could be larger gains in fiscal incentives for the rich to locate in poor communities were deductibility to be eliminated just for rich communities.

What then should be done about the tax deduction? Since both trickle down effects appear to be rather modest, a full elimination of deductibility makes good sense from both an equity and an efficiency standpoint. But if Congress should search for intermediate possibilities, there are some, different from those usually suggested, that might be investigated. One is to allow deduction of local but not state taxes. Such a measure would produce two-thirds of the revenue gained by complete elimination, with only the first of the potential trickle down effects discussed here. Even this could be neutralized at small cost by adjusting federal matching shares for those state programs that do directly affect low income people (such as AFDC and Medicaid).[15]

And it should be possible to do even better. As was suggested above, the income mixing point argues for retaining the deduction for residents of low income communities but not high income communities. These high income communities need no fiscal incentive to get rich people to live there, by almost anybody's policy objective function. Rather than spreading the deduction across all communities, why not strengthen the fiscal incentive for income mixing, and limit the federal revenue loss, by confining the deduction to residents of lower income com-

munities? A plan would have much the same goals as the President's urban enterprise zones, but in conferring the fiscal benefit to all taxpayers living within a jurisdiction (and contributing to the jurisdiction's schools), it is much more workable and less distortionary than the present urban enterprise zone proposal.

The differential elimination of deductibility may not be the best use of federal revenues under any and all circumstances. It may still be preferable to devote more funds to straightforward income support plans, or to general support of poor communities through targeted revenue sharing. And there is a definite loss of tax reform momentum whenever any subsidy, however well-intentioned, is made differential. But if compromises with full deductibility are to be made, this measure seems more likely to preserve overall efficiency and equity goals than other intermediate provisions now being discussed.

FOOTNOTES

**I would like to thank Deborah Laren for her invaluable assistance, and Daphne Kenyon for generously supplying the federal tax rate data. Discussions with Ted Bergstrom, Paul Courant, Elizabeth Gordon, Richard and Peggy Musgrave, and John Yinger have proven very helpful. My work has been financed by a grant from the Sloan Foundation.

[1]These reports are all cited in Kenyon (1985a).

[2]Table 7 in Kenyon (1985b) reports that in 1982 41 percent of all taxpayers claimed itemized deductions (weighting joint returns twice as single returns). Only 3 percent of taxpayers with adjusted gross incomes of less than $5 thousand itemized, 11 percent between $5 thousand and $10 thousand, and so on up to 97 percent of all taxpayers with incomes over $100 thousand.

[3]The main difficulty is in knowing whether the median, or decisive, voter in a community itemizes deductions. Zimmerman (1983), Noto and Zimmerman (1983 and 1984), and Ladd (1984) just assume so, even though on an aggregate basis less than half of all tax returns claim deductions. Hettich and Winer (1984) use the share of rich taxpayers as a proxy for the share of itemizers, but get the wrong sign when explaining the share of revenues made up of deductible income taxes. Inman (1985) uses an arbitrarily weighted average of marginal federal tax rates to measure the effective tax price facing the decisive voter, but still gets rather inconsistent results.

[4]Noto and Zimmerman (1983), who first made this point, did call their measures "transfer efficiency," but the adjective often gets lost as the story is retold.

[5]Another complication, not analyzed here, is that house prices in various communities may change. Sparrow (1985) shows how these could alter outcomes, but only under the standard assumption that all homeowners itemize. Yinger (1985b) deals with the case where willingness-to-pay curves are distorted by the concomitant property tax distortion in the housing market. There is no end to the fun that can be had.

[6]It might seem that there is more to it, that the expression should also include the general gain in consumer surplus from moving to the rich community where tax prices are lower. The reason such an expression has not been included is that I have assumed that this taxpayer had some other reason for wanting to live in the poor community initially that offset this apparent consumer surplus. When deductibility is eliminated, the only marginal effects are then the changes in surplus for the poor and rich communities.

[7]Inman (1985) discusses this relative impact also, arriving at apparently different conclusions than I do. The reason is that I focus on public spending, assumed to be larger in the rich community. Inman focuses on fiscal transfers to poor people, assumed to be positive in the poor community and zero in the rich community. If Inman is right about the magnitude of within jurisdiction transfers, the other steps in his reasoning could follow. But logically it is implausible that transfers would be so much higher in the poor community, and empirically it seems doubtful—see Gramlich and Rubinfeld (1982).

[8]Another issue that has been debated in the literature can be clarified by equation (10). It has been argued that deductibility encourages income stratification so that voters can mutually avail themselves of the deductibility provision. The argument is correct, but refers only to one of the factors generating relative gains and losses.

Political scientists still have not learned how to ask these types of questions. For some evidence, see Traugott (1985).

[9]This point is made by Oakland (1985). To support his argument, a direct estimate of the price elasticity of demand for overall public spending from this data set comes out to be about .05 (Gramlich and Rubinfeld (1982); while a direct estimate for one particular service, education, is about .4 (Bergstrom, Rubinfeld, and Shapiro (1982)).

[10]The results have been previously reported in Gramlich (1985). Similar ones for Massachusetts are given by Ladd (1984).

[11]Such estimates are given by Zimmerman (1983), Noto and Zimmerman (1983 and 1984), and Ladd (1984). Kenyon (1985a and 1985b) gets smaller estimates, because she reduces the change proportionately by the share of itemizers (1985a), or computes the tax price change for the partially itemizing, partially non-itemizing median income voter (1985b). Inman (1985) gets smaller estimates because he adjusts for varying marginal federal tax rates across the income distribution. These approaches are closer to the right idea.

[12]Gramlich and Rubinfeld (1982) identified this phenomenon more carefully from an econometric standpoint, and speculated on some reasons for it.

[13]It can be shown that if the income effect of grants

is negligible and if most grants are not open-ended (they are not), the marginal relative price of public goods for a typical rich taxpayer can be approximated by

$$\frac{S_r}{S_p} = \left(\frac{S_r E_r + G_r}{S_p E_p + G_p}\right)\left(\frac{E_p}{E_r}\right)$$

where G_r and G_p are per capita grants in the rich and poor community respectively.

The values used in Table 5 are taken either from the micro data tape for a rich itemizer in 1978 as described in the text, or from the 1976/77 Census of Governments (COG) for city, school, and county governments. They are as follows, all in per capita terms:

	Detroit	Detroit suburbs
E_p or E_r (COG)	1031	869
G_p or G_r (COG)	619	334
$S_p E_p$ or $S_r E_r$ (micro)	508	395

Hence

$$\frac{S_r}{S_p} = \left(\frac{395 + 334}{508 + 619}\right)\left(\frac{1031}{869}\right) = .767$$

[14]In this case there is a slight underestimate of the spending reduction. Because many other deductions are eliminated by Bradley-Gephardt, fewer voters will be itemizers. For those who switch from itemizing to non-itemizing, the tax price would jump from S(1 − t) to S, instead of to .86S as I have assumed. The estimate shown in the table can then be viewed as a lower bound estimate of the impact of the change; the upper bound estimate would be that for full elimination of deductibility.

[15]To offset a ten percent reduction in state spending, assumed to operate equally across all categories, the marginal price for AFDC and medicaid should be lowered twenty percent (if a_1 = .5). In high income states where the marginal price is now .5, the federal matching share should go from its present value of .5 to .6. In low income states where the marginal price is now .17, the federal matching share should go from it present value of .83 to .86. Across the country this offset would cost the federal government about $4 billion in fiscal 1984. The cost of replacing the lost spending by raising food stamps is about the same.

REFERENCES

Bergstrom, Theodore C., Daniel L. Rubinfeld, and Perry Shapiro (1982), "Micro Based Estimates of Demand Functions for Local School Expenditures," *Econometrica*, vol. 50, September, pp. 1183–1205.

Courant, Paul N., Edward M. Gramlich, and Daniel L. Rubinfeld (1980), "Why Voters Support Tax Limitation Amendments: The Michigan Case," *National Tax Journal*, vol. 33, March, pp. 1–20.

Gramlich, Edward M. (1985), "Fiscal Federalism: A Reform Agenda," in John Quigley and Daniel L. Rubinfeld (eds.), *American Domestic Priorities: An Economic Appraisal*, University of California Press, pp. 34–70.

Gramlich, Edward M. and Daniel L. Rubinfeld (1982), "Micro Estimates of Public Spending Demand Functions and Tests of the Tiebout and Median-Voter Hypotheses," *Journal of Political Economy*, vol. 90, June, pp. 536–560.

Hettich, Walter, and Stanley Winer (1984), "A Positive Model of Tax Structure," *Journal of Public Economics*, vol. 24, June, pp. 67–87.

Inman, Robert P. (1985), "Does Deductibility Influence Local Taxation?" Federal Reserve Bank of Philadelphia Working Paper, 85-6.

Kenyon, Daphne A. (1985a), "Federal Income Tax Deductibility of State and Local Taxes: What Are Its Effects? Should It Be Modified?" in Advisory Commission on Intergovernmental Relations, *Strengthening the Federal Revenue System: Implications for State and Local Taxing and Borrowing*, forthcoming.

Kenyon, Daphne A. (1985b), "Federal Tax Deductibility," Mimeo, Advisory Commission on Intergovernmental Relations.

Ladd, Helen F. (1984), "Federal Aid to State and Local Governments," in Gregory B. Mills and John L. Palmer (eds.), *Federal Budget Policy in the 1980s*, The Urban Institute, pp. 165–202.

Noto, Nonna A., and Dennis Zimmerman (1983), "Limiting State-Local Tax Deductibility in Exchange for Increased General Revenue Sharing: An Analysis of the Economic Effects," Prepared for the Senate Subcommittee on Intergovernmental Relations, August.

Noto, Nonna A., and Dennis Zimmerman (1984), "Limiting State-Local Tax Deductibility: Effects Among the States," *National Tax Journal*, vol. 37, December, pp. 539–550.

Oakland, William H. (1985), "Consequences of the Repeal of State and Local Tax Deductibility Under the U.S. Personal Income Tax," Mimeo, Tulane University.

Sparrow, F. T. (1985), "The Subsidy Value and Incidence of Tax Expenditures Which Benefit State and Local Governments: The Case of the Property Tax," Mimeo.

Traugott, Michael W. (1985), "Public Response to Proposal C and Income and Property Taxes in Michigan," Mimeo, The University of Michigan.

Yinger, John (1985a), "On Fiscal Disparities Across Cities," forthcoming, *Journal of Urban Economics*.

Yinger, John (1985b), "Inefficiency and the Median Voter: Property Taxes, Capitalization, Heterogeneity, and the Theory of the Second Best," Mimeo, Harvard University.

Zimmerman, Dennis (1983), "Resource Misallocation from Interstate Tax Exportation: Estimates of Excess Spending and Welfare Loss in a Median Voter Framework," *National Tax Journal*, Vol. 36, pp. 183–201.

[13]

The Impact of the Tax Reform Act of 1986 on State and Local Fiscal Behavior

Paul N. Courant and
Edward M. Gramlich

Just three years have elapsed since TRA86 was signed and most of its provisions regarding states and localities became widely known. Most of these provisions have been in effect for less than three years. One or two years of post-TRA86 aggregate data on states and localities are available, one or no years of data for some of the key micro variables. This is not very much information, given various lags in behavioral responses and the degree to which subtle effects emanating from TRA86 can be concealed by more dramatic behavioral shocks. Our purpose here then is to take a first look at whether TRA86 is having the various impacts it was thought likely to have. There is no question that these early indications may become revised or outmoded as time passes, behavior changes, and new data become available.

We investigate three main topics:

1. The impact of TRA86 on the aggregate fiscal policy of states and localities—spending, the level and composition of taxes, and asset stocks.

2. The impact of TRA86 on the economic activity, property values, and tax bases of local jurisdictions.

3. The impact of TRA86 on the market for state and local bonds.

The first topic is investigated by comparing aggregate national income accounts data for 1987 and 1988 with those of earlier years through time series regression analysis. The second is investigated by a form of event study. Rather than conducting what seemed to be a hopeless examination of mobility and property values for all jurisdictions, we focus on adjacent border jurisdictions in states that should be quite differentially affected by TRA86. We then look for shocks in a variety of indicators of population shifts, including building permits, assessed values, and county employment levels. The third topic is investigated by comparing the return on state and local bonds relative to taxable bonds, both before and after TRA86.

Paul N. Courant and Edward M. Gramlich   244

8.1   State and Local Fiscal Behavior

We first discuss a simple theory of state and local fiscal behavior in the
presence of differential federal tax treatment of different taxes and the
pre-TRA86 empirical predictions of its impact. We then give our own early
empirical estimates of what seemed to have happened and compare these
estimates with more informal reports of what is going on.

A Simple Theory

Consider a jurisdiction that levies a variety of taxes and user fees, receives
grants from other governments, and spends the money on goods, services,
and transfers. Without going into the underlying social choice mechanism,
we can posit that the jurisdiction has a demand for public spending that
varies positively with the community's resources and negatively with the
total cost to the jurisdiction's residents of a dollar's worth of public expenditure (E). Thus jurisdictions will have demands for public spending that are
downward sloping in the cost per dollar of such spending, drawn as the
MB schedule in figure 8.1.

The supply schedule for this jurisdiction's public expenditure is more
complicated. If the jurisdiction behaves rationally, this supply schedule will
be the usual horizontal sum of the marginal cost functions of the various
sources of revenue. First will come lump-sum grants (G). These are fixed in
total amount and, once this amount is reached, are supplied inelastically.
Then come the various taxes the jurisdiction can assess. To anticipate later
analysis of TRA86, these taxes will be disaggregated into those that were
deductible (D) before and after TRA86, those taxes and fees that were
nondeductible (N) before and after TRA86, and sales taxes (S) which were
deductible before but not after TRA86. The marginal cost for each of
these taxes is weakly increasing in revenue raised because of direct burden,
excess burden, or political costs. These marginal cost schedules are shown
as D, N, and S respectively in figure 8.1.

The jurisdiction will choose its revenue sources so that the three marginal costs are equalized. At this point the marginal benefits of public spending will also equal these common marginal costs, as shown in figure 8.1.
The line indicated by MC is the horizontal sum of all revenue sources
before TRA86 and E is the equilbrium level of public spending, which is
financed by the fixed level of G and the designated level of each of the
taxes.

Impact of Tax Reform Act on State and Local Fiscal Behavior

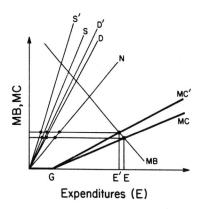

Figure 8.1
Impact of TRA86 on state and local budgets:

Budget constraint

$$\Delta E = \Delta D + \Delta S + \Delta N$$

TRA86 impact

$$D' = D\left(\frac{1 - a't'}{1 - at}\right)$$

$$S' = S\left(\frac{1}{1 - at}\right)$$

Predictions

$\Delta E < 0$

$\Delta S < 0$

$\Delta D < 0$

$\Delta N > 0$

Paul N. Courant and Edward M. Gramlich

Now assume a federal tax change such as was made by TRA86. This bill would change the fiscal position of the jurisdiction by

1. lowering the marginal federal tax rate faced by most itemizers in the jurisdiction,

2. lowering the fraction of taxpayers who itemize,

3. removing the sales tax deduction altogether.[1]

TRA86 did not affect the marginal cost schedule for nondeductible taxes and fees, so there would be no shift in the N schedule.

The standard way of representing the impact of changes such as this has become to focus on the mean voter in the jurisdiction. With this focus, even if the median voter in the jurisdiction does not itemize deductions, the loss of, say, the sales tax deduction is costly for the jurisdiction because some voters in the jurisdiction are worse off and now find public services to be more costly.[2] Letting t stand for the average marginal federal tax rate of itemizers in the jurisdiction before TRA86, t' for this rate after TRA86, a for the share of taxpayers who itemize before TRA86, and a' for the share of taxpayers who itemize after TRA86, the other two tax schedules would shift as follows:

$$D' = \frac{D(1 - a't')}{1 - at},$$ (1)

$$S' = \frac{S}{1 - at}.$$ (2)

These shifts are shown in figure 8.1, as is the shift in the horizontal sum schedule to MC'. The jurisdiction would reoptimize at the new expenditure level E' and the higher aftertax marginal tax cost of all three taxes.

One could then make the following predictions of the impact of TRA86 on state and local budgets:

State and local spending E would fall.

Nondeductible taxes and fees N would rise.

Sales taxes S would fall.

Deductible taxes D would fall.

The first two predictions would be true with any normally sloped spending demand function and marginal cost function for nondeductible taxes. These two predictions in turn imply that the sum of S and D will fall. If the pretax cost functions of these two taxes are similar, S is likely to fall by more in percentage terms because its aftertax cost increases by more. But there are some instances where either tax may not drop, although the sum still will.

One such complication is mentioned by Inman (1989), who gives a reason why sales taxes could rise in response to TRA86. Inman points out that in eliminating a tax deduction primarily used by the rich, TRA86 might have thrown the distributional balance of states and localities out of whack, forcing these governments to raise regressive sales taxes to restore their distributional balance. Another complication that works in the same direction is raised by Metcalf (1989), who shows that when sales taxes are exported to other jurisdictions, the relative cost of sales taxes could rise less than that of income taxes with TRA86: The price of the component borne at home rises more than for income taxes, but the price of the exported component does not rise. This latter effect would be shown on figure 8.1 with a very elastic S schedule, so even a higher percentage change than for the D curve might raise the marginal cost at the initial revenue mix by less.

These predictions are also only relevant for changes in the aftertax cost of certain taxes, which in effect pivot the MC curve counterclockwise. Further complications ensue when some of the schedules in figure 8.1 also shift for independent reasons. If, for example, there were an outward shift in the MB function, the new intersection would be on the MC' schedule at a higher expenditure level. The higher aftertax marginal cost and benefit would lead to greater use of all taxes, with the consequence that S and D might both rise in order to finance this higher spending. If, on the other hand, grants were cut, the MC' schedule would be shifted in, the new equilibrium would be at a lower spending level but again a higher aftertax cost of all taxes, and again all taxes could be increased to finance the cut in grants.

One final factor is what is known as the "windfall effect" of TRA86. TRA86 raised the federal tax base, and many states use this federal tax base as the base for their own tax. In such a case TRA86 could shift the D curve outward because of this windfall effect, again making it more likely that D would increase.

Pre-TRA86 Empirical Predictions

Before the fact almost everyone predicted that TRA86 would lower state and local spending. Using various estimates of marginal rates and numbers of itemizers before and after, Courant and Rubinfeld (1987), Kenyon (1988), and Gramlich (1987) predicted very slight declines in state and local spending, on the order of 1%. Using empirical estimates from a sample of local governments, Holtz-Eakin and Rosen (1988) predicted very sharp declines in local spending, on the order of 8%. Applying their elasticity estimates to state spending gives even larger percentage declines for states.[3] This is one battle to be joined.

The second prediction is that TRA86 should have raised the share of nondeductible taxes and fees. Although this prediction is clear from the theory, nobody was able to get very sensible parameter estimates before the fact. Feldstein and Metcalf (1987) obtained mixed results on the question, whereas Holtz-Eakin and Rosen (1988) and Inman (1989) estimated coefficients, albeit insignificant ones, that implied that fees would fall, not rise, in response to TRA86.

The third and fourth predictions are that the mix would shift away from those taxes where marginal costs are increased . Hettich and Winer (1984), Inman (1989), and Noto and Zimmerman (1985) found relatively small effects of TRA86 on the revenue mix. In contrast, Feldstein and Metcalf (1987) and Holtz-Eakin and Rosen (1988) found much larger effects. Feldstein and Metcalf estimated very high elasticities (with large standard errors) of revenue from deductible taxes with respect to marginal cost. At face value their estimates implied that TRA86 should reduce income taxes by at least 12% and sales taxes by 30% or more. The similar numbers for Holtz-Eakin and Rosen (with smaller standard errors) were that local deductible taxes should fall by 6% and state sales taxes by 14%. Another battle to be joined.

As mentioned above, all of this gets much more complicated when other large changes are occurring simultaneously. And there were no shortage of these. One of the most dramatic is the change in the fiscal relationship between the federal government and states and localities. Grants from the federal government have been cut significantly. A decade ago grants were 3.4% of GNP and rising as a share; by 1988 grants were 2.3% of GNP and falling as a share. Provisions on the big income distribution grants'—AFDC and Medicaid—have been tightened, general revenue sharing has been cut out altogether, categorical grants have first been converted to block form and then killed or reduced. But while these cuts were occurring, the federal government has actually mandated increased state in local spending in areas such as health care, environmental protection, and human services.

Regarding windfalls, Gold (1988) estimated the state personal income tax windfall to be $6.3 billion, of which only $1.1 billion was likely to be retained after all discretionary rate cuts took effect. Aten (1987) initially

estimated the state corporate tax windfall to be $3.4 billion, though sub-
sequent data suggest it was less (Aten and Gold 1989).

A Time-Series Model

To see whether the various theoretical and empirical predictions of the
impact of TRA86 stand up, we fit a model to aggregate time-series data.
Obviously it would have been possible to take a case study type look at
the behavior of particular state or local governments, as Chernick and
Reschovsky (1989) recently did, but there is always the problem of generalizing to the whole on the basis of particular governments. And there
are so many individual local governments (about 80,000 right now) that
one could never say anything sensible about local governments with this
approach.

Our first approach then was to do what researchers would naturally do
in investigating any other aspect of TRA86—its effect on investment,
saving, housing, or whatever. That is to use aggregate national income
accounts data. These can now be broken down by state general governments and local general governments separately, which also makes sense in
view of the fact that different taxes and types of spending are used by the
different levels of government. Separated state and local fiscal data are now
available on an annual basis from 1959 to 1988 (Levin and Peters 1986,
1987; Peters 1988). We applied a time-series model modified from Gramlich (1978) to annual time-series observations from 1959 to 1986, the
period of the old tax law, and then made out-of-sample extrapolations for
the post-TRA86 years 1987 and 1988. From these extrapolations we can
see whether the residuals moved in line with the theoretical and empirical
predictions.

The model postulates a state or local objective function made up of three
arguments:

Spending

Aftertax private income

Fund balances

The latter is included because available fund balances can be turned into
future spending or private income. Utility is maximized subject to the
budget constraint:

$$\Delta B = D + S + N + G - E, \tag{3}$$

where ΔB refers to the change in the stock of fund balances, or the surplus, of governments and all other variables are as defined above. The level or stock of fund balances B is defined as:

$$B = B_{-1} + \Delta B. \tag{4}$$

Combining equations (3) and (4), it can be seen that

$$B_{-1} + G = E - D - S - N + B, \tag{5}$$

which is the basic budget identity of the model. The left side variable of equation (5) is grants and previously unallocated balances. These can be distributed to spending E, tax cuts $-D$, $-S$, and $-N$, and currently unallocated balances B according to the actions of state or local politicians.

To focus on shifts in tax shares resulting from TRA86, we estimate separate regressions for seven or six dependent variables:

1. Direct spending (E for localities, one component of E for states).

2. Grants to localities (the other component of E for states).

3. Deductible personal taxes (one component of D, mainly income taxes, for states, mainly property taxes for localities).

4. Deductible business or corporate taxes (the other component of D).

5. Sales taxes (S).

6. Nondeductible taxes, fines, and user fees (N).

7. Currently unallocated balances (B).

Following the standard utility maximization calculation (detailed in Gramlich 1978), each of these variables can be shown to be a function of income (GNP less federal taxes plus federal transfers to persons), a price term, and grants and previously unallocated balances ($B_{-1} + G$).

A model such as this could be fit either in money or real terms. The budget identity actually works in money terms and since most state tax systems are not indexed for inflation, most tax equations should also be formulated in money terms. On the other side, spending equations are usually fit in real terms, as if voters make decisions about real spending levels. Since our main interest is on the tax side and in the budget identity—to see how impacts are allocated across all budgetary categories—we fit the model in money terms. Each dependent variable and dollar flow independent variable is measured in money terms, and each equation includes the state and local purchases deflator as a separate independent variable. Previous versions of this model disaggregated grants according to whether they reduce the prices of favored activities at the margin. But since most actual grants these days do not reduce prices at the margin (are closed-ended), and since there is little time-series variation in matching rates for open-ended grants, we simplified the model to treat all grants from higher-level governments as exogenous closed-ended grants with no price effect at the margin.

There was serial correlation in the level version of the model, so we fit the equations under the assumption that the time-series residuals for all equations u followed the first-order process

$$u = 0.75u_{-1} + e, \tag{6}$$

where e represents the new shock in any period. The coefficient 0.75 must be the same in the equations for all budgetary components to preserve the budget identity, and it was selected by examining the uncorrected residuals from all seven or six budgetary equations.

The set of identities given above requires that the sum of all dependent variable equals $(B_{-1} + G)$, so the coefficients of this variable sum to one and the constants and coefficients of all other variables sum to zero. This constraint was automatically built into the coefficient estimates by the simple expedient of including every independent variable in the equation for every dependent variable. There are more elaborate ways to incorporate constraints if some of the coefficients have to be zeroed out, but most of our coefficients made reasonable sense. Since our main interest was in the residuals anyway, we followed golfers' summer rules and played the coefficients as they lay.[4]

The estimates for state governments are shown in table 8.1. The row sum of coefficients for the constant and each independent variable other than grants and previously unallocated balances is zero and that for grants and previously unallocated balances is one, as discussed above. Hence in this first year a dollar of federal grants raises direct spending by 0.2935, grants to localities by 0.3155, causes 0.0371 worth of tax cuts and raises the surplus by 0.3538. Next year this 0.3538 goes into unallocated balances and is further distributed to spending increases and tax cuts. On the other hand, in the first year a dollar rise in GNP raises all taxes by 0.1013 (0.0312 + 0.0121 + 0.0442 + 0.0138), spending by 0.0682 (0.0473 + 0.0209), and the surplus by 0.0332. Next year this amount too causes further rises in spending and this time slight cuts in taxes. Since the spending coefficient on untied grants is well above that for private income, there is an important "flypaper" effect—funds' inflows stick where they hit. Such an effect is quite characteristic of empirical models of state and local

Table 8.1
Budget constraint model, state governments annual observations, 1960–86

Independent variable	Dependent variables						
	Direct spending	Grants to localities	Minus deductible personal taxes	Minus deductible business taxes	Minus sales taxes	Minus nondeductible taxes	Unallocated balances
Constant ($ billion)	−14.38	−2.56	4.67	−2.32	−6.78	4.44	16.96
Grants and previously unallocated balances	0.2935 (2.3)	0.3155 (4.4)	0.0617 (1.2)	−0.0113 (0.3)	0.0382 (0.6)	−0.0515 (1.1)	0.3538 (2.5)
Income less federal withdrawals	0.0473 (5.3)	0.0209 (4.1)	−0.0312 (8.7)	−0.0121 (5.4)	−0.0442 (9.2)	−0.0138 (4.3)	0.0332 (3.3)
Gross price	34.54 (1.1)	23.26 (1.3)	30.30 (2.4)	23.66 (2.8)	47.63 (2.8)	−4.67 (0.4)	−154.72 (4.4)
Residual statistics (after correction for serial correlation)							
R^2	0.9912	0.9902	0.9881	0.9318	0.9893	0.9828	0.5617
Standard error ($ billion)	2.05	1.16	0.82	0.55	1.09	0.74	2.52

Note: semi-first differences ($\rho = 0.75$); t ratios below coefficients.

behavior, and there have been many, many theoretical rationales developed to explain it.

A 1% increase in the gross price deflator raises money spending by $.58 billion, implying a price elasticity of spending demand of about -0.8 at present levels of the variables. The finding that state spending demand is inelastic is standard, though it is puzzling that a rise in the gross price and money spending is coupled with tax cuts, leading to a large decline in fund balances. But the gross price variable (the state and local purchases deflator) in a time-series analysis is certainly measured very poorly, it behaves pretty much as a trend, and it should not interfere with our attempt to discern TRA86 induced changes in residuals.

Table 8.2 gives the residuals for these equations. Since the equations were fit assuming a first-order serial correlation process, it is not straightforward to know which residuals to give. The upper part of the table contains the residuals before any correction for serial correlation, u in equation (6), for 1987 and 1988 in comparison with those for the rest of the 1980s. Up to 1986 the residuals were within the regression sample, the 1987 residuals are out-of-sample extrapolations based on 1987 values of the exogenous variables, and for two of the series—deductible personal taxes and sales taxes—this calculation could also be done for 1988. As before, the residuals sum to zero across all budgetary components for each date.

The next panel shows the component of these residuals that would have been predicted at the end of 1986, the last year before TRA86 went into effect. To measure these predicted residuals, we have used whatever information was available at the end of 1986. The uncorrected 1986 residuals were known and forecast through equation (6). Given these, the model solved for the 1987 value of B, which in turn was used to generate predicted 1988 residuals across all seven budgetary equations. As the footnote to the table explains, since the 1986 prediction of 1987 stocks was higher than actual by $2.5 billion, this $2.5 billion was allocated across all seven budgetary equations by the estimated coefficients to give predicted 1988 residuals that sum to the same amount. Then these predicted residuals were subtracted from the uncorrected residuals to give the new shocks for 1987 and 1988, shown in the bottom panel.

These new shock residuals suggest the following story about the first year impact of TRA86 on state budgets:

1. There was a positive shock in the direct spending residual of $6.6 billion for 1987. The authors who predicted a small decline in state spend-

Table 8.2
1980s residuals, state budget model (billions of current $)

Date	Uncorrected residuals (u)						
	Direct spending	Grants to localities	Minus deductible personal taxes	Minus deductible business taxes	Minus sales taxes	Minus nondeductible taxes	Unallocated balances
1980	−5.3	0	0.1	−1.9	1.0	2.0	3.8
1981	−8.1	−2.4	1.8	−1.1	2.9	0.1	6.5
1982	−4.7	−2.9	1.1	0.6	2.7	−0.6	3.6
1983	−3.0	−3.0	0.9	0.5	2.5	−0.3	1.9
1984	−3.2	−2.4	−0.7	0.5	1.5	−0.5	4.6
1985	0.0	−0.7	−1.0	0.6	−0.5	−0.8	2.1
1986	4.3	0.3	−0.1	0.2	−0.7	−1.0	−3.3
1987	9.8	2.9	−4.8	−3.4	−1.5	2.6	−6.1
1988	na	na	0.1	na	−0.7	na	na
1987 value	248.6	135.2	−83.4	−25.7	−123.8	−57.7	−23.1
Predicted as of 1986[a]							
1987	3.2	0.2	−0.1	0.2	−0.6	−0.8	−2.5
1988	3.1	1.0	0.1	0.1	−0.4	−0.7	−1.0
New shock (uncorrected less predicted)							
1987	6.6	2.7	−4.7	−3.6	−0.9	3.4	−3.6
1988	na	na	0	na	−0.3	na	na

a. Since 1986 prediction of 1987 unallocated balances was higher than actual by $2.5 billion, this amount is allocated across all seven components according to the regression coefficients.

ing, such as Courant and Gramlich, were wrong, but not nearly as far wrong as those who predicted a large decline in spending, such as Holtz-Eakin and Rosen. The shock could be partly caused by the nongrant mandating of expenditures discussed earlier, but even the extreme estimates of the governors would not peg it as this large.

2. There was a positive shock in the residual for state grants to localities of $2.7 billion. This shock could well be due to federal grant policy, because federal grants to localities were cut by the large total of $4.5 billion between 1986 and 1987. This rise in state grants to localities could then be compensating for some of the decline in federal grants to localities.[5]

3. There was a positive shock in deductible personal taxes of $4.7 billion (the residual of the negative of taxes was negative). Gold's windfall amount mentioned earlier would seem to account for only a small share of this total, but there are many reasons why our residual could be above the net calculated by Gold. States could still be benefiting from a capital gains windfall in their 1987 refunds, or their discretionary measures to return the windfall could simply not have been made yet or taken effect yet. In view of these possibilities, our shock of $4.7 billion is likely to be quite close to the mark.

4. There was a positive shock in deductible business taxes of $3.6 billion, again very close to Aten's windfall amount.

5. Sales taxes showed a positive shock of $0.9 billion. Apparently the financing effect described above outweighed the price effect, belying the predictions of those who argued the reverse.

6. Nondeductible taxes and user fees showed a negative shock of $3.4 billion, a change that does not makes sense under any of the hypotheses discussed earlier. Even Inman's ingenious account of why sales taxes might have increased cannot simultaneously explain why regressive user fees might have decreased. The simultaneous decline in oil prices could explain some drop in severance taxes, part of the reason for the decline in this catchall, but there is no obvious story for the sharp drop in "fines," which accounts for most of the drop. The only consolation is that all other pre-TRA86 estimates of user fee sensitivity also had the wrong sign.

7. The surplus showed a negative shock of $3.6 billion, the net implied by all of these spending and tax changes.

Then we move on to 1988. At present data are available for only two of the taxes; personal deductible taxes and sales taxes. But they both show that taxes are moving in the expected direction. The personal tax windfall now seems like it is down to zero, much as Gold might have forecast, and the positive shock in sales taxes is also very small. So price effects are not of the wrong sign, but they are obviously not of the right sign either. In fact the 1959–86 equation works remarkably well for these two taxes through 1988.

Given the large state spending residuals and the windfalls, it is not terribly surprising that state deductible taxes rose in the short run. And it may not even be surprising that state sales taxes rose. But what is very definitely surprising from almost any standpoint is that state nondeductible taxes and fines went down.

Regressions for localities are shown in table 8.3. The equations are presented in the same form, the only change being that there is no analogue for state grants to localities—all local spending is direct. The equations again show a powerful flypaper effect and again imply a price elasticity of spending demand in the neighborhood of −0.5, a standard result. This time rises in the gross price do not lead to any noticeable changes in taxes but are entirely financed by drawing down balances.

The residuals in table 8.4 tell a very similar story about the impact of TRA86:

1. The first year new shock for direct spending is $10.3 billion, only about $1 billion of which could be attributed to the cuts in higher government grants to localities (federal grants down by $4.5, state grants up by $2.7, and the coefficient of grants on spending is 0.6600).

2. Both types of deductible taxes show a positive new shock of $2.1 billion. Since these deductible taxes are mainly residential property taxes, there is no windfall, and the entire rise must be attributed to the need to finance the rise in direct spending.

3. There is no new shock for sales taxes. Indeed, the 1987 value of $24.9 billion shown in the table indicates that local sales taxes are pretty minor to begin with.

4. User fees have a slight positive shock of $1.4 billion.

5. Fund balances show a negative shock of $6.8 billion.

Again we have the large positive residual in spending, also observed at the state level. There is some rise in deductible taxes to finance this spending demand, and this time some rise in nondeductible taxes and fees as well. But for the most part in 1987 local governments had not gotten around to financing the spending increase but just let balances fall.

Table 8.3
Budget constraint model, local governments annual observations, 1960–86

Independent variable	Dependent variables					
	Direct spending	Minus deductible personal taxes	Minus deductible business taxes	Minus sales taxes	Minus nondeductible taxes	Unallocated balances
Constant ($ billion)	8.20	−8.48	−0.10	1.59	5.20	−6.42
Grants and previously unallocated balances	0.6600 (4.4)	0.0395 (0.4)	−0.0026 (0.7)	−0.0312 (2.7)	−0.0216 (0.5)	0.3561 (2.4)
Income less federal withdrawals	0.0097 (0.5)	−0.0289 (2.3)	−0.0009 (1.8)	−0.0049 (3.3)	−0.0176 (3.3)	0.0426 (2.3)
Gross price	151.71 (2.9)	−3.03 (0.1)	2.06 (1.5)	−0.65 (0.2)	7.53 (0.5)	−157.62 (0.5)
Residual statistics (after correction for serial correlation)						
R^2	0.9888	0.9534	0.8137	0.9890	0.9763	0.8275
Standard error ($ billion)	3.23	2.12	0.09	0.25	0.90	3.13

Note: semi-first differences ($\rho = 0.75$); t ratios below coefficients.

Table 8.4
1980s residuals, local budget model (billions of current $)

Date	Uncorrected residuals (u)					
	Direct spending	Minus deductible personal taxes	Minus deductible business taxes	Minus sales taxes	Minus nondeductible taxes	Unallocated balances
1980	-3.0	7.8	-0.2	1.0	3.7	-9.5
1981	-2.8	6.6	-0.3	0.9	3.0	-7.6
1982	-3.9	2.5	-0.3	0.2	-0.1	1.3
1983	-3.6	2.4	-0.2	0.1	-0.9	2.1
1984	-7.1	2.7	-0.2	-0.1	-0.3	4.8
1985	-6.7	0.4	-0.4	-0.5	-1.3	8.3
1986	1.9	-2.6	-0.5	-0.3	-1.6	2.9
1987	11.7	-3.6	-0.8	-0.3	-2.6	-4.6
1988	na	-3.8	na	-0.9	na	na
1987 value	368.2	-124.6	-2.2	-24.9	-62.6	29.6
Predicted as of 1986[a]						
1987	1.4	-2.0	-0.3	-0.2	-1.2	2.2
1988	-0.4	-1.6	-0.2	-0.2	-0.9	0.9
New shock (uncorrected less predicted)						
1987	10.3	-1.6	-0.5	-0.1	-1.4	-6.8
1988	na	-2.2	na	-0.7	na	na

a. Since 1986 prediction of 1987 unallocated balances was less than actual by $2.2 billion, this amount is deducted from all six components according to the coefficients in table 8.4.

By 1988 some of these tax responses begin to occur but not in directions pleasing to those who predicted large price effects. Unlike for state governments where the embarrassing positive shocks in deductible and sales taxes are at least getting smaller, at the local level these shocks seem to be getting larger. That could reflect the financing effect of continued spending pressures for higher revenue: It certainly does not confirm a change in the revenue mix due to tax price changes.

In the theory outlined above state and local spending are endogenous and are reduced by TRA86. These econometric estimates make it hard to see price impacts on the revenue mix because instead of falling, both state and local spending are rising so rapidly. To see if our results were being driven by the spending residuals, we reestimated the model, this time making state and local spending exogenous so that their residuals are constrained to equal zero. Then the equations are refit with only the tax and unallocated balances residuals adding to zero. Instead of equation (5), the constraining identity becomes

$$B_{-1} + G - E = -D - S - N + B. \tag{7}$$

This variant of the model is given in tables 8.5 through 8.8. The equations are, if anything, more sensible than before because prices can be assumed to affect spending, spending to affect taxes, and the puzzling direct link between prices and taxes can be suppressed. But the residuals tell

Table 8.5
Recursive budget constraint model, local governments annual observations, 1960–86

Independent variable	Minus deductible personal taxes	Minus deductible business taxes	Minus sales taxes	Minus non-deductible taxes	Unallocated balances
Constant ($ billion)	8.52	1.20	−1.22	4.02	−12.52
Grants—spending and previously unallocated balances	0.0621 (1.1)	0.0037 (0.1)	0.2103 (3.1)	−0.0054 (0.1)	0.7292 (5.3)
Income less federal withdrawals	−0.0168 (3.7)	−0.0055 (1.8)	−0.0140 (2.6)	−0.0165 (4.6)	0.0528 (5.0)
Residual statistics (after correction for serial correlation)					
R^2	0.9847	0.9087	0.9894	0.9817	0.5885
Standard error ($ billion)	0.91	0.62	1.06	0.75	2.14

Note: semi-first differences ($\rho = 0.75$); t ratios below coefficients.

Table 8.6
1980s residuals, state model (billions of current $)

	Uncorrected residuals (u)				
Date	Minus deductible personal taxes	Minus deductible business taxes	Minus sales taxes	Minus non-deductible taxes	Unallocated balances
1980	1.3	−0.9	1.6	1.5	−3.5
1981	2.5	−0.2	2.4	−0.3	−4.4
1982	2.6	2.1	4.7	−1.0	−8.1
1983	1.5	1.7	3.8	0	−7.0
1984	−1.4	1.0	0.9	0	−0.6
1985	−1.2	0.9	−0.8	−0.7	1.9
1986	−0.7	−0.1	−1.5	−1.1	3.4
1987	−5.0	−3.7	−0.4	−2.8	6.3
1988	−1.8	na	−3.6	na	na
1987 value	−83.4	−25.7	−123.8	−57.7	−23.1
Predicted as of 1986[a]					
1987	−0.5	−0.1	−1.2	−0.8	2.6
1988	−0.5	−0.1	−1.4	−0.6	0
New shock (uncorrected less predicted)					
1987	−4.5	−3.6	0.8	3.6	3.7
1988	−1.3	na	−2.2	na	na

a. Since 1986 prediction of 1987 unallocated balances was less than actual by $2.6 billion, this amount is deducted from all five components according to the regression coefficients.

Table 8.7
Recursive budget constraint model, local governments annual observations, 1960–86

Independent variable	Minus deductible personal taxes	Minus deductible business taxes	Minus sales taxes	Minus non-deductible taxes	Unallocated balances
Constant ($ billion)	0.55	0.36	1.84	5.48	−8.22
Grants—spending and previously unallocated balances	0.2519 (3.0)	0.0013 (0.3)	−0.0187 (1.5)	−0.0380 (0.9)	0.8036 (6.5)
Income less federal withdrawals	−0.0191 (6.3)	−0.0005 (3.0)	−0.0074 (16.4)	−0.0179 (11.9)	0.448 (10.0)
Residual statistics (after correction for serial correlation)					
R^2	0.9659	0.7848	0.9865	0.9764	0.8743
Standard error ($ billion)	1.78	0.09	0.27	0.88	2.62

Note: semi-first differences ($\rho = 0.75$); t ratios below coefficients.

Table 8.8
1980s residuals, recursive local model (billions of current $)

Date	Uncorrected residuals (u)				
	Minus deductible personal taxes	Minus deductible business taxes	Minus sales taxes	Minus non-deductible taxes	Unallocated balances
1980	8.3	0.3	0.9	3.8	−13.0
1981	7.6	0.2	1.2	3.1	−11.8
1982	4.2	0.3	0.5	0.2	−4.9
1983	3.5	0.4	0.5	−0.7	−3.4
1984	1.8	0.3	0.5	−0.1	−2.2
1985	1.3	0.1	−0.2	−1.2	3.0
1986	3.5	0	−0.4	−1.9	6.3
1987	2.0	−0.3	−0.5	−3.3	6.5
1988	−5.2	na	−0.4	na	na
1987 value	−124.6	−2.2	−24.9	−62.6	−29.6
Predicted as of 1986[a]					
1987	−2.6	0	−0.3	−1.5	4.7
1988	−3.1	0	−0.1	−1.0	0.3
New shock (uncorrected less predicted)					
1987	0.6	−0.3	−0.2	−1.8	1.8
1988	−2.1	na	−0.3	na	na

a. Since 1986 prediction of 1987 unallocated balances was less than actual by $4.7 billion, this amount is deducted from all five components according to the regression coefficients.

about the same story as before. The new state shocks in table 8.6 still show the windfall gradually dying out for deductible taxes. This time the sales tax shock begins negative and then becomes positive in 1988, exactly the reverse pattern of the earlier estimates. Nondeductible fees and fines are still down. Hence by and large the recursive model for states still gives no comfort to those who believe in large price effects.

The new local shocks in table 8.8 are generally pretty small. As in table 8.4, local user fees move the right way, and sales taxes' residuals are very small. Deductible taxes rise for some reason (the windfall effect is still inoperative for local property taxes), as do balances.

Hence as regards fiscal flows, it is frankly hard to see a big impact of TRA86 on either state or local governments. For some reason direct spending went up at both levels of government. This put pressure on governmental finances and led to some nonwindfall-induced rises in deductible taxes at both levels. Sales tax residuals were generally positive, if fairly small, indicating that the financing effect seemed to dominate the price effect. Nondeductible taxes and fees, which should have risen sharply at both levels of government, in fact did not, rising only slightly at the local level and falling at the state level. The main financing of the spending surge was then left over for fund balances. To the extent that taxes changed to finance this surge, knowing about TRA86 would not have helped one to make very good predictions of changes in the revenue mix. And the predictions of large budgetary effects by Holtz-Eakin and Rosen and Feldstein and Metcalf are simply not supported by the experience so far.

Other Evidence

These regression residuals seem quite consistent with other evidence of post-TRA86 fiscal changes for state and local governments. It is hard to document the puzzling fall in nondeductible taxes and fees made up of countless items not even recorded separately in the aggregate accounts. But sales tax changes are generally made at the state level, and there it is easier to see what is going on. According to Gold (1988), Gold and collaborators (1987, 1988), and Fabricus and collaborators (1989), the behavior of many states was consistent with the pattern of our residuals. In 1987 and 1988 seven states substantially increased their sales taxes, in 1989 five more states significantly increased sales taxes, and a number had less significant increases. Both the regression results and this more informal evidence then confirm the puzzling move toward greater use of state sales taxes.

The situation with income taxes is more interesting, and it goes beyond a simple explanation of the residuals. Even though no clear story emerges from these residuals, there does seem to be evidence of deeper structural change in state income tax systems that mirrors changes at the federal level. Gold (1988) and Fabricus and collaborators (1989) detail a number of these:

1. By 1989, 8 states had restructured their entire income tax, generally increasing conformity with the federal income tax.

2. By way of redistributing their windfall gains, 19 states reduced income tax rates and only 6 increased them as of 1989.

3. By 1988, 18 states had increased their personal exemption or credit, 20 states had increased their standard deduction, and 12 states eliminated all taxes on poor families. More states moved in these directions in 1989.

The net result of these changes is to reduce administrative costs by increasing the conformity between state and federal tax systems, and to enhance economic efficiency by generally lowering state marginal tax rates. Equity is also improved, to the extent that many poor families are removed from state as well as federal tax rolls. In the long run these structural effects of TRA86 should be much more important than the price effects economists spend much more time discussing. And we might say that even if we could find some price effects.

8.2   Mobility and Capitalization

As was seen already, TRA86 affected the tax price of state and local public expenditure differentially in different states. Tax prices rose in all states because of the drop in marginal federal tax rates and the elimination of the sales tax deduction. But because the incidence of deductible and sales taxes varies a good deal across states, the effect of TRA86 on effective tax burdens also varied a good deal. In this section we try to exploit that variation by looking at economic and fiscal behavior in adjacent cities (sometimes counties) on opposite sides of state lines before and after TRA86.

By looking at adjacent cities, we can make the convenient assumption that everything other than tax prices changed in the same way on both sides of the state boundary between 1986 and 1987. Take two cities—say, Fargo, ND, and Moorehead, MN. These cities are in the same labor market, the same grain market, and the same tractor market. Even fairly localized changes in economic environment should affect them in about the same way. But TRA86 will not: It will cause a much higher rise in effective tax burdens in high-tax Minnesota than in low-tax North Dakota.

What would then happen? A first possibility is that governments would adjust, with Minnesota, say, eliminating its sales tax. In the first part of the chapter we found minimal evidence of such adjustments to take advantage of TRA86 for states and localities as a whole, though it is always possible that there would be more adjustment in our key border towns. If there is no governmental adjustment, then the private sector may adjust its location of business or residential activity. Our basic strategy then is to pick pairs of cities where the differential effect of TRA86 on tax prices was large and to analyze a number of measures of economic behavior for each pair. The reason for looking exclusively at cases where the differential effect was large is simply that little time and less data have passed since TRA86; if TRA86 is going to have measurable effects, it is most likely to have them across these pairs of cities.

Even in this purposely biased sample, there are probably few cases where differences in the change in the local cost of public services are large enough to induce people to bear the cost of moving across a state border (the biggest differences are on the order of 0.5% of annual income for the average taxpayer). But the differences could be large enough to affect the behavior of both households and firms that are potentially moving within or into the economic area. Such effects are both a consequence of local and state fiscal policy and impose a constraint (or opportunity) on the fisc. The town on the favored side of the border will enjoy a fiscal windfall at the expense of the town on the unfavored side. Direct evidence on these fiscal effects with one year of data seems too much to hope for, but direct evidence for the economic effects has a better chance. The capitalized value of a half percent of annual income is perhaps $1,000 for the average household, much more for the average itemizing household or the average rich household.[6] If all of the change is capitalized immediately, there should be noticeable changes in property values. If some of the change remains available to new entrants, there should be noticeable increases in population and economic activity on the favored side of the border.

Ideally, we would look at changes in the market value of existing real property, which would measure the extent to which changes in local tax benefits were valued in local markets. In practice, none of the measures available is anywhere near that good. For some of our pairs we have data on changes in assessed value, but we have no idea how much the change is due to improvements and how much to revaluation of existing property, nor do we know the relationship between assessed value and market value. Moreover none of the data sets we use has complete information for every city, and this makes things especially difficult when the unit of analysis is the city pair. If, for example, data of tolerable-looking quality are available for 60% of the cities, we will only be able to use 36% of the pairs.

In order to choose pairs of cities (sometimes counties) that might be expected to show effects of TRA86, we constructed a measure of the change in the cost of state and local taxes collected from residents. As before, t stands for the mean marginal tax rate faced by itemizers in a state, a for the fraction of taxpayers who itemize, S for sales taxes, and D for deductible taxes. If governments do not change their tax structure as a result of TRA86, the increase in state and locally borne cost of tax collections as a share of state income ($\Delta C/Y$) can be expressed as

$$\frac{\Delta C}{Y} = \frac{atS}{Y} - \frac{\Delta(at)D}{Y}. \tag{8}$$

Impact of Tax Reform Act on State and Local Fiscal Behavior   265

We calculated $\Delta C/Y$ for each of the contiguous 48 states (Alaska and Hawaii did not seem promising sources of city pairs), using Metcalf's NBER TAXSIM calculations of a and t for 1985 (the most recent year available) and actual state budget data for 1986. $\Delta(at)$ was estimated by assuming that $\Delta(at)/(1 - at) = -0.46$ in all states, the average estimate that Courant and Rubinfeld (1987) derived from data used by Hausman and Poterba (1987).

Having estimated $\Delta C/Y$ for 48 states, we plotted the values on a map and looked for those pairs of states that had cities near to each other and that had the largest differences in $\Delta C/Y$. We required that there be cities of noticeable size, both because that increased the probability of finding useful data and because it enhanced the plausibility of the maintained hypothesis that the relevant labor market conditions would be the same on both sides of the border.[7]

Fourteen pairs of adjacent states had values of $\Delta C/Y$ of 0.002 or greater. The largest difference (Pennsylvania–New York) was 0.004. For each of the 14 pairs of states, we looked for adjacent cities on both sides of the border. Some (Greenwich, CT–Port Chester, Rye, NY; Portsmouth, NH–Kittery, ME) are very close indeed. Others (Billings, MT–Sheridan, WY) are much farther apart. And some simply do not exist, such as on the border between Oregon–California or, curiously, Massachusetts–New York. For some states there is more than one potentially usable pair. Pennsylvania and New York, for example, have a long border, and cities (or counties) can be matched across it in more than one place. Information about the city pairs and their data availability is given in table 8.9.

For each city (or county) pair for which data were available, we analyzed data on building permits, assessed property values, and county employment. In all cases we computed the share of the favored member of the pair in the total volume of activity in the pair and measured the change in the share between 1986 and 1987.

Usable building permit data for single-family houses are available for 11 pairs of cities; for multifamily houses, no cities. TRA86 should have caused the share of building permits to rise in the favored state. But it did so in only 4 of the 11 cases, with an average change in share of -7.5%. When these data were smoothed by subtracting the average of available 1984–86 shares from the 1987 share, the share rose in 5 of the 11 cases, with an average change in share of -4.8%. It is also possible that some building permits taken out in 1986 could have been in response to TRA86, so we compared the 1986 and 1987 average share with the share in the previous three years. In this test 6 of the 11 cases were positive, with an average

Paul N. Courant and Edward M. Gramlich

Table 8.9
Information on city and state pairs

States	$100\Delta C/Y$	City or county	Data
NY–PA	$0.73 - 0.33 = 0.4$	Jamestown–Warren	
		Olean–Bradford	
		Binghamton, Johnson City, Endicott	BP
		–Dunmore, Carbondale	
MA–NH	$0.47 - 0.12 = 0.35$	Lawrence, Lowell, Methuen–Nashua	BP
		Essex, Middlesex–Hillsborough,	CBP
		Rockingham counties	
		Dracut–Nashua	AV
		Lawrence, Methuen–Salem	AV
WA–OR	$0.61 - 0.27 = 0.34$	Vancouver–Portland	BP, AV
WY–MT	$0.47 - 0.13 = 0.34$	Sheridan–Billings	BP
NY–CT	$0.73 - 0.41 = 0.32$	Rye–Greenwich, Stamford	BP
MN–ND	$0.51 - 0.21 = 0.30$	Moorehead–Fargo	BP
		Clay–Cass counties	CBP
UT–ID	$0.58 - 0.29 = 0.29$	No places	
VT–NH	$0.39 - 0.12 = 0.27$	Brattleboro–Keene	BP
		Windham–Cheshire counties	CBP
MD–DE	$0.50 - 0.24 = 0.26$	No data	
NY–MA	$0.73 - 0.47 = 0.26$	No places	
CA–OR	$0.51 - 0.27 = 0.24$	No places	
ME–NH	$0.34 - 0.12 = 0.22$	Kittery–Portsmouth	BP, AV
		York–Rockingham counties	CBP
NM–TX	$0.42 - 0.22 = 0.20$	Las Cruces–El Paso	BP
		Clovis–Amarillo, Lubbock	BP
NJ–DE	$0.43 - 0.24 = 0.20$	Pennsville–Wilmington	BP

Note: AV = assessed value; BP = building permits; CBP = county business patterns.

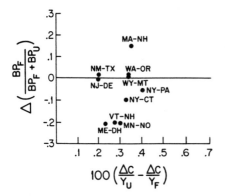

Figure 8.2
Change in building permit shares and tax costs: BP_F = building permits in state favored
by TRA86; BP_U = building permits in state not favored by TRA86; $\Delta C/Y_F$, $\Delta C/Y_U$ = as
defined in equation (8), 1985–86 data. Building permit shares are based on 1987 data
over the 1984–86 average.

change in share of 0.1%. All of this leads to the conclusion that *1986* was
an unusually good year for the favored cities, but 1987 an unusually bad
year. TRA86 could explain the first change but not the second, and certainly not the fact that the two-year average was unchanged from the
previous three-year average. One example of this relationship between
$\Delta C/Y$ and changes in the share of building permits is plotted in figure 8.2.
What should be a neat positive relationship entirely in quadrant I is in fact
a jumble.

Regarding assessed values, the use of the Moody's (1988) series for
calculations such as these can be seriously misleading if there are changes
in assessment rules from year to year. But excluding those city pairs where
neither element had a change in assessment practices between 1986 and
1987 left only four city pairs.[8] The share for the favored pair did rise in
three of them, but this is hardly a statistically significant finding.[9]

Finally, *County Business Patterns* provides extensive information on economic activity in U.S. counties and is in principle suited to shedding some
light on the problem at hand. Unfortunately, the Census Bureau has not yet
released 1987 for most regions of the country. New England and the
Mountain states are all that are available as of September 1989, giving us
three New Hampshire pairs and Montana–Wyoming. Shares of total employment and total payroll did rise in three of our four pairs, but again
these are awfully sparse data from which to generalize.

The upshot of our attempts to look at early evidence on mobility and capitalization is more randomness. In the previous section there was some suggestion from the early data that TRA86 was not having large effects on the budget position of states and localities: Here a more appropriate conclusion is that it is just too early to do analyses of this sort.

8.3   The Market for State and Local Bonds

TRA86 was also predicted to have powerful effects on the market for state and local bonds. The most important reason is that the value of the exemption of state and local bond interest is now reduced, both by the lower personal and corporate tax rates and by the fact that half of bond interest is now included in the base for the corporate alternative minimum tax. Other provisions that could have an effect are those that eliminate the interest deduction for banks that use the borrowing to buy tax-exempt securities, and those that limit the issuing of private-purpose tax-exempt bonds by state and local governments.

To see how all this works, a general expression for the impact of the interest rate on tax-exempt municipal bonds m can be written as

$$m = r(1 - bt), \tag{9}$$

where r is the interest rate on taxable securities, t is now the marginal federal tax rate applied to the taxable interest income of the highest income taxpayers, and b is an adjustment factor.[10] Were all marginal tax rates the same and state and local securities perfect substitutes for private securities, b would equal one. But if municipal bonds are held by investors with lower tax rates than this maximum, b can be less than one empirically. Poterba (1989, from whom much of the following analysis is taken) shows that over the 1980s b has been about 0.93 for short-term bonds (based on the corporate rate paid by banks, alleged to be the marginal investors in this market) and about 0.55 for long-term bonds (based on the rate paid by high income individuals, alleged to be the marginal investors in this market). The different top-bracket tax rates are used because historically there has been a good deal of segmentation between the short- and long-term markets—governments are either forced to use, or find it advantageous to use, long-term bonds to finance construction projects even though the implied interest rate is higher, and banks have been arbitrageurs in the short- but not the long-term market (Mussa and Kormendi 1979).

When m and r differ, Gordon and Slemrod (1986) point to the existence of a number of separate arbitrage opportunities involving state and local bonds:

1. Classic governmental arbitrage, where the government borrows at the tax-exempt rate m and lends at the taxable rate r. Citizens gain $r - m$ on every dollar borrowed. The Internal Revenue Service (IRS) has rules against this form of arbitrage. But Gordon and Slemrod show how difficult it is for the IRS to enforce these rules, and Metcalf (1989) shows that a lot of this form of arbitrage does seem to exist.

2. Brokerage arbitrage, where citizens use their government as a broker. Citizens borrow at $r(1 - t)$ and prepay taxes so their government can invest and earn r. Citizens must trust their friendly local government to credit them the prepaid taxes. If they are so willing, they can gain rt. Note that bonds are not involved in this transaction.

3. High-income arbitrage, where citizens borrow at $r(1 - t)$ and invest in municipal bonds at m, gaining $m - r(1 - t)$. The citizens' own local government plays no role in this transaction. The gap between m and $r(1 - t)$ also corresponds to the annual gain per dollar borrowed realized by high-income people from this sort of tax subsidy for state and local governments, in that these high-income people earn $m - r(1 - t)$ more than they would if they were the marginal investors and b were equal to one.

4. Low-income arbitrage, where low-income citizens have their government borrow at m, cut taxes, and then let the citizens invest the proceeds at $r(1 - t_1)$, where t_1 is the tax rate faced by low-income people, gaining $r(1 - t_1) - m$ in the process. Unlike the above form of arbitrage, where it is assumed that high-income citizens face a high marginal rate, these low-income citizens face much lower effective progressive marginal rates. They are able to make more in aftertax returns on taxable securities than they pay on tax-exempt municipals. Gordon and Slemrod do find that in 1977 communities with low marginal tax rates borrowed more than communities with high marginal tax rates, other things equal.

How is all this changed by TRA86? There are at least five provisions that could have an impact:

1. The reduction in individual and corporate marginal tax rates means that the gap between r and m should diminish. To state and local governments, this means that the tax-exempt rate should rise relative to other interest rates.

2. That marginal tax rates are compressed eliminates at least one of the arbitrage channels that previously benefited low marginal tax rate communities.

3. That banks can now no longer deduct interest when they buy tax-exempt securities means that they are now less likely to hold, and arbitrage, short-term state and local bonds.

4. That tax-exempt interest is now included in the base for the corporate alternative minimum tax means that municipal bonds are now not tax free for some banks, again reducing banks demand for short-term state and local securities.

5. Volume caps on private purpose tax-exempt securities should lower the supply of these.

The cut in marginal tax rates and the bank provisions should raise the tax-exempt rate relative to other rates, reducing the tax subsidy for state and local governments. This prediction has come true: According to Poterba's (1989) calculations, the short-term tax-exempt rate averaged $0.564r$ from 1982–85 and $0.685r$ in 1988; the long-term tax-exempt rate averaged $0.792r$ from 1982–85 and $0.845r$ in 1988.[11] If banks are no longer the marginal investors in the short-term market, this short-term rate could also become more volatile. Over time the reduced subsidy should show up in higher state and local interest costs and perhaps in reduced state and local construction spending. However, given all the opportunities for financial market arbitrage, it is not at all clear that m, rather than r, sets the hurdle rate for state and local physical capital formation.[12]

Second, the cut in the high-income individual rate from 0.5 to 0.28, and in the corporate rate from 0.46 to 0.34, means that all of the gaps leading to arbitrage possibilities should either diminish or disappear altogether:

1. The return to classic governmental arbitrage has fallen from $r(1 - 0.564) = 0.436r$ to $r(1 - 0.685) = 0.315r$ for short-term bonds and from $r(1 - 0.792) = 0.208r$ to $r(1 - 0.845) = 0.155r$ for long-term bonds (Poterba 1989). These declines, and the volume caps on private purpose bonds, should reduce both the reward from and the ability of governments to engage in this sort of arbitrage.

2. The return to brokerage arbitrage has fallen from $0.46r$ to $0.34r$ if done by corporations and from $0.5r$ to $0.28r$ if done by high-income individuals. Even when this return was much larger, Gordon and Slemrod found little of this sort of arbitrage, perhaps because high-income investors did not

trust their governments as brokers, but just in case the trust grows, the opportunities are now constricted.

3. The return to high-income arbitrage fell from $r(0.792 - 0.5) = 0.292r$ to $r(0.845 - 0.72) = 0.125r$ for high-income personal investors in long-term bonds, and by similar large amounts for other combinations of individual and corporate investors in long- and short-term securities. Since state and local governments play no role in this form of arbitrage, it will be hard to notice anything on state and local books, but there will, as stated, also be an implied reduction in the excess returns realized by high-income taxpayers from the tax subsidy for state and local bonds.

4. The return on low-income arbitrage is made negative. There are now no positive taxpayers for whom $r(1 - t_1)$ exceeds m. This change would seem to block out entirely this arbitrage channel and should make it difficult to replicate the Gordon-Slemrod finding that low marginal tax rate communities borrow more in the post-TRA86 world.

Third, there is at least indirect evidence that the volume caps on private purpose securities are having an impact. There was a flood of these offerings in late 1986, after TRA86 was passed but before its provisions took effect, confirming again the proposition that the best place to look for impacts of taxes on behavior is in the timing of actions that groups are planning to take anyway.

In all cases credit market efficiency is improved and both the revenue losses and the social losses associated with tax arbitrage are mitigated. One must go through financial data much more carefully than we have to make definitive quantitative estimates of the gains from this side of TRA86, but the gains could be sizeable.

8.4   Conclusions

The most widely discussed aspect of the impact of TRA86 on state and local behavior is in its alteration of the locally borne cost of different types of taxes. Sales taxes are made much more costly and income and property taxes somewhat more costly. Despite many predictions and some econometric work that suggested that these tax changes would have large effects, as of 1988 they had not seemed to have had much impact on state or local budgets as measured by out-of-sample fiscal data. Generally spending went up, contrary to both theoretical and empirical predictions, fines and user fees went down, contrary to theoretical predictions, and one has to squint very hard to make sense of the movements in deductible taxes and sales taxes. In any case the movements are quite small, even in those rare cases where they are in the expected direction.

Another way to search for effects of TRA86 is to compare activity measures for pairs of state border communities affected quite differently by TRA86 but quite similarly by everything else. Using border communities introduces a very large bias toward finding large effects, and even with this large bias, the effects on measures of activity such as building permits seem miniscule. Indeed, our point estimate is that they have the wrong sign. Here, however, we are mining early data so hard that our conclusions must be quite tentative.

So what are the effects of TRA86 on the state and local sector? In the end we are forced back to rather subtle factors. TRA86 stimulated an unusual amount of state legislative activity regarding taxes, and the result will be state income taxes that generally have lower rates, broader bases, and less taxation of the poor, mimicking the federal tax changes. TRA86 reduced the value of the tax exemption for state and local bonds, and the result will be higher interest costs for states and localities, reduced efficiency losses, reduced arbitrage revenue losses, and perhaps reduced capital spending. TRA86 may have done some other things as well, but three years after the fact its impacts are much smaller than predicted, and there is no evidence that its long-run effects will be large.

Notes

We are grateful to Steven D. Gold, Donald Peters, and Gilbert Metcalf for making available recent data, interpreting recent events, and commenting on earlier drafts of the chapter. We are also grateful to Charlotte Mack, who provided able research assistance.

1. Other changes affecting the state and local bond market will be discussed later.

2. The issue is dealt with in more depth by both Courant and Rubinfeld (1987) and Feldstein and Metcalf (1987).

3. Holtz-Eakin and Rosen's estimate of the elasticity of local spending with respect to the price of deductible taxes is -1.8. The tax price of local spending rose by 4% or 5% as a result of TRA86; that for state spending, because of the sales tax, by about 6%.

4. Using the constraint in this way does lead to one complication we have not been able to resolve. The constraining variable B is a lagged dependent variable, which means that there could be serial correlation in the residuals beyond that taken out by our correction. One might want to construct an instrument for B and use that in the estimation. Knowing what to do about the constraints is then

not straightforward, however, because in principle all dependent variables should then be recomputed.

5. A recent paper by Helen Ladd (1989) finds strong evidence of such behavior.

6. For high-income itemizers differences in the change in the local cost of public services across neighboring jurisdictions could exceed 1% of a much higher income. The annual change for high income itemizers could be on the order of $600; the capitalized value more than $10,000.

7. But we were unable to use data on the fiscal policies of the cities themselves. Each of these cities had to be assigned the average fiscal policy of all state and local governments in the state, a potential source of measurement error.

8. Although Moody's does not report a reassessment for either Billings, MT, or Portland, ME, it is clear from the numbers that there must have been one.

9. We can only interpret these data qualitatively, not quantitatively, because the denominator of the share, "total assessed value" for the pair, does not mean anything when different jurisdictions have different ratios of assessed to market value. The sign of changes in the share are still meaningful, but only when assessment rules have not changed.

10. In principle one could use either the highest marginal rate (0.33) or the rate for the highest-income taxpayers (0.28) in equation (9). That there is now a difference is one of the little nuggets of TRA86. Since most wealth available for investment in state and local bonds is in the highest income range, we will use 0.28 throughout this section.

11. In the spirit of giving all pre-TRA86 predictions however embarrassing, we should report that Courant and Rubinfeld (1987) speculated that by cutting back on other tax shelters, TRA86 "might" actually lower m relative to r. As the numbers show, it did not.

12. This could go either way, and it bears further study. If state and local governments are constrained by various antiarbitrage provisions, they would exhaust arbitrage opportunities as far as possible and then buy tangible capital to the point where the return was m. In this case TRA86 would reduce real capital formation by raising m. If the constraint were instead on the amount of debt that they could issue, they would only buy tangible capital that earned at least r, and TRA86 would have no effect on real capital formation.

References

Advisory Commission on Intergovernmental Relations. 1988. *Significant Features of Fiscal Federalism*, vol. 2.

Aten, Robert H. 1987. The Magnitude of Additional Corporate Income Taxes Resulting from Federal Tax Reform. *Tax Notes* 37 (3 August): 529–534.

Aten, Robert H., and Steven D. Gold. 1989. Where's the Corporate Tax Windfall? *Tax Notes* (2 October): 107–114.

Bureau of the Census. 1985–87. *County Business Patterns*. Washington, DC.

Bureau of the Census. 1983–87. *Housing Units Authorized by Building Permits and Public Contracts*. Washington, DC.

Chernick, Howard, and Andrew Reschovsky. 1989. The Distributional Politics of Fiscal Adjustment: A Case Study of Four Northeastern States. Mimeo. October.

Courant, Paul N., and Daniel R. Rubinfeld. 1987. Tax Reform: Implications for the State-Local Public Sector. *The Journal of Economic Perspectives* 1: 87–100.

Fabricus, Martha A., Steven D. Gold, and Corina L. Ecki. 1989. *State Budget Actions in 1989*. National Conference of State Legislatures.

Feldstein, Martin S., and Gilbert E. Metcalf. 1987. The Effect of Federal Tax Deductibility on State and Local Taxes and Spending. *Journal of Political Economy* 95: 710–736.

Gold, Steven D. 1988. Tax Reform Activity in the States. *Publius* 18: 17–35.

Gold, Steven D., Corina L. Eckl, and Brenda M. Erickson. 1987. *State Budget Actions in 1987*. National Conference of State Legislatures.

Gold, Steven D., Corina L. Eckl, and Martha A. Fabricus. 1988. *State Budget Actions in 1988*. National Conference of State Legislatures.

Gordon, Roger H., and Joel Slemrod. 1986. An Empirical Examination of Municipal Financial Policy. In Harvey S. Rosen (ed.), *Studies in State and Local Public Finance*. Chicago: University of Chicago Press.

Gramlich, Edward M. 1978. State and Local Budgets the Day after It Rained: Why Is the Surplus So High? *Brookings Papers on Economic Activity* 1: 191–216.

Gramlich, Edward M. 1987. Federalism and Federal Deficit Reduction. *National Tax Journal* 40: 299–313.

Hausman, Jerry A., and James M. Poterba. 1987. Household Behavior and the Tax Reform Act of 1986. *Journal of Economic Perspectives* 1: 101–119.

Hettich, Walter, and Stanley Winer. 1984. A Positive Model of Tax Structure. *Journal of Public Economics* 24: 67–87.

Holtz-Eakin, Douglas, and Harvey S. Rosen. 1988. Tax Deductibility and Municipal Budget Structures. In Harvey S. Rosen (ed.), *Fiscal Federalism: Quantitative Studies*. Chicago: University of Chicago Press.

Inman, Robert P. 1989. The Local Decision to Tax: Evidence from Large U.S. Cities. NBER Working Paper No. 2921. April.

Kenyon, Daphne A. 1988. Implicit Aid to State and Local Governments through Federal Tax Deductibility. In Michael G. Bell (ed.), *State and Local Finance in an Era of New Federalism*. Greenwich, CT: JAI Press.

Ladd, Helen F. 1989. State Aid to Local Governments in the 1980s. Mimeo. October.

Levin, David J., and Donald L. Peters. 1986. Receipts and Expenditures of State and Local Governments: Revised and Updated Estimates, 1959–84. *Survey of Current Business* 66: 26–33.

Levin, David J., and Donald L. Peters. 1987. Receipts and Expenditures of State Governments and of Local Governments: Revised and Updated Estimates, 1983–86. *Survey of Current Business* 67: 29–35.

Metcalf, Gilbert E. 1989. Arbitrage and the Savings Behavior of State Governments. NBER Working Paper No. 3017. June.

Metcalf, Gilbert E. 1989. A Note on the Sales Tax after Reform: Why Hasn't It Disappeared? Mimeo. June.

Moody's Investor Service. 1985–87. *Moody's Municipal and Government Manual*. Chicago.

Mussa, Michael L., and Roger C. Kormendi. 1979. *The Taxation of Municipal Bonds*. Washington, DC: American Enterprise Institute.

Noto, Nanna, and Dennis Zimmerman. 1984. Limiting State-Local Tax Deductibility: Effects among the States. *National Tax Journal* 37: 539–550.

Peters, Donald L. 1988. Receipts and Expenditures of State Governments and of Local Governments: Revised and Updated Estimates, 1984–87. *Survey of Current Busines* 68: 23–25.

Poterba, James M. 1989. Tax Reform and the Market for Tax-Exempt Debt. *Regional Science and Urban Economics* 19: 537–562.

[14]

Journal of Economic Literature
Vol. XXXII (September 1994), pp. 1176–1196

Infrastructure Investment: A Review Essay

By EDWARD M. GRAMLICH

The University of Michigan

I thank David Aschauer, Sheldon Danziger, Michael Deich, John Fernald, Charles Hulten, Alicia Munnell, Laura Rubin, Joel Slemrod, John Tatom, and two anonymous referees for helpful comments on earlier drafts.

E CONOMISTS TRY not to be faddists but they often cannot help themselves. While work on a topic should mirror the prospective importance of the topic, that situation seems to occur with disappointing frequency. Instead, the usual pattern is that some reasonably important topic will be totally ignored for the longest time, then recognized, and then the subject of a flurry of work all out of proportion to its likely long run importance.

Nowhere has this speculative bubble of economic research been more clearly illustrated than with infrastructure investment. Macroeconomists have long felt that the stock of public capital is an important factor input in the production of total output. Macroeconomists have known that U.S. productivity growth slowed dramatically in about 1973 and macroeconomists should have known that United States investment in public capital has been down since the late 1960s. Yet analysis of the U.S. productivity slowdown completely ignored infrastructure investment for the first fifteen years of this slowdown, concentrating instead on energy prices, social regulation,

the composition of the work force, research and development, different rates of obsolescence of the private capital stock, and any number of other matters. The public capital stock was hardly ever even mentioned as a potential factor in the productivity slowdown.

Aschauer changed all that. He wrote a series of papers (1989a, 1989b, 1989c) that put these two movements together econometrically—infrastructure investment turned down and aggregate productivity turned down slightly later, both in the United States and in some other developed countries. His work hit the magic button. Those who had worried about the productivity puzzle for fifteen years welcomed a new suspect. Those who were worried about low rates of U.S. national saving welcomed a new way to make their argument even more forcefully than with official figures on saving and investment, which do not count infrastructure investment as investment. Political liberals and liberal politicians saw a way to rescue government spending and projects from the assaults of Reaganism, and even a way to avoid otherwise necessary budget cuts—just call the spending infrastructure investment. All of these planets came into proper alignment, and Aschauer's papers were followed by an unusual amount of attention, from politicians and economists. Beefing up infrastructure investment became simultaneously the liberals' political war cry of the early 1990s and one of the favorite topics for econometric research, by now the subject of at least forty other econometric studies using different data and techniques.

Now that the bubble has happened and may even be beginning to burst, it is useful to stand back and ask what has been learned from this discussion. It almost goes without saying that infrastructure investment was always more important than was indicated by its lack of attention up to 1989; never as important as the intense attention since 1989 would suggest. But in the process of debate, many other matters have been clarified—about how to identify a shortage of infrastructure investment, about whether there ever was an overall shortage, and about whether this possible shortage has been a factor in the aggregate productivity decline. In this essay I review all these questions. But I then go beyond this review to ask what I think is a much more fundamental question, the question that economists should have been focusing on all along. In a word, is the country doing something wrong, and if so, what? That is, what, if any, policies regarding infrastructure investment should be changed?

I. *Basic Facts About Infrastructure Capital*

There are many possible definitions of infrastructure capital. The definition that makes the most sense from an economics standpoint consists of large capital intensive natural monopolies such as highways, other transportation facilities, water and sewer lines, and communications systems. Most of these systems are owned publicly in the United States, but some are owned privately. An alternative version that focuses on ownership includes just the tangible capital stock owned by the public sector. Broader versions include successively human capital investment and/or research and development capital. Most econometric studies of the infrastructure problem have used the narrow public sector ownership version of infrastructure capital as their independent variable. This is in large part because it is very hard to measure anything else. It is difficult to measure privately owned infrastructure capital, and even if good measures were available, it would be difficult to distinguish private infrastructure capital from other private capital. It is difficult to distinguish human investment spending for health and education from consumption spending, difficult to know whether to count all research and development expenditures as investment, and difficult to know how to depreciate either of these types of spending in defining capital stocks. Hence for these purposes I follow others in using a relatively narrow public sector ownership definition of the stock of infsmstructure capital.

Bureau of Economic Analysis (BEA) estimates of this nonresidential stock in 1991 in current dollars are shown in Table 1. The net stock of infrastructure capital, structures plus equipment, military and domestic, was $2755.8 billion, of which $2034.1 billion ($2755.8 − $514.1 − $207.6) was for nonmilitary structures and $2241.7 billion ($2755.8 − $514.1) was for nonmilitary structures and equipment. Most of this nonmilitary capital, 88 percent of the structures and 71 percent of the equipment, is owned by state

TABLE 1

PUBLIC INFRASTRUCTURE CAPITAL, 1991
(BILLIONS OF CURRENT DOLLARS)

Item	Federal	State and Local	Total
Nonmilitary structures	242.8	1791.3	2034.1
Highways	16.9	708.0	724.9
Education	1.2	318.8	320.0
Other buildings	33.7	224.3	258.0
Hospitals	11.7	50.0	61.7
Water and Sewers	—	295.5	295.5
Conservation	143.4	35.9	179.3
Industrial	25.7	—	25.7
Other	10.1	158.7	168.9
Nonmilitary equipment	61.0	146.6	207.6
Military	514.1	—	514.1
Total	**817.9**	**1937.9**	**2755.8**

Source: BEA, in Tatom (1993).

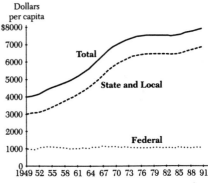

Figure 1. Real Nonmilitary Government Capital
Stock per Person (1987 prices)

Source: Tatom (1993)

and local governments. While the infrastructure problem usually is described as a problem needing federal government attention, these figures indicate that, if infrastructure investment is a problem, it may be much more a state and local problem than a federal problem. This issue will be discussed in the policy section below.

The categories shown in Table 1 suggest why economists might have trouble analyzing infrastructure capital. The services of capital such as highways and schools are generally not sold on the market (though highway user fees could be used more extensively than now, and indeed user fees will be a big focus in the policy discussion below). While infrastructure capital is purchased on the market at the time of initial construction or installation, it is rarely sold, implying that economic rates of depreciation are almost never directly measured. Depreciation measures used in the construction of infrastructure stocks are physical measures based on service lives of different

types of public structures. It would in principle be possible to measure rates of utilization of infrastructure capital— how many vehicles use roads, etc.—but in practice these measures are available only for some components of the public capital stock. And like other public goods, a large share of the benefits of infrastructure capital involve improved security, time saving, improved health, a cleaner environment, or improved outdoor recreation, magnitudes that are difficult to measure and that are not included in official measures of national output. Hence it will also be difficult to relate infrastructure investment to its goals, or changes in them. No wonder there are empirical controversies.

Measures of the stock of infrastructure capital are shown in Figures 1 and 2. Figure 1 shows total nonmilitary infrastructure capital ($2241.7 in Table 1) per capita, in 1987 dollars. The federal component of this capital, mainly for conservation structures and other buildings, has been close to $1000 per capita for more than four decades. Because this capital affects mainly the utility value of outdoor

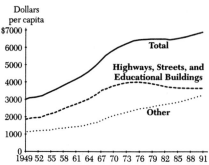

Figure 2. State & Local Net Capital Stock per Person (1987 prices)

Source: Tatom (1993)

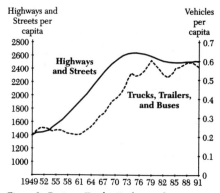

Figure 3. Business Trucks, Trailers, and Buses per Person and Highways and Streets per Person (1987 prices)

Source: Tatom (1993)

recreation, which is not counted in national output, and because it has been so constant for so long, not permitting serious time series inferences, it has generally been ignored in previous analyses of infrastructure investment and I will follow suit.

The stock of real state and local infrastructure capital per capita did grow steadily up to the early 1970s, but has leveled off since then. The implied investment numbers leading to this pattern for stocks have showed a decline in investment since the early 1970s, both absolutely and as a share of GDP (Clifford Winston and Barry Bosworth 1992; Hulten and Robert Schwab, forthcoming). Because 1973 was the watershed year beginning the overall national productivity decline, it is not surprising that simple time series analyses find a correlation between the stock of infrastructure capital and overall productivity. I will discuss a number of econometric issues in interpreting this correlation below; for now I continue just looking at the numbers to give the general patterns.

Figure 2 decomposes the total state and local capital stock into its biggest components: highways, educational

buildings, and all other—water and sewer systems, hospitals, and miscellaneous other structures. The "other" component has not been constant but has grown at a relatively steady rate over four decades, so it would again be hard to make time series inferences about the causes of productivity movements on the basis of this series. The real action comes from the two biggest components of state and local infrastructure capital; highways, streets, and educational buildings, between them accounting for 53 percent of the state and local stock in 1991.

Figure 3 shows separately the highways and streets component of the state and local capital stock. This stock rose sharply from 1955 to 1975, the period when the U.S. interstate highway system was being built, and has since leveled off as interstate construction has slowed and the previously built highways have depreciated. An additional factor is the price of gasoline, which rose sharply in the mid 1970s and could have cut into the demand for highways, though over this time both the auto stock and the

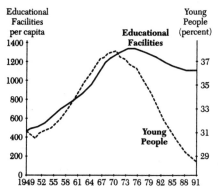

Figure 4. Stock of Educational Facilities per Person (1987 prices) and the Share of Young People in the Total Population

Source: Tatom (1993)

number of miles driven per capita has still increased. The price of gasoline apparently did cut into the number of trucks, trailers, and buses on the roads, also shown in the Figure. While one could get a shortage out of this pattern by extrapolating previous rates of investment spending, the rise in gasoline prices and the fall in numbers of heavy vehicles suggests that such an extrapolation may not be in order. It is certainly not obvious from these overall numbers that there is a highway shortage.

Figure 4 takes a similar look at public schools and other educational buildings, the second largest component of the state and local capital stock. Again the stock rose rapidly from 1950 to 1975, following by four years the rapid rise in the school and college age population also shown in the Figure. For the past two decades the school and college age population has plummeted, the share of pupils educated in public schools has been very stable, but the stock of public educational buildings has declined only gradually. If these numbers suggest one question, it is not whether there has been underinvest-

ment in educational structures, but rather whether there is now too much educational capital stock—perhaps the value of educational structures should have declined even more rapidly as the publicly educated school and college age population declined. As for productivity studies, it is also clear that educational buildings should not be part of the independent variable, because while these structures may have a very important long run productivity impact, they certainly do not have a short run impact on aggregate supply. To the extent that the rise and fall of educational structures is responsible for a correlation with national productivity trends, the correlation is probably bogus.

These simple comparisons cannot resolve difficult policy questions by themselves, but they do suggest a number of pitfalls as one gets into more careful analysis. The net real stock of state and local structures per capita has risen sharply and then leveled off. But the rise was due in part to the building of the interstate highway system and in part to the building of educational structures to meet rapid increases in the school and college age population. Apart from these movements, the federal stock of infrastructure capital has been very stable and the other components of state and local capital have grown at stable rates. It is hard to find a great need for infrastructure capital based on these numbers alone, and one might be somewhat suspicious of correlations of these numbers and national productivity without some careful corrections.

II. *Is There a Shortage of Infrastructure Capital?*

I argue below that I think the most important question involving infrastructure investment is not whether there has

been a shortage of infrastructure investment, but rather whether government
policies regarding infrastructure investment should be changed. I get to the
underlying policy issue below, but for
now I lead up to it by focusing on the
question that has been the focus of the
vast majority of papers about infrastructure—whether there is or has been a
shortage of infrastructure capital. There
have been four ways of trying to determine if there is, or was, such a shortage:

- Engineering assessments of infrastructure needs.
- Political measures based on voting
  outcomes.
- Economic measures of rates of return.
- Econometric estimates of productivity impacts.

I review each in turn.

A. *Engineering Needs Assessments*

The first clarion calls regarding the
infrastructure gap involved needs assessments (Associated General Contractors
1983; National Council on Public Works
Improvement 1988). These assessments
typically relied on engineering studies of
the condition of and need for capital facilities. The studies specified some desired
capital stock based on some arbitrary initial period when capital was presumed
to be adequate, and then measured desired investment as the gap between this
and the actual stock. There was almost
no economic reasoning anywhere in the
calculation—fixed proportions were assumed, there was no adjustment for excessive or underutilized initial capital,
and there was no recognition that citizens
may want to trade off the benefits of
greater capital against the costs.

Many of these engineering-type studies involved highways, the largest and
most volatile component of the infrastructure capital stock. Table 2, taken
from George Peterson's (1991) analysis

TABLE 2

ENGINEERING ESTIMATES OF HIGHWAY AND BRIDGE
INVESTMENT NEEDS
(ANNUAL COSTS, BILLIONS OF 1982 DOLLARS)

Study	Year	Period	Investment Need
Assoc. Gen. Contractors	1983	1983–2002	65.4
Cong. Budget Office	1983	1983–1990	27.2
Joint Economic Committee	1984	1982–2000	40.0
Fed. Highway Admin.*	1989	1987–2005	34.5
Fed. Highway Admin.**	1989	1987–2005	25.1
Capital expenditures	1982		19.1
Capital expenditures	1987		29.0

Source: Peterson (1991).
* Full constrained needs. Assumes that some urban
needs for road widening cannot be met because of the
difficulty of acquiring rights of way.
** Necessary to sustain current performance.

of the 1980s, shows that these physical
needs studies suggested smaller highway
infrastructure gaps as time passed and
as they were done more carefully. Even
though the Associated General Contractors study found actual highway investment to be less than a third of the desired
level in the early 1980s (comparing actual
investment, $19.1 billion, with "needed"
investment, $65.4 billion), by 1987 there
was no highway spending gap at all using
the U.S. Congressional Budget Office
(CBO) (1983) estimates and only a slight
gap using the FHA (1989) estimates
(comparing actual investment, $29.0 bil-
lion, with either $27.2 billion or $34.5
billion).

More up to date FHA numbers are
shown in Table 3. The Table gives estimates of the percentage of pavement
mileage needing improvement and the
percentage of peak hour vehicle miles
traveled under congested conditions. In
each case the physical needs measure—

TABLE 3

PAVEMENT RATINGS AND PEAK HOUR CONGESTION
(PERCENTAGE OF PAVEMENT MILES
OR VEHICLE MILES TRAVELED)

System and year	Needing improvement*	Congested**
Urban interstate		
1983	16.8	30.6
1987	11.1	42.0
1991	7.7	47.2
Urban and other arterials		
1983	10.0	28.5
1987	8.7	30.0
1991	6.8	28.7
Urban collectors		
1983	14.9	6.0
1987	13.6	6.0
1991	11.3	7.5
Rural interstates		
1983	13.3	3.0
1987	11.6	7.7
1991	7.6	8.8

Source: FHA (1993).
* Percent of pavement mileage rated in poor condition.
** Percent of vehicle miles travelled where the peak vehicle-capacity ratio exceeds a threshold set by FHA (0.8).

the percentage of highway miles in poor condition—declined steadily between 1983 and 1991. It is now at very low levels in all categories. The story is less clear for measures of highway congestion, which did all rise between 1983 and 1991, but congestion is still only at a high level for urban interstate and other arterials. There could be all kinds of pricing or other incentive policy changes that could reduce traffic congestion on these types of roads.

There are other needs assessments for water and sewer systems, aviation, and mass transit (Winston and Bosworth 1992). The story seems to be always the same—while one could make some case for a shortage of infrastructure capital, the shortages are not dramatic and it is

far from clear that any step up in present rates of investment is in order.

Hence in the end these needs assessments do not make a compelling case for there being an overall shortage of infrastructure capital. They make a series of arbitrary, noneconomic assumptions, and even then do not give clear evidence that infrastructure capital is significantly out of balance. Perhaps the most convincing evidence in favor of a shortage involves urban highway congestion, and there could be many other explanations for, and ways of resolving, urban highway congestion.

B. *Political Voting Outcomes*

State and local officials themselves report that their biggest hurdle in building new infrastructure capital is in gaining the approval of voters. Roughly 20 percent of all new state and local construction must now be approved by referenda, which suggests that referenda voting might prove a good way to identify and measure infrastructure shortages.

Peterson (1991) also analyzed the results of referendum voting. He constructed a model explaining the results of voter referenda on capital investment projects. He reasoned that if public officials could guess the tastes of their voters right on average, they would submit spending proposals that reflected these tastes correctly on average, and roughly half of these proposals would be approved. But political officials might not be able to guess the tastes of their voters correctly on average, and they might fear the loss in credibility and public esteem should their bond proposals fail at the polls. Hence they might be expected to let infrastructure construction fall behind its true desired level so they could submit capital spending proposals that should capture large majorities, anticipating that more than half of these proposals would generally be approved.

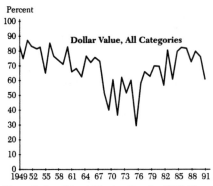

Figure 5. Local Bond Election Results, 1948–90
Percent Approved by Voters

Source: Peterson (1991)

There could be, in this political sense, a slight infrastructure shortage, but not one that policy measures should try to correct as long as there is no unhappiness with this general procedure for making infrastructure decisions. Moreover, apart from some lack of information or perception problems, there should never be a gross shortage of infrastructure capital because if this capital ever did fall far short of its desired level, vote-maximizing politicians could be expected to submit proposals to raise spending and utility-maximizing citizens could be expected to approve the proposals.

To determine whether a large gap in infrastructure investment opened up in the 1980s, Peterson analyzed the results of bond voting over time. The results, for overall capital projects for the 1948-90 period, are shown in Figure 5. Over the entire period the approval share averaged 70 percent, well above half as Peterson predicted. From 1968 to 1978, the share of construction dollars approved was below this average every single year, indicating either that voters were in an anti-public spending mood or that officials had overextended the public capital stock. Evidence in favor of the anti-

spending explanation comes from the large number of state tax or spending limitation measures passed in this period. But from 1979 to 1989, the approval share was above the historical average in all years but 1981 and 1983. One could take these outcomes as evidence that the public capital stock had fallen below the level desired by voters. But by the very end of the period, the approval share seemed once again poised to fall below its historical average, suggesting that if there ever was any underinvestment, it might have already been corrected.

As with the needs assessments, there is no clear evidence of an infrastructure shortage from these voting data. There is evidence that voters were more unfavorable to infrastructure projects in the 1968-78 era and more favorable since. This could be because infrastructure capital fell behind voters' desire for it, or there could be other causes. But even if there was a persistent gap for a time, public officials and voters may have already corrected it.

C. Economic Rates of Return

The economic approach to infrastructure investment involves computing all the benefits and costs of projects and then their rate of return. If the effective real rate of return exceeds the going real interest rate, the investment is worthwhile. Alternatively, if the net present value of project benefits evaluated at the going real interest rate is positive, the investment is worthwhile.[1]

While the methodology for computing real rates of return, and the implied present value of net program benefits, has

---

[1] The latter statement assumes that the going real interest rate is the proper rate for evaluating project benefits. In an open economy, it is the proper measure of the opportunity cost of private capital; in a closed economy, the matter is more complicated but the going pre-tax real interest rate is at least a reasonable contender (Gramlich 1990).

TABLE 4

PERCENTAGE REAL RATES OF RETURN ON HIGHWAY INVESTMENT

Investment	Rate
Projects to maintain current highway conditions	35
New urban construction projects	15
Upgrading sections not meeting minimum standards	5
New rural construction projects	Low
Fix sections above minimum standards	Negative

Source: CBO (1988).

been around in one form or another for decades, it is surprising how few careful calculations of rates of return are available for infrastructure investment. The Army Corps of Engineers and the Tennessee Valley Association have made estimates of net benefits and rates of return for various canal and dam projects, but these estimates are suspect in a number of ways (CBO 1988; Gramlich 1990). Here the usual suspicion is that these agencies load the dice in favor of infrastructure spending that is pejoratively called pork barrel spending. For our standard highway category, the most complete and acceptable calculations of prospective rates of return have come from the FHA for various types of highway expenditures done in the early 1980s. These have been analyzed by the CBO and are shown in Table 4.

A mixed picture emerges from the Table. Figure 3 showed how it was hard to make an aggregate case that highway investment was too high or too low—this investment seemed to be more or less in balance with the number of heavy vehicles that might use highways. Table 4 now shows that some types of highway investment still seem highly desirable, such as plain old maintenance and to a lesser extent urban construction. Others

do not seem as desirable, such as rural construction and improvements beyond minimum service standards. This distinction between maintenance and new construction will be important in the policy discussion below. The overall mixed picture is probably not surprising, and indeed it is the reason why economists generally prefer more disaggregated approaches in dealing with alleged capital shortages.

But even on their own terms, numbers like those shown in Table 4 may not ultimately be very informative. For one thing, rates of return were calculated in the early 1980s, when highway construction was much lower than it is now (see Table 2). By now, the pickup in highway construction could have lowered many rates of return substantially. For another, the numbers shown in the Table are not nearly disaggregated enough. There are growing and declining areas of the country, and surely infrastructure capital is more than adequate in some areas and quite inadequate in others. It is fine to disaggregate into particular categories of infrastructure capital, such as maintenance and new construction, but it would be far more useful to give particular rates of return—that on road maintenance in New York and Los Angeles, on new construction in San Francisco and Chicago, and so forth. With all the pages written on infrastructure investment, one is struck by how little there is of this sort of truly useful disaggregated information.

There are, of course, some problems even with this microeconomic approach. The most important in interpreting both the rate of return studies and the econometric studies (dealt with below) is benefit externalities. One argument for doing overall macroeconometric studies is that it is so difficult to deal with externalities in the micro studies. True, but it is also hard to know how serious the bias is.

Douglas Holtz-Eakin (1992) shows that it is unlikely that externalities would be a major problem because regional benefits do not seem to be any higher than state benefits in econometric studies. Gramlich (1990) reports data from license plate studies showing that even on major interstate highways most drivers are from within the state, and suggesting that the external benefits from highways for out-of-state drivers are not very large. Moreover, there are negative as well as positive externalities. The above estimates of high rates of return for urban road construction might be especially suspect in this regard, for often these projects impose significant external pollution and social costs on urban neighborhoods, costs that are difficult to quantify in rate of return studies.

While the picture is mixed, there are some categories of highway investment, maintenance, and possibly urban roads, that seem quite economic and where added infrastructure investment might make sense on average. There are other categories such as rural construction where added investment probably does not make sense on average. There are undoubtedly important regional differences in the value of added infrastructure investment. From this, it is hard to avoid the conclusion that while there may not be an aggregate shortage of infrastructure capital, at any time there could well be, or have been, shortages of particular types of infrastructure capital.

D. *Econometric Estimates of Productivity Impact*

Although macroeconometric studies might seem to be one of the least efficient approaches for determining infrastructure gaps, econometrics is what economists like to do, and these studies have commanded the most attention. Aschauer's initial papers have been fol-

lowed by his own supporting work (1990, 1993) and that of Holtz-Eakin (1988, 1992), Munnell (1990a), Narayana Kocherlakota and Ke-Mu Yi (1992), Fernald (1993), and Rafael Flores de Frutos and Alfredo Pereira (1993). These papers have in turn generated a raft of criticisms from such authors as Henry Aaron (1990), Charles Schultze (1990), Hulten and Schwab (1991a, forthcoming), Rubin (1991), Dale Jorgenson (1991), and Tatom (1991a, 1991b, 1993, forthcoming).

The basic idea is simple—just expand an aggregate production function to include the public capital stock. The production function is written as:

$$Q = AF(K,L) \qquad (1)$$

where K is the stock of private capital, L is the labor force, and A is an index representing total factor productivity. Aschauer and others then make A a function of the services provided by the government capital stock (G), rewriting (1) as:

$$Q = A^*F(K,L,G) \qquad (2)$$

where A^* is total factor productivity purged of the influence of the government capital stock. Using the Cobb-Douglas form and writing (2) in logs gives:

$$\ln Q = \ln A^* + a\ln K + b\ln L + c\ln G. \qquad (3)$$

Because government capital is not paid for its services, interpretation of the production elasticities, a, b, and c, is tricky. If one assumes that private capital and labor are paid their marginal products and finds c to be positive, $a + b = 1$ and $a + b + c > 1$, so that returns to scale are increasing. If one assumes returns to scale are constant and finds c to be positive, $a + b + c = 1$ and $a + b < 1$, so that labor and capital are paid more than their marginal products. When Aschauer did his macro time series regressions, he found c to be positive, from .38 to .56, forcing this choice between increasing returns and large factor rents.

It is also possible to use (3) to determine the rate of return on government capital. Differentiating the Cobb-Douglas form of (2) yields:

$$c = F_G G / Q \qquad (4)$$

where F_G is the marginal product of government capital. Given that G was $1938 billion in 1991 (Table 1) and Q was about $4800 billion (using private business output), estimates of production elasticity c from .38 to .56 result in pretty stratospheric estimates of the marginal product of government capital, 100 percent per annum or more.[2] That means that one unit of government capital pays for itself in terms of higher output in a year or less, which does strike one as implausible. When Holtz-Eakin (1988) and Munnell (1990a) followed similar procedures, they also got very high rates of return.

A number of logical criticisms have been made of this macro time series approach, and a number of econometric criticisms. On the logic side, a first question involves the definition of the variables. The usual version of public capital entered into these production regressions is the state and local stock, corresponding to the number that is $1938 billion in Table 1.[3] As was seen in discussing Table 1, 37 percent of the total stock involves highways, which could influence overall national output if better

highways lower the cost of trucking. But many of the benefits of highway investment will also involve the time saving of private individuals, which will generally not be reflected in national output. The 16 percent of the state and local stock representing education buildings, the 12 percent representing miscellaneous office buildings, the 3 percent representing hospitals, and the 2 percent representing conservation should not have much short term impact on the supply of aggregate output as it is now measured. Adding everything up, only about two-thirds of the existing state and local capital stock even purports to raise national output, so the stratospheric output rates of return for all public capital become all the more implausible.

This problem has been recognized and a number of authors have gone over to another concept called core infrastructure, defined as highways and water and sewer systems, about 60 percent of the state and local total. Both Aschauer (1989a) and Rubin (1991) have tried various definitions of the appropriate stock, and they do find that the core infrastructure component of the state and local stock has the highest production elasticity. But the rates of return for core infrastructure capital are still implausibly high, so this disaggregation is not the whole answer to the puzzle.

Another way to check on these results is used by Rubin and Fernald. If core infrastructure is to raise overall productivity, it ought to raise value added most in industries that directly benefit from the public capital stock, such as transportation. Rubin and Fernald do a number of tests of the impact of core infrastructure capital on productivity in various manufacturing industries. It is difficult to make an assessment here—Rubin does not find much pattern to the results but Fernald does.

[2] The implied marginal product of government capital is slightly less when evaluated for earlier years, but only slightly less. For example, the G/Q ratio is about .4 in 1991 and about .5 in 1970, roughly the midpoint of the time series estimation period for most authors. Had the calculations in the text been done in 1970, the marginal product of government capital would have been 75 percent or more, still pretty stratospheric.

[3] Some authors add the nonmilitary federal stock but the conclusions are little changed.

It would also be possible to check on the results by converting production functions to cost functions, as was originally suggested by Ann Friedlaender (1990). While nobody has estimated cost functions for the same data sets used in the productivity studies, Aschauer (1993) reports on a number of cost function studies that show positive social rates of return on infrastructure capital, for manufacturing industries in this and other developed countries.

Another logical problem involves the high rate of return. It is hard to see how the rate of return on public capital measured from output changes could ever lie above that of private capital. The private capital rate shows how private investors are making decisions at the margin, comparing marginal output benefits of their capital with the opportunity cost of their own funds. For public capital, these same investors would compare marginal output benefits with the opportunity cost of somebody else's funds. If public investment really were as profitable as claimed, would not private investors be clamoring to have the public sector impose taxes or float bonds to build roads, highways, and sewers to generate these high net benefits? The impact on business profits would be higher than for private capital and the cost to business far less. While it is hard to measure the clamor of private business investors, and even harder to determine whether inducing clamor is an efficient modus operandi for business investors, very little such pressure seems to have been observed, even when the implied econometric rates of return were allegedly very high. Most of the political arguments of private investors in the 1980s were that tax rates were too high, not that public investment was too low.

A final logical problem stressed by Hulten (forthcoming) might be described in various ways, either in terms of linkages or in terms of the old marginal-average problem. Simply saying that some capital has been productive in the past, which is all a production study can hope to say, does not mean that future investments will also be productive. It could be very beneficial to build up a network of highways and not very beneficial to expand this network. There could be many such examples for infrastructure investment, and there is a sense in which looking at past patterns might tell very little about future beneficial effects of public investment.

There are also a number of econometric problems with the macroeconomic time series method of estimating production functions. Perhaps the most serious involves common trends. We saw in Table 2 that the overall trend for state and local capital per capita mirrored the overall trend for national output per capita, rising rapidly up to the early 1970s and then much more slowly. There could be very different explanations for these trends—state and local capital could be influenced by the building of the interstate system and by the number of school and college age students; while overall productivity could have slowed for all the usual reasons—energy prices, environmental regulation, declining technology opportunities, and the like.

One way to deal with common trends is to use some form of differencing. When Hulten and Schwab (1991a) and Tatom (1991b) first difference macro time series observations, they get much lower estimates of the marginal product or rate of return of public capital, often not even positive and always statistically insignificant. Munnell (1992) feels that this correction may be too radical, because differencing could destroy the long term relationships in the data. Tatom (forthcoming) on the other hand tests the variables for stationarity and finds that differencing is required to make valid statistical estimates of the coefficients. Both authors agree that the proper approach is to test the variables for co-integration and adjust them before estimating the relationship. This is almost exactly what Tatom (1993) does, still finding essentially no productivity impact of infrastructure capital.

A second econometric problem involves missing variables, the obvious one being some measure of energy prices. These went up just when the stock of infrastructure capital and overall productivity stopped going up, and at a minimum one would think energy prices should be controlled for in aggregate production studies. When Tatom (1991b) makes such a control, in effect mixing production functions and cost functions, the estimated impact of infrastructure capital becomes weaker still. Tatom's approach can be criticized precisely because it does mix production functions and cost functions, and an obvious suggestion for future work is to try to pin this matter down by using measures of energy quantities in production functions.

A third econometric problem involves causality—does the levelling off of infrastructure capital reduce the growth of output, or does the reduced growth of output reduce the demand for infrastructure capital? Robert Eisner (1991) in particular has raised this question. Tatom (1993) does a series of lead-lag tests that indicate the causation may be more from output to infrastructure capital. Hulten (forthcoming) goes on to show that a plausible multi-equation growth model would make public capital an endogenous variable in the macro growth system, implying that its contribution to growth cannot be determined from a regression of output on public capital. To be sure, this type of criticism could be levelled at many production studies, many estimated production elas-

ticities for private capital, and many lead-lag tests.

There is also another form of simultaneous bias. The idea of production studies is to relate the stock of infrastructure capital to aggregate supply, but when infrastructure investment rises, aggregate demand is what changes in the short run. Even if the true aggregate supply effect of core infrastructure were zero, a rise in infrastructure investment would raise aggregate demand and output in the short run, leading to an inappropriate inference of large productivity effects of infrastructure investment.

The idea of making public capital an endogenous variable in a macro growth system has been pursued by Flores de Frutos and Pereira (1993). They correct for both common trends and simultaneity and do find that public investment is clearly endogenous, driven positively by private output changes and negatively by private employment changes. But even with all these corrections, they still find very high rates of return on public capital, almost as high as those found by Aschauer.

Another way to correct for simultaneity was used by Fernald. He first disaggregated by industry, reasoning that individual industry productivity would not simultaneously determine the overall stock of public capital. He then focused only on roads, and he interacted this stock of roads with use of roads, as measured by industrial vehicle stocks. Again, even with all of these careful corrections, Fernald still found very high rates of return on public capital, as high as those found by Aschauer. These latest two studies destroy the notion that more careful econometrics leads inevitably to lower implied rates of return on public capital.

Some of these problems of econometric interpretation could be lessened by using pooled time series, cross section data across states, as Munnell (1990b), Jose Costa, Richard Ellson, and Randolph Martin (1987), Eisner (1991), Randall Eberts (1986, 1990), Kevin Duffy-Deno and Eberts (1991), Holtz-Eakin (1992), and Hulten and Schwab (forthcoming) have all done. This approach generally gives more sensible estimates of the implied rate of return on infrastructure investment: now that rate of return ranges from the implied rate of return on private capital on the high side to zero on the low side (see Munnell's summary, 1992). While this approach takes advantage of greater variation in the infrastructure (and other) independent variables, it may still overstate infrastructure impacts by confounding intrinsic state productivity differences with variation in infrastructure capital. It still is subject to the reverse causation criticism. It may also either understate or overstate infrastructure impacts by ignoring out-of-state benefit spillovers. Some of Ohio's capital has impacts in states other than Ohio, but some of the contribution to Ohio's output is from capital lying outside Ohio which may be correlated with that lying inside Ohio. It is very difficult to deal with problems of this sort.

If it makes sense to use data from different states, it also makes sense to use data from other countries, as Aschauer (1989b) did early on. As for the basic trends, Tatom (forthcoming) shows that infrastructure investment in Canada, Japan, and five advanced European countries has followed the same basic pattern as in the United States—as a share of GDP, public capital formation has dropped off since the 1960s and 1970s. As for the econometric relationships, there is by now a massive literature that attempts to use production function analysis to find the determinants of growth rates across countries. Ross Levine and David Renelt (1992) have in effect summarized this literature by trying to make

fair comparisons of the whole list of variables suggested to influence growth rates across 119 countries. It turns out that most of the variables alleged to influence growth rates do not pass tests of statistical robustness. One of the variables that definitely does not pass their robustness test, indeed never gets significantly positive coefficients, is the government capital stock. But a similar analysis focusing just on transportation infrastructure for 96 countries by David Canning and Marianne Fay (1993) find normal to high rates of return in developed countries, high rates of return in industrializing countries, and moderate rates of return in underdeveloped countries.

Hence, while the business of estimating time series econometric relationships has preoccupied a large segment of the profession for the past five years, one cannot help but feel that there are two kinds of research bubbles here, time series and cross section. For time series, as was asserted above, public investment should never have been *totally* ignored up to 1989, and probably should not have been the focus of so much attention since 1989. On the cross-section side, compared to more detailed studies of referenda voting and benefit-cost analyses, the attention to macro time series seems way out of proportion to what ever could have been learned from inevitably low-powered comparisons of time series trends, even if buttressed by cross-sectional data.

III. *Policy Considerations*

Not only have previous studies not provided very convincing answers to whether there is or has been an infrastructure shortage, but they may not have even focused on the right question in the first place. Even if there were no doubt of an infrastructure shortage, it is not clear what infrastructure policy or policies should be changed. By the same token, finding no evidence of shortage would not mean that *no* policy should be changed. Hence rather than asking whether there is a shortage, it seems more helpful to ask what, if any, policies should be changed. In this section I switch the focus and analyze the infrastructure issue from this policy perspective.

A common way in which decisions about whether to invest in infrastructure capital are made is the one described above—states and localities propose bond issues and voters decide whether to build the structure. Because voters are deciding, it is hard to say there is a structural policy defect here. But voters are influenced by the financial and other terms of the deal, and these are set by governments and could be altered. The most important way in which this is done now is by federal grants, but other restrictions on whether and under what circumstances state and local governments can impose user charges can also be altered.

A. *Federal Grants*

Federal grants for construction purposes have followed a long swing process, ascending from less than 1 percent of GDP in the 1950s up to about 1.5 percent by 1978. At that point they began a long descent and grants are now back to close to the same percentage of GDP as in the 1950s.[4]

The standard argument for federal infrastructure grants is benefit spillovers: citizens outside of the jurisdiction receive some benefits from infrastructure projects, and if these citizens' votes are not reflected in decisions, too little infrastructure capital will be supplied. The

[4] In doing these calculations, it is important to distinguish federal grants for construction purposes from other federal grants, these days largely consisting of open-ended grants for medicaid and public welfare.

most precise way to deal with the problem is by a series of Coasian bargains between governments, but given that there are something like 80,000 state and local governments in the United States, there would be very high transactions costs to arrive at such a set of bargains. It would be simpler, the argument goes, just to have the federal government provide matching grants for infrastructure projects, with the federal match in some general way representing the appropriate contribution of outsiders.

If this is the argument for federal grants, the actual terms of federal grant programs leave much to be desired. It is helpful to distinguish types of capital. One type is new capital with large costs and potentially enormous technological benefits, say as for the super-conductor, super-collider. For such capital technological spillovers are substantial, justifying federal support. Federal matching shares should reflect the benefits, technological and other, that flow beyond state lines. It is of course difficult to determine such benefits for these advanced technology projects, but present federal matching shares on this type of capital, generally about 90 percent, are probably way too high. Rather than keeping federal matching shares this high and having states lobby intensely for projects, as now happens, one quasi-market approach for determining proper federal matching shares would be to let states bid on projects. If the state of Massachusetts really wanted the super-conductor, super-collider, let it outbid Texas. Such an approach should save on federal tax dollars and improve the statewide allocation of government projects.

A second type of infrastructure capital, by far the most common, is capital like that already in place—widened or expanded roads, improved water and sewer plants, and on down the list. Studies have shown that for most infrastructure projects of this kind the majority of the benefits, 70 percent or so, are realized by those inside the state (Gramlich 1990). Given this, the proper federal matching grant would pay about 30 percent of the costs for the typical project. Instead, the typical federal infrastructure grant pays about 80 percent of the cost of a project up to some limit, then none of the costs. In the usual case where the grant limit is small relative to typical state spending on the project, the federal money provides no price subsidy at all at the margin, and much too large an inframarginal income subsidy. These capped grants then achieve the worst of both worlds—they cost the federal government too much, hence raising the federal deficit and probably lowering national saving, and they do nothing about external benefits at the margin. The correction is obvious—lower federal matching shares and remove the caps.

The problems with overly generous inframarginal matching could be even worse than they seem. Suppose state or local officials know that there is too little of some type of public infrastructure nationally, and they think that Congress will rise to the bait and pass a new grant program. Rather than simply building the facility in short supply, the generous federal matching gives these officials a powerful incentive to wait and see if they can get a federal grant, rather than just going ahead with their own project. Exactly this seems to have happened, first with a countercyclical public works grant program passed in the late 1970s (Gramlich 1978) and later with pollution-control grants (James Jondrow and Robert Levy 1984).

Another problem involves the distinction made earlier between new construction and maintenance. Basically, maintenance investment seems to have higher rates of return but new construction gets higher federal matching subsidies. In

fact, often highway maintenance projects get little or no federal matching while new interstate construction projects get the generous treatment described above. The solution is obvious here too—while matching shares are lowered for new construction, they might actually be raised up to their proper low level for highway maintenance.

A further problem involves the financing of the federal grants. At the national level there are five dedicated trust funds—for airports, highways, aquatic resources, harbors, and inland waterways. The Department of Transportation (1990) has recently suggested creating others for the coast guard and railroads. Into each trust fund goes the dedicated revenue, such as that from the gas tax for highways, and out come the federal grants for the relevant projects. Many states have similar arrangements to finance their own infrastructure projects.

This trust fund arrangement can be useful in limiting federal subsidies by forcing the dedicated tax to pay for all or most of the spending in question. At the same time, if the arrangement is misapplied, it can lead to inefficient outcomes. One example of such a misapplication is the gas tax, which could also be rationalized as an energy conservation measure that should not have its returns sent to the highway trust fund and devoted to the construction of further highways. Recent budget bills have devoted much of the gas tax revenues to general federal revenues and not to the highway trust fund, but it was twenty years into America's energy crisis and fifteen years into America's budget crisis before this daring step was taken.

A second example of such a misapplication is that four of the trust funds, all but the one for aquatic resources, do not even limit federal subsidies by forcing trust fund revenues to cover all of the federal spending for the facilities in question (David Montgomery 1989). At a minimum they should do that. At present, whenever there is a hold-down on federal infrastructure grants for budget reasons, the revenues build up in the trust fund, again achieving the worst of both worlds—the funds are there, activating lobbyists in favor of increased spending, even though spending is already subsidized by federal general revenues. The solutions are obvious here too—finance all grants from the trust funds, and devote most gas tax revenues to general revenue.

B. *User Fees*

The above comments suggest some general reforms in federal grant programs for infrastructure investment. But if it were possible to impose user fees on infrastructure facilities, which it certainly is for highways and other transportation infrastructure, many higher education structures (the user fee is commonly known as tuition), hospitals, many water and sewer systems, some conservation structures, and some industrial structures, it would be possible to do even better than to have revamped federal grants finance the infrastructure investment.

Take the case of highway maintenance financing, perhaps the largest category of infrastructure investment where there are opportunities for desirable expansion. If these maintenance projects are eligible for federal grants, the federal government collects a gas tax, devotes a large share of it to the federal highway trust fund, and has the trust fund in turn provide grants with 80 percent federal matching to states, which probably match the federal money with revenues from their own gas tax. Suppose instead the gas tax were devoted to federal general revenues and budget deficit reduction, the federal highway trust fund were abolished, and the states were permitted

to finance their own maintenance expenditures with revenues from tolls (which in general they cannot now levy if they have used federal money to build their interstate roads). The impressive list of advantages from such a change is as follows:

- Revenue. There would be a new source of revenue to pay for the highway maintenance, lessening budget problems at both the federal and state levels.
- Allocation. Over the long run the toll revenue from highway *x* could be devoted to restoring highway *x*, thus giving public officials a better quasi-market guide on how to allocate their maintenance (and other) funds (Wallace Oates 1991).
- Politics. The nasty political debate about excessive taxation could be moderated. At least in this area it would be very clear where the toll revenues were going.
- Taxation by Willingness to Pay. This has always been the public finance dream, to devise financing schemes that tax citizens according to their willingness to pay for the facility. How better to do that than to use user fees?
- Spillovers. Rather than have federal grants, even reformed federal grants, employ inevitably crude estimates of out-of-state marginal benefits in constructing matching ratios, toll user fee finance of highway maintenance would automatically be paid by out-of-state users in proportion to their use.
- Conservation. Highway engineers report that interstate roads depreciate according to the cubic power of vehicle axle weight (Kenneth Small, Winston, and Carol Evans 1989). Rather than letting all vehicles use the road for free, tolls could be based

on true damage imposed on the road, hence encouraging heavy truckers to lighten their axle weight and extend the life of the road. Or, states could build thicker roads and charge truckers for that. Part of the economic saving here would be that less road maintenance would need to be done if tolls were set efficiently.

• Congestion. Tolls could be varied by the time of day or week, hence lessening congestion.

With so many advantages, it is hard to say no. There are clear opportunities to have user fees finance much infrastructure investment, simultaneously financing the investment and extending the life of the capital. States could be allowed to finance their road maintenance and new construction projects by tolls (generally not possible now), airports could be allowed to use ticket taxes (recently made possible) and landing charges (still not possible), higher education could charge tuition rates nearer to marginal costs (giving more aid to needy students), hospital and other structures could finance themselves with fees. There are a number of technological innovations in the collection of these fees that could keep down administrative costs (Winston and Bosworth 1992; Martin Neil Baily, Gary Burtless, and Robert Litan 1993). The revenue from the fees could also be devoted to properly designed trust funds to keep revenues and spending in balance. One radical version of this proposal is that infrastructure capital could simply be privatized, with the private owners given both the permission and incentive to set up their own fee schedules.

There are, of course, economic objections to comprehensive user fee financing of all infrastructure capital. Present day federal matching grants could still be more efficient if it were costly to collect

the user fees, if there were externalities, if there were natural monopolies with spillovers, or to complete a national network of roads and/or airports. While one can think of types of capital for which these types of objections are relevant, these exceptions to the general rule would seem to be of modest enough importance that a more extensive set of user fees should still bring about large efficiency gains. A more extensive set of user fees may in the end result in more or less infrastructure investment—that prediction is difficult to make. But the mechanism for making infrastructure decisions would be much improved. States would have a new and powerful incentive to find the optimal stock of infrastructure capital.

There could also be political objections to user fee financing of infrastructure capital. If user fees are so wonderful, why are they not used more widely? Space constraints prohibit a deep discussion of the politics of paying for government spending, a topic with many well-known subtleties. But one thing that can be said is that if the world gradually adjusts its institutions in the direction of the optimal approach, the use of user fees in the United States is growing dramatically (CBO 1993).

IV. Conclusions

As for the alleged infrastructure shortage, the evidence reviewed in the paper is decidedly mixed. The needs assessment approaches and macro time series approaches used to justify big increases in infrastructure spending are flawed in many ways. One might make some more headway by looking at more disaggregated time series, bond referenda voting, and rates of return, where there is some evidence that some types of infrastructure could have been in short supply, but even here the evidence is inconclusive and it is not clear that the overall shortage persists.

What should be done about any shortages? The best approach is not to try to analyze the numbers and tell how short the supply is and how much national or state spending or grants should be increased. A far more sensible approach is to set up institutional structures that permit state and local governments, the holders of almost all infrastructure capital, to find their own optimal stock. The way this might be done is to reform the present system of financing infrastructure investment. States could be forced to bid for costly, large-scale high technology projects. States could also be permitted or encouraged to impose user fees to finance their own capital and maintenance. And federal matching grants could be restructured and used much less intensively.

As for the contribution of economic researchers to this new understanding, there is some good news and some bad news. After years of ignoring the issue, economists led by Aschauer did finally find it, giving some more professional gloss to advocacy pieces that up to then were entirely from the infrastructure lobby. But the contributions of economists were not all they could have been—there seems to have been far too much attention to the details of macro production studies, which can never answer the relevant policy questions very well, and far too little attention to more disaggregated rate of return studies and studies of the impact of different types of policy changes.

While in some sense the problems outlined and discussed here are more at the state and local level than at the federal level, the federal government could help matters in various ways. The obvious way is to change policies to permit states to go on their own on infrastructure investment, cutting states loose from the fed-

eral grant system and giving states their own source of revenue and power to make key decisions. But there are some less obvious ways as well. Improved capital stock data would make it possible to conduct more disaggregated studies. Improved estimates of economic rates of depreciation of the infrastructure stock would also improve estimates of the size of this stock and the desirability of expansion. More importantly, the federal government might even give policy analysts something to study by doing experiments with policy changes of various sorts— permitting bidding for valued projects, permitting user fees, permitting privatization, permitting other sorts of incentive changes—to see how state and local governments and their voters will respond. Studying reactions of this sort can redirect the efforts of economists onto studies of just what policy changes are in order.

REFERENCES

AARON, HENRY J. "Why Is Infrastructure Important? Discussion," in ALICIA H. MUNNELL, ed. 1990b, pp. 51–63.
ASCHAUER, DAVID A. "Is Public Expenditure Productive?" *J. Monet. Econ.*, Mar. 1989a, 23(2), pp. 177–200.
———. "Public Investment and Productivity Growth in the Group of Seven," *Econ. Perspectives*, 1989b, 13(5), pp. 17–25.
———. "Does Public Capital Crowd Out Private Capital?" *J. Monet. Econ.*, 1989c, 24(2), pp. 171–88.
———. "Why Is Infrastructure Important?" in ALICIA H. MUNNELL, ed. 1990b, pp. 21–50.
———. "Genuine Economic Returns to Infrastructure Investment," *Policy Stud. J.*, 1993, 21, pp. 380–90.
ASSOCIATION OF GENERAL CONTRACTORS. "America's Infrastructure: A Plan to Rebuild." May 1983.
BAILY, MARTIN NEIL; BURTLESS, GARY AND LITAN, ROBERT E. *Growth with equity: Economic policymaking for the next century.* Washington, DC: Brookings Institution, 1993.
CANNING, DAVID AND FAY, MARIANNE. "The Effect of Transportation Networks on Economic Growth." Columbia U., mimeo, May 1993.
DUFFY-DENO, KEVIN T. AND EBERTS, RANDALL W. "Public Infrastructure and Regional Economic Development: A Simultaneous Equations Approach," *J. Urban Econ.*, Nov. 1991, 30(3), pp. 329–43.
EBERTS, RANDALL W. "Estimating the Contribution of Urban Public Infrastructure to Regional Eco-

nomic Growth." Fed. Res. Bank of Cleveland Working Paper No. 8610, Dec. 1986.

_____. "Public Infrastructure and Regional Economic Development," *Fed. Res. Bank of Cleveland Econ. Rev.*, 1990, 26, pp. 15–27.

EISNER, ROBERT. "Infrastructure and Regional Economic Performance," *New Eng. Econ. Rev., Fed. Res. Bank of Boston*, Sept./Oct. 1991, pp. 47–58.

FEDERAL HIGHWAY ADMINISTRATION. *The status of the nation's highways, bridges, and transit: Conditions and performance.* Washington, DC: U.S. Department of Transportation, Federal Highway Adminstration, 1993.

FERNALD, JOHN. "How Productive is Infrastructure? Distinguishing Reality and Illusion with a Panel of U.S. Industries." Federal Reserve Board Discussion Paper, Aug. 1993.

FLORES DE FRUTOS, RAFAEL AND PEREIRA, ALFREDO. "Public Capital and Aggregate Growth in the United States: Is Public Capital Productive?" U. of California at San Diego Discussion Paper 93–31, July 1993.

FRIEDLAENDER, ANN F. "How Does Public Infrastructure Affect Regional Economic Performance? Discussion," in ALICIA H. MUNNELL, ed. 1990b, pp. 108–12.

GRAMLICH, EDWARD M. "State and Local Budgets the Day after It Rained? Why Is the Surplus So High?" *Brookings Pap. Econ. Act.*, 1978, 1, pp. 191–214.

_____. *A guide to benefit-cost analysis.* 2nd ed. Prentice-Hall, 1990.

HOLTZ-EAKIN, DOUGLAS. "Private Output, Government Capital, and the Infrastructure Crisis." Discussion Paper No. 394, Columbia U., May 1988.

_____. "Public Sector Capital and the Productivity Puzzle, National Bureau of Economic Research Working Paper No. 4144, 1992.

HULTEN, CHARLES R. "Optimal Growth with Public Infrastructure Capital: Implications for Empirical Modeling." U. of Maryland Discussion Paper, 1993.

HULTEN, CHARLES R. AND SCHWAB, ROBERT M. "Is There Too Little Public Capital? Infrastructure and Economic Growth." American Enterprise Institute Discussion Paper, Feb. 1991a.

_____. "Public Capital Formation and the Growth of Regional Manufacturing Industries," *Nat. Tax J.*, Dec. 1991b, 44(4), pp. 121–34.

_____. "Infrastructure Spending: Where Do We Go From Here?" in the National Tax Association Proceedings, forthcoming.

JOINT ECONOMIC COMMITTEE. "National Infrastructure Advisory Committee Report." Feb. 1984.

JONDROW, JAMES AND LEVY, ROBERT A. "The Displacement of Local Spending for Pollution Control By Federal Construction Grants," *Amer. Econ. Rev.*, May 1984, 74(2), pp. 174–78.

JORGENSON, DALE. "Fragile Statistical Foundations: The Macroeconomics of Public Infrastructure Investment." American Enterprise Institute Discussion Paper, Feb. 1991.

KOCHERLAKOTA, NARAYANA AND YI, KE-MU. "The

Long Run Effects of Government Policy on Growth Rates in the United States." U. of Iowa/Rice U. mimeo, Sept. 1992.

LEVINE, ROSS AND RENELT, DAVID. "A Sensitivity Analysis of Cross-Country Growth Regressions," *Amer. Econ. Rev.*, Sept. 1992, 82(5), pp. 942–63.

MONTGOMERY, W. DAVID. "Statement before the U.S. Senate Committee on Appropriations." May 11, 1989.

MUNNELL, ALICIA H. "Why Has Productivity Growth Declined? Productivity and Public Investment," *New Eng. Econ. Rev.*, Jan./Feb. 1990a, pp. 3–22.

_____. *Is there a shortfall in public capital investment?* Ed.: ALICIA H. MUNNELL. Conference Series No. 34. Boston: Federal Reserve Bank of Boston, 1990b.

_____. "How Does Public Infrastructure Affect Regional Economic Performance?" in ALICIA H. MUNNELL, ed., 1990b, pp. 69–103.

_____. "Infrastructure Investment and Economic Growth," *J. Econ. Perspectives*, Fall 1992, 6(4), pp. 189–98.

NATIONAL COUNCIL ON PUBLIC WORKS IMPROVEMENT. "Fragile Foundations: A Report on America's Public Works." 1988.

OATES, WALLACE E. "Discussion." American Enterprise Institute Discussion Paper, Feb. 1991.

PETERSON, GEORGE E. "Is Public Infrastructure Undersupplied?" in ALICIA H. MUNNELL, ed. 1990b, pp. 113–30.

_____. "Historical Perspective on Infrastructure Investment: How Did We Get Where We Are?" American Enterprise Institute Discussion Paper, Feb. 1991.

RUBIN, LAURA S. "Productivity and the Public Capital Stock: Another Look." Federal Reserve Board Discussion Paper, May 1991.

SCHULTZE, CHARLES L. "The Federal Budget and the Nation's Economic Health," in *Setting national priorities: Policies for the nineties.* Ed.: HENRY J. AARON. Washington, DC: Brookings Institution, 1990, pp. 19–64.

DA SILVA, JOSE COSTA; ELLSON, RICHARD W. AND MARTIN, RANDOLPH C. "Public Capital, Regional Output, and Development: Some Empirical Evidence," *J. Reg. Sci.*, Aug. 1987, 27(3), pp. 419–37.

SMALL, KENNETH A.; WINSTON, CLIFFORD AND EVANS, CAROL A. *Road work: A new highway pricing and investment policy.* Washington, DC: Brookings Institution, 1989.

TATOM, JOHN A. "Should Government Spending on Capital Goods Be Raised?" *Fed. Res. Bank of St. Louis Rev.*, Mar./Apr., 1991a, pp. 3–15.

_____. "Public Capital and Private Sector Performance," *Fed. Res. Bank of St. Louis Rev.*, May/June 1991b, 73(3), pp. 3–15.

_____. "Paved With Good Intentions: The Mythical National Infrastructure Crisis." Policy Analysis, Cato Institute, Aug. 12, 1993.

_____. "Shifting Perspectives on the Role of Public Capital Formation," *Fed. Res. Bank of St. Louis Rev.*, forthcoming.

U.S. CONGRESSIONAL BUDGET OFFICE. *Public works infrastructure: Policy considerations for the 1980s.* Washington, DC: U.S. GPO, Apr. 1983.

———. *New directions for the nation's public works.* Washington, DC: U.S. GPO, Sept. 1988.

———. *The growth of federal user charges.* Washington, DC: U.S. GPO, Aug. 1993.

U.S. DEPARTMENT OF TRANSPORTATION. *Moving America: New directions, new opportunities.* Washington, DC: U.S. Department of Transportation, 1990.

WINSTON, CLIFFORD AND BOSWORTH, BARRY. "Public Infrastructure," in *Setting domestic priorities: What can government do?* Eds.: HENRY J. AARON AND CHARLES L. SCHULTZE. Washington, DC: Brookings Institution, 1992, pp. 267–93.

[15]

MIGRATION AND INCOME
REDISTRIBUTION RESPONSIBILITIES*

EDWARD M. GRAMLICH
DEBORAH S. LAREN

ABSTRACT

The importance of migration of AFDC beneficiaries as a determinant of
state benefit levels is examined in this paper. A pooled cross-section time-
series model fit to state data over the seventies indicates that benefit levels
in other states have a positive influence on own-state benefits and a negative
influence on recipients. This evidence is supported by that from a transition
matrix, which shows that while very few AFDC households make an interstate move in a year, when they do move they are much more likely to
go to a high-benefit state than to a low-benefit state. Both pieces of evidence
argue for more centralization of income redistribution responsibilities in
the United States.

One of the important factors determining the level of government at
which various public functions should be carried out is migration. On
the tax side, many argue for state or federal regulation of local tax-
abatement programs, fearing that local tax competition to attract industry
might stimulate no new industry in aggregate but hurt all local treasuries.
On the expenditure side, an argument against plans to return welfare and
food stamps to state governments is the feeling that states will be prevented from being as generous as they would otherwise be for fear of
attracting hordes of welfare recipients.

The importance of migration may be the central normative issue
involved in the many plans that have been suggested over the years to
centralize or decentralize income redistribution responsibilities in the

*The authors are members of the faculty of the Department of Economics and the Institute
of Public Policy Analysis, The University of Michigan.*

* Our work on this topic has been financed by a grant from the Sloan Foundation. We
have benefitted from the helpful suggestions of Ted Bergstrom, Robert Frank, Robert
Hutchens, Daniel Rubinfeld, Gary Solon, and Hal Varian. [Manuscript received May
1983; accepted May 1984.]

The Journal of Human Resources • *XIX* • *4*
0022-166X/84/0004-0489 $01.50/0

United States (the most recent, to decentralize, being that of President Reagan in 1982). Theoretical models of income redistribution such as that of Pauly [14] have also highlighted the spatial distribution of inter-dependent utility—that is, are the taxpayers of jurisdiction x made better off by a rise in minimum living standards in jurisdiction y? This question seems intrinsically impossible to answer, though Ladd and Doolittle [9] have tried to do so, using a survey of the Advisory Commission on Intergovernmental Relations (ACIR). But the migration question seems as important and is much more amenable to research.

There has been a substantial amount of research on the migration question, but it has yet to be integrated into the literature on the deter-mination of income-redistribution benefits. The early literature on the topic, summarized by Holmer [7], showed that recent migrants accounted for a very small share of recipients under the Aid to Families with De-pendent Children (AFDC) program in the late sixties. But there are three reasons why these results may not eliminate the impact of fears of mi-gration in the states' setting of AFDC benefits today. For one thing, most of the key studies were done before the Supreme Court ruled state resi-dency requirements unconstitutional in 1969. Secondly, migrants were defined to be relatively recent immigrants—generally those in the previous five years. If both the migration decision and the states' ability to change its AFDC benefit level operate sluggishly, long-term effects may dominate relatively unimpressive short-term responses. Finally, the key question is not the actual level of migration, but how important this migration is perceived to be by those in charge of setting state AFDC benefits. If migration is perceived to be important, or if statewide benefit disparities are kept just under the level that would actually stimulate migration, migration might be much more of a constraining force than the actual numbers would suggest.

Recent literature on the topic seems to be giving greater importance to migration. Both DeJong and Donnelly [3] and Cebulla and Kohn [2] took nonwhite migration as a proxy for AFDC migration and related this migration to relative state benefit levels, generally finding fairly sizable effects. An obvious problem is that only about 25 percent of the nonwhite families receive AFDC payments, and only about half of AFDC recipients are nonwhite. A more recent study by Southwick [16] corrected this prob-lem by using AFDC recipients as a dependent variable, and also worked out better ways for controlling for migration flows that might have taken place for reasons other than AFDC benefits. He still found that AFDC benefits were an important determinant of the migration of AFDC re-cipients. But his study also raised some questions. He used survey data on where AFDC recipients in a state in 1967 were born to determine migration, raising the possibility that these AFDC recipients could have migrated to a state before benefits were set at a high level (the exact reverse of the problem with the studies cited by Holmer; Southwick seems to have overcorrected). Also, Southwick's measure of migration deals only with AFDC immigration, not emigration. Still more recently, Blank [1], using microdata from the Current Population Survey, found that AFDC benefit levels exerted a fairly strong impact both on migration and on the participation in AFDC of female-headed families. She calculated results only for the change expected in location over a five-year period, however, and it is not clear from her model how much AFDC benefit levels influence the long-run equilibrium population proportions.

Apart from these gaps, all of the previous literature on migration in response to AFDC benefits has completely ignored the other side of the question. If AFDC benefit levels do partly determine migration flows, are they set so as to discourage these flows? The long literature on the determination of AFDC benefits is silent on the question. One of us has tried to deal with it (see Gramlich [4]), but this paper is meant to be a substantial extension of that treatment.

In this paper we try to add to knowledge about migration and AFDC policies in two ways. In the first part of the paper we develop a model that simultaneously determines AFDC benefits in a state and its recipient population. The model can be solved to determine how benefit levels in other states determine the own state's benefit levels. This procedure gives one estimate of this critical coefficient.

In the second part of the paper we take a different tack. The model in the first part was estimated with Social Security Administration (SSA) data on characteristics of state AFDC plans. The model in the second part uses microdata from both the 1980 Census and the Panel Study of Income Dynamics (PSID) on AFDC recipients in the seventies (after residency requirements had been made unconstitutional). Families who received AFDC benefits are surveyed to see if they made an interstate move and where. A transition matrix is constructed for these families, and solved to give the equilibrium distribution of the AFDC population for states of varying levels of AFDC payments. This distribution is compared to a hypothetical distribution that would exist if all states paid the same benefit levels, and from this an estimate of the sensitivity of migration to benefit levels is constructed.

It turns out that the estimates of the econometric model conform very well to the estimates based on the transition matrix. To anticipate our conclusions, both sets of results say that migration in response to AFDC benefit levels does seem to take place, though very sluggishly. The perception that this migration is important does seem to have a significant influence on states in their setting of AFDC benefits. Our ultimate policy implication is a conventional one, backed up by better evidence: State governments should be given less, not more, financial responsibility for determining income redistribution policies.

THE SIMULTANEOUS EQUATIONS MODEL

A model of the determination of AFDC benefits should be based on why these benefits are paid in the first place. Several rationales have been proposed in the literature. The altruism models of Hochman and Rodgers [6], Pauly [14], Orr [13], and others all make the standard public choice assumption that voters or their representatives are maximizing some collective utility function that has as arguments the disposable income of taxpayers and some notion of the living standards of transfer recipients—as if those who are well-off also care about the living standards of those who are not well-off. For this reason, these models are called interdependent utility models of benefit payments. As benefits rise, the marginal value of further increases falls and the marginal utility of the taxpayer's own income rises, leading to an optimization characterized by the usual marginal conditions. Since, in general, it is difficult to distinguish contributors to AFDC from potential recipients, one might complicate these models, in a direction suggested by Varian [17], by adding a motive for income security: Voters may be more inclined to vote for transfer benefits if they feel they may need them some day, due to uncertainty about their own income. They may even empathize more with transfer recipients if subject to uncertainty in their own income stream. When such a modification is made, the impact of community income in the benefit-determination models becomes ambiguous. The altruism view suggests a positive income elasticity for AFDC benefits (as people become richer, they have less marginal utility for their own income and would be more inclined towards redistribution), while the income security view suggests a negative income elasticity (richer people would be less fearful that they would ever need transfers and less inclined towards redistribution).

A different approach is suggested by Peltzman [15]. He follows the new trend in the public choice literature in distinguishing between voters and politicians. Rather than trying to stay in office by passing legislation favored by the median voter, Peltzman's politicians try to stay in office by earning the gratitude of transfer recipients without antagonizing most taxpayers. They do this by redistributing income from rich to poor—a small percentage change in the income of the rich can lead to sizable percentage changes in the income of the poor—again until some marginal political conditions are satisfied. Elsewhere Gramlich and Rubinfeld [5] have pointed to a problem with this strategy: As far as state elections are concerned, potential transfer recipients are few enough, with such low voter-turnout rates and such a weak propensity to vote for state spending increases, that it is hard to see how anybody could make a political career following Peltzman's rules. But if Peltzman is correct, his model also raises the possibility of an ambiguity in the migration effect. The altruism model suggests that migration, or the perception of it by state legislators, would make legislators reluctant to pay a certain level of benefits because state tax rates would become too high. The vote-buying model suggests that things might go the other way, because legislators might see the chance to gain votes from potential immigrants in other states by raising AFDC benefits. In addition to its obvious policy interest, trying to deal more carefully with the migration question also helps indicate which theoretical approach appears to be more fruitful.

For this paper we adopt the general form of the altruism model, though with enough free parameters that results could be consistent with either the income-security variant or the vote-gaining variant. We begin by postulating a general utility function for the individual who has come to be called the "decisive" voter in a state—the voter who, through a complex set of political reactions, determines state policy:

$$(1) \qquad U(i) = U(i)[X(i), B]$$

where $U(i)$ refers to the quasi-concave utility function of this ith voter, $X(i)$ to the voter's income after state taxes to pay for AFDC, and B to the average level of AFDC benefits in the state.

This utility function is maximized subject to two separate budget constraints, one for the decisive voter's household and one for the state government. The household budget constraint can be written simply as:

$$(2) \qquad X(i) = Y(i)[1 - T]$$

where T is the state income tax rate necessary to finance AFDC, here assumed to be proportional, and $Y(i)$ is before-tax income. The state budget constraint is:

$$(3) \qquad TY = (1 - M)(RB/N)$$

where Y is average per capita income, R is the number of AFDC recipients in the state, and N is the state population. The variable M stands for the federal matching rate for AFDC benefits, defined so as to include an adjustment for the fact that state benefit payments will cause some drain on the federal treasury and some federal tax cost to state taxpayers.[1]

---

1   The adjustment is computed by letting $M = m(1 - v)$, where m is the statutory matching rate and v is the ratio of state to federal income. Hence, state taxpayers pay $1 - m$ directly and then $100v$ percent of all federal matching costs, yielding a total state share of $1 - m + mv = 1 - M$. The ratio v is never very large (a maximum of .1 for California), and was taken to be constant over time for each state in our empirical procedure.

Maximizing utility subject to these budget constraints, and assuming the usual logarithmic form for the implied demand equation for the ith voter, gives the AFDC benefits equation:

$$(4) \qquad B = c_0 Y(i)^{c_1} P(i)^{-c_2}$$

where $P(i)$ is the effective relative price of AFDC benefits for this voter, and the intercept c_0 should be interpreted as varying across states according to tastes, institutions, and other factors.

To this point the maximization exercise is very standard. The complicating feature for AFDC is that the recipient population cannot be viewed as exogenous, but would vary depending on the level of benefits. Within a state, higher benefit levels will make more families eligible for welfare because of the breakeven effect—higher benefit levels raise the income breakeven level and the size of the eligible population. And also, the higher benefit levels could raise the recipient population if they induce migration. An equation reflecting these forces is:

$$(5) \qquad R = \hat{R} \, B^{b_1} \, \overline{B}^{-b_2}$$

where $\hat{R}$ is an unobservable variable representing the recipient population if own-state benefits (B) were equal to those in surrounding states ($\overline{B}$) and if the two elasticities (b_1 and b_2) were the same. If there is a breakeven effect, b_1 should exceed b_2. Because R is likely to respond to $\overline{B}$ with some lag, $\overline{B}$ should refer to benefits in surrounding states in some previous period. The final equation in the model explains the unobservable hypothetical recipient population, $\hat{R}$:

$$(6) \qquad \hat{R}/N = a_0 Y^{-a_1} U^{a_2}$$

where U is the state's unemployment rate. One could imagine many other variables, such as the state income distribution and demographic composition, being included in (6). Variables such as these are measured only intermittently and change very slowly over time within a state; hence we represent them by allowing intercepts to vary across states.

The model is solved by combining (2), (3), (5), and (6):

$$(7) \qquad X(i) = Y(i) - [1 - M][Y(i)/Y][a_0 Y^{-a_1} U^{a_2} B^{1+b_1} \overline{B}^{-b_2}]$$

and then differentiating to determine the relative price of AFDC:

$$(8) \qquad \begin{aligned} P(i) &= -\partial X(i)/\partial B \\ &= [1 + b_1][1 - M][Y(i)/Y][a_0 Y^{-a_1} U^{a_2} B^{b_1} \overline{B}^{-b_2}] \end{aligned}$$

We then substitute (8) into (4), take logs, and differentiate.[2] Letting the logarithmic derivative of a variable, X, be given by $L(X)$ ($= \partial \ln X$), we have:

---

2 Since $Y(i)$ is unobservable, at this point we must also assume that the ratio of the decisive voter's income to average income in a state $[Y(i)/Y]$ is a constant.

(9) $$L(B) = [1/(1 + c_2 b_1)][(c_1 + c_2 a_1)L(Y) - c_2 L(1 - M) - c_2 a_2 L(U) + c_2 b_2 L(\bar{B})]$$

as the reduced-form equation for AFDC benefits. The companion reduced-form equation for the endogenous recipient rate is:

(10) $$L(R/N) = [1/(1 + c_2 b_1)][(b_1 c_1 - a_1)L(Y) - c_2 b_1 L(1 - M) + a_2 L(U) - b_2 L(\bar{B})]$$

The two equations, (9) and (10), contain eight coefficients for the four exogenous variables $L(Y)$, $L(1 - M)$, $L(U)$, and $L(\bar{B})$. These can determine the six unknown parameters in the model, a_1, a_2, b_1, b_2, c_1, and c_2. The parameter of primary interest here, b_2, can be estimated from both equations. If there were common exogenous influences simultaneously affecting benefits in this state and benefits in other states, the estimate from the benefits equation (9) would be biased upwards. For equation (10) the interpretation is more complicated. The model assumes that $\bar{B}$, the benefit level in surrounding states in some earlier period, is exogenous. In this event, equation (10) will underestimate b_2—actual migration flows are very sluggish, or state legislators may perceive that migration is important and set benefit levels to discourage it. If $\bar{B}$ is not exogenous, which could happen if there is autocorrelation in the $\bar{B}$ series *and* if benefits in the own state influence those in surrounding states (something we would doubt for most states because of the "small country" assumption of international trade models), the estimate of b_2 from (10) could be too high or too low.

The overidentification of the parameters can be used to increase the efficiency of their estimates by imposing the cross-equation restrictions. An easy way to do this is to multiply (10) by c_2 and then combine the equations as follows:

(11) $$DV = IV * C$$

where DV is a $2n \times 1$ vector of the dependent variable, n observations of $L(B)$ stacked on top of n observations of $c_2 L(R/N)$; IV is a $2n \times 6$ matrix of independent variables; and C is a 6×1 vector of coefficients. The reason there are six independent variables in this form is that after (10) is multipled by c_2, $L(\bar{B})$ and $L(U)$ both have coefficients that are the negative of each other in the two stacks, so these variables can be combined into one stacked variable with the cross-equation restrictions explicit.

As an additional comment on the model, the impact of migration on AFDC benefits is here described as occurring solely on the benefit side—that is, the migration of potential AFDC recipients. Another channel by which AFDC benefits could influence R/N is through the migration of positive taxpayers. While the dictates of rational analysis would suggest this to be a much less important channel (at today's levels, a 30 percent increase in average AFDC benefit levels would raise the disposable income of AFDC recipients approximately this amount, but would reduce the disposable income of average income taxpayers by only one-third of 1 percent), to the extent that positive taxpayer migration does matter, it will provide another explanation for any discovered importance of migration.

Data

The data used to estimate this simultaneous equations model are the same as used for estimating just the benefits equation in Gramlich [4]. Many of the more detailed empirical issues were discussed at some length there and will only be alluded to here. The equations were fit to pooled time-series cross-sectional data for states from 1974 to 1981, a period after residency requirements were eliminated. Tastes, institutions, and the other shift factors affecting both benefits and recipients were accounted for by letting each state have its own intercept in each logarithmic equation and then eliminating all these intercepts by first-differencing all variables. This means that time-series variation in the variables determined the coefficients. Alternative trials in which cross-sectional variation was also introduced by the use of only regional shift dummies gave reasonably similar coefficients for the central variables.

The benefits variable has until now been described simply as average benefits in a state, but in fact it is more complicated. Both guarantee levels and tax rates vary widely across states, the latter because of state differences in administering the AFDC law (see Lurie [10], Hutchens [8], and Moffitt [12]). If labor supply is endogenous, these variations could lead to endogenous measurement bias in observed average benefit levels, thereby obscuring the true measure of state policy. We tried to circumvent this problem by constructing a one-dimensional measure of state AFDC policy, defined as:

$$(12) \qquad B = G - S(1)E(1) - S(2)E(2)$$

where G is the guarantee level for a family of four; $S(1)$ and $S(2)$ are AFDC tax rates on earned and unearned incomes, respectively, as estimated by Moffitt [11]; and $E(1)$ and $E(2)$ are average real values of the relevant incomes for all states based on PSID data. Constructing the variable in this way allows it to reflect both state guarantee levels and tax rates, yet still be unaffected by endogenous changes in labor supply. The only cost is that the sample is whittled from all 51 states (including the District of Columbia) to the 35 states for which Moffitt has estimated AFDC tax rates.

Federal matching rates play a key role in the model. In earlier years AFDC operated according to a convex grant schedule under which the federal sharing rate declined as B rose. When Medicaid was introduced in 1965, states were given the option of being reimbursed by the older convex AFDC schedule or the flat, open-ended Medicaid reimbursement schedule that just paid states at a constant rate depending on their income, but with no statutory federal share lower than .5. By 1974 (the start of our estimation period), 41 states had switched to the Medicaid formula (27 in our sample), and by 1979 49 had switched (33 in our sample). To avoid difficult problems in estimating price elasticities with kinked price schedules, we confined the sample to those states on the Medicaid formula. This left a total sample of 201 (27 states times 7 first differences for each plus 6 midterm switchers times 2 first differences for each).[3]

Other problems involve the definition of B in the own and surrounding states. Most AFDC recipients also draw food stamp benefits, with a complex set of arrangements whereby food stamps tax away AFDC benefits and AFDC taxes away food stamps. In the predecessor to this paper, Gramlich tried to estimate displacement coefficients for food stamps (how much do states lower AFDC benefits when food stamps are raised?), but this attempt did not prove very successful because of the lack of independent variation in food stamp levels. For this paper we simply define B alternatively as excluding or including food stamps. When food stamps are included, we also allow for the appropriate taxing arrangements. The $\bar{B}$ variable is handled similarly.[4]

For the $\bar{B}$ variable, we also tried three variants. One is the average level of B (with or without food stamps) in all other states, as if moving costs are largely fixed. The second is the average level of B in all states contiguous to the particular state, as if moving costs depend on the distance moved. The third is the maximum level of B in the contiguous states. Hence, we actually ran each version of the model six times, with and without food stamps and with all, contiguous, or the maximum of contiguous states defined as the comparison state. As suggested above, the $\bar{B}$ variable was defined as a rectangular lag over the two previous years to reflect the fact that legislators will not know current $\bar{B}$ when they set their own level.

Otherwise all definitions are standard. All dollar values are in real terms deflated by a national average price level (which was found to work just as well as regional prices in the earlier paper).

---

3   Moffitt [12] does show how AFDC equations could be estimated in the presence of kinked budget lines, for 1970 data. By now, such a technique is unnecessary.

4   Because food stamps are fully paid for by the federal government, the budget constraint must be rewritten when $B + F$ replaces B, and this leads to a nonlinearity in the model. Gramlich [4] discusses the issue and attempts to deal with it.

Estimates

OLS estimates of the reduced-form equations (9) (for benefits) and (10) (for the recipient-population ratio) are given in Table 1. The basic model seems to fit quite well, with all eight coefficients except one (which is not large) taking on the expected sign and standard errors of less than 10 percent of the dependent variable. The fits are virtually the same for the six versions of the recipient-population ratio equation, but the versions with more comparison states and with food stamps included in the definition of benefits seem to fit better for the benefits equation (after adjusting the dependent variable to the standard errors on a common basis).

The underlying parameters of the model are also fairly stable across the six versions. There is no unique set of estimates for the parameters. In what follows we use the expression for $c_2b_1/(1 + c_2b_1)$ to find the denominator for all expressions and then solve. The parameter that determines how rises in state income reduce AFDC recipients, a_1, is estimated to be about .6 in all versions, and while there is some range for the unemployment-to-recipients parameter, a_2, it is always a good deal smaller. The parameter that might be called the pure income elasticity for AFDC benefits, c_1, is estimated to be fairly low, averaging .15 in all versions, perhaps being this low because of the income-security effect. According to these estimates, the main reason why state AFDC benefits seem to rise with income is the recipient effect: higher income implies fewer potential AFDC recipients, relaxes the budget constraint, and allows states to pay higher benefits. The absolute price elasticity for AFDC benefits, c_2, is estimated to average .67, a reasonable number for public expenditure programs. Estimates of the mobility parameters do vary across the versions, with b_1 ranging between .11 and .83 and b_2 between .02 and 3.41.

Estimates using the cross-equation restrictions are given in Table 2. Since the parameter c_2 is used in the construction of the dependent variable in (11), we estimated the model by an iteration scheme. We inserted the average estimate for c_2 in Table 1, estimated (11), recomputed c_2, reestimated, and so forth. The final estimates are shown in the table.[5] The range for b_2 is whittled substantially, now going from .18 to 1.14 with an average of .61. The range for b_1 is also narrowed—now it runs from .16 to .89 with an average of .47. It is not clear why b_2 is greater than b_1 (according to the model it would be less), but the difference is not very large in all versions. The only other change of note is that now c_1, the pure income elasticity, becomes negative, as the security effect

---

5 As a simple check as to whether the values of c_2 that emerged from this iterative process might be local, rather than global, maxima, we tried starting c_2 at illogically high values and got the same final values.

apparently dominates the normal income effect. Regarding the central theme of the paper, the migration effect is strong and significant no matter how the model is estimated.

To eliminate the possible problem that b_2 is estimated to be greater than b_1, in violation of our theory, we then restricted the two parameters to be equal ($b_1 = b_2 = b$). We estimated the model using this new coefficient restriction along with the others. The results, shown in Table 3, are not much different from those in Table 2. The effect of the unemployment rate on the number of recipients does rise some, and the pure income elasticity falls slightly to a more negative number. What seems to be a robust result is that state income has a weak impact on AFDC benefits. What seems to be difficult to discern is how this impact can be decomposed into an income-elasticity and a budget-constraint effect. But our main object of interest is the now more tightly restricted migration parameter b. It falls in the same .18 to 1.19 range as before, with an average of .61.

TRANSITION MATRICES

Another way to estimate the impact of actual or potential migration on AFDC benefits is by the use of microdata on AFDC families. We used microdata from two sources, a subsample of the 1980 Census and the PSID. The Census surveyed all families on the amount of public assistance income received in 1979 and half of the families on their state of residence in 1975. The PSID has annually recorded the amount of AFDC received and the state of residence. Both these sets of data can be used to estimate the moving behavior of AFDC families.

With these data it is also possible to resolve at least three problems with Southwick's results cited above. First, these surveys were conducted after residency requirements were rescinded and the large-scale north-south migration had ceased. Second, since we are looking at migration over a relatively short period, our benefits measure is a much clearer reflection of the actual benefits at the time of the move. Third, since we can tell who left as well as who entered a state, we can measure net migration flows better than did Southwick.

In this section we make use of a transition matrix. We divide states into those with fairly generous AFDC benefits (the "Highs"), those with average benefits (the "Mediums"), and those with low benefits (the "Lows"). Using these groupings, we construct the transition matrix, P:

		State of Residence in t		
		High	Medium	Low
State of residence	High	p_{11}	p_{12}	p_{13}
in $t - 5$:	Medium	p_{21}	p_{22}	p_{23}
	Low	p_{31}	p_{32}	p_{33}

TABLE 1

OLS ESTIMATES OF EQUATIONS (9) AND (10)

201 Pooled State Observations, 1974–1981

(Absolute *t*-ratios below coefficients)

Food Stamps Surrounding States	I no all	II yes all	III no contiguous	IV yes contiguous	V no contig, max	VI yes contig, max
			Equation (9)			
$\dfrac{c_1+c_2a_1}{1+c_2b_1}$	.497 (1.8)	.249 (2.0)	510 (1.8)	.285 (2.1)	.653 (2.1)	.597 (3.6)
$\dfrac{c_2}{1+c_2b_1}$	.542 (1.7)	.293 (2.0)	.643 (1.9)	.413 (2.6)	.684 (1.9)	.847 (1.3)
$\dfrac{c_2a_2}{1+c_2b_1}$	−.075 (2.0)	−.026 (1.5)	−.052 (1.3)	−.017 (0.9)	−.024 (0.6)	−.029 (1.3)
$\dfrac{c_2b_2}{1+c_2b_1}$	1.151 (9.4)	.999 (14.1)	.794 (7.5)	.787 (11.8)	.440 (5.1)	.313 (5.1)
R^2	.199	.417	.122	.340	.100	.156
SE	.093	.042	.098	.046	.105	.057
			Equation (10)			
$\dfrac{b_1c_1-a_1}{1+c_2b_1}$	−.473 (2.7)	−.425 (2.4)	−.468 (2.7)	−.430 (2.5)	−.482 (2.8)	−.481 (2.7)
$\dfrac{c_2b_1}{1+c_2b_1}$	.102 (0.5)	.244 (1.2)	.132 (0.6)	.277 (1.1)	.153 (0.7)	.094 (0.5)

Continued overleaf

TABLE 1 (continued)

$\dfrac{a_2}{1+c_2 b_1}$	.093 (3.8)	.083 (3.5)	.091 (3.8)	.084 (3.5)	.093 (3.9)	.094 (4.0)
$\dfrac{b_2}{1+c_2 b_1}$	.026 (0.3)	.225 (2.2)	.065 (1.0)	.191 (2.2)	.057 (1.1)	.014 (0.2)
R^2	.274	.295	.278	.294	.279	.275
SE	.060	.060	.060	.060	.060	.060
Parameter Estimates[a]						
a_1	.567	.632	.573	.587	.628	.547
a_2 (from 9)	-.138	-.089	-.081	-.041	-.035	.034
a_2 (from 10)	.104	.110	.105	.109	.110	.104
b_1	.188	.833	.205	.551	.224	.111
b_2 (from 9)	2.124	3.410	1.235	1.915	.643	.370
b_2 (from 10)	.029	.298	.075	.247	.067	.015
c_1	.212	.084	.163	.056	.264	.147
c_2	.604	.388	.741	.533	.808	.935

a   There is no unique set of estimates for the parameters. These were derived by using the expression for $c_2 b_1/(1 + c_2 b_1)$ to find the denominator for all expressions and then solving.

TABLE 2

STACKING ESTIMATE OF EQUATION (11)

201 Pooled State Observations, 1974-1981

(Absolute t-ratios below coefficients)

Food Stamps Surrounding States	I no all	II yes all	III no contiguous	IV yes contiguous	V no contig, max	VI yes contig, max
$\dfrac{c_1 + c_2 a_1}{1 + c_2 b_1}$	.244 (1.0)	.142 (1.0)	.228 (1.0)	.162 (1.1)	.308 (1.3)	.345 (2.2)
$\dfrac{c_2}{1 + c_2 b_1}$	.827 (2.7)	.541 (2.8)	.859 (2.8)	.610 (3.1)	.867 (2.8)	.897 (4.4)
$\dfrac{c_2 a_2}{1 + c_2 b_1}$	.020 (0.8)	.031 (1.9)	.030 (1.2)	.036 (2.2)	.045 (1.8)	.064 (3.8)
$\dfrac{c_2 b_2}{1 + c_2 b_1}$	.592 (7.0)	.618 (9.3)	.437 (6.3)	.494 (8.4)	.255 (4.7)	.163 (3.5)
$\dfrac{b_1 c_1 - a_1}{1 + c_2 b_1}$	-.694 (3.8)	-.530 (3.9)	-.696 (3.7)	-.549 (3.9)	-.761 (4.0)	-.724 (4.8)
$\dfrac{c_2 b_1}{1 + c_2 b_1}$	.333 (1.4)	.438 (2.6)	.306 (1.2)	.417 (2.3)	.300 (1.2)	.142 (0.7)
SE[a] (for 9)	.098	.046	.102	.049	.107	.058
SE[a] (for 10)	.066	.062	.064	.062	.062	.062
Parameter Estimates						
a_1	.783	.656	.777	.660	.868	.778
a_2	.024	.057	.035	.059	.052	.071
b_1	.402	.892	.357	.683	.346	.159
b_2	.716	1.142	.509	.810	.294	.182
c_1	-.635	-.412	-.634	-.413	-.635	-.412
c_2	1.239	1.046	1.239	1.046	1.239	1.046

a Computed directly from the residuals for each equation.

TABLE 3

STACKING ESTIMATE OF EQUATION (11)

b_1 Set Equal to b_2 and Labeled b

201 Pooled State Observations, 1974–1981

(Absolute t-ratios below coefficients)

Food Stamps Surrounding States	I no all	II yes all	III no contiguous	IV yes contiguous	V no contig., max	VI yes contig., max
$\dfrac{c_1 + c_2 a_1}{1 + c_2 b}$	.075 (0.3)	.047 (0.3)	.158 (0.6)	.121 (0.8)	.329 (1.4)	.340 (2.2)
$\dfrac{c_2}{1 + c_2 b}$	.838 (2.3)	.525 (2.2)	.853 (2.6)	.600 (2.8)	.872 (2.8)	.897 (4.4)
$\dfrac{c_2 a_2}{1 + c_2 b}$	.053 (1.7)	.048 (2.5)	.044 (1.6)	.043 (2.5)	.041 (1.6)	.065 (3.8)
$\dfrac{c_2 b}{1 + c_2 b}$	.541 (5.7)	.626 (7.9)	.435 (5.9)	.501 (7.9)	.253 (4.8)	.163 (3.5)
$\dfrac{b c_1 - a_1}{1 + c_2 b}$	-.673 (4.5)	-.549 (4.4)	-.682 (4.2)	-.554 (4.2)	-.762 (3.9)	-.715 (4.9)
SE[a] (for 9)	.100	.046	.102	.049	.107	.058
SE[a] (for 10)	.063	.069	.067	.070	.063	.061
Parameter Estimates						
a_1	.722	.605	.763	.655	.857	.777
a_2	.065	.091	.052	.072	.047	.072
b	.646	1.192	.510	.835	.290	.182
c_1	-1.154	-.724	-.872	-.545	-.560	-.427
c_2	1.826	1.404	1.510	1.202	1.167	1.072

a Computed directly from the residuals for each equation.

where each row sum equals one. This transition matrix can be solved to give the equilibrium distribution of the AFDC population, X, with the property that:

$$(13) \qquad\qquad X * P = X$$

where X is a 1×3 row vector with its elements summing to one.

X is the vector describing the long-run distribution of AFDC recipients with existing AFDC benefit programs. It can then be compared with a hypothetical vector Z that might obtain if all states paid the same AFDC benefits. This assumption allows us to estimate equation (5) above by

$$(14) \qquad x_1/z_1 = B_1^{b_1}\overline{B}^{-b_2} \quad \text{and} \quad x_3/z_3 = B_3^{b_1}\overline{B}^{-b_2}$$

where x_1 and x_3 stand for the first and third elements in the equilibrium AFDC distribution X; z_1 and z_3 stand for the corresponding elements in the hypothetical equal-benefits distribution Z; B_1 and B_3 are high- and low-benefit state average benefits, respectively, and $\overline{B}$ refers to the overall average of benefits. In effect, the elements of X and Z are being taken as measures of R and $\hat{R}$ in the model of the first section of the paper.

Data

For this test we used data from both a .1 percent subsample of the 1980 Census, covering almost 100,000 households, and the PSID, which has followed some 5000 families for 15 years now.[6] We looked at interstate mobility over a five-year period, confining our attention to female-headed families who received public assistance payments in their state of residence in year t. In the Census data, state of residence is recorded for 1975 and 1980. In the PSID we compared state of residence over two five-year periods, 1976–1981 and 1971–1976.[7]

The combined sample size of movers and nonmovers was 1220, 706 from the Census and 514 from the PSID. The large majority of our observations were for nonmovers. Each observation constituted an entry into the transition matrix; entries for the nonmovers, of course, were made in the principal diagonal.

We ranked the states using the five-year average of state benefits (for the respective period) and then divided the states into three groups based

---

6 Panel Study of Income Dynamics, Survey Research Center, Institute for Social Research, The University of Michigan. Census of Population and Housing: Public Use Microdata Sample A, Bureau of the Census.

7 This calculation ignores some information that could be gained on "reentrants," those who moved out of, but back again to, their original state within the five-year period. This may not be much of a loss, however, since the two moves that would have been entered in the transaction matrix for each reentrant would cancel out.

on this distribution. The groupings for the 1975–1980 period, with their average real B values (in 1981 dollars) are shown in Table 4.[8]

Estimates

Estimates of the transition matrix are given in Table 5. Panel 5a shows estimates for the 706 Census observations, Panel 5b for the 706 Census and 514 PSID observations combined, making for a total of 1220. Although the PSID observations alone give similar results, we do not show them separately because the off-diagonal cell sizes get fairly small.

The main fact of interest in the table is how few AFDC beneficiaries move from one group of states to another in a five-year period—only about 7 percent for those in the low-benefit states and 3 percent for those

TABLE 4

FIVE-YEAR AVERAGE OF STATE BENEFITS,

1975–1980

High $540 < B < 720$	Medium $330 < B < 510$	Low $115 < B < 320$
Hawaii	Rhode Island	Maryland
Wisconsin	New Hampshire	Nevada
Connecticut	Idaho	Missouri
Vermont	Kansas	Ohio
Oregon	Utah	Kentucky
New York	South Dakota	West Virginia
Alaska	Maine	New Mexico
California	Nebraska	Arizona
Michigan	Illinois	Arkansas
Minnesota	District of Columbia	North Carolina
Washington	Virginia	Florida
Iowa	Oklahoma	Georgia
Massachusetts	Wyoming	Louisiana
North Dakota	Montana	Tennesse
Pennsylvania	Delaware	Alabama
New Jersey	Colorado	South Carolina
	Indiana	Texas
		Mississippi

---

8 Ideally, one would like to correct for regional price differences, but the only regional price index available is a 25-city consumer price index. This index obviously gives no values at all for more than half of the 51 states (some of the 25 cities are in the same state), and imperfect values for the others. Experimentation with this index in the earlier paper proved notably unsuccessful. Here we just ignored the issue.

TABLE 5

ESTIMATES OF AFDC TRANSITION PROBABILITIES

	State of Residence in 1980			Observations
	High	Medium	Low	
	a. Census Estimates, 1975–1980			
State of residence in 1975				
High	.971	.016	.013	374
Medium	.050	.909	.041	121
Low	.043	.028	.929	211
	b. Census and PSID Estimates, 1971–1981			
	State of Residence in *t*			
State of residence in $t-5$				
High	.975	.011	.014	571
Medium	.032	.944	.024	248
Low	.035	.030	.935	401

Note: t is 1980 for the Census; either 1981 or 1976 for the PSID.

in the high-benefit states. Certainly whatever the impact of migration, the process is very sluggish, as reported in the findings cited by Holmer [7]. But our interpretation of the findings is not the same as his.

A closer inspection of the matrix indicates that while interstate migration is indeed a rare event, its impact is not unimportant. For since the entries below the principal diagonal are proportionately more than twice as large as those above the diagonal, the probabilities indicate that if AFDC families should happen to make an interstate move, they are much more likely to go to a state with higher AFDC benefits. In the long run, even this sluggish and apparently unimportant mobility can alter the interstate distribution of the AFDC population substantially.

The question of exactly how much the population will be altered can be answered formally simply by computing the steady-state AFDC population distribution according to (13). These distributions, the X row vectors, are shown in Table 6. There they are compared with three different estimates of the Z vector, the hypothetical AFDC distribution were benefits in all states equal.

Panel 6a corresponds to Panel 5a, giving the calculations for the Census data. The first row gives the actual X vector over the 1975–1980 period, as a standard of comparison. The second row gives the equilibrium distribution of the AFDC population calculated from the transition matrix of Panel 5a. The correspondence with the actual distribution is reasonably close for the medium-benefit states, though the equilibrium calculations indicate that for prevailing benefit levels there will be more

TABLE 6

HYPOTHETICAL EQUILIBRIUM DISTRIBUTION
OF THE AFDC POPULATION

	High	Medium	Low	b_1	b_2	t(High)
		a. Census				
X, Actual distribution	.549	.159	.292	—	—	—
X, from Panel 5a	.611	.173	.216	—	—	—
$Z(1)$ Control	.310	.194	.496	1.730	1.718	2.667
$Z(2)$ Population only	.468	.180	.352	.864	.870	1.482
$Z(3)$ Equation (6)	.446	.178	.376	.996	1.001	1.692
		b. Census and PSID				
X, Actual distribution	.549	.159	.292	—	—	—
X, from Panel 5b	.572	.222	.206	—	—	—
$Z(1)$ Control	.310	.194	.496	1.708	1.706	2.987
$Z(2)$ Population only	.468	.180	.352	.844	.860	1.222
$Z(3)$ Equation (6)	.446	.178	.376	.973	.989	1.556

migration into high-benefit states (from .549 to .611) and out of low-benefit states (from .292 to .216).

The next three rows of Panel 6a give the different estimates of the Z vector. The first estimate, $Z(1)$, simply repeats the transition matrix procedure for a sample of 23,747 nonaged, non-AFDC recipient, two-parent families from the Census. The aged two-parent families were omitted from this comparison test because most of the female-headed families eligible for AFDC were nonaged; the AFDC recipients were omitted to avoid contaminating the comparison. The Z vector derived in this way can be thought of as allowing *all* influences on location to work through the transition matrix, as if all influences but AFDC were held constant. This calculation sends significantly fewer families to high-benefit states and significantly more to low-benefit states than for the AFDC transition matrix.[9]

The next two estimates do not use the transition matrix solution for the Z vector. The $Z(2)$ estimate simply uses equation (6) but assumes that income and unemployment rates are the same in all states; this is tantamount to assuming that the AFDC population is distributed the same as the total population. The third estimate, $Z(3)$, uses population, income, and unemployment rate averages over the period exactly as given

---

9 As with the AFDC transition matrix, most observations fall on the principal diagonal {.937, .900, .951}. For both populations, interstate moving is a very rare event and changes in population distribution, if any occur, are determined by the direction of the moves that do take place.

in equation (6), with assumed values of $a_1 = .7$ and $a_2 = .05$ based on the estimates of Table 2. Unemployment has very little effect, but the generally higher income in the high-benefit states and the lower income in the low-benefit states does crowd a few more AFDC recipients into the low-benefit states.

When we compare the X and Z distributions, we can see that the low-benefit states do appear to be doing something that, in equilibrium, will give them many fewer AFDC beneficiaries than they might otherwise have been predicted to have. It is not clear from this transition probability analysis what the "something" is, but presumably the level of benefits is the important part of the story. If that is the whole story, the average state benefit levels and elements of the X and Z vectors can be combined in a way described by equation (14) to give new estimates for the migration parameters, b_1 and b_2. These are in the .86 to 1.73 range, as shown in the table, agreeing rather well with the regression estimates in the first part of the paper. Indeed, there is even agreement on the puzzling phenomenon that the outside elasticity, b_2, is slightly greater than the inside elasticity, b_1.

Two other calculations can be made from the table. One involves significance levels. Each Z vector gives an estimate of how many AFDC recipients would locate in a group of states if all benefit levels were equal. We can then treat these Z values as representing the number of AFDC recipients in a group of states if benefit levels had no effect on migration and test this null hypothesis against its alternative that benefit levels do affect migration. For each of the values of z_1, the null hypothesis is that $x_1 - z_1 = 0$ and the t-statistic is $(\hat{x}_1 - z_1)/\sigma_{x_1-z_1}$, where $\hat{x}_1$ represents the share of AFDC recipients in high-benefit states as calculated from the transition matrix, and σ_{x-z} represents the standard error of the difference as calculated from the binomial probability formula (assuming the shares in medium- and low-benefit states can be aggregated). The t-values shown indicate that the estimated value of x_1 ($= .611$) is different from the null hypothesis value of .310 with a 99.9 percent probability, and from the null hypothesis value of .446 with a 94 percent probability (in one-tailed tests).[10]

The second calculation involves half-lives. We have mentioned already that the migration we are talking about here is a very slow process.

---

10 These calculations are done as follows: Assume for simplicity that we divide the world into high-benefit states and all other. The solution of the transition matrix (equation (13)) in this case is just $x_1 = p_{21}/(p_{12} + p_{21})$, $x_2 = p_{12}/(p_{12} + p_{21})$, $x_1/x_2 = p_{21}/p_{12}$. If H_0 is true, $x_1/x_2 = z_1/(1 - z_1)$. This implies that $p_{21} = [z_1/(1 - z_1)]p_{12}$ or $p_{21} - [z_1/(1 - z_1)]p_{12} = 0$. The t-statistic given is then the estimated adjusted difference, $\hat{p}_{21} - [z_1/(1 - z_1)]\hat{p}_{12}$, divided by its standard error, $[(\hat{p}_{21})(1 - \hat{p}_{21})/n_2 + (z_1/(1 - z_1))^2(\hat{p}_{12})(1 - \hat{p}_{12})/n_1]^{.5}$, where n_2 and n_1 refer to the appropriate row totals in Table 5.

How slow? Suppose we started from a situation where all AFDC benefits were equal and x_1 equalled, say, .310. Then benefits are assumed to be exogenously placed at their actual values, implying that the share of recipients in high-benefit states would go to .611. The transition matrix can be solved repeatedly to compute the half-life of the change—how long it would take for $(.611 - .310)/2$ of these recipients to shift. The answer, for all three Z vectors, is about 45 years. The process we are describing here is indeed slow and sluggish.

Panel 6b repeats all of these calculations with the X vector that comes from Panel 5b, the combined Census-PSID sample. Most of the results are essentially the same, except that in equilibrium we would predict more AFDC recipients going to medium-benefit states (from .159 to .222). The implied b values are close to those of Panel 6a, and the significance levels are very similar.

As a final remark, the twin suggestions here that b_2 is strong and significant and that migration is sluggish leads to the following thumbnail sketch of the postwar history for AFDC. Somehow in the sixties the prevailing liberal optimism, the War on Poverty, community action programs, or the fact that generous states may have felt protected by residency requirements, encouraged about one-third of the states to raise benefits to high levels, another third of the states to raise benefits to medium levels, and the remaining third of the states to keep them low. This set in motion a very sluggish migration process towards high-benefit states, which is gradually reducing the real level of AFDC benefits as it becomes perceived. The rise in food stamps in 1974 may have accelerated the reductions. In any one snapshot, migration appears to be unimportant; over the long run it is perhaps quite important and should lead to continuing erosion in real benefit levels, particularly in states where benefits are now relatively high.[11]

CONCLUSIONS

Both methods used to try to infer the importance of migration among the AFDC population and what that does to state benefit levels have their deficiencies. The regression model is subject to the criticism that both

---

11   This thumbnail history would be more convincing if real AFDC benefits were dropping more in the high-benefit states than the low-benefit states. In fact, the percentage decline is about the same. If food stamps should be considered part of the benefit level, the mathematics imply that real benefits are dropping more in high-benefit states, and that the story works. If food stamps should not be so considered, the story must be amended to allow for the possibility of Cournot-Nash type behavior in the low-benefit states as well—the high-benefit states are chasing a moving target downward, and this could ultimately take real AFDC benefits close to zero (see Gramlich [4]).

the dependent and independent variables could be influenced by common outside trends, making for an overestimate of the migration effect, or the criticism that sluggish migration effects might be very hard to discern in a finite time-series sample, making for an underestimate of the migration effect. The transition analysis is subject to the criticism that separate impacts of other independent variables have not been formulated and estimated.

Despite these criticisms, the fact that both widely different ways of estimating the migration effect show that it is very strong, statistically significant, and of the same order of magnitude is surely worth something. Our tentative conclusion is that migration of AFDC beneficiaries does appear to be an important phenomenon, though only in the very long run. It does appear to be perceived that way by state legislatures, who appear to be very much conditioned by what other states are doing when they set AFDC benefits. In normative terms, a federal system of benefit determination for AFDC scores poorly because voters in a state cannot afford to set the benefit levels they want: they must keep in step with their neighbors. This provides a strong argument against turning financial responsibility for redistribution policy completely over to state governments, as is now proposed by President Reagan. Indeed, it is an argument for altering the present AFDC financial arrangements in quite the opposite direction and letting the national government set a benefit level that more closely approximates that which would be desired by state voters were migration not such an important factor.

REFERENCES

1. Rebecca M. Blank. "Welfare, Wages, and Migration: An Analysis of Locational Choice by Female-Headed Households." Princeton University Working Paper No. 170, November 1983, mimeo.
2. Richard J. Cebula and Robert M. Kohn. "Public Policies and Migration Patterns in the United States." *Public Finance* 30 (1975): 186–96.
3. Gordon F. DeJong and William L. Donnelly. "Public Welfare and Migration." *Social Science Quarterly* 54 (September 1973): 329–44.
4. Edward M. Gramlich. "An Econometric Examination of the New Federalism." *Brookings Papers on Economic Activity* (2:1982): 327–60.
5. Edward M. Gramlich and Daniel L. Rubinfeld. "Voting on Public Spending: Differences Between Public Employees, Transfer Recipients, and Private Workers." *Journal of Policy Analysis and Management* 1 (Summer 1982): 516–33.
6. Harold M. Hochman and James D. Rodgers. "Pareto Optimal Redistribution." *American Economic Review* 59 (September 1969): 542–57.
7. Martin Holmer. "AFDC Policy and Migration: A Review." Chapter 2 in

"Economic and Political Causes of the Welfare Crisis." Ph.D. dissertation, MIT, 1975.

8. Robert M. Hutchens. "Changes in AFDC Tax Rates, 1967–1971." *Journal of Human Resources* 13 (Winter 1978): 60–74.

9. Helen F. Ladd and Fred C. Doolittle. "Which Level of Government Should Assist the Poor?" *National Tax Journal* 35 (September 1982): 323–36.

10. Irene Lurie. "Estimates of Tax Rates in the AFDC Program." *National Tax Journal* 27 (March 1974): 93–111.

11. Robert A. Moffitt. "An Economic Model of Welfare Stigma." University of Wisconsin, October 1981, mimeo.

12. ————. "The Effects of Grants-in-Aid on State and Local Expenditures, The Case of AFDC." Paper presented at an NBER workshop, November 1982, mimeo.

13. Larry L. Orr. "Income Transfers as a Public Good: An Application to AFDC." *American Economic Review* 66 (June 1976): 359–71.

14. Mark V. Pauly. "Income Redistribution as a Local Public Good." *Journal of Public Economics* 2 (February 1973): 35–58.

15. Sam Peltzman. "The Growth of Government." *Journal of Law and Economics* 23 (October 1980): 209–87.

16. Lawrence Southwick. "Public Welfare Programs and Recipient Migration." *Growth and Change* 12 (October 1981): 22–32.

17. Hal R. Varian. "Redistributive Taxation as Social Insurance." *Journal of Public Economics* 14 (August 1980): 49–68.

309-23

(87)

[16]

I38 9100
U. S.

Cooperation and Competition in Public Welfare Policies

Edward M. Gramlich

Abstract

Present public welfare policies and various proposals for reforming them do not often exploit the advantages of cooperation between otherwise competing altruists. The article examines this principle from a number of perspectives. It shows first how the advantages of the existing cooperative payments structure could be lost in some widely-publicized welfare reform proposals, and it makes a suggestion for retaining these advantages. The article next shows how the same principle could be used to improve existing incentives for private giving. Finally, it uses the same logic to rationalize newly evolving notions of sharing responsibility between governments and the recipients themselves.

INTRODUCTION

It has become almost trite to call for a reexamination of the public welfare system. Welfare reform has, in one form or another, been proposed by every President since John F. Kennedy. The number of books on the topic from academics, Congressional staffers, and think tanks run into the fifties. The number of journal articles on the topic far exceeds that. And the number of newspaper articles far exceeds even that. One might think that the field has been worked over enough.

Yet with all this attention, an important principle in the design of public welfare policies has by and large escaped explicit notice. Sometimes actual policies are consistent with the principle, sometimes inconsistent; sometimes suggestions for reform of these policies are consistent with the principle, sometimes they are inconsistent—no uniform pattern exists. The principle, one of the most basic in game theory, is that joint utility maximization can be achieved by the cooperation of interested parties in some activity, not by competition between them. In the case at hand, this means that the utility of all concerned, givers and recipients of public welfare, can be increased by policies and arrangements that encourage cooperation between otherwise

Journal of Policy Analysis and Management, Vol. 6, No. 3, 417–431 (1987)
© 1987 by the Association for Public Policy Analysis and Management
Published by John Wiley & Sons, Inc.   CCC 0276-8739/87/020417-15$04.00

competing governments or between governments and recipients of transfer payments.

I try to show how this very intuitive principle can be applied to a series of difficult policy issues that arise in the design of public welfare programs. I first demonstrate the principle with a simple model, and then I apply it to four important problems in the design of welfare policies:

1. financial sharing arrangements between higher and lower levels of government;
2. relative support levels in competing states;
3. financial sharing arrangements between public and private charities;
4. implicit contractual relationships between governmental payment agencies and recipients of transfer payments.

I review each example and show how it raises the underlying principle, describe current policy, and assess the degree to which it (or its reform) does or does not exploit the advantages of cooperation.

A SIMPLE MODEL OF CHARITABLE GIVING

The simple model that illustrates the basic principle follows one used first by Harold Hochman and James Rodgers, recently modified by Russell Roberts.[1] Assume that we have a society made up of two altruists and one poor person (these stylized individuals could be thought of as groups to make the model more realistic). The model makes a standard assumption of what might be called partial utility interdependence—both altruists care about utility levels of the poor person, but neither altruist cares about the utility of the other altruist.

Suppose first that transfers from altruist B are zero. Then the set of consumption possibilities facing altruist A are shown by the "No gift from B" locus in Figure 1. A has initial income of Y_A, spends G_A of it on a gift to C, retains $Y_A - G_A$ for private consumption, and C consumes the gift by spending C_C, all as shown in the figure. Now suppose that B independently decides to make a gift of G_B to the poor person. A switches to the new "Gift from B" locus in Figure 1, implying higher consumption for C at every consumption level for A in just the amount G_B.

The new situation from A's standpoint can be described either in terms of an old economist's tool—indifference curve analysis, or one that is growing in popularity in many social sciences—game theory. From the indifference curve standpoint, the gift of B can be viewed as an increase in A's income: A can in effect spend this gift as he would any other source of outside income by reducing his gift to C and using that reduction for his own consumption. He moves to the point given by C_C' and $Y_A - G_A'$ in the figure. Note that at this point both A and C have higher consumption levels because of B's gift. Because A has reduced his gift in response to B's gift, A could be viewed as free-riding on B's gift.

This free-rider problem brings in game theory. Game theory elements exist whenever there are small independent groups that can either compete or cooperate in some activity, such as aiding C. Both A and B want to see C supported, but they prefer to have the other altruist do the supporting. A lives better when B's gift is increased, and vice versa. Using the above illustration, the noncooperative equilibrium can be found by having A take B's

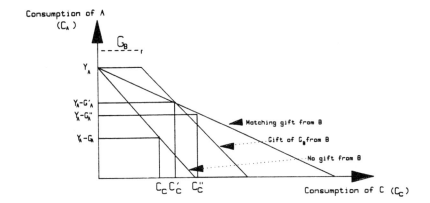

When B makes a gift of G $_B$ A's gift falls from G $_A$ to G' $_A$
and C's consumption rises by less than the gift

When B and A match gifts. the "price" of giving is
reduced for A. A gives more. C consumes more. and all
three get higher utility

Figure 1. The cost of giving and the free rider problem.

gift as given and then determine his own. B then takes A's gift as given and
determines her own. A recomputes, then B, and so forth until a noncooperative equilibrium is reached. The result is an equilibrium because both parties
are actually doing what they are assumed to do. It is noncooperative because
each party is acting independently, responding to the other's actions but not
planning actions jointly.

But cooperation can improve on the equilibrium from the standpoint of all
players. Suppose A and B agree to cooperate by sharing equally all costs of
aiding C. Then A's consumption line is shifted to the "Matching gift from B"
locus, with an absolute slope just half as large as before. Hence a dollar's
sacrifice in consumption for A now buys $2 of increased consumption for C,
instead of $1 along either of the previous loci. As contrasted with the old
equilibrium at C'_C, C's consumption increases to C''_C because it is cheaper for A
to raise C's consumption. Obviously the change raises C's utility. Less obvious is the fact that A's utility will generally increase too, because to the right
of C'_C there is more consumption for C at every consumption level for A, and A
values the increase in C's consumption.[2] The very same argument shows why
B's utility is also increased. In game theory terms, the matching arrangement enables A to exploit the fact that he is made better off by B's contribution and to induce more of it by making his own. In the noncooperative game,
when A contributes more, B contributes less. In the cooperative game, when
A contributes more, B does too. A no longer has an incentive to take a free
ride on B's gift; nor does he any longer fear that his gift gives B a free ride.

VERTICAL COOPERATION: THE FEDERAL GOVERNMENT AND THE STATES

I now try to apply the lessons of this simple model to a series of policy problems in the welfare area. The first of these involves the relationship between the federal government and state governments. The governments are altruistic in the sense that they give public assistance transfers. They compete in the sense that they can strive to free-ride on the transfers of the other government. Taxpayers may think of themselves as being simultaneously state and federal taxpayers. Yet states and the national government can be represented as independent competing altruists because most national taxpayers live outside of, not within, a particular state. For example California, the largest state, is home to only ten percent of the national taxpayers.

Present assistance programs for low income recipients involve both competitive (nonmatching) and cooperative (matching) assistance. The important nonmatching programs are for food stamps and public housing, in-kind programs accounting for about \$12 billion in fiscal year 1987. Neither of these programs requires matching by states, and both can be represented as the fixed income transfers described above. As such, they both should be vulnerable to the free-riding problem.

First, do national taxpayers free-ride on state benefit levels by reducing national payments when state payments rise? Basic benefit levels for food stamps and public housing were determined prior to and independently of state benefit programs. Yet this sort of free-riding is nonetheless present in the way actual payments are determined. For both programs, payments depend on hypothesized food or housing expenditures for the recipient family, less cash income. If the state adds to cash income by making higher public assistance payments, then federal benefits are reduced (in both cases by \$.30 on the dollar). There is, in effect, automatic national free-riding on state payment levels.

Next, do state taxpayers free-ride on national taxpayers by reducing state payments when national payments rise? For public housing a good deal of this sort of free-riding might be expected, given the explicit mingling of federal and state payments. Federal payments usually go to a state housing agency that develops its own "needs" standards independently of whatever federal grants are available. If federal payments rise while needs standards are fixed, state payments necessarily fall. In this sense, higher federal payments benefit state taxpayers and not public housing recipients, just as in the free-riding scenario.

Proving the case for free-riding with food stamps is more difficult because federal funds are not explicitly mingled with state funds. Food stamps go directly to recipients, as with the grant G_B in Figure 1 (where the federal government is altruist B and the state government is altruist A). If a state makes payments along the downward-sloping portion of the "Gift from B" schedule, alterations in food stamp levels should cause free-riding. Empirical studies of state public assistance payments have shown that the marginal propensity of states to spend income on public transfer programs is very low (less than 0.05).[3] If these results apply to the food stamp program, states will devote very little of any marginal increases in food stamp aid to increased assistance for poor people, and the main beneficiaries of rises in food stamp support levels will again be the free-riding states.

But this does not give the full story for food stamps because many states could desire to pay very low benefits. These states would find themselves on the horizontal portion of the "Gift of G_B" schedule, in which case they could expand benefit payments to the kink point with no sacrifice in their own consumption. For such states, marginal rises in food stamp benefits will generate much less free-riding.[4]

The second type of assistance operates through a matching grant, as in the Aid to Families with Dependent Children (AFDC) and medicaid programs. The federal government pays as much as 0.78 of all AFDC costs for poor states such as Mississippi, and as little as 0.50 of all AFDC costs for high-income states such as California and New York. These programs then operate just like the matching grants in the previous model. Past studies have indicated that while states are not very responsive to income changes in setting public benefit levels, they are quite responsive to price changes brought about by matching.[5] Federal government costs are expected to be $26 billion for medicaid and $8 billion for AFDC in fiscal year 1987, with state government costs being estimated at another $22 billion for medicaid and $7 billion for AFDC.

As might be expected, the fact that states are free to set their own AFDC support levels (though influenced by the matching federal grant) leads to wide disparities in support levels. In 1985, combined AFDC-food stamp benefits ranged from 90 percent or more of the poverty level in twelve states to slightly less than half of the poverty level in states such as Alabama and Mississippi. Econometric studies cannot explain a large share of this cross-sectional variation with variables such as income, unemployment, matching rates, regional prices, and migration. No matter how one does the econometrics, the role of nonquantifiable differences in "tastes" is large.[6]

The present system thus contains some noncooperative programs involving free-riding as well as some cooperative programs. In view of the argument for cooperation given above, it might seem that reform proposals would focus on the noncooperative elements, trying to reorient the structure in a more cooperative direction. In fact, the major welfare reform proposals now under debate generally move in the opposite direction.

On one side President Reagan, concerned that the federal government is imposing its desires on the obviously diverse states, has wanted to decentralize. His widely-advertised but never-enacted "new federalism" proposal would have converted both food stamps and AFDC to state programs with no matching. It also would have made fiscal transfers in order to eliminate any income changes to states in the various switches. On the other side most past Secretaries of the Department of Health and Human Services (HHS), supported by many other poverty analysts, have been more concerned with the large statewide differences in support levels among the recipient population.[7] They have wanted to centralize the system. A typical proposal would retain food stamps and public housing as nonmatching assistance (but converted from in-kind programs to cash) and convert AFDC and medicaid from straight matching grant programs to programs with a uniform national benefit floor. Optional state supplementation of benefits would be permitted, but the proposals have been unclear about the federal matching arrangement above this floor.[8]

Between these two, I will suggest an intermediate system. It reconciles the HHS Secretaries' interest in nationwide minimum benefits with Reagan's interest in state option above this national floor. And in keeping with my argument, it does so without sacrificing the advantages of the cooperative payment structure that now exists. The system would accomplish these goals by combining food stamps, public housing, and AFDC into one federal grant with no state matching up to some base level (as in food stamps), and then progressively more state matching or less federal matching, as benefit levels increase. In effect, the national government would pay all of the costs of the first segment on the benefits schedule and lesser amounts thereafter. This matching schedule would serve to reduce interstate variation in benefits as well as to maintain a cooperative payment structure.

A graphical analysis of the three plans for a representative high- and low-benefit state is given in Figure 2. Current law establishes a budget line with a kink at F_0, the food stamp benefit level, and then a gradual downward slope because of AFDC matching (here assumed to be at the same rate for both states). High-benefit states now make payments at H_0 and low-benefit states at L_0. Reagan's new federalism plan simply eliminates these matching arrangements and returns the revenue to the states. If this revenue is the same for both states, both operate on the "New federalism" budget line. The high-benefit state reduces benefits to H_1 (because of the lower grant and the substitution of an income grant for a price grant) and the low-benefit state to L_1 (because of the switch in grant from the present kinked schedule.[9] As compared with the present system, then, the new federalism plan probably

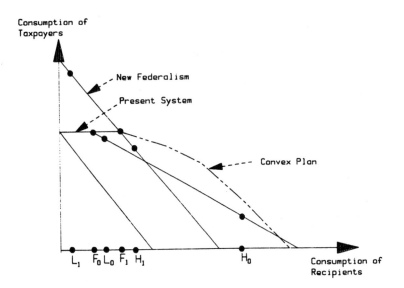

Figure 2. Proposed changes in low income support programs.

F_0 = present food stamp guarantee level
H_0 = benefit level in high benefit state, present system
H_1 = benefit level in high benefit state, new federalism plan
L_0 = Benefit level in low benefit state, present system
L_1 = benefit level in low benefit state, new federalism
F_1 = benefit level in low benefit state, national floor plan

would feature reduced benefit levels in all states and quite low benefit levels in some states.

The HHS benefits floor plan would raise benefits from L_0 to F_1 in low-benefit states. If the plan simply institutes a floor with no matching above this floor, high-benefit states would operate on the new federalism plan to the right of F_1. Benefits in the high-benefit state would be the same as in the new federalism plan, at H_1, again implying a substantial reduction from present levels because of the elimination of the price subsidy. In these terms, such a change would convert grants from cooperative matching grants to noncooperative income grants, with consequent losses in both benefit levels and utility.

The "convex plan" I suggest is also shown in the figure. How the results compare to the other two plans obviously depends on the parameters of such a plan—I have drawn it to make the horizontal portion is the same as with the HHS floor plan, with segments showing progressively less federal matching as benefits rise. As with the floor plan, benefits in the low-benefit state will be at the first kink point F_1, an increase over present levels. The high-benefit state experiences a rise in both its income and its effective price for AFDC. What happens to its benefit levels is unclear; should the price effect outweigh the income effect, as is suggested by most empirical evidence, these benefits will be cut back slightly below the present level at H_0. But they should be well above H_1, the level in both of the other plans, because the matching or cooperative payment structure is retained for these high-benefit states.

Two further points deserve emphasis. In this era of federal deficit-watching, I should confess that my convex plan lies almost everywhere to the northeast of the present system. This means that unlike the other two plans, it will entail a shifting of some of the cost of supporting AFDC from states to the federal government. Using the same AFDC eligibility standards as are now in effect, a relatively generous convex plan raises benefit levels in about half the states and shifts about $5 billion in state costs upward in 1985.[10] These revenue-shifts could be reduced by phasing out the federal matching more quickly, by altering matching rates on other categorical grants, or by changing the income tax deductibility of state-local taxes.[11]

As a final note, historians will recognize the convex plan as quite similar to the grant arrangement when AFDC was first passed back in the 1930s (although no national floor existed then). In the 1960s, a change allowed states to choose between their convex grant schedule and a flat rate schedule determined by their income in the then newly introduced medicaid program. Since then inflation has sharply eroded the brackets defining the shift in matching rates, and all states have now gone over to this flat rate schedule. In that sense, the reform I suggest simply eliminates the recent flattening of matching rates for states in order to raise the national floor without losing the advantages of cooperation between altruists.

HORIZONTAL COMPETITION: THE WAR BETWEEN THE STATES

The fact that states now set their own AFDC benefit levels raises the cooperation-competition issue in another way. States can free-ride on the benefit payments of other states by the simple expedient of paying lower benefits so that recipients will move across the border to get higher benefits. Competing state governments could then engage in a competitive benefit-cutting process, driving benefit levels in both states far below the levels desired in either state in the absence of migration.

The underlying convention in such a process is that states have no responsibility for supporting people not residing within their borders. Once recipients emigrate, they are no longer entrusted to the care of the state of origin. One could imagine states of immigration refusing to pay benefits to new immigrants; indeed, many states did so until the Supreme Court struck down welfare residency requirements in 1969. Now states must support even-handedly all recipients inside their borders.[12]

The process is diagrammed in Figure 3, showing altruist *A* as a state with a taste for high benefit levels and altruist *B* as a state with a taste for low benefit levels. As mentioned above, combined support levels are now roughly half as high in low benefit states (reflected in the fact that point *X*, showing actual levels, is on a ray from the origin with a slope equal to 0.5). Point *C* refers to the level of benefits that these states would prefer in a closed economy, with no migration of beneficiaries across state lines and no federal matching. For high-benefit states, the two influences offset each other—federal matching raises benefit levels compared to a closed economy, but the threat of migration of beneficiaries from low benefit states lowers benefit

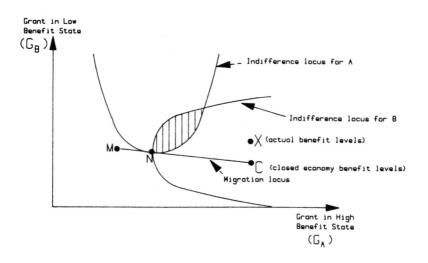

M = Benefit levels if recipients were completely
sensitive to differentials (G_A = G_B)

N = Noncooperative equilibrium point (G_A > G_B)
(assuming no matching)

Area of potential joint utility gain from
coordinating policies

Figure 3. Competition between the states to keep benefits low.

levels. These two influences seem to have roughly equal effects, so point C is drawn with the same abscissa as point X.[13] But for low benefit states, the two effects work in the same direction—federal matching raises benefits, as does being part of a migration system with a state paying higher benefits. So point C is drawn with a lower ordinate than point X.

The importance of migration in this process depends on how sensitively beneficiaries react to their living standards. If recipients were never to move (no matter how badly they fared in a state), or if rigid residency requirements were enforced, states would go to their desired closed economy benefit levels. But as migration becomes more sensitive to relative benefit levels, state benefits become similar: it becomes increasingly costly to pay benefits higher than those in other states for fear of attracting hordes of welfare recipients. In the limit, when migration is perfectly sensitive to benefit disparities, payments in the two states will be driven to equality at point M. At any other level, the state paying the highest benefits will get all the AFDC recipients.

The noncooperative equilibrium, with no federal matching or coordination but with whatever degree of migration exists, can be found by locating the actual degree of migration on the migration locus. At this point, N, each state is at the minimum point on an indifference curve—which is to say it is at the point of tangency between its highest indifference curve and the line set by the assumed fixed level of benefits in the other state. To the right of N, state B is better off because it can free-ride on the higher benefit levels in A. Above N, A is better off because it can free-ride on higher benefit levels in B. Point N represents both an equilibrium (because each state is doing what it was expected to do) and noncooperation (because each state is taking as given the other's action and not trying to coordinate behavior). As the noncooperative maximum with no federal matching, point N also represents the outcome under President Reagan's new federalism welfare reform plan.

The shaded area gives the space in which both states could gain by coordinating behavior. They could coordinate on their own; but with many states paying benefits, such coordination is likely to be costly and difficult to enforce. More practically, states would receive the gains from coordination in a federal system if the central government were to create incentives for higher benefits by the matching grant program discussed. As was mentioned, my convex plan is one variant of such a scheme. It would probably result in a northward movement from point X (higher benefits in low benefit states and roughly unchanged benefits in high benefit states). Federal matching has the effect of offsetting the "externality" that comes about with migration when the benefit payments in one state have an effect outside that state. Just as federal matching introduces vertical cooperation between the federal government and state governments, it offsets the effects of horizontal competition between state governments.[14]

VERTICAL COOPERATION: PRIVATE CHARITIES

Charitable contributions comprise another source of spending on social services in the U.S. Although we know less about private than public spending, both raise similar analytical issues. Again the federal government gives both income and price support grants to private charities, one type of assistance that has free-rider problems and one does not, and improvement in the structure of these grants is possible.

As before, consider the federal government altruist B and some private charity altruist A. Private social welfare agencies get much of their money directly from the federal government—about sixty percent in the 1980s.[15] These funds, totalling about $5 billion in 1987, come from a variety of programs that seem to be structured like matching grants but in reality are not because total transfers are limited. The private social welfare charities are nonprofit enterprises, which means that they cannot use the federal money for non-welfare purposes but must pass it through in the form of direct spending. These passed-through federal funds can then be considered nonmatching grants like the G_B variable in Figure 1—they ultimately go to recipients, but they are limited in amount.

The vehicle for matching contributions is the income tax, which allows deduction of personal and corporate charitable contributions at the relevant marginal tax rate (up to fifty percent through 1986 and generally thirty three percent afterwards). As with state public assistance programs, econometric researchers have found that the price effect for charitable giving seems to be far greater than the income effect. Thus a switch from nonmatching to matching assistance would raise charitable contributions significantly.[16]

An important difference exists between private charitable giving and public assistance. For the latter, matching rates can be determined internally according to what makes programmatic sense. If a convex matching schedule is appropriate, it can be adopted. For charitable contributions this degree of freedom is not present because the matching rate, or marginal income tax rate, serves many other goals of the tax system.[17] This means, for example, that if base-broadening tax reform is adopted, the implied reduction in marginal tax rates will cause an adverse price effect on charitable giving.

My suggested policy improvement in this area follows the same logic of my proposal for vertical cooperation between the federal government and the states. There I criticized the notion of switching from price to income transfers and of losing the virtues of cooperation. For private charities, a logical approach would be just the opposite. Rather than retaining limits on grants to private charities, hence making them operate like nonmatching grants at the margin, the federal government could convert all grants to flat rate matching form. Such a switch would enhance the advantages of the cooperative payment structure already contained in the income tax. Federal budget costs could be controlled by keeping the matching rates on these grants much lower than is now the case.[18]

COOPERATION BETWEEN GOVERNMENTS AND RECIPIENTS

Existing models of cooperative and competitive behavior refer to relationships between various altruistic governments. While the models have not been applied to relationships between altruists and recipients of transfer programs, the underlying logic seems perfectly applicable. If altruists become frustrated when they feel other altruists are free-riding, they should become even more frustrated if they feel the recipients themselves are free-riding. In this section I try to apply the basic model to these types of relationships—relationships where the recipient wears two hats. He is both a recipient and an altruist partly responsible for his own support, in a position either to free-ride on the efforts of the government or to share responsibility with the government. Most interesting policy changes in public assistance are taking place in this area.

Most past analyses of income support programs have focused on technical aspects of the "plan"—the guarantee level, the tax rate, the earned income disregard, and the like? Following Lawrence Mead and Irwin Garfinkel,[19] analysts should also examine another dimension of these plans—the implicit obligations recipients incur, or are perceived by taxpayers to incur, once they receive benefits. Formerly, many social scientists viewed it as intrusive to impose any obligations at all on recipients. Any attention received by implicit obligations in the scholarly literature was likely to be negative. As an example, a commonly cited goal of the negative income tax experiments was to see whether a work requirement was "necessary". But politicians never have considered it intrusive to impose obligations on recipients, and taxpayers certainly have not. Poll after poll has indicated that while taxpayers are willing to support the needy, they are unwilling to support the lazy or the irresponsible.[20]

Two such obligations stand out. First, recipients have an obligation to work. As a condition of AFDC eligibility, most recipients with children over six years of age have been required to register for work and training. But recipients could be denied benefits only if they refused available and suitable jobs, and until recently few provisions existed for actually creating such jobs. This was changed in 1981, when states were permitted to give the work requirement new teeth by operating public employment or private wage subsidy programs. Recipients could be denied benefits if they refused to participate. Since that time over forty states either have set up or applied to set up such programs. It could become quite costly for states to run these programs—either providing the jobs themselves or subsidized day care. The speed with which states have initiated work programs gives impressive evidence that state taxpayer-altruists seem to think an effective work requirement should be attached to income support benefits.

Perhaps even more surprising, recipients seem to agree with the idea. Surveys of recipients indicate that an overwhelming majority sees the work requirements as fair, or at least is "satisfied" with the notion of working for their welfare benefits.[21]

The second obligation involves the support of one's children. This obligation is difficult to enforce because many people receiving public assistance are in single-head households where the father is absent with whereabouts often unknown. Under the Child Support Enforcement program, states are now required to establish paternity, locate absent parents, and obtain child support (financed by federal matching funds). If need be, Internal Revenue Service collection procedures, the federal parent locator service, and the federal courts can be used in this process, thus making it easier for states to collect from fathers who try to escape their support obligations by moving to a different state (a new twist on the migration problem).

The two contrasting approaches—states are permitted to make their work requirements effective but required to enforce child support obligations— bring up an interesting interaction with the federal structure of welfare policies discussed earlier. Of the two contrasting approaches, the logic of cooperation favors permissiveness. Under a permissive but not compulsory approach, states would be able to take into account peculiarities of their own labor market and population of recipients (well-trained or not, geographically dispersed or not, English speaking or not, etc.) in designing either jobs or child support enforcement programs. Moreover, there would be no requirement for strict enforcement of obligatory measures if the state taxpayer-altruists were not very concerned about enforcing these obligations, perhaps because of their potential costs. This logic suggests that state taxpayers should be allowed to design their own approach, including the option of not having an enforcement program.

But in granting states the option not to enforce these obligations, analysts need remember that some external costs may be generated. If it ultimately saves the taxpayers money to enforce work or child support obligations (as seems to be the case with work requirements),[22] federal taxpayers lose their matching funds whenever states opt not to have an obligation-enforcing program. To preserve the efficiencies of the matching grant system in this case, states should reimburse the federal government for whatever states are costing it by not having a program. At least rough estimates of this cost can be made,[23] and the implied reimbursements appear to be modest. In any case, it is probably less important to get the numbers exactly right than to establish the principle that states are not entirely on their own in determining whatever enforcement obligations they will impose. In addition, to prevent certain states from becoming a haven for parents fleeing financial responsibility for supporting their children, states should be obligated to cooperate in tracking down the absent parents of other states' welfare recipients, even if they choose not to track down their own absent parents.

At this point it is hard to determine if welfare recipients are being generally perceived to be shirking their obligations, and if this perception explains the oft-noted political unpopularity of public assistance.[24] Moreover, if the perception exists, is it changeable now that public assistance programs are changing to require more on the part of recipients? What does seem clear, however, is that a program of income support that does not entail some responsibility-sharing by recipients will never rank highly on the joint utility maximization criterion used above. The competitive and cooperative solutions cannot be neatly diagrammed here; but it is probably much more important to work out satisfactory solutions.

Conclusion

The straightforward implication of all of these seemingly unrelated issues is that in a wide range of public welfare applications, cooperation works better than competition. Designing satisfying public welfare policies has proven so difficult in the United States that it may be time to focus on gaining the advantages of cooperation as consistently as possible. One way that this can be done is by coupling all welfare reform plans that institute a national floor with benefit-matching for some range above that floor, so as not to lose the advantages of cooperation. Another way is to remove limits on grants to private charitable social services in order to increase the financial cooperation between public and private givers.

A third way this can be done, the most intricate of all, is to continue an ongoing reform by introducing more recipient responsibilities in the design of welfare policies. Without such changes, welfare seems sure to frustrate and disappoint taxpayers and to stigmatize and impoverish recipients. Just as financial sharing among governments makes sense in paying for the programs, responsibility sharing with recipients makes sense in designing the programs.

EDWARD M. GRAMLICH is Professor of Economics and Public Policy at the University of Michigan. Since January, 1986, he has been on leave as Deputy Director of the Congressional Budget Office. Any opinions expressed here are his own and not those of the budget office.

I would like to thank Henry Aaron, Gina Adams, Nancy Gordon, Robert Hartman, Deborah Laren, Rudolph Penner, Janice Peskin, Ralph Smith, and Roberton Williams for helpful comments on an earlier draft. Much of my work was financed by a grant from the Ford Foundation.

NOTES

1. See Harold M. Hochman and James D. Rodgers, "Pareto Optimal Redistribution," *American Economic Review*, September 1969, vol. 59, pp. 542–557; and Russell D. Roberts, "A Positive Model of Private Charity and Public Transfers," *Journal of Political Economy*, February 1984, vol. 92, pp. 136–148.
2. A continuous indifference curve drawn through the C_C' point generally lies below that drawn through the C_C'' point, unless the slope of the indifference curve changes rapidly to the right of C_C'.
3. See Edward M. Gramlich and Deborah S. Laren, "Migration and Income Distribution Responsibilities," *Journal of Human Resources*, Fall 1984, vol. 19, pp. 489–511.
4. It would be nice to have independent confirmation of these predictions, but such evidence is difficult to come by because there has been little real variation in the food stamp program. Since it was nationalized in the early 1970s, benefits have been constant in real terms, and the program has applied uniformly across states.
5. Gramlich and Laren, *op. cit.*, and Larry L. Orr, "Income Transfers as a Public Good: An Application to AFDC," *American Economic Review*, June 1976, vol. 66, pp. 359–371.
6. Gramlich and Laren, *op. cit.*, and Orr, *op. cit.*
7. Eight past Secretaries of HHS made a widely publicized proposal for a national floor on benefits in 1982. Earlier the Advisory Commission on Intergovernmental Relations had made a similar proposal, and later a group of economists from the Brookings Institution did likewise. See Alice M. Rivlin (ed.), *Economic Choices 1986*, Washington: The Brookings Institution, 1984, p. 166.
8. Using Figure 2, to the right of the floor level of benefits at F_1, a national floor plan could have no matching at all and revert to the New federalism benefit schedule. Or it could drop down to the old schedule, in which case there would be what is known as a "notch," or a range where states could sacrifice their own consumption without raising benefits at all. Or there could still be matching, as in the convex plan I am about to discuss.
9. The constant revenue assumption minimizes benefit disparities that would result from such a switch. A different possibility is that each state would get the same amount of dollars as it got before the change, in which case benefits would be even lower than L_1 in the low benefit state and higher than H_1 in the high benefit state.
10. The illustrative generous plan referred to would pay all support costs up to sixty percent of the poverty line, seventy five percent of all support costs up to eighty

percent of the poverty line, and fifty percent of all support costs up to the poverty line. Such a plan would raise support payments to the poor by $2.7 billion in 1985 (a six percent increase), and switch $5 billion from state costs to national government costs (a twenty-five percent increase in national government support costs). As noted in the text, these numbers are illustrative, and there are many ways in which they could be reduced.

11. Edward M. Gramlich, "Reforming U.S. Fiscal Federalism Arrangements," in John M. Quigley and Daniel L. Rubinfeld (eds.), *American Domestic Priorities: An Economic Appraisal*, Berkeley: University of California Press, 1985, pp. 34–69, lists a number of ways in which this could be done.

12. Conventions have varied widely here. Charles C. Brown and Wallace E. Oates, "Assistance to the Poor in a Federal System," mimeo, 1986, give a fascinating look at how the English handled this problem with their poor laws as early as the 1600s.

13. See Gramlich, *op. cit.*

14. There is no general rule for whether the actual point X should be within or without the shaded area. In Gramlich, *op. cit.*, I found it to be outside, indicating that present matching rates more than compensate for migration-induced inefficiencies. This does not mean that matching rates are too high, because there could be other reasons for raising benefits in various states. Brown and Oates, *op. cit.*, have derived a convex plan based only on these migration inefficiencies.

15. See Lester M. Salamon, "Nonprofit Organizations: The Lost Opportunity," in John L. Palmer and Elizabeth V. Sawhill (eds.), *The Reagan Record*, Washington: The Urban Institute, 1984, pp. 261–285.

16. See Charles T. Clotfelter and C. Eugene Steuerle, "Charitable Contributions," in Henry J. Aaron and Joseph A. Pechman (eds.), *How Taxes Affect Economic Behavior*, Washington: The Brookings Institution, 1981, pp. 403–436.

17. To be sure, there are ways in which the after-tax price of charitable giving can be altered without altering the rest of the income tax, most recently with the non-itemizer deduction for charitable gifts (no longer in the tax code after the 1986 changes).

18. At present most grants to charitable organizations contain federal matching rates of eighty percent or more, up to a limit on the total grant. My suggestion is to lower matching rates to, say, twenty or thirty percent but to remove the limit on the grant. The marginal incentive to spend would be increased, and for normal elasticities, the federal government would save money.

19. See Lawrence M. Mead, *Beyond Entitlement: The Social Obligations of Citizenship*, New York: Free Press, 1986; and Irwin Garfinkel, "The Role of Child Support Insurance in Antipoverty Policy," *Annals*, American Academy of Political and Social Science, May 1985, vol. 479, pp. 119–131.

20. See Hugh Heclo, "The Political Foundations of Antipoverty Policy," in Sheldon H. Danziger and Daniel H. Weinberg (eds.), *Fighting Poverty: What Works and What Doesn't*, Cambridge: Harvard University Press, 1986, pp. 312–340.

21. See Joseph Bell, *West Virginia: The Demonstration of State Work Welfare Initiatives*, New York: Manpower Demonstration Research Corporation, 1984. It should be noted, of course, that a work requirement is not the only way to encourage work. The approach that has received the most attention up to now has been the incentive approach—that is, to keep tax rates in support plans as low as possible. While the low tax rate approach makes sense in terms of the logic of cooperation, I do not stress it here because there is another problem with it. If guarantee levels in a support plan are high, low tax rates mean that vast numbers of people are potential transfer recipients. The numbers can only be controlled by cutting guarantee levels, and then those without much earnings capacity are supported at very low levels.

22. See Judith M. Gueron, *Work Initiatives for Welfare Recipients*, New York: Manpower Demonstration Research Corporation, 1986.

23. Based on data such as those given in Barbara Goldman, Daniel Friedlander, and David Long, *California: The Demonstration of State Work Welfare Initiatives*, New York: Manpower Demonstration Research Corporation, 1986.

24. The political unpopularity of welfare has been noted in at least three recent extensive voter surveys. For California see Jack Citrin, "Do People Want Something for Nothing: Public Opinion on Taxes and Government Spending," *National Tax Journal*, June, 1979, vol. 32, no. 2, pp. 113–130; for Michigan see Paul N. Courant, Edward M. Gramlich, and Daniel L. Rubinfeld, "Why Do Voters Support Tax Limitation Amendments: The Michigan Case," *National Tax Journal*, March, 1980, vol. 33, pp. 1–20; and for Massachusetts, see Helen F. Ladd and Julie Boatwright Wilson, "Why Voters Support Tax Limitation: Evidence from Massachusetts' Proposition 2½," *National Tax Journal*, June, 1982, vol. 35, pp. 121–148.

[17]

5

A Report on School Finance and Educational Reform in Michigan

Paul N. Courant, Edward Gramlich, and Susanna Loeb*

In late 1993 Michigan Governor John Engler signed into law a radical educational reform bill. The bill passed with both Republican and Democratic support and implemented a shift from local taxes to state taxes and from property taxes (especially residential property taxes) to a variety of other revenue sources. It also lengthened the number of school days, instituted curriculum and testing requirements, and permitted the formation of charter schools—schools of choice within the public education system. The bill was also noteworthy because it mandated a ballot amendment in which the voters could choose between two different plans to replace most of the lost local property tax revenues. The primary difference between the plans was that one would have increased sales taxes, while the other would have increased income taxes. The ballot proposal was voted on in March 1994, and the sales tax increase won handily.

The Michigan legislation raises any number of interesting issues and presumably will be studied and evaluated for years. This paper is one of the first of these evaluations. Because the law is taking effect as we write, we cannot do much before and after data analysis but, we can use other sources of information to predict various outcomes and impacts of the bill.

We begin by describing Michigan's system of educational finance before and after the new law. We then use state education data to see what the substitution of state for local taxes does to the interdistrict distribution of per pupil expenditures on schools, both nominally and after adjusting for variation in costs among districts. We predict the effect of this substitution on the financial support of public education over time, in both low- and high-spending districts. We then examine new and unique provisions for charter schools and speculate on the impact of these on education in the state. Finally, since the bill substitutes state for local property taxes and sales taxes for property taxes, we examine its likely impact on property values and economic activity in the state. We conclude with a research agenda and a summary of the open questions raised by this experiment.

*Paul N. Courant and Edward Gramlich are professors of economics and public policy in the Department of Economics and the Institute of Public Policy Studies at the University of Michigan. Susanna Loeb is a graduate student in the Department of Economics at the University of Michigan.

Educational finance before and after the change

Historically, education finance in Michigan has relied more heavily on both local taxes and property taxes than most other states. In the 1990-91 school year, Michigan, a state with average levels of overall taxes, was third among states in the share of school spending financed locally (65.2 percent), behind New Hampshire, which has virtually no state taxes, and Oregon, which has since changed its school financing.[1] Michigan property taxes as a share of personal income also rose from 4.3 percent of personal income in 1978 to 5.0 percent by 1991.

Whether the differences between Michigan and national norms should have warranted a perpetual property tax rebellion, they clearly did so. Over the past two decades there have been more than ten property tax cut initiatives placed on statewide Michigan ballots. Only one of these ballot initiatives actually passed—the relatively mild Headlee Amendment in 1978[2]—but the property tax cut fervor was usually strong enough that new ballot initiatives for cutting property taxes were being cranked up even as the old ones were going down to defeat. Property tax reform, rather than reform of the school system itself, has been the dominant statewide political issue for at least two decades.

Finally, in 1993, the local property tax cutters won. In the summer of that year the legislature passed, more or less out of the blue, a bill that simply abolished, with no source of revenue replacement specified, all use of local property taxes for school operating expenditures.[3] Taken literally, the state imposed a local tax cut of over $6 billion with no offsetting tax increase. To put it mildly, this changed the nature of the game for Michigan school finance. The default position was no longer the status quo, but one in which there was no way in which local districts were permitted to raise revenue for schools and in which the total resources for K-12 education were at about a quarter of their previous level. Clearly, those who wanted to cut property taxes had the upper hand in the ensuing legislative battles. In late December, on the last day of the legislative session, both houses passed, and the governor signed, a financing bill that contained two options, either of which would have radically changed the system of school finance in Michigan and either of which would have replaced approximately all of the lost revenue.[4] Here are the main provisions of the new system, as passed by the voters in March.

- A combination of an increased state sales tax, a statewide property tax on all property, a local property tax on non-homestead property,[5] a sharp increase in the tobacco tax, and a real estate transfer tax. These revenues (most of which derive from property taxation of one kind or another) approximately replace the lost local property taxes for schools. Under the new system, 79 percent of state and local revenues for schools will be raised by the state,[6] as compared with 31 percent under the old system.

■ A system of state foundation grants to school districts that would, when fully implemented, put a floor under spending of $5,000 per pupil in 1994-95, indexed by a formula that we describe later. The system of grants also tends to preserve, in nominal terms, differences in spending per pupil for districts that currently spend $5,000 per pupil or more and greatly limits the extent to which such districts can change the amounts they spend relative to a state-imposed formula.

■ Strengthened requirements for an academic core curriculum, pupil performance standards, and minimum numbers of school days.

■ Provisions for charter schools, schools of choice, that would be subject to the statewide curriculum and testing requirements but would not have to use certified teachers. If students were to transfer from their normal public school to charter schools, the charter schools would get the foundation allowance of the district in which the school is located or $5,500 per pupil (indexed), whichever is less. The public school then would lose the per pupil state revenue for any students who attended charter schools.[7] (At this writing, the charter schools have been declared in violation of the state constitution. Our strong expectation is that the law will be revised to re-establish charter schools.)

In the parlance of educational finance, the new law switched Michigan from a modified power equalization system of state aid for public schools to a modified foundation system.

Power equalization in Michigan—The Ancien Regime

Under the power equalization system that was in effect through the 1993-94 school year, the state permitted local school districts to assess whatever property tax millage rates they wanted, but then supplemented the revenue raised by low wealth districts, thus moving the system towards wealth neutrality across districts. Typically, the formula determining the state grant per-pupil in district j was as follows:

(1) $F + t_j [(SEV/N)^* - (SEV_j/N_j)]$,

where t_j is the millage rate in district j, SEV_j is the state equalized value of taxable property (the property tax base, defined as one-half of market value in Michigan) and N_j is the number of pupils in the district.[8] The amount $(SEV/N)^*$ in this formula is the target for equalization and was chosen by the state legislature each year. In 1992-93, $(SEV/N)^*$ was $96,260. The formula assures that any district whose property per pupil was less than the target amount would, if it levied property taxes at millage rate t, receive revenue as if its actual property per pupil were $(SEV/N)^*$. F, in the formula, was a relatively small foundation grant, $310 per pupil in 1992-93, giving a total of roughly $3,470 per pupil at an average millage rate ($3,671 in 1994 dollars).

8

Districts whose *SEV* per pupil exceeded the target amount had their state grants taxed away, according to the formula, up to *F*. Once the net grant was zero, there was no further grant. Thus, the richest districts (approximately 33 percent in 1992-93) were termed "out of formula" and became powerful lobbyists against the system of state aid.

Michigan's system of power equalization did not lead to equal spending per pupil across districts. One reason is that discussed above—the system of power equalization itself was incomplete, so that the yield per mill of tax rate was higher for the richest districts than for those "in-formula." More important is the well-known result [Reschovsky (1994)] that the wealth elasticity of demand for public education exceeds the price elasticity in absolute value. Thus, even if all districts received the same marginal tax revenue per pupil for levying a mill, richer districts would generally choose to buy more education. And so they did, as we shall see later.

The foundation grant system—Brave New World

In the old system, a district's spending per pupil was determined by the millage rate, and, for richer districts, local *SEV* per pupil. In the new system, the connection between current local policy and spending is almost entirely absent, except in a small number of districts. The new system works differently for three different sets of districts, with each defined by its per pupil spending in 1993-94.

All of the allocation formulas in the foundation grant system are derived from two numbers. One is the *basic foundation allowance*, which is $5,000 per pupil for 1994-95. The other we term the School Aid Fund Index (SAFI), which is used to determine the basic foundation allowance in future years. The SAFI for year *t* will be computed by total statewide revenues per pupil for all taxes that are earmarked for the school aid fund, divided by the 1994-95 level of this ratio.[9]

The 365 districts, which include 786,994 students, that spent less than the $4,772 per student in 1993-94 will be brought up to basic foundation allowance over the next few years under a formula that allows these districts to "catch up."[10] There were 122 districts, with 713,285 students, that spent between $4,772 and $6,500 per pupil in 1993-94. In 1994-95, all of these districts received small real increases in spending per pupil according to an ad hoc formula that was designed to assure that everyone was made better off by the reforms in the short run.[11] After 1994-95, per pupil spending in these districts will increase by the same dollar amount as the basic foundation grant.[12]

The third group comprises 37 districts, with 162,202 pupils, which spent more than $6,500 per pupil in 1993-94. All of these districts get the same revenue per student[13] ($6,500 in 1994-95, increased by the same absolute amount as the basic foundation grant in subsequent years) as districts that spent $6,500 in 1993-94. However, these high-spending districts are allowed to supplement their foundation grant by levying local taxes on homestead property, provided that their revenue per pupil does not exceed the 1993-94 level, plus $160 dollars for 1994-95, plus the dollar increase in the basic foundation grant in future years.[14]

While the new system increased per pupil revenue in each district, it also removed an indirect source of state aid. Prior to 1994-95, districts were required to put the equivalent of five percent of their expenditures on salaries into a retirement fund. The state then paid the additional money needed for that fund, a contribution that varied from year to year depending on need, ranging from about four percent to seven percent of salary expenditures. Under the new system, districts are required to pay the full retirement amount. This will add an additional cost to each district of, on average, $200 per student (1994-95 dollars).

The effect of all this, even with the additional retirement fund spending, will be to dramatically increase the spending of the lowest-spending districts, to freeze the nominal dollar differences in spending per pupil for all of the districts currently spending between $5,000 and $6,500, and, for reasons given later, probably to lower spending in districts currently spending above $6,500 per student.[15] Over time, this implies a reduction in the real spending of the highest-spending districts (slower when inflation is low) and a smaller reduction or possible increase (depending on the relationship between SAFI and inflation) in the real spending of districts in the middle range, thus slowly eroding the real differences in spending across districts.

The cross–sectional variance of per pupil spending

We begin our analysis of the old and new systems by showing the cross-sectional distribution of school operating expenditures per pupil as compared to property tax wealth per pupil under the old power equalization system. Figure 1 shows the data for 523 Michigan K-12 school districts (excluding those with incomplete data) for 1992-93, expressed in 1994 dollars.[16]

While there is a great deal of random variation in per pupil spending, there is also a clear positive relationship between per pupil spending and per pupil wealth (the univariate regression coefficient is 0.0083 with a t-ratio of 21). This suggests that in the old power equalization regime Michigan fell far short of wealth neutrality. For districts in the lower ranges of the wealth distribution this deviation from wealth neutrality in spending levels can be explained by the fact that the millage subsidy was not great enough given the underlying price and wealth elasticities for public education spending. In the upper ranges of the wealth distribution the districts were "out of formula" and there was no effective power equalization at all.

Controlling for cost differences

The school operating expenditures plotted in figure 1 are in money terms. As is well known, the price of public education can vary across a state like Michigan—it is likely to be much more costly to operate schools in large cities such as Detroit than in smaller towns and suburbs. To adjust for this problem, we estimate the costs of operating public schools and compute real operating expenditures per pupil.

It is not easy to measure the costs of public schooling. Ideally, differences in costs across districts would be directly observable and exogenous with respect to district choices, and there would be a price index of the goods and services that districts buy. Such is not the case, and there is an enormous literature that tries to determine how to proceed when neither condition is satisfied (Ratcliffe, Riddle, and Yinger 1990; Downes and Pogue 1994).

The simplest way to address the cost problem is to run a reduced form regression of per pupil spending on some demand variables and some cost variables. Demand variables are typically measures like income and wealth per pupil. Cost variables are typically measures of cost—distance from major cities, share of disadvantaged pupils, urbanization, etc. The regression controls for demand influences and allows us to use these controls to isolate cost factors. But there are several problems of interpretation with the approach:

- Not all independent variables can be neatly compartmentalized into those influencing demand and those influencing costs.

- Two important independent variables, federal and targeted state grants, both raise demand directly and also reimburse districts for high costs.

- There are market effects—cost decreases move a district down its demand function and then raise output by an amount that depends on demand and supply elasticities and may not be easily ascertained.

- There generally will be a residual that will have some demand components and some cost components.

Given these difficulties, we have adopted several ways to correct for costs. We regressed per pupil operating expenditures on a set of independent variables across the 523 Michigan school districts for 1992. The equation is shown in table 1 with those variables that we interpret as cost variables designated by an asterisk. Both income and wealth, which we take to be demand variables, have positive and significant coefficients.[17] Federal grants go largely to reimburse districts for extra education costs that are imposed by specific populations and were considered a cost variable. State grants for restricted purposes are largely for cost reimbursement and were also considered a cost variable. The small and large district dummies display a U-shaped average cost curve for Michigan school districts and were considered cost variables. The various

FIGURE 1

Operating expenditures per student under the old system in 1994 dollars: money terms
523 Michigan school districts

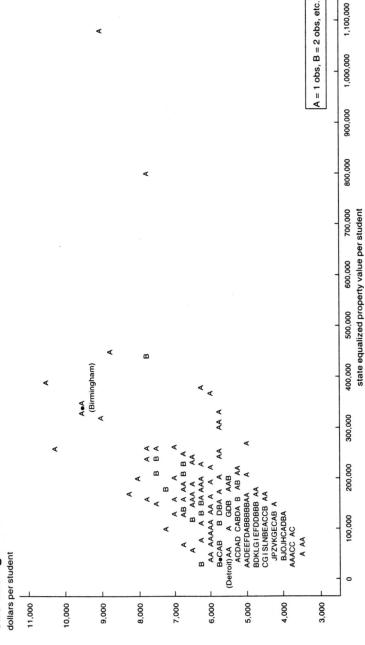

12

TABLE 1

The cost equation and OLS regression results

Current operating expenditures per pupil = $\alpha + \beta_1$(state equalized valuation per pupil)
    $+ \beta_2$(district income per pupil)
    $+ \beta_3$(revenues from federal sources)* $+ \beta_4$(restricted revenues from state sources)*
    $+ \beta_5$(small district dummy)* $+ \beta_6$(large district dummy)* $+ \beta_7$(urban district dummy)*
    $+ \beta_8$(rural district dummy)* $+ \beta_9$(south lower peninsula district dummy)*
    $+ \beta_{10}$(north lower peninsula district dummy)* $+ \beta_{11}$(upper peninsula district dummy)* $+ \varepsilon$.

Variables	Mean (standard deviation)	Regression coefficient (t-statistic)
SEV per pupil	102471.3 (84,034)	0.0059 (17.82)
Income per pupil	60840.8 (32,891)	0.0076 (8.14)
Federal revenues*	194.75 (202.74)	1.056 (8.25)
Restricted state revenues*	150.80 (102.41)	0.904 (3.88)
Small*	0.023 (0.150)	926.65 (5.31)
Large*	0.128 (0.334)	182.60 (2.26)
Urban*	0.031 (0.172)	241.38 (1.64)
Rural*	0.489 (0.500)	-101.70 (-1.89)
South lower peninsula*	0.565 (0.496)	-607.39 (-8.27)
North lower peninsula*	0.174 (0.379)	-938.39 (-9.99)
Upper peninsula*	0.099 (0.299)	-728.03 (-7.04)
Intercept		3,905.94 (36.12)
R-Square		0.749 (F Value = 138.60)

Note: Variables followed by * are cost variables.

regional dummies—spending is high in Detroit, high in other metropolitan areas, low in rural areas, low in the upper peninsula, low in the northern part of the lower peninsula—were also considered cost variables.

We first considered the variables designated above as cost variables, subtracted them times their coefficients from the dependent variable, and defined the remainder as real per pupil operating spending on schools. This procedure increased our estimate of mean spending by about five percent. In the reported figures, we proportionally renormalized the data so that mean real spending, in any cross-section, is the same as mean nominal spending.[18] This version of spending, called Real1, probably undercorrects for price differences for two reasons. It does not correct for the fact that cost changes might work through the implicit price term to change spending, an issue we deal with below. In addition, it implicitly assumes that the residual does not pick up any cost factors. The data plot for the Real1 version is given in figure 2.

We then recalculated under the assumption that the entire residual was picking up unmeasured cost differences and subtracted the residual to define a new version of real spending, Real2. This procedure still makes no adjustment for the effect of interdistrict differences in cost on the demand for education, but now overestimates the presence of cost factors in the residual. Just as Real1 undercorrects for costs, Real2 probably overcorrects for interdistrict cost differences.

We can also take account of the response of real spending to differences in costs. We do that by assuming a price elasticity of demand for education spending of -.5, at the upper end of standard estimates in the literature.[19] Under this assumption, it is straightforward to show that real spending (defined here as Real3) is given by [(nominal spending) / (nominal spending / Real1)²]. This procedure yields smaller "price" adjustments and larger "quantity" adjustments than does Real1. We show spending defined by Real3 in figure 3. Real4 is constructed from Real2 analogously to the way Real3 is derived from Real1. Thus, Real4 adjusts for the effects of cost on demand and assumes that the residuals in the original regression can all be attributed to costs.

The statewide standard deviations for nominal per pupil spending and all four variants of renormalized real per pupil spending under the old law are given in table 2. In addition, table 3 contains all the measures for two sample districts, Detroit and Birmingham, a high-income suburb of Detroit. Because costs are in general lower in low-spending districts in Michigan's upper peninsula and northern lower peninsula, correction for these cost differences greatly lowers the standard deviation of per pupil spending. As table 2 reports, the standard deviation falls from $1,036 per pupil (.21 coefficient of variation) for nominal spending to $826 per pupil (.17 coefficient of variation) for Real1, to $652 per pupil (.13 coefficient of variation) for Real2, to $802 per pupil (.16 coefficient of variation) for Real3, and to $797 per pupil (.16 coefficient of variation) for Real4. Conceptually, both Real3 and Real4 should be preferred to Real1 and Real2, because they allow for demand effects. We think that Real3 underadjusts somewhat for cost differences, because it attributes all of the residual to factors other than cost. Still, it is arguably the best estimate that we have, and we concentrate on it for the remainder of the discussion.

No matter how we do it, correcting for cost factors already lowers the coefficient of variation of real spending from about .21 to about .16, a reduction on the order of one-quarter. Correction for cost factors also lowers the univariate

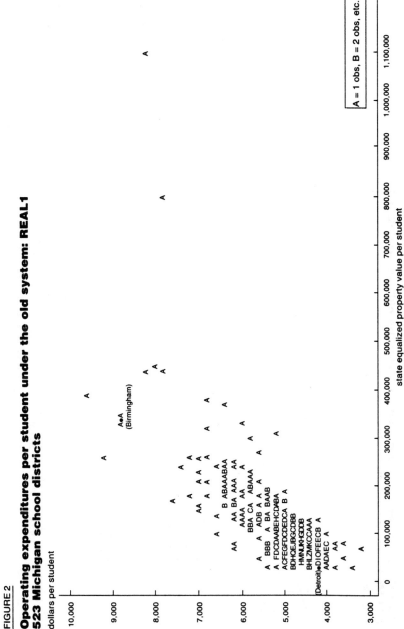

FIGURE 2

**Operating expenditures per student under the old system: REAL1
523 Michigan school districts**

FIGURE 3

Operating expenditures per student under the old system: REAL3 523 Michigan school districts

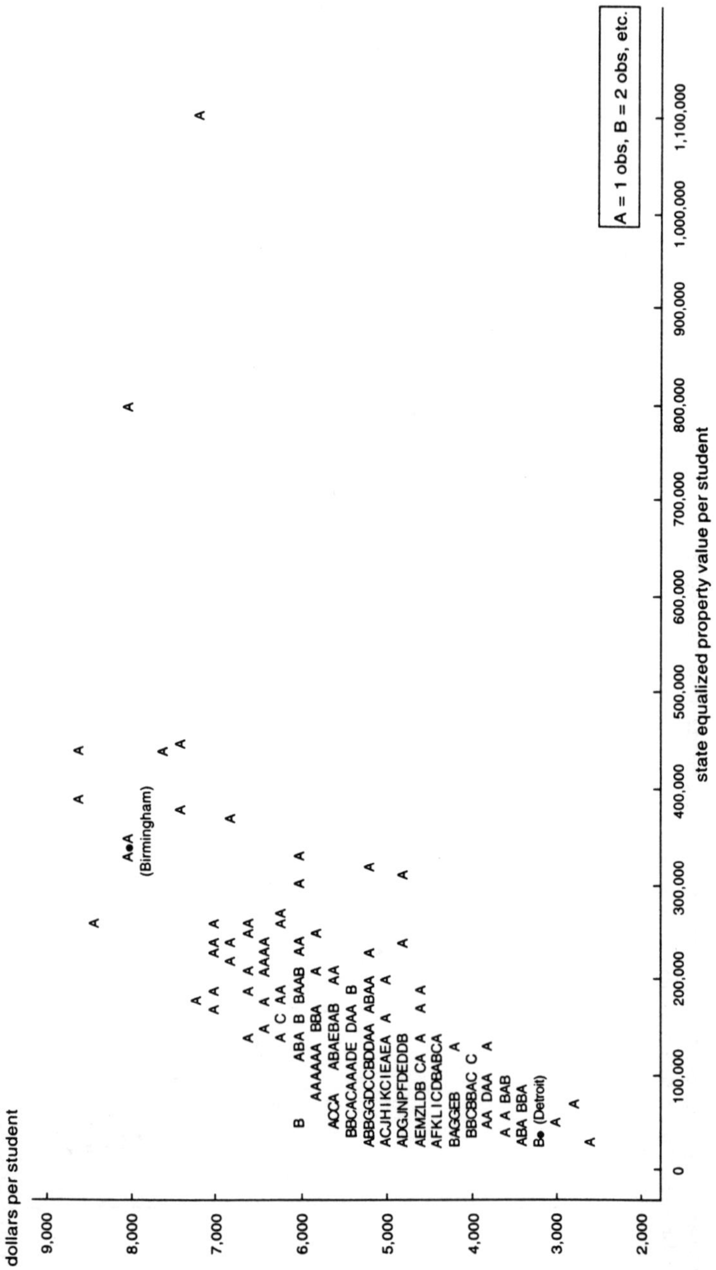

16

TABLE 2

Predicted per pupil spending in 1994 dollars

Measure	Mean	Standard deviation	Coefficient of variation	Regression coefficient SEV / pupil (t-statistic)
Under the old system				
Money terms	4,948.04	1,036.40	0.209	0.0083 (20.79)
Real1	4,948.04	825.72	0.167	0.0073 (25.36)
Real2	4,948.04	652.34	0.132	0.0073 (60.77)
Real3	4,948.04	802.28	0.162	0.0064 (20.33)
Real4	4,948.04	796.60	0.161	0.0067 (22.11)
Under the new system: Assuming richer districts spend maximum allowed				
Money terms	5,668.07	683.23	0.121	0.0056 (21.46)
Real1	5,668.07	575.07	0.101	0.0047 (21.78)
Real2	5,668.07	529.22	0.093	0.0047 (25.43)
Real3	5,668.07	720.33	0.127	0.0040 (11.87)
Real4	5,668.07	935.20	0.165	0.0043 (9.43)
Under the new system: Assuming a -0.5 price elasticity of demand for education in higher-spending districts				
Money terms	5,603.96	459.46	0.082	0.0033 (17.29)
Real1	5,603.96	417.57	0.075	0.0026 (13.64)
Real2	5,603.96	464.52	0.083	0.0025 (11.63)
Real3	5,603.96	667.50	0.119	0.0019 (5.61)
Real4	5,603.96	958.36	0.171	0.0023 (4.77)

regression coefficient by about the same one-quarter. In this sense, both the spread of school spending and the deviation from wealth neutrality under the pre-reform system are not as dramatic in real terms as they appear in money terms, though there is still both a big spread and a big deviation from wealth neutrality.[20]

Real spending differences under the new law

The new law will change the distribution of spending through a variety of mechanisms. First, it will bring spending up to the basic foundation allowance ($5,000 per pupil in 1994-95, as indexed by SAFI) for all districts currently spending below that amount. Second, it preserves nominal spending differences among all other districts, unless districts now spending more than $6,500 per pupil choose to spend less than the amounts they are permitted. Third, since it takes non-homestead property off the local tax base for supplementation

TABLE 3

Predicted per pupil spending in 1994 dollars:
Two sample districts

Measure	Detroit (*SEV* per pupil = $31,616.09)	Birmingham (*SEV* per pupil = $345,127.75)
Under the old system		
Money terms	5,844.43	9,556.33
Real1	4,337.85	8,782.80
Real2	4,392.70	7,876.55
Real3	3,197.66	8,016.79
Real4	3,251.26	6,393.11
Under the new system: Assuming richer districts spend maximum allowed		
Money terms	6,016.86	9,412.77
Real1	4,529.03	8,697.36
Real2	4,584.10	7,785.43
Real3	3,391.71	7,995.31
Real4	3,452.42	6,365.50
Under the new system: Assuming a -0.5 price elasticity of demand for education in higher-spending districts		
Money terms	6,016.86	7,579.28
Real1	4,526.92	6,935.60
Real2	4,581.97	6,023.70
Real3	3,388.23	6,313.60
Real4	3,446.60	4,728.84

purposes, it can greatly increase the tax price facing homeowners in some of the districts that will spend more than $6,500 per pupil in 1994-95, which may result in cut backs on spending. We consider the static effects first—looking at the distribution of spending that can be expected in 1999-2000, by which time all districts will be spending at least the basic foundation allowance. We present all of the analysis in 1994 dollars, assuming, with the Congressional Budget Office (1994), that nominal income will grow at 5.1 percent per year for the next five years, and the CPI will grow at an annual rate of 2.6 percent.

Static effects—assuming no behavioral response

Assuming that current law stays in effect, changes in the levels and distribution of real spending will be almost entirely determined by the relationships among SAFI, changes in the student population, and inflation.[21] Extrapolating from the period 1979 to 1992, the taxes used to compute SAFI have an elasticity of .937

18

TABLE 4

Predicted per pupil spending in 1994 dollars weighted by enrollment

Measure	Mean	Standard deviation	Coefficient of variation
Under the old system			
Money terms	5,360.77	1,074.86	0.2005
Real1	4,973.31	897.15	0.1804
Real2	4,991.52	654.24	0.1311
Real3	4,642.53	1,001.26	0.2157
Real4	4,668.56	43.94	0.1808
Under the new system: Assuming richer districts spend maximum allowed			
Money terms	5,848.63	754.23	0.1290
Real1	5,470.81	758.60	0.1387
Real2	5,489.07	599.48	0.1092
Real3	5,147.91	1,036.80	0.2014
Real4	5,177.67	1,032.75	0.1995
Under the new system: Assuming a -0.5 price elasticity of demand for education in higher-spending districts			
Money terms	5,757.23	487.23	0.0846
Real1	5,380.64	549.67	0.1022
Real2	5,398.88	530.75	0.0983
Real3	5,059.29	927.84	0.1834
Real4	5,090.22	1,066.31	0.2095

with respect to nominal income. Using the CBO prediction of 5.1 percent nominal GDP growth over the next five years and adjusting for growth in the student population,[22] we project the nominal basic foundation grant to be $6,122 per pupil in 1999, or $5,385 in 1994 dollars according to the CBO's inflation projection for the period. Thus, the basic foundation grant grows somewhat more slowly than real income (1.5 percent per year versus 2.6 percent per year)[23] over this period. During a recession, given any inflation and any population growth at all, the elasticity of .937 with respect to nominal income implies that real spending per-pupil would fall.

Figure 4 shows the estimated distribution of spending for 1999-2000. With a floor of $5,385 (1994 dollars) under per pupil spending and nominal spending differences among districts preserved, mean spending will be $5,668 and the standard deviation will be only $683.23 for a coefficient of variation of only .12, a substantial drop from the current value of .21. The lowest-spending district will

Paul N. Courant, Edward Gramlich, and Susanna Loeb

19

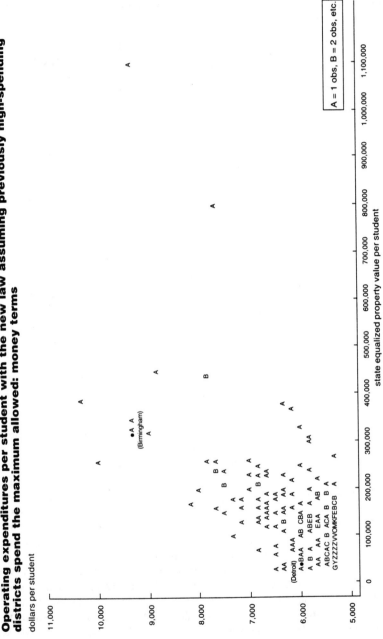

FIGURE 4

Operating expenditures per student with the new law assuming previously high-spending districts spend the maximum allowed: money terms

have increased per pupil spending by $1,850, and the highest-spending district will have increased spending by about $250. By any measure, this constitutes a radical reduction in the dispersion of per pupil spending.

Because there is no recognition of cost differences in the new law, many low-spending districts in the upper and northern lower peninsulas will be pulled up beyond the foundation level in real terms, implying that the standard deviation will be lower when looked at in real than in money terms. Using Real3 to adjust for costs, as seen in figure 5, the standard deviation falls to $720 (1994 dollars), implying a coefficient of variation of .13, compared to a value of .16 under current law.

The new plan reduces the variance of per pupil spending largely by increasing the spending of the poorest districts. As a result, some districts will gain nearly $2,000 per pupil. Because this change in revenue is so great, the value of an extra dollar for operating expenditures will not be worth a dollar for many of these districts. We expect to see attempts at fiscal substitution in these income-rich districts, disguising other expenditures as school operating expenditure. For example, schools may operate parks for the community or use "maintenance" expenditures to purchase capital. Some districts may even sell school buildings to raise money that could be used for non-school expenditures and then rent back the building with their increased state revenue. In addition, we expect the emergence of entrepreneurs with the latest educational products competing for the extra funds of these newly rich districts.

As we have pointed out, for districts currently spending between $5,000 and $6,500, the state foundation grant will preserve the nominal differences in spending among districts. This feature, given a positive income elasticity of demand for education, means that in general, the state foundation grant in this range will be higher, the higher is the district's income. The ability to hold the middle-income districts harmless during the reform comes at the price of substantial regressivity in the pattern of state spending per pupil.

Dynamic effects—pressure to reduce supplemental millages in high-spending districts

The new financing rules generally increase the tax price facing voters in districts above $6,500 spending per pupil, these being the only voters that have the option of raising supplemental millage locally. In the old days, these districts could change their spending by varying the property tax rate on *all* taxable property in their districts. Now, however, the margin is entirely homestead property. As long as the tax rate on homestead property is below 18 mills (the mandatory rate on all other property) any supplemental millages apply only to homestead property. Thus, the tax price facing homeowners will rise by the reciprocal of the share of homestead property in total taxable property in the district.[24] Where the share of homestead property is low, the

FIGURE 5

Operating expenditures per student with the new law assuming previously high-spending districts spend the maximum allowed: REAL3

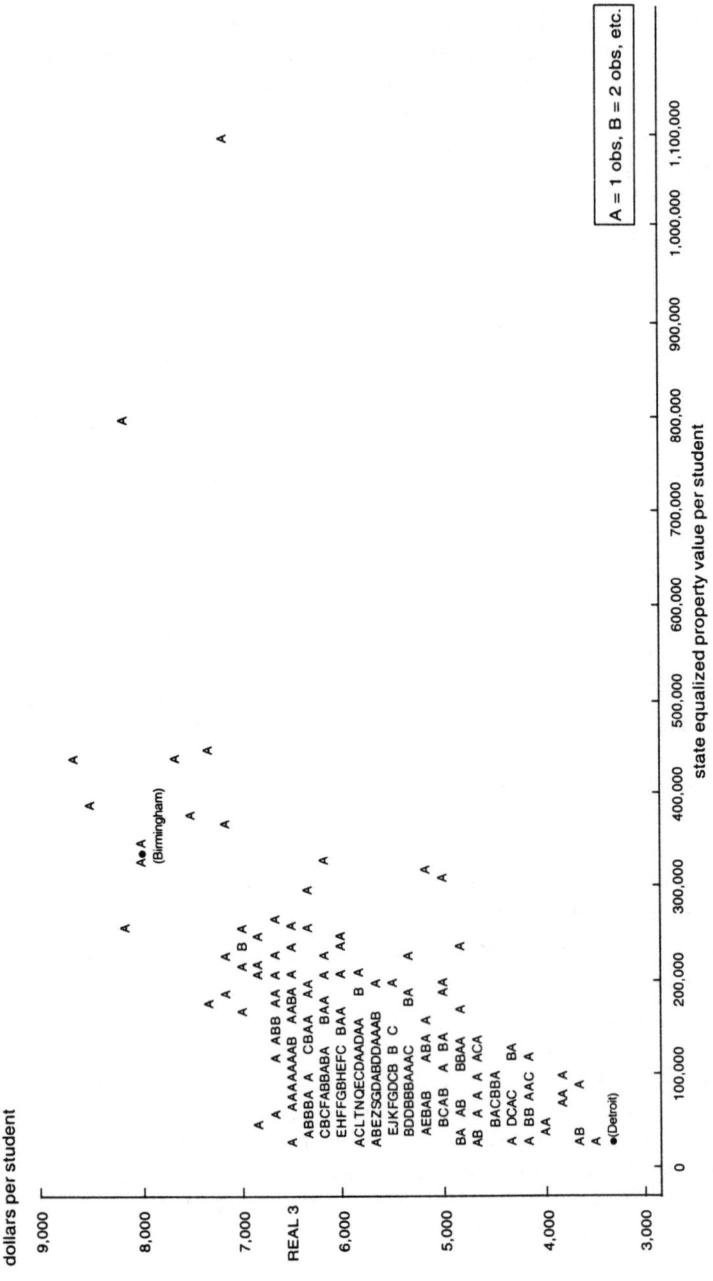

dollars per student

A = 1 obs, B = 2 obs, etc.

state equalized property value per student

increase in tax price will be very large. For 23 of the 37 districts (including Ann Arbor) the share is less than 50 percent, implying more than a doubling of the tax price of education for homeowners.

In order to estimate the effect of these increases, we assumed that the change in law has no effect on the after-tax incomes of households in districts that do not change their locally raised millages (sales taxes went up, property taxes went down, there was a loss in deductible taxes; on average, given that the change was approximately balanced-budget, the assumption is not terrible.) Thus, all we have to worry about is moving along the demand function. We assume, as before, that the price elasticity of demand for public education is -0.5. For spending above SAFI-adjusted $6,500, the price of education for homeowners changes by a factor equal to the reciprocal of the share of owner-occupied housing in total property. For spending below SAFI-adjusted $6,500, the price is zero. Taking the static spending estimates for 1999 as a starting point, we incorporated estimated price change and assumed price elasticity of demand. Then we predict each district's spending to be either the resulting amount or SAFI-adjusted $6,500 ($7,045), whichever is more.

Results of this exercise are shown in figure 6 and the bottom panel of table 2, under which there is both somewhat lower mean spending ($5,604 versus $5,668, 1994 dollars) and substantially lower maximum spending ($8,836 versus $10,376) than under the static assumptions. Moreover, because spending at the top is reduced so much, the coefficients of variation are considerably smaller than in the static case: .08 for nominal spending and .12 for REAL3 (see figure 7). The effects that we estimate here seem quite large, and we are not confident of them. We are confident, however, that when voters in districts discover (to their surprise, and, near as we can tell, the surprise of everyone involved with designing and implementing Michigan's finance reforms) the sharp increases in tax prices, some millages will fail, and spending will fall, even if not as much as our assumptions imply.

Pressures for change in the basic foundation allowance

So far, our analysis assumes that the reforms stay in place indefinitely (or at least until the year 2000). At least as interesting and perhaps more important, we think, is the possibility that the basic foundation allowance will be changed. The basic foundation allowance is a statutory creation of the state legislature, and the taxes earmarked for schools account for only about 82 percent of state grants to local districts. Thus, every year, the state will have to appropriate extra money, out of general revenues, in order to fully fund the 1993 formula. Moreover, because average real spending rises considerably more rapidly than do these taxes, during the period that the lowest-spending districts see their real spending climb to that of the basic grant, these taxes will account for only about 78 percent of formula-mandated state spending on education. The question will then arise, every year, whether the state will provide more, less,

FIGURE 6

Operating expenditures per student with the new law assuming a -0.5 price elasticity of demand for public education: money terms

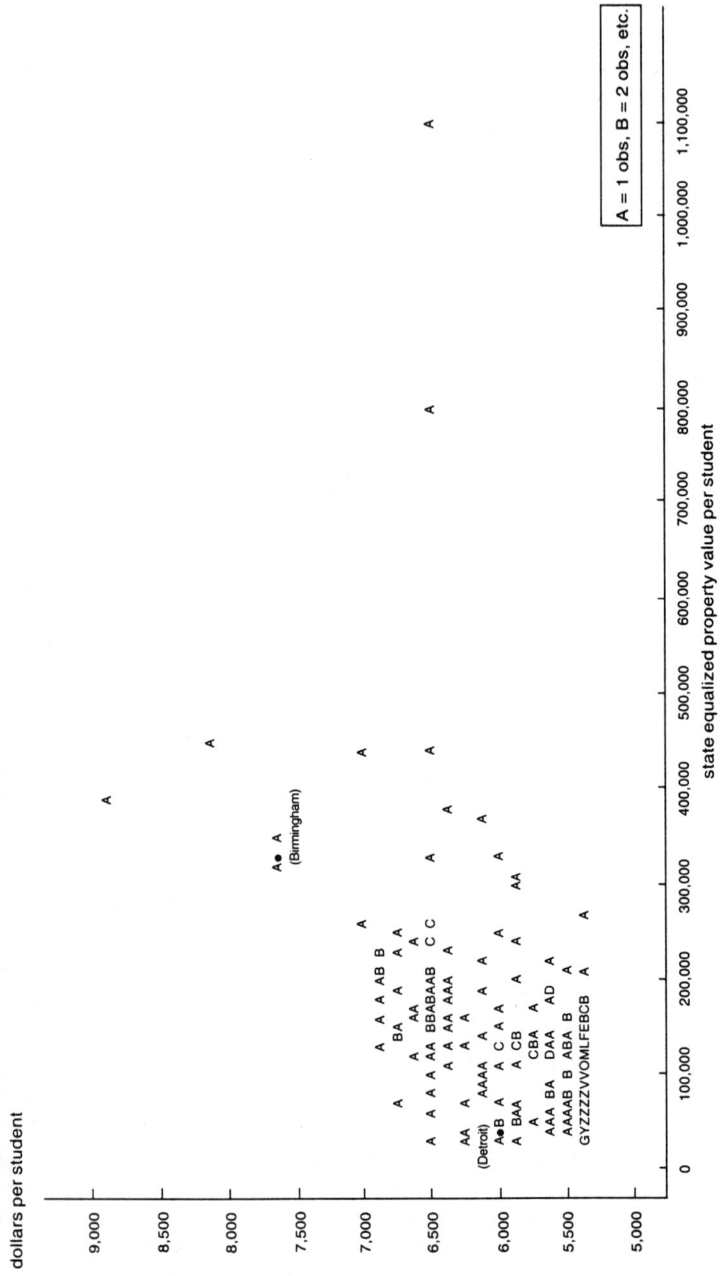

dollars per student

state equalized property value per student

A = 1 obs, B = 2 obs, etc.

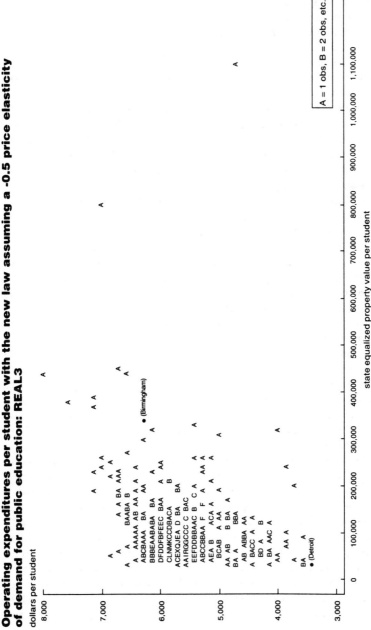

FIGURE 7

Operating expenditures per student with the new law assuming a -0.5 price elasticity of demand for public education: REAL3

or the same amount as the current formula dictates. There is also a serious question of where the remaining money will come from. In 1994-95, it comes largely from accumulated surplus. That source will be exhausted by next fiscal year. In the current political climate, it is virtually unthinkable that taxes will be raised; the unidentified revenue needed to fund the formula amounts to about $1.5 billion or 18.0 percent of all state spending on K-12 activities and 13 percent of state spending on other activities that are supported with state raised revenues.

Suppose that over time the state does have difficulty coming up with the funds necessary to make the new formula work. The law allows for many alternative legislative actions—the basic grant could grow by less than SAFI, the differential could grow less than even the nominal amounts, or the state-mandated millages could rise. At this point it is hard to predict the response. This is one of the many open-ended dynamic issues of the new legislation.

In California, which preceded Michigan by fifteen years in going to a foundation plan for financing elementary and secondary education, Silva and Sonstelie (1993) have observed that per pupil education spending rose much less rapidly than in the rest of the country. Silva and Sonstelie provide a social choice argument for the relative decline in California spending that depends mostly on the fact that a uniform foundation plan forces high-income taxpayers off their demand curves for public education. Prior to the *Serrano* decision, which mandated uniform spending per pupil across the state, high-income people tended to cluster together (leaving low-income people clustered, as well) and chose to purchase relatively high amounts of education, because the income elasticity of demand for education is high. With perfect income sorting, the average level of education expense in the state would be equal to the amount demanded by a household with average income. All households, according to the Tiebout mechanism, would be (approximately) on their demand curves. When disparate California school districts were effectively merged into one district with common financing, people were forced off their demand curves.

Silva-Sonstelie make the usual assumption that the amount of education spending will be determined by the median voter, in a statewide system. In California, as everywhere, the median of the income distribution is below the mean, because there is a long upper tail of the income distribution. Thus, for the median-income household, assumed to be the decisive voter, income will be lower than the old average, but the tax-price of education will also be lower.[25] In principle, the net of lower income and lower prices could lead demand to go either way, but in practice the income effect is stronger in the Silva-Sonstelie analysis. This is not surprising—it is well established that the income elasticity of demand for education is greater in absolute value than the price elasticity. Silva-Sonstelie find that this fairly straightforward social choice model accounts for about half of the decline in spending per pupil in California relative to other states over the past 20 years. Silva and Sonstelie did not make the point, but they might have added that the loss of local control of financing might have tended to move things in the same direction and that this effect could have worked for both rich and poor districts.

While the Silva-Sonstelie prediction could come true in Michigan, there is a key difference between the Michigan and California reforms. The Michigan reform preserves a great deal of the existing inequality in spending per pupil, especially at the upper end of the spending distribution. This greatly weakens the Silva-Sonstelie mechanism. Still, it remains interesting to ask what is likely to happen to the basic foundation level, given the rules that permit ongoing inequality of spending in Michigan. In the standard model, the educational demand of the statewide median voter is determined, not for a uniform level of education spending, as in California, but for the *minimum* level, the basic foundation grant, recognizing that under the current Michigan formula, all districts receive, dollar for dollar, any increases (or lose, dollar for dollar, any reductions) in the basic foundation allowance. Thus, quite unlike the California situation, the choice facing voters at the margin is whether they want to increase or decrease their current (as of when the law is fully phased in, and other behavioral adjustments made) levels of spending, via the foundation grant. We have not attempted to model this social choice process. We note one further implication is that school millages were decided in local elections with low turnouts whereas the basic foundation allowance will be set by the state government which is elected by a larger, on average, different voter population.

The formula itself

There could be even more radical change. The key parameters of the Michigan system post-reform are the basic foundation allowance and the "frozen" differences among the middle group of districts. Plainly, poorer districts would like the basic foundation grant to be high, but low enough so that the median voter wants to stay in the system, rather than return to a system of local finance. The inflexible nature of interdistrict differences will surely lead to political problems. In the short run, everyone is getting about what they got last year, although, generally, if districts were on their demand curves they are now off, incomes and tax prices both having changed as a result of the reforms. Thus, there will be immediate pressure, we expect, for districts to have some flexibility at the margin—either to raise spending with locally raised revenue or to cut spending, cut local taxes, and keep the change, depending on the circumstances of individual districts. Over time, as some districts get richer and others poorer, this pressure will get stronger. Districts with rising income will want to increase real spending, and, under the current formula, will not be allowed to. This will lead to pressure for changing the formula. To the extent that these pressures induce the legislature to permit local financing at the margin, the basic foundation system itself could tend to unravel.

Charter schools

There is one important wild card in all of this—charter schools. Michigan's charter school provisions allow considerable potential for publicly supported schools of choice within Michigan districts. The charter school provision is similar to a within public school voucher system. Private groups can be authorized to set up charter schools and accept students, with a maximum state grant of $5,500 pupil[26] (and no local supplementation funds) transferred from the public schools to the charter schools. Charter schools would not be allowed to supplement these funds on their own.[27] The charter schools would have to obey all the state curriculum and testing requirements placed on other schools, and, according to the Michigan constitution, the charter schools could not be religious schools. The charter schools would have some limited ability to hire noncertified teachers, though this provision may be tested in court. While charter schools can determine their own capacity, if over-subscribed they must accept students at random from their application lists to prevent racial or income segregation.

The Michigan legislation lets four different groups authorize and sponsor charter schools—the state department of education, the local school boards, the intermediate school districts, and the state public universities. In the early going, the state public universities seem to be the main authorizing body—approximately ten charter schools opened in Michigan in September 1994, nearly all of which have a state public university as an authorizing body. On the other hand, only a handful of state public universities have gotten into the charter school business. In the short run, it is costly for universities to set up separate groups to authorize charter schools, and not all questions of legal liability have been worked out.[28]

If one were to do an evaluation of the charter school provisions after enough time had passed, one would first look into the supply conditions—how many charter schools open in what areas, offering what programs, and at what cost? Since it is cheaper to teach elementary than secondary student pupils, and the reimbursement schedule is on a flat per pupil basis, we might expect there to be more charter elementary schools than secondary schools. If the charter elementary schools are successful, we expect that this might lead to pressure to increase the charter school grant so that students could move on to charter high schools.

Evaluation of charter schools should also include a quasi-experimental comparison of students in charter schools with students in the normal public schools. Since charter schools must admit students at random if oversubscribed, such studies may be able to avoid some of the usual selection bias. In addition, given both the new and previously existing testing requirements in Michigan, there should be rich enough test data to do meaningful comparisons.

Charter schools respond to longstanding claims by advocates of school choice that money is not enough (Hanushek and Chubb 1990). They also raise a host of potential problems—will the separation of church and state be maintained, will they be truly integrated along racial and income lines, will they be more effective teachers than the normal public schools, will they be drowned in legal-contractual problems? In the case of Michigan, charter schools may also change the nature of the education debate. For years, Michigan legislators, educators, and policy analysts have been debating educational reform as if financial reform were the only issue. Now that financial reform has been more or less addressed, at least for a time, and the system has been opened up to permit competition among publicly supported schools, perhaps the discussion will turn to the content of education and how to make schools more effective. The questions raised by charter schools may both stimulate and focus this discussion.

Other economic effects of the reforms

The finance reforms change the incidence of the state tax system in complicated ways. We choose not to go into detail here in characterizing the changes, but we will briefly address two issues. One issue that figured prominently in the governor's rhetoric when he spoke in favor of the reforms was the question of incentives to business location. In this area, the reforms will probably have only modest effect on interstate business-location decisions, although they clearly reduce the amount of intrastate variation in taxes that would affect the spatial allocation of business capital.

Interstate effects will be small for a simple reason. Under the old regime, as under the new, it was easy for industrial facilities to obtain a 50 percent property tax abatement, lasting for twelve years. The abatements were granted by the local city council, but it applied to all local taxing jurisdictions, including school districts. In other work in progress, Carolyn Fischer and Paul Courant have estimated that about half of all potentially eligible capital obtained these abatements. Presumably, the other half found some benefit in locating in places without abatements. Consider a school district that levied 32 mills, approximately the average millage, for school operating expenditures. Under the old system, if the district offered abatements, new capital would pay 16 mills. Under the new system, local taxes for schools are reduced to 18 mills, which might be abated to 9; the state levies 6 mills, which it probably will not abate. The total is again 15, essentially no change. Districts in jurisdictions that offered abatements but that levied less than 30 mills for school operations could see an increase in effective tax rates on capital. Those with higher millages will see a decrease. But, overall, the effects appear to be small.[29]

Overall the interstate effects look small, but the uniform local tax plus state tax of 18 plus 6 mills will greatly reduce intrastate variation in tax rates on industrial capital. Jurisdictions that abate will charge, effectively, 15 mills. Those that do not abate will charge 24 mills. The range is truncated at both ends, relative to the old law.

A second issue involves the well-known concept that taxes on mobile capital exceeding the level consistent with benefit taxation must fall on immobile factors. Arguably, local schools are not of much direct benefit to mobile capital, so the taxes on mobile capital in the new law are probably too high. Even to the extent that good schools encourage firms to recruit employees who value good schools, there are important spillover effects across jurisdictions. The schools in a high-income suburb can be good, even as the schools across the street from the factory are not. From this perspective, by cutting taxes on homesteads to six mills while mandating 24 mills for businesses, the Michigan reforms got it exactly backwards.

Conclusion

At this point it is still early to evaluate the effects of the far reaching educational reforms in Michigan. These reforms substantially changed the structure of school financing in Michigan moving it away from local-level financing to a system of primarily state-level financing and from a modified power equalization system to a modified foundation grant system. In doing this, the reforms seem likely to reduce the variance in education spending, both by increasing the revenues of low-spending districts and by decreasing the spending of richer districts. By substituting slowly growing state taxes for local taxes, they may reduce overall state spending on education in the long run, as seems to have happened in California. However, unlike California's foundation grant system, the Michigan system preserves substantial interdistrict variation in school financing which both allowed the law to be politically feasible and may reduce the extent to which overall school spending is reduced.

The rigidity built into the system could lead to problems. Assuming districts were on their demand curve for education under the old system, under the new system, they are off. Thus, there could be pressure from these districts to have more flexibility in their school funding. This pressure should increase as district wealth changes over time and seems likely to lead to revisions in the structure of the new law. Yet, the new system, by decreasing the inequality in educational expenditures across Michigan and replacing much local funding with state funding, still should create a much more equitable system of school financing for Michigan students. The final passing of a finance reform bill after 20 years of attempts, along with the introduction of charter schools, also may help to refocus the education debate away from finance on to questions of effective schools.

Notes

[1] U.S. Department of Education, National Center for Education Statistics, *Common Core of Data Survey.*

[2] The Headlee Amendment requires that local governments, including school districts, roll back millages when property values rise by more than the Consumer Price Index (CPI), so that spending can increase only at the rate of inflation unless there is a specific vote to authorize more rapid increases.

[3] The governor and the Republicans had proposed a 20 percent cut in property taxes, with the revenue shortfall to be made up with vaguely specified cuts in other spending and increases in taxes. A prominent Democrat in the Senate (Senator Debbie Stabenow) made what appeared to be a rhetorical proposal that if 20 percent was a good cut, 100 percent would be better. Her proposal passed, with minimal debate and bipartisan support, in one day, leaving the legislature, according to the newsmagazine *The Economist,* in the position of having jumped out of an airplane with the hope that it would be able to stitch together a parachute before it hit the ground.

[4] Although the *New York Times* and other national media characterized the March vote as substituting sales taxes for property taxes, this was quite inaccurate. The local property tax was abolished in the summer of 1993, nearly a year before the ballot proposal came to voters. Voters chose between two financing systems, both of which replaced a hefty amount of the abolished local property taxes with other, mainly state, property taxes. The major difference in the financing schemes involved about a third of the total revenue involved, and the choice there was between an income tax increase and a sales tax increase.

[5] Districts may choose not to levy this tax, which must be 18 mills or the 1993-94 millage rate, whichever is less. However, there is no alternative source of local revenue available to districts that do not levy the 18 mills. The millage must be approved by voters. Currently, all but one district have approved the millage. The one district that did not initially approve the 18 mills has a re-vote scheduled.

[6] In fact, almost all of the of revenues that will be raised at the local level are accounted for by the 18 mills on non-homestead property. Because of this, 21 percent overestimates the role of local decisionmaking in school funding issues under the new system.

[7] We are unsure whether those richer districts that raise additional funds through local homestead property taxes are required to return to the taxpayers the local revenue for students who choose to attend charter schools. Since millage rates are voted on before actual per pupil counts can be taken, the student population used to set an allowed millage rate for richer districts are estimates. Districts may gain or lose funding as a result of inaccuracies in these estimates.

[8] These and other facts about school finance in Michigan came from Philip C. Kearney, *A Primer on Michigan School Finance*, University of Michigan (1994), an extremely useful and much more detailed description of the new system.

[9] The relationship of this index (57 percent of which is sales taxes, 15 percent of which is property taxes, and a bit over 12 percent of which is income taxes) to growth in prices and real income is discussed later in the paper.

[10] All districts will be brought up to at least $4,200 in 1994-95. After that, districts that are between $4,200 and $5,000 will have their per pupil spending increase at a considerably greater rate than the basic foundation allowance itself, until all districts reach at least the basic foundation allowance.

[11] Under the formula, the lowest-revenue districts get an increase of $250 and the highest-revenue districts are permitted to increase spending by $160 per pupil. Any district spending more than $6,500 in 1994-95 must raise local revenue to cover the amount in excess of $6,500.

[12] For example, if district A spends $5,780 in 1994-95, district B spends $6,430, and the proportionate increase in SAFI times $5,000 is $180, district A will receive a grant from the state of $5,960, and district B will receive $6,610 for 1995-96.

[13] School district revenues come from a combination of state funds and the 18 mill local tax on non-homestead property. The state finances districts so that this combined revenue reaches the levels specified by the new law.

[14] Districts that are allowed to spend more than $6,500 in 1994-95 must tax homesteads (principal residents of owner-occupants) up to the point where the local tax on homesteads reaches 18 mills, which is the mandatory tax on non-homestead property. If a homestead millage of 18 mills or less does not raise all the revenue that is both permitted and desired by local voters, the district may tax all property more, at a uniform rate. But, no district may ever spend more than twice the basic foundation allowance.

[15] There is more flexibility to the program than we have suggested. Districts are allowed to levy an enhancement millage of 3 mills, and spend that locally raised money, until 1996-97. After that, they can still vote enhancement mills, but these must be redistributed across the relevant intermediate school district (usually a county, and always much larger than a local school district), implying a form of regional tax-base sharing. In any case, the amount of local control over spending levels, for the vast majority of school districts, is very small.

[16] District-level information on Michigan schools comes from *The Integrated Database on Michigan Education*, a resource of the School of Education, University of Michigan.

[17] Following Bradford, Malt, and Oates (1969) income could also be a negative indicator of cost. We do not deal with this possibility here.

[18] The means used are means of districts, not of students. Student means are higher than districts means.

[19] See Rosen (1988), p. 94. Real1 invokes the implicit assumption that the elasticity is zero; therefore, Real3 and Real1 bound the plausible range of effects.

[20] Table 4 shows the distribution of spending with district sizes weighted by number of pupils. For Real3 and Real4, adjusting for costs has little effect on the distributions. We think that the reason for this is that, under those measures, Detroit has very low real spending, and hence leads to a large weight at the low end of the distribution, increasing the variance in real spending across pupils. Thus, under Real3 and Real4 different districts' places in the distribution change greatly, while the summary statistics overall are fairly stable.

[21] The difference between entirely and "almost entirely" is the optional 3 mill enhancement that may be levied at the district level, though revenues must be shared with the entire intermediate school districts to which the levying district belongs.

32

[22] Estimates of student population growth come from *Enrollment Projects for Michigan Public School Based on 1982-83 through 1992-93 Membership Data*, prepared by Frederick R. Ignatovich, Department of Educational Administration, College of Education, Michigan State University. Since estimates of kindergarten and first grade enrollment were not given for 1999-2000, the year in question, we substituted the 1998-99 estimate for first grade and the 1997-98 estimate for kindergarten in our calculations.

[23] The elasticity implies that the foundation grant would grow at 4.8 percent in nominal terms and 2.2 percent in real terms if the size of the student population remained the same. Including the predicted growth in numbers of students, the foundation grant should grow at 1.5 percent in real per student terms.

[24] This assumes that homeowners believe that non-homestead property does not change in response to changes in tax rates. For sophisticated voters the perceived change in tax price will be smaller, because they will recognize that taxes levied on mobile capital, before and after the reforms, fall on immobile factors.

[25] Taxes are roughly proportional to income, and the median voter has below-average income. With uniform spending per pupil, then, this voter pays less than her or his share of all spending. In a Tiebout world, each person would pay about his or her share of spending in a district. This would be true of districts containing median-income people, so their tax price will have fallen.

[26] The $5,500 is indexed by the same dollar amount as the $5,000 basic foundation allowance. In districts that spend less than $5,500 in 1994-95, the charter schools would receive the same as district spending per pupil.

[27] Downes (1992) points out that richer districts in California got around the *Serrano* rules, at least to some degree, by private supplementing of the uniform public spending amount and using various schemes to raise non-tax revenue. Although charter schools are not allowed to charge tuition, it is hard to see how they can be prevented from having bake sales, accepting donations, and doing the other things that public schools do to raise extra resources.

[28] One charter school received a considerable amount of attention (*The Wall Street Journal*, September 16, 1994). The Noah Webster Academy—authorized by a financially struggling district with a two-room elementary school, 20 students, and one teacher—planned to install an advanced computer network for instruction, an unusual combination of advanced technology and potentially fundamentalist religious beliefs. It has attracted 2,000 students, primarily home schooled, drawing in approximately $11 million of state money from per pupil foundation grants. The American Civil Liberties Union and Michigan's largest teachers' union then sued successfully to block funding for Noah Webster and unsuccessfully to have the entire state charter law ruled invalid.

[29] Under the new aid formula the state will pay the full cost of abatements for schools. However, the other elements of local government will still incur costs when abatements are granted.

References

Bradford, David, Richard Malt, and Wallace Oates, "The rising cost of local public services: Some evidence and reflections," *National Tax Journal*, Vol. 22, June 1969, pp. 185-202.

Congressional Budget Office, *The Economic and Budget Outlook: Fiscal Years 1995-1999*, 1994, summary table 2.

Downes, Thomas A., "Evaluating the impact of school finance reform on the provision of public education: The California case," *National Tax Journal*, Vol. 45, December 1992, pp. 405-419.

Downes, Thomas A., and Thomas F. Pogue, "Adjusting school aid formulas for the higher cost of educating disadvantaged students," *National Tax Journal*, Vol. 47, March 1994, pp. 89-110.

Hanushek, Eric A., and John E. Chubb, "Reforming educational reform," in *Setting National Priorites*, H. Aaron (ed.), Washington, DC: Brookings Institution, 1990, pp. 213-248.

Ignatovich, Frederick R., *Enrollment Projects for Michigan Public Schools Based on 1982-83 through 1992-93 Membership Date,* Lansing, MI: Michigan State University, College of Education, Department of Educational Administration, 1994.

Kearney, Philip C., *A Primer on Michigan School Finance*, Ann Arbor: University of Michigan, 1994.

Ratcliffe, Kerri, Bruce Riddle, and John Yinger, "The fiscal condition of school districts in Nebraska: Is small beautiful?" *Economics of Education Review*, Vol. 9, No. 1, 1990, pp. 81-99.

Reschovsky, Andrew, "Fiscal equalization and school finance," *National Tax Journal*, Vol. 47, March 1994, pp. 185-197.

Rosen, Harvey S., *Public Finance*, Homewood, IL: Irwin, 1988.

Rothstein, Paul, "The demand for education with 'power equalizing' aid: Estimation and simulation," *Journal of Public Economics*, Vol. 49, 1992, pp. 135-162.

Silva, Fabio, and Jon Sonstelie, "Did *Serrano* cause a decline in school spending?" University of California at Santa Barbara, mimeo, 1993.

Stecklow, Steve, "Acadamy in Michigan severely tests the idea of 'charter' schools," *The Wall Street Journal*, September 16, 1994, p. A1.

[18]

Reforming U.S. Federal Fiscal Arrangements

Edward M. Gramlich

Economists have written any number of articles calling for tax and expenditure reform. There have been briefs for reforming the income tax, integrating it with the corporate tax, switching to a consumption tax, moving away from or toward a more progressive rate structure. There have been just as many normative treatises about expenditures—arguing for constitutional limits on total expenditures, reforming the social insurance trust funds, replacing certain expenditures with negative income taxes or vouchers. In a discipline that is alleged to emphasize the positive over the normative, public finance economists have certainly bucked the trend.

But not in one area. In contrast to many other developed countries, the United States has a very decentralized system of fiscal relationships. Over $180 billion is given as intergovernmental grants from higher to lower levels of government, and many promising revenue sources are left completely to local governments. These arrangements, loosely termed a fiscal federalism system, have not received much normative, reformist attention from economists. Politicians have certainly become aware of the potential of the federalism issue, and presidents Nixon and Reagan have both advanced well-publicized reform proposals.[1] The quasi-governmental Advisory Commission on Intergovernmental Relations (ACIR) has noticed the system and has its own reform proposals.[2] Economists have done a multitude of theoretical and empirical studies on various aspects of federalism, trying to determine optimal governmental arrangements, predicting the effects of grants or taxes, estimating the degree to which fiscal decisions are "capitalized" into property values, and the like. Unlike studies of other aspects of public finance, however, these analyses have not provided very pointed statements of what is wrong with the present federal arrangements and how they might be changed to further various goals.[3] In this paper I try to come up with such a statement.

There are obvious risks in such an attempt—one person's item to be reformed may be another person's ideal. And the theoretical basis for many of these supposed improvements is, as always, in doubt. However, a number of aspects of the present United States federal system seem unlikely to appeal either to those economists who worry primarily about efficiency or to those who worry primarily about equity. For all the positive papers analyzing the empirical impact of federalism, most of these features have not gotten the criticism they deserve from economists.

Two apologies are necessary at the outset. One is that a complete discussion of all aspects of federalism in need of major or minor reform would require a lengthy treatise. There have been two very extensive reviews of federal theory and present-day arrangements in the past decade—by Oates (1972) and Break (1980). Obviously, in one paper I cannot cover all the ground covered by these books and by countless shorter articles. I am forced to be selective both in choice of topics and in the treatment of arguments bearing on the topics. Readers desiring a more comprehensive, and undoubtedly more balanced, discussion can refer to these earlier sources. I must also mention that none of the items I single out for reform is original. I have made a stronger case for many of these measures than is typically found in the literature, but I am certainly not the first to use the relevant arguments.

The second apology is for the omission of a topic that should be fundamental to any discussion of fiscal federalism—that of reforming the structure of governments themselves. The United States has an extremely eclectic structure, with strong historical roots. Some states are large and diverse, others are small; some states conduct extensive expenditure operations of their own, other states leave these operations to localities or special districts; in some areas cities and counties overlap, in others they do not; in some areas special districts are organized to conduct functions, in others they are not; in some areas there is freedom for cities to annex suburbs, in other areas there is not. In all areas it is quite difficult to change whatever arrangements do exist. Economists such as Buchanan (1965) have developed some theories for understanding these arrangements, but there is as yet a wide gap between these theories and their practical applications. I do not even try to fill the gap here, but—as will become apparent—the optimality or lack of optimality of a set of budget-ary arrangements among existing governments depends very much on the existing structures. The two questions should ideally be studied simulta-neously, not separately.

THE THEORY OF FEDERALISM
AND THE UNITED STATES SYSTEM:
THE MUSGRAVE TRICHOTOMY

Twenty-five years ago Musgrave (1959) advanced his now-famous tri-chotomy that divided governmental functions into their allocation, distri-bution, and stabilization components. The Musgrave trichotomy is not always very helpful in making particular decisions—almost every tax has both allocative and distributional implications, and most expenditures do too, but it serves a useful function as an organizing device in the area of federalism.

ALLOCATION

Two separate traditions apply to public spending decisions within a federal system. Tiebout (1956) proposed a consumer choice model, ac-cording to which rational consumers would select a jurisdiction, and its menu of public goods, that would maximize consumer utility. Jurisdic-tions would then be led to provide the optimal menu; if not, residents would move to other jurisdictions until utility was maximized.

The second tradition follows Breton's (1965) notion of "perfect map-ping" of jurisdictions. According to this notion, jurisdictional boundaries would be set to include only that set of individuals who obtain benefits from the relevant public good. In principle there could be as many juris-dictions as public goods, though in later work Breton and Scott (1978) rationalized a lesser number of jurisdictions by taking into account the costs of organizing and coordinating jurisdictions, and the costs to con-sumers of relocating.

These two traditions have been combined in various ways by various authors. Oates (1972) showed how jurisdiction size can be determined by the balance between two competing forces—the welfare loss from taste differences, which would argue for small jurisdictions, and the welfare gain from benefit spillovers, which would argue for large jurisdictions. His "decentralization theorem" called for public goods to be provided by the jurisdiction covering the smallest area over which benefits are distributed, so that public goods efficiencies are maximized and the effect of taste differences minimized. Breton and Scott worked out a more general theory of public goods benefits and organizational costs, but they did not formulate any general theorems, on the grounds that it might always be possible to reduce total costs by various kinds of intergovernmental transfers. Atkinson and Stiglitz (1980) built a series of models that included mobility, changes in the marginal product of labor as labor crowds into a jurisdiction, and income differences. The "results" they got were again very agnostic. Sometimes large jurisdictions were appropriate, sometimes small; sometimes there was a stable local public-goods equilibrium, sometimes not.

In light of this theoretical indeterminacy, it is no wonder that little progress has been made in attempting to determine which levels of government should provide what public services for allocation reasons. It is first necessary to adopt what seem to be reasonable simplifying assumptions and then derive the implications of the relevant model. A plausible set of such assumptions might be that organizing any new government is expensive, that mobility is costly, that changes in the marginal product of labor are small, and that income differences can be ignored (so as to focus only on considerations of efficiency). In this case one is led to the pragmatic conclusion that allocation responsibility for providing public services should be meted out to jurisdictions in accordance with Oates' decentralization theorem. But one should recognize that this conclusion is rather specialized and pertains at best only to marginal changes in the administrative structure and the pattern of production.

Turning to the actual numbers, the distribution of expenditures by function and level of government (Table 2.1) seems more or less in accord with the decentralization theorem. Those expenditures that appear to provide benefits over a wide area—national defense and energy—are conducted almost exclusively at the national level. Those that appear to provide benefits over a narrow area—elementary and secondary education and civilian safety—are carried out at the local level.[4]

The one mystery in this type of analysis involves state governments. These governments make 60 percent of all government purchases at the national or the local level, but it is not clear what public services convey benefits over as large an area as that covered by most states. I will argue below that at least some of the types of expenditure made by state governments—purchases and transfers for income support and health and hospitals—are better left to other levels of government.

Of the remaining state purchases, transportation is probably the one

TABLE 2.1

Government Expenditures by Functional Level, 1981 (billions of current dollars)

Function	Federal Government			State Governments			Local Governments	
	Purchases	Transfer, interest, subsidy	Grants	Purchases	Transfer, interest, subsidy	Grants	Purchases	Transfer, interest, subsidy
Defense & veterans	$169.3	$ 20.2	$ 1.4	—	—	—	—	—
Civilian safety	2.1	—	0.2	$ 7.1	—	$ 0.6	$ 21.7	—
Education	1.4	6.0	7.9	33.8	$ 2.5	62.2	116.8	—
Health & hospitals	5.9	0.7	3.4	18.5	0.1	2.2	19.3	—
Income support	5.2	258.2	39.9	32.4	11.1	10.8	7.3	$ 9.0
Housing & community service	0.4	6.4	8.2	0.9	0.4	0.8	13.3	-3.5
Recreation & culture	1.2	0.4	0.3	1.2	—	—	5.5	—
Energy & utilities	11.1	-1.4	1.1	0.4	-0.2	—	2.6	-2.5
Agriculture	6.7	4.9	0.8	2.0	—	—	—	—
Natural resources	4.9	—	1.1	2.0	—	0.7	1.3	—
Transportation	6.5	2.3	11.7	17.7	0.9	4.6	15.1	0.2
Post office	0.5	0.9	—	—	—	—	—	—
Economic development	1.7	-0.1	0.9	1.9	—	—	1.0	—
Labor training	1.6	0.6	5.9	3.0	0.6	—	—	1.0
Commercial activities	—	—	—	—	-1.9	—	0.1	0.2
General purpose	10.5	73.1	5.0	17.0	-2.2	11.5	25.8	1.5
Total[a]	229.2	372.2	87.9	138.0	11.2	93.4	230.0	5.9

[a]Because of rounding, details may not add to total.
SOURCE: "The U.S. National Income and Product Accounts," *Survey of Current Business*, July, 1983, table 3.16; and Levin (1983).

public service that does have natural statewide benefits, through the geographical linking of road networks. Education, specifically purchases for higher education by state university systems, may also give benefits statewide, but these benefits do not seem as "natural," since they are strongly influenced by the tuition and admissions policies followed by the state universities. Most such universities offer a large tuition reduction and perhaps relaxed admissions standards to in-state students and then find, unsurprisingly, that in-state students attend in very high numbers. One could argue that the benefits are statewide, but that begs the deeper question of whether the tuition reduction should have been granted in the first place.

To make one suggestive test of the degree of intrinsic statewide benefits, I examined data on University of Michigan (UM) freshmen accepted for admission. The results of this test, in the form of a logit regression explaining students' acceptance probabilities, are given in Table 2.2. They show that once the tuition differential has been eliminated, the probability that in-state residents who were accepted for admission will attend UM is no higher than for the accepted out-of-state residents. That sounds like an example of an unnatural statewide benefit.

DISTRIBUTION

For this governmental function, the basic theoretical analysis was done by Pauly (1973). The Pauly model determines income distribution by the interdependent utilities of individuals—higher living standards for poor transfer recipients make richer taxpayers better off. In most of his cases Pauly arrives at conclusions close to those of the decentralization theorem—that distributional policies should generally be determined by lower levels of government. Two very strong assumptions must be made to arrive at the result, however, and those assumptions are open to question.

The first assumption involves the geographical linking of utilities. The Pauly model assumes that the welfare of donors can be improved only by raising living standards in the donors' own jurisdictions, as if donors are affected by the sight of, and externalities attendant on, poor people. Some survey evidence analyzed by Ladd and Doolittle (1982) sheds doubt on this assumption. Ladd and Doolittle find that an overwhelming majority of respondents to two separate ACIR polls (1981)—respondents who are assumed to be like those who would ordinarily pay for redistribution programs—believe that the national government should retain an impor-

TABLE 2.2

Probability of Attendance as Freshman of Residents (No Alumni/ae Relatives)
Accepted by the University of Michigan, 1981

Academic ability percentile (%)	Parent's income above median?	Differential tuition reduction ($)	Probability of attending (%)	Estimated probability of attending without differential tuition reduction (%)*	Probability of nonresident attending
Top 25	yes	$2640	53%	27%	18%
Top 25	no	3090	46	21	20
Next 25	yes	3260	55	28	28
Next 25	no	3130	54	28	28
Bottom 50	yes	3370	61	35	37
Bottom 50	no	3170	59	32	41

*From a logit regression
SOURCE: "Report of the Task Force on Undergraduate Student Aid," University of Michigan, 1984, mimeo.

tant role in supporting needy people. Ladd and Doolittle interpret these results as implying that poor people throughout the nation ought to be the beneficiaries of income support programs, as if donors' preference functions contain no state-line distinction.

The other assumption involves the potential migration of beneficiaries. Even if particular states wanted to be generous, they would not be able to be if prospective beneficiaries of transfer programs were highly mobile. Mobility would raise the tax price of redistribution in all states and would prevent states from following the basic redistribution choices of their donors, for fear of attracting hordes of welfare recipients. The prevailing view seems to be that migration is not, practically speaking, a problem, because only 1 or 2 percent of transfer recipients make interstate moves in a year (see Holmer 1975). But this view is belied by transition matrix calculations given in Table 2.3 which indicate that when transfer recipients (most of whom are not working) do move, they are much more likely to move to states with more generous income-support systems. In the long run, even the low degree of mobility pointed to in the prevailing view can lead to major population shifts among the beneficiary population, as is shown in Table 2.3. This evidence provides another argument for retaining some national interest in income redistribution policies.

But it is not obvious how the national interest should be retained. Tresch (1981) views the federal aspect of redistribution policy as an either/or choice: either the national government would determine an income distribution, or a lower government would. For various reasons he favors having lower governments make the determination, and this leads him to advance a hierarchical redistribution plan. Under this plan, the national government would redistribute income among states, the states among localities, and the localities among households. Legislators at any level could vote for as much or as little redistribution as they wanted. Migration of beneficiaries and positive taxpayers alike could be stabilizing in such a system, if generous localities were entitled to greater transfers from higher levels of governments when low-income families immigrated and high-income families emigrated. But if migration were costly, this system would represent the national interest no better than a fully decentralized system, because there would be no way for national legislators representing national preferences to insure that low-income people were taken care of in particular states. Moreover, even if migration were not costly, the outcome might be socially undesirable, because it could lead to extreme differences in state and local incomes.

An alternative view is taken by Boadway and Wildasin (1984). They

TABLE 2.3

Transition Probabilities, Panel Survey of Income Dynamics (PSID) and the Decennial Census, 1970–1980

Individual characteristic	Number	Transition probabilities[a]				Initial share of AFDC or unemployment in high AFDC or unemployment state	Ultimate share[b]	Half-life (years)[c]
		High AFDC or unemployment state in t		Low AFDC or unemployment state in t				
		p_{11}	p_{12}	p_{21}	p_{22}			
AFDC recipients[d]	1220	.975	.025	.034	.966	.446	.572	45
Most unemployed workers[e]	2722	.986	.014	.018	.982	.583	.563	21
Long term unemployed[f]	525	.973	.027	.016	.984	.634	.372	16

[a] Five-year transition probabilities for AFDC recipients; one year for unemployed workers.
[b] The steady-state distribution of the relevant population, given the transition matrix. Let x be the equilibrium share of the population residing in high AFDC (unemployment) states. Then $x(1-p_{12}) + (1-x)p_{21} = x$, or $x = p_{21}/(p_{12} + p_{21})$.
[c] The length of time it takes for repeated multiplications by the transition matrix to give x halfway between its postulated initial value and its computed ultimate value.
[d] Non-aged female family heads receiving AFDC in period $t + 1$. Data from PSID and the Census are aggregated.
[e] Non-aged male family heads in the labor force with more than 170 hours (one-twelfth of a year) of unemployment, from PSID.
[f] Non-aged male family heads in the labor force with more than 1040 hours (one-half of a year) of unemployment, from PSID.
SOURCES: First row, Gramlich and Laren (1984), tables 4, 5. Other rows, Gramlich (1984), table 1.

Reforming U.S. Federal Fiscal Arrangements   43

do not see the national-subnational question as an either/or choice but, rather, analyze the question as a matter of benefit spillovers, where the spillover represents both the fact that donors may care about recipients from all states and the fact that when one state raises support levels and attracts migrants, other states benefit. In this logic, taxpayers outside the jurisdiction are willing to contribute to support levels in the jurisdiction, and the appropriate policy would be to allow subnational units to set support levels, partly financed by open-ended matching grants from the federal government. That, as it happens, is close to the present arrangement used in the United States for two of the main general programs for redistributing income, Aid to Families with Dependent Children (AFDC) and Medicaid. Both programs contain the added stipulation that the matching rates are more favorable for low-income states. The third main general redistribution program, food stamps, is a national program with minimum nationwide support levels.[5]

While the structure of income support programs receives extensive criticism, the Boadway–Wildasin analysis suggests that it is not so obviously in need of repair. I disagree. In the Appendix I give an analysis that shows, first, that any inefficiencies caused by migration spillovers are small, and, second, that present matching grants greatly over-correct for these inefficiencies. Yet even with these overly generous matching grants, AFDC support levels are extremely low in the states of residence of slightly more than half of AFDC beneficiaries. The basic reason is that voters in these low-benefit states appear to have little taste for redistribution, as is readily inferred from their low benefit levels in spite of generous federal matching and upward pressure from the higher support levels in other states.

That leads me to a somewhat paternalistic position, carefully spelled out in the Appendix. I would like to see a uniform national minimum standard somewhere near the level that now obtains in the states of residence of slightly less than half of the AFDC beneficiaries, roughly the Health and Human Services poverty living standard. Certainly this minimum standard could be supplemented by states, and perhaps there should even be a slight federal match for supplementation. My reason for desiring minimum standards is the simple one that I am bothered by the fact that support levels in states paying low benefits are so low. Given the numbers, there is no reasonable way to raise these support levels substantially with Boadway–Wildasin-type matching grants, and no reasonable way to justify national standards by resorting to migration inefficiencies.

STABILIZATION

The prevailing view as of a decade ago was that national governments should try to stabilize the economy by manipulating taxes and expenditures; subnational governments should not attempt to do so. Over the past decade the first statement has come under a series of withering attacks: the criticism of Mundell (1963) and Fleming (1964) that with flexible exchange rates, foreign capital flows will automatically crowd out fiscal changes; the criticism of Lucas (1972) and Sargent and Wallace (1975) that flexible prices and rational expectations render ineffective any systematic macro-policy changes; the criticism of Barro (1974) that households with long horizons expect to pay the cost of government at some point in history, and hence that the actual timing of tax liabilities (and the split between debt and taxes) has no impact on consumption. There are still unreconstructed Keynesians around (like me), but the faith in activist fiscal policy is substantially less than in former times.

Even in the fiscal activist's heyday, Oates (1972) was arguing that subnational fiscal policies were pointless. In part, his argument was based on the belief that national stabilizing fiscal policies presented a realistic alternative to subnational fiscal policy—now not so readily accepted. In part, the argument was based on a belief that the debt of subnational governments was external and that of national governments internal—a distinction now viewed as obsolete. To the extent that debt is floated on a national or worldwide capital market at a predetermined interest rate, bondholders are no better off by virtue of getting a particular interest payment, all debt is effectively external, and there is no differential advantage in having the national government float the debt.[6]

In part, the lack of faith in subnational fiscal policy was also based on a view that either the mobility of labor or goods in a country was very high. If the mobility of goods in response to spending demand was high, movements in aggregate demand throughout a country would be highly positively correlated and demand stimulation in one area would not cause extraordinary income changes there. If the mobility of labor was also high, whatever differential movements in demand might occur would inspire offsetting by changes in labor supply.

The last two rows of the transition matrix (Table 2.3) try to verify the latter of these critical assumptions, the assumed mobility of labor. Here the topic is the movement of unemployed workers, either short or long term, between states of high and low aggregate unemployment. The message is certainly to downgrade the importance of labor mobility for any but the longest run. As with the transfer recipients discussed earlier, in the short run very few workers, even when unemployed for as long as half a year, move from a high to a low unemployment state.

The upshot of all these considerations is that perhaps the question of subnational fiscal policy should be reopened. If most demand shocks these days are ultimately due to relative price shifts that benefit some areas of the country and hurt others (see Medoff 1983 for some evidence on the importance of these), if these shocks are largely transitory, if labor is immobile across regions of the country in the short run, and if currency value changes weaken national fiscal policies, then use of subnational fiscal policies may present a sensible way to decentralize responsibilities for this function of government. In another paper (Gramlich 1984) I make this argument in more detail. Most states have constitutional provisions that prevent them from running current-account-budget deficits, but they are not prevented from altering taxes and expenditures in response to income changes in their areas, and it appears to me that they should follow such policies.

TAX ASSIGNMENT

Two basic questions arise in any examination of the federal structure of taxation. The first involves the levels of taxes raised by national and subnational governments; the second, the types of tax used.

NATIONAL VS. SUBNATIONAL TAXES

While the presumption on the expenditure side of the budget is that expenditure programs should be conducted by subnational governments whenever possible, there is an opposite presumption on the tax side. Partly because of a belief that the administrative costs of levying taxes are higher for subnational than national governments, partly because of a fear of tax competition, the standard belief is that tax collection should be centralized whenever possible.

As on the expenditure side, this presumption can at least be said to be specialized, perhaps appropriate in some cases but certainly not in general. For one thing, it totally ignores a point brought out by the new "rent-seeking" literature: that inefficiencies due to lobbying for the grants may dwarf conventional economic inefficiencies. When expenditure programs are decentralized and taxes centralized, large-scale general-purpose transfers (which actually exist in other federal countries such as Canada

46   Edward M. Gramlich

and Australia) are needed to balance budgets at both governmental levels. These large transfers place a premium on local politicians who can lobby for grants from the federal government and very little premium on those who are effective managers of their governments—a common complaint in countries that rely heavily on tax-sharing grants (Walsh 1983). The rent-seeking literature should then alert us to a competing principle— that, as a rule, those governments that buy government services should impose their own taxes.

Moreover, the administrative cost argument given in favor of tax centralization seems quite weak. Perhaps in less developed countries it may be true that the national government can administer tax laws more effectively than can subnational governments, but there is no research supporting such a proposition in the United States. And it would be strange if such research could be found, since all states have to do to lower their own administrative costs and the compliance costs of their taxpayers is to use the federal tax base and apply their own rate.[7]

The question of competition among various governments for desirable tax bases is more complicated. In a Tiebout model with costless migration, competing governments at the same level should strive to eliminate what Buchanan (1950) called *fiscal residuals*: the difference between taxes paid to a local government and expenditure benefits received from it. The threat of tax competition among subnational governments will then limit the extent to which any of these governments can tax either industry or well-off individuals in their own community, for if these groups are asked to pay extra costs, they will simply leave the community. There is then relatively little scope for assessing redistributive taxes at any but the national level.

This innate limitation on redistributive taxes at the subnational level does not require fiscal transfers from higher to lower levels of government for redistributive spending, as long as the redistribution is done mainly by the federal government, as I have previously argued that it should be. But it could justify such transfers for spending done for allocation reasons. Gordon (1983) points out that horizontal tax competition eliminates an opportunity for a decentralized government to assess completely nondistorting taxes, if there are some factors that are in highly elastic supply to subnational jurisdictions and completely inelastic supply to the nation. In principle Gordon's point is important, but I would be more worried about it if I could determine what such productive factors are— in today's open-economy models, a routine assumption is that capital and perhaps even entrepreneurship are in elastic supply to the whole country (called the "small country" assumption, for obvious reasons). Pending illumination on this point, my tentative position on this issue is that while it is theoretically possible that principles of tax assignment would call for having certain taxes levied by national governments and accompanied by grants to the subnational governments actually doing the spending, there is no clear evidence that such an arrangement is appropriate for the United States.

Another form of tax competition would also call for more centralization of the revenue-raising function than the spending function. This form is not very common in the United States, though it exists in resource-rich countries such as Australia. It involves the vertical tax competition among all levels of government that could lay claim to taxing profitable resource deposits. Cassing and Hillman (1982) tell a story about rail freight for coal in Queensland, the most resources-rich Australian state. The federal government tries to gain its return from Queensland coal by imposing an export duty. The state of Queensland tries to gain its own return by charging exploitive rail freight rates. As the federal government raises its rates to gain revenue, the profitability of coal is reduced, as is the monopolistic freight rate Queensland can charge. Similarly, by raising its freight rates Queensland can reduce revenues available to the federal government. If the two were to compete, they would tax coal excessively and generate suboptimal tax revenues for both governments. This is one case where it would make sense to centralize taxes and have one government distribute a share of the optimal tax revenue to the other.

Whatever the resolution of these typically complex normative issues, the previously reported data on general-purpose grants suggest that there is in fact broad adherence to the levy-your-own-taxes principle in the United States. Table 2.1 shows that only $5 billion of the $88 billion in federal grants to state or local governments in 1981 were for general purposes, and only $11 billion of the $93 billion in state grants for local governments.

TYPES OF TAXES

The two basic principles for organizing a tax system are the ability-to-pay and the benefit principles. In a federal system we would expect that migration among subnational jurisdictions would be an important factor in the long run (as the tax competition argument and the evidence on AFDC benefits, described above, suggested), which in turn implies that subnational jurisdictions ultimately have only one feasible taxing ar-

Edward M. Gramlich

TABLE 2.4

Government Revenues by Type of Tax or Grant,
1981 (billions of current dollars)

Revenue item	Federal government	State governments	Local governments
Personal income taxes	$291.7	$62.7	$25.9
Estate and gift taxes	7.0	–	–
Corporate profits taxes	67.5	13.2	0.6
Excise taxes	41.7	–	–
Customs duties	8.6	–	–
Fees and charges	6.1	19.0	8.3
Sales taxes	–	76.3	14.1
Property taxes	–	2.7	72.4
Contributions for social insurance	204.5	26.7	7.1
Federal grants	–	65.7	22.0
State grants	–	–	93.4
Total*	627.0	266.2	244.0

*Because of rounding, details may not add to total.
SOURCE: "The U.S. National Income and Product Accounts," *Survey of Current Business*, July, 1983, table 3.16; Levin (1983).

rangement, the benefit principle. If they try to make well-off individuals or industry pay taxes that will be spent in the form of programs that benefit others in the jurisdiction, these groups will move out of the jurisdiction.

It follows that in a federal system, most ability-to-pay, or redistributive, taxes will be imposed at the national level, while most benefit taxation will be done at the state or local level. An examination of actual tax data for the United States (Table 2.4) shows this to be generally the case. Income and corporate taxes, the most important ability-to-pay taxes, are imposed mainly at the national level. Contributions for social insurance, used to finance trust funds such as social security, Medicare, unemployment insurance, and the like, are also assessed at the national level. Those state or local contributions that are assessed are for pension systems for the employees of these governments, and should be viewed as a component of the wages of these employees. Those taxes that are mainly benefit taxes, fees and charges and property taxes, are assessed at the local level.[8] As on the expenditure side, the taxes of state government represent a mixed bag, with some ability-to-pay taxes, some benefit taxes, and the state sales tax, which is hard to classify.

TAX EXPORTATION

One important source of inefficiency in this division of taxing responsibility involves the possibility of exporting taxes. A standard claim on the expenditure side of the budget, routinely advanced as a rationale for categorical grants from the federal to lower governments, is that spending can be too low if some benefits from an expenditure program are realized outside the community. There is a similar, though less commonly heard, argument on the tax side (first made by McLure 1967). If taxes can be exported from a jurisdiction to individuals outside the jurisdiction, without a concomitant transfer of expenditure benefits, local citizens are not internalizing all the costs of public services, and they will spend too much on these public services. Just as we have categorical subsidies for those types of expenditures with benefit spillovers, we should in principle also assign public-service excise taxes for whatever spending is financed by exportable taxes.

The difficulties of matching expenditures and the taxes used to pay for them probably make any formal excise-tax scheme impractical, but there may be other arrangements that should be made to deal with tax exporting. One is to have the federal government assume all tax sources that can easily be exported. It is sometimes argued that this is why the federal government should take over responsibility for the corporate tax (as it largely has), but that view does not accord with prevailing views on the incidence of the corporate tax. That tax is now generally considered to be a tax on a mobile factor, capital, which would drive it, and ultimately labor, out of a jurisdiction, leaving the tax to be paid by the locationally fixed factor, land. Hence in general the corporate tax would not be exported. What would be exported are capital taxes on factors within a jurisdiction owned by outsiders (such as on resources) and excise taxes on travelers with a low price elasticity of demand.

As a practical matter, tax exporting inefficiencies do not seem to be of overriding practical importance in the United States. A recent study by Mutti and Morgan (1983) finds the revenue implications of excise-tax exporting to travelers to be very small, even for states, such as Florida, for which tourism is very important. Beyond that, though the decisions have been made on constitutional grounds, a long series of Supreme Court rulings have effectively prevented the taxation of outsiders and have thereby kept down the distortions that could have arisen from exporting (Hellerstein 1977).

Although the Supreme Court is of course concerned with legal tradi-

50   Edward M. Gramlich

tions and not economic inefficiencies, there is one way an alleged constitutional restriction does cause tax exportation. As a result of court rulings in the early 1940s, the federal government now does not tax state and local bond interest payments. This treatment lowers state and local bond interest rates to about 80 percent of the rate for comparable-risk corporate securities, and subsidizes state and local investment in all communities affected by cost-of-capital. There seems to be no economic point to such a subsidy—if there are spillover benefits, matching grants can be used—and its elimination would improve the overall allocation of capital in the United States, as well as improving the equity of the federal income tax. If the subsidy really is rooted in constitutional constraints, this distortion will be with us as long as we have an income tax, though it could still be removed by moving to an expenditure tax, which taxes return to capital only when it is consumed. But there is enough confusion about the ultimate origin of the subsidy that one might also argue for another court ruling on the constitutionality of having the federal government tax state and local interest payments.

While the courts have generally tried to limit tax exporting, congressional actions have generally gone the other way. In one significant case, Congress explicitly encourages a form of tax exporting through the income-tax deduction for state and local taxes paid. This federal deduction lowers the marginal tax price for local public goods for those voters who itemize deductions, and represents exactly the sort of tax exporting that should be prevented from the standpoint of efficiency.[9]

An examination of the impact of this tax deduction within a state suggests that its effects might be considerably more pernicious than are commonly supposed. A first point is that not all state and local revenues are deductible—in general, fees and charges, the revenues that most closely conform to the benefits principle and hence cause least deadweight loss, are not deductible, while the less efficient income and sales taxes are. A second point is that only 30 percent of all tax returns claim itemized deductions. If the median, or decisive, voter in a community does not itemize, then the deduction does not affect state or local spending but merely represents an unwarranted tax break for the high-income taxpayers who do itemize.

But that is not the end of it. Although only 30 percent of *all* tax returns claim itemized deductions, it may still be that a high percentage of the tax returns filed by voters itemize deductions. Table 2.5 presents data from a survey of Michigan voters. The bottom row of the table shows that of all 2001 survey respondents, 862, or 43 percent, claim itemized deductions.

TABLE 2.5

Voters Who Itemized Deductions on Their Federal Tax Returns
(Michigan Voter Survey, 1978)

| | | | | Share itemizing | |
Residence	Respondents	Voters	Itemizers	Voters	Nonvoters
Detroit	270	164	94	.409	.255
Detroit suburbs	583	356	304	.607	.388
Lansing	54	28	21	.357	.423
Lansing suburbs	38	30	19	.533	.375
Other urban counties	242	156	107	.519	.302
Rural counties	814	514	317	.432	.317
Total	2001	1248	862	.490	.332

SOURCE: Survey data are described in Courant, Gramlich, and Rubinfeld (1980).

The difference between the 30 percent share from overall statistics and this 43 percent share is apparently due to tax returns filed on behalf of minors and others not likely to appear in a voter survey sample. The bottom row also indicates that among voters, the share of itemizers rises to 49 percent. And some of the disaggregated numbers in the table show that among voters in high-income areas, such as the Detroit and Lansing suburbs, the share rises to 60 percent.

Assume for the moment that the median voter model gives a reasonably accurate picture of how public-spending decisions are made in local jurisdictions. The numbers in Table 2.5 indicate the maximum number of voters who would be swayed by the state-local tax deduction to switch their vote in favor of higher expenditures. Using the overall statistics as an example, say that 49 percent of the voters itemize, and that voting turnout decisions are unaffected by the deduction provision. Then up to 49 percent of the voters could have their desired size of public spending increased by the tax deduction. If not too many of these voters had previously favored big governments (in which case they would have already voted for high spending), public spending would be likely to rise in the community. Reasoning in this way, we can see that the effective tax price for public spending is more likely to fall, and public spending to rise, the richer the community.

The tax price for public spending on such social investment services as education is already relatively low in these richer areas because of their high tax base. Now this basic advantage is compounded by the federal tax deduction. Indeed, a firm believer in migration will also argue that the tax deduction sets up incentives for rich people to live together so that they can export their taxes to others. It is hard to imagine a consciously designed public-policy measure having worse impacts on both efficiency and equity, in the short and the long run, than the federal income-tax deduction for state and local taxes.

INTERGOVERNMENTAL GRANTS

The other important financing mechanism in a federal system involves intergovernmental grants. As the previous numbers made clear, the United States has a very extensive grant system at both the national and the state level. While most existing grants are categorical, there are separate rationales for categorical grants and for general-purpose grants.

THE RATIONALES FOR GRANTS

Grants from higher to lower levels of government can be of a form that alters relative prices facing the recipient government, or that does not. With general-purpose grants the price structure is not altered: these grants affect community income only, and stimulate local consumption of public services according to the income effect. With open-ended categorical grants the price structure is altered: these grants lower relative prices for certain types of expenditures, have both income and substitution (price) effects, and stimulate local consumption of public services according to the uncompensated price elasticity of demand. Since the substitution effect expands spending, if anything, it is easy to establish that open-ended price reduction grants stimulate more spending on the public service in question per dollar of the federal grant.

Whether one type of grant or the other is appropriate depends on the type of problem being corrected by the grant. If there are externalities that imply that social benefits from public services exceed those realized within a community, open-ended price subsidies are appropriate—just the reverse of the tax exportation argument. If the mismatch of expenditure and revenue responsibilities described above is present, general-purpose transfers are appropriate. Indeed, Breton and Scott (1978) point out that there may be any conceivable mismatch of administrative responsibilities for taxes or expenditures at any level of government, making any set of transfers, from higher to lower governments (as most now are), or from lower to higher governments, appropriate.

But the most commonly discussed rationale for general-purpose transfers, and the one that is potentially most relevant in the United States, involves income differences across communities. Should these exist, there will be one of two outcomes. If benefit taxation is not complete, rich people will be net contributors to the public budget and poor people will receive some transfers through the public budget (in Buchanan's [1950] terms, the rich have positive fiscal residuals and the poor negative ones). If benefit taxation is complete, poor people will gain from the higher demand by rich people for public goods.[10] Either way, the tax price for public services in a community will depend on how many rich people there are or, crudely, on community income.

The argument often stops there, but it should not. Differing tax prices do not necessarily constitute a social ill, though they can if they lead poor communities to under-consume (relative to rich communities) merit public services such as education. One of many ways to eliminate these tax price differences across communities is through general-purpose transfers. But the general-purpose transfers must be compensatory, that is, they must be given in greater per-capita amounts to poor than to rich communities. And it is by no means obvious that general-purpose transfers are the best way to deal with these community income differences. Yinger (forthcoming) points out that two separate notions of equity could be applied in problems such as this: (a) fair compensation, under which all communities would have access to the same bundle of all goods; or (b) categorical equity, under which the expected expenditures on designated public services would be equalized. Under the former notion, general-purpose grants would be appropriate and would have to be given in the amount of income differences among communities. Under the latter, general-purpose grants could be given, but it would be possible to achieve the same end with fewer grant dollars by using Feldstein's (1975) variant of the power equalization approach.

Say that expenditures on public services in the ith community were determined by the linear equation

(1) $E_i = a_0 + a_1 Y_i + a_2 G_i + a_3 P_i + u_i$

where E_i is real consumption of public services, Y_i is community income (here used as a proxy for community living standards), G_i is general-purpose grants received by the community, P_i is the dollar size of price-reduction (open-ended matching) grants received by the same community, and the residual u_i refers to all other reasons why spending might differ across communities. With normal preference functions, $a_3 > a_2$; that is, the price-reduction grants would provide an added impetus to spending. If there exist what are known as "flypaper" effects, whereby general-purpose grants stimulate more spending than income, $a_2 > a_1$.[11] To achieve fair compensation through general-purpose grants, $\partial G_i / \partial Y_i$ must equal -1, that is, all income deviations must be compensated dollar for dollar by larger general-purpose grants. To achieve categorical equity, it is merely necessary to insure that expected spending is equal across communities. This is done simply by taking the total derivative of (1) with respect to income, arriving at $\partial G_i / \partial Y_i = -a_1/a_2$ if equalization is accomplished through general-purpose grants, and $\partial P_i / \partial Y_i = -a_1/a_3$ if through open-ended matching grants. The first derivative is greater than or equal to -1; the second is clearly greater than -1. In these latter cases, because the price sensitivity is relied on to stimulate public spending, and because the standard is not to eliminate all spending deficiencies but only the public-services spending deficiency, less grant money is needed to achieve categorical equity.[12] Another advantage of this form of matching grants, not shown in the analysis, is that the stimulated public spending could be limited to those public services that really are merit goods.

The upshot of all this is that the usual rationales for general-purpose grants are all quite limited. One rationale could be the assignment-of-responsibilities mismatch described above, though it seems that American subnational governments are able to raise enough revenue to pay for their spending programs without resorting to obviously inefficient taxation. One could be the income-differences argument, though if the categorical-equity standard is used, categorical grants can achieve the same objective with fewer grant dollars.[13]

ACTUAL GRANTS

Table 2.6 shows real levels of intergovernmental grants at the federal level over the past decade, disaggregated by type of grant. In principle, a similar analysis of state grants to local governments should be done, but I do not show these data because nobody has developed disaggregations based on the type of grant, and those distinctions are crucial in the analysis.

The table shows that a decade ago, in 1972, there were almost no general-purpose grants, fairly large grants for income support, and even larger categorical grants for other, benefit spillover programs. Over the decade, general-purpose grants rose until 1980 because of the introduction of the Nixon administration's general-revenue-sharing program,

Reforming U.S. Federal Fiscal Arrangements   55

TABLE 2.6

Federal Grants by Type, 1972, 1980, and 1983
(billions of 1983 dollars)

	1972*	1980*	1983
General purpose	$ 1.2	$ 10.6	$ 6.5
Block	6.7	12.7	12.9
Income support	29.1	42.3	44.8
Categorical	44.2	47.3	28.8
Total	81.2	112.9	93.0

*Deflated by the national accounts deflator for state and local purchases
(1972 = 0.423, 1980 = 0.809).
SOURCE: *Budget of the United States Government, Fiscal Year 1985*, Special
Analysis H, tables H.8 and H.9.

then dropped back in real terms when the Carter administration eliminated general-revenue-sharing for state governments. Categorical grants
remained stable until 1980, then dropped back when the Reagan administration killed some of them and converted others to what are known as
block grants—grants that are nominally categorical (money has to be
spent on a designated function), but effectively for general purposes (the
designated functions are so broad, and enforcement so limited, that recipient governments can effectively do what they want with the grant
money). Income-support grants have grown from 1972 levels due to the
exploding costs of Medicaid, offset by a real drop in AFDC grants.

GENERAL-PURPOSE GRANTS

The present general-revenue-sharing program goes only to local governments, basically on a per-capita formula. There are provisions in the
law that have the effect of giving slightly more funds to poorer areas, but
the redistribution is minimal and haphazard.[14] Even if the redistribution
were effective and systematic, however, there would seem to be little cause
to retain general revenue sharing. The program violates the levy-your-
own-taxes principle described above, in a way that has never been defended in terms of administrative cost saving. And even if redistribution
were a more important objective of the program than it apparently is,
open-ended matching grants with federal matching rates depending neg-

atively on community income or positively on needs could accomplish
the goals of categorical equity with fewer grant dollars.

BLOCK GRANTS

These grants appear to represent a political compromise: conservatives
would like to kill many categorical grant programs altogether but, lack-
ing the muscle to do that, they settle for converting the grant to block
form. As said above, this effectively makes the grant into a general-
purpose grant. But the allocation of funds for the grant program is based
on whatever categorical program just got cashed out—miles of highway,
numbers of dilapidated houses, or whatever. Since the grants now are for
general purposes, the random elements in the grant distribution formula
make the funds allocation even more haphazard than for general revenue
sharing. There are also excess administrative costs to maintain the fiction
of the block grant. Finally, as argued above, there is no very good argument for general-purpose grants anyway. For all these reasons, these
grants should either be terminated or converted to categorical-equity-
matching grants for poorer communities. Block grants may provide a
useful political compromise, but it is hard to see why an economist who
worries about efficiency and equity would ever favor such programs.

INCOME-SUPPORT GRANTS

I argued above in favor of replacing federal grants for income support
with a national program paying basic income-support levels. This should
consist of a basic national benefit level (say somewhat above the present
average level of AFDC and food stamps). States should be allowed to
supplement this level, perhaps with slight (say 25 percent) federal matching support.

In 1983, federal matching grants for all income-support programs
totalled $45 billion (see Table 2.6). States spent another $13 billion of
their own funds on Medicaid and yet another $6 billion on AFDC. Were
the federal government simply to assume these expenditures, federal costs
would rise by about $19 billion. Then there should be some reallocations,
with most of the $6 billion going to raise AFDC benefits in low-benefit
states in the South. The total amount of funds devoted to AFDC can be
greater than $6 billion because of the fact that Medicaid is a program
much in need of cost-saving reform apart from the federal aspects focused

on here, and various cost-sharing measures should be able to reduce expenditures on it.

OTHER CATEGORICAL GRANTS

Until the recent introduction of general revenue sharing, conversion to block grants, and rapid growth of Medicaid, the main form of federal intergovernmental transfer has been categorical matching grants in areas such as transportation, education, community services, environmental protection, and hospital construction. These grants appear to have as their rationale benefit spillovers across jurisdictional lines,[15] but in fact the grants are structured so that they are unlikely to achieve any such objectives.

A first fact about these grants is that legal federal matching shares are very high, averaging 80 percent across the present $29 billion of other categorical grants.[16] While there may be some benefit spillovers, at the margin the ratio of internal to total benefits for these programs seems to be much higher than 20 percent. This gives states an incentive to overspend, and overspend they probably will. To prevent grant levels from becoming very large, the federal government is forced to impose limits on the size of the grant—overall program limits enforced by the Office of Management and Budget, formula limits for individual governments or groups of governments, and agency limits for application grants. Standard indifference-curve analysis next shows that the price reduction is not effective at the margin, and that the grants have effects much like those of general-purpose grants.[17] Then budget-cutters such as David Stockman come along and argue that the grant should be either terminated or converted to block form.

This political cycle is designed to end in the termination of the categorical-grant program. Perhaps many of these grants should never have been passed—that is a question for the benefit-cost analysts. But if there is a valid spillover rationale for categorical grants, a better way to improve the grant than by simply converting it to block form and effectively killing it can easily be found. That better way is simply to lower federal matching shares until the ratio of internal to total program costs at the margin equals the ratio of internal to total program benefits at the margin.

In making such a cavalier proposal, I realize that it will often be difficult, if not impossible, to estimate the critical marginal ratio very precisely. But it should not be difficult to come closer than the 20 percent that is now the standard. My own preference would be to assume an internal

Edward M. Gramlich

share of 80 percent unless it could be shown to be significantly lower. If this is the appropriate share, a very simple demand analysis indicates that such a change should reduce federal categorical grants by about $11 billion, increase expenditures on public services with benefit spillovers, and eliminate a dead-weight loss that appears to be about 1 percent of the level of expenditures.[18]

THE REFORM AGENDA

Rather than summarize the paper, I will try to maintain its spirit by listing what seem to me to be the major problems with present-day United States fiscal federal arrangements. These problems and the proposed remedies are stated very bluntly, without even trying to list the many compromises and intermediate reforms that could work in the right direction.

1. Given the inability of the national government to stabilize demand shocks, or to stabilize them in different regions simultaneously, states should undertake limited use of stabilization policies. They can do this by creating rainy-day funds, building up these funds (running budget surpluses) in boom years, and running down the funds in recession years.

2. The federal deduction for state and local taxes paid should be abolished. This change will raise federal revenue by an estimated $26 billion (see the summary in Table 2.7), it should affect tax prices and public-spending levels relatively little in rural jurisdictions and central cities, but it should raise marginal tax prices and lower public-spending levels in high-income suburbs. I would have made a similar recommendation, for a similar reason, about the income-tax exclusion for state and local interest, but I am assuming that the provision exists for constitutional reasons, and even my reform proposals do not go that far.

3. Federal grants for income-support programs should be replaced by direct federal income-support programs with uniform national benefit levels and optional state supplementation, perhaps with limited matching support. At today's levels, a reasonable package would raise federal budget expenditures by $20 billion.

4. Federal general-purpose grants and block grants should be replaced by categorical-equity matching grants to poorer communities for merit public services such as education, health, and housing. At

Reforming U.S. Federal Fiscal Arrangements   *59*

TABLE 2.7
Summary of Reform Changes
(billions of 1983 dollars)

Item	Reduction in federal deficit
Eliminate deduction for state-local taxes:	26.0
Property tax[a]	8.0
Other[a]	18.0
Impose uniform national income-support benefits:	− 20.0
Raise AFDC in low-benefit states[b]	− 10.0
Assume state Medicaid expenses[b]	− 10.0
Revamp general-purpose grants:	7.5
Eliminate general-revenue-sharing[c]	4.6
Eliminate broad-based grants[c]	12.9
Introduce categorical-equity grants[a]	− 10.0
Lower federal matching share on categorical grants:	10.8
Eliminate present limited categorical grants	28.8
Introduce open-ended grants with 20% matching	− 18.0
Total impact	24.3

[a]From *Special Analysis G of the Budget*, table G.2.
[b]Author's estimate.
[c]From *Special Analysis H of the Budget*, tables H.8, H.9.
SOURCE: *Budget of the United States Government, Fiscal Year 1985*, Special Analyses G and H.

today's levels, $17.5 billion of federal grants would be saved, and perhaps $10 billion could be used for the categorical-equity grants.

5. Federal categorical grants should be altered by lowering federal matching shares to a level that better corresponds to the ratio of internal to total benefits and by eliminating limits on the size of the grant. At today's levels, such a change is likely to reduce federal budget expenditures by about $11 billion.

The measures are not advanced as a package—any one of them could be adopted with or without any of the others. If the whole package were passed, Table 2.7 suggests that all changes combined should reduce the federal budget deficit by about $24 billion—a saving equal to about one-seventh of the enormous present level of the deficit. The short-run impact of the package would be to raise income-support levels greatly for low-income people in the South; the long-run impact should be to raise support levels for all low-income people. People in low-income communities should benefit further through increased consumption of merit public services. But not everybody will be better off. For a change, high-income itemizers will be made worse off.

APPENDIX: DECENTRALIZATION OF
INCOME DISTRIBUTION RESPONSIBILITIES

In the text I asserted that the twin forces of beneficiary migration and the diverse levels of AFDC benefits desired by different states argue for a more centralized system of income support. In this appendix I give the exact nature of this argument. The appendix uses real numbers and parameters from Gramlich and Laren (1984).

Suppose we had a country consisting of two states, one that preferred to pay relatively generous AFDC support levels (B_1) and one that preferred to pay very low support levels (B_2). Each state determines benefits by maximizing the utility function for its decisive voter:

(1) $U_i = U_i [Y_i(1 - T_i), B_i]$

subject to the constraint that

(2) $T_iY_i = (1 - M_i) (B_iR_i) (B_i/B_j)^b$

where i indicates the state determining benefits, j indicates the other state, U_i the utility value for the state's decisive voter, Y_i this voter's pre-tax income (for which I will use average per-capita income), T_i the proportional state income tax rate to pay for AFDC, M_i the federal matching rate for the state, and R_i for the level of recipients per capita if state i paid the same benefits as state j. If state i benefit levels exceed those in the other state $(B_i>B_j)$, recipients would rise according to the migration-sensitivity parameter b. There are cross-state transmission effects whenever $b>0$.

Determination of benefits in this two-state country is shown in the well-known bargaining diagram Figure 2.1. At the Nash point N each state is maximizing utility under the assumption that all federal matching rates are zero and that benefits in the other state are fixed. At this point we have, for state 1,

(3) $\partial U_1/\partial B_1 = -[R_1 (1+b) (B_1/B_2)^b] + u_1 = 0$

where u_1 is the partial derivative of U_1 with respect to B_1, and where the partial derivative of U_1 with respect to after-tax income in state 1 has been normalized at unity. At the Nash point there is no first-order impact of changing benefits on utility, because the state has already maximized by

Reforming U.S. Federal Fiscal Arrangements   61

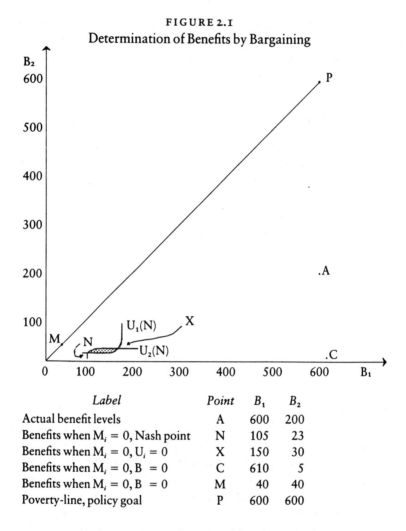

FIGURE 2.1
Determination of Benefits by Bargaining

Label	Point	B_1	B_2
Actual benefit levels	A	600	200
Benefits when $M_i = 0$, Nash point	N	105	23
Benefits when $M_i = 0, U_i = 0$	X	150	30
Benefits when $M_i = 0, B = 0$	C	610	5
Benefits when $M_i = 0, B = 0$	M	40	40
Poverty-line, policy goal	P	600	600

equating the marginal value of benefit increases (u_1) to the marginal cost of income losses (the term in brackets). Hence the indifference curve passing through this point, U_1, is horizontal there.

But we also know that at the Nash point B_2 increases will raise U_1, because they attract AFDC recipients into state 2 and raise after-tax income in state 1 for every level of B_1. This can be seen by differentiating the utility function with respect to B_2:

(4) $\partial U_1/\partial B_2 = R_1 b \ (B_1/B_2)^{1+b} > 0$

This result shows why the U_1 curve is concave from the horizontal axis:

as B_1 is, say, raised above its optimal level at N, increasing rises in B_2 are necessary to keep the state on its indifference level.

The same results are true for state 2. The equation analogous to (3) shows that the U_2 curve is vertical at Nash point N. The equation analogous to (4) shows that benefit increases in state 1 raise utility in state 2. And the curve is concave to the vertical axis because increasing rises in B_1 are necessary to compensate for non-maximizing changes in B_2.

The fact that indifference curves cross at N implies that utility can be raised simultaneously in both states by bargaining, or by having the central government simply set benefits in both states at some level that raises utility in one state without lowering it in the other. Such a contract curve solution could be found by maximizing the joint utility function

(5) $\quad J = wU_1 + (1 - w)U_2$

for some arbitrarily specified weight w, assumed to lie between zero and one. But for reasons that will become apparent shortly, that is not going to be my argument for greater centralization. Another proposition is that the Boadway and Wildasin (1984) solution of federal matching could in principle be used to arrive at a contract curve solution, by effectively externalizing some of the cross-state gains of higher benefit levels in a state. Shortly we will also see that if this is the justification for federal matching, actual matching rates turn out to be far too generous to achieve this limited goal.

The diagram gives the area of possible gains from greater coordination as the shaded area. The northeastern limit of this area, denoted by X, can be approximated by reasoning that U_1 becomes vertical when rises in B_1 no longer raise utility in the state, that is, when B_1 is so high that u_1 is zero. Similarly, U_2 becomes horizontal when u_2 is zero. These points can be located with the equations

(6) $\quad (\partial U_1 / \partial B_1) \ \partial B_1 + (\partial U_2 / \partial B_2) \ \partial B_2 = 0$

where the solution is just as before except that the derivatives are used to solve for the levels of B_1 and B_2 where the indifference curves become vertical and horizontal respectively. It can be seen from the graph that the exact crossing point is at a B_1 value less than that at which U_1 is vertical and at a B_2 value less than that at which U_2 is horizontal. I could locate this point exactly if I were willing to assume a specific form for the utility functions, but we will shortly see that such a step is not necessary.

This is all the positive theory that is required; I now try to find the various points with real-life values. The values for B_1 and B_2 will be state monthly AFDC guarantee levels for a family of four in 1981 dollars, assuming food stamps at a standard national level. Given this level, AFDC guarantee levels of about $600 would have been necessary to keep a family out of poverty status in 1981 (labeled P on the diagram).

The first step is to locate actual benefit levels in the presence of federal matching and migration. Data from Gramlich and Laren (1984) show that in typical high-benefit states, covering nearly half of AFDC recipients, B_1 ranged from $540 to $720 with a mean close to $600. In low-benefit states, B_2 ranged from $115 to $510, with a mean close to $200. These values are indicated on the diagram by point A.

Values at the Nash point N are determined from the equations given in Gramlich and Laren. Equation 9 there shows benefits to be determined in the two states by the relationships

(7a) $L(B_1) = [1/(1+cb)][Z_1 - cL(1-M_1) + cbL(B_2)]$

(7b) $L(B_2) = [1/(1+cb)][Z_2 - cL(1-M_2) + cbL(B_1)]$

where $L(x)$ denotes the log of a variable, c is the price elasticity of demand for AFDC benefits, and the Z_i terms represent the influence of all other variables. The Nash point is found by using the actual values listed above and reasonable parameter estimates from the paper ($b=0.65, c=1.8$) to evaluate the Z_i. Then these figures replace Z_i, the M_i are set at zero, and the values at point N are computed. B_1 falls from $600 to $105, B_2 from $200 to $23. The sharp drops are caused by three factors.

1. There is a sharp change in matching ratios, from $M_1 = 0.5$ and $M_2 = 0.75$ to zero.

2. The estimated price elasticity is high.

3. The estimated migration effect is high, causing the fall in B_1 to lower B_2, this to lower B_1, and so forth as in a multiplier.

Whether these estimates are believable is, of course, not as obvious. The paper finds both estimates to be highly significant, and it does confirm the all-important migration parameter with two different bodies of data.

The next step is to locate point X, the approximation for the northeastern crossing point. Because u_2 is already found to be very low (that is why the group 2 states pay so little AFDC, even when most costs are financed by the federal government), U_2 becomes horizontal when B_2 rises to 30; the same type of calculation makes U_1 vertical when B_1 equals 150. These two values are shown as point X on the graph; the true crossing point is slightly to the southwest. That these AFDC levels are so low explains why I do not use this lack of coordination argument for greater centralization: the rises in benefits due to improved coordination would not be very high.

Two other points are shown on the graph. Point C, for a closed economy, shows the solution to the model given in Equation 7 when there is no matching and when there is no migration effect. What migration does is to bring benefits in the two states together; when b is set at zero, states diverge to what might be thought of as their true preference benefit levels—close to the actual value for B_1 but close to zero for B_2. In this sense the present matching-grant system is about right for preserving the closed economy solution for the B_1 states but much more generous than is necessary for preserving the closed economy solution for the B_2 states. Finally, the point labeled M goes the other way, showing the equilibrium values for benefits when migration is infinitely sensitive to benefit disparities, as might be assumed in extreme versions of the Tiebout model. In this case benefits must be equal in the two states, by my calculation at about $40.

Hence the results here are dominated by the low intrinsic desire on the part of the group 2 states to pay benefits. These states now pay benefits of only $200 a month for a family of four, roughly one-third of the poverty line. And this in the presence of a price reduction by the federal government that averages 75 percent, a large estimated price elasticity of demand, a large migration sensitivity, and benefits in other states over three times as high. When the federal matching is eliminated to find the Nash point, benefits in these group 2 states fall to very low levels, and in the presence of the migration sensitivity, this pulls down benefits in the other states. With a Nash point anchored at this low a level, none of the normal federal policy measures aimed at improving coordination will have much effect—even at point X, benefits will be less than $30 in the low-benefit states.

To be candid, then, my policy suggestions are not aimed at preserving tastes in these low-benefit states. My goal is that benefits in all states be set at something like the poverty level of $600 per month, which also happens to be the preferred level in the high-benefit states. The much-maligned present system does bring about this result in these high-benefit states; its defects are highly overrated. But it still does fall short of my goal because of the low benefits in the other states. The easiest way to achieve the goal is simply to have the federal government establish uniform national benefit levels, with optional state supplementation.

As a final matter here, one might ask about two types of sensitivity tests. First, does the low intrinsic "taste" for AFDC benefits among low-benefit states reflect their low income? The answer is *no*. The Gramlich–Laren paper also estimates income elasticities as part of the model, and even when these are complicated by the fact that low-income states are likely to have more AFDC recipients, other things being equal, the income elasticities are extremely low. Redoing the Figure 2.1 analysis with all incomes standardized would lead to only trivial changes. AFDC benefits are low in low-benefit states for reasons that are not captured in the income term: many of these states have high incomes.

The other type of sensitivity test refers to the migration parameter b. It is already high enough that the Nash point is geometrically closer to M than to C. But it is also true that if b were underestimated for any of a number of reasons (the opposite of the usual criticism of the Gramlich–Laren paper), point X could stretch to cover point A. Unfortunately, it would take a b value close to 10 (15 times the value now estimated) to get X up to A, and close to 26 (40 times the value now estimated) to get X up to P. Theoretically, more sensitive migration could relieve the strain of the paternalistic argument for centralization: realistically, it cannot.

ACKNOWLEDGMENTS

I would like to thank the editors of the volume, along with Henry Aaron, Harvey Brazer, Theodore Bergstrom, Paul Courant, Roger Gordon, Wallace Oates, David Wildasin, and John Yinger for helpful comments. Deborah Laren and Marieka Klaiwitter produced some of the numbers, and some of the work was financed by a grant from the Sloan Foundation.

NOTES

1. Various administrations have issued numerous government documents containing these proposals. Barfield (1981) gives a good summary of them and an analysis of what happened to them.

2. The first ACIR report, *Fiscal Balance in the American Federal System*, was issued as early as 1968. Break (1980) and Barfield (1982) cover a series of subsequent reform documents.

3. One exception must be noted: Ladd (1982). While many of Ladd's arguments are similar to mine, her reform agenda is different in certain important ways.

4. In confining the benefits of elementary and secondary education to a small area, I am assuming that the primary beneficiaries of education are students and/or their parents. Once these students complete their education and move away from the area, other areas benefit from the initial area's schooling expenditures. It is difficult, however, to ascertain the extent of such benefits. For me to wade into that issue here would serve no purpose; if there

Edward M. Gramlich

are appreciable geographical spillovers of this sort, education should be struck from the second list.

5. The numbers in Table 2.1 appear to suggest that income support transfers are given mainly at the federal level. Those numbers, however, are misleading: the federal transfer item consists of social security, unemployment, disability, and Medicare payments, all financed by social insurance trust funds where the ultimate beneficiaries (as a class) are making the contribution. These programs are not income redistribution in the sense of this class of people transferring income to other people.

6. Then Barro complicates the question further by arguing that, if the present generation will ultimately pay for government expenditures, it does not matter for consumption whether this generation pays now or later; the consumption loss implied by the external debt is offset by an equal (in present value terms) present-day consumption gain. If the present generation can escape payment by dying and not adjusting bequests, the present-day consumption gain may exceed the future consumption loss implied by the external debt.

7. Some attempts to coordinate tax policies and apply rates to the same base are discussed by Break (1980).

8. There is a great deal of dispute about exactly what sort of tax the property tax is. It can be thought of as a benefit tax to the extent that local public services are related to home values and financed by a property tax on these home values. But under certain conditions property taxes on homes or businesses may be shifted onto others and hence not be true benefit taxes.

9. Mutti and Morgan's (1983) analysis of the impact of this provision concentrates on other aspects. They work out the implications of tax importing and of having the federal government raise the revenue lost through the tax deduction by higher marginal rates on all taxpayers. Since I am concerned with the efficiency aspects of exporting, I focus only on it. Tax importing, and the higher marginal rates necessary to pay for everybody else's deduction, will be exogenous to the public-spending decisions of a particular subnational jurisdiction.

10. This statement may require some explanation. In a world of complete benefit taxation, all taxpayers are assessed Lindahl taxes. If the income elasticity of demand for public goods is positive, two poor people living together will have a lower sum of marginal benefits at each public-spending level than will a rich and a poor person living together. If the physical cost of providing public services is constant, the heterogeneous community will spend more than will the homogeneous poor community, and the Lindahl tax price of the poor person will be lower in the heterogeneous community. The poor person in the heterogeneous community gets more consumer surplus even if there is complete benefit taxation.

11. The *flypaper* moniker is occasioned by the fact that money may stick where it hits. If income rises, governments have to tax it away. But if general-purpose grants rise, governments seem to be able to cut taxes less than proportionately, and retain more of the funds for public spending. The issue is discussed at length in Mieszkowski and Oakland (1979).

12. Yinger (forthcoming) has a much more complicated model that includes need and cost factors as well. The logic used here is applicable in this more general case, but the particular allocations of grant funds will obviously change.

13. Another well-known argument is being ignored here. This is that general-purpose grants are more efficient from the standpoint of subnational governments precisely because they do not constrain subnational choices. Here I am assuming that categorical equity implies a social interest in spending on the particular service, which in turn means that subnational tastes are not the dominant concern.

14. The distribution of general-revenue-sharing funds, far and away the largest federal general-purpose transfer, is examined in Nathan, Manvel, and Calkins (1975).

15. Schultze (1974) shows how even this appearance might be viewed as wishful thinking by those with faith in the rationality of the political process.

16. This share was computed from numbers given in the *Budget of the United States, Fiscal Year 1982*, Special Analyses, p. 255.

17. A theoretical analysis can be found in Wilde (1971). An econometric analysis that gives these results is Gramlich (1982).

18. Suppose the true ratio of external to total marginal benefits was 0.2 and federal

grants were made open-ended at this matching rate. Most observers estimate the price elasticity of demand for state and local public services to be about 0.5 and the income elasticity to be very low. If so, a conversion to open-ended grants would raise state and local spending by about 0.1 and reduce (linearized) dead-weight loss by about $(0.5)(0.2)(0.1) =$ .01, or 1 percent of the present level of public spending. What this change does to grant levels is more uncertain. A rough estimate based on the numbers in Table 2.1 indicates that there is perhaps $80 billion of state and local expenditures in the functional categories in which the present $29 billion of closed-ended categorical grants (Table 2.6) is given. Converting these categorical grants to open-ended matching grants with a federal share of 0.2 will raise state and local spending to about $88 (based on the above elasticity), of which about $18 will be federal grant expenditures. In principle, the change should reduce federal grant outlays by $11 billion; in practice, I admit that everything hinges on how large state and local expenditures are in the grant categories, a number that (among others in this example) is very difficult to ascertain.

REFERENCES

Advisory Commission on Intergovernmental Relations. 1981. "Changing Public Attitudes on Governments and Taxes, 1981." S-10. Washington, D.C.

Atkinson, Anthony B., and Joseph E. Stiglitz. 1980. *Lectures on Public Economics.* New York: McGraw-Hill.

Barfield, Claude E. 1981. *Rethinking Federalism: Block Grants and Federal, State, and Local Responsibilities.* Washington, D.C.: American Enterprise Institute.

Barro, Robert J. 1974. "Are Government Bonds Net Wealth?" *Journal of Political Economy* 82: 1095–1117.

Boadway, Robin W., and David E. Wildasin. 1984. *Public Sector Economics.* Boston: Little, Brown.

Break, George E. 1980. *Financing Government in a Federal System.* Washington, D.C.: Brookings Institution.

Breton, Albert. 1965. "A Theory of Government Grants." *Canadian Journal of Economics and Political Science* 31: 175–87.

Breton, Albert, and Anthony Scott. 1978. *The Economic Constitution of Federal States.* Toronto: University of Toronto Press.

Buchanan, James M. 1950. "Federalism and Fiscal Equity." *American Economic Review* 40: 583–99.

———. 1965. "An Economic Theory of Clubs." *Economica* 32: 1–14.

Cassing, J. H., and A. L. Hillman. 1982. "State-Federal Resource Tax Rivalry: The Queensland Railway and the Federal Export Tax." *Economic Record* 58: 235–41.

Courant, Paul N., Edward M. Gramlich, and Daniel L. Rubinfeld. 1980. "Why Voters Support Tax Limitation Amendments: The Michigan Case." *National Tax Journal* 33: 1–20.

Feldstein, Martin S. 1975. "Wealth Neutrality and Local Choice in Public Education." *American Economic Review* 65: 75–89.

Fleming, Marcus. 1964. *Domestic Financial Plans under Fixed and Flexible Exchange Rates.* Washington, D.C.: International Monetary Fund Staff Papers.

Gordon, Roger H. 1983. "An Optimal Taxation Approach to Fiscal Federalism." *Quarterly Journal of Economics* 98: 567–86.

Gramlich, Edward M. 1982. "An Econometric Examination of the New Federalism." *Brookings Papers on Economic Activity* 2: 327–60.

———. 1984. "Subnational Fiscal Policy." Mimeo. Ann Arbor: University of Michigan.

Gramlich, Edward M., and Deborah S. Laren. 1984. "Migration and Income Redistribution Responsibilities." *Journal of Human Resources* 19: 489–511.

Hellerstein, Jerome R. 1977. "State Tax Discrimination against Out-of-Staters." *National Tax Journal* 30: 113–34.

Holmer, Martin. 1975. "Economic and Political Causes of the Welfare Crisis." Ph.D. dissertation. Cambridge, Mass.: MIT.

Ladd, Helen F. 1982. "Financing Public Services in the Federal System." Pp. 31–44 in *Federalism: Making the System Work*. Washington, D.C.: Center for National Policy.

Ladd, Helen F., and Fred C. Doolittle. 1982. "Which Level of Government Should Assist the Poor?" *National Tax Journal* 35: 323–36.

Levin, David J. 1983. "Receipts and Expenditures of State Governments and of Local Governments, 1968–81." *Survey of Current Business* 63: 25–38.

Lucas, Robert E. 1972. "Expectations and the Neutrality of Money." *Journal of Economic Theory* 4: 103–124.

McLure, Charles. 1967. "The Interstate Exporting of State and Local Taxes: Estimates for 1962." *National Tax Journal* 20: 49–77.

Medoff, James L. 1983. "U.S. Labor Markets, Imbalances, Wage Growth, and Productivity in the 1970s." *Brookings Papers on Economic Activity* 1: 87–120.

Mieszkowski, Peter, and William H. Oakland. 1979. *Fiscal Federalism and Grants-in-Aid*. COUPE Papers on Public Economics 1. Washington, D.C.: Urban Institute.

Mundell, Robert A. 1963. "Capital Mobility and Stabilization Policy under Fixed and Flexible Exchange Rates." *Canadian Journal of Economics and Political Science* 29: 475–85.

Musgrave, Richard A. 1959. *The Theory of Public Finance: A Study in Public Economy*. New York: McGraw-Hill.

Mutti, John H., and William E. Morgan. 1983. "The Exportation of State and Local Taxes in a Multilateral Framework: The Case of Household Type Taxes." *National Tax Journal* 36: 459–76.

Nathan, Richard P., Allen D. Manvel, and Susannah E. Calkins. 1975. *Monitoring Revenue Sharing*. Washington, D.C.: Brookings Institution.

Oates, Wallace E. 1972. *Fiscal Federalism*. New York: Harcourt, Brace, Jovanovich.

Pauly, Mark V. 1973. "Income Redistribution as a Local Public Good." *Journal of Public Economics* 2: 35–58.

Sargent, Thomas J., and Neil Wallace. 1975. "Rational Expectations, the Optimal Monetary Instrument, and the Optimal Money Supply Rule." *Journal of Political Economy* 83: 241–54.

Schultze, Charles L. 1974. "Sorting Out the Social Grant Programs: An Economist's Criteria." *American Economic Review* 64: 181–89.

Tiebout, Charles M. 1956. "A Pure Theory of Local Expenditures." *Journal of Political Economy* 64: 416–24.

Tresch, Richard W. 1981. *Public Finance: A Normative Theory.* Plano, Texas: Business Publications.

U.S. Department of Commerce. *Survey of Current Business,* various issues.

U.S. Office of Management and Budget. *Budget of the United States Government,* various issues.

Walsh, Cliff. 1983. "Reforming Federal Financial Relations: Some Radical (Or Are They Conservative?) Proposals." Paper presented at the Federal Finances Symposium, Hobart, Australia.

Wilde, James A. 1971. "Grants-in-Aid: The Analytics of Design and Response." *National Tax Journal* 24: 143–56.

Yinger, John. Forthcoming. "On Fiscal Disparities across Cities." *Journal of Urban Economics.*

FEDERALISM AND FEDERAL DEFICIT REDUCTION†

EDWARD M. GRAMLICH*

BETWEEN fiscal years 1980 and 1985, when the federal budget deficit rose from 2.7 percent of GNP to 5.3 percent, grants and tax expenditures benefitting state and local governments fell from 4.4 percent of GNP to 3.7 percent. Between fiscal years 1985 and 1987, when the federal deficit is expected to decline to 3.9 percent of GNP, grants and tax expenditures are expected to fall again to 3.4 percent of GNP. Over the entire period from 1980 to 1987 the rise in the deficit would have been twice as great had it not been for the cuts in grants and tax expenditures. For the 1980s, at least, that little federal budget-cutting that has been done has been done on the backs of state and local governments.

The political question emerging from these numbers is what has happened to the lobby for state and local governments, a lobby that was responsible for rapid expansions in grants and tax expenditures of all sorts up to 1980. I leave aside that issue, but turn to some interesting economic questions involving deficit reduction and the cuts. The paper examines the cuts in grants and tax expenditures, along with other developments that have occurred simultaneously, to see what these developments mean for federal-state-local fiscal relations in the United States. I focus first on the impact of the cuts for the overall saving-investment balance, and then on more basic allocative efficiency, equity, and stabilization considerations.

Federal Grants and the Cuts

The federal government now engages in five types of transactions that directly or indirectly benefit state and local governments. All have been scaled back in the 1980s, though the pattern has been uneven and the rationales have differed. These types are listed as follows, with dollar amounts and shares of GNP given in Table 1.

*Congressional Budget Office.

1. A Grants.

The first type, called case A grants, consists of open-ended matching grants for states to fund a series of low income programs, mainly Aid to Families with Dependent Children (AFDC) and Medicaid. For these two programs federal matching shares run from fifty to eighty percent of program costs, depending on state income. As Table 1 shows, these A grants now cost the federal government $54.2 billion, 1.2 percent of GNP. In the recent period there have been a number of administrative efforts to cut these grants, but the share has not declined much because Medicaid grants continue growing due to rising relative costs of health care.

2. B Grants.

Whereas open-ended A grants can be thought of as reducing prices for states, B grants are closed-ended unconditional grants that raise spendable resources without influencing relative prices. There are, or were, two important types of B grants. The first type was general revenue sharing, a straight unconditional grant amounting to almost $7 billion back in 1980, but now killed off because of the recent budget cuts. The second type is called a block grant. These grants are really consolidations of grants that formerly were categorical for much narrower programs. The grant consolidation process has proceeded in two stages since the early 1970s. Many grants have been converted to block form, but in the 1980s some of the early block grants, particularly under the Comprehensive Employment and Training Act (CETA) and the Community Development Block Grant (CDBG) have been sharply cut back. The net effect of the conversion to block grants and the elimination of various programs has been that case B grants now total $13.4 billion, dropping from 0.6 to 0.3 percent of GNP in the 1980s.

1. Federal Transactions Benefitting States and Localities

Fiscal years, 1950 through 1990

By type listed in text[1]

Year	A	B	C	D	E	Sum
(Billions of current dollars)						
1950	1.3	-	1.0	0.1	0.1	0.3
1960	2.5	-	4.5	2.9	0.8	10.7
1970	8.6	-	15.5	7.7	2.2	34.0
1980	31.9	17.1	42.5	22.0	7.5	121.0
1985	48.1	16.6	41.2	31.0	12.8	149.7
1987	54.2	13.4	42.3	26.2	12.8	148.9
(Share of GNP)[2]						
1950	0.4	-	0.3	-	0.1	0.9
1960	0.5	-	0.9	0.6	0.2	2.1
1970	0.8	-	1.5	0.8	0.3	3.3
1980	1.2	0.6	1.6	0.8	0.3	4.4
1985	1.2	0.4	1.0	0.8	0.3	3.7
1987	1.2	0.3	1.0	0.6	0.3	3.4

1. A refers to A grants, B to B grants, C to C grants, D to the tax deduction, and E to the tax exemption.

2. Share of the sum may not equal sum of the shares because of rounding error.

Source: OMB (various years)

3. C Grants.

These grants are a hybrid form, categorical with federal matching, but limited in total amount by the federal government. Numerous past studies have indicated that grant limits are small relative to state-local desired spending on a program, which is to say that the price reduction seems generally to be ineffective at the margin. Hence the economic effects of C grants should be similar to those of B grants despite the nominal categorization. These grants have dropped from 1.6 to 1.0 percent of GNP in the 1980s, partly because of the consolidations into B grants referred to above, and partly because of budget cuts. There have also been occasional reductions in federal matching shares.

4. Tax Deductions.

Federal income tax law permits the deduction of most taxes paid to state and local governments, thereby giving a separate price subsidy to state and local spending. This subsidy has gradually been lessened in the 1980s through the cuts in marginal income tax rates in both the Economic Recovery and Tax Act of 1981 (ERTA) and the Tax Reform Act of 1986 (TRA), and by the reduction in numbers of itemizers under TRA. TRA also eliminated the sales tax deduction, which may induce some alteration in state revenue patterns. Once all rate cuts and tax base changes of TRA are phased in, the tax deductions are still expected to be worth about $25 billion in federal revenue, 0.5 percent of GNP, by 1990.

5. Tax Exemptions.

The federal income tax base excludes interest paid by state and local governments. State and local bond rates are thus lower than they would otherwise be, and bond-financed construction spending is subsidized. Because of the income tax exemption of state and local interest payments, it is also possible for states and localities to divert this subsidy into general support through bond arbitrage. Both the marginal tax rate cuts and other restrictions on private purpose bond exemptions in TRA greatly restrict these possibilities, but the interest exemption is still expected to be worth $13 billion, 0.2 percent of GNP by 1990.

Saving, Investment, and the Surplus

The first question is whether cuts in these items benefitting state and local governments will serve their long-run macroeconomic purpose. The most convincing reason for opposing continuing structural federal deficits is that they seem likely to reduce, and have reduced, the

share of U.S. national output devoted to wealth accumulation. In a closed economy this reduction takes the form of direct crowding out of investment; in an open economy it takes the form of reductions in the trade balance and increased foreign borrowing.

However the crowding out takes place, the share of output devoted to wealth accumulation can be measured either by subtracting foreign borrowing from net investment to derive domestically-financed net investment, or by summing public and private saving to derive net national saving. The second approach is taken in Table 2. Since all saving and/or investment shares are cyclical, it would be misleading to look at particular years, as was done above for grants and tax expenditures. Rather, Table 2 shows decade averages since 1950, focusing particularly on the 1980s.

The Table shows first that net national saving, in the right column, has dropped sharply, from 7.4 percent of GNP in the 1950s and 1960s to only 2.7 percent of GNP in the 1982–86 period. Of the three sectors, the state and local sector actually saves more now than it did in the 1950s and 1960s, because of the large current surplus in pension accounts for state and local employees. State and local general governments have never saved or dissaved to any degree. Net private saving has fallen, by roughly the amount that state and local pension saving has increased. If the distinction between private and state and local saving is viewed as artificial because pension fund surpluses should really be allocated to the private saving of state and local employees, the meaningful number is their sum, nonfederal saving. This has averaged about 7.7 percent of GNP throughout the entire period since 1950.

What has differed between the 1950s and 1960s and the 1980s is federal saving, the negative of the federal deficit. In the early period the federal budget was balanced on average, now it runs deficits approaching 5 percent of GNP. These deficits have subtracted from the pool of funds available for wealth accumulation and driven down national saving rates, just as

2.   Aggregate Saving Rates, 1950-86

Decade averages, percent of GNP

Period	Priv	StLoc	Fed	Sum[1]
1950-59	7.5	-0.2	0.1	7.4
1960-69	8.1	0.1	-0.3	7.9
1970-79	8.1	0.8	-1.7	7.1
1980-81	6.5	1.1	-2.2	5.4
1982-86	6.1	1.5	-4.9	2.7

1.   Share of the sum may not equal sum of the shares because of

rounding error.

Source: Bureau of Economic Analysis.

neoclassical economists would have predicted. Not only have the rising federal deficits seemed to have caused the drop in net national saving; they have not been offset by rises in private saving as would have been predicted by those believing in Ricardian equivalence.

Given this background, how will cuts in grants or tax benefits for state and local governments help solve the problem of deficient national saving? Barring other changes in the federal budget, cuts in grants or tax benefits will reduce federal deficits. They might appear to lower the state and local surplus a like amount, but that cannot happen. These grants or tax benefits go entirely to general governments. These governments not only do not run large deficits or surpluses, as said above, but they cannot. Virtually all general governments are constrained by their constitutions to balance their operating budgets. Hence when federal grants fall, states and localities must either cut spending or raise revenues. When federal tax deductions fall, states and localities that cut taxes must also cut spending. When state and local interest exemptions are reduced, states and localities that cut borrowing must either cut spending or raise taxes. So the cut in grants or tax benefits should reduce federal dissaving, leave unchanged state and local saving, and raise net national saving.

Of course, if cuts in grants do increase national saving, they very likely will not achieve another objective sometimes imputed for them. It is often argued that cuts in grants are necessary to avoid federal tax increases. But to the extent that grant cuts force states and localities to make budget adjustments such as tax increases, cuts in grants do not avoid the necessity for tax increases, they merely change the form.

Interpretation of the actual numbers is hampered by delays in getting disaggregated data, but such figures as are available suggest that states and localities have been able to make the necessary budget adjustments without serious difficulty. Despite the fact that grants were rising sharply in the 1970s, there were a steady stream of reports of impending municipal bankruptcies and defaults. In the 1980s, sharp cuts in grants have been accompanied by less, not more, reports of financial problems. The aggregate state and local general government budget surplus rose to a high level of $20 billion in 1984, and though it has slipped back since then, by the end of 1986 it was still roughly in line with historical cyclical patterns. The National Association of State Budget Officers (NASBO (1987)) reports that most states will have positive fund balances by the end of fiscal 1987, though the balances are generally fairly small and highly negative for two states (Texas and Alaska). Bahl (1987) describes a number of recent reports on local government financial conditions that suggest no major problems.

The necessary belt-tightening seems to have been done largely on the revenue side. By the end of 1986, aggregate state and local spending was the same share of GNP as in 1980, the beginning of the cutback period. Taxes as a share of GNP have risen by more than the cuts in grants. For the future, the NASBO survey reports that 28 states are considering discretionary tax increases in 1987, far more than are considering decreases. Only two of these states are relying on the "windfall" revenue that falls into state coffers as a result of the base-broadening provisions of TRA—all others are making a discretionary increase in some kind of tax. As predicted above, the cuts in grants avoided federal tax increases, but not state and local tax increases.

Hence it now appears that the federal deficit reduction strategy has limited what would otherwise have been a sharper drop in national saving. Federal dissaving has been curbed without a concomitant reduction in state and local saving, because of state and local tax increases. I now turn to the deeper impacts of these changes on efficiency and equity aspects of U.S. fiscal federalism relations.

Allocation

The normative rationale for having the federal government play any role at all in influencing state and local spending and taxing decisions involves benefit spillovers. If some public spending program benefits households residing outside the taxing-spending jurisdiction, these outsiders should pay some of the cost. If they do not, the particular spending and taxing district will devote too few resources to the program.

While this rationale has been well known for at least fifty years and is still accepted in principle, actual federal price subsidies for state and local spending seem to have greatly exceeded the amount called for by the spillover rationale. Table 3 provides a breakdown of the $42.3 billion in federal type C grants in fiscal 1987. Only three of the large programs have federal matching shares below 75 percent, and the overall average matching share is 81 percent. If this were not enough of a price subsidy, in particular circumstances the federal income tax deduction and interest exemption add to it.

These very high subsidies can be contrasted with the much lower estimates of true benefit spillovers. Spillover rates are not easy to estimate, but Office of Management and Budget (OMB, 1985) figures indicate that most federal infrastructure investments went for projects that were of local and regional interest. A Congressional Budget Office (CBO, 1982) study of the federal highway program, far and away the largest of the grant programs listed in Table 3, found that prospective construction projects of primarily local interest greatly outnumbered those of primarily national interest. Even on the Interstate Highway System, supposedly of clearly national interest, a Department

3. A Breakdown of Categorical (Type C) Grants

Fiscal 1987

Type	Amt[1]	F[2]
Highways	12.3	.83
Compensatory education	3.1	1.00
Employment and training	2.9	.94
Sewage treatment	2.6	.55
Mass transit	2.0	.80
Human development services	1.9	.83
Public housing	1.9	1.00
Unemployment trust fund admin.	1.6	1.00
Food donations	1.4	1.00
Rehabilitation services	1.3	.83
Education for handicapped	1.2	.99
Vocational education	1.0	.58
Employment service	0.9	1.00
Social services	0.9	.54
Discretionary transit grants	0.9	.75
Airports	0.9	.80
Educational impact aid	0.8	1.00
Special education	0.6	1.00
Forest service	0.6	1.00
Miscellaneous	3.5	nc
Sum	42.3	.81

1. Billions of current dollars.

2. Federal matching share up to the funds limit.

Source: Unpublished OMB data.

of Transportation traffic survey found that almost all interstate highways had less than thirty percent out-of-state drivers, as opposed to the ninety percent federal matching rate for building and resurfacing these roads. Across the board, Netzer (1986) estimates that national marginal benefits are in the range of ten to twenty percent of total marginal benefits for most subsidized state and local programs.

For categorical grants, both the positive results and the normative prescriptions are obvious. The positive results are that states and localities facing highly subsidized prices for particular public services will overspend on these services. To control state and local spending in the presence of this high subsidy, the federal government must then resort to bureaucratic limits—limits on funds available, rationing through selection of only certain project applications, effort maintenance restrictions, and the like. These limits turn what otherwise might be an open-ended price subsidy into its present hybrid form. When the limits are binding at a level of spending that is small relative to that that states would otherwise have done, this hybrid structure achieves the worst of both worlds—there is *less* state and local spending than would be desired from a normative standpoint, because the initial price subsidy is too *high* and therefore the price subsidy at the margin too *low*. It follows logically that a fall in federal matching shares can simultaneously improve economic efficiency and reduce federal spending.

Despite the intrinsic appeal of such a change in an era of fiscal austerity, reductions in federal matching rates have actually been quite rare. Most recent changes in categorical grants have been either to consolidate type C categorical grants into type B block grants, or to cut the funds limit on type C grants. Neither corrects the present inefficiency that benefit spillovers go unrecognized at the margin. But there have been occasional reductions in matching rates. The Omnibus Water Bill of 1986, for rivers, harbors, and other "pork barrel" type projects, for the first time requires state and local cost matching on new projects. If

these projects have so few local benefits that localities do not want to put up their share (generally about forty percent), there will at least be some price rationing of inefficient projects. The two Clean Water Acts passed in the 1980s, for waste water treatment, have also reduced federal matching shares from 75 percent at the start of the decade to a much lower number at the end by converting categorical grants to a subsidized loan revolving fund. The Highway Act of 1982 also lowered some federal matching rates. As a final straw in the wind, OMB data show that the aggregate federal matching share on all case C categorical grants has dropped from 86 percent in 1980 to 81 percent in 1986.

Another price subsidy for state and local spending that operates in particular circumstances is that involved in the deductibility of state and local taxes. Two changes in TRA will scale this, or its impact, back. On one hand, the cut in marginal tax rates for many taxpayers lessens the price subsidy. On the other hand, the fact that the number of itemizers is reduced by other base-broadening measures decreases numbers of voters voting for large state-local budgets because of the tax deduction.

Empirical research on the impact of deductibility on state and local spending has found surprisingly small effects. One approach used by Kenyon (1987) is called the average voter model. According to this model the proportional change in overall state and local spending, G, from eliminating deductibility provisions can be approximated by

$$dlnG = epti, \qquad (1)$$

where e is the tax price elasticity of demand for public spending with respect to a change in the price and the next three terms determine how this price changes when deductibility is eliminated. The proportional change depends on the proportion of taxes that are deductible, p, the marginal federal income tax rate faced by the average itemizing taxpayer, t, and the share of itemizers, i.

Kenyon uses what has now become a

standard elasticity estimate of −.5 for making her calculations. She also argues that the share of deductible taxes benefitting individuals is only .4, because so much state and local spending and taxes are devoted to business. Before TRA the marginal tax rate, t, averaged .31 for all itemizing taxpayers and the share of itemizers, i, was only .32. Hence the impact of a complete elimination of deductibility was a mere −.02, or a two percent drop in overall state and local spending. Once all changes are made, TRA is expected to cut the average marginal tax rate for itemizing taxpayers to .19, the itemization share to .25, and the predicted drop in spending to −.01, a one percent drop. We can infer, then, that TRA will reduce state and local spending by the difference, one percent. According to this average voter method, the impact of deductibility on state and local spending is surprisingly slight, and the impact of the restriction of deductibility under TRA is similarly slight.

An alternative way to make the calculations, which focuses on a different aspect of deductibility, uses a median voter model. This approach, used by Gramlich (1985), requires micro data on the spending and tax desires of individual voters, along with their tax prices and incomes with and without deductibility. The impact of the deductibility is computed voter by voter, and then old and new medians are computed. The calculations are done for a sample of Michigan voters, with an elasticity estimate of −.5 and a share of deductible taxes set at 1, to determine the percentage changes in just the spending and taxes affecting individuals.

The results are shown in Table 4. Complete elimination of deductibility results in a reduction of the local spending and taxes desired by the median voter of between one and five percent, much as in Kenyon's calculations (particularly if one multiplies these changes by her p of .4).

The Table 4 calculations bring out another interesting aspect of deductibility. Because high income voters are much more likely to itemize than low income voters, and because they tend to live in high income communities, changes in deductibil-

ity provisions have very slight impacts on the spending desires of the median voter in low income communities such as Detroit, Lansing, and the rural communities. On the other hand, the changes have major impacts in high income urban suburbs. The deductibility changes in TRA would thus cause an uneven pattern of reductions—large in high income communities, very slight in low income communities, making for Kenyon's slight overall reduction. As such, the social attractiveness of the change is greatly enhanced—not only are the overall reductions slight, but they occur in communities that ought to be able to get along without the federal price subsidy.

TRA makes two further changes that could have significant allocative effects. One involves the fact that the deductibility of sales taxes is eliminated, which should inspire states to raise more revenue through other sources—user charges (nondeductible before and after TRA) and income and property taxes for households and businesses (deductible before and after TRA, though at lower rates). Shifts into user charges would generally enhance economic efficiency, shifts into income and property taxes would generally worsen it.

The question is how large these shifts will be. Because sales taxes have not been treated separately under the federal income tax until now, empirical researchers are forced back onto inference of response elasticities from other ways in which the burden price of sales taxes differs from that of other revenue sources—specifically the degree to which sales taxes can be exported out of the state. Among those researchers who have tried to distinguish separate response elasticities for sales taxes, Inman (1986) reports the counterintuitive finding that removing the deduction will *raise* reliance on sales taxes, Gade (1986) estimates that it will *lower* reliance on sales taxes, and Kenyon (1987) predicts little change. The NASBO (1987) survey indicates that of the twenty-six states planning a discretionary tax increase apart from the TRA windfall, half are planning to respond by raising sales taxes. For this to happen just as TRA is eliminating sales tax deductibility is re-

4. Desired Local Government Spending under different Tax
        Deductibility Provisions

Number of voters desiring specified percentage changes in local
spending and taxes, from a sample of Michigan voter-taxpayers[1]
                Median voter class underlined

Place	>10	6-9	1-5	NoCh	1-5	6-9	>10	Sum
			1980 Tax Law					
Detroit	7	5	2	87	3	27	18	149
Det.sub.	20	16	9	229	3	30	25	332
Lansing	2	2	-	17	-	3	4	28
Lan.sub.	1	1	1	18	-	3	2	26
Oth.urb.	11	8	11	79	-	14	7	130
Rural	40	31	28	314	3	41	48	505
Total	81	63	51	744	9	118	104	1170
			TRA of 1986					
Detroit	23	6	15	56	8	26	15	149
Det.sub.	65	26	81	100	21	27	12	332
Lansing	3	4	1	13	2	3	2	28
Lan.sub.	4	1	8	8	-	4	1	26
Oth.urb.	27	9	30	42	3	13	6	130
Rural	84	44	87	202	16	44	28	505
Total	206	90	222	421	50	117	64	1170
			Full elimination of deductibility					
Detroit	37	14	6	54	4	21	13	149
Det.sub.	165	32	14	93	3	17	8	332
Lansing	5	8	-	11	-	2	2	28
Lan.sub.	12	1	1	8	-	3	1	26
Oth.urb.	54	12	9	43	1	7	4	130
Rural	163	65	37	188	4	25	23	505
Total	436	132	67	397	12	75	51	1170

1. Methodological details are given in Gramlich (1985).

Source: Gramlich (1985) and further calculations.

markable in and of itself, and seems to verify Inman's counterintuitive prediction. It also suggests that the impact of TRA on the composition of state revenues may not be very large.

The final allocative change made by TRA is through its tightening of restrictions on bond arbitrage. Gordon and Slemrod (1986) identify four ways in which this arbitrage can take place:
1. Communities can borrow at the tax exempt rate m and invest at the taxable bond rate r, gaining r − m.
2. Citizens can borrow at r(1 − t) and invest through their governments at r, gaining rt.
3. High income citizens can borrow at r(1 − t) and invest in municipal bonds at m, gaining m − r + rt.
4. Low income citizens can have their government borrow at m, lower taxes, and the citizens can then invest the proceeds at r(1 − t), gaining r − rt − m.

Before TRA the marginal tax rate for most investors was in the neighborhood of .5 and m was about .7r. TRA makes the marginal tax rate for all taxpayers close to .3, and a simulation of its impact by Galper, Lucke, and Toder (1986) finds m to be close to .9r. These changes close off or alter the four types of arbitrage as follows:
1. The spread between r and m falls from .3r to .1r, hence reducing the profitability of this direct arbitrage channel. In addition, a series of limitations on the degree to which states and localities can use the tax-exempt market to finance private purpose and industrial development projects further blocks the channel.
2. The spread between r and r(1 − t) falls from .5r to .3r, restricting the profitability of this channel.
3. The spread between m and r(1 − t) stays at .2r, making for no change here.
4. There are no citizens for which r(1 − t) exceeds m, so this channel disappears altogether.
One of the channels is gone altogether, two have greatly reduced rewards, one of these has added administrative barriers, and one is unaffected. Overall, there should be much less arbitrage, and uneconomic paper-shuffling, as a result of TRA.

All of these changes should make for modest efficiency improvements, as they save the federal government money. Reductions in federal matching rates for some types of projects should make marginal cost shares better reflect true benefit spillovers. Limitation of the value of the state and local tax deduction should reduce a price subsidy that now goes mainly to high income communities. Reductions in possibilities for bond arbitrage should lessen uneconomic tax and credit transactions.

Distribution

State governments have an impact on the distribution of income in the United States because they determine benefit levels and eligibility in some important programs. Of the four main programs benefitting low income individuals, food stamps and Supplemental Security Income (for the aged poor) are straight federal programs, while AFDC and Medicaid are state-run programs where the federal government provides matching assistance through the type A grants referred to above.

This income support system has been the subject of intense criticism, from academics and politicians, liberals and conservatives, recipients and taxpayers. With so many criticisms from so many quarters it is hard to sort out exactly what is wrong, but a general listing, where different observers would emphasize different points, would run as follows:
1. Low income support programs have appeared to encourage recipients to become dependent on the welfare system.
2. Because of that, these public programs have become almost uniquely unpopular with taxpayer-voters (see Citrin (1979) for California voters, Courant, Gramlich, and Rubinfeld (1980) for Michigan voters, and Ladd and Wilson (1982) for Massachusetts voters).
3. Because of that, support levels have gotten very low, with many recipients getting less than half of the poverty line in some states and less than the poverty line in all states.

4. Because of that, poverty is rising, from slightly over 10 percent of all families in 1980 to 11.5 percent in 1985 (years in which the overall unemployment rate was close to 7 percent).

Just as there are many criticisms of the present welfare system, there are many suggestions for reforming it. One of the aspects most often singled out for programmatic reform is its federalist structure. In the 1980s the Reagan Administration made a widely-publicized "New Federalism" proposal for decentralizing the welfare system by turning its management and financing over to state governments, with compensatory revenue sharing to neutralize the implicit costs. Eight past Secretaries of the Department of Health and Human Services (HHS), along with many others, proposed going in exactly the reverse direction—centralizing the system by establishing a uniform national benefits floor. Neither the Administration plan nor its opposite national floor plan was ever seriously considered by Congress.

A disagreement among economists has paralleled this policy disagreement. Pauly (1973) and Tresch (1981) have argued that income support should be primarily a subnational government responsibility, while Ladd and Doolittle (1982) have argued that it should be primarily a national government responsibility. Apart from the well-known migration issue, which clearly argues that income support should be a national responsibility but may be of secondary empirical importance (Gramlich (1985)), the key issue in this debate has been whether taxpayer-donors should try to raise the incomes of the poor throughout the country, or only the poor in their own area. Even with clever analysis of polling data, it seems essentially impossible to answer this question.

But there is another issue that economists have tended to ignore. One argument for the decentralized approach is that states and localities can serve as laboratories for testing national policy changes—systems can be tested on a small scale and perhaps better tailored to local conditions. There has been a quiet revolution in welfare policy in the 1980s in which

states have actually played this role quite successfully.

The revolution began in 1981. The Reagan Administration, wanting to reduce welfare costs and dependency, tried to force states to tighten work requirements. Congress resisted a compulsory approach, but at least permitted states to experiment with different ways of making benefits conditional on enrollment in various kinds of public job, training, and wage subsidy programs, often combined with public day care programs for mothers with small children. More than half the states have now developed their own "workfare" programs, and these programs have generally proved to be successful—enrollees have been placed in jobs and earned more income than would otherwise have been the case, state welfare costs have been reduced, the programs have generally passed a full benefit-cost test, and they appear to be popular with both state governors and welfare recipients themselves (Gueron (1986)).

Should these early promising results hold up, rises in the earned income of enrollees should reduce their dependency on the transfer system, the first of the four problems listed above. In reducing dependency, welfare could become more popular, as seems to be indicated by the fact that many state governors are now boasting about the program changes they have made, or making highly publicized proposals for changing the system in this direction (Cuomo Task Force, 1986). This increased popularity could inspire an increase in benefit levels, or at least forestall continued real erosion in benefit levels. That, and the rise in recipient earnings, should reduce poverty. In other words, the workfare type changes made by the states as a result of the permissive 1981 legislation have the potential to unravel the entire welfare impasse.

This is one case where the decentralization strategy appears to have worked beyond almost anyone's expectations. States were permitted to try out new approaches to welfare, they did, the approaches have seemed to work, and the welfare mess now appears less intractable. It is ironic that the Reagan Administration's widely trumpeted New Federalism initiative did very little to revitalize federalism—the initiative was briefly debated and then dropped—but the little known and perhaps unintended impact of the permissive workfare changes may in the end prove responsible for quite fundamental changes.

Stabilization

The conventional wisdom, argued most cogently by Oates (1972), is that the national government and not the states should be responsible for short term macroeconomic stabilization policy. This belief rests on three important propositions:
1. The shocks that a stabilization authority is counteracting are assumed to be national shocks, where spending demands rise or fall throughout the whole nation.
2. The national government is assumed to have more leverage in counteracting cycles—aggregate demand responds more to national policy changes.
3. Any debt that is created in the course of Keynesian type stabilization policies is internal for the national government, external for a state government.

Modern macroeconomic developments, particularly the opening of national economies to foreign trade and capital flows, have greatly weakened each proposition. First, 1970s and 1980s style spending shocks have not been national but rather regional—energy price increases and decreases have helped one part of the country and hurt another; rises and falls in the value of the dollar have done likewise. In the presence of such "zero sum" shocks, it is hard to know what a national stabilization authority would do, increase or decrease fiscal stimulus?

Second, in the open economy, flexible exchange rate model of Mundell (1963), national fiscal policies have a very weak impact on aggregate demand, because any fiscal stimulus is offset by an exchange rate appreciation and a worsening of the trade deficit. State fiscal stimulus in response to zero sum shocks, on the other hand, would not lead to an appreciation of the currency for the whole country, because these state policies are mutually-offsetting just as the shocks they respond to are mutually-offsetting. For these purposes, then, individual states can be thought of as still being on fixed exchange rates.

Third, if the open world capital markets are competitive, capital is assumed to be in highly elastic supply at a nearly constant real rate of interest. In the strict version of this model, there is absolutely no difference in the debt floated by national and state governments—both have economic effects like those of external debt, because in both cases citizen-bondholders gain no income from these interest payments. They earn the fixed world rate of interest whatever debt they hold, they do not gain from any debt being floated, and all debt for both governments has a full annual future costs set by the fixed rate of interest.

The other recent development does not reflect any opening of the world economy, but rather the large American budget deficits of the 1980s. These have become such a large and intractable problem that even if the U.S. still lived in the old closed economy, policy-makers would have serious reservations about adding any more Keynesian-type debt in response to a recession. Portfolios may not accept any more debt without sharp rises in interest rates, and the political problems in eliminating the deficit once the recession is over are multiplied.

The upshot is that it is now much less wise for the U.S. national government to engage in old-style Keynesian countercyclical policies. The demand stimulus is likely to be quite weak, the lasting interest cost quite large, and it may not even be clear which way to turn the dials.

What about state countercyclical policies—should they too be forsworn, or do they now take on increased responsibility to fill the vacuum? A convenient way to answer the question is in terms of an equation Marston (1985) used to explain unemployment rates within a state

$$U = U + Z + av_{-1} + w \qquad (2)$$

where U is a state's unemployment rate, U is the national rate, Z is a constant state differential, a is an autoregression coefficient, and v and w are residuals.

If state unemployment rates were to change because U changes, stabilization would be the task of national policy. State policies could not be rescued by the fixed exchange rate argument used above, because then all states would be moving in the same direction, and the national currency would appreciate just as if the national government stabilized. The variable Z refers to a permanent differential, the result of state wages, labor market conditions, unemployment insurance, and so forth. Variations in U caused by Z should not be counteracted by stabilization policies at any level of government, but rather by underlying structural policies. Variations due to w are typically assumed to be beyond the scope of stabilization policy because of the action-recognition lag—these movements come and go before an authority can act. A *necessary* condition for the desirability of state stabilization policy, then, is that an important component of state unemployment movements be in the av_{-1} term—a particular state cyclical deviation lasting long enough to be offset by state policy.

This is a necessary condition. To develop sufficient conditions, it must also be established that state policies have a significant impact on state incomes, that labor is immobile, and that state incremental external debt costs are small enough that the exercise of state stabilization policies raises some measure of state utility. All of this is worked out in Gramlich (1987), for a variety of states and macroeconomic models. The general conclusion is that it is optimizing for states to try to offset spending shocks, by from two-fifths to one-tenth of the shock, depending on the size of the state, the state's import leakage, and other factors. This is not an enormous degree of stabilization, but it is some, and it does seem enough to call for a revision in the conventional wisdom

that stabilization should not be a state responsibility.

While the balanced budget restriction that almost all states and localities operate under may seem to rule out state stabilization policies, in fact it does not. There are several ways in which such state stabilization policies could be pursued, even within existing legislative and constitutional restrictions. One is that the balanced budget restriction operates on the operating budget only; there is nothing to prevent bond-financed countercyclical construction spending. A second is for states to raise their sales tax rates in an expansion, build up a rainy day fund, and use the proceeds to finance cuts in sales tax rates in a recession. Whether households are simple-minded cash flow consumers or careful life cycle consumers who know that sales tax rates will vary over time, households will reallocate their spending to stabilize state incomes. NASBO (1987) reports that thirty-two states now have such rainy day funds to buffer their finances, and ultimately their economies. The funds are small as yet, with a cumulated stock balance of just one percent of expenditures, but that is one percent more than a decade ago.

A third stabilization mechanism is for states to borrow from the federal unemployment insurance trust fund in a recession and pay back in a subsequent expansion. Burtless and Vroman (1984) report that a different set of thirty-two states did borrow fairly large amounts from the national unemployment trust fund in the 1980–84 recessionary period. They are now using the expansion to repay this debt.

Implications

The halting steps to try to rein in federal deficit growth in the early part of the 1980s and then reduce them later has turned out to have an important impact on the development of fiscal federalism in the United States. Almost all of the budget-cutting that was done over the decade was in terms of various grants and tax expenditures benefitting state and local governments, a sharp contrast from the previous decades of rapid growth. And for a variety of reasons detailed in the paper, these cuts, and other developments, appeared to have triggered generally desirable long term changes.

One desirable change is the simple one that states and localities have shown themselves able to manage the cuts without piling up great amounts of debt or claiming bankruptcy. In this area, they have seemed to perform much better than in the 1970s, and much better than the national government.

In terms of longer-run goals, for efficiency cuts in grants and changes in tax laws have both made for modest improvements in the price structures facing state and local governments, to make them better conform to underlying benefit-spillovers. For distribution, changes states were permitted to make on their own show promise of untangling the long-standing impasse regarding United States welfare policy. For stabilization, new macroeconomic developments and the large federal deficits have meant that the federal government is pretty much forced to forswear Keynesian-type anti-recessionary policies for the foreseeable future. Any counter-cyclical policies that will be conducted will have to be conducted by states, and in recent years the states have began to take just such steps.

In each area, grant and tax expenditure cutbacks, along with other developments, have forced states and localities to accept more responsibilities with less money. The set of fiscal federalism relationships existing in the United States is much better for the experience. At least there is one positive result of America's high budget deficits.

FOOTNOTE

†Acting Director of the Congressional Budget Office, on leave from the University of Michigan. Kathy Ormiston did the research on grants underlying Table 3 and Deborah Laren the simulations underlying Table 4. Harvey Galper, Larry Hush, Helen Ladd, Rudolph Penner, and Eric Toder also made helpful comments.

REFERENCES

Bahl, Roy, "Urban Government Finance and Federal Income Tax Reform," *National Tax Journal*, vol. 40, March, 1987, pp. 1–18.

Burtless, Gary and Wayne Vroman, "The Performance of Unemployment Insurance since 1979," *Industrial Relations Research Association Series*, December, 1984, pp. 138–146.

Citrin, Jack, "Do People Want Something for Nothing: Public Opinion on Taxes and Government Spending," *National Tax Journal*, vol. 32S, June, 1979, pp. 113–130.

Congressional Budget Office, *The Interstate Highway System: Issues and Options*, 1982.

Courant, Paul N., Edward M. Gramlich, and Daniel L. Rubinfeld, "Why Do Voters Support Tax Limitation Amendments: The Michigan Case," *National Tax Journal*, vol. 33, March, 1980, pp. 1–20.

Gade, M. N., *Optimal State Tax Design*, Michigan State University Ph.D. dissertation, 1986.

Galper, Harvey, Robert Lucke, and Eric Toder, "Revenue Effects and Portfolio Behavior: A Simulation of the TRA of 1986," *National Tax Association Proceedings*, 1986.

Gordon, Roger H. and Joel Slemrod, "An Empirical Examination of Municipal Financial Policy," in Harvey S. Rosen (ed.), *Studies in State and Local Public Finance*, The University of Chicago Press, 1986.

Gramlich, Edward M., "Reforming U.S. Fiscal Federalism Arrangements," in John M. Quigley and Daniel L. Rubinfeld (eds.), *American Domestic Priorities: An Economic Appraisal*, University of California Press, 1985.

Gramlich, Edward M., "The Deductibility of State and Local Taxes," *National Tax Journal*, vol. 38, December, 1985, pp. 447–465.

Gramlich, Edward M., "Subnational Fiscal Policy," in John M. Quigley (ed.), *Intergovernmental Fiscal Relations in an Era of New Federalism*, JAI Press, 1987.

Gueron, Judith M., *Work Initiatives for Welfare Recipients*, Manpower Demonstration Research Corporation, 1986.

Inman, Robert P., "Does Deductibility Influence Local Taxation?" *Federal-State-Local Fiscal Relations: Technical Papers*, vol. 1, Treasury Department, 1986.

Kenyon, Daphne A., "Implicit Aid to State and Local Governments through Federal Tax Deductibility," in John M. Quigley (ed.), *Intergovernmental Fiscal Relations in an Era of New Federalism*, JAI Press, 1987.

Ladd, Helen F. and Fred C. Doolittle, "Which Level of Government Should Assist the Poor?" *National Tax Journal*, vol. 35, September, 1982, pp. 323–336.

Ladd, Helen F. and Julie Boatwright Wilson, "Why Voters Support Tax Limitation: Evidence from Massachusetts Proposition 2 1/2," *National Tax Journal*, vol. 35, June, 1982, pp. 121–148.

Marston, Stephen T., "Two Views of the Geographic Distribution of Unemployment," *Quarterly Journal of Economics*, vol. C, February, 1985, pp. 57–80.

Mundell, Robert A., "Capital Mobility and Stabilization Policy under Fixed and Flexible Exchange Rates," *Canadian Journal of Economics and Polit-*

ical Science, vol. 29, November, 1963, pp. 475–485.

National Association of State Budget Officers, *Fiscal Survey of the States*, March, 1987.

Netzer, Dick, "Effect on State and Local Government," *Economic Consequences of Tax Simplification*, Federal Reserve Bank of Boston, 1986.

Oates, Wallace E., *Fiscal Federalism*, Harcourt, Brace, Jovanovich, 1972.

Office of Management and Budget, *Budget of the United States Government: Special Analysis H*, various years.

Pauly, Mark V., "Income Redistribution as a Local Public Good," *Journal of Public Economics*, vol. 2, February, 1973, pp. 33–58.

Task Force on Poverty and Welfare, Governor Mario Cuomo, *A New Social Contract*, 1986.

Tresch, Richard W., *Public Finance: A Normative Theory*, Business Publications Inc., 1981.

[20]

NEW YORK: RIPPLE OR TIDAL WAVE?

The New York City Fiscal Crisis: What Happened and What is to be Done?

By EDWARD M. GRAMLICH*

The New York City fiscal crisis as it was played out in the nation's newspapers this year had all the elements of a first class drama. There was first of all the tension—would the city make it through its periodic financial hurdles, would the Ford Administration blink, what would happen if the city defaulted? Then there were the accusations—was it the fault of Wagner, Lindsay, Beame, Rockefeller, Ford, the unions, or economic and social forces beyond the city's control? Then the controversy—the issue seemed ideally suited to split deficit spenders from budget balancers, soft-headed liberals from hard-headed accountants, eastern establishment intellectuals from the silent majority. Finally, though it did not capture as much press coverage, the crisis also graphically illustrated several basic issues in the economics of federalism that are now creeping into public finance textbooks—the proper role of local and national governments in stabilizing the economy and redistributing income, whether the federal or the state government has an obligation to protect the financial integrity of local governments, whether public expenditures can be effectively controlled in the short run. This paper discusses the city's fiscal plight in the context of all of these issues.

* The Brookings Institution and Cornell University. I have benefited from discussions with Robert Reischauer and Harvey Galper and the assistance of Jack Whiting.

I. How Big are the Deficits?

Local governments borrow for three reasons, two of which are generally acceptable to bond holders and one dangerous. The first acceptable reason is to finance long-term capital investment projects—if a locality is building a school that will last for many years, it does not have to pay the entire bill in any one year but can spread the cost over the lifetime of the school by floating long-term debt. The second acceptable reason is to smooth out seasonal fluctuations in revenues and expenditures by short-term borrowing. The final reason, which generally is not acceptable either by a city's laws or in the eyes of bondholders, is to cover a current account deficit.

The first fact to recognize about the New York City fiscal plight is that unfortunately the city has borrowed to cover current account deficits continuously ever since fiscal 1960–61. How this was allowed to happen is still something of a mystery, but the relevant data, from the official U.S. Census figures, are given in Table 1. The first column lists the gross revenue of the city—taxes, charges and fees, grants from the federal government and New York State, and revenue from the water and transit authorities (which have been combined with the general government in this analysis). The second column lists the current general government expendi-

TABLE 1—NEW YORK CITY BUDGET DATA, FISCAL 1960-1974
(Millions of current dollars)

Date	Revenue	Current Expenditures Plus Debt Retirement	Current Account Surplus	Capital Expenditures	Net Borrowing
1960	2,769.6	2,726.5	43.1	528.3	485.2
1961	2,901.0	2,948.2	− 47.2	542.0	589.2
1962	3,119.5	3,170.0	− 50.5	582.0	632.5
1963	3,408.4	3,459.0	− 50.6	667.4	718.0
1964	3,688.8	3,788.5	− 99.7	657.6	757.3
1965	3,961.1	4,015.4	− 54.3	657.7	712.0
1966	4,367.5	4,537.0	−169.5	561.3	730.8
1967	5,174.8	5,176.0	− 1.2	554.8	556.0
1968	6,085.8	6,144.1	− 58.3	658.0	716.3
1969	6,864.7	6,945.6	− 80.9	698.3	779.2
1970	7,233.9	7,775.4	−541.5	797.0	1,338.5
1971	8,274.8	9,053.9	−779.1	1,135.1	1,914.2
1972	9,501.5	10,119.6	−618.1	1,192.9	1,811.0
1973	10,774.9	10,807.2	− 32.3	1,371.5	1,403.8
1974	11,291.5	11,779.1	−487.6	1,709.6	2,197.2

Source: U.S. Bureau of the Census, City Government Finances; various issues.

tures for all functions, including water, transit, contributions to the pension retirement system, and expenditures to retire maturing debt (which can be considered as the measure of capital consumption expenditures when investment is financed by long-term debt). The deficits are in the third column, the level of capital expenditures in the fourth, and net borrowing in the fifth. The large current account borrowing, particularly in recent years, was not backed up by capital formation; as a consequence it had to be done in the short-term market, and the city now has both extraordinary levels of outstanding short-term debt and extraordinarily high "uncontrollable" expenses simply to roll over this short-term debt every year. In 1973-74, for example, the outstanding short term debt was $485 per capita, much higher than any other large city, and it would now claim 32 percent of current expenditures—almost the entire controllable portion of the expenditure budget—to pay it off if new lenders cannot be found.[1]

[1] Extensive data on levels of short-term debt per capita can be found in Data Resources, Inc., "New

While these are certainly not reassuring figures, they are based on the latest available Census information and understate the magnitude of the current fiscal problem in three important ways. The first is that budget data are only available up to fiscal 1973-74, which is before the onset of the current recession that cost the city dearly. Had the city's unemployment rate in 1973-74 been what it is today (11 percent instead of 6.5 percent), the deficit would have been larger by about $500 million.[2] The second is that the Census

York City Default: Some Economic Implications." Only two cities, Rochester and Yonkers, have higher levels of short-term debt per capita. Rochester has a high credit rating and seems in fairly sound position; Yonkers has also been flirting with default all year.

[2] This estimate is derived as follows. Nationally incomes are reduced by 2.8 percent for every 1 percent increase in the unemployment rate. Were this to be the case in New York City, 1973-74 incomes would have been lower by 12.6 percent in this hypothetical recession. If income and sales tax revenues decline proportionately and property tax revenues and charges slightly, the revenue loss from lower income would have been about 7.5 percent, or $400 million. On the expenditure side, the increase in unemployment translates into a 130 thousand loss of private jobs. Nationally it has been estimated that one private job loss raises the poverty population by one person—were

basically takes the city's word on the breakdown between current and capital expenditures, and it has been admitted by city officials that many current expenditures were inappropriately classified as capital items. Were the more realistic Municipal Assistance Corporation (*MAC*) figures used, roughly $700 million would come out of the capital account and go into current expenditures, raising the current deficit by the same amount. The third is that it is generally conceded that the retirement pension funds, based actuarially on mortality tables from many years ago, are underfunded, meaning that present general government contributions do not cover the annual increase in liabilities of the funds. There is no good estimate of the extent of this bias, but it is perhaps not unreasonable to say that the true contributions should be larger by 25 percent, or $200 million. Were all of these changes made, the measured current account deficit of $488 million in 1973–74—already a very large number—might have been realistically estimated to increase by about $1,400 million, giving a predicted "low employment" current account deficit of nearly $2 billion, or about seventeen percent of revenues. The anticipated deficit for fiscal 1975–76 is somewhat smaller than this—approximately $800 million for the New York City version of the current account deficit, another $600 million of operating expenditures in the capital budget, and a still unknown shortfall in pension contributions—in part because of the cutbacks mandated by the New York State Financial Emergency Control Board.[3] Even with these cutbacks, however, the general picture is one of large and growing

current account deficits, persisting for long periods of time, and bound to frighten prospective lenders and threaten default sooner or later.

II. The Composition and Growth of the Deficits

The hypotheses that have been advanced to explain these deficits can be divided loosely into two groups. One type of explanation focuses on the power of the public employee unions in New York City, the bargaining concessions that have been won over the years, and the sheer size and ability to control votes of public employee unions.[4] A second focuses on the fact that the city finances an ambitious social welfare program on its own—it funds expensive welfare, higher education, public hospital, and public housing programs, along with a persistently large transit deficit and generous contributions to employee pension funds. In other large cities these programs are either not undertaken at all by the public sector, completely financed by grants or user charges, financed by the tax revenues of independent special districts, done by an overlapping county government or done by the state. Though all programs might be desirable at the national level, and in fact many argue that the city is doing a job made necessary by the lack of adequate national or state policies in these areas, it remains an inescapable fact of federalism that if localities try to redistribute income to a much greater extent than the other locali-

<hr>

this true in New York, the private job loss would raise the welfare population and net expenditures by about 13.5 percent, or $100 million.

[3] See the Joint Economic Committee Report, *New York City's Financial Crisis*, November 3, 1975, p. 30 ff.

[4] A long catalogue of the bargaining concessions is given by Raymond D. Horton. An indication of the sheer size effect is given by the fact that there are now about 450,000 full and part-time city government employees in New York City. If each was married, lived in the city, and had one close friend or relative who would vote alike on city issues, conceivably 1,350,000 votes, 30 percent of the entire voting age population and roughly half of the probable number of voters, could be marshalled in favor of making some strategic concession to, or dealing leniently with, unions.

TABLE 2—COMPOSITION OF NEW YORK CITY BUDGET DEFICIT, FISCAL 1974
(Millions of current dollars)

Revenues	11,291.5	Current expenditures	11,779.1
Grants	5,076.3	Normal functions	3,769.5
Normal functions plus untied	1,442.2	Schools	1,726.3
Schools	872.4	Marginal functions	6,283.3
Marginal functions	2,761.7	Welfare	2,587.4
Welfare	2,393.1	Higher education	490.1
Higher education	196.0	Transit	989.7
Public hospitals	135.5	Public hospitals	1,088.1
Public housing	37.1	Public housing	294.3
Own revenues	6,215.2	Pension contributions	833.7
Taxes plus normal charges	5,186.0		
Marginal functions	1,029.2		
Higher education	72.0		
Transit	629.5		
Public hospitals	147.3		
Public housing	180.4		
Current account deficit	487.6		
Normal revenues	6,628.2	Normal expenditures	3,769.5
School grants	872.4	School expenditures	1,726.3
Current account deficit	487.6	Marginal functions deficit	2,492.4
		Welfare	194.3
		Higher education	222.1
		Transit	360.2
		Public hospitals	805.3
		Public housing	76.8
		Pension contributions	833.7

Source: U.S. Bureau of the Census, *City Government Finances*, 1973–74.

ties, or if they run abnormally large deficits and incur subsequent high interest and debt retirement costs, there is a good risk that the taxpaying population will simply pick up stakes and leave the locality in a fiscal situation that much more precarious.

These competing hypotheses can be tested very loosely by examining the city's budget in more detail. Table 2 decomposes expenditures into a normal component—expenditures for functions normally undertaken by city governments—school expenditures—which are usually financed out of the budgets of independent school districts in other large cities—and the net deficit of each of these six "marginal functions"—marginal in the sense that they do not normally drain revenue from the city government. The total deficit on these marginal functions came to the enormous total of $2,492 million in 1973–74, almost

five times the measured current account deficit.[5] It is of course true that often the deficits in the accounts of these marginal programs are related to union pressure, particularly in the case of pensions but also in the case of transit, hospitals, and higher education, but as an overall impression it does appear that the city's problems stem

[5] The Census gives total public welfare expenditures of $2,587 million and grants of $2,393 million in 1973–74, leading to a net deficit on the welfare account of only $194 million. Adjusting this figure to a 1975–76 basis would perhaps add another $100 million. This Census estimate of the drain due to welfare is just one-third of that given by a recent Congressional Budget Office report on New York City, which relied both on program information and on information from *MAC*. The difference is apparently caused by the fact that Census must be putting some medicaid expenditures into the public hospital category, but not medicaid grants. Correcting this problem with the Census data would alter the composition of the marginal functions deficit between welfare and public hospitals, but not the overall total. See Congressional Budget Office.

TABLE 3—THE GROWTH OF THE NEW YORK CITY BUDGET, FISCAL 1960–74
(Millions of current dollars)

Fiscal Year	Normal Revenue plus School Grants	Normal Expenditures	School Expenditures	Marginal Functions Deficit	Current Account Surplus
1960	2,154.5	1,170.3	415.0	526.1	43.1
1970	4,956.5	2,655.5	1,284.6	1,557.9	−541.5
1974	7,500.6	3,769.5	1,726.3	2,492.4	−487.6
		Per Annum Growth Rates (%)			
1960–70	8.3	8.2	11.3	10.8	—
1970–74	10.6	8.8	7.4	11.8	—
1960–74	8.9	8.4	10.2	11.1	—

Source: U.S. Bureau of the Census, *City Government Finances*, various issues.

more from the fact that it subsidizes a broad array of functions than from the fact that the employees are gaining very high wages for performing normal public services.

This point is reinforced by examining growth rates over the 1960–74 period, as is done in Table 3. Over this time the net marginal functions deficit has grown by 11.1 percent per annum, more than expenditures either on the normal functions or on schools. Normal expenditures have grown by 8.4 percent, roughly 2.1 percent of which is a growth in employment, 2.4 percent is a growth in real wages per employee, and 4.0 percent is a growth in prices in New York City. School expenditures have grown by 10.3 percent—3.7 percent employment, 2.6 percent real wages, and 4.0 percent prices.[6]

III. Comparison with Other Cities

It is also instructive to compare the New York City budget with that of the twenty nine other largest cities. This comparison can illustrate first the degree to which New York City is unique, and secondly the risk that the New York fiscal

[6] If the city's contribution to the pension fund were added into wages, the growth in real wages per employee would be slightly higher—2.6 percent and 2.8 percent respectively for normal and school categories.

disease may spread to other cities.

Budget data for the general governments of the thirty largest *U.S.* cities for 1973–74 are given in Table 4. The budgetary items are grouped into normal and marginal functions categories, as was done in the bottom panel of Table 2, and are all expressed in per capita terms. Per capita expenditures on schools in the city are also shown in the table, even though New York City, Washington, Buffalo, Baltimore, Boston, and Memphis are the only other cities where school expenditures are actually in the general government budget.[7]

The table indicates first that only two large cities had current account deficits in 1973–74—New York City and Washington. But where New York City had to finance its deficit by borrowing from the bond market, Washington did not at the time have home rule and could borrow with federal guarantees (though this situation has changed as of January 1, 1976). Of the other cities, only Philadelphia had

[7] In the remaining cities schools are financed by an independent school authority. The data for schools comes from a different Census source that is not yet published for fiscal 1973–74. Thus data for the previous fiscal year are used throughout. Note that Honolulu has no local expenditures of any sort for schools because in Hawaii the schools are run by the state government.

TABLE 4—COMPARATIVE BUDGETS, THIRTY LARGEST U.S. CITIES, FISCAL 1973–74
(Dollars per capita)

	Normal Revenue	Normal Expenditures	School Expenditures	Marginal Functions Deficit	Current Account Surplus
New York City	962.1	493.0	207.0	325.9	−63.8
Buffalo	660.3	318.0	272.0	17.1	53.2
Baltimore	796.1	358.6	207.9	40.6	189.0
Boston	835.8	487.3	188.1	117.4	43.0
Philadelphia	637.4	369.5	202.5	54.0	11.4
Pittsburgh	523.9	233.9	220.6	13.7	55.7
Washington	1,223.4	823.1	227.7	324.1	−151.5
Chicago	512.2	247.1	219.0	20.9	25.2
Cleveland	628.7	350.7	214.0	8.3	55.7
Columbus	423.8	225.6	160.2	0.5	37.5
Detroit	702.9	334.2	219.9	98.4	50.4
Indianapolis	450.4	177.7	191.4	40.4	40.9
Milwaukee	564.2	260.9	217.0	25.3	61.0
St. Louis	572.3	299.1	173.3	60.3	39.6
Kansas City	568.3	292.1	173.4	38.0	64.8
Atlanta	674.8	294.8	204.2	25.9	149.9
Jacksonville	561.6	208.4	199.8	27.7	125.7
Memphis	489.8	204.4	168.0	20.4	97.0
New Orleans	487.7	253.0	138.8	24.1	71.8
Dallas	474.5	236.4	167.9	13.1	57.1
Houston	366.9	178.1	158.1	8.7	22.0
San Antonio	342.0	128.8	136.5	6.1	70.6
Denver	723.0	350.1	208.0	50.3	114.6
Los Angeles	607.4	242.5	224.7	50.9	89.3
San Francisco	956.4	466.2	194.7	225.0	70.5
San Diego	467.3	181.2	217.9	23.4	44.8
San Jose	492.4	163.1	282.0	14.4	32.9
Phoenix	480.1	210.0	208.8	5.9	55.4
Seattle	672.7	314.9	250.9	36.7	70.2
Honolulu	304.6	242.5	—	2.5	59.6

Source: U.S. Bureau of the Census, *City Government Finances*, 1973–74.

TABLE 5—NEW YORK CITY BUDGET IN RELATION TO THAT OF 27 OTHER LARGE CITIES
(Dollars per capita)

	Normal Revenue	Normal Expenditures	School Expenditures	Marginal Functions Deficit	Current Account Surplus
New York City	962.1	493.0	207.0	325.9	− 63.8
Mean of 27 cities*	580.5	273.6	200.8	39.5	66.6
NYC—Mean	381.6	219.4	6.2	286.4	−130.4
New York City	962.1	493.0	207.0	325.9	− 63.8
Unconstrained regression prediction*	681.1	372.0	213.3	97.8	− 2.0
NYC—Reg. Pred.	281.0	121.0	−6.3	228.1	− 61.8
New York City	962.1	493.0	207.0	325.9	− 63.8
Constrained regression prediction*	758.3	361.5	225.9	98.6	72.3
NYC—Reg. Pred.	203.8	131.5	−18.9	227.3	−136.1

Source: U.S. Bureau of the Census, *City Government Finances*, 1973–74.

* Excluding New York City, Washington, and Honolulu from sample.

a current surplus that was small enough relative to revenues that it would have been converted to a deficit had the city's 1973–74 unemployment rate been as high as it is now.

In terms of composition, it is again the marginal functions where New York City stands out. The net deficit on these marginal functions was $326 per capita in New York City, roughly the same as Washington, which is also a state government and therefore has a large budget for welfare, higher education, and public hospitals. The only other cities that have marginal functions deficits of more than $60 per capita are San Francisco (large transit subsidies and pension contributions), Boston (large pensions and public housing), and Detroit (large pensions).

Table 5 makes this comparison more systematically. The top panel compares New York's per capita budget figures with the mean for the twenty-seven other large cities (all those listed in Table 4 except New York, Washington, and Honolulu). New York's normal expenditures are $219 more than average, school expenditures are above average, and the marginal functions deficit is $286 more than average. Revenues are fortunately also $382 more than average, but the current account deficit is still $130 more than average.

It can be argued that these comparisons are misleading because New York City is not an average large city. Its racial composition, income levels, employment growth, and age are not extraordinary as cities go, but its population size and density clearly are (the population density in New York City of 25,000 per square mile is 2.5 times as great as the next highest). One way to correct for those factors in making budgetary comparisons is to run regressions for the twenty-seven city sample, explaining budgetary variables as a function of independent variables such as population size and density, income and

poverty levels, federal and state grants, and regional and governmental structure dummy variables. Values for New York City can then be inserted in the regressions and budgetary totals "predicted" for a hypothetical city with all of New York's properties.

When this comparison is made, it cuts down but does not eliminate the deviations of New York's actual budgetary values from their predicted values. Information in the second panel of Table 5, based on regressions explaining the four right-hand budgetary variables, leads to a positive residual of $121 for normal expenditures, $228 for marginal functions, and $62 for the current account deficit. Information based on regressions for all five budgetary variables, estimated in a way that insures the budget identity is preserved, leads to positive residuals of $132 for normal expenditures, $227 for marginal functions, and $136 for the current account deficit.[8] However this comparison is made, New York runs a substantially greater current account deficit than is predicted on the basis of other cities, has somewhat greater expenditures on normal functions, virtually no greater expenditures on schools, and much greater deficits for marginal functions.

IV. The Bond Ratings

One of the interesting sidelights in the gradual progression of the city toward default was that an investor looking solely at the ratings of New York City bonds would have gotten rather misleading information. Back in the early 1960's, when the city first experimented with current account deficit spending, the city's bonds were rated *A* by both Moody's and Standard and Poor's Investors Services— of "upper medium" quality. In 1965–66, when the deficits had persisted for five

---

[8] The two sets of regressions are reported in Appendix A.

years, both services downgraded the city's bond rating to *Baa*—of "lower medium" quality (the classification is labelled *BBB* by Standard and Poor's, but it means the same as *Baa* for Moody's). This caused a 50 to 75 basis point increase in borrowing costs and raised a continuing popular outcry by city officials and congressmen against the private rating services, even despite the fact that the market itself was at this time forcing New York to borrow at much higher rates than other *Baa* borrowers.[9] The lengthy political campaign eventually seemed to pay off, however, and in December 1972, Moody's upgraded the city bonds again to *A*, despite the fact that the very large current account deficits were just then beginning. Standard and Poor's behaved even more curiously, holding out against upgrading the city until December 1974, but then upgraded the city's bonds to *A* just as the early signs of a potential default were being raised.[10]

The rating services are private agencies, and though they publish voluminous information on the budget of borrowing governments, it is impossible to tell exactly how they arrive at their ratings. A statistical attempt to explain their ratings by Carleton and Lerner turned up population size, the debt-assessed value ratio, the average tax collection rate, and whether or not the borrowing agency was a school district as statistically significant independent variables, but still left a large random component to the ratings.[11] The school dummy and population variables

were only included to measure the lower rating given smaller and more unknown borrowers—if the examination was confined to a sample of large city general governments, the ratio of gross outstanding debt to the assessed value of property in the district would be the only controlling factor. While it is certainly one good indication of credit worthiness, this measure is not fully adequate for several reasons—it contains no adjustment for grants from state or the national government, no adjustment for changes, income, or sales taxes, no account of the ability of the city to alter tax rates on assessed value, and it only recognizes indirectly whether the city is or is not actually running current account deficits.

It is possible to estimate whether, or when, Moody's was being fair to New York City by their own standards in much the same way as before. A regression was fit to data from the 19 other largest cities (excluding New York and Washington), using pooled cross-section data for 1955, 1965, 1970, and 1974. The dependent variable was a rating index (1 for *Baa*, 2 for *A*, 3 for *Aa*, and 4 for *Aaa*) and the independent variable was the debt-assessed value ratio. The results, in Table 6, indicate that *by their standards* Moody's did indeed appear to be penalizing the city in the 1965–72 period—the "predicted" rating throughout this time was *A*. In retrospect, of course, this penalty was quite deserved. However, even *by their standards*, the value of New York City securities began dropping in 1972, just when the city's rating was upgraded, and this *A* rating was retained right up until the city could no longer market any securities in April 1975. This shift in the rating was difficult to justify then, impossible now.

The more fundamental question, of course, regards the standards. It is difficult and possibly unfair to make a very

---

[9] In 1971 New York was forced to pay 7.75 percent for twenty-year *Baa* bonds, while Greenwood, Mississippi, paid only 5.8 percent for twenty-year bonds of the same quality. A fascinating account of this whole experience is contained in a "Background Paper" by John E. Petersen.

[10] This situation is described in more colorful terms by a news release of Senator Thomas Eagleton, November 26, 1975.

[11] See William T. Carleton and Eugene M. Lerner. Their results are corroborated in broad detail by other studies (see Petersen, Ch. 7).

TABLE 6—PREDICTED AND ACTUAL RATINGS, NEW YORK CITY BONDS
(Current dollar totals in millions)

Date	Gross Debt Outstanding	Assessed Value of Property	Ratio of Debt to Assessed Value	Actual Rating[a]	Predicted Rating[b]	Predicted Less Actual
1955	4,845.8	20,277.8	.239	2.0	2.30	0.30
1965	7,459.2	29,752.7	.251	1.0	2.27	1.27
1970	8,690.8	34,292.3	.253	1.0	2.27	1.27
1974	13,508.7	38,529.2	.351	2.0	2.05	0.05

Source: U.S. Bureau of the Census, *City Government Finances;* various issues. Moody's Rating Service, various issues.

[a] Scale used is as follows:
$$Baa = 1.0$$
$$A = 2.0$$
$$Aa = 3.0$$
$$Aaa = 4.0$$

[b] On basis of the regression:

Predicted Rating = $2.824 - 2.197$ (Debt/Ass. Val.), $R^2 = .03$
     (1.6) $SE = .85$.
                     sample size = 76

The dependent variable was measured in the scale used in footnote a, and the regression was fit to pooled cross-section observations on the nineteen largest cities, excluding New York City and Washington, in 1955, 1965, 1970, and 1974.

forceful criticism of the rating services—no general obligation bonds rated by the services have defaulted in the postwar period, and their information and stamp of approval has surely played a role in that good record. As the New York City case illustrates, however, there is always a first time, and in retrospect the information provided by the rating services in this particular case was not so good. They correctly penalized the city in the 1965–72 period, but incorrectly backed down in 1972. This faulty information may reflect a possible weakness in the criteria apparently used by the rating services—specifically, the fact that the deficit position of the current account budget appears to have little or no direct role in the ratings—or it could also reflect the possibility that the ratings may have been influenced by political pressures from city officials.

V. Impact on the Economy

The present fiscal difficulties of New York and other cities arise in part because of the economic recession, but there is also some reverse feedback. If the city defaults, or flirts with default, this may set in motion a chain of events that will threaten the recovery from the recession. It then becomes important to try to determine whether there are any such multiplier effects for the New York situation.

The most immediate problem is the capital losses on bonds in default. If the city were to be unable to meet all its obligations, in all likelihood bondholders would be the ones to take the first losses. A large share of the outstanding bonds are held by banks in New York, and there was for a time thought to be a risk that the losses would be so great as to trigger a flight of deposits from the city banks. Most of the risk from this quarter seems to have passed, however. It never was highly likely,[12] and now that the federal government has agreed to make short-term loans to the city, and the Federal Reserve to make discount loans to any banks in difficulty, the risk of a chain reaction col-

[12] See the Congressional Budget Office Report, p. 19, and Robert Samuelson, "Troubled· Friend at Chase Manhattan," *The New Republic,* November 15, 1975.

lapse of banks because of the New York fiscal crisis is relatively slight.

A second possible way in which the New York fiscal situation could retard the recovery is through the direct cutbacks or tax increases required to balance the city's budget. The New York State Emergency Financial Control Board plan for balancing the city's budget calls for expenditure cutbacks of about $100 million in fiscal 1975–76, $500 million in fiscal 1976–77, and $700 million in fiscal 1977–78. This comes on top of a previous 6 percent expenditure cutback and 7 percent revenue increase already made by the city, and a further $200 million tax increase as part of the package which induced the Administration to agree to short term federal loans to the city. New York State, with its own financial problems, has also recently raised taxes by $600 million. The net effect of all of these actions seems likely to reduce the aggregate demand stimulus contributed by state and local governments by about $2 billion, leading to a reduction in *GNP* of approximately $4 billion below what would otherwise be the case.[13]

A third factor that must be considered is the impact on the state and local bond rate. This impact can be tested as follows. A regression was fit of the form

$$CORP \ (1-t) - RATE = a_0 + a_1 U + a_2 TIME,$$

where *CORP* is the corporate *Aaa* rate, *RATE* is the municipal bond rate in the appropriate risk class (*Aaa, Aa, A,* or *Baa*), *t* is the estimated average personal and corporate marginal tax rate among state and local bondholders, *U* is the unemployment rate, and *TIME* is a time trend. The regression explains the rate differential between the after-tax corporate bond rate and the relevant municipal

[13] These estimates accord with those of the Joint Economic Committee, p. 55.

rate as a function of the unemployment rate (since state and local governments must borrow relatively more in a recession, their rate would rise relative to the corporate rate) and time (since municipal rates have been falling relative to the corporate rate over time). The equation was fit to halfyear data from 1955–74, and then extrapolated to 1975 to see how values predicted by the regression compare with actual municipal rates in 1975.

The comparisons are given in Table 7. For the *Aaa* rate, the actual municipal rate has averaged 13 basis points above the predicted rate throughout 1975, 20 basis points in the third quarter. For bonds in the more risky categories, the residuals are much larger, rising to a total of 103 basis points in the third quarter for *A* bonds and 96 for *Baa* bonds. This difference in risk spread demonstrates what Treasury Secretary William E. Simon calls a "flight to quality" in these hard times.[14] The problem, of course, is that in many cases the lack of quality might not be a function of the locality's own fiscal behavior but reflect the impact of outside uncontrollable forces such as the economic recession.

It is not clear whether the entire residual in 1975 actual municipal bond yields can be blamed on New York City, but it seems likely that a large component can. The residual is greatest in the higher risk borrowing classes the city is typically classified in and has become greatest when the news about the city's fiscal problems was the most alarming. If we make the extreme assumptions that the entire residual is caused by the New York situation and that the corporate rate is not *lowered* by

[14] See Simon's statement of September 24, 1975. Among other things, the statement is ironic for the degree to which it downplays the risk that state and local interest rates will rise for high quality borrowers. Simon spent the first half of the year warning of the danger that federal deficits will raise interest rates for all borrowers and crowd them out of credit markets.

TABLE 7—PREDICTED AND ACTUAL STATE AND LOCAL BOND RATES, 1975
(In percentage points, by months)

Month	Aaa Bonds			Aa Bonds			A Bonds			Baa Bonds		
	Actual	Predicted[a]	Difference	Actual	Predicted[a]	Difference	Actual	Predicted[a]	Difference	Actual	Predicted[a]	Difference
Jan.	6.39	6.25	0.14	6.57	6.42	0.15	7.13	6.55	0.58	7.45	6.76	0.69
Feb.	5.96	6.08	−0.12	6.11	6.24	−0.13	6.53	6.38	0.15	7.03	6.59	0.44
March	6.28	6.12	0.16	6.49	6.29	0.20	6.79	6.42	0.37	7.25	6.63	0.62
April	6.46	6.34	0.12	6.82	6.51	0.31	7.09	6.64	0.45	7.43	6.85	0.58
May	6.42	6.29	0.13	6.76	6.47	0.29	7.13	6.59	0.54	7.48	6.81	0.67
June	6.28	6.19	0.09	6.72	6.35	0.37	7.36	6.48	0.88	7.49	6.70	0.79
July	6.39	6.24	0.15	6.80	6.40	0.40	7.50	6.54	0.96	7.60	6.74	0.86
Aug.	6.40	6.33	0.07	6.80	6.49	0.31	7.55	6.62	0.93	7.71	6.83	0.88
Sept.	6.71	6.33	0.38	7.10	6.49	0.61	7.81	6.62	1.19	7.96	6.84	1.12
QI	6.21	6.15	0.06	6.39	6.32	0.07	6.82	6.45	0.37	7.24	6.66	0.58
QII	6.39	6.27	0.12	6.77	6.44	0.33	7.19	6.57	0.62	7.47	6.79	0.68
QIII	6.50	6.30	0.20	6.90	6.46	0.44	7.62	6.59	1.03	7.76	6.80	0.96
9 mo. avg.	6.37	6.24	0.13	6.68	6.41	0.27	7.21	6.54	0.67	7.49	6.75	0.74

[a] From the equation

$$CORP\,(1-t) - RATE = a_0 + a_1 U + a_2\, TIME,$$ where $CORP$ is the Aaa corporate rate, $RATE$ stands for the four risk classifications above, U is the unemployment rate, $TIME$ is a time trend, and t is an estimated average income tax rate. The equation was fit by half years from 1955–74. In all categories a value of $t = .2$ gave the lowest standard errors. The estimated coefficients (with t-ratios in parentheses) were as follows:

RATE	a_0	a_1	a_2	R^2	SE
Aaa	.021	.003 (.1)	.038 (7.2)	.58	.19
Aa	−.096	−.014 (.4)	.042 (7.5)	.78	.21
A	−.424	—	.046 (7.6)	.78	.23
Baa	−.857	−.015 (.4)	.064 (9.1)	.83	.26

these troubles in the municipal market, the New York situation will reduce the extent to which state and local governments borrow to finance capital construction projects. Weighting the third quarter residuals by the proportion of borrowing in each risk class leads to an increase in the state and local bond rate of 63 basis points, which should by itself reduce state and local construction by about $4.5 billion.[15] The *GNP* impact of this would be about $9 billion in the first year or two, and when added to the impact of the direct cuts discussed above, both together would reduce *GNP* by .7 percent and raise the unemployment

rate by about .25 percentage points over what it would otherwise be.[16] This is quite a large effect for the fiscal difficulties of just one city, large enough by itself to offset the tax cut recently passed by Congress.

Moreover, focusing only on this surprisingly large macroeconomic impact can obscure two points. The first is that if the city does default, and if that default does threaten the solvency of major New York

[15] Using an estimate derived in Gramlich and Galper, Table 4. This estimated construction effect is about the same as that given by F. Gerard Adams and James N. Savitt, though they anticipate a larger rise in state and local interest rates and use a smaller interest rate elasticity for construction.

[16] The interest rate effects are larger than those found by Ronald W. Forbes and John E. Petersen, because I have allowed the municipal Aaa rate to be affected by the New York City problem. I have not included observations from 1975 in the regression (as they did), and I have worked in the impact of the tax exemption of state and local interest payments (as they did not). The analyses also differ in that my calculation focuses on the probable effect on state and local borrowing and investment, whereas theirs focuses on the rise in interest payments, assuming that borrowing is unaffected.

banks and cause a loss of deposits, the situation becomes much more uncertain and the risk of a general collapse of borrowing and investment much greater. In this context, one great advantage of bailing out the city is precisely this—it keeps the general economic risks predictable and manageable.

The second point is that this estimate of the impact of any New York default is only manageable for the country as a whole—the impact on the economy and the citizens of the city itself will be extremely painful. Table 5 showed that per capita taxes are already much higher in New York than in other cities, and the measures taken to put the city on a sounder fiscal footing will raise them further, increasing the risk of a flight of the taxpaying businesses and households to other localities. On the expenditure side, the *MAC* figures project that by fiscal 1978 55 percent of the city's expenditures will be "uncontrollable"—mandated for interest, debt service, welfare, and pension payments. This forces very deep cutbacks in the remaining controllable portion, estimated by the Joint Economic Committee to be 18 percent in real terms. Even with a freeze on money wages, these are severe cutbacks. And even these severe cutbacks might not be adequate to balance the city's budget by 1978 if they lead to other reductions in federal and state grants mandated for the programs cut back or if they reduce levels of economic activity and revenues in the city.

VI. What is to be Done in the Short Run?

It is generally easier to analyze what went wrong than to say what to do about it. Several principles do emerge from the preceding facts, however, and I will try to highlight the pertinent ones.

The first is that the city itself is ultimately responsible for its financial woes—the budget deficits started long ago, in part

because of official underestimates of the severity of the problem; the deficits were large even before the current recession, and not caused by any one particular program but a host of them. The second is that even though the problem is of the city's own making, things have reached such a point that now the city simply cannot correct the problem by itself—tax burdens in the city and state are already extremely high, uncontrollable expenditures are extremely high, and the cash expenses necessary to roll over the short-term debt when the market will not are excruciating. Even with the severe cuts in expenditures mandated by the Emergency Financial Control Board, it will take the city three years to restore balance in its budget, and only then under relatively optimistic assumptions regarding future revenues.

The question facing the national government is whether to take steps to avoid the city's having to default on the bonds it must retire in the near future.[17] If this were not done, there is at least some chance that a financial panic could develop, and some chance that the economic recovery could be aborted even if a panic did not develop. There is also an excellent chance that the delivery of vital services in the city—police, fire, sanitation, health, education—could be temporarily or permanently disrupted by default, and that it would be very difficult to pick up the pieces. Minimizing each of these fears is essentially the rationale for not allowing the city to default.

On the other side, the advantage of a default is that the city has in fact signed certain contracts that it is simply unable to meet, it has to improve its budget pro-

[17] Default in this sense means having the court, and not the Emergency Financial Control Board, take over the reconciliation of inconsistent claims on the city. In a narrow legal sense, one could argue that the recent state action to substitute *MAC* bonds for some of the maturing city debt implies that the city is already in default.

cess and reduce its deficits, and it never will unless it is forced to go through the default process. The last assumption is the key one—by this time the state itself and through its Emergency Financial Central Board has exerted so much control on the city that it effectively lost its budgetary autonomy and will have to abrogate some contracts, whether or not there is a default. Given this, these marginal benefits of a default are probably unimportant and it seems almost foolish to risk the possible severe dangers of allowing the city to go under. By this time, all but the most hard-nosed conservatives appear to agree with this position.

VII. Long-Term Measures

The city's plight does illustrate several more long-term issues, however, and it is well to emphasize them before such crises recur. The first is that better state and local financial accounting is urgently needed. There is no obvious reason why the budgets of large state and local governments could not be more quickly made available to the financial community, tabulated in standard form, using official conventions on what is current and what capital spending, on the increase in pension fund liabilities, on the size and maturity of outstanding debt. Whether the bond rating authority is then brought under the Securities and Exchange Commission, as Senator Eagleton wishes, there should also be much more explicit statement of why bonds are rated as they are, the criteria used, and the data behind these criteria.[18] As a specific suggestion, the rating agencies have apparently relied solely on stock figures such as the ratio of debt to assessed property values; it would seem that flow figures such as the recent size of current account surplus, the controllable portion of the budget, and the dangers in not be-

ing able to roll over short term debt should also enter in.

A second point regards the intrinsic financial difficulties of state and local governments when macroeconomic conditions change. State and local revenues are now composed largely of income and sales taxes—those two sources comprised 60 percent of own revenue in 1973—and net expenditures for welfare and medicaid have also become very large. When aggregate conditions change, state and local budgets will tend to operate in an automatically stabilizing manner just as will the federal budget. The only difference is that the inability to run current account deficits at the state and local level forces the stabilizers to be offset by other spending costs or tax increases. It can, of course, be argued that governments should have had the foresight to build up a stock of liquid assets for just such an emergency. This argument is not terribly persuasive in a time like the present, however, when the business cycle decline is so much steeper than any government could possibly have anticipated. In any case to illustrate the problem, a special Joint Economic Committee survey of eighteen large cities found only five that did not raise taxes or cut spending in the past year.[19] This is both counterproductive from a macro standpoint and, more importantly, it leads to instability in the delivery of services at the state and local level. A sensible remedy would be to give out revenue sharing money on a countercyclical basis, as Senator Muskie wants to do. It was emphasized above that the recession was not at the heart of New York's woes, and these woes would have only been modestly ameliorated by a countercyclical revenue sharing program, but they would have been ameliorated and the program would still seem to have appeal in a cyclical economy.

---

[18] See, for example, the Twentieth Century Fund.

[19] Joint Economic Committee, p. 29.

A final point involves the redistributive nature of the city's social programs. As was argued earlier, New York's difficulties can in large part be traced to the fact that it was doing too much on its own. In some cases—pension contributions, higher education, transit subsidies, public hospitals—the choice was the city's own; in others—welfare and medicaid—the choice was made by the state and mandated on the city's budget. Laudable as these choices may be from a social standpoint, local governments do have to be careful in a federal system, first, not to laden taxpayers with too much debt and forced debt service payments, and, second, not to undertake too much redistribution at the local level. If these programs are to be done, they must at least be financed on a national scale. In this sense, the New York experience can also be interpreted as something of a setback for the new federalism, which some advocates interpret as turning functions such as income redistribution back to the states and localities.

TABLE A.1—UNCONSTRAINED REGRESSIONS PREDICTING BUDGETARY VARIABLES
(*t*-ratio below coefficient)[a]

Dependent Variable	Inter-cept	Popula-tion	Disposable Income	Poverty	Non-white	Normal Grants	Density	Midwest	South	City–County	R^2/SE
Normal expenditures	−426.0	−29.6	.075	1,163.9	—	.472	12.3	—	—	—	.665
		(−1.5)	(3.1)	(2.7)		(1.8)	(3.3)				56.5
School expenditures[b]	317.0	—	—	−525.5	56.1	—	—	−42.4	−44.0	—	.689
				(−4.0)	(1.3)			(−3.9)	(−4.0)		21.3
Marginal functions deficit	−356.8	−13.0	.059	468.5	—	—	5.4	—	—	27.2	.657
		(−1.3)	(4.6)	(2.1)			(3.1)			(2.0)	29.9
Current account surplus	42.7	—	—	—	—	.576	−6.0	—	—	—	.619
						(5.8)	(−4.4)				25.6
Normal Revenue[c]	−423.1	−42.6	.134	1,106.9	56.1	1.048	11.7	−42.4	−44.0	27.2	—

Source: U.S. Bureau of the Census, *City Government Finances;* Sales Management, *1974 Survey of Buying Power,* U.S. Dept. of Commerce, *Statistical Abstract of the U.S., 1973.*

[a] Each dependent variable is in per capita terms. Population is the gross size of the city's 1973 population in billions, Disposable Income (*DI*) is the average disposable income for the city in per capita terms in 1973, Poverty is the 1973 ratio of households with *DI* below $5000 to the total number of households in the city, Nonwhite is the 1973 ratio of the nonwhite population to the total, Normal Grants is the per capita total for normal functions and untied in 1973, Density is the number of thousands of people per square mile in the city, all the remaining variables are one for the indicated category and zero otherwise.

[b] Using slightly different data, where the first five variables are defined for the county area in accordance with school district boundaries.

[c] Implied by the summation of coefficients in the other four rows.

TABLE A.2—CONSTRAINED REGRESSIONS PREDICTING BUDGETARY VARIABLES
(*t*-ratio below coefficient)[a]

Dependent Variable	Intercept	Population	Disposable Income	Poverty	Normal Grants	Density	Midwest	South	City–County	R^2/SE
Normal expenditures	−429.8	−25.6	.074	1,236.7	.445	10.0	16.4	−21.0	15.2	.682
		(−1.2)	(2.7)	(2.5)	(1.6)	(2.0)	(0.6)	(−0.5)	(0.5)	59.5
School expenditures	291.3	−2.0	−.004	−336.8	.223	1.2	−31.7	−32.9	−28.9	.666
		(−0.2)	(−0.4)	(−1.7)	(2.0)	(0.6)	(−2.6)	(−1.9)	(−2.5)	24.4
Marginal functions deficit	−380.7	−12.3	.062	436.2	.117	5.1	11.3	9.3	25.6	.677
		(−1.1)	(4.3)	(1.7)	(0.8)	(1.9)	(0.7)	(0.4)	(1.7)	31.3
Current account surplus	41.4	11.1	−.003	44.0	.557	−6.5	−11.8	1.2	10.4	.684
		(1.1)	(−0.3)	(0.2)	(4.5)	(−2.9)	(−0.9)	(0.1)	(0.8)	26.9
Normal revenue	−477.8	−28.8	.129	1,380.1	1.342	9.8	−15.8	−43.4	22.3	.797
		(−1.0)	(3.6)	(2.2)	(3.8)	(1.5)	(−0.4)	(−0.8)	(0.6)	77.3

Source: U.S. Bureau of the Census, *City Government Finances;* Sales Management, *1974 Survey of Buying Power;* U.S. Dept. of Commerce, *Statistical Abstract of the U.S., 1973.*

Specification is the same as in Table 6, except that Nonwhite variable is dropped from all equations. Every other independent variable is entered in all equations to insure consistency.

REFERENCES

F. G. Adams and J. N. Savitt, "Statement of the House Budget Committee," Oct. 23, 1975.

W. T. Carleton and E. M. Lerner, "Statistical Credit Scoring of Municipal Bonds," *J. Money, Credit, Banking*, Nov. 1969.

Congressional Budget Office, "New York City's Fiscal Problem, Its Origin, Potential Repercussions, and Some Alternative Policy Responses," Oct. 10, 1975, 13, 19.

R. W. Forbes and J. E. Petersen, "Costs of Credit in the Municipal Bond Market," Municipal Finance Officers Association 1975.

E. Gramlich and H. Galper, "State and Local Fiscal Behavior and Federal Grant Policy," *Brookings Papers*, 1973, *1*.

R. D. Horton, *Municipal Labor Relations in New York City: Lessons of the Lindsay-Wagner Years*, 1973.

J. E. Petersen, *The Rating Game*, Twentieth Century Fund 1974, 125.

Sales Management, *1974 Survey of Buying Power.*

R. Samuelson, "Troubled Friend at Chase Manhattan," *The New Republic*, Nov. 15, 1975.

U.S. Bureau of the Census, *City Government Finances*, 1973–74.

U.S. Dept. of Commerce, *Statistical Abstract of the U.S.*, 1973.

[21]

EDWARD M. GRAMLICH

"A Fair Go": Fiscal Federalism Arrangements

THE Australian belief in equality and apparent fear of market outcomes are evident in the system of fiscal relations between the commonwealth and the state governments. From the standpoint of equality Australia has the most equalizing federalist system in the world. Grants intended to remove disparities in incomes and to alleviate the enormous costs of providing public services are large, respected, and longstanding; such grants have existed in some form for over fifty years. But from the standpoint of protection from market outcomes there are many inefficiencies in the Australian system, many cases in which bureaucratic controls are used to allocate resources in preference to market-like

I am indebted to Fred H. Gruen for his advice and help in arranging interviews, and to my conference discussants, Professors Russell L. Mathews and Clifford Walsh, for their helpful (and extensive) comments. Among the federal officials who were helpful at the interview stage were Carol J. Austin, Vincent C. Blackburn, Ian Castles, Judge R. Else-Mitchell, V. W. J. Fitzgerald, Peter D. Jonson, and William E. Norton. Among the state treasury officials were Peter Emery, John Hall, Barry Nicholls, and Norman Oakes. Among the academic economists were Peter D. Groenewegen, Nanak Kakwani, Ronald Lane, Russell L. Mathews, Michael G. Porter, Jeff Richardson, Peter L. Swan, Thomas J. Valentine, and Clifford Walsh. Among the economists from private business were James Catterall, John Donovan, Brian Hamley, John McLeod, and Donald Stammer. I owe special thanks to those who read and commented on early drafts of the manuscript—Ted Bergstrom, Peter D. Groenewegen, Brian Hamley, Peter J. Lloyd, Barry Nicholls, John Niewinghuysen, Joseph A. Pechman, John Yinger, and the other authors whose chapters appear in this book. Finally, I thank the Alfred P. Sloan Foundation for financing some of my work on the project.

231

Edward M. Gramlich

mechanisms, and many other instances in which the system does not let public officials bear the full responsibility for their decisions. As Russell Mathews, the guru of Australian federalism, puts it: "The Australian fiscal system which has evolved since World War II may then be seen as one which maximises the amount of political noise and minimises the degree of electoral accountability, financial responsibility, economic efficiency and effective policy choice."[1]

These two partly conflicting themes imply that the Australian system will have a better score when evaluated on grounds of equality than on economic efficiency. In this paper I develop this theme. I first discuss fiscal federalism in general—in contrast to a purely centralized scheme for the provision of public services, what does a federal scheme try to accomplish? I then describe the Australian system, with relatively little emphasis on the historical origins of the system, a topic amply covered by others.[2] I also discuss a particularly interesting, and underresearched, question, the extent of diversities in the Australian system—how federal is it?

The next sections of the paper turn to various policy considerations. I first analyze the Australian system of intergovernmental grants. I also address a series of selected tax issues that illustrate close involvement with fiscal federalism. Several suggestions for reforming or improving Australia's fiscal arrangements are made and evaluated in both of these sections.

Fiscal Federalism

Most countries have adopted a centralized system of government for the financing and provision of public services. A few—prominently Australia, Canada, the United States, and West Germany—have opted for more decentralized provision, here called fiscal federalism. As compared to a centralized system, a federal system will typically entail less equal provision of public services. Subnational governments, free

1. Russell Mathews, "The Commonwealth-State Financial Contract," in Jennifer Aldred and John Wilkes, eds., *A Fractured Federation? Australia in the 1980s* (Sydney: George Allen & Unwin for the Australian Institute of Political Science, 1982), p. 48.
2. One of the best sources is U.S. Advisory Commission on Intergovernmental Relations, *Studies in Comparative Federalism: Australia* (Washington, D.C.: US ACIR, 1981), especially the articles by Russell Mathews, R. Else-Mitchell, and W. R. C. Jay.

to decide how much to tax their citizens and spend on public services, typically select dissimilar amounts, so that citizens in different jurisdictions receive different amounts of public services. Since preferences for public services vary, a more decentralized system should achieve a higher rating on grounds of economic efficiency. Citizens in subnational jurisdictions can decide on their preferred array of public services. They can also move to jurisdictions that provide arrays closest to the ones they prefer.

It follows that a federal system can be evaluated for the equality and efficiency with which it provides public goods. On the question of equality, in Australia, as in many other countries, there is a basic tax-transfer redistributive system that is operated almost entirely by the central government to reduce the variance of spending power among individual families. But as long as income, wealth, and relative prices vary by community or by state, the income, sales, or property tax rates necessary to provide a standard menu of public services (the so-called tax price of public services) also vary. One problem this introduces is that it creates an incentive to move to affluent communities where public goods are cheap, bidding up land prices, pricing the poor out of these communities, and increasing the amount of income segregation of communities. Another problem is that the basic economic and social opportunities available to citizens—such as for education and health care—may depend on public services because the variance in tax price may cause poor areas to spend less on education and health than more affluent areas, thereby adding to the other disadvantages faced by the poor. Hence the variance in tax prices provides a rationale either for centralized financing and provision of public services, or for decentralized provision with equalizing transfers among communities. How well the transfers do equalize opportunities among communities or states is the first criterion by which a federal system can be evaluated.

The second criterion is economic efficiency. In market economies governments should seek to minimize unnecessary distortions in the pattern of resource allocation and relative prices. One way to minimize these distortions is for local governments to provide the array of public services desired by their electorates. The closer is the array to that desired by voters, the more efficient the system. A second way is to select taxes that involve minimum economic distortions to pay for these public services. A third way is to avoid wasteful duplication and

Edward M. Gramlich

inconsistency on both the tax and expenditure sides of the budgets that can result when the actual providers and financers of public services are subnational governments. Rail lines extending across state lines can be standardized; one state's highways can start where another state's leave off; taxing conventions can minimize compliance and paperwork costs for the private sector.

Subsequent sections of the paper analyze the Australian federal system in terms of the one equality criterion (how well it equalizes the tax price, or expected expenditures on public services, in the face of income and wealth differences) and the three efficiency criteria (how large the excess burden is in the provision of public services, how distortionary the tax system is, and how significant duplication and coordination costs are across states).

The Australian Federal System

The basic outlines of the Australian federal system were set down in the Constitution of 1901. The Constitution gave the central government (Commonwealth of Australia) responsibility for defense, foreign affairs, international and interstate trade and commerce, maritime activities, currency and banking, and old-age and invalid pensions. An amendment in 1946 extended this pension responsibility to cover all forms of social security payments to families. The six signatory states retained most other responsibilities such as the provision of education, health, public safety, transport, and community and social services. States were also given control of their local governments and to this day have retained that control, though localities had some responsibility delegated to them for road systems, recreation and cultural services, and services to property.[3]

3. One examining a map of Australia may be confused by exactly what areas are states and what are not. There have always been six official states in Australia. Ordered as they usually are in government documents (by population, except in one case), and with the capitals in parentheses, they are New South Wales (Sydney), Victoria (Melbourne), Queensland (Brisbane), South Australia (Adelaide), Western Australia (Perth), and Tasmania (Hobart). The Northern Territory (Darwin) will eventually be independent, but not before the mid-1980s. Because administrative and financial arrangements for the Northern Territory are sui generis, I generally do not discuss Northern Territory relationship in this chapter.

The Australian Constitution empowered the central government to impose all forms of taxation, but not to discriminate among states. States were given concurrent powers of taxation, except that they were not permitted to collect customs and excise duties. In later years this exclusion was interpreted by Australia's High Court to mean that virtually all forms of sales or other indirect taxes on goods were considered to be excise duties and were unavailable to the states, a fact that takes on fundamental importance in an evaluation of the Australian system.[4]

The system of grants from the central to state and local governments has changed over time much more than the tax system. In the early days the Constitution made provision for the sharing of customs and excise duties with the states. Under Section 96, it also empowered the commonwealth to grant financial assistance to any state, basically on any terms. This provision was eventually interpreted to enable the central government to provide both general-purpose equalization grants among the states and specific-purpose, or categorical grants, to achieve particular expenditure objectives.[5]

This granting authority has its origin in the period just before World War I when the states of Tasmania and Western Australia sought and obtained special grants to help balance their budgets; they were joined by South Australia just before the Great Depression. When economic disparities widened in the depression, the commonwealth responded to threats of secession by creating in 1933 a unique body, the Commonwealth Grants Commission (CGC).[6] The CGC, an independent statutory authority, was to report on application of any state for special assistance. Over time this authority has developed into a responsibility to recommend the level of equalization grants to be paid to individual states. Currently this commission computes what are known as grant "relativities," the ratios that determine the relative amounts of general-purpose

4. R. Else-Mitchell, "Constitutional Aspects of Commonwealth and State Taxing Laws," in Dean Jaensch, ed., *The Politics of "New Federalism"* (Adelaide: Australasian Political Studies Association, 1977), pp. 37–42.

5. R. Else-Mitchell, "The Australian Federal Grants System and Its Impact on Fiscal Relations of the Federal Government with State and Local Governments," in US ACIR, *Studies in Comparative Federalism: Australia*, p. 30.

6. Western Australia went so far as to vote for secession by a two-thirds margin, but the petition was denied by the British parliament because the rest of Australia had not approved.

assistance received by states to equalize their tax prices for public services.

World War II brought another important change. To finance the war the government passed the Uniform Tax Scheme, which excluded states from individual and company income taxes. In return, the central government supplemented and eventually replaced the previous special-assistance grants with unconditional grants that are now referred to as tax-sharing grants. These grants have grown through time and are now the main form of central government aid to states; they also constitute the means by which interstate equalization is accomplished. As noted above, the CGC became the agency that made recommendations about relativities for tax-sharing grants and its importance has grown along with those grants.

This evolution of the grant system was paralleled by an increase in central government supervision of the capital accounts of states and localities. In the 1920s there were fears that certain states would not be able to repay their large outstanding debts (with New South Wales later defaulting on some bonds in the 1930s), and that the Commonwealth would become liable for these repayment obligations. For this reason, and also to rationalize and coordinate state offshore borrowing, in 1928 a constitutional amendment created another unique body, the Australian Loan Council (ALC), to regulate the floating of this debt. Although the prime minister is represented on the ALC (with the treasurer normally serving as chair), and the six state premiers also serve, the central government has increasingly dominated the ALC. Through the ALC, the central government now does all the borrowing for state general governments, and these governments repay the ALC. The central government domination of the ALC began in the 1950s, when it began to make special loans to the states to finance their capital projects. By the early 1970s the states had become heavily in debt to the central government, which then took over $1 billion of state debt and the interest charges on it. In 1975 this arrangement was transformed into an interest-free capital grant to state governments of one-third of the ALC borrowings on their behalf.

The ALC also regulates the borrowing of most "semigovernmental" authorities (quasi-governmental bodies engaged in revenue-raising operations for electric power, public utilities, and transportation) under what is known as the "gentlemen's agreement" of 1936. This control has been gradually relaxed in very recent years.

The modern history of the Australian grant system resembles that of the U.S. grant system. During the 1972–75 regime of Labor party Prime Minister Gough Whitlam, specific-purpose grants grew from 2.1 percent of GDP to 5.8 percent in three short years (similar to what happened in the United States during the Great Society years). This growth reflected the declared intention of the Labor party to standardize public services among states with highly restrictive specific-purpose grants even in functional areas for which states had formal constitutional responsibility.

Just as the Great Society was eventually followed by a retrenchment labeled "the new federalism" in the United States, similar events occurred in Australia. In 1976 the Liberal-Country party government of Malcolm Fraser proposed a series of measures to decentralize the system by insuring automatic growth of tax-sharing grants, computing relativities for all states (not just those that had been applying for special assistance), and cutting out or scaling back many of the rapidly growing specific-purpose grants (similar to the proposals for special revenue-sharing and block grants made by Republican Presidents Nixon and Reagan in the United States). States were also given more revenue-raising capability by being allowed to attach a surcharge or a rebate onto the national income tax rate, though for good economic and political reasons to be discussed below, no state has ever used this power. As a result of Fraser's initiatives, the growth of tax-sharing grants has far exceeded that of specific-purpose grants since 1975, and by 1981 the former accounted for about 4.5 percent of GDP. But the specific-purpose grants were not cut back either, at least in nominal terms, and they still constitute 4 percent of GDP (the lack of a sharp cutback in these grants is also similar to what the United States has experienced). Hence attempts to change the system by both the Labor party and Liberal-Country party prime ministers have expanded the system—specific-purpose grants grew and tax-sharing grants did not decline under Whitlam, and the latter grew while the former did not decline under Fraser.

Some broad summary indicators of this growth and development in the postwar period are given in table 1. During the 1970s direct (nongrant) expenditures by the central government increased by 2.6 percentage

Table 1. *Government Expenditures, Grants, Taxes, and Surplus, by Level of Government, Selected Years, 1950–80*

Year	Commonwealth government					State and local governments			State and local taxes as percent of revenue[d]
	Expenditures	Grants	ALC advances[a]	Taxes	Surplus[b]	Expenditures	Taxes	Surplus[c]	
Amount ($ millions)									
1949–50	763	202	36	1,000	−1	651	196	−217	45.2
1959–60	1,794	649	397	2,827	−13	1,979	842	−91	44.6
1969–70	4,551	1,637	680	7,157	289	4,935	2,256	−362	49.3
1974–75	9,992	5,194	1,225	15,272	−1,139	11,876	4,622	−835	41.9
1979–80	20,023	10,662	896	29,627	−1,954	22,894	9,186	−2,150	44.3
Share of GDP (percent)									
1949–50	15.0	4.0	0.7	19.6	−0.0	12.8	3.8	−4.3	...
1959–60	13.1	4.7	2.9	20.6	−0.1	14.4	6.1	−0.7	...
1969–70	14.9	5.4	2.2	23.4	1.0	16.2	7.4	−1.2	...
1974–75	16.2	8.4	2.0	24.7	−1.9	19.2	7.5	−1.4	...
1979–80	17.5	9.3	0.8	25.9	−1.7	20.0	8.0	−1.9	...

Source: W. E. Norton, P. M. Garmston, and M. W. Brodie, *Australian Economic Statistics, 1949–50 to 1980–81:1. Tables*, Occasional Paper 8A (Canberra: Reserve Bank of Australia, May 1982), tables 2.16, 2.17, 2.19, 2.20, 5.1, pp. 47–48, 50–51, 116.
a. Australian Loan Council advances.
b. Net of ALC advances—that is, commonwealth taxes minus the sum of commonwealth expenditures, grants, and ALC advances.
c. Net of ALC advances—state and local taxes plus commonwealth grants ALC advances minus state and local expenditures.
d. State and local taxes divided by the sum of grants, ALC advances, and state and local taxes in percentage terms.

points of GDP, and grants increased by 3.9 percentage points of GDP as a result of the developments discussed above. The 1970s brought economic pressures to limit government borrowing, so the ALC has tightened up, and ALC advances have actually fallen as a share of GDP. Both the central and the state and local government taxes have risen as a share of GDP, but not as much as expenditures, and particularly at the central government level the deficit has grown. The other fact to note is how small state and local taxes are. By 1980 they accounted for only 23 percent of total tax revenue and only 44 percent of the revenue available to the states and localities (that is, the sum of grants, ALC advances, and taxes). This latter phenomenon has led many observers to suggest that the heavy reliance on grants eliminates some of the responsibilities for sound budgetary management at the subnational level.

The Extent of Diversity

The historical evolution of Australian federalism toward a more centrally controlled system might imply that state and local differences in services are gradually being eliminated. Those observers, mainly in the Labor party, who believe in standardizing public services across areas will generally not lament the passing of these differences; those firmly committed to the federalism goal of accommodating differences in tastes for public services on the part of citizens will lament the passing.

But before any funerals are held, it makes sense to see just how great are these differences in public services. And, for all the rhetoric about the growth in central control and the standardization of public services, the differences in these public services levels turn out to be surprisingly great. Table 2 shows public consumption outlays per capita by state. The overall national average in the first row is $761 per capita, ranging from a high of $1,010 in Tasmania to a low of $659 in Queensland. Tasmanians spend 50 percent more on public services than do Queenslanders. Although it might be thought that income differences could explain some of the disparities, they do not. To begin with, state incomes do not vary much in Australia—Victoria, the highest income state, has a personal income per capita 1.05 times the national average, while

Table 2. Expenditures for Public Services, by State, 1980–81
Dollars per capita unless otherwise indicated

Item	Weighted average[a]	New South Wales	Victoria	Queensland	South Australia	Western Australia	Tasmania	Comparative statistics		
								Weighted standard deviation[b]	Coefficient of variation[c]	Standardized coefficient of variation[d]
Total public consumption outlays[e]	761.0	738.0	755.0	658.7	850.4	889.0	1,010.0	76.9	0.101	0.077
Primary and secondary education	229.1	218.3	260.7	181.1	257.0	226.0	266.5	28.2	0.123	0.098
Public safety	76.5	78.3	66.0	73.2	83.5	93.5	97.5	8.7	0.114	0.135
Health and hospitals	202.2	206.0	186.9	165.7	218.0	269.4	248.2	27.8	0.138	0.143
Social services	13.5	9.6	15.3	17.4	16.0	14.4	13.9	3.1	0.230	...
Community development	2.2	2.2	3.7	...	3.1	1.4	1.6	0.9	0.409	...
Recreation and culture	10.7	7.7	8.5	8.6	18.7	18.5	31.5	5.4	0.505	...
Total public consumption outlays as a share of disposable income (percent)	12.7	12.0	12.0	12.0	14.6	15.5	17.9	1.5	0.118	0.057
Addendum										
Percentage share in the United States[f]	11.8	...	...	...	...	...	...	2.1	0.175	...

Sources: State expenditures—Australian Bureau of Statistics. *State and Local Government Finance in Australia, 1980–81* (Canberra: ABS, 1981), tables 17, 26, 35, 44, 53, 62; population—Treasury Department, *Payments to or for the States, the Northern Territory, and Local Government Authorities, 1982–83.* Budget Paper 7 (Canberra: Australian Government Publishing Service, 1982), table 6, p. 19. Also Russell Mathews, "Federalism in Retreat: The Abandonment of Tax Sharing and Fiscal Equalization," reprint 50 (Canberra: Australian National University, Centre for Research on Federal Fiscal Relations, 1982), table 3, p. 26; Russell Mathews, "Regional Disparities in Australia," in U.S. Advisory Commission on Intergovernmental Relations, *Studies in Comparative Federalism: Australia* (US ACIR, 1981), table 1, p. 3; "National Income and Product Accounts Tables," *Survey of Current Business*, vol. 62 (August 1982); and Norton, Garmston, and Brodie, *Australian Economic Statistics*, table 5.18, p. 147.
a. Weights based on population shares.
b. Square root of weighted average squared error.
c. Weighted standard deviation divided by the weighted mean.
d. All calculations redone with public spending standardized for differences in population structure and dispersion, climate, and topography.
e. Components do not add to total because only selected consumption items are shown.
f. Total public consumption as a share of U.S. personal income, excluding Alaska and Hawaii.

Queensland, the lowest income state, is at 0.91 of the national average.[7] In the case at hand, Queensland, with low spending, does have the lowest income; but Tasmania, with high spending, has the second lowest income. The comparison can be made more formally by computing public consumption as a share of disposable income, as in the last row. When this is done, Tasmania is still spending 50 percent more than three other states, and the coefficient of variation actually increases.

The other rows of the table show that this variation is not a result of the functional aggregation scheme, but exists across the board. For every category of public consumption the coefficient of variation exceeds 0.1, and it rises to quite high levels exactly where it might be expected to—in the less standard categories like community development and recreation and culture where statewide taste differences might be significant.[8]

As a standard for comparison, the last row of table 2 gives the statewide coefficient of variation of public consumption divided by income for the United States, a country in which public spending differences are perceived to be very great. The standard deviation and coefficient of variation are greater in the United States than in Australia, but not by very much. Roughly there appears to be about two-thirds as much expenditure diversity in supposedly homogeneous Australia as in the supposedly heterogeneous United States.

It is impossible to compare Australian statewide figures with those in the United States beyond this point, but it is possible to refine the Australian calculations. As part of its calculations for grant relativities, the CGC measures public spending as standardized for differences in population structure and dispersion, climate, topography, and other factors. The last column in table 2 repeats the Australian calculations with these standardized expenditures, both gross and as a share of

7. Russell Mathews, "Regional Disparities in Australia," in US ACIR, *Studies in Comparative Federalism: Australia*, table 1, p. 3.

8. Some critics have objected to these calculations because they ignore equalization transfers. Although this is true, one would think that eliminating them would make my point even stronger—if anything, there should be more of a difference between high- and low-income states and even more diversity. On the other side, there is one sense in which the variation does depend on the aggregation scheme. Since Queensland is the normal outlier, calculations done with Queensland excluded do lower the coefficient of variation, usually by about 15 percent.

Table 3. *Measures of Local Government Diversity in Expenditures, Australia and the United States, 1979–80*
Dollars

Suburban area[a]	Mean current expenditure	Standard deviation	Coefficient of variation
Sydney, New South Wales	145	33	0.228
Brisbane, Queensland	99	28	0.282
Victoria	155	48	0.310
Detroit, Michigan[b]	223	70	0.312

Sources: For Australia—Australian Bureau of Statistics, *Local Government Finance: New South Wales, 1980* (ABS, New South Wales Office, 1981); *Local Government: Victoria, 1980–81* (ABS, Victoria Office, 1981); and *Local Government: Queensland, 1980–81* (ABS, Queensland Office, 1981). For the United States—U.S. Bureau of the Census, *1977 Census of Governments*, vol. 4: *Governmental Finances*, and *Finances of Municipalities and Township Governments* (GPO, 1979).
a. Suburban areas with populations of 20,000 or more, excluding central cities.
b. Excludes two cities with their own public hospitals and a domed sports center.

disposable income.[9] While the coefficient of variation does increase for certain types of spending, it declines for the largest public education category and for the overall total, and especially for the overall total as a share of income. It is clear that these other factors do partly explain interstate expenditure diversity. But whether the two-thirds ratio would be raised or lowered with these added controls will remain a mystery until the same calculations are done for the United States.

Of course, the reason for having diverse public services is to accommodate differences between citizens' tastes. When a comparison of services is made among Australian states, one cannot be sure that is the proper inference. Australia's states are large and far apart, with dramatically different labor markets (so that many households do not have a realistic option of whether to live in various states). A more meaningful comparison would then be to show diversity within cities in the same area, or the same labor market. Such a comparison cannot easily be made for Australia because only three states publish data on local government expenditures, and no states publish data on local incomes. But those data that are available, shown in table 3, for the suburbs of Sydney, Brisbane, and the large cities of Victoria still indicate significant diversity. Now the coefficient of variation has risen to between 0.23 and

9. The figures are taken from Russell Mathews, "Federalism in Retreat: The Abandonment of Tax Sharing and Fiscal Equalization," reprint 50 (Canberra: Australian National University, Centre for Research on Federal Financial Relations, July 1982), table 3, p. 26.

0.31, the latter being just that for the Detroit suburbs.[10] Adjusting for income differences might lower the coefficient of variation (though surprisingly it does not for Detroit), but such an adjustment could not possibly eliminate the large amount of expenditure diversity shown.

It is easier to report these numbers than to interpret them. One point is obvious. Despite most commentators' emphasis on the centralist drift of Australian federalism, this system is federalist in more than name. Expenditure differences between states and communities are quite large, almost as large as in the diverse United States, and the dislocations involved in moving to a much more centralized system would be nontrivial. Beyond that, state expenditure differences seem by and large to be unexplained by differences in incomes or spending power or by differences in population structure and climate. That is a healthy sign, for it indicates that the system appears to be accommodating taste differences and is not just passing along income or cost differences. Moreover, if anything, differences are largest in areas in which tastes might be expected to vary and play a strong role, such as culture and community development, and for localities within urban labor markets. While fiscal federalism in Australia is perhaps a shadow of the system that might have existed in 1901, it is still thriving, and in some gross sense it might even be reasonably efficient in accommodating taste differences that apparently do exist in Australia.

The System of Intergovernmental Grants

The centerpiece of any federalist system, Australia's included, is the system of intergovernmental transfers from the central to subnational governments. There are three basic components of the grant system: unrestricted tax-sharing grants (4.8 percent of GDP in 1982), advances from the ALC (0.9 percent of GDP, 0.7 percent when repayments are excluded), and categorical specific-purpose grants (3.4 percent of GDP). With each component a set of policy issues has developed in recent years, and this section comments on these issues.

---

10. I hesitate to call Detroit a typical U.S. city, but it is one for which I have data readily available.

Tax-Sharing Grants

As described above, these grants are the lineal descendants of the sharing of customs duties originally envisaged by the Australian Constitution. Two important issues keep reappearing in discussions of them— their size and how they are distributed among states.

A series of conferences for the premiers of the six states held at the onset of the Liberal-Country party administration in 1975 established that the tax-sharing grants would be equal to 40 percent of personal income tax collections in the previous year. Although the number of these grants has grown at a reasonably adequate rate since that time (holding steady as a share of GDP), the central government has moved unilaterally to reduce them below the 40 percent standard. This was costly to the states in two ways: there was a loss of money and, since the level of funding is now considered by many as not guaranteed, there was also a loss of financial autonomy. This unilateral action has worked, in a small way to be sure, to enhance what is perceived as domination of the system by the central government. This point is brought up again below in the discussion of the appropriate government body to take responsibility for imposing taxes.

But the procedure for splitting up this grant money is what gives the Australian federalism system its unique character. The Personal Income Tax Act of 1978 provides one of the clearest imaginable statements of the objective of equalizing the tax price of public services:

the respective payments to which the states are entitled . . . . should enable each state to provide, without imposing taxes and charges at levels appreciably different from the levels of *taxes and charges imposed by the other States*, government services at standards not appreciably different from the standards of the government services provided by the other States (italics added).[11]

The question of how these equalizing payments are to be determined has been given to the CGC, and then to the premiers of the states for agreement. Because equalizing payments by their very nature involve taking from some states and giving to others, gaining agreement on a set of relativities has been difficult. But in 1982 the commonwealth did institute changes in the relativities written into the 1976 act, and by 1985

11. *Payments to or for the States, the Northern Territory, and Local Government Authorities, 1982–83*, Budget Paper 7, prepared by the Treasurer of the Commonwealth of Australia (Canberra: Australian Government Publishing Service, 1982), p. 13.

the shares will be adjusted in part according to the plan recommended by the CGC.

To understand how the CGC establishes relativities, some algebra is necessary. The CGC tries to equalize what it calls (mistakenly, I argue below) fiscal capacity. If the per capita revenue base in the ith state is denoted by Y_i and that for the commonwealth average is $\overline{Y}$, the CGC defines a concept of revenue needs, T_i, that is approximately equal to

$$(1) \qquad T_i = \overline{t}(\overline{Y} - Y_i),$$

where $\overline{t}$ is the average tax rate applied to the base in all states (with $\overline{t}\overline{Y}$ then yielding the revenue of a standard tax system, or "taxes and charges imposed by the other states" in the above quotation). Expenditure needs, E_i, are approximately equal to

$$(2) \qquad E_i = \overline{e}(C_i - \overline{C}),$$

where $\overline{e}$ is a standard level of public services, C_i is a vector of the costs of providing these services in a particular state, net of specific-purpose grants, and $\overline{C}$ is the representative cost vector for all states.[12]

Tax-sharing grants could be open-ended, as was the case in earlier days when particular states could apply for special assistance; in that case the CGC just computed the deficit for each state as the sum of revenue and expenditure needs, added a basic entitlement constant across all states, G^*, and determined each state's tax-sharing grant, G_i, by

$$(3) \qquad G_i = E_i + T_i + G^*.$$

Because of budgetary stringency, these grants have not been treated as open-ended by the central government, and it has been necessary to scale back G_i so that the sum of these grants is consistent with desired overall budgetary totals for the central government. One way to do this is simply to reduce G^* by an appropriate amount, thereby giving a

12. The exact formulas used by the CGC are not always written down and change from time to time. In one recent year, for example, the CGC defined $\overline{t}$ and $\overline{e}$ by first doing the calculations with each state excluded and then defining standardized tax revenues or costs as a population-weighted average of these values. My formulas give numbers very close to theirs but are simplified approximations.

246   *Edward M. Gramlich*

constant per capita reduction in all states.[13] Another way is to make proportional reductions by the factor $(1 - \alpha)$; thus

(4) $$A = \overline{G}N / \sum_{i=1}^{6} G_i N_i,$$

where $\overline{G}$ is the predetermined amount of assistance per capita made available by the central government, N is total population, and N_i is population in each state. After lengthy arguments, what the CGC has in fact done is to take the average of the two amounts.[14] Even these shares are only those recommended by the CGC—the commonwealth and the premiers of the states then negotiate the final shares.

This attempt to equalize public spending capacity across states is the most explicit and comprehensive in the world, and after fifty years the CGC now has extensive experience at trying to measure true cost differences, as opposed to policy or efficiency differences that are not adjusted for. Moreover, while CGC members and economists often are frustrated by the slowness of changes,[15] the fact is the CGC is powerful, is listened to, and even makes fairly significant changes in the equalizing provisions that are eventually adopted. Any flaws in the system should then be viewed against a background of its notable achievements.

Nonetheless, the system is not perfect, and various kinds of criticisms can be made. The most basic has been raised by Walsh, and it involves the G^* term in equation 3.[16] He argues that the mix of expenditure diversity and revenue centralization creates a revenue cartel that damages effective government. If states had to rely more on revenues that they themselves raised, consistent with any overall level of equalization, they would spend more time and effort managing their government and less lobbying for their relativity or their basic entitlement. To put this point in terms of the new "rent-seeking" literature, while the basic

13. A supporting argument is given by Nicolaas Groenewold, "The 'New Federalism' and Horizontal Equalization," *The Economic Record*, vol. 57 (September 1981), pp. 282–87.

14. As described in Commonwealth Grants Commission, *Report on State Tax Sharing and Health Grants, 1982*, vol. 1 (Canberra: AGPS, 1982), pp. 23–24.

15. See, for example, the lengthy and detailed complaints of one of the CGC's two economists, Russell Mathews, in "Federalism in Retreat."

16. Clifford Walsh, "Reforming Federal Financial Relations: Some Radical (or Are They Conservative?) Proposals," presented at the Federal Finances Symposium, Hobart, Tasmania, August–September, 1983.

entitlement G^* has been treated above as predetermined, in fact it is a political rent-seeking variable; resources are used up in determining it; and there is no reason why it will be set at the level that maximizes satisfaction in various states. Walsh's solution would be to set G^* equal to zero (or drastically reduce it), and have the central government return appropriate taxing authority to the states. As will be seen below, the latter suggestion is one that makes sense even if G^* is not reduced at all, but in Walsh's argument it becomes that much more important to deal with vertical tax assignments.

A second problem can be termed the "Woop Woop" problem, after a (possibly mythical) sparsely settled town in Western Australia where the main activity after dark is listening to the "woop woop" of the frogs. There are many towns like this in Australia, and the cost of supplying them with public services is very high. The CGC mechanically tries to eliminate these cost differentials by its equalization formulas. But that just removes a disincentive that would otherwise encourage citizens to move away from these high-cost areas and in the long run raises the overall cost of providing public services (and private goods too, for that matter). When differential tax prices result from divergent resource costs, it may be better for the CGC to avoid equalizing every cost difference. Doing so mechanically obscures what should be a matter for a policy debate on equality versus efficiency.

A final criticism, perhaps mainly semantic but one about which there is a fair amount of misunderstanding in Australia, is that the CGC scheme is ultimately not an equalization scheme at all. The argument is as follows. Assume that the costs of providing public services are equal across states but that one state has an income of $900 per capita, $100 below the national average. Assume further that the tax rate in this state equals the average rate of 0.1. Without any equalization grants, the state spends $90 on public services, $10 less than the national average. The CGC then gives the state $10 (see equation 1), based on the reasoning that if the state devoted the entire $10 to the public sector, its spending would be up to the average. The CGC claims that the $10 grant gives the state "the capacity" to provide an average menu of public services. But the CGC grant is unconditional, and surely the state will use some of it (probably about $9) to cut taxes and provide more private goods and raise public spending only about $1. The CGC scheme, then, has equalized neither true fiscal capacity (which is still lower in the state, $910 versus $1,000 as conventionally measured) nor expected public expenditures ($91 versus $100). It may be a sensible scheme, but because it does not make any important variable equal, it cannot be called an equalization scheme.[17]

Should the CGC take a further step and recommend grants that make some variable equal across states? There are, as it turns out, three ways in which that could be done that are consistent with CGC traditions and logic and that seem to be consistent with Australian politics. One way that works through the price term was suggested by Martin Feldstein in his work on local school finance in the United States.[18] According to this approach, suppose that state expenditures are determined by the following illustrative expression (the logic works for any other hypothesized relation):

(5) $E_i = a_0 + a_1 Y_i + a_2(G_i + R_i) + a_3 S_i - a_4 P_i + u_i,$

where all symbols are as defined above, S_i represents specific-purpose grants received by the ith state, assumed to be uncorrelated with income, R_i refers to royalty payments for mineral resources, also assumed to be exogenous and uncorrelated with income, P_i is the price of public services to a state, and u_i is a random residual with a mean of zero. Feldstein's approach is to use open-ended matching grants to vary the price facing states according to

(6) $P_i = \overline{P} + b_1(Y_i - \overline{Y}),$

where $\overline{P}$ is the average price facing all states. According to equation 6, the grant formula would be such that prices are higher in states with high income. The way to determine exactly how much higher the prices would be is to find the price that makes expected state expenditures independent of state incomes. Formally, that amounts to substituting equation 6 into equation 5, differentiating the expression with respect to state income, setting that derivative equal to zero, and solving to find b_1, the coefficient that tells how much a state's price should be raised as its income

17. This example has focused on capacity, but one could obviously construct a symmetric example for cost.

18. Martin S. Feldstein, "Wealth Neutrality and Local Choice in Public Education," *American Economic Review*, vol. 65 (March 1975), pp. 75–89.

increases. Doing all this yields a simple expression,

$$(7) \qquad b_1 = a_1/a_4.$$

The equalizing scheme thus gives more price aid to poorer states the higher the sensitivity of expenditure demand is to income (because this sensitivity would otherwise lead to large spending differentials), and the lower is the implied price sensitivity of demand (because more aid is necessary to get the state to spend more to offset its income deficiency). It is important to note that this scheme equalizes only expected expenditures on public services, not actual expenditures. In that sense, it is independent of the state's own fiscal policy, just as is the present CGC procedure.

The second approach follows the same logic but is adapted to the CGC tradition of giving only unconditional aid. It involves simply altering G_i to neutralize the income effect by replacing equation 3 with

$$(8) \qquad G_i = \overline{G} - b_2(Y_i - \overline{Y}),$$

so that states with higher income have lower unconditional grants. Solving in the same way as before yields

$$(9) \qquad b_2 = a_1/a_2.$$

A more general approach, in keeping with the CGC tradition of neutralizing all differences—income, resource income, prices, and specific-purpose grants—makes the expression for tax-sharing grants

$$(10) \qquad G_i = \overline{G} + \frac{a_1}{a_2}(\overline{Y} - Y_i) + (\overline{R} - R_i) + \frac{a_3}{a_2}(\overline{S} - S_i) + \frac{a_4}{a_2}(P_i - \overline{P}).$$

In either case (equation 9 or 10), if a state has a revenue need, as defined by $(\overline{Y} - Y_i)$, it should be reimbursed by a_1/a_2 of this need, as contrasted to t times the need (now granted by the CGC). In general, a_1/a_2 will be closer to unity than t, implying more aid to states with lower income. Indeed, in many cases a_1/a_2 will equal unity.[19] On the other hand, if a

---

19. The a_1/a_2 may not equal unity—that is, unconditional grants may be spent at a higher rate than income—because of what has come to be known as the "flypaper" effect (money sticks where it hits). For a discussion, see Edward M. Gramlich, "Intergovernmental Grants: A Review of the Empirical Literature," in Wallace E. Oates, ed., *The Political Economy of Fiscal Federalism* (Lexington, Mass.: D. C. Heath, 1977).

250   *Edward M. Gramlich*

Table 4. *Tax-Sharing Grants Implied by Various Distribution Formulas, by State*[a]
Dollars per capita

Item	New South Wales	Victoria	Queens- land	South Australia	Western Australia	Tasmania
1982 relativities	426.6	415.4	575.3	630.2	675.0	825.0
1982 CGC report[b]	431.9	424.3	649.6	594.9	580.4	674.2
1982 premiers' agreement	429.1	421.5	647.0	613.3	578.7	693.8
Power equalization						
Price only[c]	482.7	469.5	556.1	517.1	529.6	538.9
Income only[d]	475.1	455.9	581.8	525.1	543.4	556.8
Income and exogenous revenue[e]	496.7	435.1	634.7	511.5	445.5	536.5

Sources: Present relativities, specific-purpose grants, and population—Treasury Department, *Payments to or for the States, the Northern Territory, and Local Government Authorities, 1982–83*, Budget Paper 7 (Canberra: Australian Government Publishing Service, 1982), esp. table 6, p. 19; income—Russell Mathews, "Regional Disparities in Australia," table 1, p. 3; resources royalty—David Nellor, *Taxation of the Australian Resources Sector* (Clayton, Victoria: Monash University, Centre of Policy Studies, 1983), table 2.2, p. 2.4.
  a. Assuming $500 per capita is to be distributed.
  b. Commonwealth Grants Commission.
  c. Based on $G - \overline{G} = 0.11\,(\overline{Y} - Y)$, where the coefficient of 0.11 comes from Blackburn's work (see note 20).
  d. Based on $G - \overline{G} = 0.16\,(\overline{Y} - Y)$, where the coefficient of 0.16 also comes from Blackburn's work.
  e. Based on $G - \overline{G} = 0.16\,(\overline{Y} - Y) + (\overline{R} - R) + 1.68\,(\overline{S} - S)$, where the 1.68 coefficient also comes from Blackburn.

state receives fewer exogenous royalty payments or specific-purpose grants, or pays higher prices for its public services, it should receive more G_i, again with a higher multiplier.

These formulas determine the extra payments made to a particular state: as with the present system, the basic entitlement can then be determined by taking the total amount of grant money made available by the central government, determining needs-related payments, and spreading the remaining funds among all people to determine the G^*.

Table 4 shows how all these approaches work in practice. All six rows show results for an overall distribution of $500 per capita, roughly the amount to be allocated in 1982 once specific-purpose grants for health are converted to general-purpose assistance. The first row shows the results of distributing these funds by the 1982 relativities, close to those initially agreed on in 1976. These relativities ranged from a low of 1.0 for Victoria to a high of 1.87 for Tasmania, and the results reflect that fact, giving almost twice as much per capita to Tasmania. The second row shows what the distribution would have been if the relativities proposed by the CGC had been in existence. The CGC relativities reduce the variance of the distribution somewhat: Victoria is still normalized at 1.0, but now Tasmania is cut to 1.59. Both Western Australia and South Australia have reduced shares under this scheme, and more money is left for Victoria. The third row gives the results of the political compromise established at the 1982 Premiers' Conference, to be phased in gradually by 1985. The numbers are fairly close to the CGC recommendations, though the gap between those recommendations and the pre-existing relativities is not closed entirely.

The last three rows give some illustrative calculations that show how my suggested equalization approaches work. The fourth row is based on the price version of equalization described in equation 6. To present numbers comparable to the rest of the table, I show only how much money would go to various states to offset the impact of income on spending for public services: as described by equation 6, the effect on the price itself would be inversely related to the sensitivity of expenditures to price, a_4. The fifth row is based on equation 8, in which unconditional grants adjust only for the income differentials. There is a slightly wider range between the high- and low-income states in this row than in the fourth row because unconditional grants have a smaller effect per dollar on spending for public services, and hence more money is necessary to bring the spending of low-income states up to the average.[20] Were the impact of unconditional grants on spending even lower, on the order of that for income, this disparity would become wider still. The bottom row of the table makes allowance for exogenous sources of funds such as specific-purpose grants and minerals royalties, as described by equation 10. Although some observers believe that such an adjustment would help Victoria, the state with the highest income, and hurt Queensland, with the lowest income but the home of large deposits of resources, the ironic result is that funds go the other way because Victoria receives

20. The coefficients used in the calculations are based on pooled state budget data, given in V. C. Blackburn, "The Effect of Commonwealth Payments on the Financial Position of State Governments in Australia," presented at the Fiftieth Conference of the Australia and New Zealand Association for the Advancement of Science, Adelaide, May 12–16, 1980, appendix 2, p. 42. They are $a_1 = 0.11$, $a_2 = 0.68$, and $a_3 = 1.14$. According to these coefficients, there is a significant "flypaper effect." A similar set of coefficients, based on estimation of tax functions, is given by P. Bernd Spahn, "Federal Grant Policy and State-Local Taxation," in Russell Mathews, ed., *State and Local Taxation* (Canberra: Australian National University Press for the Centre for Research on Federal Financial Relations, 1977), table 7-3.

specific-purpose grants that are above average and Queensland, grants that are well below average.[21]

The criticisms raised in this section about present CGC procedures thus involve each of the terms of the basic CGC equation 3. One proposed improvement is to have the central government remove itself, partially or completely, from the revenue-raising business by allowing each state to raise more of its basic entitlement, G^*, on its own. Another is to weigh efficiency against equality in determining the public service cost-adjustment terms, E_i. A third is to alter the capacity-adjustment terms, T_i, to make expected expenditures on public services independent of state income; so if the authorities decide the optimal equalization scheme should be partial, it should at least be described as that.

The Loan Council

The second fifty-year-old unique institution in the Australian grant system is the Australian Loan Council (ALC). As stated above, this was started in 1928 to regulate the borrowing of state and local governments. But despite this rationale, it is probably true that any agency established to deal with a problem that happened once fifty years ago had better be reexamined. The ALC is essentially a credit-rationing scheme operated by the central government on one set of borrowers who happen to be in the public sector, leaving alone all other borrowers who happen to be in the private sector. The usual argument against such a scheme would be that capital markets are efficient, and that rationing by price incentives (that is, high interest rates) is effective not only in limiting the overall amount of debt floated, but in channeling them to those borrowers most willing to pay. Formal, government-imposed credit rationing schemes such as the ALC would have no role in such a view of the world. Are there any redeeming features of the ALC?

21. I argued above that public-service price differentials could be ignored in these calculations and followed that convention here. A question remains about private-goods price differentials. Should they be used to deflate money incomes? One argument might be to use them and do all adjustments in real terms. Another might be to adopt the same view as for public-service prices, to discourage households from moving to areas having high transportation and distribution costs, and hence to ignore private-goods prices. If I were a member of the CGC, I would probably vote for splitting the difference. As an author, I was not able to find such numbers by state, so I ignored the problem and simply used money values everywhere.

Three years ago the Campbell Committee of Inquiry investigated this matter and gave a mixed verdict. They recommended that semigovernments—those public authorities engaged in commercial operations such as for transport, harbors, rail, and electricity and brought under the ALC by a gentlemen's agreement—be released from it and allowed to borrow on their own. As a response to this recommendation, in 1982 state electric power authorities were given such freedom for a three-year trial period, and in 1983 the ALC relaxed its constraints on other semigovernmental borrowing. For state and local general governments that would still come under the ALC, the Campbell Committee recommended that the so-called 30–20 rule be eliminated. It required certain financial institutions to hold 30 percent of their assets in public securities, of which 20 percent had to be commonwealth securities. This change has not yet been implemented, though the growth in so-called noncaptive holdings of government securities has been so rapid since that time that such a change would probably have little effect on the pattern of interest rates today.[22] But the Campbell Committee still called for continuation of the ALC, mainly because it believed that without the ALC there would be no discipline on the borrowing of state general governments.[23] The most commonly heard justification is that politicians (in state governments) have short horizons and cannot be relied upon to worry about overborrowing when they themselves will not be in office when the interest is due. A subsidiary rationale is that foreign borrowing must be controlled by the commonwealth.

One could certainly question control of foreign borrowing and arguments on its behalf. Free capital markets for subnational securities do seem to work well in other countries, such as the United States. And although a large share of state and local funds comes from grants, the size of the state need not imply less discipline: *at the margin* states do have to finance their expenditures and borrowing by raising taxes. Their central government grants are fixed in amount, and cannot be boosted to cover unwise capital investments. The profligate state must raise taxes. The incentive for sound capital investments is therefore stronger than might at first be apparent. And this is doubly true if states borrow

22. The data for this statement were supplied by Donald Stammer of Bain & Co., Sydney.
23. See Australian Financial System Inquiry, *Final Report of the Committee of Inquiry* (Canberra: AGPS, 1980), chaps. 10, 12, and the recommendations there.

from abroad. If states do not hedge against exchange rate risk (the risk they will have to repay in appreciated currency if the Australian dollar depreciates), they will have to pay for this gamble.

A related matter that receives remarkably little attention in these debates (not even mentioned by the Campbell Committee) is that since 1975 the commonwealth has given capital grants equal to one-third of the total amount borrowed on behalf of state general governments. Hence if a state requested a $100 million capital program and the request was approved, the ALC would borrow $100 million for the state and the state would actually repay only $66 million to the ALC. Not only is the borrowing done at subsidized interest rates because the central government guarantees repayment of the bond, but the state also receives $34 million free and clear, with no interest or repayment obligations. It is no wonder that state general government borrowers have to be rationed through nonprice methods. If the goal is to convince states to pay attention to the market, a first step might be to eliminate these large subsidies for capital borrowing.

One final point, also not stressed by the Campbell Committee, seems to grow more important every day. The more stringent are the ALC restrictions on governmental borrowing, the more do states contrive creative financing schemes to circumvent the ALC. Queensland has always led in this area. One of its favorite schemes involves "security deposits." When a rail or other capital facility is to be built to transport resources to port, Queensland may force the company to make a loan of the construction costs, called a security deposit, to the state. The state then builds the facility and nominally repays the principal and interest out of freight rates. Mining companies allege that Queensland in fact raises its rates to provide revenue to repay the company's loan. The result of all this paper shuffling is not a reduction in borrowing at home or offshore—private companies have to do that to provide their security deposit—but a form of hidden taxation of resources companies; these companies must provide capital to build a railroad but do not own it or receive a return on it.

An even more creative scheme was devised by New South Wales. Called "leverage leasing," it is a first cousin to the recently limited safe-harbor leasing in the United States. When a public facility is to be built, a private company is formed to build and own it. Since this company is private, it can claim depreciation allowances and the investment allowance on the new construction expenses. It then leases the facilities to the government, which charges rates in the usual way. Again the ALC has been circumvented—the private company had to borrow internally or externally to build the facility, and total borrowings are unaffected. But this time a tax loophole is created; it costs the federal treasury in company tax reductions that would not have been made had the facility been built by public borrowing. Again there is no reduction in total borrowing, but some new tax loopholes are created by the government's attempt to regulate borrowing.[24]

When these kinds of factors are added, the normative case for the ALC seems weak and becoming weaker. The recent relaxation of the gentlemen's agreement seems a step in the right direction, and this agreement could be abolished altogether. And to put it in even more radical terms, while the ALC itself cannot be abolished without a constitutional amendment, the treasurer could, on his own, begin providing more routine approvals for state general government borrowing— and at the same time eliminate the large subsidy so that states themselves would be more concerned about borrowing costs and would ration themselves.

Specific-Purpose Grants

The other leg of the Australian grant triad is the set of specific-purpose grants. While there are many of these specific-purpose grants, the largest sums are concentrated in primary and secondary education, higher and technical education, housing, roads, and, until recently, health. These grants, like categorical grants in other federal countries, are characterized by tight categorical requirements on how the money is spent. Except in the case of health, specific-purpose grants have always been limited in amount by the central government.

Both in the United States and in Australia the main problem with categorical grants is that they are not set up so as to lead to efficient spending outcomes. In the United States federal matching shares are quite high—the federal government pays about 80 percent of the cost of a project on a typical grant, much more than the share of marginal

24. Tax authorities eventually disallowed the tax advantages on the leased equipment, but this still does not stop circumvention of the ALC.

benefits likely to be realized by citizens in other states. Thus states find
these grants advantageous, tend to subscribe very heavily to them, and
even establish offices in Washington to seek out and lobby for more
grants. The federal government then must limit the size of the grants
administratively, usually to an amount that is small relative to what the
states would otherwise have spent in the relevant program area. It
becomes easy for states to claim that the expenditures they would have
incurred in the case were under the supposedly categorical grant and
then divert the grant money to their own purposes. This phenomenon,
known as grant displacement, explains why most U.S. federal categorical
grants result in state-local tax reduction, and why the efforts of Presidents
Nixon and Reagan to convert the grants to general-purpose assistance
have probably resulted in little real change in state-local spending.[25]

In Australia, circumstances are much the same. Australian federal
matching ratios are even higher than they are in the United States, 100
percent for most specific-purpose grants, and the incentives for states to
overspend are that much greater. Again, the central government is forced
to limit spending administratively, though this time to amounts that seem
to be larger relative to the normal expenditures of state governments.
Observed grant displacement is thus less, at least as perceived by two
authors who have studied the problem, V. C. Blackburn and Bernd
Spahn. Their results indicate a lack of displacement for specific-purpose
grants. A dollar of these grants raises state spending by more than a
dollar and hence raises state taxes a small amount, while a dollar of
general-purpose assistance raises state spending less than a dollar and
lowers state taxes.[26]

But although the observed level of displacement is smaller in Australia,
that changes only the symptoms of the problem, not the problem itself.
In Australia, as in the United States, the central difficulty with specific-
purpose grants is that the matching shares of the central government are
too high, so that states have no incentive to limit their use of the grants

25. See Edward M. Gramlich, "An Econometric Examination of the New Federalism," *Brookings Papers on Economic Activity, 2:1982*, pp. 327–70.

26. The relevant numbers for Blackburn were given above in note 20. He finds that
$1.00 of specific-purpose grants raises spending by $1.14 and (implicitly) raises taxes
by $0.14, while $1.00 of general-purpose aid raises spending by $0.68 and (implicitly)
lowers taxes by $0.32. Spahn finds that $1.00 of specific-purpose grants raises taxes by
$0.36 and (implicitly) spending by $1.36, while $1.00 of general-purpose aid lowers taxes
by $0.12 and (implicitly) raises spending by $0.88.

and overspend unless arbitrary limitations are imposed by the central government. The obvious solution to the problem is for the central government to lower its own matching shares until the marginal external-internal cost ratio corresponds to the marginal external-internal benefit ratio—hence taking the pressure off administrative mechanisms to ration expenditures. If this is not done, the block-grant approach followed in the United States may still be preferred to making no changes at all, but it is definitely a second-best reform if specific-purpose grants are being used in project areas in which there are some out-of-state benefits.

While the Australians have not adopted the block-grant solution on anything approaching the scale used in the United States, they have followed the model in one crucial program area—health. In this case the reform does appear likely to succeed, for reasons that are somewhat idiosyncratic but nevertheless instructive.

By the early 1970s Australia had developed a system whereby state governments ran inexpensive public hospitals (free, without any means test, in Queensland), and the central government made a small payment to the hospitals based on numbers of patients. During the Whitlam administration this policy was changed to require Australian states to provide free care regardless of means in the standard care wards of their public hospitals, with the central and state governments each paying half of the expenses. In the jargon of grants, this amounted to a categorical open-ended grant with a central government matching share of 50 percent. The free hospital care led to a rapid escalation in costs, which caused central government outlays for specific-purpose health grants to triple as a share of GDP (0.4 percent to 1.3 percent) in just one year.[27] This also led to another commission of inquiry, the Jamison Committee, to find ways of improving the efficiency of the system.

The Jamison Committee recommendations, most of which were adopted by the Fraser government, were to put a cap on the specific-

27. Similarly, it might be imagined that health expenses would have been higher in Queensland, where public hospitals have been free since World War II, than in other states. This is clearly not the case. Queensland has the lowest per capita expenditures on this budget item by a large amount, as is shown in table 2. Moroever, nobody has yet produced any quantitative evidence that service levels of public hospitals in Queensland are substandard, or even below those in other states. Since Queensland hospitals have always been free, that state has learned how to manage hospitals more cheaply by centralizing control, putting doctors on salaries, and reimbursing hospitals by group session hours and not by the number of visits.

purpose grant and to convert it to a general-purpose grant. The aggregate amount of the grant would eventually be indexed for cost changes in some way, and its distribution would be determined in a manner like that used by the CGC.[28] But while their funds would be set in this manner, states themselves would continue to operate their public hospitals. Under the subsequently passed States (Tax Sharing and Health Grants) Act of 1981, states were not required to spend their health grants on hospitals—these were general-purpose grants—but they had to make free health care available to low-income groups, pensioners, and others in special need. Implicitly states were free to devise fee schedules for others.[29]

Soon after the Jamison Committee made its recommendations, as a result of an election, Fraser was out of office and Labor party prime minister Robert Hawke was in. One of the important election campaign platforms of the Labor party was to return to the 1975 scheme of free health care in the public hospitals, this time to be financed by an income tax surcharge of 1 percent. Such a change is now being planned and is slated to be made in early 1984. There is an important difference, however, between the Whitlam health grant and the plan presently envisaged by the new Labor government. As under the Fraser administration the health grant will still be capped, but it will be larger by an amount equal to the 1 percent income tax surcharge. States will still be responsible for their public hospitals and now will be free to control everything but the fee schedule. Hence states will still have an incentive to manage their hospitals cheaply—they still save $1 if they can cut costs by $1.

28. See Commission of Inquiry into the Efficiency and Administration of Hospitals, *Report of the Commission of Inquiry into the Efficiency and Administration of Hospitals*, vol. 1 (Canberra: AGPS, 1981).

29. A much more detailed examination of these issues is given in a joint paper by the Commonwealth Treasury and Health Departments, "Hospital Funding Arrangements: A Historical Perspective," paper presented at the Research Advisory Committee Seminar of the Centre for Research on Federal Financial Relations (Canberra: Australian National University, May 19, 1983). See also the discussion in George Palmer, "Commonwealth/State Fiscal Relationships and the Financing and Provision of Health Services," in P. M. Tatchell, ed., *Economics and Health, 1981*, Proceedings of the Third Conference of Australian Health Economists (Canberra: Australian National University, 1982).

Table 5. *Tax Revenues for Governmental Units, 1981–82*
Millions of dollars

Item	Common-wealth	States	Localities	Total
Individual income tax	21,224	. . .	. . .	21,224
Company income tax	5,215	. . .	. . .	5,215
Excise duties[a]	6,090	. . .	. . .	6,090
Sales tax	2,854	. . .	. . .	2,854
Customs duties	2,060	. . .	. . .	2,060
Payroll tax	16	2,398	. . .	2,414
Stamp duties	11	1,350	. . .	1,360
Motor taxes	10	1,009	. . .	1,020
Property taxes	21	370	1,718	2,109
Other	491	1,976	88	2,555
Total	37,992	7,103	1,806	46,901

Source: Russell Mathews, "Federal-State Fiscal Relations in Australia," paper presented to Workshop on Australia's Federal System, Resource Development and Resource Trade (Canberra: Australia-Japan Research Centre and the Australian National University, November 1983), table 1, p. 9.
a. Includes natural gas and crude oil levy and coal export duty.

Taxation Responsibilities

The other important aspect of Australia's fiscal federalism system is the sharing of tax responsibilities. The broad detail on how taxing responsibilities are shared is given in table 5. Commonwealth taxes amounted to four-fifths of total taxes in 1981–82. The Constitution, along with subsequent High Court interpretations, gave the central government exclusive right to impose customs, excise, and sales duties. The Uniform Tax Scheme of the World War II years gave the central government control over both the individual and company income tax. Partly because of this revenue imbalance, states were given exclusive access to the payroll tax (on employers only) in the early 1970s. In addition, states impose various types of stamp duties and other miscellaneous taxes. Just as in the United States, local Australian governments have one main tax, the property tax.

In this section, I discuss three tax-policy questions with strong federalism overtones. I first discuss a problem that has arisen in connection with the individual income tax, the largest and most important tax in Australia. This problem turns out to be related to the lack of death duties in Australia, so I then do an autopsy on the death of these death duties. Finally, I examine some options for taxing Australia's significant earnings from natural resources.

Individual Income Taxes

For many years now the individual income tax has been Australia's primary means of raising revenue. One virtue usually attributed to the income tax is that it has desirable consequences both for horizontal equity—taxpayers with the same incomes are treated equally—and for vertical equity—since the progressivity of the schedule can be varied, any amount of income redistribution can in principle be accomplished. The individual income tax is also acknowledged to distort people's choices between work and leisure and between consumption and saving, but this distortion is not obviously larger than the distortion implicit in other taxes.

None of this is inappropriate for Australia, but there is a cancer that is greatly eroding support for the income tax, or at least support for further increases in the income tax. The problem is that Australia's income tax is one with fairly high marginal rates—now 30 percent of income up to a level just above the median income, then 46 percent, then 60 percent. In addition to this there is a state payroll tax, paid by the employer at a rate of 5 percent in most states. But there are almost no other supporting taxes. There is no capital gains tax for assets held more than a year. There is no death duty. There is no broad-based retail sales tax. That means that a very strong economic incentive is created for avoiding or evading the income tax. If one can convert income from relatively completely taxed wage and salary income to capital gains income, one can save up to $0.60 on each $1.00 ($0.65 with the payroll tax included). In the United States, no model for an ideal system, the differential is less than half that.[30]

How important are tax avoidance and evasion? The figures available are sparse for avoidance (legal activities) and even sparser for evasion (illegal underreporting). There are some data, however, and several

---

30. A taxpayer in the highest marginal income tax bracket in the United States pays $0.50 out of each dollar; the same taxpayer pays $0.20 in capital gains tax. From the remaining $0.30 of the dollar, another few cents are lost to the retail sales tax.

Australian economists have come up with numbers suggesting that a striking share of the tax base is lost through simple tax evasion, either illegal underreporting of income or overreporting of deductions.

Using time-series data, Russell Mathews gives figures indicating that between 1965 and 1979 the share of tax revenues resulting from wage and salary income has risen steadily, from 67 percent to 81 percent. Had this share not changed at all, income tax revenues would have been $2.7 billion, or 21 percent higher.[31] Such a calculation could be biased high or low. On the one hand, it may be an underestimate of the amount of evasion because it assumes there was no evasion in 1965. On the other hand, it could be an overestimate because it attributes all change in the distribution of tax revenues to the tax law, and there could be a number of alternative explanations.

But the results obtained by Mathews are supported by two different calculations of Neville Norman. Norman first modifies a procedure that has been used to estimate the size of the underground economy in the United States—analyzing changes in the currency-deposits ratio, which in Norman's case is corrected for changes in that ratio due to inflation. The currency-deposit ratio has risen from 27 percent to 43 percent in Australia since 1965. On the basis of his econometric analysis Norman estimates that 10 percentage points of this increase are due to inflation, leaving 6 percentage points to be explained by the shift toward nonreportable income activities. Applying the same money velocity for the nonreported sector as for the reported sector, Norman then gets an estimate of lost income tax revenues of $3.5 billion in 1981, 21 percent of revenues, exactly the same share that Mathews found for an earlier year.[32]

Norman also has one other method, which makes inferences on the basis of the commissioner of taxation's "honors list"—a sample of returns of apprehended evaders. Using this sample, Norman found that detected evaders did not report about half of their income in 1973–74. Extrapolating this forward and assuming on the basis of other calculations that 7 percent of potential taxpayers were evaders, Norman finds

31. Russell Mathews, "The Structure of Taxation" (Canberra: Australian National University, Centre for Research on Federal Financial Relations, 1980), table 4.

32. See Neville R. Norman, "The Economics of Tax Evasion," paper presented at the Eleventh Conference of Economists (Bedford Park, South Australia: Flinders University, August 1982).

a 1978–79 income tax loss of $2.7 billion, again just Mathews's 21 percent share.

Each of these methods has its weaknesses, but the fact that all three suggest one-fifth of potential income tax revenues is being lost through simple tax evasion is surely meaningful. And one-fifth is a large share indeed. If the true amount of tax revenue lost through simple evasion is anything like this, many of the claims usually made on behalf of the income tax have a very hollow ring. Because Norman also found evasion to be concentrated at the top of the income scale, the tax is promoting less vertical equity than might be imagined. Because many evaders are not apprehended, the tax is not conferring horizontal equity. And because resources are devoted both to evasion and to entirely legal avoidance schemes, the tax also seems to be generating substantial economic inefficiencies.

There might then be some sense in altering the overall mix of Australian taxes to place less reliance on the income tax (implying lower marginal rates for those who pay), and more reliance on other taxes (implying higher tax rates for those who evade). Recently at least four economists, two from the right and two from the left, have so argued in Australia.[33]

It may seem that evasion of the federal income tax would have little to do with fiscal federalism. Nothing could be further from the truth. Because states are excluded by a constitutional interpretation from imposing broadly based retail sales taxes, they can raise more revenue only through a surcharge to the income tax, a higher payroll tax, or various narrowly based, nonneutral taxes such as stamp duties, financial assets charges, or taxes and charges on the resource industry. Given the taxing situation, all options are likely to generate economic inefficiencies.[34] The obvious solution is either to change the constitutional interpretation or otherwise empower states to use a retail sales tax.

---

33. The two convervative authors are Geoffrey Brennan, "Tax Reform Australian Style" (Canberra: Australian National University, 1980); and Peter L. Swan, "Reforming the System: An Economist's View," address given to the Economic Society of Australia, Sydney, March 4, 1983. The two liberal authors are Russell Mathews, "The Case for Indirect Taxation," Endowed Lecture in Taxation Law and Policy, Taxation Institute of Australia, May 5, 1983; and Peter D. Groenewegen, "Rationalizing Australian Taxation Revisited," Shann Memorial Lecture (Nedlands, Western Australia: University of Western Australia, 1983).

34. Given the high rates of income tax, one might at least imagine that states would make use of their freedom to lower these rates and recover the revenue in other ways.

The "Death" of Death Duties

While the main problem today in the Australian federalism arrangements seems to be the states' lack of access to desirable sources of revenue on equity or efficiency grounds, there is one potential counter-example. Formerly the states imposed death duties; in 1977–78 the states raised $240 million from this source, about 5 percent of their revenue. But then states began lowering their death duties until finally, in 1982, the last one was abolished. Why?

An important lesson of local public finance is that income redistribution cannot be done at the subnational level. If one state imposes higher death duties than another without correspondingly augmenting public services, the high-income elderly tend to migrate to the low-tax state, thereby reducing revenues in the high-tax state and effectively forcing it to lower its death duties. Although migration between subnational districts is normally desirable for efficiency, it can frustrate attempts of subnational governments to redistribute income. Hence most income redistribution needs to be done at the national level.[35] For this reason, of all the taxes that the Australian central government could have left to states, the death duty was precisely the wrong one.

The lesson was borne out quite predictably. Most Australian states in the late 1970s had rather imperfect systems of death duties that were potentially evadable by the very wealthy with clever lawyers. These states imposed fairly stiff taxes on small estates and featured long waiting periods and unexpected fluctuations in real tax levels as asset values fluctuated. An early salvo in the campaign against death duties was fired in 1970, when Sydney Negus was elected senator from Western Australia as one of the first single-issue candidates. He ran on a shoestring and had one campaign platform, to try to abolish death duties.

State treasury officials gave two political reasons why they would not seriously entertain such a measure. One is that states would be worried that the CGC would think they had enough money. Another is that states would be prevented from advertising the income tax as that tax paid to Canberra (as they do now). As soon as states cut rates once, it would become apparent to voters that they could do so again, and they could no longer insulate themselves from criticism of the income tax.

35. A colleague, Deborah Laren, and I have tried to show the truth of this lesson for some policies operating on the other side of income and age distribution (for U.S. public assistance policies) on the other side of the globe in "Migration and Income Redistribution Responsibility," *Journal of Human Resources* (forthcoming, Fall 1984).

264   *Edward M. Gramlich*

The election of Negus resulted in no legislation, but soon afterward
the premier of Queensland (ever the maverick in the Australian federation), Joh. Bjelke-Peterson, picked up the issue. At the time, high capital
gains on family farms were causing both farmers and other small
entrepreneurs to fear the loss of family holdings to death duties. Rather
than index brackets for inflation or make other incremental changes, as
his own treasurer urged, Bjelke-Peterson pushed ahead and by 1977 had
totally abolished Queensland's death duties. Parts of Queensland have
some of the nicer beaches and climate in Australia, and either for this
reason, the lack of death duties, or some combination, the elderly began
to flood from the other states to Queensland. A study of Australian
migration patterns by Graeme Hugo shows that between 1976 and 1981
Queensland was the only Australian state to have a net gain of persons
over fifty years old as a result of internal migration, with a large share of
those migrants coming from New South Wales and Victoria.[36]

At that point the other states began tripping over one another to follow
Queensland's lead and abolish their own death duties. The game of
"follow the leader" is shown in table 6, which shows death tax rates
from 1976, when Queensland made its move, to 1983, when Victoria's
duty was finally phased out. Since the central government also lowered
its own smaller death duties over this time (for reasons not explained by
my story), Australia now stands without any death duties. Untaxed long-
term capital gains and estates and the possibility for nonwage earners to
avoid the income tax poke a large hole in the achievement of the equality
objective that many Australians hold so dear. As the tax system stands
now, those beginning life with wealth can accumulate even more by
capital gains and pass it through to the next generation without ever
being taxed. But those who start without much wealth and work in wage
or salaried jobs may never get ahead because of the high marginal income
tax rates. For these groups, it is not such a "fair go."[37]

36. Graeme Hugo, "Interstate Migration in Australia, 1976–81," *Australian Bulletin
of Labour*, vol. 9 (March 1983), pp. 102–30.
37. So, at least, was the argument given by several different tax commissions
analyzing the Australian system in the mid-1970s. See, for example, Australian Treasury
Taxation Paper, *Estate and Gift Duty, Purposes and Rationale 14*, December 1974; or
Taxation Review Committee, *Full Report of the Taxation Review Committee*, January
31, 1975 (Canberra: AGPS, 1976).
In a paper written about that time, Geoffrey Brennan argues a contrary case. See
H. G. Brennan, "On the Incidence of Estate and Gift Duties: A Theoretical Analysis,"

Table 6. *State Estate Tax Rates, 1976–83*[a]
Percent

Type of inheritance and state	1976	1977	1978	1979	1980	1981	1982	1983
Estate passing to spouse								
New South Wales	27.0	...	...	...	...	...	...	...
Victoria	26.0	...	...	...	...	...	...	...
Queensland	20.0	...	...	...	...	...	...	...
South Australia	27.5	...	...	...	...	...	...	...
Western Australia	25.0	25.0	...	...	...	...	...	...
Tasmania	26.0	26.0	...	...	...	...	...	...
Estate passing to child								
New South Wales	27.0	27.0	27.0	27.0	27.0	27.0	...	...
Victoria	26.0	26.0	26.5	26.5	26.5	34.0	22.0	...
Queensland	20.0	...	...	...	...	...	...	...
South Australia	27.5	27.5	27.5	27.5	...	...	...	...
Western Australia	25.0	25.0	25.0	12.5	...	...	...	...
Tasmania	26.0	26.0	26.5	26.5	26.5	26.5	...	...

Source: Commonwealth Grants Commission, *Report on State Tax Entitlements* (Canberra: AGPS), appendixes, 1977–82.

a. Data for years shown are for June. For June 1976, June 1977, and June 1978 a child is defined as under age twenty-one. Beginning in June 1979 no age distinction is given.

Two interpretations are possible. One was given above: an attempt to devolve redistribution responsibilities to the subnational level was totally frustrated by migration or the anticipation of it. But an alternative explanation holds that the prevailing death duty was simply unpopular: Senator Negus and Premier Bjelke-Peterson showed how unpopular. The speed of events and the coarseness of migration data probably preclude finding the true explanation. But one tax that states apparently cannot use is the death duty.

As a postscript on this matter, a recent development does give signs of mitigating the imbalance in the way income from labor and capital are taxed, at least for those with a long-run view of things. Henry J. Aaron's

in R.L. Mathews, ed., *State and Local Taxation* (Canberra: Australian National University Press, 1977). He makes the point that if the income of the donor was subject to income tax, estate taxes could be viewed as a form of double taxation, with concomitant inefficiencies. While Brennan's model seems convincing as far as it goes, there are two practical problems with the argument: to the extent that estates are accumulated by long-term capital gains, they would not have previously been subject to any tax at all; and efficiency is not everything. One of the goals of estate taxation is to even out disparities in economic opportunities across generations. Hence even a double tax may at times be appropriate.

chapter in this book describes the Hawke government's recent law to raise taxes on superannuation payments — private lump-sum pension benefits — to rates of 15 percent on the first $50,000 and 30 percent thereafter for all accumulations, beginning in 1984. Revenues from this tax will obviously grow quite slowly. But it should gradually close a major loophole in the income tax law by, in effect, giving taxpayers the option of choosing expenditure tax treatment. If workers want to save in the form of private pensions (currently their contributions to super-annuation are limited, but the employers' contributions are not), they will be taxed henceforth at 30 percent on their accumulations, or at their marginal income tax rates if they convert their lump sums to annuities. The 30 percent tax treatment resembles a flat rate expenditure tax applied also to bequests; the marginal rate treatment, a progressive income tax. In either case, the lack of a death duty is made irrelevant and a major gap in the present revenue system of Australia is closed.[38] But this neat device for closing the loophole still does not solve the revenue problems of the states.

Resources Rent Taxes

One important actual and potential source of revenue for the states is that derived from exploitation of natural resources. All six states have some mineral resources and gain revenue from them. The second row of table 7 indicates that in 1978–79, the latest year for which complete data are available, the states raised between $3 and $43 per capita through various charges and bidding fees paid by the mineral resources industry, amounting to between 2 and 20 percent of their total revenues. The central government taxes exploration of mineral resources too and thus raises $137 per capita, 9 percent of its revenues, through schemes for leasing offshore oil drilling rights, company taxes on resource developers, a coal export duty, and a natural gas and crude oil levy. Moreover, the Hawke government is now considering proposals for replacing the natural gas and oil levy with what is known as a resources rent tax on the petroleum sector.

The question of the proper taxation of rents from natural resources raises many issues—defining rents and proper deductible expenses, determining discount rates, international harmonization of taxation of

38. This point was called to my attention by John F. Helliwell.

Table 7. *Resources Taxes and Royalties, by State, 1978–79*
Dollars per capita

Item	Commonwealth duty[a]	State royalty	Total
Weighted average, all states	137.1	16.8	153.9
New South Wales	137.1	6.7	143.8
Victoria	137.1	22.1	159.2
Queensland	137.1	24.9	162.0
South Australia	137.1	3.2	140.3
Western Australia	137.1	43.0	180.1
Tasmania	137.1	5.1	142.2
Addenda			
Weighted standard deviation	. . .	11.7	11.7
Coefficient of variation	. . .	0.697	0.076

Sources: Nellor, *Taxation of the Australian Resource Sector*, tables 2.2 and 2.3; pp. 2.4 and 2.8 (inflated to 1978–79 prices by using an inflator of 1.487); and Treasury Department, *Payments to and for the States, the Northern Territory, and Local Government Authorities, 1982–83*, table 6, p. 19.
    a. Includes company taxes (34 percent), natural gas and crude oil levy (60 percent), coal export duty (5 percent), and a small amount of royalties.

multinational resources companies—and I make no pretense of giving this complex subject a careful treatment. Some of these topics are considered in the chapter by John F. Helliwell. But in the Australian context, the resources tax is complicated by two factors: there are a lot more earnings from resources to tax than there are in most countries; and the federal-state tax issue is unusually complex.

Even the discussions that do try to come to grips with the optimal tax treatment of resources rents typically assume the existence of one government, something that must strike practical persons in Australia as akin to the economist's "can opener" assumption. In fact, there are two governments that impose a tax, the state and the commonwealth, and makers of resources tax policy must worry about how the two fit together, a matter infrequently addressed by Australian economists.

The reason both governments can impose taxes is a provision in the Australian Constitution of 1901 that gives states title to mineral rights located within their borders—the state in effect becomes the landowner. To a limited degree the commonwealth is a landowner too—it holds title to resources in the mineral-rich Northern Territory and offshore oil properties, but most of the commonwealth revenue derives from its power to assess company income taxes, export duties, and other special imports. As long as this fundamental aspect of property rights in Australia is not changed and there are income taxes, there will be two governments that tax.[39]

Dual taxing authorities create two types of inefficiencies. First, both domestic and international resource companies must incur the numerous practical problems of dealing with the disparate taxing procedures of seven governments instead of one. Second, the state and federal governments compete for these apparently rich sources of revenue. Cassing and Hillman have developed one realistic example to illustrate what can happen. They assume that the commonwealth wants to maximize revenue from a coal export duty, the optimal rate of which depends negatively on the rail freight that Queensland charges coal producers to transport coal to port. The state of Queensland (always Queensland!), the home of this coal deposit, finds that its monopolistic price for these rail services depends negatively on the federal duty. As long as the two governments do not cooperate, the state and federal governments will compete for tax revenues, and this competition increases deadweight inefficiencies, drives down total output, and reduces joint federal-state revenues.[40] Vertical tax competition yields many similar inefficiencies.

If a mine or a well could be made operational with no uncertainty, it would be possible to design efficient schemes of taxation—schemes that tax away some revenue without interfering with the pattern of development. But there is a great deal of uncertainty in the resources sector—about the geological information, about world prices once the resources are produced, and about production costs—and any taxation scheme for resources (unless it confers full tax credits for losses, which are not even feasible if drillers go broke and leave the industry) will then lower the net expected return from a venture and provide some disincentive to exploration and development. Although Australia's interest is generally in maximal exploration and development (the reasons, and caveats, are given in the chapters by John F. Helliwell and by Rudiger Dornbusch and Stanley Fischer), one could not argue seriously that the earnings from these resources should go untaxed. If other forms of income are

39. Indeed, there is also a third. Local governments also assess taxes and charges on minerals companies, but to keep the discussion manageable, I consider those charges as user fees and do not include them.

40. J. H. Cassing and A. L. Hillman, "State-Federal Resource Tax Rivalry: The Queensland Railway and the Federal Export Tax," *The Economic Record*, vol. 58 (September 1982), pp. 235–41.

taxed, presumably earnings from resources should be too. The important question is how these earnings can be taxed with the least inefficiency.

If there were just one government imposing a tax and certain strong assumptions held, the most efficient tax would be none at all on earnings from production. Firms should bid for rights to explore property, and in the competitive limit they will bid away all their expected profits.[41] But such a scheme may not be practical in Australia for two reasons. First, a bidding scheme implies releasing mineral resources firms from the company tax—something that is again likely to be politically infeasible and certainly will cause difficult problems of transfer pricing for firms that are engaged in mining and other industries. Second, a complete royalty bidding scheme may not raise much revenue in Australia because the mining companies do not appear to trust the states. Repeatedly the representatives of mining companies point to the fate of minerals properties that proved more lucrative than expected: rather than let the firms keep the winnings from their gamble, the states boosted rail charges or imposed some other tax, hidden or not.[42] As long as firms expect this behavior to be possible, and governments cannot commit themselves to forswear it, firms will underbid on the competitive auctions and revenues from resources will not be maximized.

Another possibility, called a Leland tax in Australia, is a two-part tariff. One part, the bid tax, should be independent of the profits of mining firms. The other part, the profits tax, should be a function of the present discounted value of expected profits from minerals.[43] As before, the royalty bid is to compensate the landowners for their property. But, as returns are earned, the government also receives a share of these

41. This point is argued by Ted Bergstrom, "Property Rights and Taxation in the Australian Minerals Sector," in L. Cook and M. G. Porter, eds., *The Minerals Sector and the Australian Economy* (Sydney: George Allen & Unwin, 1984).

42. This point was made most forcefully by John MacLeod of CRA Ltd., an Australian mining firm. Bergstrom recognizes and discusses it. See ibid.

43. The scheme takes its name from H. Leland, "Optimal Risk Sharing and Leasing of Natural Resources, with Application to Oil and Gas Leasing in the OCS," *Quarterly Journal of Economics*, vol. 92 (August 1978), pp. 413–38. It is also described in detail by Craig Emerson and Peter Lloyd, "Improving Mineral Taxation Policy in Australia," Discussion Paper 36 (Canberra: Australian National University, Centre for Economic Policy Research, October 1981); and by Peter L. Swan, "A Review of the Northern Territory Government's Green Paper on Mining Royalty Policy for the Northern Territory," Discussion Paper 39 (Canberra: Australian National University, Centre for Economic Policy Research, December 1981).

earnings from the profits tax. Although the Leland scheme formally taxes the present discounted value of present and future minerals profits, in the real world a tax system that cannot tax future values can come very close just by taxing profits as properly defined.[44]

Australian taxes on minerals are imposed variously on volume, value, or profits, based on royalties at the state level and company duties and special duties at the commonwealth level; all are assessed at widely disparate rates.[45] Nobody would describe them as efficient or neutral. But it does not seem difficult to move from this hodge-podge system to an efficient set of taxes and straighten out the state-federal problem simultaneously. The strategy would be to allow states, the landowners, to assess royalties as lump-sum amounts, bid competitively. The federal government could then assess its present proportional company tax, allowing deduction of all royalties, expensing other capital and exploration costs, but *not* allowing the deduction of interest payments (because the proceeds of the loan for which interest is paid are not taxable). The company tax should allow full loss offsets—that is, potential tax credits— to maintain neutral treatment over time.[46] Applying the same marginal

44. This can be seen as follows. According to the Leland scheme, there is a tax on the present and future value of profits, V,

$$V = \sum_{j=0}^{L} v_j/(1 + r)^j,$$

where v_j represents annual profits in real terms, r is the real interest rate (or the nominal interest rate if v_j is expressed in money terms), and j designates the year until the resource is exhausted in year L. To simplify the algebra, set $L = 1$ and assume that profitability is expected to grow at rate g in this second year. If taxes are levied at the proportional rate, t, the present value of a Leland tax is $\hat{T} = tV$; the present value of all present and future company taxes, T, is

$$T = tv_0 + \frac{tv_0(1 + g)}{1 + r} = t\left[V_0 + \frac{V_0(1 + g)}{1 + r}\right] = tV = \hat{T}.$$

45. See, for example, two interesting tables that try to characterize the schemes in Emerson and Lloyd, "Improving Mineral Taxation," tables 2 and 3.

46. These ideas go back to the work of E. Cary Brown, "Business Income Taxation and Investment Incentives," in Lloyd A. Metzler and others, *Income, Employment, and Public Policy: Essays in Honor of Alvin H. Hansen* (Norton, 1948). Because any loan has a present market value of zero, the discounted tax liabilities on it should also be zero. This can be accomplished by adding the proceeds of the loan to taxable income and then later allowing the deduction of interest and principal payments from taxable income, or by not adding the proceeds of the loan and then not allowing for any interest or principal deductions. Both the Australian company tax and the U.S. corporate tax do not add loan proceeds but do allow for interest deductions, so they both can be said to subsidize debt finance at the expense of equity finance.

company tax rate of 46 percent imposed on other sectors would then attain neutral treatment among all sectors of Australian industry.[47] A more pragmatic reason for keeping the same marginal rate is to avoid the transfer pricing difficulty. The central government's particular levies such as those on natural gas, crude oil, and coal would have no place in such a scheme and should be abolished.[48] The scheme would reasonably approximate the Leland tax, and the lines of taxing authority between the states and the commonwealth would be clear.

If such a scheme were adopted, the CGC could operate just as it does now. Already states earn royalty income that the CGC takes into account in determining its needs variable, T_i. The CGC does not compensate deficiencies in the tax base dollar for dollar, although it does attempt to compensate deficiencies in potential royalties dollar for dollar. But note the word "potential." The CGC correctly realizes that if it compensated actual royalties dollar for dollar, states would have no incentive to maximize their actual resource earnings. Hence the CGC goes through a complex calculation to estimate potential royalties on the basis of the underlying profitability of a resource deposit, and it even tries to calculate whether states are assessing hidden royalties in setting unusually high rail charges. All these procedures could and should remain in this version of the Leland tax scheme.

The final option worth considering is the resources rent tax (RRT), tentatively described in a December 1983 discussion paper published by the Hawke government. The RRT is planned to apply only to natural gas and oil, and to replace the admittedly cumbersome excise taxes the commonwealth now imposes. The present tax requires a distinction between new and old oil (new oil is that discovered after 1975 and taxed at a lower rate to encourage production), and is based on production levels instead of profitability. As such, it discourages production from wells that are marginally profitable.

The RRT, on the other hand, is designed to tax only extraordinary

47. In the strictest sense, the optimal tax literature does not suggest tax rates that are constant across all sectors, but rather rates that vary depending on elasticities of supply. In real world applications, however, the one-tax-rate standard is usually defended as the best that can practically be done.

48. Two papers have recommended reforms along these lines, although not identical to these. See Craig Emerson and Peter Lloyd, "Improving Mineral Taxation"; and David Nellor, *Taxation of the Australian Resources Sector* (Clayton, Victoria: Monash University, Centre of Policy Studies, 1982), chaps 6 and 7.

profits from resources, those beyond the level necessary to encourage production, in a way that represents an "equitable sharing of economic rents between the community and investors in the petroleum sector."[49]

The government provides some calculations that illustrate the basic idea, if not the precise details. In the illustrations tax rates vary between 10 and 40 percent, with early year losses carried forward at a "threshold" rate or rates (interest rates, for purposes of calculating tax liability) that vary between 20 and 40 percent. In other respects, the tax base closely resembles that of the Leland tax. An important decision yet to be made is whether to apply one threshold rate and one tax rate to all projects, or to use multiple rates, designed in effect to tax more profitable projects but at the cost of added administrative difficulties.

To the extent that the loss offsets in the RRT are incomplete, and it is too early yet to tell how much, there will be an inevitable reduction in the net profitability of petroleum development and in the development itself. On the other hand, the RRT will rationalize petroleum taxation, base taxes on underlying profitability, and provide tax reductions and incentives for greater development of marginal wells.

The RRT, if and when adopted and extended to other resources, will raise some difficult issues of fiscal federalism. In setting heavier taxes for the most profitable wells, the RRT will in all likelihood reduce the states' potential royalty earnings. Were just one state affected, but not the average, the CGC would compensate the state dollar for dollar and that would be the end of it. But in this case average potential royalties for all states will decline, and even with present compensation arrangements, states in the aggregate will lose revenue from the RRT. The Hawke government has promised to negotiate further compensation arrangements with the states, presumably increasing the G^* (in equation 3) by an appropriate amount, but at this point states might be forgiven for fearing that a bird in the hand is worth two in the bush. Moreover, with the G^* raised appropriately, the disparity between revenue respon-

49. The Hawke government's tentative proposal can be found in Treasury Department, *Discussion Paper on Resource Rent Tax in the Petroleum Sector*, December 1983. It follows a long discussion in the Australian literature, initially started by Ross Garnaut and Anthony Clunies-Ross, "Uncertainty, Risk Aversion, and the Taxing of Natural Resource Projects," *The Economic Journal*, vol. 85 (June 1975), pp. 272–87, and later, "The Neutrality of the Resource Rent Tax," *The Economic Record*, vol. 55 (September 1979), pp. 193–201.

sibility and expenditure responsibility is made that much greater, with possibly damaging consequences for states' abilities and capabilities to manage their own affairs.

Summary—Equality and Efficiency Reconsidered

Overall the Australian system of fiscal federalism receives high marks for equality, although not for efficiency. The CGC is a remarkable institution for the amount of equalization it achieves, for its respectability and longevity, and for the degree to which analysts and politicians work together until agreements are reached. One can quibble with its precise procedures, arguing that there should be less equalizing for the cost of public services and more with regard to income, but these are relatively minor criticisms.

The system is less admirable from an efficiency standpoint. The CGC's basic entitlement is set at a high level, divorcing taxing responsibility from expenditure responsibility and placing an extraordinary premium on states' ability to lobby for grants. Moreover, its equalization for public service price differences can cause people to locate in areas quite costly to supply, and there are vast stretches of such areas in Australia. The ALC, while it still has its Australian defenders, has the look of an anachronism, emphasizing as it does nonprice political rationing and encouraging costly schemes to circumvent it. The specific-purpose grants have matching shares designed to encourage their over-utilization by states and intended to force the commonwealth into still more administrative rationing schemes. The taxing imbalance almost ensures that state taxation will cause excessive distortion. And the mélange of competing resource taxes and unclear lines of demarcation between the state and federal authorities risks overburdening one of Australia's most promising growth industries.

Postscript

As an outsider from the United States, a country that worries perhaps excessively about its federalist institutions, I could not help but be struck by how little most public servants and economists in Australia appear to

274   *Edward M. Gramlich*

care about fiscal federalism. Many observers seem to want a centralized system, even though the historical differences between states, the vast distances, and the existing spending disparities suggest that such a hope is a pie in the sky. Thoughts about whether states are given enough freedom to manage their own budgets rarely come up. Perhaps this explains why the same people who trust federal bureaucrats in Canberra to control public spending and borrowing do not trust state authorities because they have "short horizons," and why some proposals for taxing mineral resources have not considered the state-federal ramifications of their proposals. With a few notable exceptions, very little economic research is done on federalism. The Australian federal system has its strong points, it could be improved, and there is no shortage of interesting analytical issues. Somebody ought to take it seriously.

Rethinking the Role of the Public Sector

EDWARD M. GRAMLICH

SWEDEN has one of the most extensive welfare states in the world. By 1982 the consolidated expenditures of all levels of government amounted to two-thirds of the country's GDP. Public expenditures covered all the usual items—defense, police and fire protection, schools, roads, health, unemployment insurance, old-age pensions, and occupational injuries. Expenditures also covered many items that would raise eyebrows in other countries—an extensive public employment program that guarantees near full employment, tuition-free higher education, highly subsidized public day care, large industrial subsidies to bail out failing firms, child-rearing allowances, government-paid parental leave, and many more.

Although the negative incentive effects from such a large public sector are well known and widely advertised, for years the Swedish economy grew at rapid rates, spurred by a very high ratio of investment to GDP. But beginning about 1970 the rosy statistics became harder to find. Sweden's real growth rate was sliced in half; its investment-GDP ratio fell by one-quarter. Indicators of labor mobility showed a downward trend. Anecdotal evidence of a flourishing "gray market" of activities to avoid the tax collectors became widespread. Polls reported large majorities of Swedes feeling that taxes were unfair, and there were brief tax revolts.

Swedish economists jumped on the bandwagon too. After a series of laudatory tracts on the Swedish model in the 1960s, modern bookshelves have been filled with such attention-getting titles as *The Welfare State in Crisis: The Case of Sweden*, "Work Disincentives in the Welfare State," "Emerging Arteriosclerosis of the Western Economies: Consequences for the Less Developed Countries," "The Swedish Welfare State in Trouble: Transition to Socialism or Enhancing Private Ownership," and "The Rise and Fall of the Swedish Model."[1]

Very recently signs of recovery have appeared. Since a successful devaluation in 1982, the annual growth rate of real GDP is up slightly, the government deficit has been reduced, and the share of output devoted to capital formation has increased slightly. The share of GDP devoted to government expenditures has declined, and marginal income tax rates have been cut. Is this the spring following a long Swedish winter?

In this chapter I will examine the development of Swedish budget policy and its impact on the economy. I begin with a short factual summary to show how remarkable the Swedish experiment is. In its level of public spending and commitment to full employment and income redistribution, Sweden differs dramatically from the United States and other countries in the Organization for Economic Cooperation and Development (OECD).

The second section focuses on the budget deficit: its magnitude, why it developed, and its impact on the economy. Looking backward, one sees that deficits increased, or public-sector saving decreased, because of very rapid growth in the noninvestment components of public spending from 1970 to 1982. Looking forward, one sees that Sweden now has an urgent need to increase its public-sector saving. The consequent growth in outstanding debt and interest payments is making it increasingly difficult for Sweden to control deficits.

The chapter next examines Sweden's tax system, made extensive to finance expenditures amounting to two-thirds of GDP. Sweden has a 19 percent value-added tax (VAT), a 36 percent payroll tax, a 52 percent corporate tax, a personal income tax with marginal rates rising to 70 percent, excise taxes, wealth taxes, inheritance taxes, and user fees.

1. See Per-Martin Meyerson, *The Welfare State in Crisis: The Case of Sweden*, (Stockholm: Federation of Swedish Industries, 1982); Assar Lindbeck, "Work Disincentives in the Welfare State" in *Nationalökonomische Gesellschaft Lectures 79–80* (Vienna: Manz, 1981); Assar Lindbeck, "Emerging Arteriosclerosis of the Western Economies: Consequences for the Less Developed Countries," *India International Centre Quarterly*, no. 1 (1982); Gunnar Eliasson, "The Swedish Welfare State in Trouble: Transition to Socialism or Enhancing Private Ownership," working paper (Stockholm: Industriens Utredningsinstitut, April 1984); and Erik Lundberg, "The Rise and Fall of the Swedish Model," *Journal of Economic Literature*, vol. 23 (March 1985), pp. 1–36.

With so many taxes imposed at such high rates on so many forms of activity, it is hard to see how public-sector saving could be increased by raising taxes further, as is advocated for the United States. But modest changes could definitely improve the Swedish revenue system. Since interest deductions outweigh taxable capital income, Sweden manages to lose revenue by taxing capital income. One way to increase public-sector saving would be to limit these interest deductions. Another change that would increase economic efficiency without obvious cost in terms of equity would be to shift revenues from the income tax to the VAT.

The next section examines expenditures. Given the infeasibility of increasing public-sector saving, these spending programs are examined with an eye to seeing which ones could be cut without serious equity problems. The most eligible programs in this sense are subsidies for low-cost consumption, transfers to failing firms, certain kinds of social insurance transfers, and various types of grants to local governments. In aggregate, possible cutbacks in these eligible programs add up to much more than a generous estimate of the public-sector saving deficiency. In a word, Sweden can resolve its public-sector saving deficiency entirely on the spending side, with an increase in economic efficiency and no obvious losses in equity.

Overview

A central government, some social insurance funds financed through payroll taxes, and a large number of local government units provide Sweden's public services. The central government carries responsibility for national defense and transfers to households, firms, and local governments. The social security funds, which finance retirement, unemployment, and health insurance payments, are often shown separately from the other central government funds in budgetary presentations.

Sweden is divided into 23 counties, covering the entire country except Gothenburg, Malmö, and the island of Gotland. These counties are responsible for providing medical services (though there is a small group of private doctors). Two hundred and eighty municipalities have responsibility for most other public services—education, nursing homes, day care, housing allowances, relief aid, transportation, sewage, and various cultural and recreational facilities. As recently as 1950 there were 2,500

Table 7-1. *Tax and Spending Levels for the Consolidated Government Sector, 1982*
Billions of kronor

Item	Central	Social security funds	Local	Total
Expenditures	241.8	46.4	134.6	422.8
Consumption	52.2	2.8	130.5	185.5
Investment	5.6	...	18.8	24.4
Interest	37.7	− 19.4	...	18.3
Grants, local	44.0	...	− 44.0	...
Grants, social security	5.4	− 5.4	...	...
Transfers	97.0	68.4	29.4	194.6
Revenues	182.4	65.0	135.6	383.0
Direct taxes	41.2	...	97.4	138.6
Indirect taxes	89.4	...	...	89.4
Social security contribution	29.1	57.5	...	86.6
Other	22.6	7.5	38.2	68.3
Net financial saving	− 59.4	18.6	1.0	− 39.8
Addendum: contribution to capital formation	− 53.8	18.6	19.8	− 15.4

Source: Ministry of Finance, *The Swedish Budget* (Stockholm, various years).

municipalities, but the central government has forced them to consolidate to their present number. With these mergers have come increased responsibilities—in 1950 local governments accounted for about half of Sweden's public consumption; today they account for three-quarters.

Some numerical detail is given in table 7-1, showing tax and spending levels for the three types of government bodies in 1982, the year when both expenditures and the budget deficit peaked as a share of GDP. For the consolidated governmental sector, expenditures totaled about Skr 423 billion (a krona is worth about $0.13), two-thirds of Sweden's GDP. The central government makes most of the transfers (including social security); the local governments account for most of the public consumption and investment. The central government still levies most of the taxes, the only significant local tax being a proportional individual income tax at a rate that averages 30 percent.

Although many of the social welfare programs date from the turn of the century, most of the growth in spending has occurred within the last two decades.[2] As late as 1960, just before a new contributory old-age

2. The development of the Swedish welfare state is discussed in Lundberg, "Rise and Fall of the Swedish Model."

Figure 7-1. *Total Public Expenditures as a Percent of Gross Domestic Product, Selected Countries of the Organization for Economic Cooperation and Development, 1960 and 1981*[a]

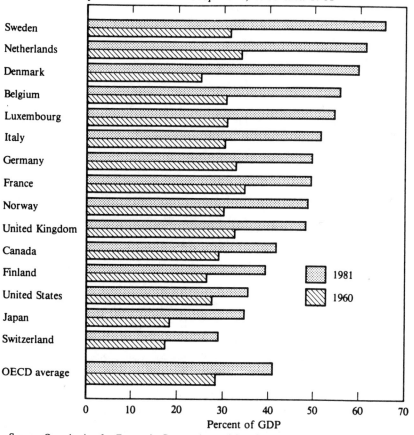

Source: Organization for Economic Cooperation and Development, *Historical Statistics 1960–1982* (Paris: OECD, 1984), p. 64, table 6.5.

a. Total expenditures include current disbursements plus gross capital formation and purchases of land and intangible assets. Luxembourg expenditures shown at 1980 level (1981 level not available). Switzerland expenditures include current disbursements only.

pension plan was introduced, Sweden's public expenditures were only 31 percent of GDP, roughly average for OECD countries (see figure 7-1). From then until the early 1980s the public sector grew rapidly. While it is claimed that part of the reason for the rapid growth in the public spending share is that GDP growth slowed in the 1970s, the main reason is the straightforward one that public spending just grew at extraordinary rates during this period. By 1981 the share of GDP devoted

ROLE OF THE PUBLIC SECTOR   255

Table 7-2. *Consolidated General Government Accounts for Sweden and the United States, 1983*
Percent of GDP

Expenditures	Sweden	United States	Difference
Total	61.0	36.4	24.6
Consumption	28.5	19.3	9.2
Defense	3.0	6.8	-3.8
Health[a]	7.3	1.2	6.1
Welfare	4.9	0.7	4.2
Education[b]	5.9	4.7	1.2
Other	7.4	5.9	1.5
Social security	14.8	7.8	7.0
Subsidies	5.2	0.7	4.5
Other transfers	5.6	4.5	1.1
Net interest	1.9	3.0	-1.1
Net investment[c]	5.0	1.1	3.9

Source: Author's calculations based on Organization for Economic Cooperation and Development, *National Accounts, 1971–1983*, vol. 2: *Detailed Tables* (Paris: OECD, 1985).
a. In total public and private spending for health, the United States outspends Sweden, 9.9 percent of gross domestic product (GDP) versus 8.2 percent of GDP.
b. In total public and private spending for education, the United States outspends Sweden, 6.0 percent of GDP versus 5.9 percent of GDP.
c. Investment here includes depreciation expense because the *National Accounts* do not elsewhere include depreciation as a current expense.

to public spending had become higher than for any other OECD country, 24 percentage points above the OECD average, 30 percentage points above that in the United States.

To see how meaningful the differences are, table 7-2 provides a comparison of public expenditures for Sweden and the United States for 1983.[3] The gross difference, equal to 24.6 percent of GDP, illustrates the disparate approaches to public policy in the two countries, with Sweden obviously much more inclined to finance services publicly and to provide a wider range of transfer payments.

To interpret the table, one should keep two special factors in mind. On the one hand, as a percentage of GDP the United States spends more on national defense than does Sweden. In this sense, the table underestimates proclivities for public spending—were Sweden saddled with a defense burden as large as that of the United States (as a percentage of GDP), its public sector would no doubt be even larger than it now is. On the other hand, the apparent difference in health spending overstates the

3. The data are compiled on a common basis by the Organization for Economic Cooperation and Development. There are slight discrepancies between these numbers and those published by the governments of both Sweden and the United States.

true difference. In Sweden virtually all health spending is financed by the public sector, while in the United States private health insurance bears most of the costs. But even though private health insurance is important in the United States, many of the supposed advantages (care provided below cost to the poor and aged) and disadvantages (inadequate incentives to economize on care) of public provision of health care seem as prevalent in the United States as in Sweden. As the footnote to table 7-2 suggests, the share of GDP devoted to spending on health is even higher in the United States.

In other areas, however, the data indicate real differences in approach between the two countries. While total spending on education as a share of GDP is again almost identical in the two countries, the United States finances less of it in the public sector. Spending on welfare and social security is proportionately much higher in Sweden because of a stronger commitment to income redistribution. Subsidies are also a much more significant component of the budget. The most striking difference between the two countries is the emphasis in Sweden on expenditure programs that reflect strong concerns about equity. Two fundamental objectives have guided development of the so-called Swedish model from the beginning: full employment and income redistribution.

The Swedes have constructed an ambitious set of labor market programs, public employment programs, and regulations to hold down unemployment. Since World War II "open" or official unemployment has never been very high in Sweden. It averaged less than 2 percent between 1960 and 1980, and only lately has it risen to 3 percent—still only 40 percent of the average OECD unemployment rate for 1983. However, the official unemployment rate is held down by a wide range of labor market programs, such as relief work, sheltered workshops, and vocational training. In 1983, while 150,000 workers were reported as unemployed (3.5 percent of the labor force), another 165,000 (3.9 percent) were enrolled in these labor market programs. The cost of the labor market programs in 1983 was about 4 percent of GDP. An additional 1 percent of GDP was paid out in unemployment compensation, and another 2 percent in industrial subsidies to prevent unemployment.[4] It is certainly unique for a country to devote resources on this scale to ensuring full employment.

The Swedish commitment to income redistribution is even more

4. Jan Johannesson and Inga Persson-Tanimura, *Labour Market Policy under Reconsideration* (Stockholm: Arbetsmarknadsdepartementet, 1984), pp. 11, 14, 47.

remarkable. The importance of this objective is most evident in the statistics on the distribution of income. A Lorenz curve–Gini coefficient calculation does not show complete equality for Sweden; but as Assar Lindbeck points out, the standard way of presenting the figures is misleading when the tax-transfer system is as focused on vertical inequities as it is in Sweden.[5] Lorenz curves and Gini coefficients rank households from bottom to top based on whatever income concept is being studied: factor income, disposable income, or some other. In Sweden the redistribution is so extensive that it totally rearranges households in the income distribution. Although equality is not perfect when all these public rearrangements have been made, there is also relatively little correspondence between pre- and postpolicy incomes. The income redistribution policies eliminate much of the vertical inequality but then introduce some horizontal inequality.[6] In such a case, it is only meaningful to examine distribution measures when families are ranked by their original factor income. To begin with, the system of "solidaristic" wage bargaining, described in chapter 5 in this volume, results in a more equal distribution of factor incomes, even before taxes and transfers come into play, than in the United States. But figure 7-2 shows that taxes and transfers also do significant equalizing. Households in the bottom decile have essentially no factor income, in the second decile a slight amount, and in the top decile sixty-six times as much as in the second decile.[7] Taxes and transfers bring the ratio of the top to the second decile down to 4 to 1. Since the number of earners (and consumers) for each household rises with income, it may be more meaningful to do the calculations for each consumer unit. When this is done, the ratio becomes 2.2 to 1.

Many further adjustments could be made. Since individuals in the lower-income groups spend less time working, Lindbeck does a further calculation in terms of hours of work and reaches the remarkable conclusion that the hourly wage rate, after adjusting for taxes and transfers, declines in the upper-income brackets.[8] Another study that

5. Assar Lindbeck, "Interpreting Income Distributions in a Welfare State: The Case of Sweden," *European Economic Review* (May 1983), pp. 227–56.

6. Vertical equity refers to the after-tax incomes of individuals with different pretax incomes; horizontal equity refers to the after-tax incomes of individuals with equal pretax incomes.

7. This distribution is heavily influenced by the inclusion of the retired, who have little or no factor income.

8. Lindbeck, "Interpreting Income Distributions," p. 253.

258   THE SWEDISH ECONOMY

Figure 7-2. *Income Distribution in Sweden, Deciles of Factor Income, 1979*

Thousands of kronor

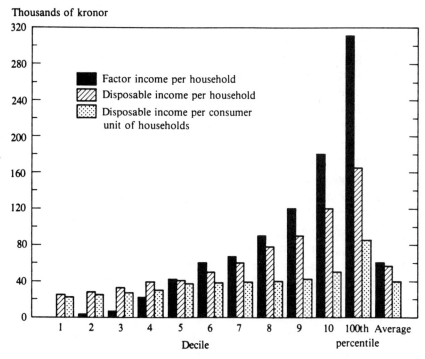

Source: Assar Lindbeck, "Interpreting Income Distributions in a Welfare State: The Case of Sweden," *European Economic Review* (May 1983), p. 232.

attempts to take account of the distributional benefits of government consumption programs showed even more equalizing tendencies.[9]

Whether one examines Sweden from the point of view of its high level of public expenditures, commitment to full employment, or extensive degree of equalizing tax and spending measures, the natural question that arises is whether too much economic efficiency is being sacrificed for the sake of the equity goals. What are the costs of the Swedish welfare state?

Deficits

When public expenditures rise rapidly and hit high levels, budget deficits often result. It is, after all, easier to administer to voters the

9. Thomas Franzen, Kerstin Lövgren, and Irma Rosenberg, "Redistributional Effects of Taxes and Public Expenditures in Sweden," *Swedish Journal of Economics*, vol. 77, no. 1 (1975), pp. 31–55.

sugar of public services than the salt of taxes. Indeed, referring again to table 7-1, Sweden clearly has a budget deficit problem. In 1982 the net financial deficit of the central government reached Skr 59 billion, 9.5 percent of GDP; and despite the recent efforts to reduce it, the deficit was 5.7 percent of GDP in 1985.

During the 1970s the growth of the budget deficit was defended on the grounds that fiscal stimulus was required to maintain employment, and concern about unemployment continues to inhibit efforts to reduce deficits. It may be a mistake, however, to place so much emphasis on the employment benefits of large budget deficits. One reason is that in modern, open economies, fiscal policy has very weak impacts on aggregate demand. For a small country such as Sweden it is not clear whether large deficits will raise, lower, or leave unchanged unemployment, inflation, and interest rates. Furthermore, continuous structural budget deficits will ultimately result in a lower national saving rate, less Swedish-owned capital stock, and lower Swedish living standards.[10] Hence any short-term employment benefits of large and continuing government deficits are likely to be offset by their longer-term adverse impact on the accumulation of wealth in the Swedish economy.[11] The numbers in table 7-1 can be rearranged to show this impact better.

First, on a consolidated basis the government deficit is smaller than that of the central government deficit alone because the trust funds have a consistent surplus. Thus the consolidated deficit in 1982 was Skr 40 billion compared with a central government deficit of Skr 59 billion.[12] Second, some of the Swedish expenditures go for public-sector capital

10. These statements follow what are by now standard postulates in the macroeconomics literature. The point about short-term open economies follows a model first laid out by Robert A. Mundell, "Capital Mobility and Stabilization Policy under Fixed and Flexible Exchange Rates," *Canadian Journal of Economics and Political Science,* vol. 29 (November 1963), pp. 475–85. The observation about long-term effects follows a whole series of models of the economic growth process by Robert M. Solow. Paul N. Courant and Edward M. Gramlich summarize the entire argument in "Fiscal Responsibility: The Nerds are Right," in *The Economic Outlook for 1985: Papers Presented to the Economic and Social Outlook Conference* (Ann Arbor: University of Michigan, 1984), pp. 325–70.

11. In keeping with the improved performance on budget deficits, the official rhetoric on economic goals now contains a much stronger statement linking budget deficits to reduced capital formation. See, for example, Ministry of Finance, *The Swedish Budget, 1986–87* (Stockholm, 1986), pp. 7–12.

12. In fact, it was even slightly less than this amount, for Swedish budgets do not correct for capital gains on government debt when exchange rates change. I have not made this correction either because, to be consistent, one must also recompute interest payments for capital gains with domestic inflation, as in Robert Eisner and Paul J. Pieper, "A New View of the Federal Debt and Budget Deficits," *American Economic Review,* vol. 74 (March 1984), pp. 11–29.

formation. The government's contribution to capital formation is more accurately measured by excluding public investment from the measure of government expenditure. When this is done, the deficit for 1982 is much smaller—Skr 15.4 billion, or 2.5 percent of GDP.

The focus on a single year, however, ignores the historical importance of the government as a major source of saving in the Swedish economy. The government's contribution is most evident within the national income accounting identity, by which economywide gross investment, public and private, must equal the sum of private saving, foreign capital inflow, and the government's contribution to capital formation. In symbols,

$$(7\text{-}1) \qquad I + I_g = S + (M - X) + (T_g - C_g),$$

where I is gross private investment, I_g is gross public investment, S is gross private saving, $M - X$ is the current account foreign trade deficit, or the net inflow of capital from foreign sources, T_g is all taxes less all transfers, C_g is public consumption, and $T_g - C_g$ is the government's contribution to capital formation.

In figure 7-3 these magnitudes are plotted for 1950 through 1985. The top line shows gross fixed public and private investment, the left side of equation 1, as a share of GDP. Both the numerator and denominator are measured in constant 1980 dollars; inventory investment has been removed from the investment series to eliminate erratic movements. The bottom line shows the government contribution to capital formation, the number in the bottom righthand corner of table 7-1.[13] As is made clear by equation 7-1, the difference between the top line $(I + I_g)$ and the bottom line $(T_g - C_g)$ equals the sum of private saving (S) and foreign capital inflows $(M - X)$.

Figure 7-3 illustrates three, or perhaps two and a half, broad epochs of change in the Swedish economy. From 1950 to 1967 the share of GDP devoted to capital formation generally increased from 18.7 percent to a peak of 24.8 percent. At that point, things went into reverse, and the share dropped back to 18.5 percent by 1982. The share recovered to 19.5 percent in 1985.

Most important, figure 7-3 highlights the strong correlation between

13. Because there is no available price deflator for total government expenditures and taxes, government's contribution to capital formation is measured as net financial saving in nominal terms divided by gross domestic product (GDP) in nominal terms, plus the ratio of real public investment to real GDP.

ROLE OF THE PUBLIC SECTOR   261

Figure 7-3. *Gross Investment and Government Contribution to Capital Formation Relative to GDP, 1950–85*

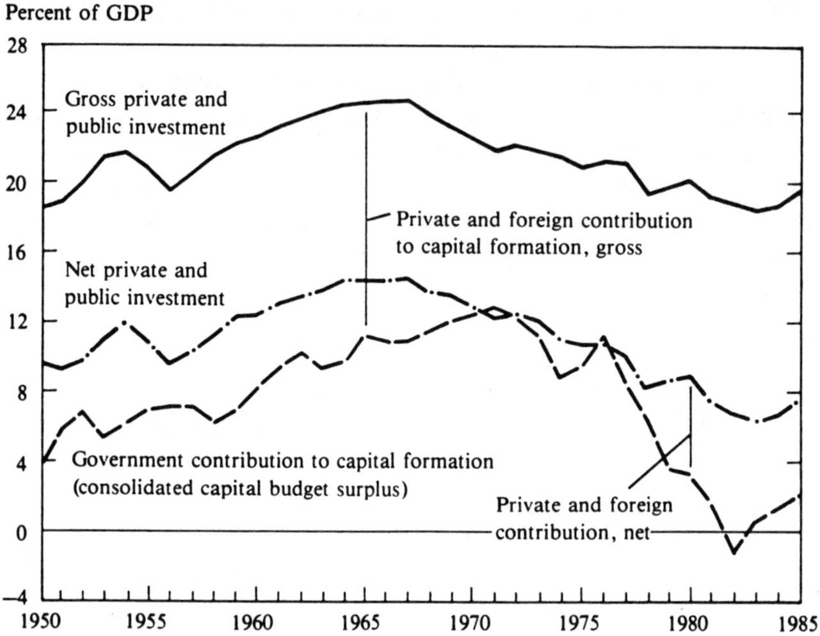

Percent of GDP

Source: Ekonomifakta Databank (1985); and Hans Tson Söderström, "Imbalances in the Swedish Economy from a Financial Perspective," *Skandinaviska Enskilda Banken Quarterly Review*, no. 2 (1984), p. 47.

domestic investment and fiscal policy. The government's contribution to capital formation was 3.9 percent of GDP in 1950, 12.8 percent in the peak investment year of 1971, −2.5 percent in 1982, and has now recovered to 3.6 percent in 1985. When the government contributed more, as it did in the 1950–70 and 1982–85 periods, net investment as a share of output rose. When the government contributed less, as it did from 1970 to 1982, the net investment share fell. In this period Sweden followed a progressively more consumption-oriented fiscal policy, diverting resources from future-oriented investment and toward present-oriented consumption.[14]

14. The correlations are not perfect for several reasons well known in the macro-economics literature. For one thing cyclical effects operate differently on total investment and the budget contribution. For another, depreciation allowances form a component of gross investment but not of the budget contribution. Third is the open economy offset—as the budget contribution rises, foreign capital flows out and the current account trade deficit decreases. A fourth is the interest effect—as the budget contribution rises,

Of course, the key question here is whether it was appropriate to divert resources from investment to consumption, as was done in Sweden in the 1970s and the United States in the 1980s. The question is hard to answer objectively because it involves a trade-off in living standards between the present and the future. But from two standpoints, it can be argued that the shift was as unwise in Sweden as it is generally conceded to be in the United States. One is that by the "golden-rule" consumption-maximizing standard, both Sweden and the United States moved farther from their optimal investment ratios.[15] A second, more pragmatic, is that for countries trying to compete in international trade and contending with falling productivity, it is not healthy to devote fewer resources to investment, particularly in high-technology equipment. Remedying the role of fiscal policy in this saving shortfall underlies the policy suggestions I make in the following pages.

Why Did the Deficits Rise?

As figure 7-3 shows, for much of the postwar period Swedish fiscal policy demonstrated a strong commitment to capital formation and economic growth.[16] Over a twenty-year period from the early 1950s to the early 1970s the Swedish public sector was the driving force behind an accelerating rate of capital formation. If nothing else, this record puts the lie to the claim that countries with large public sectors are intrinsically unable to generate capital.

But things did fall apart in Sweden in the early 1970s. The 1972–82 period was a disaster for the government's contribution to capital formation; twenty years of increased accumulation was more than undone in only ten. The turnaround in the mid-1980s has managed to restore only about one-third of what was lost in the prior decline.

The enormous expansion of government expenditures stands out as the most evident cause of the growth in the budget deficit. From 1970 to 1982, when deficits grew, nominal GDP grew at an annual rate of 10.8 percent. But as table 7-3 shows, those government expenditures that do

---

interest rates fall and there is less private saving. A fifth is the Ricardian equivalence effect—as the budget contribution rises, farsighted and altruistic households may save less.

15. The golden-rule standard, if maintained for a long period, leads to the highest standard of living in a country. Edmund S. Phelps worked out the logic of the rule. See "The Golden Rule of Accumulation: A Fable for Growthmen," *American Economic Review*, vol. 51 (September 1961), pp. 638–43.

16. In doctrine as well as in fact. One early Social Democratic deputy finance minister who worried much about growth and capital formation was Dag Hammarskjöld.

ROLE OF THE PUBLIC SECTOR   263

Table 7-3. *Growth in Swedish Public Consumption Expenditures,*
Selected Years and Periods, 1970–86

Expenditures	1970	1982	1986	Annual growth rate 1970–82	Annual growth rate 1982–86
	Billions of kronor				
Expenditures detracting from capital formation	64.3	398.4	562.2	15.2	8.6
Local government consumption	22.9	130.5	187.1	14.5	9.0
Central government transfers, households	11.6	61.6	82.4	13.9	7.3
Central government transfers, business	2.3	31.0	34.8	21.7	2.9
Social security transfers	6.0	68.4	108.8	20.3	11.6
Interest	1.2	18.3	36.5	22.7	17.3
All other	20.3	88.6	112.6	12.3	6.0
	Percent of GDP				
Expenditures detracting from capital formation	37.3	63.5	61.1	4.4	1.0
Local government consumption	13.3	20.8	20.3	3.7	0.6
Central government transfers, households	6.7	9.8	9.0	3.2	2.1
Central government transfers, business	1.3	4.9	3.8	11.1	6.4
Social security transfers	3.5	10.9	11.8	9.5	2.0
Interest	0.7	2.9	4.0	11.8	8.0
All other	11.8	14.1	12.2	1.5	3.6

Source: Ministry of Finance. *The Swedish Budget,* various years.

not contribute to capital formation grew at an annual rate of 15.2 percent,
rising from 37.3 percent of GDP in 1970 to a peak of 63.5 percent in 1982.

Of course, whenever deficits grow relative to GDP, there is a possibility that the "cause" will not be in excessive expenditure growth but
in taxes (if tax rates have been cut) or reduced growth of GDP, which
could have grown less rapidly. In Sweden, however, taxes also rose
sharply, from 48 percent of GDP in 1970 to 61 percent in 1982. Yet the
government contribution to capital formation still declined by 13 percent
of GDP. And while the real GDP growth rate did dip by 2 percentage
points after 1970, had it continued its former growth, the expenditure
share would still have increased by 2.2 percent annually between 1970
and 1982, rising above 50 percent of GDP. Hence it is impossible to
avoid the conclusion that the fall in capital formation occurred primarily
because of the rapid rise in public noninvestment expenditures.[17]

17. One may also ask whether real noninvestment expenditures grew at a faster rate

The categories of expenditures that grew most rapidly are also shown in table 7-3. Local government consumption, central government transfers to households and business, social security transfers, and interest payments rose sharply as a share of GDP from 1970 to 1982. These five items, representing 68 percent of total expenditures in 1970, accounted for more than 90 percent of the increase in the share of GDP represented by government spending.[18]

The Interest Burden

One of the five rapidly growing items in table 7-3 is the net interest payments of the consolidated public sector. These rose from 0.7 percent of GDP in 1970 to 4.0 percent of GDP in 1986. Interest payments have played a critical role in the development of the budget deficit, both because they are uncontrollable in the short run and because of the dynamics of the link between past budget deficits, the outstanding debt, and future interest payments. The cumulative buildup of debt creates the potential for explosive growth in future deficits.

The role of debt accumulation can be illustrated with a slight rearrangement of the definition of the budget deficit to separate interest expenses from other government outlays:

$$(7\text{-}2) \qquad dD = E' - T + rD,$$

where dD is the change in the outstanding debt, E' is government expenditures other than interest payments, T is taxes, and rD is the average interest rate on government debt.[19] The difference between E' and T is often referred to as the primary deficit, and it is a measure of the extent to which taxes are sufficient to cover the current level of public services. Dividing equation 7-2 by D, and rearranging terms yields

$$(7\text{-}3) \qquad \frac{dD}{D} = \frac{E' - T}{D} + r = r + z,$$

---

in the 1970s than previously. The answer is yes. From 1970 to 1982 real noninvestment spending grew by about 7 percent a year, about 25 percent faster than in the previous decade.

18. This calculation is done as follows: had noninvestment expenditures remained at 37.3 percent of GDP in 1982, they would have totaled Skr 234 billion. In fact, they totaled Skr 398 billion, an excess of Skr 164 billion. The increase in the share of GDP accounted for by the five items represented Skr 150 billion, 91.5 percent of the total.

19. This formulation ignores non-interest-bearing debt, such as money creation, but since money creation was small relative to the deficit, the simplification has no effect on the basic analytical points.

ROLE OF THE PUBLIC SECTOR   265

where z equals the ratio of the primary budget deficit to the outstanding debt. If Sweden's capital market is open to international flows, as it almost certainly is in the long run, the nominal interest rate on government debt can be viewed as exogenously determined by world markets.[20] In that case, elimination of the primary deficit implies that the public debt will grow at the nominal interest rate, and the interest burden relative to GDP, rD/Y will grow if the nominal rate of GDP growth falls short of the nominal interest rate.

The dynamics of the relationship between the growth in the public debt and the interest burden for 1974–84 are shown in figure 7-4.[21] The numbers are taken from a recent International Monetary Fund report on Sweden that shows consistent debt, interest rates, and interest payments since 1974.[22] The top line in figure 7-4 gives the nominal rate of growth of interest-bearing debt, the left side of equation 7-3. The growth in debt has exceeded the nominal interest rate, implying consistent primary budget deficits. However, the nominal rate of growth of GDP (dY/Y) fell below the nominal interest rate in the early 1980s. In theoretical growth models dY/Y should be less than r for countries that are undersaving, as Sweden has been in recent years. Since the growth of debt is greater than r and the rate of growth of nominal GDP is less than r, it is obvious that D/Y will rise over time. If r does not decline, the interest burden, rD/Y, will also rise. That it has can be observed by the bottom line in figure 7-4.

Figure 7-4 highlights the difficulties of bringing the budget deficit under control in Sweden. Even if it were possible to eliminate the primary budget deficit, the outstanding debt, and thus the interest burden, would continue to increase as a share of GDP because the growth of income is less than the rate of interest. In future years an increasing portion of

20. This condition is only true when Sweden's inflation rate is approximately equal to that of its major trading partners, but the impact of my simplification is slight. If nominal interest rates are given by world capital markets but they are variable, the question becomes more complicated because any induced change in r should be factored in. And if r is determined in a capital market sealed off from foreign capital flows, the question becomes still more complicated because now higher deficits might influence r, and the higher income of domestic bondholders would return new tax revenue to the Treasury.

21. All the numbers in the figure are averaged over three-year periods from 1974 to 1983 to smooth out erratic variation.

22. The report identifies Sweden as one of the countries with the worst interest payment growth problem. See Martin J. Fetherston, "Aspects of the Growth of Budgetary Interest Payments," working paper DM-85-2 (Washington, D.C.: International Monetary Fund, 1985), p. 11.

Figure 7-4. *Dynamics of Interest Growth, Three-Year Averages,*
1974–84

Percent

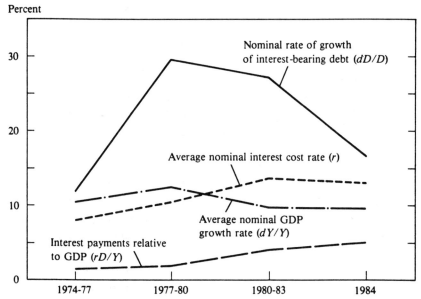

Source: Martin J. Fetherston, "Aspects of the Growth of Budgetary Interest Payments, 1974–81," working paper DM-85-2 (Washington, D.C.: International Monetary Fund, 1985), p. 11.

taxes must be diverted from financing current public services to pay interest on old debt. Were it not for the growing interest burden, Sweden's recent progress in reducing deficits would have been much more noticeable. The problem will only get worse unless the deficit is cut even further.

The Ownership Question

I have argued that Sweden's fiscal policy could be, and should be, altered to promote more capital formation. Since a high share of the requisite saving is generated by the public sector, and since Sweden has a long history of debate on the split of income shares between labor and management, it is perhaps inevitable that the issue of capital formation gets confused with the issue of ownership. If there is going to be more capital, do workers or capitalists get to own it? This issue is a red herring. There is no intrinsic reason why either group should own whatever stock of capital exists, and however this ownership issue is resolved, the

debate about it should not be allowed to prevent the desired accumulation
in the first place.

In principle the government's contribution to capital formation could
be used in either of two ways. The government could run a surplus,
retire government debt, and provide new funds for privately owned
capital. Or the surplus could be used to create publicly owned capital.
Indeed, at any point the government can sell or buy capital and privatize
or socialize the existing stock with no impact on the national income
accounts budget. Logically, the accumulation issue and the ownership
issue are totally separate. Any rate of accumulation can be consistent
with any ownership pattern.

Accumulation and ownership have also been totally separate in
practice. Figure 7-3 shows that most of Sweden's net saving has been
generated by the public sector. But most new capital has been owned by
the private sector. Private investment, I, was three-quarters of total
investment, $I + I_g$, in the peak years around 1970, about 78 percent in the
trough year 1982, and 85 percent in 1985.

Although the issue is a red herring from both a logical and empirical
standpoint, confusion over it may have done some damage. It is sometimes alleged that a political stalemate over ownership has reduced
accumulation—conservatives have opposed government investment
and liberals have opposed private investment. If this is so, it is a
regrettable example of unresolved political disputes in the present
diverting resources from the future.

Summary

While it may be stretching things to describe the growth of the budget
deficit as a crisis, one cannot help but view the Swedish fiscal policy
during the 1970s with some concern. In 1970 Sweden's investment share
was high, its fiscal policy promoted capital formation, and there was no
problem of an interest burden. In the space of a decade, all these
advantages were squandered. In making budget decisions about spending, taxation and ownership, a regrettable tendency to load the costs of
political disagreements onto the future recurred. Recently, Sweden has
started on the road back, but the road is harder because a large potential
increment to the capital stock has been lost in the meantime and because
the interest burden has grown. One can admire the Swedes for making
the turnaround, much more established and advanced than the still

incipient U.S. fiscal turnaround, but regret that the consumption binge in both countries made the road so much harder.

Taxes

By international standards Swedish taxpayers face a truly enormous annual tax bill, 61 percent of GDP. Total revenues have grown from 24 percent of GDP in 1950 to their present level; and while the greatest growth has been in social insurance payroll taxes, all types of taxes have increased greatly as a share of GDP.

Most of the controversy over tax policy concerns the high marginal rates embedded in the income tax and the distorting influences it has had on the Swedish economy. A study by Ingemar Hansson found that the marginal rate for the average Swedish wage earner rose from 31 percent in 1955 to 55 percent by 1980 (30 percentage points of that 55 percent go to local governments).[23] Figure 7-5 provides cross-sectional estimates of marginal tax rates that vary between 30 percent and 70 percent for the income tax alone, between 60 percent and 70 percent when means-tested spending programs are added, and between 70 percent and 80 percent when the payroll tax and the VAT are included.[24] Marginal rates can surely not be any higher for such a large share of the population anywhere else in the world.

While marginal tax rates seem incredibly high now, a short time ago they were even higher. In 1985 the government completed a three-year tax reform package that, among other things, lowered marginal tax rates for most taxpayers. Whereas in 1982 almost half of all taxpayers faced marginal tax rates of 80 percent (and more than that when the other taxes were considered), by 1985 the share was down to 10 percent. A further reform will lower the top bracket rate to 75 percent.

Incentive Effects

The natural question that arises about these high tax rates is their effect on incentives for work, saving, paying taxes, and even living in

23. Ingemar Hansson, "Skattereformen och de Totala Marginaleffekterna," *Economisk Debatt*, no. 1 (1983), p. 19.

24. Assar Lindbeck, "How Much Politics Can Our Economy Take?" Unpublished manuscript, 1986.

ROLE OF THE PUBLIC SECTOR   269

Figure 7-5. *Marginal Tax Rate of Income Taxes and Benefits*
(Tenant without Income of Capital)

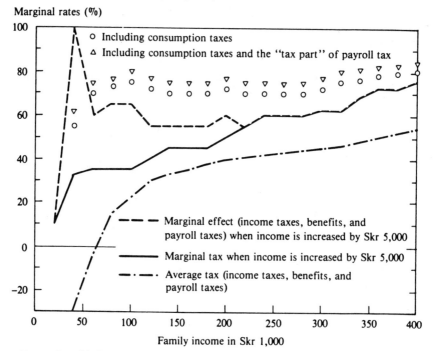

Marginal rates (%)

Family income in Skr 1,000

Source: Assar Lindbeck, "How Much Politics Can Our Economy Take?" Unpublished manuscript, 1986.

Sweden. As Gary Burtless points out in chapter 6, the effect on labor supply is complex because of offsetting provisions in the tax laws. The antiwork provisions, by and large, come into full force for those workers already in the labor force. The high marginal tax rates that emerge from the tax and transfer system do discourage long hours of work. The average number of hours worked each year is low in Sweden compared with hours worked in the United States. The disincentives are also reflected in increased absenteeism. Between the early 1960s and the late 1970s, paid absenteeism increased from 8 percent to 14 percent for male employees, from 11 percent to 18 percent for females, and from 14 percent to 28 percent for women with children under seven years of age.[25] Furthermore, all firms must grant five weeks of vacation. There

25. Lindbeck, "Work Disincentives in the Welfare State," p. 48.

may be many other subtle effects on intensity of work, willingness to gamble on a new profession or work in a new region, and so forth.

But along with these disincentives are very strong incentives for people to be in the labor force in the first place. Parents do not benefit from the highly subsidized day care and parents' insurance unless both are employed. Labor force programs make it attractive for the handicapped and disabled to work. And there are programs for teenagers. Spouses considering entry into the labor force are given one additional fillip—earnings are taxed separately, with an added child-care deduction, to prevent the lower-earning spouse from being taxed at the high marginal rate of the higher-earning spouse.

There are other potential disincentives. One possibility is that of tax-induced emigration from Sweden. People have not emigrated in large numbers, but that is partly because the government makes it difficult to avoid taxes by leaving. It is presumed that an emigrant's income is subject to tax for five years, unless the person can show that he or she has no strong link to Sweden, such as relatives or a summer home. Several well-known public figures, however, have emigrated to avoid the high taxes. There are also reports that up to Skr 3 billion a year are transferred out of the country in the form of capital exports.

Finally, high taxes can stimulate growth of the gray economy, an economy consisting of transactions that are either illegal or semilegal and are inspired by the desire to avoid taxation. If the size of the gray economy could be easily measured, taxes could be collected on it, so it is almost intrinsic that estimates of its size will range widely. Many believe it is not very large. Tax cheating is difficult in Sweden because all returns are audited, income and payroll tax returns are compared, and individuals' social security numbers are used in almost all transactions—for bank loans, rent contracts, subscriptions, and so forth.

But some economists have come up with larger estimates that challenge the conventional wisdom. One is based on a theoretical model built by Ingemar Hansson.[26] Hansson has two sectors, one producing measured (taxable) and the other unmeasured (untaxed) output, with taxes causing resources to flow from the former to the latter. In equilibrium, after-tax earnings are equal in the two sectors; but because of the tax wedge, the productivity of factors is higher in the taxed sector.

26. Ingemar Hansson, "Marginal Cost of Public Funds for Different Tax Instruments and Government Expenditures," *Scandinavian Journal of Economics*, vol. 86, no. 2 (1984), pp. 115–30.

Hansson then inserts parameters in the model that fit Swedish data in 1979 for all observable variables and elasticities, the key ones being the response of labor supply to after-tax wages and the response of capital (saving) to after-tax interest rates. His model implies that Swedish income tax rates are very close to the point at which a further increase in rates actually reduces tax revenue because of the shift of output to the gray economy.

A second empirical attempt to measure the gray economy comes from Edgar Feige.[27] He notes that despite the growth of a very advanced mechanism for settling accounts in Sweden, currency demand has increased sharply since 1972 (before then it had fallen, when controlled for other independent factors). He then develops a model to estimate how much this unexplained rise would have raised effective transactions in the quantity theory identity, arriving at a residual of about 25 percent of GDP. While there is no direct proof that the residual is entirely or even largely caused by the growing gray economy, Feige makes the attribution. Given the differences in productivity between the measured and unmeasured sectors, Feige's estimate implies that even more than 25 percent of resources, as opposed to output, is employed in the underground economy.[28]

Whatever the accuracy of these estimates, much productive activity could be diverted from the market either to illegal activities or to legal but less productive, or at least untaxed, activities. Rather than relying on comparative advantage and working in the market in their most productive professions, Swedish workers have a powerful incentive to work for themselves as, for example, household repair persons. Impersonal transactions such as household repairs are thus diverted from the market to the home. Lindbeck cannot resist pointing out that what goes with this is a movement of very personal activities such as child rearing from the home to subsidized public services, a bizarre possible manifestation of the welfare state.[29]

Because of this diversion, Hansson's model suggests that a clear gain in economic efficiency would result from reducing the maximum marginal

27. Edgar L. Feige, "The Swedish Payments System and the Underground Economy" (Stockholm: Industriens Utredningsinstitut [Industrial Institute for Economic and Social Research], 1985).
28. No allowance of this magnitude is made for underground activity in the Swedish national accounts. Thus, by implication, Feige believes that the standard of living in Sweden is even higher than that implied by international comparisons of GDP per capita.
29. Lindbeck, "Work Disincentives in the Welfare State," pp. 44–45.

tax rate from, say, 80 percent to 50 percent. The estimates of revenue loss are not large, only about Skr 5 billion to Skr 7 billion, and the revenue could be recovered with a rise in the VAT rate to 20.5 percent. While there would be a loss of vertical redistribution for those now in the tax base, the figures indicate that overall redistribution would still be extensive.

Finally, another kind of redistribution should be considered—between the evaders not in the tax base and those unwilling or unable to evade. When evaders earn income in the gray market and spend in the real market, they pay only the VAT rate of 19 percent. When full taxpayers earn income they are subject to tax rates of 70 to 80 percent. If marginal income tax rates were reduced and the VAT increased, the gap between the two groups would be reduced and the tax system would be much fairer.[30]

Capital Income

Sweden now taxes income from capital in several ways. In the personal income tax, capital income received by high-income families is added to the income of the highest-earning spouse and taxed at that marginal rate. At lower ranges capital income is treated just like labor income. As in the United States, nominal income from dividends and interest is fully taxable, and 40 percent of nominal income from long-term capital gains is taxable. The rules for interest deductions are complicated; most interest income is now deductible, but only at a maximum rate of 50 percent. In one interesting contrast to U.S. procedures, Sweden taxes the imputed income from owner-occupied homes, though at a low rate. Most homeowners are assumed to earn imputed income equal to 2 percent of their homes' value, with a higher rate being used for expensive houses.

Sweden has a corporate tax that looks much like that in the United States. As in the United States, it does not raise very much revenue (only 1 percent of GDP in recent years). Corporations pay the national tax at a 52 percent rate, but, after a recent change, no local corporate

30. A recent paper by Jonathan R. Kesselman discusses all of this with regard to Australia where similar suggestions have been made. See "The Role of the Tax Mix in Tax Reform," paper prepared for the Conference on Changing the Tax Mix, Monash University, Melbourne, Australia, 1985. Kesselman points out that the horizontal equity claim is overstated if the flow into evading activities lowers returns there (though of course there would still be an efficiency gain from raising the VAT).

tax. Firms are allowed to deduct dividends on new shares for twenty years following the new issue to reduce the double taxation of income from dividends. Historical cost accounting is used to measure both capital gains from inventory and capital depreciation. But to prevent inflation-induced increases in tax rates, firms are allowed to deduct up to 60 percent of the value of inventories purchased, and as in the United States accelerated depreciation rules are generous.

The Swedish tax system has other interesting components. An investment fund system is intended to stabilize investment over the business cycle. Each year a firm can deduct up to half of its taxable profits for an investment fund, depositing half this amount interest-free at the Central Bank and being allowed to use the other half for any purpose. The central government then releases these investment funds in recessions, and firms are allowed to withdraw funds equally from the Central Bank and non-Central Bank reserve for investments.

A second component affects Sweden's wealth tax. Individuals are taxed on their wealth at nominal rates that go from 1 percent at the bottom to 2.5 percent at the top. The wealth tax is not deductible within the income tax. There is also a tax on inheritances and gifts.

In the aggregate, taxes on labor income totaled 49 percent of GDP in 1982. In contrast, aggregate taxes on capital barely yield positive revenues, only 1 percent of GDP. The corporate income tax brings in 1 percent of GDP, and the personal income tax on capital income actually loses as much revenue as wealth and inheritance taxes gain. The net tax on capital income is low because firms and individuals deduct interest expenses at high rates while most of the interest income accrues to tax-exempt institutions. In addition, individuals are able to borrow funds, deduct the interest expenses at high marginal tax rates, and invest the proceeds in lightly taxed assets such as housing and capital gains. One striking result is that the government would actually gain revenue by not taxing the capital income of individuals, provided that the interest deduction was also eliminated.

Despite the low overall tax on capital income generated within Sweden, the income tax imposes a large penalty on the incentive for households to save. Users of borrowed funds receive generous tax deductions, while savers must pay large taxes on interest and dividend income. This is particularly true when inflation is high because the income tax base is not indexed. In recent years there have been attempts to promote saving by creating accounts in which taxes on interest are deferred. As with U.S. individual retirement accounts, however, individuals are not prevented from shifting previously existing assets into these accounts, and they do not necessarily add to personal saving at the margin. Moreover, because of the interest deduction, it is possible to borrow funds to deposit in the tax-free account, claim an interest deduction, and hence thwart the purpose of the tax deferral.

On the investment side, the most salient feature of the Swedish tax structure is that it has a highly distorting effect on the allocation of capital. Because of the investment credit and depreciation provisions, the tax rate is lower on equipment than on structures and inventories. Because nominal interest is deductible, debt-financed investment is taxed at lower rates than new equity-financed investment. Because of the new share dividend deduction, equity-financed investments are taxed at a lower rate than investments financed from retained earnings. Because new firms cannot carry over all their eligible deductions for interest and depreciation, investment in old firms is subsidized more than investment in new firms. All of these distortions get worse with inflation, because most capital income is not indexed. A study by Jan Södersten and Thomas Lindberg found variations in effective tax rates on different types of investment in 1980 that ranged from −52 percent to 105 percent.[31] The exact numbers and features of the tax system are different from those in the United States, but the general inefficiencies in taxing income from capital are serious in both countries.

In evaluating proposals for tax reform it is important to take account of the increasingly open structure of Swedish capital markets. If savers are free to invest in a world capital market at world rates of interest and investors are free to borrow in that same world market, wealth accumulation in Sweden depends only on the sum of private and government saving. Any changes in private investment are offset by changes in the trade balance, leaving domestic wealth accumulation unaffected even in the short run. In such a world, investment subsidies make very little sense. The government is, in effect, diverting saving that could be invested at the world real interest rate to subsidized investment in Sweden that pays less than this rate. Or it is compensating foreign savers to invest in Sweden at returns less than the world real interest rate. In

31. The results of the study can be found in Mervyn A. King and Don Fullerton, eds., *The Taxation of Income from Capital: A Comparative Study of the United States, the United Kingdom, Sweden, and West Germany* (University of Chicago Press, 1984), pp. 87–148.

general, tax-induced distortions in capital allocation generate dead-weight losses without affecting the overall supply of wealth that determines long-run living standards.[32]

In view of the undesirability of capital income subsidies, an obvious remedy would be to abolish the personal income tax on capital income, and along with it the personal interest deduction. The most extreme version of such a change would be a thoroughgoing consumption tax, and indeed that has been suggested.[33] Without repeating that proposal, which among other things requires reform of the corporate tax, there is a simpler alternative that accomplishes many of the same ends: prohibit taxpayers from deducting more interest than the amount of capital income of all sorts that they claim. According to numbers from Krister Andersson, aggregate revenue and aggregate saving would rise by about 0.5 percent of GDP under such a measure, and that estimate may understate the true effect on aggregate saving if the disappearance of arbitrage opportunities increases the impact on personal saving of the tax-deferred accounts. Andersson also shows that such a measure would improve the distribution of income because for low-income people capital income taxes exceed interest deductions, while for high-income people it is the reverse, particularly for the very rich.[34]

Summary

Four major conclusions emerge from this brief overview of the Swedish tax system. First, the taxation of labor income has increased to the point that it is imposing major costs on the economy in lost efficiency. It is distorting the allocation of labor, promoting the growth of a gray economy, and undermining public support of the tax system. These grounds alone constitute a powerful argument for continuing the rollback of marginal income tax rates.

Second, the taxation of capital income generates very little net revenue, yet it has had major distorting effects on the allocation of capital

32. There is one slight exception to this statement. High investment taxes on foreign investment could deter capital inflows. This point is likely to be relevant in a high-tax country like Sweden, because even if Swedish taxes are credited against host country taxes, they may exceed host country taxes.

33. See Sven-Olof Lodin, *Progressive Expenditure Tax—An Alternative?* Report of the 1972 Government Commission on Taxation (Stockholm: Liber Förlag, 1978).

34. Krister Andersson, "The Swedish Tax System," (University of Lund, 1986), p. 45.

among sectors of the economy. The distortions result from the failure to adjust the taxable income base for inflation, inconsistencies in the treatment of interest as an expense and as income, and tax preferences granted to specific types of investment, such as housing.

Third, Swedish policymakers need to rethink the issue of capital income taxation in what is becoming an increasingly open world capital market. In such circumstances, subsidizing investment in Sweden is inefficient in replacing foreign investments yielding higher returns with domestic investment yielding lower returns. On the other side, excess taxation of capital employed in Sweden is also counterproductive, as it drives investment abroad. There is an urgent need to undertake a thorough reform of the whole system of capital income taxation, including the corporate and individual income tax and the wealth tax.

Fourth, while tax reform is important, that reform is unlikely to yield either a significant increase in tax revenues or generate significant improvement in savings and investment. To a large extent reform will mean a shift in emphasis among different taxes, such as lower income tax rates financed by an increase in the VAT or removals of various kinds of distortions. Most significant efforts to reduce the budget deficit must focus on expenditures.

Expenditures

One could examine Sweden's extensive expenditures from a positive standpoint. Why are expenditures so high? Why have they grown so rapidly? Does either their level or growth reflect the true tastes of Swedish voters or the many types of political distortions that have been pointed out in recent years?[35] While each topic could make for a fascinating discussion, my main focus is on controlling spending. I argued earlier that deficits should be cut; I have also argued that at least certain tax rates should be cut. Hence I will not adopt the positive approach here but instead follow the more normative approach of

---

35. There are many such theories. Some involve the motives of bureaucrats and politicians and how these lead to growth in public consumption; some involve political bribes and how these lead to growth in either transfers or public wages. It is ironic that most theories have been developed by U.S. economists and tested, with only indifferent success, with U.S. data. One suspects that should the researchers focus on Sweden, they could claim more convincing successes for their theories.

examining the list of spending programs to find those with particularly tenuous rationales.

In principle one should search for these dubious spending programs everywhere on the spending side of the budget, but I will follow the further simplification of focusing on the rapid-growth items identified in table 7-3 as primary causes of the rising deficits. Four of these programs— the three types of transfers and local consumption—are discretionary. It makes sense to focus on them for possible cutbacks: they are where the big money is, and a short time ago, when the Swedish economy was growing more rapidly, they were much less extensive. It also turns out that each of these programs is large by world standards.

Transfers to Households

Two of the transfers listed in table 7-3, those from the central government and those from the social security trust funds, go to households. These more than doubled as a share of GDP between 1970 and 1986, growing from 10.2 percent of GDP to 20.8 percent sixteen years later. From a programmatic standpoint it makes sense to discuss the two together, because the largest of each type of transfer is a pension payment for the aged. From a fiscal standpoint, spending cuts will have differential effects. The 10.9 percent of GDP devoted to social security transfers is financed by payroll taxes paid into trust funds that have been running surpluses. Cuts here will result in payroll tax reductions over a long period of time, with little short-term impact on the deficit. The 9.0 percent of GDP devoted to central government transfers to households is only partially financed by payroll taxes of the central government. Should spending be cut here, with no change in payroll tax rates, there will be a cut in the deficit.

The oldest of these programs, known as the basic pension, was enacted in 1913. Benefits are paid by the central government at a flat rate that is now about 32 percent of average disposable income for single people and 50 percent for couples, with this flat rate being adjusted as income grows. On top of this basic pension there is a national supplementary pension (ATP) paid by the social insurance fund and financed by payroll taxes on a pay-as-you-go basis. Initially, benefits were tied to the individual's prior contributions, but in recent years the tie to prior contributions has been frayed, and the program incorporates some redistribution.[36] Perhaps because of this, Sweden is beginning to see growth in private pensions.

That Sweden funds the future liabilities of the ATP system through current taxes explains some of the budgetary trends discussed earlier. To qualify for the maximum ATP benefit (60 percent of pensionable income over a person's highest-paid fifteen years in the labor force), a worker has to have employer contributions made for thirty years. Hence the system does not fully reach maturity until the mid-1990s. That is also the period in which, given Sweden's demographics, the expenditures will peak as a share of GDP.[37] In the meantime, the payroll contributions are running ahead of benefit payments, and the system is in substantial surplus.

The obvious policy change recommended by those who write about pension programs in Sweden is to reduce the generosity of the system.[38] There are numerous ways in which this could be done: replacement rates could be lowered, disability provisions could be tightened, retirement ages could be raised, and the discount for early retirement could be increased. Depending on how these cuts were distributed among the programs paid for by the central government and by the social security funds, and on what was done to payroll tax rates, such changes could either cut deficits or cut payroll tax rates. In either case the changes would simultaneously increase the work incentives for older workers.

The social security fund also includes two other significant social insurance programs. One affects health insurance. Health insurance benefit payments are not very large in Sweden, only about 2.5 percent of GDP, because the main health costs occur elsewhere in the budget. The municipal governments run all the hospitals and clinics. What is meant by health insurance is thus only a payment for income losses when not working because of sickness, and for a "parental insurance" program. Both programs have obvious rationales, but neither contains any cost-cutting incentives. Tax rates under the sickness plan do not depend

36. Additional details are provided in chapter 6 in this volume. Complete descriptions of these and other programs are provided by Per Gunnar Edebalk and Åke Elmér, "Social Insurance in Sweden," in Lars Söderström, ed., *Social Insurance: Papers Presented at the 5th Arne Ryde Symposium* (Amsterdam: North-Holland, 1983), pp. 53–79; and Sven E. Olsson, "Welfare Programs in Sweden," in Peter Flora, ed., *Growth to Limits—The West European Welfare States Since World War II* (New York: W. de Gruyter, 1986).

37. Ann-Charlotte Stahlberg, "Transfereringar Mellan den Förvärvsarbetande och den Äldre Generationen" (Stockholm: Institutet för Social Forskning, 1984). See also the chapter by Gary Burtless for a more detailed discussion.

38. Ibid.

on an employer's experience, and there is no incentive for employers to police claims. The parents' insurance plan, introduced in 1974, gives payments to new parents for up to one year based on a measure of income loss for days taken off because of infant care. This is one of the programs that complicate the work incentive issue. There is a large incentive to be in the labor force and collect the benefits if one expects to become a parent.

The other major program is for unemployment insurance. The main program is financed by a payroll tax. As with the other transfers, unemployment compensation payments are taxable, and the effective replacement rate is about 85 percent of after-tax wages.[39] The most interesting features of the unemployment insurance program are the long length of the benefit period—up to sixty weeks for those less than age fifty-five and ninety weeks for those older—and again the lack of any experience rating in setting employer tax rates. There is also a small program, financed through general revenue, with much lower wage replacement rates (about 50 percent) for new and disadvantaged workers who have not worked in covered employment long enough to qualify for regular benefits.

Obvious savings could be made in this part of the budget: introducing experience rating into the tax for the unemployment and sickness plans and trimming the extremely generous parents' insurance plan. Perhaps the budget savings would be small in the short run because of the quasi-contractual nature of these benefits, but the savings would increase over time.

Transfers to Business

While household transfers grew relative to GDP, much of that growth could be explained by demographic changes and the maturation of the large Swedish pension. Transfers to business also grew sharply, from just 1.3 percent of GDP in 1970 to 4.9 percent of GDP by 1982, but without the rationales.

Slightly more than half of the total includes price subsidies, regular continuing payments to hold down the cost of some consumption item. They illustrate the tendency in Sweden to pile redistributional programs

39. Greater detail on effective tax rates is provided in Anders Björklund and Bertil Holmlund, "Unemployment Compensation in Sweden" (Stockholm: Industrial Institute for Economic and Social Research, 1984).

on top of one another—to the point that today they create horizontal inequities rather than increasing vertical equity.

One such payment is an interest subsidy for housing. Because subsidies are based on nominal interest rates, they have grown sharply (from zero in 1970), and they magnify the distortions already present in the uneven set of capital income taxes. Drugs, medical and dental care, and public transportation in Stockholm all receive hefty subsidies. And although the cost is not large, in some ways the most curious subsidy of all is for daily newspapers. The point of the subsidy is to keep alive different political points of view, a goal that, while laudable, seems grossly inconsistent with the fact that Sweden does not permit private television channels.

The other major category of business transfers has evolved out of Sweden's industrial policy: subsidies of losses, investment grants, and other special transfers for struggling firms. A large share of the subsidies went to the shipyards, steel, and forest product industries located in the sparsely populated north of Sweden, which produces for the export market. Before 1975 such subsidies were almost nonexistent. But since then the standard Swedish full-employment guarantee has apparently been supplanted by a more ambitious regional full-employment guarantee.[40] If a wage agreement, movement in terms of trade, change in technology, or something else threatens large-scale layoffs in particular firms, the government has simply bailed out the firm with large transfers. These subsidy programs became very costly, reaching 2 percent of GDP in 1982. The consequences for promoting wage discipline were harmful. The redundancy of government subsidies is again exemplified in the response to unemployment. Sweden not only has an unemployment compensation system with very complete coverage, which includes a costly and extensive set of programs for training unemployed workers and giving them public employment, but the government also bails out failing firms.

As table 7-3 shows, these transfers to business have been reduced as a share of GDP in recent years, and the magnitude of the industrial subsidies has been cut in absolute amount. Subsidies for steel plants and forestry products have disappeared entirely from the budget, subsidies for mining are down to less than Skr 0.5 billion, and the subsidies for shipbuilding, about Skr 3 billion a year, are being phased out.

40. Lundberg, "Rise and Fall of the Swedish Model."

Local Government Consumption

By most political standards Sweden's governmental system would not be described as highly decentralized. But ironically, the general level of public spending has become so large that in terms of some basic considerations, such as the importance of local spending, grants, and taxes, Sweden's local governments play a bigger role in the economy than do the local governments in other countries with much more decentralized systems.

Central government consumption of goods and services, as opposed to transfers, has declined as a share of GDP since 1970. Local consumption, now 74 percent of the total, has more than taken up the slack, being one of the main areas of spending growth identified earlier. This growth reflects a large expansion in all the domestic functions under the responsibility of local governments, even though there has been an offsetting trend within each of these functional areas to shift responsibility from local governments to the central government.[41]

Spending by local governments has not attracted the attention of Swedish economists, and very little analysis is available in English.[42] The 23 county governments make about 36 percent of the consumption expenditures, mainly to operate the large Swedish health and hospital systems, to provide some social welfare services, and occasionally to run county high schools (table 7-4). The 280 municipal governments do just about everything else—they oversee the public schools, day care centers, housing, recreation, public safety, roads, and so forth.

While consumption by local governments is now more than 20 percent of GDP, there are various ways in which the central government restricts local decisionmaking. For one thing, the central government has merged many local governments out of existence. There were 2,500 municipalities in 1950, and now there are only 280. The reason given for these combinations, worked out by city planners and geographers, was that the municipalities needed to be strengthened to take on their big responsibilities, or that there were certain economies of scale in running school systems and the like. However, in the earlier period, the many municipalities had developed extensive networks for sharing the costs

41. Richard Murray, "Central Control of the Government Sector in Sweden" (Stockholm: Industrial Institute for Economic and Social Research, 1984).
42. There are Swedish papers on this topic, but the only one I could find in English, as of now unpublished, was the one by Murray.

THE SWEDISH ECONOMY

Table 7-4. *Local Government Consumption and Grants, 1983*[a]
Billions of kronor

Level of government	Local consumption	Grants	
		General purpose	Special purpose
Total	146.3	7.4	39.0
Municipalities[b]	93.5	4.3	31.5
Counties[c]	52.8	3.1	7.5

Source: *National Accounts, Appendix 1.*
a. Disaggregated data are not available for 1982.
b. General responsibility for education, social welfare, housing and community amenities, public safety, business promotion, culture and recreation, sewage, roads, and public utilities.
c. General responsibility for health and hospitals, with some high schools and some social welfare services.

of certain public services. It is not clear whether the resulting economies of scale have outweighed one new deadweight loss. Diverse tastes are submerged into a common level of public spending as governmental units get larger.

The next limitation on the freedom of action of local governments lies in an extensive system of mandating. Murray has calculated that about 44 percent of the expenditures of local governments are obligatory, for activities such as supporting a public school system; about 25 percent of expenditures are voluntary but in some way regulated, such as housing allowances; and the remaining activities, such as town planning, parks and recreation, and public transportation are voluntary.[43]

Finally, the central government controls the financing. Local governments cannot run deficits and can impose virtually no indirect taxes. Their revenue comes from income taxes, grants, and user fees, as table 7-1 shows. The proportional income tax raised Skr 97 billion, more than twice as much as the income tax raised for the central government. Although local governments set their own tax rate, the central government determines the tax base, collects the tax, and redistributes the revenue (with a two-year delay).[44] In recent years the central government has raised the minimum taxable income and removed corporations from the local income tax base.

43. Murray, "Central Control of the Government Sector."
44. There is one point of interest in light of the recent U.S. debate on tax reform. The U.S. federal income tax permits the deduction of state and local taxes. President Ronald Reagan proposed eliminating this deductibility as a means of broadening the tax base. The change was largely successfully resisted, in part because of fears that eliminating deductibility would reduce state and local spending. It may be reassuring to those holding such fears to note that in Sweden, where local spending exploded in recent years, local income taxes are not deductible.

Further details on Sweden's grant system are given in table 7-4. In 1983 special purpose grants constituted 84 percent of all grants; the remainder were general purpose grants. The general purpose grants are supposed to be redistributive, but, as in the United States, many question exactly how redistributive, because of problems in defining local tax bases. Since these are general purpose grants, they have no marginal effect on prices facing local governments.

The special purpose grants are given out for functions such as education and day care on a per student or per worker basis. Since they depend on numbers of students, they are not open-ended with respect to spending per student and usually have no price effect on spending for public services.[45] This is just as well because the normal justification for such grant-induced price reductions—benefit spillovers across community lines—is probably as absent in Sweden's remote communities as it is anywhere in the world.

Since the usual rationales for central government grants—externalities and community income differences—seem not to be germane in the Swedish context, one might wonder why these grants should not be cut back, perhaps drastically. Were this to be done, it might be possible to improve local decisionmaking by increasing accountability, for at least three reasons.

Rather than having outside grants finance one-third of local consumption, communities would have to foot a greater share of the bill. They would then be more economical in their use of tax dollars and more vigilant in guarding against spending programs that could not pass a public choice test. These political incentives to economize would be increased still more if localities were to start collecting their own income taxes.

The second source of greater accountability is at the level of the individual. If grants were reduced, there would be pressure either to reduce uneconomic expenditures or to increase user fees. To the extent that user fees were increased, gains would be likely in both efficiency and horizontal equity. At present, for services such as health care, day care, and nursing homes, user fees are low, and there are large and often

45. Grants are referred to as open-ended when the central government matches a constant share of local spending, thus lowering the price of those services to local government. Grants are closed-ended when central government matches local spending only up to a point and after that forces the local government to pay the entire cost of the added service. I am arguing here that both types of grants operate like closed-ended grants without price effects.

unsatisfied demands for services. These unsatisfied demands lead to horizontal inequalities and long queues—queues that could be cut back were the price system to do more rationing.[46] A commonly stated reason for not raising user fees is the impact on vertical equity, but this rationale seems particularly weak. For one thing, other redistributional policies are already so extensive that further efforts are redundant. For another, the existence of queues raises the possibility that scarce slots will be allocated to the rich and powerful by factors other than prices.[47]

A third way cutting back grants could improve accountability and efficiency is that it would encourage governments to seek out cheaper sources of supply of public services. One possibility is to permit competition by licensing, for example, parents' cooperatives to run day care centers. Another is through a voucher system. Under such a scheme, consumers are given a voucher that can be spent either at public agencies or at licensed private suppliers. Consumers could be required to pay a portion of the cost of the voucher.

There are still other possibilities. In the United States one promising solution to burgeoning health costs is the health maintenance organization, in which consumers pay, or are given a voucher for, a predetermined premium, and there is an economic incentive for the supplier to maintain the consumer's health as cheaply as possible.[48] Another possibility is for explicit contracts with private suppliers for trash collection, cleaning parks, and so forth. Unlike the permanently franchised public agencies, the private suppliers have an incentive to keep costs down in order to renew their franchise.

Summary

This discussion of expenditures can be summarized numerically. The analysis of deficits, particularly in figure 7-3, showed that Sweden's public contribution to capital formation is now 2 percent of GDP, about 8 percentage points less than in the high-saving days between 1962 and

46. Marten Lagergren and others, "Care and Welfare at the Crossroads" (Stockholm: Secretariat for Futures Studies, 1982).

47. If vertical equity were still a serious concern, it would always be possible to differentiate the user fees so that lower-income groups could consume public services at a lower price.

48. Ingemar Ståhl, "Can Equality and Efficiency Be Combined? The Experience of the Planned Swedish Health Care System," in Mancur Olson, ed., *A New Approach to the Economics of Health Care* (Washington, D.C.: American Enterprise Institute, 1981), pp. 172–95.

1977. The analysis of taxes showed that the most that could be recovered on the tax side, by the limitation of interest deductibility, was about 0.5 percent of GDP. That leaves about 7.5 percent of GDP to be made up by spending cuts. Of course, in a high-tax country like Sweden there is independent justification for spending cuts. Even if deficits were not cut at all, spending cuts might arguably increase efficiency, as Hansson and others have been saying.

I have discussed a few of the possible spending cuts. All can be defended on grounds of efficiency, and most would appear feasible with little or no cost in terms of equity. Central government transfers now amount to 9 percent of GDP, 4 percent of GDP more than the social security transfers levied to pay for them. There does not, of course, need to be exact pay-as-you-go financing for these transfers, but it is still true that many of them seem generous by world standards, and the share of effective general revenue financing is large. Business subsidies have been cut sharply in recent years, but they still amount to 4 percent of GDP, and further cutbacks would seem to make sense. Grants to local governments do not seem to fulfill the usual rationales for such grants; they amount to 7 percent of GDP, and they could be trimmed as well. Were this to be done, local governments would be forced by their budget limitations either to cut spending or raise fees, resulting in more public-sector saving in the consolidated accounts. These three numbers alone indicate that there is much scope for achieving the desired reductions in spending.

Conclusion

Since World War II the Swedes have constructed a very ambitious welfare state. The goals are laudable—to even out income distribution, provide for full employment, give effective social insurance for unforeseen and damaging events, and provide a full menu of public services. But there are also costs in tax distortions, redundant subsidies, and declining public saving. It is not clear that the dire predictions of some Swedish economists are in order, but certain things need fixing to combat some of the economic problems that Sweden is now having.

Deficits should be reduced, marginal taxes on earned income should be lowered, local accountability should be increased, transfer programs should be experience rated, redundant transfers and capital subsidies should be eliminated, and user fees should be increased. The distinguishing feature of these remedies is that they are reasonably straightforward: the problems caused by the inappropriate policies are well known, and the remedies can be implemented without big sacrifices in the distributional and employment goals that have guided Swedish policy. Indeed, in recent years some of the necessary actions have been taken.

This analysis suggests that what is really needed, in Sweden as elsewhere, is a willingness to think about and experiment with policies from a broader perspective. To solve the problem of deficits, the political debate must move beyond the budgetary stalemate to a recognition that if changes are not made, serious burdens will be placed on future generations, and the economic growth that has made the Swedish model work will be threatened. In rethinking their policy on marginal tax rates, the Swedes should consider what equitable redistribution really means when vertical redistribution is already extensive and horizontal redistribution haphazard, and when the status of those able and not able to avoid income taxes is compared. Transfer programs are evidence of the problem of redundant subsidies. It is not necessary to have more than one systematic program to protect against social ills. The focus on public consumption must take account of efficiency as well as equity and of the fact that expenditures cannot keep rising at past rates, or even stay at past levels, without causing serious distortions in both taxes and expenditures. Particular policies can readily be changed if these broader perspectives are taken and if the more subtle and long-term costs can be made part of the debate.

[23]

Canadian Fiscal Federalism: An Outsider's View

Edward M. Gramlich*

The practice and study of fiscal federalism probably takes on more importance in Canada than anywhere else in the world. West Germany and Austria have federal systems, but they are of more recent vintage, with more centralization, and for more homogeneous populations than Canada's. Switzerland has an old federal system with a reasonable degree of decentralization, but it is a much smaller country than Canada. Australia and the United States are large countries with long federal traditions, but again the populations are more homogeneous and there is less at stake than in Canada. Average Australian and American economists, let alone laypeople in those countries, are simply not aware of the issues of federalism to anything like the degree realized in Canada.

An outsider asked to comment on the Canadian system can take two tacks. One is comparative study, examining what the Canadians do vis-à-vis what the Americans, Australians, Swiss, and Germans do. That approach has been pursued quite intensively in Canada—by my count there are at least four recent comprehensive studies of fiscal federalism systems elsewhere and their relevance for Canada.[1] The other is to resort to theory, comparing what the Canadians do with the orthodox canons of public finance. Some of that approach is scattered in the voluminous Canadian literature on fiscal federalism, but comparative studies are much more frequent.

In this paper I use an eclectic blend of comparative analysis and invocation of theory.[2] I even try to correct the theoretical canons where I think

---

*I am indebted to Richard Bird, Thomas Courchene, and Melville McMillan for helpful comments.

[1] Richard M. Bird, *Federal Finance in Comparative Perspective* (Toronto: Canadian Tax Foundation, 1986); Herman Bakvis, *Federalism and the Organization of Political Life: Canada in Comparative Perspective*, Queen's Studies on the Future of the Canadian Communities, no. 2 (Kingston, Ont.: Institute of Intergovernmental Relations, Queen's University, 1981); John A. Hayes, *Economic Mobility in Canada: A Comparative Study* (Ottawa: Supply and Services, 1982); and Wayne R. Thirsk, "Fiscal Harmonization in the United States, Australia, West Germany, Switzerland, and the EEC," in Michael J. Trebilcock, J. Robert S. Prichard, Thomas J. Courchene, and John Whalley, eds., *Federalism and the Canadian Economic Union* (Toronto: Ontario Economic Council, 1983).

[2] The format follows one I have previously used in discussing the federalism situation of my own country: Edward M. Gramlich, "Reforming US Fiscal Federalism Arrangements," in John M. Quigley and Daniel L. Rubinfeld, eds., *American Domestic Priorities: An Economic Appraisal* (Berkeley: University of California Press, 1985), 34-69.

they are inappropriate or dated. The goal of the enterprise is to see what can be learned from a study of Canada that is of value to that country and also to the other federal countries.

Roughly following Richard Musgrave's[3] famous triad of fiscal functions—allocation, distribution, and stabilization—I begin with the way in which the Canadian federal system assigns spending responsibilities. I next turn to taxing powers and then to the structure of the grant system. As a final matter, I discuss the split of stabilization responsibilities between government levels. This is the third and least discussed leg of Musgrave's triad, the one for which I think the conventional wisdom is most seriously in error.

The Assignment of Spending Responsibilities

Compared with spending assignments in the other federal countries, Canada's system is distinctive in the important role assigned to provincial governments. I show this with respect to the first two legs of Musgrave's triad, allocation and distribution.

Allocation

The theory of public finance offers two separate traditions for determining how spending programs should be assigned to different levels of government in a federal system:

1) Charles Tiebout[4] poses the question in terms of a consumer choice model in which rational consumers select a jurisdiction and its menu of public goods to maximize utility. Jurisdictions then compete to provide the optimal menu; if they do not, citizens move around until utility is maximized.

2) Another way of putting the matter follows Albert Breton's[5] notion of perfect mapping of jurisdictions. Jurisdictional boundaries mark off just that set of individuals who obtain benefits from the relevant public good or service. In principle, there could be as many jurisdictions as public goods, though, in later work, Breton and Anthony Scott[6] rationalized a smaller number of jurisdictions by including the costs of organizing and coordinating them and the costs to consumers of moving.

---

[3]Richard A. Musgrave, *The Theory of Public Finance: A Study in Public Economy* (New York: McGraw-Hill, 1959).

[4]Charles M. Tiebout, "A Pure Theory of Local Expenditures" (October 1956), 64 *Journal of Political Economy* 416-24.

[5]Albert Breton, "A Theory of Government Grants" (May 1965), 31 *Canadian Journal of Economics and Political Science* 175-87.

[6]Albert Breton and Anthony Scott, *The Economic Constitution of Federal States* (Toronto: University of Toronto Press, 1978).

These two traditions have been combined in various ways by various authors. Wallace Oates[7] synthesized them by showing how jurisdiction size can be determined by the balance between two competing forces: the welfare loss from taste differences, which argues for small jurisdictions, and the welfare gain from minimizing benefit spillovers, which argues for large jurisdictions. His "decentralization theorem" called for public goods to be provided by the jurisdiction covering the smallest area over which benefits are distributed; that way the efficiencies of public goods are maximized and the impact of taste differences is minimized. Breton and Scott[8] worked out a more general theory of the benefits and organizational costs of public goods, but they did not formulate any general theorems because they thought it was always possible to reduce total cost by some sort of intergovernmental transfer. Anthony Atkinson and Joseph Stiglitz[9] made things even more complicated and indeterminate by introducing complications on the production side (though many of these complications take on less importance when jurisdictions are open to trade and commuting).

In light of this theoretical indeterminacy, economists have been reluctant to take strong positions about which public functions should be carried out by which levels of government. Practical politicians, in Canada and elsewhere, lack the luxury of being able to avoid decisions. They seem to have made choices roughly in line with Oates's decentralization theorem. Those services that provide benefits over a wide area—for example, national defence and international affairs—are responsibilities of the national government. Those that provide very localized benefits—for example, schools, road maintenance, waste removal, police and fire protection, parks—are provided by local governments. Thus far, the Canadian spending assignments are fairly standard.

The Canadian system is distinctive, however, in the important role played by the provincial governments. In 1981, Richard Bird[10] reported, provincial government spending averaged 38 percent of all public spending in Canada, as opposed to 36 percent in Australia, 30 percent in Switzerland, 25 percent in Germany, 22 percent in the United States, and 14 percent in Austria. Canadian provinces are responsible for the health care system, the social service system, institutions of higher education, a range of economic development and agricultural programs, and other matters that are national responsibilities in other federal countries. Although the gross numbers may give a misleading impression of provincial powers in some instances—for example, Canadian institutions of higher education, in contrast to many in the United States, have no out-of-province tuition fees—in others, the gross numbers understate provincial powers. To my

---

[7]Wallace E. Oates, *Fiscal Federalism* (New York: Harcourt Brace Jovanovich, 1972).

[8]Supra footnote 6.

[9]Anthony B. Atkinson and Joseph E. Stiglitz, *Lectures on Public Economics* (London, Eng.: McGraw-Hill, 1980).

[10]*Federal Finance in Comparative Perspective*, supra footnote 1, at 7, table 1.2.

knowledge, the Canadian provision that allows provinces to opt out of public programs and receive compensating revenues or taxing authority is unique. It is true that no other country has a province as jealous of its powers as Quebec (Australia's Queensland may be the closest imitation), but that is the point.

Distribution

The importance of Canadian provincial governments can be seen even more clearly on the distribution side. Most federal systems have centralized distribution programs conducted by the national government. Canada and the United States are important exceptions to this pattern, with both retaining significant roles for their provincial or state governments.

Given the prevalence of centralized distribution systems, it may come as a surprise that public finance economists are split on whether income redistribution should be handled at the national or the subnational level. Mark Pauly and Richard Tresch[11] have argued that redistribution should be a subnational function, primarily because they see the benefits occurring locally and not nationally—that is, the taxpayer-donors of one province feel better off if the poor in that province are helped, but they see no benefit to themselves if the poor in some other province are helped. Helen Ladd and Fred Doolittle[12] make the reverse argument, but only for the United States and on the basis of admittedly vague survey evidence that US voters see redistribution benefits as fulfilling national more than subnational needs.

An additional point is the possibility that beneficiaries migrate across jurisdictional lines in search of higher income-support benefits. If there is much of that, decentralization carries a form of external cost: high income-support benefits in one jurisdiction can lead to the immigration of poor people and thus to lower welfare costs in other jurisdictions. The United States seems to have some cross-state beneficiary migration, but by my count it is not enough to alter one's predisposition on the centralization issue.[13] In any case, recognition of this theoretical point led Robin Boadway and David Wildasin[14] to argue for a middle-of-the-road approach to financing welfare benefits, with subnational governments operating redistribution programs that are partly financed by open-ended matching grants from the national government to account for the spillovers.

---

[11] Mark V. Pauly, "Income Redistribution as a Local Public Good" (February 1973), 2 *Journal of Public Economics* 35-58; and Richard W. Tresch, *Public Finance: A Normative Theory* (Plano, Tex.: Business Publications, 1981).

[12] Helen F. Ladd and Fred C. Doolittle, "Which Level of Government Should Assist the Poor?" (September 1982), 35 *National Tax Journal* 323-36.

[13] Gramlich, supra footnote 2.

[14] Robin W. Boadway and David E. Wildasin, *Public Sector Economics*, 2d ed. (Boston: Little-Brown, 1984).

I do not intend to magnify the role of economic theory in explaining real world institutions, but it is true that both the United States and Canada follow this matching-grant scheme. The most important distributional program in the United States, public assistance, is operated by state governments with an open-ended federal grant; the matching rate ranges from 50 percent for high-income states to 78 percent for low-income states. There is also a national food stamp program, which sets minimum benefits across all states. Even with this standardization, benefit levels vary widely across states, and one common policy suggestion in the United States is that the system be further centralized, either by raising minimum benefits or by altering the provisions of the grant schedule to compact the statewide distribution of benefits (say, by providing more federal matching for the first x dollars of benefits). In recent years, however, the decentralized structure has offered real advantages because the states have been innovators in the area of combining work with welfare.

The Canadian situation looks similar. The most important distributional program is the Canada assistance plan (CAP), under which the provinces receive an open-ended welfare grant with a flat 50 percent matching rate. There is no explicit minimum benefit, but a province is eligible for the matching grant only if it has a plan that covers the basic requirements of recipients.

One question worthy of study in Canada, as in the United States, is whether the flat-rate grant system leads to the desired degree of benefit compression across the provinces. Should the program be supplemented with a more explicit minimum benefit provision or some similar change in the grant schedule? Another question is whether the CAP's decentralized structure provides some program innovation advantages, as there seem to be in the United States.

Tax Assignment

Although the Canadian system is truly federal in its assignment of spending responsibilities, it appears to be less so on the tax side. This greater tax centralization can be defended from a theoretical standpoint (though again I do not want to place undue reliance on theory as an explanation for institutions).

The strongest argument for *decentralizing* taxing authority is that of political accountability, a point made most fervently by Australian economists such as Cliff Walsh.[15] When expenditure programs are decentralized and taxing authority is centralized, as they happen to be in Australia, large

---

[15] Cliff Walsh, "Reforming Federal Financial Relations: Some Radical (or Are They Conservative?) Proposals," paper presented to the Federal Finance Symposium, Hobart, Australia, 1985. Walsh is considered a rightist in Australian politics, but a very similar complaint is made by a leading spokesperson on the political left: see Russell Mathews, *Federalism in Retreat: The Abandonment of Tax Sharing and Fiscal Equalization*, Reprint Series no. 50 (Canberra: Centre for Research on Federal Financial Relations, Australian National University, 1982).

central government grants to subnational governments are required to balance the books. The existence of these large grants places a premium on subnational politicians who can lobby successfully for grants from the central government and reduces the value of politicians who can simply manage programs well and balance spending benefits and taxpayer costs. Yet to realize the underlying Tiebout efficiencies of government competition (the basis for desiring decentralized spending responsibilities in the first place), subnational governments should pay for their own spending programs and compete by way of offering citizens attractive spending and tax packages.

On the other side, arguing for centralizing taxation, are a number of considerations:

• If tax administration is cheaper at the national level than at the provincial level, centralization offers administrative efficiencies.

• If some factors of production are mobile across provincial boundaries but not national boundaries, decentralization may involve dead-weight inefficiencies.[16] (This point is the analogue of the one made above about the external cost of income redistribution if potential recipients can move from jurisdiction to jurisdiction.)

• If one province has monopoly power in the supply of some resource, that province can exploit others by taxing the resource and thereby exporting some of its tax burden. It is both more efficient and more equitable to centralize and let all citizens reap the returns from the resource.

• If both the province and the national government are in position to levy a tax on an exportable resource, decentralization can lead to vertical tax competition and to suboptimal production from the resource.[17]

What is the reality in Canada of the centralization and decentralization of taxation? One can answer the question using several criteria.

Accountability

On the matching of spending and revenue for accountability, the answer is mixed. Bird's cross-country comparisons have shown that Canadian provincial governments raise a relatively high share of their own revenue and thus must be relatively accountable, but that local governments raise a relatively low share. In 1981, for example, provincial governments in Canada raised 81 percent of their own-source revenue, in contrast to 78 percent in the United States, 72 percent in Germany and Switzerland, 55 percent in Austria, and 39 percent in Australia, the home of economists who complain most about the issue of political accountability. Yet Cana-

---

[16]For a model that works out this point formally, see Roger H. Gordon, "An Optimal Taxation Approach to Fiscal Federalism" (November 1983), 98 *Quarterly Journal of Economics* 567-86.

[17]For an Australian illustration of the point, see J.H. Cassing and A.L. Hillman, "State-Federal Resource Tax Rivalry: The Queensland Railway and the Federal Export Tax" (September 1982), 58 *Economic Record* 235-41.

dian local governments raised only 49 percent of their own-source revenue; the comparable amount was more than 60 percent in all other federal countries including Australia.[18] Thus, if Canada has a problem of governmental accountability, it seems to be that local governments do not have to raise as much of their own funds—by property taxes, user fees, or whatever— as might be warranted.

Administration

For tax administration, Canada seems to have worked out a reasonable compromise between the administrative efficiencies of centralization and the economic efficiencies of decentralization. The federal government and each province levy a personal income tax, but all the provinces except Quebec use the federal income tax base and collection apparatus. Thus, each province can decide how much to tax—setting its rate as a separate percentage of the basic federal tax to yield its own revenue—but its taxpayers are spared the difficulty of preparing two forms, having separate deductions, and the like. A similar arrangement exists for the corporate tax, except the provincial revenue is generated by a tax credit, and three provinces assess their own tax. All the provinces except Alberta impose their own sales taxes, which are soon to be supplemented with a national value-added tax.[19] On this count, the Canadian arrangements seem preferable to the arbitrary delegation of tax bases that occurs in Australia and to the decentralized systems used in the United States and Switzerland.

Despite the Canadian uniformity of tax systems and bases, which should reduce the administrative costs of paying and collecting taxes, the actual tax rates need not be the same across jurisdictions. Some Canadians advocate harmonization of tax rates along with tax bases, but they may be going too far; after all, the basic virtue of a federal system is that different governments are free to pursue their own fiscal goals. Moreover, although it is difficult to sort through the plethora of taxing conventions to measure rate differences, my general impression is that there is a surprising degree of similarity.[20] One wonders whether this similarity of tax rates reflects the fact that factor supplies are so elastic to the provinces or a more prosaic unwillingness to practise true federalism.

Use of Revenue

The next issue is which government gets to use which tax revenue. The principle of factor mobility suggests that the jurisdictions over whose boundaries factors are the most mobile—localities—should use either taxes

---

[18]Supra footnote 10.

[19] See the discussion by J.A. Johnson, "Issues in Provincial Sales and Excise Taxation," in this volume.

[20]For more discussion, see Robin Boadway and Frank Flatters, "Federal-Provincial Fiscal Relations Revisited: Some Consequences of Recent Constitutional and Policy Developments," Thomas J. Courchene and Arthur E. Stewart, "Provincial Personal Income Taxation and the Future of the Tax Collection Agreements," and John Bossons, "Provincial Taxes on Corporations," all in this volume.

that are closest to benefit taxes or taxes on locally fixed factors. In practice, the backbone of own-source local tax revenue in both Canada and the United States turns out to be the property tax. Economists have written volumes about the optimality of this assignment, a literature I will not even try to summarize other than to say that the consensus seems to be that the arrangement is not a bad one. Part of the property tax certainly falls on a fixed factor, land, and to the extent that better schools, parks, and police services raise local property values, the property tax is certainly a benefits tax. Yet to the extent that the property tax falls on business, it is a tax on mobile capital, and thus there may be tax competition driving property tax rates below the optimal level. In the United States, this competition takes the form of pressures for local abatement of business property taxes (a competition that is often regulated by state governments just to prevent localities from competing away all business tax revenue). This phenomenon appears to be less widespread in Canada—non-residential property bears a higher burden than residential property in most provinces—but it is certainly a possible side effect of what otherwise seems a sensible assignment of revenue sources for local governments.

For other taxes, the principle of factor mobility seems unlikely to help much in judging tax assignment in the Canadian setting. Since most of the country's provinces are so large, since it has so few populous cities near provincial borders, and since there is a province with a primarily franco-phone population almost in the middle of the country, it is hard to think of factors that would be mobile across provincial boundaries but not across national boundaries, the basis for determining what government should use what tax. In essence, both the provinces and the national government have the choice of taxing a reasonably immobile factor, labour, and a reasonably mobile factor, capital, and it is hard to see how the relevant parameters in this choice would differ much between the provinces and the national government. Perhaps this is why there is so little mention of underlying factor mobilities in Canadian discussions of tax assignment. It is certainly a reason for expecting careful political compromises to replace underlying economic realities in working out the arrangements to share income, corporate, and perhaps eventually consumption taxes.

Underlying economic realities definitely do matter, however, in one form of taxation: that of taxing the returns from natural resources. Both the tax exporting and the vertical tax competition arguments given above argue that the central, not the provincial, government should reap the returns from the exploitation of natural resources. Australia already has high national taxes on resource returns, and there are discussions of raising them even further.[21] The United States imposed a national windfall profits tax after the 1970s burst in oil prices, and there are continuing efforts to get

---

[21]Edward M. Gramlich, " 'A Fair Go': Fiscal Federalism Arrangements," in Richard E. Caves and Lawrence R. Krause, eds., *The Australian Economy: A View from the North* (Washington, DC: The Brookings Institution, 1984), 231-74.

states to reduce or eliminate their own severence taxes on resources. Yet in Canada, resource taxes are imposed by the provinces, apparently without much discussion of nationalization of this revenue source. There is discussion of how the equalization formulas should be adjusted for the fact that provinces have uneven resource bases.[22] There is also extensive debate on federal price controls and the like which have nationalized a good share of the oil and gas rents by non-fiscal means. Yet national taxation of the returns from resource exploitation might be a better solution to the problem of how to share rents across the country, and the area of resource taxation seems a surprising exception to the otherwise strong trend toward tax harmonization in Canada.

The Grant System

Grants from the national government to lower levels of government have two broad rationales: to deal with income differences among regions, and to deal with benefit spillovers across jurisdictions. All federal countries try to deal with benefit spillovers by special purpose or categorical grants from the central government to lower governments. Most deal less frontally with income differences; if there is a concern, the response is usually either to institute centralized services so that all regions get at least a minimum level or to alter matching rates on special purpose grants so that poorer jurisdictions can consume public services on more favourable terms. Canada and Australia go much further by giving large equalization grants to their poorer provinces. These general purpose grants, unlike special purpose grants, can be used in any way the recipient government wants—there is no attempt to influence marginal choices by the provisions of the grant.

General Purpose Equalization Grants

One can think of two rationales for equalization grants:

1) Fair compensation. Under this standard, all jurisdictions would have access to the same bundle of all goods.

2) Categorical equity. Under this standard, grants would be calculated to equalize expected spending on designated important public services that are the responsibility of subnational governments, services such as health care and education.

Neither the Canadian system nor the Australian system is geared to fit either rationale precisely. Grants designed to meet the first objective would be general purpose, as both the Canadian and Australian grants are, but they would be given in amounts that equalized jurisdictional incomes. Both the Canadian and the Australian grants are on a lesser scale. Grants designed to meet the second objective would be special purpose with matching rates varied across provinces, so that expected spending was independent of

---

[22]Thomas J. Courchene, *Equalization Payments: Past, Present, and Future* (Toronto: Ontario Economic Council, 1984), chapter 8.

income (by having the post-grant price term in the spending equation fully offset the income or cost term). In the United States, such grants are termed "power equalization" grants; in principle, state governments use them to even out public school tax price disparities across local governments, but in practice almost all states fall well short of this goal.

Both the Canadian and the Australian equalization grants are given in amounts less than would be necessary to achieve the fair compensation standard. Suppose that average per capita income in one province is $100 less than the standard, and that the province spends 20 percent of its income on public services. A strictly fair compensation grant would be $100 per capita; the Australian and Canadian grants are for $20. The rationale behind this apparently low amount is that with it the province can raise spending to the average while still imposing the average national tax rate on the rest of income. Yet, on the one hand, the province is unlikely to devote all of its unconditional grant to public services, so there will still be a disparity in the level of service consumption. On the other hand, even if the government were to devote the entire grant to public services, it is hard to see why precise equalization of average tax rates should be so important. Hence the rationale is not entirely convincing.

Although the rationale underlying equalization grants may be suspect, the actual approach followed is reasonable. Like redistribution on the tax side, exact equalization of income differences under a fair compensation standard would present major incentive problems. Without such differences, what would provide market incentives for factors to migrate to better-endowed areas? Although Canada does not attempt to introduce cost factors into its equalization formulas, Australia does that too, and economists there often criticize the procedure as blunting the incentives in areas where the cost of supplying public services is high (and large, sparsely populated countries such as Canada and Australia can have some very high-cost areas).

Hence, although the Canadian and Australian general purpose grants may not completely meet either the fair compensation or the categorical equity standard, they still seem a reasonable compromise on the goals of regional efficiency and regional equity.

Special Purpose Grants

Although Canada's main special purpose grants are nominally for post-secondary education and health care—they are labelled that way in the official accounts and their amounts are related to the amounts given under antecedent categorical programs—they now seem to be special purpose in name only. The amounts received by the provinces are independent of provincial spending on the relevant functions, which means that the grants do not affect relative prices at the margin.[23] In theoretical parlance, a pro-

---

[23]Richard A. Musgrave, Peggy B. Musgrave, and Richard M. Bird, *Public Finance in Theory and Practice*, 1st Canadian ed. (Toronto: McGraw-Hill, 1987), chapter 24.

vincial government's spending response to the grants depends only on income effects, not on relative price or substitution effects.

Other countries have similar grants. In the United States in the 1980s, for example, there has been a trend to using what are known as "block grants," which are grants that are independent of state spending and thereby do not affect relative prices at the margin. Although such grants may somewhat reduce the grant bureaucracy, they are not likely to stimulate spending on the relevant public services nearly as much as would open-ended matching grants, and thus they are no answer to the benefit spillover issue. I have computed that if present block grants and close-ended matching grants in the United States were replaced by open-ended matching grants with the central government's matching share equal to the estimated share of marginal benefits received by out-of-state citizens, economic efficiency would be enhanced and the federal government budget deficit could be cut substantially.[24] I cannot tell whether the same would be true in Canada, but the preconditions are certainly there—very large block grants and the likelihood of some substitution or relative price sensitivity in the spending demands of provincial governments.

Stabilization

One of the least controversial propositions in both public finance and macroeconomics is that only the national government should attempt to conduct stabilization policy. The conventional view, exposited by Oates[25] 15 years ago and never seriously challenged since, supposes that demand conditions in a province mirror those in the national economy, that fiscal multipliers for national budget changes are higher than those for provincial budget changes, and that provincial debt is external and national debt internal. The inference from these premises is that it is unwise for a provincial or subnational government to run its own fiscal stabilization policy.

Although the premises may have been accurate 15 years ago, each can now be seriously questioned.[26] There are four points to consider:

1) Relative price shocks. The new importance of relative price shocks, whether from the energy sector or exchange rates, implies that demand conditions may not be highly correlated across provinces. They may not even be positively correlated, which means that expansionary and contractionary policies may be simultaneously called for in different parts of the country.

2) Fiscal multipliers. Now that the world is on floating (or at least "dirty" floating) exchange rates, national fiscal changes are largely offset

---

[24]Gramlich, supra footnote 2.

[25]Supra footnote 7.

[26]And have been in Edward M. Gramlich, "Subnational Fiscal Policy," in John M. Quigley, ed., *Perspectives on Local Public Finance and Public Policy: A Research Annual*, vol. 3 (Greenwich, Conn.: JAI Press, 1987), 3-27.

through trade balance crowding-out. Subnational fiscal changes, in contrast, are likely to be too small and too uncoordinated to cause such crowding-out. In effect, subnational economies are still on fixed exchange rates.

3) Nontradeable goods and services. The rapid growth of the nontradeable sector, especially services, implies that a large share of value added is now produced and consumed inside a province.

4) Open capital markets. The opening of international capital markets and the consequent highly elastic supply of capital imply that all debt, whether provincial or national, is external and imposes costs on the jurisdiction.

The first and second of these points constitute arguments for conducting fiscal stabilization policy at a subnational level, not a national one. The third and fourth neutralize what had previously been felt to be advantages for stabilizing with national budgets.

These points have taken on a great deal of importance in the United States because of the federal budget paralysis of the 1980s. What is to happen, some ask, if there should be a recession? The large and continuing federal budget deficits have proved so difficult to cut that there is likely to be little sentiment for antirecession fiscal stimulation. Yet, in theory, states could do their own stimulation, especially in areas hardest hit by recession. In practice, this approach might be difficult to take because many states have depleted their assets ("rainy day funds") and because US states are generally prohibited from borrowing on current account. (Given this prohibition, building up asset stocks in good years is necessary, but doing so demands foresight of a type that seems to be in short supply in the United States these days.)

Things sound easier in Canada. Although local governments are generally prohibited from borrowing on current account, provincial governments are not.[27] Moreover, the federal-provincial arrangements include national stabilization grants to provincial governments explicitly to cover shortfalls in revenue due to recession. These grants permit relatively easy decentralization of stabilization policy. Perhaps more should be done, but in this area Canada seems well ahead of the United States.

Summary

Canada has long had a system that is federal in actuality as well as in name. Its outstanding feature is probably the important role played by provincial governments—they have more important allocative and stabilization functions than the subnational governments in all other federal systems and more important distributional functions than those in all others but the

---

[27]The various arrangements are described in *Provincial and Municipal Finances, 1987* (Toronto: Canadian Tax Foundation, 1988), chapter 14.

United States. This is an attractive package, especially to one such as me who is fairly well persuaded of the advantages of a federal structure.

Yet there are four important Canadian deviations from what public finance theorists would describe as the ideal federal structure:

1) Canada gives the harmonization of tax systems across the provinces such an unusual weight that not only tax bases but even tax rates are much the same from province to province.

2) Resource taxes are left to the provinces, in spite of both efficiency and equity advantages to the contrary.

3) Local governments rely more on grants and less on taxes than one would think desirable from the viewpoint of accountability.

4) National special purpose grants have been so consolidated that there are now no marginal price incentives and no real advantage to using this form of fiscal support.

I am an outsider and in no position to weigh carefully all the pros and cons of these four deviations from what the theorists might consider optimal. Yet they are clearly deviations, and there are clear costs to the present arrangements.

Name Index

..